Lotus® 1-2-3®
A Tutorial

Second Edition

Includes coverage of
Releases 2, 2.01, 2.2, 2.3, 2.4, 3.0, 3.1+, and Windows

Ruth Yaron Cicilioni
University of Scranton

West Publishing Company

Minneapolis/St. Paul   New York   Los Angeles   San Francisco

WEST'S COMMITMENT TO THE ENVIRONMENT
In 1906, West Publishing Company began recycling materials left over from the production of books. This began a tradition of efficient and responsible use of resources. Today, up to 95% of our legal books and 70% of our college texts are printed on recycled, acid-free stock. West also recycles nearly 22 million pounds of scrap paper annually—the equivalent of 181,717 trees. Since the 1960s, West has devised ways to capture and recycle waste inks, solvents, oils, and vapors created in the printing process. We also recycle plastics of all kinds, wood, glass, corrugated cardboard, and batteries, and have eliminated the use of styrofoam book packaging. We at West are proud of the longevity and the scope of our commitment to our environment.

Production, Prepress, Printing and Binding by West Publishing Company.

COPYRIGHT © 1993 by   WEST PUBLISHING CO.
610 Opperman Drive
P.O. Box 64526
St. Paul, MN 55164–0526

Dedicated to my twin sons,
John and Fred,
with Love

Brief Contents

Section I Mandatory Lessons

Section II Recommended Lessons

Section III Optional and Independent Lessons

Appendices

Contents

The lessons are designed to give the instructor maximum flexibility. The first four lessons, covering the basics, are mandatory and must be covered in order. Lessons 5, 6, and 7 are optional, although strongly recommended. Lessons 8 through 23 and the Appendices are optional, independent, and can be covered in any order. A detailed table of contents can be found at the beginning of each lesson.

Section I Mandatory Lessons

The student builds a simple worksheet using the basics of 1-2-3: cell pointer, pointer movement, control panel, ranges, entering and editing data, values VS labels, label-prefixes, menus, choosing menu options, function keys, global VS local settings, erasing the worksheet, @SUM, saving files, and /Quit.

Range, Go, Line, Page, Align, and As-Displayed VS Cell-Formulas format.

Copying and moving a single cell, row and column range, and two-dimensional range, pointing to a range, [F3/NAME], /Data Fill, and all range name commands.

All formats for values including Percent and Currency, hiding data, hiding zeroes, Help, and /System. The student practices pointing to ranges using [End].

Section II Recommended Lessons

Relative, absolute, and mixed addressing with [F4/ABS]. @PMT is used in an addressing example.

@AVG, @COUNT, @MAX, @MIN, @STD, and @VAR using a gradebook example. @ABS, @INT, @RAND, @ROUND, and precedence of mathematical operators. Trigonometric @ functions and other complex mathematical @ functions are listed.

@IF is covered in detail. @TRUE, @FALSE, @ROWS, @COLUMNS, @CELL, AND @CELLPOINTER are mentioned.

Section III Optional and Independent Lessons

What-if and sensitivity analysis is demonstrated using a home mortgage example. Optionally, @PMT, @FV, @PV, @NPV, and other financial @ functions are covered.

Graphing is covered in depth with many graph figures.

For Releases 2.x, Image-select, size, fonts, action, save settings in PrintGraph. For Releases 3.x, /Print Printer Image, Range *, and Options are included.

The entering of dates and times for use in computations of birthdays, payment due dates, hours passed, etc.

String functions including @LEFT, @RIGHT, @MID, @LENGTH, @REPEAT, @PROPER and concatenation of data. Optionally, ASCII codes and associated @ functions.

Quick macros with Learn for Releases 2.x and Record for Releases 3.x. Simple macros are manually created using standardized procedures. Examples are progressive and build up to user-defined menus. Included are \0, AUTO123, subroutine macros, and pausing for user input.

Includes a list of macro commands with explanations. Numerous advanced macro examples are presented.

Appendices

Hardware and software requirements for each release. Listed are the add-ins included in each release. File extensions and worksheet compatibility between releases is discussed.

This appendix is meant to be a convenient summary list of the new features in this release over previous releases. Release 2.2 features are explained and demonstrated throughout the text.

Similar to Release 2.2 Summary.

Similar to Release 2.2 Summary.

Similar to Release 2.2 Summary. Multiple worksheets and files are discussed with their corresponding pointer movement keys and addressing schemes.

Similar to Release 2.2 Summary.

Lotus for Windows is briefly introduced. A list of menu pulldown commands with explanations follows. A mapping from Release 3.1+ commands to the new Windows commands is included.

How to attach, invoke, and automatically attach and invoke an add-in. Command summaries and sample sessions for the Viewer, Tutor, MacroManager, Auditor, and Backsolver Add-ins.

A full command summary is included. A sample session allows the student to practice most of WYSIWYG's features. Exercises are included.

A command summary and sample session are included.

A command summary and sample printout are included.

Menu trees of 1-2-3 and WYSIWYG commands.

Pictures of the icons with descriptions of their functions.

To the Instructor

This tutorial is a tool the student can use to teach him/herself Lotus. It uses a "hands-on" approach in a manner which requires almost no intervention from the instructor. An instructor's explanations are necessary only for special case situations, such as network-specific commands.

Each instructor has their own agenda in mind, therefore the lessons are designed to give the instructor maximum flexibility. The instructor decides on the subject matter to be covered, assigns appropriate independent lessons, and assigns exercises which determine the depth of coverage. Numerous exercises at levels of increasing difficulty are included after each lesson to allow the instructor to vary assignments over the span of several semesters. In addition, four cumulative exercises are included at the end of most lessons.

This manual can be used alone or as a supplement to other books in courses where Lotus knowledge is required. Because the lessons are designed to be general in nature, a student in any field of study may use this tutorial. No knowledge of college-level science or business courses is assumed, therefore any student from the freshman to the graduate level may use this tutorial. Because of the extensive use of Lotus in business applications, specifically in the fields of accounting, economics, and finance, optional exercises are included which may be ignored by non-business majors.

PC time at most universities is sometimes scarce. Although this manual is a tutorial and is meant to be read while simultaneously using the computer, it functions well as a stand-alone text when no computer is available. 1-2-3 commands are given as full words rather than initials. A considerable number of figures depicting screen displays is integrated into the text so the student can easily picture the results of the commands.

For years, my colleagues and I have searched for a good Lotus tutorial. We found that too much class time was devoted to covering Lotus 1-2-3 commands, leaving little time for subject-specific applications. LOTUS: A TUTORIAL will give you the freedom to teach problem-solving, instead of keystroking, in the classroom.

The Second Edition

Additions to the text include:

Coverage of the new releases of Lotus--2.3, 2.4, and 3.1+--along with releases 2, 2.01, 2,2 and 3.0.

An appendix on Lotus for Windows.

Additional coverage of quick macros in Lesson 22.

An appendix on WYSIWYG including exercises.

An appendix containing summary menu trees of 1-2-3 and WYSIWYG commands.

An appendix containing pictures of the SmartIcons and descriptions of their functions.

An expanded table of contents and index.

Four cumulative problems at the end of most lessons and the WYSIWYG appendix.

A instructor's disk including worksheet files of all exercises.

Instructional Materials

The **instructor's manual** contains answers to all exercises, teaching tips, written test questions, on-computer tests, and additional exercises.

The **exercise disk** contains worksheet files of all exercises.

To the Student

The only way to learn Lotus is to use it. This tutorial uses a "learn by doing" approach and requires you to be using the computer while simultaneously reading the text. Instead of just passively reading, you will DO, and this will greatly aid your comprehension. Do not just follow the steps by rote, but think about what you are doing.

The basics of Lotus are covered in the first few lessons. Subsequent lessons delve further into Lotus's capabilities. The examples get increasingly more complex, requiring you to use previously covered concepts in useful application in order to maximize retention. The more often I think a Lotus feature is used, the earlier it appears in the tutorial. This progression will enable you to implement Lotus very quickly. You don't need to know everything about Lotus before it becomes useful to you.

I have tried to make the lessons as easy-to-follow, thorough, and as clear as possible. If you have any suggestions, I would appreciate your correspondence. I'm sure that you will find many uses for Lotus in your business and home. Good luck!

Ruth Yaron
University of Scranton
Scranton, PA 18510

Acknowledgements

I thank the people at the University of Scranton who have helped in the development of this book. My gratitude to Dr. Robert McCloskey, Anne Marie Stamford, Charles Taylor, Vince Merkel, and Karl Johns.

I express many thanks to the dedicated professionals at West Publishing, especially Nancy Hill-Whilton and Richard Fenton.

My appreciation to the reviewers, whose suggestions and criticisms have greatly improved this manuscript: Bob Autrey, Mesa Community College; Lloyd J. Buckwell, Jr., Indiana University Northwest; Janice Burke, South Suburban College; Dominic Ciaccio, Kankakee Community College; Charmayne B. Cullom, University of Northern Colorado; Bill Cummings, Northern Illinois University; Diane Drozd, College of DuPage; Patricia L. Duckworth, Metropolitan State College; Chana Edmond-Verley, Davenport College; Lois Graff, George Washington Univeristy; Paul N. Higbee, University of North Florida; Nancy Hogg, Davenport College; Richard Leon Howe, Orange Coast College; Eric Jaede, College of St. Thomas; Marlyce Johnson, Milwaukee Area Technical College; James E. LaBarre, University of Wisconsin - Eau Claire; Linda R. Lang, Pima Community College - West Campus; Kathleen J. Lorencz, Oakland Community College; Laura H. Murphy, Sampson Community College; Scott H. Rupple, Marquette University; Steve Samuels, DePaul University; David Skougstad, Metropolitan State College; Charles G. Strattan, Miami-Dade Community College; Kathleen Tesker, St. Louis Community College; Maureen Thomas, Bemidji State University; and Michael R. Williams, Kirkwood Community College.

I also wish to acknowledge my family, especially Johnny, Freddy, and my mother, who were very supportive in this project.

GETTING STARTED

Contents:

Getting Started explains how to install and start Lotus.

Installing Lotus

The Install program puts Lotus on your hard drive so that you can use it. It also sets up drivers for your printer, so that Lotus will know exactly how to send data to that particular brand of printer. If Lotus is already installed on your system, you can skip this section.

First, make sure that your hard drive has enough space for Lotus. Issue the DOS directory command (DIR) on your C: drive (or whatever drive you're using for Lotus) and verify that the number of bytes free is greater than the space required. See Appendix A Summary of Releases for the hard disk space required for your particular release.

Put the disk labelled Disk 1 Install in drive A:. Change the default drive to A: by typing A: at the DOS prompt. Type install and follow the directions on the screen.

Lotus for Windows: To install this release, run Windows, put the Install disk in drive A:, select File Run, and type A:Install. Start Lotus by opening the Windows Program Manager, opening the program group window labelled "Lotus Applications" and selecting the 1-2-3 for Windows icon. Please read the appendix on Windows before you begin Lesson 1.

Release 3.1+: WYSIWYG is installed with the Install program you have just completed. You must install the other add-ins -- Auditor, Backsolver, Solver, and Viewer -- separately, using the Enhancement Add-ins Disks. These add-ins are explained in the Add-ins Appendix and are not necessary to do the lessons in this text. You may install them now or sometime in the future. If you choose to install them now, put the Enhancement Add-ins Disk 1 in the drive and type AINSTALL.

Releases 2 and 2.1: To install these releases on a hard disk, a different procedure is necessary.

Create a directory on the hard disk called 123:

md \123 [Return]

Change the current directory to 123:

cd \123 [Return]

copy all files from all disks in the Lotus package using the command:

copy a:*.* [Return]

The System disk is required in drive A when you run Lotus on your hard disk unless you issue the **copyhard** command in Release 2.01 (**copyon** command in Release 2). This command prevented people from making multiple copies of Lotus on different systems. It could only be done once, unless you undo it with the **copyhard** command to move it to another system.

Run install by entering the command:

install

and follow the instructions.

Now that Lotus is installed, you can run INSTALL again from your hard drive if you change hardware. For instance, if you get a new printer, run INSTALL from the directory on the C: drive where Lotus is installed and choose the Changing Selected Equipment option.

Starting Lotus

Change the directory to the one where Lotus is installed by using the DOS cd or chdir command and enter Lotus. Figure GS-1, the Lotus Access System, should be on your screen.

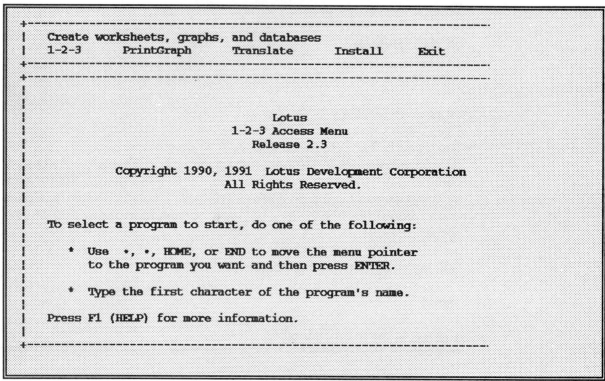

```
+-------------------------------------------------------------
|  Create worksheets, graphs, and databases
|  1-2-3        PrintGraph      Translate      Install     Exit
+-------------------------------------------------------------

+-------------------------------------------------------------
|
|
|
|                             Lotus
|                        1-2-3 Access Menu
|                          Release 2.3
|
|            Copyright 1990, 1991  Lotus Development Corporation
|                        All Rights Reserved.
|
|
|  To select a program to start, do one of the following:
|
|     *  Use  *, *, HOME, or END to move the menu pointer
|        to the program you want and then press ENTER.
|
|     *  Type the first character of the program's name.
|
|  Press F1 (HELP) for more information.
|
+-------------------------------------------------------------
```

Figure GS-1. The Lotus Access System.

You are ready for Lesson 1.

Starting 1-2-3

You can "skip over" the Lotus Access System and go directly into the worksheet part of Lotus by entering 123 at the DOS prompt instead of Lotus. A blank worksheet will appear on your screen, as in Figure 1-1, page 8.

WORKSHEET BASICS

Contents:

Lesson 1 covers most of the basics of creating a worksheet. It is rather lengthy because many concepts must be covered to create even a simple worksheet. Breakpoints are inserted at places in the text where you can stop, take a break, and return without concern of losing the continuity in the lesson.

It is necessary for you to be using a computer to do these lessons. You should now be sitting in front of your PC with the Lotus Access System Menu (Figure GS-1, page 4) on the screen. If this menu is not on your screen, get it there by following the directions in the GETTING STARTED section.

Lotus Access System Functions

The second line on the screen:

1-2-3 Printgraph Translate Install Exit

consists of all functions or options available on the Lotus Access System Menu. Everything else on the screen is helpful information whose only purpose is to instruct or remind. Lotus consists of many functions which do different tasks.

1-2-3 is the worksheet program or the electronic spreadsheet part of Lotus and is probably the part you will use most often.

Printgraph allows you to make printouts of graphs which have been created in 1-2-3.

Translate allows you to take files created by other software programs and convert them to a Lotus-compatible format and vice-versa.

Install tailors the Lotus system for your particular use.

Exit takes you back to DOS.

Releases 2 and 2.1: The View option shows you the capabilities of Lotus.
Releases 3.0 and 3.1+: Menu is on second line with
1-2-3 Install Translate Exit only.

For now, note that the two options **1-2-3** and **Exit** exist.

1-2-3 is highlighted by a reverse-video rectangular bar. Typing the [Return] key (same as the Enter key or the Carriage Return key) will cause you to enter the 1-2-3 program of Lotus:

You enter: **[Return]**

After a few seconds a copyright notice appears followed by a blank worksheet as shown in Figure 1-1.

Releases 2.2: UNDO is shown on the bottom of the screen.
Releases 2.3 and 2.4: If you have a mouse, icons are shown on the right of the screen.
Releases 3.0 and 3.1+: On the first line is A:A1: and above the 1 there is another A. These extra A's are explained in the Appendix. For the rest of this lesson please ignore them.

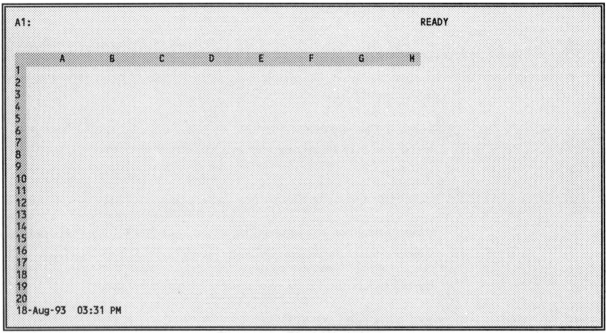

Figure 1-1. Blank Worksheet.

The date and time are shown on the bottom line of the screen. If yours are incorrect, use the DOS commands DATE and TIME to correct them.

The **worksheet** is a matrix of rows, designated by numbers, and columns, designated by letters. The intersection of each row with each column is a **cell** which can contain data. Each cell has an address consisting of the letter of its column and the number of its row, such as A1 or D14.

Cell Pointer

The highlighted bar, which is referred to as the **cell pointer** or just **pointer**, is now in the cell A1. It designates the cell with which you are currently working.

Special Keys

There are several keys on the keyboard which have words on them, such as Esc, Home, End, PgUp, NumLock, ScrollLock, etc. When I tell you to enter a word in brackets, you should tap the key with that word on it once. For example, if you are told to enter [Home], do NOT type the word "Home". Instead tap the key with the word "Home" on it once. The same follows with [Esc], [PgUp], etc.

Two keys with a plus sign between them means to hold down the first key while tapping the second key once. For example, [Shift] + [Tab] tells you to hold down the [Shift] key and while it is still depressed, tap the [Tab] key once.

[Esc]

One of the most important keys on the keyboard is the one marked Esc. The Escape key will let you "escape" from keystroke errors while using 1-2-3, and you will use it very frequently. Find it on your keyboard now and remember to use it if you want to "undo" a keystroke mistake. I will give specific examples later.

Arrow Keys

One of the ways to change the pointer's position is to use the arrow keys. Find the four arrow keys, [Right], [Left], [Up], [Down], on your keyboard. These four keys do not have the words "Right", "Left", etc. on them, they have pictures of arrows pointing in those directions. Use these arrow keys now to move the highlighted pointer around the worksheet.

You enter: **[Right] [Down] [Left] [Up]**

WARNING: If there is a NUM displayed on the bottom line of the screen, these arrow keys will not move the pointer and, instead, will put numbers on the second line of the screen. To correct this, tap the [NumLock] key to turn off the NUM indicator. Now tap [Esc] to clear the numbers and try the arrow keys again.

Releases 2.3 and 2.4: The mouse can be used to change the pointer's position. Try clicking on another cell.

While moving the pointer, note that the cell address in the upper left corner of the screen shows the current pointer position.

Worksheet Dimensions

There is more to the worksheet than can fit on the screen. Move off the right edge of the screen.

You enter: **[Right] 10 times.**

There are actually 256 columns to the worksheet labelled A, B, C, ..., Z, AA, AB, AC, ..., AZ, BA, BB, BC, ..., BZ, CA, CB, CC, ..., CZ,..., IV. There are 8192 rows. Most keys will repeat if you hold them down.

You: **Hold [Down] key continuously.**

Pointer Movement Keys

Besides using the four arrow keys, there are other pointer movement keys.

[Home] moves pointer to cell A1.

[PgDn] moves 20 rows down.

[PgUp] moves 20 rows up.

[Tab] moves a screen to the right.
        ([Tab] is usually the key under [Esc] with two opposite arrows drawn on it.)

[Ctrl] + [Right] also moves a screen to the right.
(See Special Keys, page 9 if you forgot how to handle the +.)

[Shift] + [Tab] moves a screen to the left.

[Ctrl] + [Left] also moves a screen to the left.

You: **Try all pointer movement keys above.**

Now move to cell A1 which is referred to as the **home cell**.

You enter: **[Home]**

Function Keys

Find the 10 keys on your keyboard marked F1, F2, F3, ..., F10. (Most newer keyboards actually have 12 function keys.) Each of these 10 function keys has a special task in 1-2-3. I will instruct you to tap one of these function keys by putting F and the number followed by a / and the key's function in brackets. For example, [F5/GOTO] means to tap the key with the F5 on it once; do not type "F5/GOTO". There is a summary of these 10 function keys on page 128.

[F5/GOTO]

The [F5/GOTO] key is a quick way to get to a remote cell in the worksheet.

You enter: **[F5/GOTO]**

Prompts and other screen messages from 1-2-3 will be shown in this book as below:

Computer message: Enter address to go to: A1

1-2-3 is now prompting you for the cell address you want to move to.

Releases 3.0 and 3.1+: Ignore the A: before the A1.

Defaults

1-2-3 will always give you a default address as it does here with the A1. A **default** is some setting, in this case a cell address, which will be taken unless you specifically state that you want something else. Don't be concerned with this A1 right now, although you should remember what a default is. "A default is what you get if you don't state otherwise."

You enter: **BQ1000 [Return]**

It doesn't matter whether the BQ is typed in uppercase or lowercase. The pointer is now in cell BQ1000.

Control Panel

The first 3 lines of the screen are called **window lines** and show information about tasks currently being accomplished. These 3 lines are known as the **control panel**. The first line shows the current pointer address on the left, which is currently BQ1000, and the **mode indicator** on the right, which currently shows READY. In **READY mode**, 1-2-3 is waiting for you to either enter data into a cell or issue a command.

The final product of the first lesson will be Figure 1-2. Keep a marker on this page so that you can easily flip to Figure 1-2 and Figure 1-3 for future reference.

	A	B	C	D	E
1		SCRANTON HARDWARE COMPANY, INCORPORATED			
2					
3			Sales	Tax	Total
4					
5	1 Nuts		$437.50	$26.25	$463.75
6	2 Bolts		$899.64	$53.98	$953.62
7	3 Screwdrivers		$76.23	$4.57	$80.80
8			------------------	------------------	------------------
9		TOTAL	$1,413.37	$84.80	$1,498.17
10					

Figure 1-2. Scranton Worksheet.

You'll build Figure 1-2 piece by piece, beginning with the part shown in Figure 1-3.

	A	B	C	D	E	F	G	H
1	437.5							
2	899.64							
3	76.23							
4								

Figure 1-3. Part I of Scranton Worksheet.

You enter: **[Home]**

Verify that the cell address A1 is shown in the control panel.

Entering Data into a Cell

After reading this paragraph, you will type 437.5 into cell A1 as in Figure 1-3. As you do, notice that the characters are shown on the input line (the second line) in the control panel. The data is not entered into the cell until the [Return] key is typed.

You enter into A1: **437.5 [Return]**

The number is displayed both in the control panel and in cell A1. There is a reason for this redundancy as you will discover later.

Correcting Mistakes

If [Return] has not yet been typed, the [BackSpace] key will erase the last character entered. If [Return] has not yet been typed, the [Esc] key will erase all characters.

Become familiar now with these two keys by entering data with mistakes into cell A2.

You enter: **[Down]**

As you enter the keystrokes below, watch the results of each on the screen.

You enter into A2: **123 [BackSpace] [Backspace] 456 [Esc]**

You enter: **899.64 [Return]**

If [Return] has already been typed, simply type the correct entry and [Return] again. The new correct number will take the place of the previous data.

You enter: **[Down]**

You enter into A3: **77.23 [Return]**

This number is incorrect as you see in Figure 1-3 and [Return] has already been typed. Correct it by simply entering the correct number as if there is nothing in A3.

You enter into A3: **76.23 [Return]**

Your screen should look like Figure 1-3.

Releases 2.2, 2.3, 2.4, 3.0, and 3.1+:
UNDO is a nice feature used to undo mistakes. You can UNDO most commands using [Alt]+[F4]. If you accidentally erase your worksheet, this is a way to get it back. UNDO must be enabled (see UNDO in index). Note that the UNDO feature uses a lot of memory; if you have memory problems, try disabling this feature.

Ranges

One of the most important concepts in 1-2-3 is a range. A **range** is a rectangular array of cells. In Figure 1-4, each group of x's is a valid range. A range can be part of a row, part of a column, a single cell, or a multiple row-multiple column part of the worksheet.

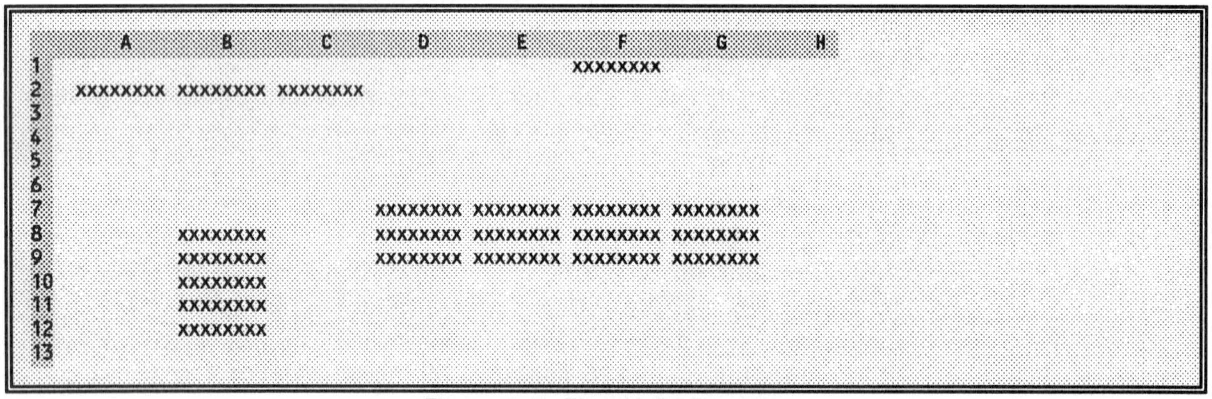

```
       A          B          C          D          E          F          G          H
 1                                                           XXXXXXXX
 2   XXXXXXXX   XXXXXXXX   XXXXXXXX
 3
 4
 5
 6
 7                                    XXXXXXXX   XXXXXXXX   XXXXXXXX   XXXXXXXX
 8              XXXXXXXX               XXXXXXXX   XXXXXXXX   XXXXXXXX   XXXXXXXX
 9              XXXXXXXX               XXXXXXXX   XXXXXXXX   XXXXXXXX   XXXXXXXX
10              XXXXXXXX
11              XXXXXXXX
12              XXXXXXXX
13
```

Figure 1-4. Four Valid Ranges.

Figure 1-5 has examples of invalid ranges because they are not shaped like rectangles.

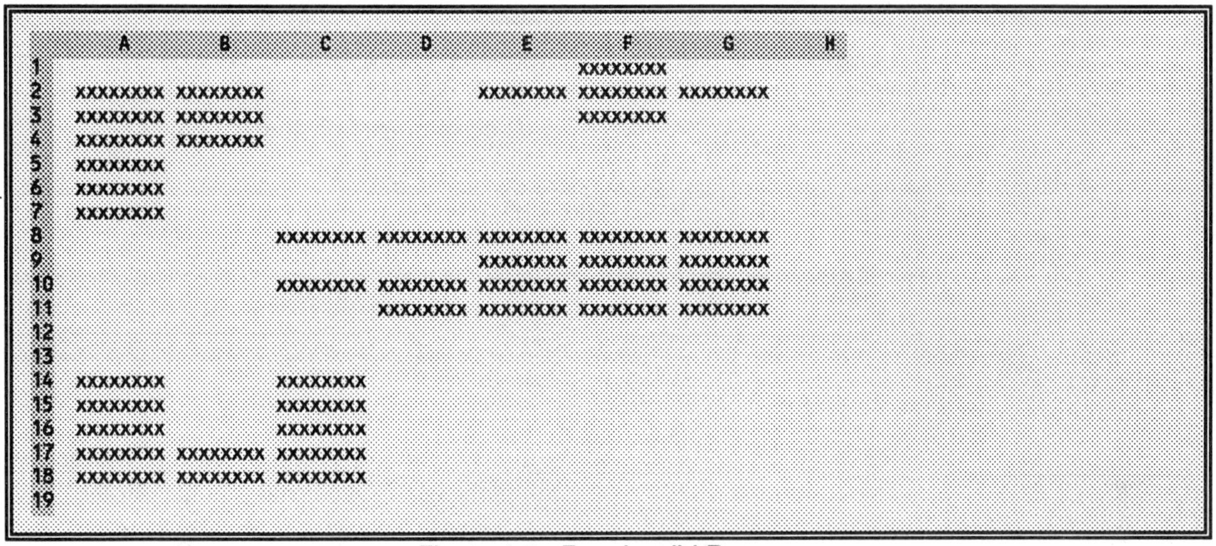

Figure 1-5. Four Invalid Ranges.

Below is the multiple row-multiple column range shown in Figure 1-4 consisting of 3 rows and 4 columns:

           D7 E7 F7 G7
           D8 E8 F8 G8
           D9 E9 F9 G9

Designating a Range by Typing

Picture a diagonal line cutting through this rectangle from D7 to G9. To designate this range to 1-2-3, type the two cell addresses at the endpoints of a diagonal and separate them by two periods. D7..G9 is one possible designation for this range. The other three possible designations are G9..D7, D9..G7, and G7..D9. Do you see that all four designations cannot possibly be any other range? They all specify this unique range. For the row range in figure 1-4 below:

               A2 B2 C2

there are two possible designations: A2..C2 and C2..A2.

For the column range in Figure 1-4, the designations would be B8..B12 and B12..B8.

For the range with only a single cell in Figure 1-4, the designation would be F1..F1.

When you type a range designation, you may actually use any number of periods to separate the endpoints. Therefore D7.G9, D7...G9, or D7.......G9 are all acceptable. I will use two periods in this manual to be consistent with the way 1-2-3 displays ranges on the screen.

Releases 2.3 and 2.4: Hitting [Del] will erase the contents of the current cell.

/Range Erase

To erase a single cell, use the 1-2-3 command /Range Erase. To practice this command, first put some data into cell A4 so that you have something to erase.

You enter into A4: **1234 [Return]**

1-2-3 is a **menu-driven** program which means that to perform most tasks, you choose an option from a menu. In non-menu driven programs, you type in command words. Pull up 1-2-3's main menu.

You enter: **/**

WARNING: Make sure you typed the forward slash key (/) which is below the ? on most keyboards. Do not type the backward slash key (\).

Your screen should look like Figure 1-6.

```
A4: 1234                                              MENU
Worksheet  Range  Copy  Move  File  Print  Graph  Data  System  Quit
Global, Insert, Delete, Column, Erase, Titles, Window, Status, Page, Hide
        A        B        C        D        E        F        G        H
1     437.5
2     899.64
3      76.23
4      1234
5
```

Figure 1-6. Main Menu.

Releases 2.2, 2.3, and 2.4:
An additional option, Add-In, is between the System and Quit options.

Note that the mode indicator in the control panel shows MENU indicating that 1-2-3 expects you to choose an option. The options available to you now are displayed on the second line of the screen:

Worksheet Range Copy Move File Print Graph Data System Quit

Choosing Options by Highlighting

One way to choose an option from a menu is by the Highlight and [Return] method. Move the highlighting to the option you want by using the [Right] and [Left] arrow keys and type [Return].

You enter: **[Right] [Right] [Right]**

The highlighting moves right.

You enter: **[Right] several times.**

You enter: **[Left] several times.**

Keep using these arrow keys until you get the idea that the highlighting never moves off the second line in the control panel. [Home] and [End] can also be used to move the highlighting.

You enter: **[Home] [End] [Home] [End]**

To continue issuing the /Range Erase command, choose the Range option by highlighting Range and typing [Return]:

You enter: **[Home] [Right] [Return]**

The Range sub-menu appears on the screen. Choose Erase from this menu:

You enter: **[Right] [Right] [Return]**

Computer message: Enter range to erase: A4..A4

Releases 3.0 and 3.1+:
A:A4..A:A4 is the range. Again, Ignore the A:'s.

The prompt asks you for a range and assumes you want the range consisting of the single cell the pointer is currently in. A4..A4 is the **default range**. Just enter [Return] and the default range will be erased.

You enter: **[Return]**

Your worksheet should look like Figure 1-3 again. Of course, you could have entered any range of any size to be erased.

You have just issued your first 1-2-3 command. All 1-2-3 commands will be issued by first bringing up the main menu with the / and then choosing options from menus. As you are going through this tutorial, focus only on the option which we are currently covering and ignore any other options in the menus. Don't allow yourself to get confused about the other options and concentrate only on the one with which you're immediately working.

[Esc] in Menu Mode

[Esc] "undoes" the last option chosen and allows you to escape from a sub-menu and return to the previous higher level menu.

You enter: **/ [Right] [Return] [Esc] [Esc]**

Remember to use [Esc] if you've accidentally chosen an incorrect option.

Third Line of Control Panel

The third line of the control panel displays either a sub-menu or an explanation of the highlighted option.

You enter: **/ [Right]**

Range is highlighted and the third line displays the Range sub-menu from which you have just chosen the Erase option. Move to the Copy option.

You enter: **[Right]**

Copy is highlighted and the third line displays an explanation of the Copy option's function which is to

Copy a cell or range of cells

Some commands have several layers of submenus through which you must navigate to complete the command. Others, such as this copy command have no submenus. An explanation of what the command will do is displayed under the lowest submenu, or last step, of each command.

You enter: **[Esc]**

You're back to READY mode.

Choosing Options by First Letter

The options in each menu have unique first characters which allows you to choose an option by simply typing its first character. Issue the /Range Erase command by typing the first letters of the two chosen options:

You enter: **/ R E**

This has the same effect as highlighting and [Return] but, in my opinion, is much faster, especially if you are a touch typist. From here on, I will instruct you to issue commands this way:

You enter: **/ Range Erase**

You may either highlight and [Return] or type each option's first character. The first time you enter a new command unfamiliar to you, I suggest that you take a few seconds to highlight the options and read the third line explanations. Reading these explanations initially should help you recall the commands. Take a minute now to look at Appendix L Menu Commands Quick Reference. The /Range Erase command can be found on page 720.

Return to READY mode.

You enter: **[Esc] 4 times.**

Releases 2.2, 2.3, and 2.4: Simply placing the mouse pointer in the control panel area causes the main menu to appear. Options can then be chosen with a mouse click.

Although you only have the 3 entries shown in Figure 1-3 at this point, you will now save a copy of this file out to disk.

/File Save

Your worksheet on the screen is stored in a temporary memory called **RAM**. RAM storage is volatile which means that it would be erased if you turned off your PC right now or lost power to it. The /File Save command will place a more permanent copy of your worksheet on disk in a file. A **file** is a group of logically related data which is treated as a unit. As you go through this tutorial, you will create several worksheet files on your disk. Each one will need a designator called a filename so that you can specify to 1-2-3 which file you want. You will now save your worksheet in a file named SCRANTON:

You enter: / **File Save**

Computer message: Enter name of file to save:

Some earlier releases display the computer message: Enter save file name:

The computer message or prompt is asking you for a filename. A default subdirectory is displayed after the prompt, which you can ignore for now. See /File Directory in Lesson 16 File Operations for information on changing the default directory.

Releases 3.0 and 3.1+: 1-2-3 uses a default file name C:\123R3\FILE0001.WK3. 123R3 is the name of the subdirectory. FILE0001.WK3 is the file name. Enter the keystrokes as instructed below.

While typing the filename SCRANTON, use [BackSpace] or [Esc] to correct any typos you might make. Uppercase or lowercase or any combination will do.

You enter: **SCRANTON [Return]**

You should see the drive's light on, indicating activity to the disk.

WARNING: It is important that you do not attempt to remove a disk from a drive when it is active, as you may damage the drive and/or the disk.

/File List

The /File List command enables you to see the files on disk.

You enter: / **File List Worksheet**

The mode indicator shows FILES.

If SCRANTON.WK1 is not highlighted, use the arrow keys to do so:

You: **Highlight SCRANTON.WK1**

The third line of the screen should be similar to:

SCRANTON.WK1   09/08/92   15:11   1456

Releases 3.0 and 3.1+: WK3, instead of WK1, is the extension for these releases.

SCRANTON is the filename; WK1 is the extension. This extension is automatically added to classify the file as a worksheet file created by 1-2-3. File extensions are useful in classifying files by type, and 1-2-3 and some other software packages have standard extensions for easy file identification.

The second and third items on that line are the date the file was created (09/08/92) and the time the file was created (15:11). The time is in military format, therefore 15:11 is 3:11 pm. (If yours are not correct, use the DOS DATE and TIME commands to set the clock properly). The last item (1456) is the number of bytes the file is using on disk. You can think of a byte as the amount of storage it takes to store one character of information. Your byte count may differ slightly from mine, although you and I have what seems to be the same worksheet file.

The second line should be similar to:

Name of files to list: c:\123r24*.wk1

c:\123r24*.wk1 designates that the files listed are those stored on the C: drive in the subdirectory \123r24 with extensions wk1. The * is a wildcard indicating that any filenames are included in the file list. For more information on directories or wild cards, see a DOS manual.

Releases other than 2.4 will have different default subdirectories. For example, Release 2.3 has c:\123r23*.wk1. Release 2 uses .wk? for its default extension. The ? is a wildcard matching any single character. (* matches any characters and any **number** of characters.) Release 2 is upwardly compatible with the very old version of 1-2-3, version 1A, which saved worksheet files with the extension .wks. Therefore *.wk? will match all files with extensions wk1 and wks.

Upward compatibility means that newer software releases can use files and command keystroke sequences from older versions of that software. So if you created worksheet files in Lotus Release 2.01, you can retrieve them and use and modify them in Lotus Release 3.1+ with virtually the same keystrokes as you were familiar with in 2.01. However, the opposite is not necessarily true, which makes the adjective "upwardly" in upwardly compatible necessary. See Worksheet File Compatibility in Appendix A for information on retrieving worksheet files from other releases into your release.

Other worksheet files in this subdirectory are listed below the third line of the screen. The arrow keys can be used to move the highlighting to their file names to display dates and times of creation and size in bytes.

Return to the worksheet:

You enter: **[Return]**

/Worksheet Erase

To clear the worksheet of all entries, use the /Worksheet Erase command.[1]

You enter: / **Worksheet Erase**

This **No Yes** menu is asking, "Are you sure you want to wipe out the worksheet on the screen and in RAM?" Choose Yes:

You enter: **Yes**

Newer releases will ask you again if you're sure. Answer yes.

Releases 3.0 and 3.1+: These releases allow you to work with more than one worksheet in RAM at a time. The message "Erase all worksheets and files in memory" refers to only those in RAM; don't worry, none will be erased on your disk by this command.

You're back to a blank worksheet. It is important that you realize that the worksheet has been erased in RAM only. You still have a copy on disk under the name SCRANTON which you can retrieve back to RAM to work with further.

/Quit

To return to the Lotus Access System Menu, choose the Quit option from the main menu.

---

[1]For information on how to erase a file from disk, see /File Erase in index.

You enter: / **Quit**

This menu should be on your screen:

No Yes

You enter: **Yes**

WARNING: In Releases 2 and 2.01, don't forget to save your files before you /Quit. This is so easy to do in these two releases. Although I'm warning you about this now, no doubt you will experience it with the resulting shock and dismay. The newer releases try to prevent this by requiring you to confirm and confirm again.

Releases 2.2, 2.3, 2.4, 3.0, and 3.1+:
If you try to /Quit from a worksheet into which changes have been made, these releases remind you to save it by requiring you to choose Yes from yet another menu.

The Lotus Access System Menu as in Figure GS-1 should be on your screen. Choose the Exit option to return to DOS.

You enter: **Exit**

When your attention span has been exceeded, it is important that you take a long break before continuing with the lessons. You are human and cannot learn when you are tired. I therefore will put frequent marks in the lessons at points where you can stop and not be concerned about losing the continuity of the lesson. Of course, you can also stop at the end of any lesson.

- - - If you need a break, stop at this point. - - -

You can now enter Lotus at the DOS prompt to enter the Lotus Access System to get back to 1-2-3, the electronic spreadsheet part of Lotus. Or, you can "jump over" the Lotus Access System and go directly to the 1-2-3 program by typing 123 at the DOS prompt.

You enter: **123 [Return]**

You should have a blank worksheet on your screen as in Figure 1-1.

/File Retrieve

The /File Retrieve command is used to pull a copy of a disk file into RAM. Bring the SCRANTON worksheet into RAM:

You enter: / **File Retrieve**

Computer message: Name of file to retrieve:

The prompt above is asking for the filename. Again you should have the drive, directory, etc. after the prompt. Give it the filename.

You enter: **SCRANTON [Return]**

The file is now being brought in from the disk. The original file on disk is not erased or changed by this command. Only a copy of it is brought in. The original remains on disk and still looks like Figure 1-3.

Your screen should also look like Figure 1-3. Note that the pointer position is exactly where you left it right before you did the /File Save, in cell A4.

Let's continue now to build Figure 1-2. Note that the numbers in column C in Figure 1-2 all have dollar signs and two digits after the decimal point; the format is different from that of the numbers in your worksheet.

General Format

By default, numbers are displayed in **General** format. "It's the format you get if you don't state otherwise." It is what is known as the **initial global display format** or the format which is set up for you when you enter 1-2-3 (initial) and the format which holds for each cell in the worksheet (global). These settings can, of course, be changed if you "state otherwise". In General format, trailing zeroes are suppressed after the decimal point, so that the entry 437.50 in General format displays as 437.5.

Determining Global Settings

It is nice that Lotus assumes many default settings for your worksheet, such as the format of numbers, the width of columns, etc.; otherwise you would have to set all of them up yourself. Of course, you will want to change some of them.

Releases 2.3 and 2.4:

When I ask you to view the global settings,

You enter: /Worksheet **G**lobal

Global settings are shown on this screen. Ignore everything except the Format: General shown in the lower right.

Releases 2, 2.01, 2.2, 3.0, and 3.1+:

When I ask you to view the global settings,

You enter: /Worksheet **S**tatus

The mode indicator shows STAT for status and the global settings are shown on this screen. Ignore all lines except these two:

Cell Display:
Format. . . . . . (G)

The G designates General format.

You: **Return to READY mode by using [Esc].**

Currency Format

Currency format displays a dollar sign before each number and displays negative values in parentheses, as is common in the accounting field.

Most of Figure 1-2's numbers are displayed in Currency format with 2 decimal digits and therefore that's what the global format for this worksheet should be.

/Worksheet Global Format

The /Worksheet Global Format command changes the global format.

From READY mode:

You enter: / **W**orksheet **G**lobal **F**ormat **C**urrency

Computer message: Enter number of decimal places (0..15): 2

You can have any number of decimal places in the range 0 through 15 as the prompt above says. The 2 after the colon is the default, if you just hit [Return]. It so happens that we do want 2 decimal places.

You enter: **[Return]**

Your entries now look like those in Figure 1-2, column C. All numbers that you enter from now on will be displayed in Currency format with 2 decimal places.

View the global settings and note that the new global setting for format is Currency 2.

Releases 2, 2.01, 2.2, 3.0, and 3.1+:
(G) has been changed to (C2), Currency with 2 decimal places.

Continue by entering the words in column B of Figure 1-2.

Labels

Words and other data which will never be used in computations are referred to as **labels** in 1-2-3. You cannot yet begin entering the labels in column B of Figure 1-2 until you add a column to the left of your entries in column A of your worksheet.

/Worksheet Insert Column

The /Worksheet Insert Column command adds one or more blank columns to the left of the range that you designate. You will now add one column to the left of column A. The pointer should be in cell A4.

You enter: / **W**orksheet **I**nsert **C**olumn

Computer message: Enter column insert range: A4..A4

The number of columns added will be equal to the number of columns in the range you designate. The default range is perfect for your needs in this case because it contains one column and is in the proper position. The added column will be to the left of A4..A4. So accept this default range:

You enter: **[Return]**

If you just hit [Return], one column is added to the left of the pointer.

Your worksheet should look like Figure 1-7.

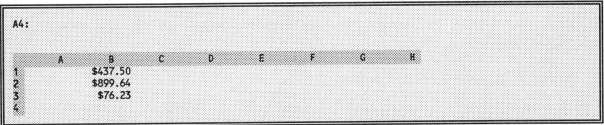

Figure 1-7. Worksheet with Inserted Column.

Position the pointer to cell A1 and enter Nuts Uppercase and lowercase DO matter when entering labels.

You enter: **[Home]**

You enter into A1: **Nuts [Return]**

Look carefully at the first line in the control panel which shows the contents of cell A1. The ' before Nuts is automatically placed there by 1-2-3 and is called a label-prefix.

Label-prefixes

A **label-prefix** is a character which signifies how a label will be positioned in a cell. The four label-prefixes are:

'	left-aligned
"	right-aligned
^	centered
\	repeat

The initial global default setting for label-prefixes is left-aligned ('). Verify this by viewing the global settings. (See page 25 if you forgot how to view the global settings).

Releases 2.3, 2.4, and 3.1+:

Note the asterisk before Left in the Labels box.

Releases 2, 2.01, 2.2, and 3.0:

Under Cell Display: you see:

Label-prefix..... '

Nuts therefore is flush left in cell A1 as all labels will be "unless stated otherwise".

WARNING: Beginning 1-2-3 users often make the mistake of using ' (on the ~ key) instead of ' (on the " key) for the left-aligned label-prefix.

You: **Return to READY mode.**

Enter the next two labels.

You enter into A2: **Bolts [Return]**

You enter into A3: **Screwdrivers [Return]**

Your worksheet should look like Figure 1-8.

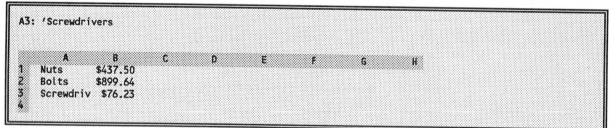

```
A3: 'Screwdrivers


        A         B         C         D         E         F         G         H
1    Nuts      $437.50
2    Bolts     $899.64
3    Screwdriv $76.23
4
```

Figure 1-8. Label Too Large for Column-width.

/Worksheet Global Column-Width

The initial global column-width is 9 characters, which can be seen if you view the global settings. Change the global column-width to 20:

You enter: / **Worksheet Global Column-Width**

Computer message: Enter global column width (1..240): 9

The range of possible column-widths shown in the prompt is 1 to 240 characters wide. Screwdrivers can fit in a column-width of 20:

You enter: **20 [Return]**

This is a global command and, therefore, all columns are set to 20 characters wide because none have been "set otherwise". Actually, we want only column A to be of width 20 and all other columns to remain width 9. Let's change the global column-width back to 9.

You enter: / **Worksheet Global Column-Width 9 [Return]**

/Worksheet Column Set-Width

The /Worksheet Column Set-Width command changes the column-width of an individual column. Make sure that the pointer is in the column whose width you want to change before you initiate this command. In this case, position the pointer in column A. Your pointer is probably still in cell A3 which is fine, although any row of column A would be ok.

You enter: / **Worksheet Column Set-Width**

At this point, you can type in a number for the column-width. However, a nice feature of 1-2-3 is the ability to use the arrow keys to see which width would work well.

You enter: **[Right] several times. [Left] several times.**

With each keystroke the column widens or thins by one character and the number after the prompt is changed for you accordingly. Use width 15 so that we'll be consistent with each other:

You enter: **Use arrow keys to set width to 15 and hit [Return].**

Your screen should look like Figure 1-9.

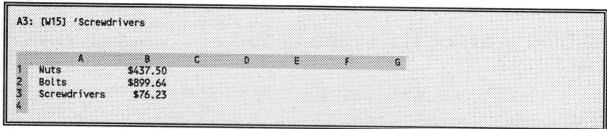

Figure 1-9. Column A's Width = 15. Global = 9.

In the control panel you see [W15]. This tells you not only that the width is 15, but also that this column is not taking the global column-width. Therefore if you change the global column-width, this column will not be affected. Try it.

You enter: **/ Worksheet Global Column-Width 50 [Return]**

All columns have width 50 except those "stated otherwise" with a /Worksheet Column Set-Width command, in this case, only column A. Change the global column-width back to 9 again.

You enter: **/ Worksheet Global Column-Width 9 [Return]**

Your next step is to enter TOTAL so that it is centered in cell A5 as in Figure 1-2, cell B9. It is easier to type all uppercase letters if [CapsLock] is turned on.

You enter: **[CapsLock]**

A CAPS indicator is shown on the bottom line of the screen.

To override the current global label-prefix of left-aligned ('), first type the center label-prefix (^), which can usually be found above the 6 key.

You enter into A5: **^ TOTAL [Return]**

You enter: **[CapsLock]**

Toggle Keys

[CapsLock] is one of several toggle keys on the keyboard. A **toggle key** alternates a setting between two states. It is similar to a light switch which changes a typical household light bulb between the two states on and off. If you type [CapsLock] repeatedly, you will see the CAPS indicator on the screen go on and off.

/Worksheet Insert Row

/Worksheet Insert Row is very similar to /Worksheet Insert Column; it adds one or more blank rows to the worksheet above the designated range. The number of rows added is equal to the number of rows in the range. You will add two rows because you need a blank row between the column header row and the Nuts row.

You enter: / **Worksheet** **Insert Row** **A1..A2 [Return]**

Your worksheet has two new blank rows as shown in Figure 1-10.

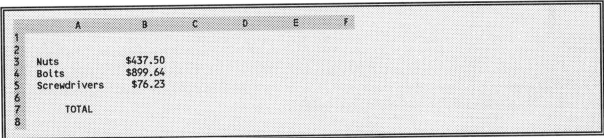

	A	B	C	D	E	F
1						
2						
3	Nuts	$437.50				
4	Bolts	$899.64				
5	Screwdrivers	$76.23				
6						
7	TOTAL					
8						

Figure 1-10. Two Inserted Rows.

Enter the three column headers:

You enter into B1: **Sales [Return]**

You enter: **[Right]**

The [Return] keystroke is not necessary if you are going to move the pointer immediately after making an entry.

You enter into C1: **Tax [Right]**

You enter into D1: **Total [Return]**

Oops! Those labels should actually be right-aligned instead of left-aligned, as you can see if you look closely at Figure 1-2. It is not necessary to re-enter the labels because of the existence of the next command.

/Range Label

To change the label-prefixes of labels WHICH HAVE ALREADY BEEN ENTERED, use /Range Label.

Releases 2, 2.01, 2.2, and 3.0: In these releases, this command is /Range Label-Prefix.

Change the labels in the range B1..D1 to right-aligned (").

You enter: **/ Range Label Right B1..D1 [Return]**

Place the pointer into each of the three cells and note that the control panel shows the label-prefixes as ".

Local VS Global Commands

It's important that you understand that some commands can be thought of as **global** and some as **local**. Global commands affect all parts of the worksheet which do not have some specific local setting. A global setting will be taken unless that setting has been "stated otherwise" with a local-type command. For instance, a column will take the global column-width, unless it has been set locally with a /Worksheet Column Set-Width command. When entering labels, the global label-prefix will be taken unless a label-prefix is typed before the label, as when you typed ^ before TOTAL. As you have just seen, existing label-prefixes can be changed with a local /Range Label command.

/Worksheet Global Label

This is the global counterpart to /Range Label and changes the setting of the global label-prefix.

Releases 2, 2.01, 2.2, 2.3, and 2.4: In these releases, this command is /Worksheet Global Label-Prefix.

Change the global label-prefix to right and verify it.

You enter: **/ Worksheet Global Label Right**

You: **View the global settings.**

This global command is different from /Worksheet Global Format in that it does not change already existing label-prefixes. Note that the labels Nuts, Bolts, Screwdrivers, and TOTAL still have their previous label-prefixes. This command will only affect label-prefixes entered after its issuance.

To confirm the results, erase cell B1 and re-type it with no label-prefix.

You enter into B1: **/ Range Erase [Return] Sales [Return]**

The control panel shows that right-aligned (") was automatically assumed as the label-prefix. From now on, any new labels will also be given right-aligned by default.

Your worksheet should look like Figure 1-11.

```
B1: "Sales


              A              B         C       D        E         F         G
1                          Sales      Tax    Total
2
3      Nuts                $437.50
4      Bolts               $899.64
5      Screwdrivers         $76.23
6
7          TOTAL
8
```

Figure 1-11. Part II of Scranton Worksheet.

It is a very good practice to save your worksheets to disk often. Right now, if you were to lose power or if you happen to be on a network and the network went down, you would lose all the work you have done since the last /File Save. The SCRANTON file on disk still looks like Figure 1-3. All additions made to the worksheet since then do not automatically go to the disk. They are in RAM only which, again, is temporary and volatile. Save the file again under the same name.

You enter: **/ File Save**

Computer message: Enter save file name: B:\SCRANTON.WK1

1-2-3 is assuming you want the file saved under SCRANTON again and, in this case, this is a good assumption. Take the default filename by just tapping [Return].

You enter: **[Return]**

This Cancel Replace menu is reminding you that the file currently out on disk named SCRANTON (Figure 1-3) will be wiped out and replaced with the worksheet now in RAM and on the screen. 1-2-3 is making sure that you really want to erase the existing disk file and overwrite it. Choose the option Replace to do just that.

Releases 2.2, 2.3, 2.4, 3.0, and 3.1+:
An additional option exists on this menu - Backup. Choosing this option causes a copy of the old file on disk (Figure 1-3) to be written to a file named SCRANTON.BAK before this file is written to disk. In other words, the previous version of the file is saved as a backup as is common with other software packages, such as word processors.

You enter: **Replace**

The file which looked like Figure 1-3 is gone forever[2] and a file like Figure 1-11 has taken its place.

You enter: **/ File List Worksheet**

You: **Highlight SCRANTON.WK1**

The date, time and size in bytes have been updated.

You enter: **[Return]**

━━

WARNING: Some of you may be familiar with other software packages, such as word processors, that automatically keep the previous file version in a backup file on disk. Release 2.0 and 2.01 do NOT do this so be careful.

━━

I find that students who have never saved files on disk before have a tough time picturing files' contents and understanding file handling at first. If you feel this way, realize that with a little practice you will soon catch on. For you, I will make a few statements about files. You just saved a newer version of a file over an older version. If during the last /File Save command, instead of entering the filename SCRANTON, you entered a different filename, two files would then exist on the disk. One would look

---

[2]Actually, the file might not be gone forever if you use one of the special software programs available on the market today for recovering deleted files.

like Figure 1-3 under the name SCRANTON, the other like Figure 1-11 under the different filename. You would enter a different filename if you wanted to keep a copy of the older version of the file on the disk for future use. I saw no use in keeping Figure 1-3 around, so you overwrote it. Your disk has a finite storage capacity which, you'll find, gets used up too quickly. Therefore it's a good idea not to keep unneeded files around to clutter up space.

- - - If you need a break, stop at this point. - - -

If you are returning from a break, bring the SCRANTON file back into RAM by using /File Retrieve. Your screen should look like Figure 1-11.

Values

Values are numerical entries or formula entries which can be used in calculations. So, basically, there are two different types of entries: values and labels. You can think of labels as those entries which will not be used in computations such as words, titles, column headers, or even social security numbers. 1-2-3 treats values and labels differently and distinguishes between them by the first character that you type into the cell. If you type one of these characters first

$$0 \; 1 \; 2 \; 3 \; 4 \; 5 \; 6 \; 7 \; 8 \; 9 \; + \; - \; . \; (\; @ \; \# \; \$$$

1-2-3 assumes that you are entering a value. Any other character will cause 1-2-3 to assume the entry is a label.

While you enter 26.25 into cell C3, note that the mode indicator is set to VALUE immediately after you type the first character, 2.

You enter into C3: **26.25 [Return]**

$26.25 is displayed in the cell because the current global format is Currency with 2 decimal places.

Values are always right-aligned in cells, unlike labels which can be left-aligned, right-aligned, or centered.

Erase cell C3.

You enter into C3: **/ Range Erase [Return]**

NEVER ENTER A CONSTANT INTO A CELL WHEN THAT ENTRY DEPENDS UPON A VALUE IN ANOTHER CELL. Cell C3 depends on the contents of cell B3. This cell should contain a formula with an arithmetic operator showing the dependency.

Arithmetic Operators

The four arithmetic operator characters in 1-2-3 are as follows: addition, +; subtraction, -; multiplication, *; and division, /. Other operators and the order in which operations are done are described later in the text (see Precedence of Operations).

In Scranton, Pennsylvania, sales tax is 6%, therefore cell C3=6% of B3 or .06*B3. Enter this formula, recalling that its first character, . , is one of the characters which cues 1-2-3 that this is a value.

You enter into C3: **.06*B3 [Return]**

The B in B3 can be upper or lower case. B3 is called a cell address, or **cell reference**. B3 is the referenced cell. The cell containing the formula, cell C3, is called the formula cell.

Change the contents of B3.

You enter into B3: **500 [Return]**

Note that C3 is changed to reflect the new sales figure in B3. Your worksheet should look like Figure 1-12.

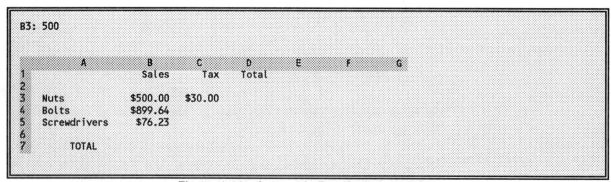

Figure 1-12. Automatic Recalculation of C3.

WARNING: Values should never be entered as labels.

This warning cannot be stressed enough! Many beginning Lotus users may enter the number 500 as [SpaceBar][SpaceBar]500[Return]. The first [SpaceBar] tells 1-2-3 that the entry is the label space space 500 which is completely different than the value 500. When used as a reference in other formula cells, the entry will be treated as the value 0, as all labels are, and the computation will be invalid.

Restore the original sales figure.

You enter into B3: **437.5 [Return]**

Continue entering the tax formulas.

You enter into C4: **.06*B4 [Down]**

You enter into C5: **.06*B5 [Return]**

Your worksheet should look like Figure 1-13.

In Lesson 3, you will learn that copying formulas is a much easier way to do these last two entries.

```
C5: 0.06*B5


              A              B        C        D        E        F        G
    1                     Sales      Tax    Total
    2
    3  Nuts             $437.50   $26.25
    4  Bolts            $899.64   $53.98
    5  Screwdrivers      $76.23    $4.57
    6
    7      TOTAL
```

Figure 1-13. Part III of Scranton Worksheet.

The Totals in column D are sums of Sales and Tax.

You enter into D3: **B3+C3 [Return]**

Surprise! What happened? Recall that 1-2-3 distinguishes between values and labels by the first character that you type. The first character here is a B, which causes 1-2-3 to assume label, not value. It thinks this is a word so it doesn't try to compute anything and displays it literally as entered. One possible remedy is adding a + before the B. + is one of the set of characters which cue 1-2-3 that this is a value, not a label.

You enter into D3: **+B3+C3 [Down]**

You enter into D4: **+B4+C4 [Down]**

You enter into D5: **+B5+C5 [Return]**

Again, it's a good idea to save your worksheet often.

You enter: **/ File Save [Return] Replace**

- - - If you need a break, stop at this point. - - -

Your worksheet should look like Figure 1-14.

```
D5: +B5+C5


          A              B         C         D        E        F        G
1                       Sales      Tax      Total
2
3    Nuts              $437.50   $26.25   $463.75
4    Bolts             $899.64   $53.98   $953.62
5    Screwdrivers       $76.23    $4.57    $80.80
6
7       TOTAL
```

Figure 1-14. Part IV of Scranton Worksheet.

Continue building Figure 1-2. What's wrong with entering B6 as shown below? Make sure you use the minus sign (-), not the underline character (_).

You enter into B6: **---------- [Return]**

The first character, -, cues 1-2-3 that this is a value which it actually is not. 1-2-3 tries to make sense of it and compute its value and gets confused. It puts you into EDIT mode, which you can see by the mode indicator.

EDIT Mode

When you make an entry which confuses 1-2-3, you are automatically placed in EDIT mode. EDIT mode allows you to modify the contents of a cell without having to re-type the entire entry. The blinking underline character on the input line is called a cursor and designates where the next typed character will be placed on the screen. In EDIT mode, you can edit the entry by moving the cursor with the [Right], [Left], [Home], and [End] keys to the position where characters are to be deleted or inserted. [BackSpace] and [Esc] work as stated before. The [Del] key can also be used, and deletes the character under the cursor whereas

[BackSpace] deletes the character before the cursor. [Ins] is a toggle key which causes an overlay indicator, OVR, to appear at the bottom of the screen. OVR signifies that characters typed will overlay and delete existing characters. By default (no OVR) existing characters to the right of the cursor move right as typed characters are inserted. ([F2/EDIT] can be used to enter EDIT mode and will be covered later in this lesson.)

1-2-3 is waiting in EDIT mode for you to remedy the problem. Move the cursor to the beginning (several [Left]'s or [Home] will do this) and add a label-prefix, such as right-aligned ("), before this entry to tell 1-2-3 that this is a label, not a value.

You enter: **[Home] " [Return]**

After all this, I now say that this label is less than desirable and should be thrown away.

You enter into B6: **/ Range Erase [Return]**

Realize that having a constant number of dashes will cause problems in the appearance of a flexible worksheet. Picture how it would look if column B's width had to be changed to 30. It would be cumbersome to have to edit that cell to add more dashes. (This is purely an aesthetic consideration and would really not cause logic or validity problems.) However, there is a label-prefix which takes care of this. The repeat label-prefix (\) is used to repeat the characters after it for the length of the cell. Re-enter the dashes using the \. Be careful not to type the forward slash (/) which you have previously used to pull up the main menu.

You enter into B6: **\- [Return]**

FLEXIBILITY IS VERY IMPORTANT TO GOOD WORKSHEET CONSTRUCTION. Worksheet structures will probably have to be changed occasionally, if not frequently, and it is good practice to build modifiability into them. Now column B can be changed to any width without having the worry about changing cell B6.

You enter into C6: **\- [Right]**

You enter into D6: **\- [Return]**

Other examples of how the repeat label-prefix works are as follows:

Contents of Cell	Cell Display
\a	aaaaaaaaa
\abc	abcabcabc
\-.	.-..-..-.
\ IBM	IBM IBM

You may enter the above into your worksheet if you wish. Do a /Range Erase to clear the cells you used.

What should the formula in B7 be?   +B3+B4+B5 is a possibility. However, let's be realistic here. Scranton Hardware would probably have hundreds, if not thousands, of items on the shelves. Who has time to type in a formula with that many terms? For this case, the @SUM function would be a more practical approach.

@ Functions

1-2-3 has many built-in functions to save you time and typing. To enter them, type @ (usually above the 2 on the keyboard) followed by the function name and a list of arguments separated by commas.

@functionname(argument1,argument2,...)

Some functions have no arguments. Arguments can be constants, cell addresses, ranges, labels, formulas, and other @ functions.

@SUM Function

For the moment, you will skip cell B7 and move to C7. In C7, you want the sum of the cells in the range C3..C5.

You enter into C7: **@SUM(C3..C5) [Return]**

Again, SUM can be typed in upper or lower case. It is important that you add no spaces before or after SUM or you will be placed in EDIT mode.

Your worksheet should look like Figure 1-15.

Release 2.4: This release is more accommodating to the problem that is discussed next. Set your global column-width to 7.

You enter: / Worksheet Global Column-Width 7 **[Return]**

```
C7: aSUM(C3..C5)


         A              B        C        D        E        F        G
                      Sales      Tax    Total
1
2
3   Nuts            $437.50   $26.25  $463.75
4   Bolts           $899.64   $53.98  $953.62
5   Screwdrivers     $76.23    $4.57   $80.80
6                            ------------------------------
7        TOTAL                 $84.80
```

Figure 1-15. @SUM Used for Tax TOTAL.

You enter into B7: **@SUM(B3..B5) [Return]**

The asterisks displayed in B7 signify that the value is too large to be displayed in a column of this width. Column B is taking the current global column-width of 9. You can locally set its width by using /Worksheet Column Set-Width or change the global column-width with /Worksheet Global Column-Width. The Total column, column D, will also need to be larger because cell D7's value will necessarily be greater than B7's. Therefore, use the global command.

You enter: / **Worksheet G**lobal **C**olumn-Width **15 [Return]**

I used a column-width of 15, which was larger than necessary to get rid of the asterisks, in order to allow for even larger numbers. Scranton Hardware's sales will probably increase in the future causing more digits in the sales figures. You want your worksheets to be as flexible as possible. If a secretary inexperienced in Lotus is keypunching numbers into your worksheet, you don't want asterisks to mysteriously appear. This can cause quite a stir in a office where nobody knows Lotus well.

You enter into D7: **@SUM(D3..D5) [Return]**

You enter: / **F**ile **S**ave **[Return] R**eplace

- - - If you need a break, stop at this point. - - -

Your worksheet should look like Figure 1-16.

Other types of arguments which can be used in @SUM are shown with their cell display results below. Use the worksheet in Figure 1-16 for values of cell references in the arguments. You may wish to type them into your worksheet and then erase them with /Range Erase.

```
D7: @SUM(D3..D5)


           A              B             C             D
1                       Sales          Tax         Total
2
3    Nuts              $437.50        $26.25       $463.75
4    Bolts             $899.64        $53.98       $953.62
5    Screwdrivers       $76.23         $4.57        $80.80
6                    -------------------------------------
7        TOTAL       $1,413.37        $84.80     $1,498.17
```

Figure 1-16. Part V of Scranton Worksheet.

Contents of Cell	Cell Display in Currency Format
@SUM(10,20,5)	$35.00
@SUM(B3,C3)	$463.75
@SUM(B3..B5,C3..C5)	$1,498.17
@SUM(B3,B4,10,B5,C3..C5)	$1,508.17

Table 1-1. Possibilities for @SUM Argument.

Insert a column to the left of column A in order to enter 1, 2, and 3 as shown in Figure 1-2. Perhaps you are concerned that the cell references in your formulas will have to be changed because of the movement of the cells after the column insertion. Not to worry. 1-2-3 will automatically adjust all cell references.

You enter: / **Worksheet Insert Column A1..A1 [Return]**

Your screen should look like Figure 1-17.

```
           A              B             C             D
1                                     Sales          Tax
2
3                    Nuts           $437.50       $26.25
4                    Bolts          $899.64       $53.98
5                    Screwdrivers    $76.23        $4.57
6                                 --------------------------
7                    TOTAL        $1,413.37       $84.80
```

Figure 1-17. Column Inserted to Left of Worksheet.

Column E scrolled off the right edge of the screen.

You enter into A3: **1 [Down]**

It is displayed as $1.00 due to the global format of currency. We'll correct this later.

You enter into A4: **2 [Down]**

You enter into A5: **3 [Return]**

Your screen should look like Figure 1-18.

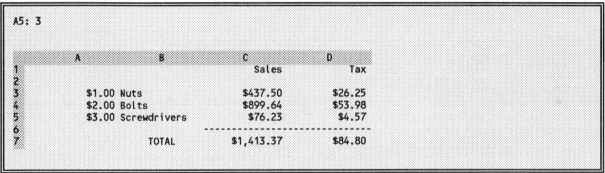

Figure 1-18. Column A Taking Global Format.

/Range Format

For the 3 cells in the range A3..A5, you must override the global currency format with the local command /Range Format. This command formats values within a specified range only.

Fixed Format

Fixed format is used to display values with a fixed number of decimal places. You need integers in A3..A5 which is the same as zero decimal places. Do a /Range Format command choosing Fixed format with 0 decimal places.

You enter: / **Range Format Fixed 0 [Return] A3..A5 [Return]**

Change column A's width to 3.

You enter into A5: / **Worksheet Column Set-Width 3 [Return]**

The only thing that must be added to your worksheet to complete Figure 1-2 is the title. Add two rows to the top of the worksheet.

You enter: **/ Worksheet Insert Row A1..A2 [Return]**

Observe Figure 1-2. The title is too large to fit in cell B1 because column B is only 15 characters wide. If you widen column B to 40 in order to fit the title, your spreadsheet would look as unbalanced as Figure 1-19 looks.

```
      A     B                      C              D         E
1           SCRANTON HARDWARE COMPANY, INCORPORATED
2
3                                   Sales       Tax      Total
4
5           1 Nuts                $437.50    $26.25    $463.75
6           2 Bolts              $899.64    $53.98    $953.62
7           3 Screwdrivers        $76.23     $4.57     $80.80
8                                 ------------------------------
9               Total          $1,413.37    $84.80 $1,498.17
```

Figure 1-19. Column B with width 40.

To remedy this problem, 1-2-3 lets labels "run into the next cell" if the next cell is empty.

Type the title. The label-prefix doesn't matter because the title is too long to be centered either way into B1. Label-prefixes only take affect when the label is smaller than the column width.

You enter into B1: **SCRANTON HARDWARE COMPANY, INCORPORATED [Return]**

Because cells C1 and D1 are empty, the title "runs over" into them. Although it is displayed in those cells, IT IS NOT STORED IN THOSE CELLS. Move the cell pointer back and forth in the first row while looking at the control panel until you are convinced that the entire title is stored only in cell B1. None of it is stored in cells C1 or D1 although it is displayed there.

You: **Move pointer into B1, C1, and D1 observing control panel.**

If you're not using WYSIWYG in the newer releases of 1-2-3, centering titles in worksheets is a pain in the neck. Note that your title is too far to the left. To move it farther right, you must add spaces before SCRANTON.

[F2/EDIT]

You have used EDIT mode before when 1-2-3 got confused about the dashes (---------) and automatically placed you there. To enter EDIT mode on your own in order to change the contents of a cell, the function key marked F2 is used. Find it on your keyboard and remember that I will use brackets and the function name, [F2/EDIT], to instruct you to depress it. Again, the most commonly used keys in EDIT mode are [Home], [End], [Right], [Left], [Esc], [BackSpace], [Del], and [Ins].

You enter into B1: **[F2/EDIT]**

Note that the mode indicator shows EDIT and a copy of cell B1's contents is placed on the input line with the cursor at the end.

Add spaces before SCRANTON to push it right.

You enter: **[Home] [Right] [SpaceBar] [SpaceBar] [Return]**

The title has been moved right two characters and is still far from being centered. Add more spaces.

You enter: **[F2/EDIT] [Home] [Right] [SpaceBar] 7 times. [Return]**

Releases 2.3 and 2.4, and 3.1+: In these new releases, WYSIWYG does a beautiful job of centering text. See appendices.

Finally your worksheet should look like Figure 1-2.

Save it under SCRANTON.WK1.

You enter: **/ File Save [Return]** Replace

When designing your worksheets, be wary of values that may need to be changed in the future. For example, in the SCRANTON worksheet, you may want to set up the tax rate in its own cell and compute the taxes using a cell reference to that cell. If the company changed states or the tax rate changed, it would only be necessary to change the entry in that one tax cell.

Did you ever sit through a movie twice? You pick up a lot more details the second time that you missed the first. Lesson 1 covers many new concepts. Because they are so vital to the rest of the text and to becoming proficient at 1-2-3, I strongly suggest you do Lesson 1 again.

You may think that it would be a waste of time, but in the long run you'll gain time and a deeper understanding while doing the other lessons.

NEW COMMAND SUMMARY

[F5/GOTO]	Causes pointer to jump to designated cell.
[BackSpace]	Erases character before the cursor.
[Esc]	In EDIT mode, erases entire entry. In MENU mode, returns to previous menu/READY mode.
/Range Erase	Erases a cell or range of cells.
/File Save	Save a copy of the current worksheet to disk.
/File List	Lists disk files.
/Worksheet Erase	Erases the entire worksheet.
/Quit	Returns to the Lotus Access System Menu.
/File Retrieve	Retrieves a worksheet file from disk.
/Worksheet Status	Displays status information of worksheet.
/Worksheet Global Format	Changes the format of all cells in the worksheet except those under control of a /Range Format command.
/Worksheet Insert Column	Inserts blank column(s) into the worksheet to the left of the designated range. The number of columns added is the same as the number of columns in the designated range.
/Worksheet Global Column-Width	Sets the column-width of all columns in the worksheet except those under control of the /Worksheet Column Set-Width command.
/Worksheet Column Set-Width	Sets the column-width of the single column the pointer is in.
/Worksheet Insert Row	Inserts blank row(s) into the worksheet above the designated range. The number of rows added is the same as the number of rows in the designated range.

/Range Label   Changes the label-prefixes in the designated range in cells that already contain labels.

/Worksheet Global Label   Sets the global label prefix. Only labels entered after this command is issued are affected; existing label-prefixes are not affected.

/Range Format   Changes the format of values in the designated range.

[F2/EDIT]   Allows the contents of the pointer cell to be changed.

EXERCISES

PART 1 EXERCISES

WORK - 2

Part 1 Exercises require the use of the 4 label-prefixes, at least 2 different formats, column-width adjustments, simple formulas, and @SUM.

1A. Create the worksheet below and save under the file name PROFIT. Adjust column widths when necessary. Use the repeat label-prefix in row 5. Enter constant values in B2..C4 and format them to Currency. Enter the proper formulas in D2..D4 which depend upon the values in columns B and C. Use @SUM in the TOTAL row.

	A	B	C	D	E
1	Period	Revenue	Expenses	Gross Profit	
2	1	$120,000	$89,000	$31,000	
3	2	$134,000	$94,000	$40,000	
4	3	$167,000	$102,000	$65,000	
5		---			
6	TOTAL	$421,000	$285,000	$136,000	

After saving the file, increase the value in B2 to $200,000. What other cells are affected by this change?

1B. Create the worksheet below and save under the file name RENT. Adjust column widths when necessary. Use the repeat label-prefix in row 7. Enter constant values in B4..C6. Enter the proper formulas in D4..D6 which depend on the values in columns B and C. Use @SUM in row 8.

	A	B	C	D
1		Square Feet	Rent per	Total
2	Department	Occupied	Square Foot	Rent
3				
4	Marketing	2500	$7.00	$17,500.00
5	Personnel	3000	$6.50	$19,500.00
6	Research	4700	$12.00	$56,400.00
7			-----------	-----------
8	TOTAL	10200	$25.50	$93,400.00

After saving the file, decrease the value in C6 to $10.00. What other cells are affected by this change?

1C. Create the worksheet below and save under the file name MAGZAD. Adjust column widths when necessary. Use the repeat label-prefix in row 8. Enter constant values in B4..C7. Enter the proper formulas in D4..D7 which depend on the values in columns B and C. Use @SUM in C9.

	A	B	C	D
1		Copies	Cost of	Cost per
2	Magazine	Sold	Ad	Copy
3				
4	Bicycles Illustrated	20000	$3,400	$0.17
5	Gardens and Terraces	13000	$1,600	$0.12
6	Chimneys Weekly	2100	$1,000	$0.48
7	Meadow and Creek	46000	$4,200	$0.09
8			------------	
9	TOTAL on Magazine Ads		$10,200	

After saving the file, increase the value in C5 to $2,000. What other cells are affected by this change?

1D. Create the worksheet below and save under the file name COOKIE. Adjust column widths when necessary. Use the repeat label-prefix in row 8. Enter constant values in B4..B7 and D4..D7. Each box of cookies costs $1.50; enter the proper formulas into C4..C7 which will depend on this cost and column B. Enter the proper formulas in E4..E7 which depend on the values in columns C and D. Use @SUM in row 9.

	A	B	C	D	E
1		Boxes	Total Price	Money	Balance
2	Girl Scout	Taken	of Boxes	Received	Due
3					
4	Alexis Tamkus	25	$37.50	$30.00	$7.50
5	Mary Buxton	30	$45.00	$45.00	$0.00
6	Anne Fisher	20	$30.00	$0.00	$30.00
7	Pattie Loughney	35	$52.50	$15.00	$37.50
8			-------	-------	-------
9	TOTAL	110	$165.00	$90.00	$75.00

After saving the file, decrease the value in D4 to $10.00. What other cells are affected by this change?

1E. Create the worksheet below and save under the file name VACUUM. Adjust column widths when necessary. Use the repeat label-prefix in row 10. Enter constant values in B7..D9. Enter the proper formulas in E7..E9 which depend on the values in columns C and D. Commission earnings are $40 for each unit sold (net); enter the proper formulas into F7..F9 which will depend on this commission amount and column E. The total earnings depend on the base salary and commission earnings. Use @SUM in row 11.

	A	B	C	D	E	F	G
1			ACME VACUUM CLEANER COMPANY				
2							
3					Net		
4		Base	Units	Units	Units	Commission	Total
5	Rep	Salary	Sold	Returned	Sold	Earnings	Earnings
6							
7	Smith	$240	10	2	8	$320	$560
8	Kochis	$190	2	2	0	$0	$190
9	Thorsten	$300	6	1	5	$200	$500
10				----			
11		$730	18	5	13	$520	$1,250

After saving the file, increase the base salary for Kochis to $250. What other cells are affected by this change? Increase Thorsten's Units Sold by 3. What cells are affected?

1F. Create the worksheet below and save under the file name JOURNAL1. Adjust column widths when necessary. Use the repeat label-prefix in rows 2, 4, 6, AND 16. Enter constant values in E7..G15. Use cell references in H7..I15. Use @SUM for totals. (See lesson on Dates and Times for the proper way to enter dates into 1-2-3 worksheets.)

	A B	C	D	E	F	G	H	I
1				JOURNAL				
2	==							
3					General		Cash	
4			Doc.	----------------		Sales	----------------	
5	Date	Account Title	No.	Debit	Credit	Credit	Debit	Credit
6	--							
7	July 1	Supplies	C1	15.50				15.50
8	1	Prepaid Ins.	C2	149.75				149.75
9	1	XYZ Comp.	C3	100.00				100.00
10	1	J. Smith, Capital	R1		400.00		400.00	
11	1	Daily Sales	T1			328.49	328.49	
12	1	Rent Expense	C4	400.00				400.00
13	2	Utilities Expense	C5	25.00				25.00
14	2	Daily Sales	T2			250.90	250.90	
15	2	Totals		$690.25	$400.00	$579.39	$979.39	$690.25
16				==				

1G. Create the worksheet below and save under the file name TRIAL. Adjust column widths when necessary. Use the repeat label-prefix in rows 5,7, and 19. Enter constant values in C8..D18. Use @SUM in row 20.

	A	B	C	D
1		BLAKELY GAS AND ELECTRIC		
2		WORKSHEET		
3		For Month Ended October 31, 1989		
4			Trial Balance	
5			---------------------	
6		Account Title	Debit	Credit
7		---		
8	1	Cash	47560.00	
9	2	Supplies	9130.00	
10	3	Prepaid Insurance	1300.00	
11	4	Acme Supply Company		10000.00
12	5	J. Smith, Capital		40000.00
13	6	J. Smith, Drawing	10000.00	
14	7	Sales		37890.00
15	8	Advertising Expense	5700.00	
16	9	Rent Expense	3500.00	
17	10	Supplies Expense	7900.00	
18	11	Utilities Expense	2800.00	
19			---------------------	
20			$87,890.00	$87,890.00

PART 2 EXERCISES

Part 2 Exercises require the knowledge of the difference between labels and values. They demand much use of label-prefixes to prevent 1-2-3 from assuming value-type data because of the first character entered into the cell. Formulas required are a little more complex than Part 1. Titles must be centered. Students are required to resolve which cells should contain formulas and constants.

2A. Create the worksheet below and save under the file name INVNTORY. If you are having trouble entering data into A5..A7 or F3, re-read the section from the lesson on Values.

	A	B	C	D	E	F
1			INVENTORY REPORT			
2						
3	Part	Beginning	Quantity	Ending	Cost per	$ Amount in
4	Number	Stock	Used	Inventory	Unit	Inventory
5	12A	102	21	81	3.49	$282.69
6	13B	56	4	52	5.00	260.00
7	14A	78	57	21	2.19	45.99
8						===============
9						$588.68

2B. Create the worksheet below and save under the file name ARCHBALD. If you are having trouble entering data into A7 or A9, re-read the sections from the lesson on Values and Label-Prefixes.

	A	B	C	D	E
1		ARCHBALD STATIONERY STORE			
2					
3		Price per	Units	Item	
4	Item	Unit	Sold	Total	
5					
6	Erasers	0.50	238	$119.00	
7	12-Pack Ink Pens	0.25	117	$29.25	
8	Lined Paper	2.30	62	$142.60	
9	"Hello" Buttons	1.99	175	$348.25	
10				-------------	
11	TOTAL SALES			$639.10	

2C. Create the worksheet below and save under the file name ADEXP. If you are having trouble entering data into A5..A7, re-read the sections from the lesson on Values and Label-Prefixes.

	A	B	C	D
1		ADVERTISING EXPENSES		
2				Cost per
3	Medium	Cost	Exposure	Exposure
4				
5	1st Radio News	$1,500	25000	0.060
6	"Howdy" Magazine	$2,400	13000	0.185
7	1989 County Fair	$5,400	100000	0.054
8		=======================		
9	TOTAL	$9,300	138000	

2D. Create the worksheet below and save under the file name POOL. If you are having trouble entering data into A7..A10, re-read the sections from the lesson on Values and Label-Prefixes.

	A	B	C	D	E	F
1		BLUE WATER				
2		POOL EQUIPMENT				
3						
4		Selling	Cost to	Gross	Quantity	Cost of
5	Item	Price	Store	Margin	On Hand	Inventory
6		===				
7	5 Oz. Chlorine Tabs	$16.95	$12.71	$4.24	100	$1,271.00
8	4000-Bristle Brush	29.99	17.24	12.75	24	413.76
9	PH Balance	5.99	4.49	1.50	35	157.15
10	"Hawaii" Lanterns	59.99	44.99	15.00	62	2789.38
11						===========
12						$4,631.29

2E. Create the worksheet below and save under the file name XYZEXP. If you are having trouble entering data into A7..A8, re-read the sections from the lesson on Values and Label-Prefixes.

	A	B	C	D
1	XYZ CORPORATION EXPENSE SHEET			
2				
3	Expense	Actual	Estimated	Difference
4				
5	Parts and Supplies	$2,394	$2,000	$394
6	Labor	1420	1500	-80
7	200 Main St. Utility Bills	755	800	-45
8	"Pocket" Change	472	200	272
9		=================================		
10	TOTAL	$5,041	$4,500	$541

2F. Create the worksheet below and save under the file name MAIL. If you are having trouble entering data into D6..D8 or A6..A7, re-read the sections from the lesson on Values.

	A	B	C	D	E	F	G
1			MAILING LIST				
2							
3	Soc Sec	Last	First				
4	Number	Name	Name	Address	Town	St.	Zip
5							
6	178-76-9527	Nagle	Sean	418 Cherry St.	Olyphant	PA	18447
7	016-36-5639	Cheney	Wilbur	214 Chestnut Ave.	Jessup	PA	18434
8	820-57-2876	Shelski	Lois	RD 3	Greentown	NJ	23987
9	174-43-1805	Zingle	Delores	Rear 507 Main St.	Hawley	PA	83564

PART 3 EXERCISES

Part 3 Exercises have formulas which are slightly more complicated than Part 2.

3A. Create the worksheet below and save under EMPPAY. Income tax cells contain constants. State tax is 2.1% of gross wages.

	A	B	C	D	E	F	G	H
1			NATIONAL SCAFFOLDING CORPORATION					
2			EMPLOYEE PAYROLL					
3								
4			Gross	Income	State	Other	Total	Net
5	Employee	Exemption	Wages	Tax	Tax	Deduct	Deduct	Pay
6								
7	Nagle	3-S	$450.00	32	9.45	30.00	71.45	$378.55
8	Cheney	1-M	$300.00	26	6.30	2.64	34.94	$265.06
9	Shelski	7-M	$239.71	12	5.03	13.47	30.50	$209.21
10	Zingle	0-S	$742.00	85	15.58	150.00	250.58	$491.42

3B. Create the worksheet below and save under STOCK.

	A	B	C	D	E	F
1			STOCK PORTFOLIO			
2						
3		NUMBER OF	PURCHASE	CURRENT	MARKET	
4	SYM	SHARES	PRICE	PRICE	VALUE	GAIN
5						
6	NBR	200	59.75	64.33	$12,866.00	$916.00
7	UGA	10	184.25	182.50	$1,825.00	($17.50)
8	WshW	500	49.66	55.00	$27,500.00	$2,670.00
9						------------
10						$3,568.50

3C. Create the worksheet below and save under PROJECT. Formulas in the projected column use the percentage difference between the two previous years.

	A	B	C	D	E
1		Projected 1989 Sales for Quarter 1			
2					
3		Actual	Actual	Projected	Division
4		1987 Qtr 1	1988 Qtr 1	1989 Qtr 1	Totals
5					
6	1st Division	$43.00	$44.50	$46.05	$133.55
7	2nd Division	37.00	37.00	$37.00	$111.00
8	3rd Division	58.00	54.00	50.28	$162.28
9		----------	----------	----------	----------
10	Total	$138.00	$135.50	$133.33	$406.83
11					

CUMULATIVE EXERCISES

The following worksheets will be modified and extended throughout the lessons. They are cumulative with regard to the first four lessons only. Cumulative exercises in Lessons 5 and beyond will require you to retrieve a worksheet created in one of the first four lessons. You don't have to worry about doing ALL previous lessons. For example, if you're doing a cumulative exercise in Lesson 11, you need only to have previously done the same exercise in Lessons 1-4. (Sometimes only Lesson 1's worksheet is required.)

C1. Create the worksheet below and save under TOFU1. Column E and rows 16 and 17 contain formulas, all other values are constants. Commission is 6% of sales. Name the 10 data rows (range A5..E14) REPS.

	A	B	C	D	E
1		IMITATION TOFU, INCORPORATED			
2					
3		SalesRep	Division	92 Sales	Commission
4		===			
5	1	Saxe, J.	2	$40,500	$2,430
6	2	Gress, R.	3	$77,000	$4,620
7	3	Cosner, L.	3	$23,400	$1,404
8	4	Smith, A.	1	$150,000	$9,000
9	5	Smith, B.	1	$54,700	$3,282
10	6	Kirlin, K.	2	$75,000	$4,500
11	7	Wodak, F.	1	$29,800	$1,788
12	8	Reese, J.	3	$111,300	$6,678
13	9	Gruss, M.	1	$88,200	$5,292
14	10	Boyle, T.	2	$67,600	$4,056
15				-----------------------	
16			Total	$717,500	$43,050
17			Average	$71,750	$4,305
18					
19		Total Sales minus Commissions =			$674,450
20					

C2. Create the worksheet below and save under FISH1. Enter all values as constants except those in columns F and G. Negative numbers under quantity sold designate returns. There was one turtle sold in the previous period which was returned by an irate father and a sad little girl, because the turtle died 20 minutes after they got it home and into its little bowl.

	A	B	C	D	E	F	G
1		HAPPY TROPICAL FISH STORE					
2	Item		Quantity	Retail	Wholesale	Profit	Total Pr.
3	#	Item Name	Sold	Price	Price	per Item	per Item
4		----------------					
5	273	7-inch fish net	63	$1.99	$0.70	$1.29	$81.27
6	238	1-lb. decorative rocks	49	$2.99	$1.30	$1.69	$82.81
7	130	underwater fern	13	$2.29	$0.90	$1.39	$18.07
8	281	40-gallon aquarium	14	$39.99	$22.00	$17.99	$251.86
9	162	goldfish	241	$0.59	$0.10	$0.49	$118.09
10	192	20-inch eel	4	$8.99	$4.00	$4.99	$19.96
11	274	2-gallon fish bowl	25	$4.99	$2.00	$2.99	$74.75
12	256	8-vitamin fish food	57	$1.79	$0.80	$0.99	$56.43
13	198	turtle	-1	$3.99	$1.50	$2.49	($2.49)
14	111	piranha	3	$10.99	$5.00	$5.99	$17.97
15	================						
16					Total Profit		$718.72
17							

PROFIT   D1 - E1

TOTAL PR   C1 * D1

C3. Create the worksheet below and save under BILL1. The values in B4..C12 are constants, all others are formulas.

	A	B	C	D	E
1		MONTHLY BILLS FOR MARCH			
2					
3		Actual	Budgeted	Over/(Under)	
4	Food	$238	$220	$18	
5	Rent	$550	$550	$0	
6	Phone	$39	$30	$9	
7	Electric	$43	$50	($7)	
8	Gasoline	$56	$45	$11	
9	Car Payment	$345	$345	$0	
10	Insurance	$55	$55	$0	
11	Charge Cards	$250	$100	$150	
12	Entertainment	$150	$100	$50	
13		---------			
14	Total	$1,726	$1,495	$231	
15					

C4. Create the worksheet below and save under GOLF1. All values are constants except those in column K and row 10.

	A	B	C	D	E	F	G	H	I	J	K
1			J & F	GOLF	COURSE	SCORE	SHEET				
2	Hole	1	2	3	4	5	6	7	8	9	Total
3	Par	4	5	4	3	5	4	4	3	4	36
4											
5	Joe	8	5	6	4	4	5	6	4	4	46
6	Mary	4	6	5	4	6	4	5	5	3	42
7	Mike	3	7	6	4	5	5	6	5	4	45
8	Sheila	5	5	6	4	3	3	4	6	5	41
9											
10	Average	5	5.75	5.75	4	4.5	4.25	5.25	5	4	43.5
11											

PRINTING WORKSHEETS

Contents:

Lesson 2 covers printing worksheets and parts of worksheets. The basic commands to get plain printouts are demonstrated. A printing problem I am sure you will run into is mentioned along with the solution. For more elaborate printing, see Lesson 19. Release 2.3, 2.4, and 3.1+ users have the WYSIWYG add-in for producing great output. See the WYSIWYG Appendix.

A **printout** of a worksheet is also called a **hard copy**. In this lesson, you will learn to send a hard copy of your worksheet to your printer. I assume that you are running stand alone (you are not on a network) with a printer connected directly to your PC. If your PC is on a network, the printouts will not be done immediately because you are sharing the network printers with other users. You should still follow my instructions, but you will have to observe the figures in order to determine exactly what is getting "printed" or sent to the network printer with each command.

If Figure 2-1 is not on your screen, retrieve the SCRANTON file.

	A	B	C	D	E
1		SCRANTON HARDWARE COMPANY, INCORPORATED			
2					
3			Sales	Tax	Total
4					
5		1 Nuts	$437.50	$26.25	$463.75
6		2 Bolts	$899.64	$53.98	$953.62
7		3 Screwdrivers	$76.23	$4.57	$80.80
8			--------------------------------------		
9		TOTAL	$1,413.37	$84.80	$1,498.17

Figure 2-1. Scranton Worksheet (Duplicate of Figure 1-2).

/Print Printer

Position the pointer to cell A1 and pull up the print menu.

You enter: **[Home] / Print Printer**

The print menu below should be on your screen:

Range Line Range Options Clear Align Go Quit

Releases 3.0 and 3.1+: There are 3 additional options between Go and Quit: Image, Sample and Hold.

Align

Position the paper to the top of the page in the printer or to just below the perforation if you are using continuous paper. Choose Align from the print menu.

You enter: **A**

1-2-3 keeps track of how many lines have been printed from the top of each page in order to tell when to eject the page. The Align options informs 1-2-3 to start counting at line 1.

Sticky Menus

The print menu is different from menus you have used before in that it remains on the screen. It is called a **sticky menu** because it sticks around in order to allow you to issue more than one option from it.

Range

1-2-3 does not assume you want the whole worksheet or all non-empty cells printed. You can print any range, from a single cell, to a row, to the entire worksheet. Let's start by printing the entire active worksheet or the range A1..E9. Choose the Range option.

You enter: **R**ange

Computer message: Enter Print range: A1

You enter: **A1..E9 [Return]**

Go

Now that the print range is designated, the only other option that MUST be issued for a hard copy is the Go option.

You enter: **G**o

Figure 2-2 has been sent to your printer. If it is a dot matrix, the print has already been done on the paper. If it is a laser, probably nothing happened because a complete page has not been filled. In other words,

```
          SCRANTON HARDWARE COMPANY, INCORPORATED

                      Sales          Tax         Total

     1 Nuts          $437.50       $26.25       $463.75
     2 Bolts         $899.64       $53.98       $953.62
     3 Screwdrivers   $76.23        $4.57        $80.80
                    ----------------------------------------
        TOTAL       $1,413.37      $84.80     $1,498.17
```

Figure 2-2. Part I of Scranton Printout.

Figure 2-2 is large enough to fill only about one quarter of a standard piece of paper. The laser would have printed just now if your worksheet was large enough to fill a whole page. Rest assured, Figure 2-2 will be at the top of the next printed page; for now, refer to the figures. (Some lasers are set up to eject a page after each Go and, if this is your case, a page has already been printed.) If you are on a network, you probably have to Exit from Lotus back to the operating system before any of your prints come out. Refer to the figures.

If your printer should be turned off or there is another problem, the mode indicator will flash **ERROR** and an error message will be displayed on the bottom line of the screen. Correct the problem, use [Esc] to return to **READY** mode, and issue Go again.

It should make sense to you, that the column headers A, B, C, etc. and row numbers are not included in the hard copy.

The two absolutely necessary commands which must be issued from the print menu to get a hard copy are Range and Go. I have found that one of the most common mistakes that students make is to forget to designate the range.

Each and every time the Go is issued a print is done. Issue Go again.

You enter: **Go**

The range is printed again immediately after the last print as is shown in Figure 2-3.

```
           SCRANTON HARDWARE COMPANY, INCORPORATED

                   Sales          Tax          Total

1 Nuts              $437.50        $26.25        $463.75
2 Bolts             $899.64        $53.98        $953.62
3 Screwdrivers       $76.23         $4.57         $80.80
                ------------------------------------------
        TOTAL      $1,413.37        $84.80      $1,498.17
           SCRANTON HARDWARE COMPANY, INCORPORATED

                   Sales          Tax          Total

1 Nuts              $437.50        $26.25        $463.75
2 Bolts             $899.64        $53.98        $953.62
3 Screwdrivers       $76.23         $4.57         $80.80
                ------------------------------------------
        TOTAL      $1,413.37        $84.80      $1,498.17
```

Figure 2-3. Parts I and II of Scranton Printout.

Note that no blank lines are automatically inserted by 1-2-3. The page is not automatically ejected to start each print on a new page. (On some configurations, the page might be ejected with each Go.)

Printing a Blank Line

Choosing the Line option from the print menu sends a blank line to the printer. Choose Line and follow it with another Go.

You enter: **Line Go**

Your printout should look like Figure 2-4.

```
         SCRANTON HARDWARE COMPANY, INCORPORATED

                    Sales           Tax          Total

1 Nuts             $437.50        $26.25        $463.75
2 Bolts            $899.64        $53.98        $953.62
3 Screwdrivers      $76.23         $4.57         $80.80
                 --------------------------------------
       TOTAL     $1,413.37        $84.80      $1,498.17
         SCRANTON HARDWARE COMPANY, INCORPORATED

                    Sales           Tax          Total

1 Nuts             $437.50        $26.25        $463.75
2 Bolts            $899.64        $53.98        $953.62
3 Screwdrivers      $76.23         $4.57         $80.80
                 --------------------------------------
       TOTAL     $1,413.37        $84.80      $1,498.17

         SCRANTON HARDWARE COMPANY, INCORPORATED

                    Sales           Tax          Total

1 Nuts             $437.50        $26.25        $463.75
2 Bolts            $899.64        $53.98        $953.62
3 Screwdrivers      $76.23         $4.57         $80.80
                 --------------------------------------
       TOTAL     $1,413.37        $84.80      $1,498.17
```

Figure 2-4. Parts I, II, and III of Scranton Printout.

Ejecting the Page

To move the printer carriage to the top of the next page, issue the Page option.

You enter: **Page**

As-Displayed Print Format

Observe cell D9 in the printout. Do you see that you really cannot tell what the actual contents of the cell is? It can be the constant 84.8, the formula +D5+D6+D7, the function @SUM(D5..D7), or even the label "$84.80. This print format is referred to as As-Displayed, because it looks similar to the worksheet as it is displayed on the screen.

Cell-Formulas Print Format

To see what is actually in cell D9, you could use the Cell-Formulas format, which prints formulas and local cell settings. Cell-Formulas format for the Scranton worksheet looks like Figure 2-5.

```
B1: [W15] "          SCRANTON HARDWARE COMPANY, INCORPORATED
C3: "Sales
D3: "Tax
E3: "Total
A5: (F0) [W3] 1
B5: [W15] 'Nuts
C5: 437.5
D5: 0.06*C5
E5: +C5+D5
A6: (F0) [W3] 2
B6: [W15] 'Bolts
C6: 899.64
D6: 0.06*C6
E6: +C6+D6
A7: (F0) [W3] 3
B7: [W15] 'Screwdrivers
C7: 76.23
D7: 0.06*C7
E7: +C7+D7
C8: \-
D8: \-
E8: \-
B9: [W15] ^TOTAL
C9: @SUM(C5..C7)
D9: @SUM(D5..D7)
E9: @SUM(E5..E7)
```

Figure 2-5. Cell-Formulas Format for Scranton Worksheet.

In Cell-Formulas format, each non-empty cell is printed on a separate line in a row by row fashion. In the Scranton worksheet, starting in cell A1 and going to the right through the first row, the first non-empty cell is B1. Figure 2-5's first line shows B1's contents including the label-prefix. The column-width indicator, [W15], shows that this column is of width 15 and will override the global column-width (whatever it may be). Note that column-width indicators are shown only in cells not taking the global column-width setting. Continuing in this row-wise fashion, the next non-empty cells are C3, D3, E3, etc.

The format display (F0) in cell A5 signifies that the 1 will be displayed in Fixed format with zero decimal places. Format displays are only shown in cells that have been /Range Formatted and are not taking the global format. Cells C5, D5, E5, etc. do not have format displays and are taking the global format (whatever it may be).

There really is no way of telling what the global settings, such as format and column-width, are by looking at a Cell-Formulas printout; only the local settings changed by commands such as /Range Formats and /Worksheet Column Set-widths are shown.

To print in Cell-Formulas format, you must go through a few sub-menus. The print menu should be on your screen.

You enter: **Options Other Cell-Formulas Quit**

You are back at the print menu. Issue Go and eject the page.

You enter: **Go Page**

Your printout should look like Figure 2-5.

Unless you change the print format setting, all printouts from now on will be in Cell-Formulas format.

WARNING: Don't forget to reset the Cell-Formulas format back to As-Displayed for the next print, if indeed you wish to print in As-Displayed format.

Change the print format setting back to As-Displayed.

You enter: **Options Other**

The menu below should be on your screen.

As-Displayed Cell-Formulas Formatted Unformatted

Releases 3.0 and 3.1+: Blank-Header is a new option on this menu. It allows or prevents the printing of blank lines in the margin at the top of a worksheet printout.

The As-Displayed and Cell-Formulas options on this menu are opposites of each other and choosing one automatically disables the other. The print format always takes on one of these two states; it's either one or the other. I will refer to options like this as **adjacent opposite options**.

You enter: **As-Displayed Quit**

Prints will now be displayed in As-Displayed format.

Print only the Sales and Tax columns of the worksheet. Choose Range and change the print range to C3..D9.

You enter: **Range**

Computer message: Enter Print range: A1..E9

The default range is the one most recently specified and is shown both after the prompt and highlighted on the screen.

You enter: **C3..D9 [Return]**

You enter: **Go**

Your printout should look like Figure 2-6.

```
        Sales           Tax

       $437.50        $26.25
       $899.64        $53.98
        $76.23         $4.57
    --------------------------------
     $1,413.37        $84.80
```

Figure 2-6. Part of the Scranton Worksheet - As-Displayed.

Send a blank line to the printer.

You enter: **Line**

Print the same range in Cell-Formulas format and eject the page.

You enter: **O**ptions **O**ther **C**ell-Formulas **Q**uit **G**o **P**age

Your printout page should look like Figure 2-7.

```
              Sales            Tax

            $437.50          $26.25
            $899.64          $53.98
             $76.23           $4.57
        - - - - - - - - - - - - - - - - - -
          $1,413.37          $84.80

        C3: "Sales
        D3: "Tax
        C5: 437.5
        D5: 0.06*C5
        C6: 899.64
        D6: 0.06*C6
        C7: 76.23
        D7: 0.06*C7
        C8: \-
        D8: \-
        C9: @SUM(C5..C7)
        D9: @SUM(D5..D7)
```

Figure 2-7. Part of the Scranton Worksheet - As-Displayed and Cell-Formulas.

/File Save saves all print settings, including the current print range and format. If you did a /File Save now and retrieved the file at a later time, a /Print Printer Go would produce the printout in Figure 2-8.

```
        C3: "Sales
        D3: "Tax
        C5: 437.5
        D5: 0.06*C5
        C6: 899.64
        D6: 0.06*C6
        C7: 76.23
        D7: 0.06*C7
        C8: \-
        D8: \-
        C9: @SUM(C5..C7)
        D9: @SUM(D5..D7)
```

Figure 2-8. Print with Current Settings.

With the print settings as they currently are, you would have to change the range and print format if you wished to make a hard copy like Figure 2-2 again.

Page-break Problem

You may sometime run into a problem in your printout similar to the one depicted in Figure 2-9.

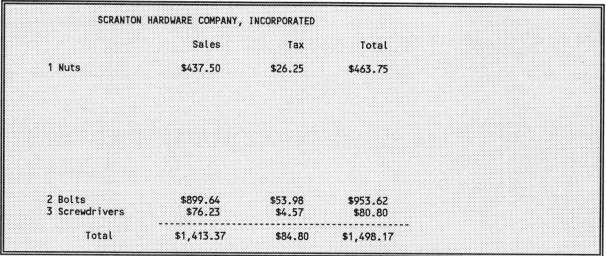

Figure 2-9. Page-break Problem in Formatted Printing.

Formatted and Unformatted Printing

The unwanted blank lines inserted into your printout are caused by 1-2-3 ejecting the page. When 1-2-3 thinks it is at the bottom of a page, it prints blank lines for the bottom margin, ejects the page, and prints more blank lines for the top of the next page's margin. If you wish to prevent page-breaks, you can go to the Options Other menu and choose Unformatted. This option sets an infinite page length and also suppresses headers and footers (see Advanced Worksheet Printing Lesson). Look at the Options Other menu:

You enter: **Options Other**

The menu below should be on your screen:

As-Displayed Cell-Formulas Formatted Unformatted

Recall that the As-Displayed and Cell-Formulas options are adjacent opposite options. Formatted and Unformatted are also adjacent opposite options. By default, printing is initially set to Formatted.

Return to the print menu.

[Esc] Quit

Other printing problems you may encounter are discussed in the Advanced Worksheet Printing Lesson.

Clear Print Settings

The Clear option will change the print settings from their current settings back to the default settings. The defaults are As-Displayed format and no range.

Choose Clear from the print menu:

Clear

You have a choice to clear all print settings or just some as you can see by this menu. Choose All:

[Return]

Return to ready mode:

Quit

Your spreadsheet is now exactly as it was when you began this lesson.

Those using a network might now have to exit 1-2-3 and Lotus and return to DOS to get your printouts.

NEW COMMAND SUMMARY

/Print Printer	Pulls up main print menu. Print will go to printer.
/Print Printer Align	Resets the line number to 1. Paper should be at the top of the page.
/Print Printer Range	Sets up the range to be printed.
/Print Printer Go	Prints a copy of the selected range on the printer according to all current print settings.
/Print Printer Line	Prints a blank line on the printer.
/Print Printer Page	Ejects the page on the printer so that the next print will start on the top of the next page.
/Print Printer Options Other As-Displayed	Prints the range in As-Displayed format or as it is displayed on the screen.
/Print Printer Options Other Cell-Formulas	Prints the range in Cell-Formulas format or one entry per line with local settings and formulas displayed.
/Print Printer Options Other Formatted	Printing is done with page-breaks, headers, footers, borders, and margins.
/Print Printer Options Other Unformatted	Printing of page-breaks, headers, footers, border, and margins is suppressed.
/Print Printer Clear	All print settings are reset to the defaults.

EXERCISES

PART 1 EXERCISES

Part 1 Exercises include printing in both As-Displayed and Cell-Formulas format.

1A. Print the PROFIT worksheet from the Lesson 1 exercises in both As-Displayed and Cell-Formulas format. Print only the range A1..B6 in both As-Displayed and Cell-Formulas format.

1B. Print the RENT worksheet from the Lesson 1 exercises in both As-Displayed and Cell-Formulas format. Print only the range A1..B8 in both As-Displayed and Cell-Formulas format.

1C. Print the MAGZAD worksheet from the Lesson 1 exercises in both As-Displayed and Cell-Formulas format. Print only the range D1..D7 in both As-Displayed and Cell-Formulas format.

1D. Print the COOKIE worksheet from the Lesson 1 exercises in both As-Displayed and Cell-Formulas format. Print only the range A1..B9 in both As-Displayed and Cell-Formulas format.

1E. Print the VACUUM worksheet from the Lesson 1 exercises in both As-Displayed and Cell-Formulas format. Print only the range F1..G11 in both As-Displayed and Cell-Formulas format.

PART 2 EXERCISES

Part 2 exercises require the use of the Page print command as well as As-Displayed and Cell-Formulas format.

2A. Make a hard copy of the INVNTORY worksheet from the Lesson 1 exercises in both As-Displayed and Cell-Formulas format beginning on separate pages.

2B. Make a hard copy of the ARCHBALD worksheet from the Lesson 1 exercises in both As-Displayed and Cell-Formulas format beginning on separate pages.

2C. Make a hard copy of the ADEXP worksheet from the Lesson 1 exercises in both As-Displayed and Cell-Formulas format beginning on separate pages.

2D. Make a hard copy of the POOL worksheet from the Lesson 1 exercises in both As-Displayed and Cell-Formulas format beginning on separate pages.

2E. Make a hard copy of the XYZEXP worksheet from the Lesson 1 exercises in both As-Displayed and Cell-Formulas format beginning on separate pages.

2F. Make a hard copy of the MAIL worksheet from the Lesson 1 exercises in both As-Displayed and Cell-Formulas format beginning on separate pages.

PART 3 EXERCISES

Part 3 exercises require the use of the Line print command as well as As-Displayed and Cell-Formulas format.

3A. Print the EMPPAY worksheet from the Lesson 1 exercises unformatted in both As-Displayed and Cell-Formulas format with 2 blank lines between the two different formats.

3B. Print the STOCK worksheet from the Lesson 1 exercises unformatted in both As-Displayed and Cell-Formulas format with 2 blank lines between the two different formats.

3C. Print the PROJECT worksheet from the Lesson 1 exercises unformatted in both As-Displayed and Cell-Formulas format with 2 blank lines between the two different formats.

CUMULATIVE EXERCISES

C1. Print the TOFU1 worksheet from Lesson 1 in both As-Displayed and Cell-Formulas format on two separate pages. Then print only the range C16..E17 in both formats with two blank lines between the formats.

C2. Print the FISH1 worksheet from Lesson 1 in both As-Displayed and Cell-Formulas format on two separate pages. Then print only the range A3..G5 in both formats with two blank lines between the formats.

C3. Print the BILL1 worksheet from Lesson 1 in both As-Displayed and Cell-Formulas format on two separate pages. Then print only the range A12..D14 in both formats with two blank lines between the formats.

C4. Print the GOLF1 worksheet from Lesson 1 in both As-Displayed and Cell-Formulas format on two separate pages. Then print only the range A7..C10 in both formats with two blank lines between the formats.

COPYING AND MOVING RANGES

Contents:

This lesson covers the copying and moving of cells, which are two of the most essential commands in the use of 1-2-3. Definition of a range and how to designate a range by both the endpoint method and point mode is illustrated. Range names and the /Range Name commands are explained. Earlier than most Lotus books, /Data Fill is introduced in order to set up activity worksheets with a minimum of typing.

Start with a blank worksheet. Remember that /Worksheet Erase should be used, not /Range Erase, because it clears everything including "unseen" settings.

	A	B	C	D	E	F	G
1	1	5	9				
2	2	6	10				
3	3	7	11				
4	4	8	12				

Figure 3-1. Worksheet for Practicing Copies and Moves.

/Data Fill

Figure 3-1 can be built very easily with the /Data Fill command, which is used to enter values in a sequence where each number differs from the previous number by a constant.

You enter: **/ Data Fill**

Computer message: Enter Fill range: A1

You enter: **A1..C4 [Return]**

Computer message: Start:

The start value is the beginning number in the sequence which will be placed in the first cell of the range. In Figure 3-1, 1 should be placed into cell A1.

You enter: **1 [Return]**

Computer message: Step: 1

The step value is the incremental value by which the successive numbers will differ. Figure 3-1's differ by 1, therefore hit [Return] to take the default in the prompt.

You enter: **[Return]**

Computer message: Stop: 8191

The stop value in the figure is 12.

You enter: **12 [Return]**

Your screen should look like Figure 3-1.

The /Data Fill command stops when either the end of the range is reached or the stop value is reached, whichever comes first. Therefore you could have taken the default stop value of 8191 with the same results, because it would have stopped at cell C4. Note that if there is more than one column in the range, the numbers are entered in a column by column fashion.

The three values given to the /Data Fill command need not be positive or integer. Formulas and @ functions can be used for the values.

Place the pointer in cell A1, if it is not already there, because I'm going to assume that pointer position when you retrieve the file later in this lesson.

You enter: **[Home]**

Save the worksheet as it exists now in a file names LES3.

You enter: / File Save **LES3 [Return]**

/Copy

The /Copy command is used to make copies of a cell or cells to other cells in the worksheet.

Copying a Single Cell

To become familiar with the /Copy command, copy a single cell, B1, to another single cell, E7.

You enter: / **Copy**

Releases 2.3 and 2.4:
Computer message: Copy what? A1..A1
Releases 2, 2.01, 2.2, 3.0, and 3.1+:
Computer message: Enter range to copy FROM: A1..A1

1-2-3 is asking what range you want a copy of, which I'll call the FROM range. You're copying from B1.

You enter: **B1 [Return]**

Releases 2.3 and 2.4:
Computer message: To where? A1
Releases 2, 2.01, 2.2, 3.0, and 3.1+:
Computer message: Enter range to copy TO: A1

Your "TO range" is the single cell, E7.

You enter: **E7 [Return]**

Cell E7 now contains the value 5.

Copy a single cell, A3, to a range of cells, B10..G18.

You enter: / **Copy A3 [Return] B10..G18 [Return]**

Your worksheet should look like Figure 3-2.

```
A1: 1


          A         B         C         D         E         F         G         H
1         1         5         9
2         2         6        10
3         3         7        11
4         4         8        12
5
6
7                                                 5
8
9
10                  3         3         3         3         3         3
11                  3         3         3         3         3         3
12                  3         3         3         3         3         3
13                  3         3         3         3         3         3
14                  3         3         3         3         3         3
15                  3         3         3         3         3         3
16                  3         3         3         3         3         3
17                  3         3         3         3         3         3
18                  3         3         3         3         3         3
```

Figure 3-2. Copying a Single Cell.

Copying a Row Range

Retrieve LES3.

You enter: / **File** Retrieve **LES3 [Return]**

Releases 2.3 and 2.4: A No Yes menu pops up to warn you that you have made changes to the worksheet which have not been saved. A /File Retrieve command first clears the worksheet before it retrieves a file, thereby losing your changes. Answer **Yes** to this menu now and for the rest of this lesson.

Your screen should look like Figure 3-1 again. Note that the /File Retrieve command actually does a /Worksheet Erase when it retrieves the file.

WARNING: In Releases 2, 2.01, 3.0, and 3.1+, don't forget to save your files before you retrieve a file. Again, you will eventually make this mistake. Live and learn. The newer releases prevent this by requiring you to confirm.

Copy the row range, A2..C2, to E1.

You enter: / Copy **A2..C2 [Return] E1 [Return]**

Copy the row range, A2..C2, to the range B8..H10.

You enter: / Copy **A2..C2 [Return] B8..H10 [Return]**

Your worksheet should look like Figure 3-3.

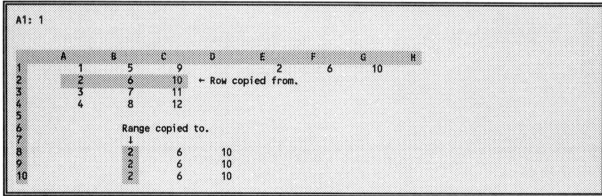

Figure 3-3. Copying a Row Range.

When copying a row range, the number of copies generated is equal to the number of rows in the TO range. The number of columns in the TO range is irrelevant. In the previous example there were 3 rows, 8, 9, and 10, in the TO range B8..H10, therefore 3 copies were made even though 3 more copies could have fit in E8..G10. If the TO range were B8..B10, the same copy would have resulted.

Copying a Column Range

Retrieve the LES3 file again.

You enter: / **File Retrieve LES3 [Return]**

The rules for copying a column range are similar to those for copying a row range. The number of copies generated is equal to the number of columns in the TO range; the number of rows in the TO range is insignificant.

You enter: / Copy **B1..B4 [Return] F2 [Return]**

You enter: / Copy **C1..C3 [Return] A10..E10 [Return]**

Your screen should look like Figure 3-4.

```
A1: 1

         A        B        C        D        E        F        G
  1      1        5        9
  2      2        6       10                          5
  3      3        7       11  ← Column copied from.    6
  4      4        8       12                          7
  5                                                   8
  6
  7
  8
  9
 10      9        9        9        9        9      ← Range copied to.
 11     10       10       10       10       10
 12     11       11       11       11       11
```

Figure 3-4. Copying a Column Range.

Start again with a fresh Figure 3-1. Begin to issue a /File Retrieve but do not type the file name yet.

You enter: **/ File Retrieve**

Note that the names of all files you have created are shown on the third line in the control panel. Instead of typing "LES3 [Return]", you can use the highlight and [Return] method to choose the file you want to retrieve. This method is similar to the highlight and [Return] method for choosing options from a menu. Use the [Right] or [Left] arrow key to highlight LES3.WK1 and hit [Return].

You: **Highlight LES3.WK1. [Return]**

Some releases come with several sample files. You may have to hit the [Right] arrow key several times to find LES3. Hitting [F3/NAME] will cause the file names to be displayed full screen. Try it.

Releases 2.3 and 2.4: LES3.WK1 can be picked by using the mouse.

Copying a Two-dimensional Range

When you copy a range with more than one row and more than one column, one copy will be generated in the TO range regardless of the size of the TO range.

You enter: **/ Copy A1..C4 [Return] B9..G19 [Return]**

You enter: / **Copy A1..C4 [Return] E4 [Return]**

Your screen should look like Figure 3-5.

	A	B	C	D	E	F	G	H
1	1	5	9					
2	2	6	10					
3	3	7	11					
4	4	8	12		1	5	9	
5					2	6	10	
6					3	7	11	
7					4	8	12	
8								
9		1	5	9				
10		2	6	10				
11		3	7	11				
12		4	8	12				

Figure 3-5. Copying a Two-dimensional Range.

WARNING: Be careful when copying large ranges as you might unintentionally copy over some important cells in the TO range.

You enter: / **Copy A1..C5 [Return] B7 [Return]**

Cells B9..D11 in the TO range were wiped out. The blank cells in row 5 of the FROM range were copied over cells B11..D11.

Your screen should look like Figure 3-6.

```
A1: 1


        A        B        C        D        E        F        G        H
1       1        5        9
2       2        6        10
3       3        7        11
4       4        8        12                1        5        9
5                                          2        6        10
6                                          3        7        11
7                1        5        9        4        8        12
8                2        6        10
9                3        7        11
10               4        8        12
11
12               4        8        12
```

Figure 3-6. Copying over Non-empty Cells.

- - - If you need a break, stop at this point. - - -

/Move

/Move is used to move a range of cells. Retrieve the LES3 file.

You enter: / **File Retrieve   Highlight LES3.WK1 [Return]**

Move the range A2..B3 to C7.

You enter: / **Move**

Releases 2.3 and 2.4:
Computer message: Move what? A1..A1
Releases 2, 2.01, 2.2, 3.0, and 3.1+:
Computer message: Enter range to move FROM: A1..A1

The FROM range is A2..B3.

You enter: **A2..B3 [Return]**

Releases 2.3 and 2.4:
Computer message: To where? A1
Releases 2, 2.01, 2.2, 3.0, and 3.1+:
Computer message: Enter range to move TO: A1

The TO range begins at cell C7.

You enter: **C7 [Return]**

Your worksheet should look like Figure 3-7.

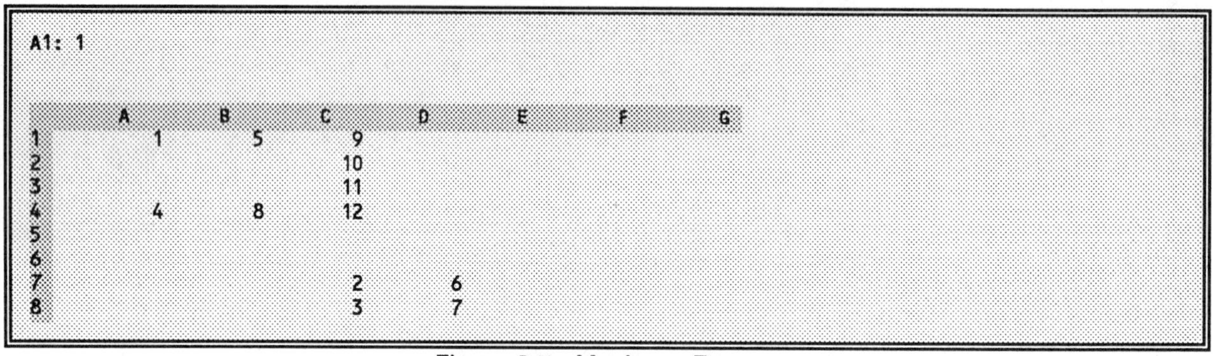

```
A1: 1

         A         B         C         D         E         F         G
1        1         5         9
2                            10
3                            11
4        4         8         12
5
6
7                            2         6
8                            3         7
```

Figure 3-7. Moving a Range.

The /Move command differs from the /Copy command in that the FROM range has been erased with /Move but remains intact with /Copy.

It is also possible, of course, to move a single cell or a very large range.

———

WARNING: Be careful when moving large ranges as you might unintentionally wipe out important cells in the TO range.

———

You enter: **/ Move A1..A2 [Return]   C7 [Return]**

Cells C7 and C8 were cleared and replaced with the previous contents of A1..A2. When blank cells are moved, they clear the corresponding cells in the TO range, as A2's contents cleared C8's in this last example. Your worksheet should look like Figure 3-8.

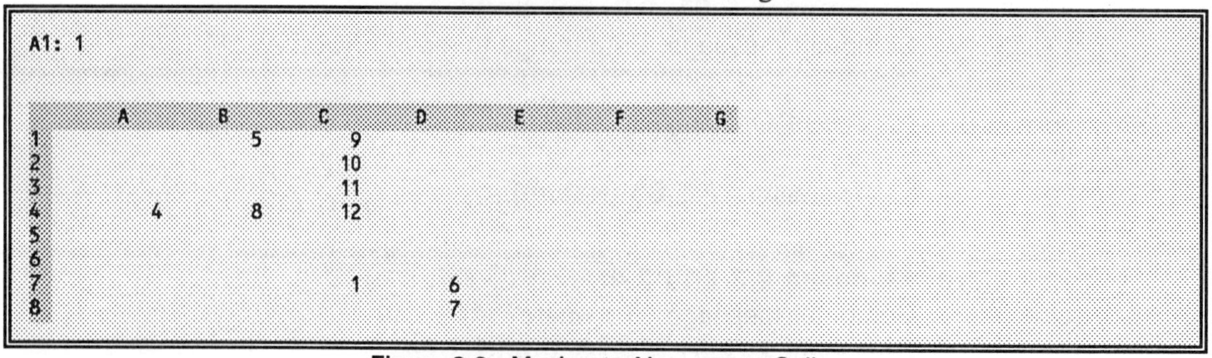

```
A1: 1

         A         B         C         D         E         F         G
1                  5         9
2                            10
3                            11
4        4         8         12
5
6
7                            1         6
8                                      7
```

Figure 3-8. Moving to Non-empty Cells.

- - - If you need a break, stop at this point. - - -

Pointing to Ranges

1-2-3 is a visually oriented program. You have seen evidence of this when using the Highlight and [Return] method of choosing an option from a menu. Highlighting options using the arrow keys plays on your sense of sight. The pointing method for ranges does this also.

Pull up the LES3 file again.

You enter: **/ File Retrieve LES3 [Return]**

Begin to make a copy of A1..C4 to E4 but don't type the range designation yet.

You enter: **/ Copy**

The mode indicator in the control panel shows POINT.

To point to ranges, the pointer movement keys such as [Right], [Left], [Up], [Down], and [Home] can be used. Use the [Down] arrow key to begin highlighting the FROM range A1..C4.

You enter: **[Down]**

Note that the default range in the prompt has changed to A1..A2 to correspond to the highlighted range. Finish highlighting the FROM range by using the arrow keys.

You enter: **[Down] [Down] [Right] [Right]**

It is very clear to the eye exactly which range will be copied. [Return] tells 1-2-3 you are finished pointing to the FROM range.

You enter: **[Return]**

Use the arrow keys to move to the TO range, E4.

You enter: **[Right] [Right] [Right] [Right]**

You enter: **[Down] [Down] [Down]**

The pointer should now be in cell E4 and the default range in the prompt should say E4.

You enter: **[Return]**

Your screen should look like Figure 3-9.

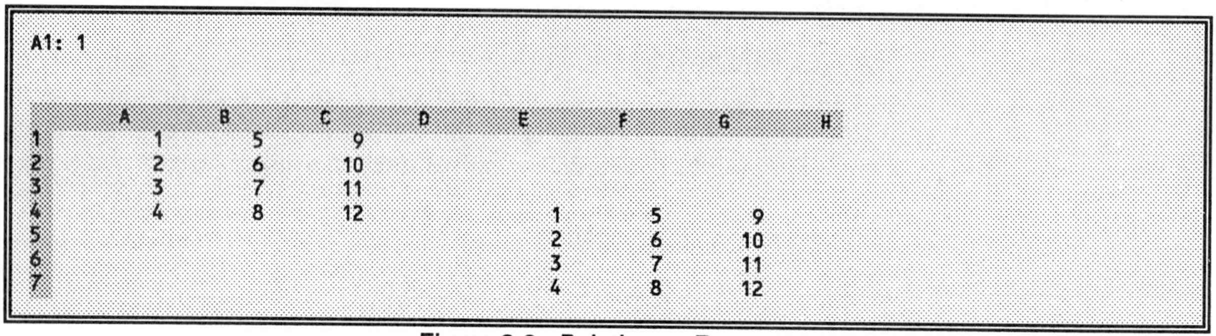

Figure 3-9. Pointing to Ranges.

Let's point to the range A1..C4 again in order to gain a full understanding of how POINT mode works.

You enter: / **Copy [Down] [Down] [Down] [Right] [Right]**

The range in the prompt should be A1..C4.

Recall from Lesson 1 that the endpoints of the diagonal of the range are the two cells which uniquely determine the range. The first endpoint listed in the prompt A1..C4, in this case the A1, is called the **anchor cell**. The second endpoint, in this case C4, is called the **free cell** and is the cell which moves and expands or contracts the highlighted range when the pointer movement keys are typed. The free cell will always be listed second in the prompt and will also always have a blinking cursor shown in the cell.

Releases 3.0 and 3.1+: Cursor is shown in free cell but does not blink.

While you enter the next few arrow keys, note that the second endpoint (designating the free cell) changes in the prompt as the cell with the cursor moves.

You enter: **[Right] [Down] [Up] [Left]**

Let's say at this point you wish to point to the range A2..C4. Do you see that it would be impossible to do so with just the arrow keys? Actually, you need to change the anchor or first endpoint from A1 to A2.

The period (.) key is used to move the anchor to another corner of the range. Try it.

You enter: **.**

Note that the cursor has moved to an adjacent corner and the prompt has been updated to show the new anchor and free cells. Remember that the anchor cell is always diagonally across from the blinking cursor in the free cell. Repeatedly hit the . key while watching the default range in the prompt until you get the hang of it.

You enter: **. several times.**

Releases 2.3, 2.4, 3.0, and 3.1+: The reverse video (or colored) bars on the borders clearly show the row and column of the free cell.

Our purpose is to highlight A2..C4, so use the . until the default range is C4..A1.

You enter: **. until C4..A1 is shown in prompt.**

Move the free cell into cell A2.

You enter: **[Down]**

Voila! A2..C4 is the FROM range. Actually it is shown as C4..A2 which is the same unique range.

For a little practice, let's start again with the range A1..C4 as the highlighted range and default range in the prompt.

You enter: **[Esc] [Esc]**

The main menu should be on your screen. Choose Copy.

You enter: **Copy**

You enter: **[Down] [Down] [Down] [Right] [Right]**

The range in the prompt should be A1..C4. Now take some time and try to highlight B2..C3.

You: **Highlight B2..C3 in POINT mode.**

Below is one possible series of keystrokes to accomplish the above highlighting.

You enter: **[Esc] [Esc] Copy**

You enter: **[Down] [Down] [Down] [Right] [Right]**

The range in the prompt should be A1..C4.

You enter: **[Up] . . [Down] [Right]**

The range in the prompt should be C3..B2.

To change C3..B2 to B2..C3, use the period.

You enter: **. .**

You enter: **[Esc] [Esc] Copy**

The range in the prompt should be A1..A1.

An easier way to highlight B2..C3 is to use [Esc] to clear the default anchor and free cell.

You enter: **[Esc]**

The range in the prompt should be A1.

The [Esc] key cleared both the anchor and free cells as you can see in the prompt. Move the pointer to cell B2.

You enter: **[Down] [Right]**

The range in the prompt should be B2.

To set the anchor cell to the current pointer cell, type the period key.

You enter: **.**

The range in the prompt should be B2..B2. Now move the free cell to C3.

You enter: **[Down] [Right]**

B2..C3 should be the highlighted range.

If you should again want to clear the anchor and free cells to start from scratch, use the [Esc] key.

You enter: **[Esc]**

You can now move the pointer to a new anchor cell and use the . key to anchor it.

You: **Return to READY mode using [Esc].**

The point method can be used with many other commands. You can point to a range anytime 1-2-3 asks for a range designation. You can also point to cell references in formulas and @ functions. To see examples of this, pull up the SCRANTON worksheet.

You enter: **/ File Retrieve SCRANTON [Return]**

Erase cell E5.

You enter into E5: **/ Range Erase [Return]**

Recall that the formula in cell E5 is +C5+D5. Enter the first character of the formula, +.

You enter into E5: **+**

Now use the left arrow key to point to the first cell reference in the formula, C5.

You enter: **[Left] [Left]**

To tell 1-2-3 that this cell is the one, type the next character in the formula, the second +.

You enter: **+**

In the control panel, the formula so far is **+C5+**. Point to the last cell reference, D5.

You enter: **[Left]**

Enter this formula with the [Return].

You enter: **[Return]**

You'll now do the same with the @SUM(E5..E7) in E9.

You enter into E9: **/ Range Erase [Return]**

You enter into E9: **@SUM([Up] [Up] [Up] [Up] . [Down] [Down])
[Return]**

Once you get some practice pointing to ranges, you may find that you much prefer this method instead of typing in the endpoints. For most of the text, I will state the range designations as I have been doing, but you may point to them. In fact, I would prefer that you point to them rather than type them, because it is easy to see mistakes in range designations by looking at the highlighting. In my opinion, you become a more proficient and effective user of 1-2-3 by using the point method.

Releases 2.3 and 2.4:

In these new releases, a range could be preselected with the fourth function key, [F4/POINT]. The preselected range will be used in subsequent commands. The range is unselected with pointer movement or [Esc].

In the SCRANTON worksheet place the cell pointer in cell B5.

You enter: **[F4/POINT]**

Computer message: Range: B5..B5

You enter: **[Down] [Down]**

The range in the prompt should be B5..B7.

You enter: **[Return]**

Note that the range B5..B7 is highlighted. Commands issued now will take this range as the default until the cell pointer is moved or [Esc] is pressed.

You enter: /Copy **[Return]**

The control panel shows: Copy what? B5..B7   To where? B5

The default FROM range is B5..B7. You must now designate only the TO range.

You enter: **B15 [Return]**

The default range was copied. Now enter a few more commands (how about /Range Label or /Move) and note that the default range will be remembered until you move the cell pointer or hit [Esc]. Don't save the SCRANTON file; leave it on disk as it was.

Release 2.3 and 2.4: Mouse users can point to ranges by clicking on the anchor cell and dragging to highlight the range. Try it with the two formulas you just entered.

- - - If you need a break, stop at this point. - - -

/Range Name Create

Pull up the LES3 file again.

You enter: / File Retrieve **LES3 [Return]**

It is possible to give names to ranges. Name the range A1..C4 KERMIT.

You enter: / **Range Name Create**

Computer message: Enter name:

Releases 3.0 and 3.1+: Computer message: Enter name to create:

You enter: **KERMIT [Return]**

Upper or lower case is irrelevant.

Computer message: Enter range: A1..A1

You enter or point to: **A1..C4 [Return]**

Although there is no indication on the screen, the range A1..C4 is known as KERMIT to 1-2-3 and KERMIT can be used as a range designation.

You enter: / **Move**

You can now enter the range name rather than typing or pointing to the range.

You enter: **KERMIT [Return]**

Move the range to B6.

You enter or point to: **B6 [Return]**

Your screen should look like Figure 3-10.

	A	B	C	D	E	F	G
1							
2							
3							
4							
5							
6		1	5	9			
7		2	6	10			
8		3	7	11			
9		4	8	12			

Figure 3-10. Moving a Named Range.

The name KERMIT is now associated with B6..D9. It moved with the range.

Of course you can use KERMIT for any command needing a range designation.

You enter: **/ Copy KERMIT [Return] A12 [Return]**

You can enter a range name in formulas and functions.

You enter into A1: **@SUM(KERMIT) [Return]**

Your worksheet should look like Figure 3-11.

A1: @SUM(KERMIT)

	A	B	C	D	E	F	G
1	78						
2							
3							
4							
5							
6		1	5	9			
7		2	6	10			
8		3	7	11			
9		4	8	12			
10							
11							
12	1	5	9				
13	2	6	10				
14	3	7	11				
15	4	8	12				

Figure 3-11. Named Range Copied and Used in @SUM Function.

The range name remains with the FROM range after a /Copy. B6..D9 still as the name KERMIT, not A12..C15.

Range names can be used to jump to a cell quickly with the [F5/GOTO].

You enter: **[F5/GOTO]**

Computer message: Enter address to go to: A1

You enter: **KERMIT [Return]**

The pointer jumps to the upper left corner of the named range, B6.

/Range Name Labels

/Range Name Labels sets up labels as range names to cells adjacent to them. Enter the labels shown in Figure 3-12.

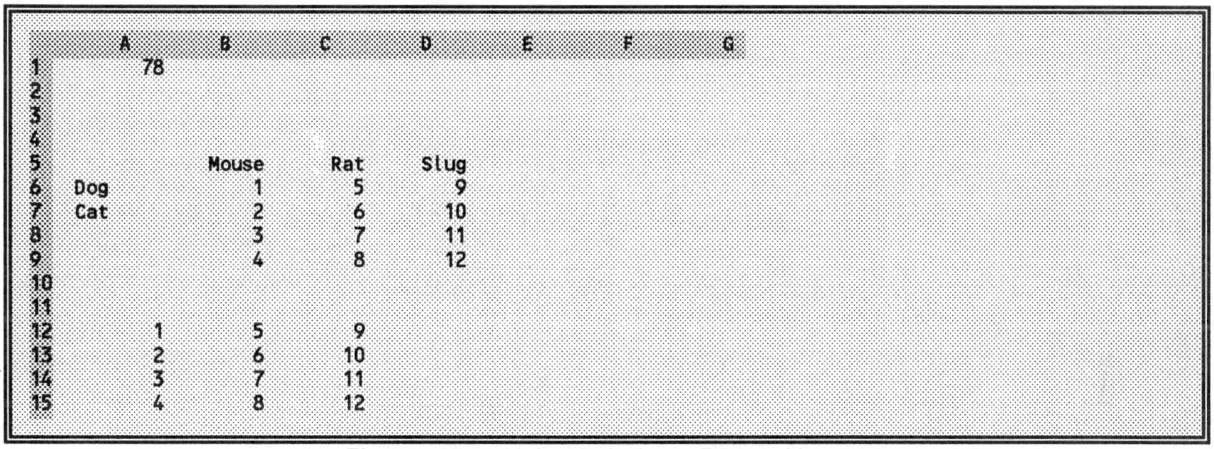

	A	B	C	D	E	F	G
1	78						
2							
3							
4							
5		Mouse	Rat	Slug			
6	Dog	1	5	9			
7	Cat	2	6	10			
8		3	7	11			
9		4	8	12			
10							
11							
12	1	5	9				
13	2	6	10				
14	3	7	11				
15	4	8	12				

Figure 3-12. Using Labels as Range Names.

You enter into A6: **Dog [Down]**

You enter into A7: **Cat [Return]**

You enter: / **W**orksheet **G**lobal **L**abel-Prefix **R**ight

You enter into B5: **Mouse [Right]**

You enter into C5: **Rat [Right]**

You enter into D5: **Slug [Return]**

After the next command, B6 will be named DOG and B7 will be named CAT.

You enter: / **R**ange **N**ame **L**abels **R**ight

Computer message: Enter label range:

You enter: **A6..A7 [Return]**

The labels in the designated range are used as names for the cells to their right.

The following command will associate Mouse with B6, Rat with C6, and Slug with D6.

You enter: **/ Range Name Labels Down B5..D5 [Return]**

/Range Name Table

/Range Name Table is used to get an alphabetized list of all range names and their associated cells.

You enter: **/ Range Name Table F2 [Return]**

Your screen should look like Figure 3-13.

	A	B	C	D	E	F	G
1	78						
2						CAT	B7
3						DOG	B6
4						KERMIT	B6..D9
5		Mouse	Rat	Slug		MOUSE	B6
6	Dog	1	5	9		RAT	C6
7	Cat	2	6	10		SLUG	D6
8		3	7	11			
9		4	8	12			
10							
11							
12	1	5	9				
13	2	6	10				
14	3	7	11				
15	4	8	12				

Figure 3-13. Table of Range Names Beginning in F2.

Releases 3.0 and 3.1+: Both endpoints are given in the table, even if the range is a single cell.

A quicker way to ascertain which range is associated with a name is to issue a /Range Name Create and note the default range.

You enter: **/ Range Name Create Cat [Return]**

Computer message: Enter range: B7

The B7 in the prompt is the range currently associated with CAT. You may have noticed that a list of current range names is listed on the third line in the control panel after the /Range Name Create was issued. Instead of typing "CAT", you could have used the highlight and [Return] method for choosing names.

You: **[Esc] back to READY mode.**

If the labels used to create range names with /Range Name Labels are deleted, the range names still exist. For example if you erased B5..D5, B6 would still have the name MOUSE, C6 would still have the name RAT, and D6 would still have the name SLUG.

/Range Name Delete

/Range Name Delete is used to clear a range name.

You enter: **/ Range Name Delete Mouse [Return]**

Instead of typing, you could have used the highlight and [Return] method for designating the name. The name MOUSE no longer exists. Verify it by trying to move it.

You enter: **/ Move Mouse [Return]**

Computer message: Invalid cell or range address

Releases 2.3, 2.4, 3.0 and 3.1+: When errors occur in these releases, the computer message adds a prompt to use the on-screen HELP facility by hitting [F1/HELP]. Help about the error will be shown on the screen. Try it.

The mode indicator flashes ERROR and the error message above is displayed on the last line of the screen. Clear ERROR mode with [Esc].

You enter: **[Esc]**

[F3/NAME]

When 1-2-3 is prompting you for a range, the [F3/NAME] key can be used to bring up a list of current range names on the third line in the control panel.

You enter: / **Copy**

The copy command is prompting you for a range.

You enter: **[F3/NAME]**

All current range names appear below the prompt. You may now type the name or use highlight and [Return] to designate it. [F3/NAME] is probably used more commonly to remember what a range is named, rather than for the convenience of using highlight and [Return]. Of course, anytime 1-2-3 is prompting your for a range, not just during the /Copy command, [F3/NAME] can be used.

Releases 2.2, 2.3, 2.4, 3.0, and 3.1+: At this point, hitting [F3/NAME] again will show a full screen of range names. You can see where this would come in handy if you had several dozen range names in a worksheet. Try it.

[F3/NAME] will work only when 1-2-3 is prompting you for a range.

You: **[Esc] back to READY mode.**

You enter: **[F3/NAME]**

An error beep is issued because 1-2-3 is not currently prompting you for a range.

Releases 2.2, 2.3, 2.4, 3.0, and 3.1+: [F3/NAME] will also show a full screen of file names when typed after /File Retrieve.

/Range Name Reset

The Reset option erases ALL existing range names and therefore should be used with much caution.

NEW COMMAND SUMMARY

/Data Fill	Enters a sequence of numbers which differ by a constant into a range.
/Copy	Makes a copy of a cell or cell range.
/Move	Moves a cell or cell range.
/Range Name Create	Associates a name with a range of cells.
/Range Name Labels	The labels in a range are used to name cells adjacent to them. The range designated contains the labels, and the cells to be named are either above, below, to the right, or to the left of the designated label range.
/Range Name Table	Creates a table of all existing range names in the worksheet, beginning at the designated range.
/Range Name Delete	Deletes an existing range name associated with a range of cells.
[F3/NAME]	Lists all existing range names on the third line of the screen when 1-2-3 is prompting you for a range. Also used to list filenames during /File Retrieve command.
/Range Name Reset	Deletes all existing range names. Be careful with this command.

EXERCISES

PART 1 EXERCISES

Part 1 Exercises can be considered "finger exercises".
They allow practice of the copy command.

1A. Create the worksheet below and save under L3ONEA. Change the global column width to 3 and issue only 2 copy commands. (The values 1 and 2 should be entered only once each.)

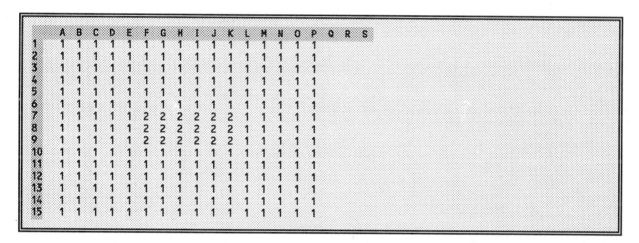

1B. Create the worksheet below and save under L3ONEB. Change the global column width to 3. Enter 1, 2, and 3 exactly once and issue only 3 copy commands.

1C.   Create the worksheet below and save under L3ONEC. Set the global column width to 1, enter the 3 characters exactly once, and use only 3 copy commands.

```
    ABCDEFGHIJKLMNOPQRST
1   <.><.><.><.>
2   <.><.><.><.>
3   <.><.><.><.>
4   <.><.><.><.>
5   <.><.><.><.>
6   <.><.><.><.>
7   <.><.><.><.>
8   <.><.><.><.>
9   <.><.><.><.>
10  <.><.><.><.>
```

1D.   How could you enter the values in column B in the worksheet blow if you wanted to save time and keystroking?

```
         A              B
1   COURSE          CREDITS
2   Accounting         3
3   Biology            4
4   Chemistry          3
5   Economics          3
6   Marketing          3
7   Physics            4
8   Basket-weaving     3
9   Tennis             3
10  Engineering        3
11  Psychology         3
12  Art                3
13  Reading            3
14  Writing            3
15  Arithmetic         3
```

PART 2 EXERCISES

Part 2 exercises require the use of /Data Fill and /Copy.

2A.   Create the worksheet below and save under L3TWOA. Use /Data Fill, /Copy, and the repeat label-prefix.

```
    A B C D E F G H I J K L M N
1        1 2 3 4 5 6 7 8 9 10
2         +---------------------------
3     1   |
4     2   |
5     3   |
6     4   |
7     5   |
8     6   |
9     7   |
10    8   |
11    9   |
12   10   |
```

2B.   Create the worksheet below and save under L3TWOB. Use /Data Fill, /Copy, and the repeat label-prefix.

```
       A         B         C         D         E         F
1     1985      1986      1987      1988      1989      1990
2  -----------------------------------------------------------
3
```

2C.   Create the worksheet below and save under L3TWOC. Use /Data Fill, /Copy, and the repeat label-prefix.

```
       A       B    C    D        E         F         G
1                            Quarter
2                       1        2         3         4
3                   +-------------------------------------
4             1985  |
5             1986  |
6             1987  |
7             1988  |
8    Year     1989  |
9             1990  |
10            1991  |
11            1992  |
12            1993  |
13            1994  |
```

PART 3 EXERCISES

Part 3 exercises require /Move and /Range Name Create as well as other previously used commands. Some require the movement of columns as well as rows.

3A. Create the worksheet below and save under L3THREEA. Use one /Data Fill, one /Copy, and one /Move command. Name the range to be moved and use its name during the issuance of the /Move command.

	A	B	C	D	E	F
1	10	10	10	10	10	10
2	20	20	20	20	20	20
3	30					
4	40					
5	50					
6	60	60	60	60	60	60
7	70	70	70	70	70	70
8	80	80	80	80	80	80
9	90	90	90	90	90	90
10	100	100	100	100	100	100
11						
12		30	30	30	30	30
13		40	40	40	40	40
14		50	50	50	50	50

3B. Create the worksheet below and save under L3EMPPAY. Retrieve the EMPPAY worksheet from Lesson 1 and modify it to look like the worksheet below. Do not re-enter any data; instead, use /Move and insert and delete rows and columns. Name any ranges to be moved and use their names during the issuance of the /Move command.

	A	B	C	D	E	F	G	H
1			NATIONAL SCAFFOLDING CORPORATION					
2			EMPLOYEE PAYROLL					
3								
4		Gross		Other	Total	Income	State	Net
5	Employee	Wages	Exemptions	Deduct	Deduct	Tax	Tax	Pay
6								
7	Cheney	$300.00	1-M	2.64	34.94	26	6.30	$265.06
8	Nagle	$450.00	3-S	30.00	71.45	32	9.45	$378.55
9	Shelski	$239.71	7-M	13.47	30.50	12	5.03	$209.21
10	Zingle	$742.00	0-S	150.00	250.58	85	15.58	$491.42

3C. Create the worksheet below and save under L3STOCK. Retrieve the STOCK worksheet from Lesson 1 and modify it to look like the worksheet below. Do not re-enter any data; instead, use /Move and insert and delete rows and columns. Name any ranges to be moved and use their names during the issuance of the /Move command.

	A	B	C	D	E	F
1			STOCK PORTFOLIO			
2						
3		CURRENT	PURCHASE	NUMBER OF	MARKET	
4	SYM	PRICE	PRICE	SHARES	VALUE	GAIN
5						
6	WshW	55.00	49.66	500	$27,500.00	$2,670.00
7	UGA	182.50	184.25	10	$1,825.00	($17.50)
8	NBR	64.33	59.75	200	$12,866.00	$916.00
9						------------
10						$3,568.50

3D. Create the worksheet below and save under L3PROJ. Retrieve the PROJECT worksheet from Lesson 1 and modify it to look like the worksheet below. Do not re-enter any data; instead, use /Move and insert and delete rows and columns. Name any ranges to be moved and use their names during the issuance of the /Move command.

	A	B	C	D	E
1		Projected 1989 Sales for Quarter 1			
2					
3		Projected	Actual	Actual	Division
4		1989 Qtr 1	1988 Qtr 1	1987 Qtr 1	Totals
5					
6	3rd Division	50.28	54.00	58.00	$162.28
7	2nd Division	$37.00	37.00	37.00	$111.00
8	1st Division	$46.05	$44.50	$43.00	$133.55
9		----------	----------	----------	----------
10	Total	$133.33	$135.50	$138.00	$406.83

3E.   Create the worksheet below.

```
        A              B          C
1  ART PREACHER'S SEAFOOD RESTAURANT
2
3  Department        1987       1988
4  --------------------------------
5  Appetizers        $900     $1,100
6  Fish               $70        $80
7  Desserts           $53        $43
8  Beverages          $17        $15
9  Soup               $30        $37
10 Salad             $250       $305
11                          --------------
12                   $1,320   $1,580
```

Save it on disk. Now change the above worksheet to look like the one below without re-entering any data. Name any ranges to be moved and use their names during the issuance of the /Move command.

```
        A              B          C
1  ART PREACHER'S SEAFOOD RESTAURANT
2
3  Department        1987       1988
4  --------------------------------
5  Appetizers        $900     $1,100
6  Soup               $30        $37
7  Salad             $250       $305
8  Fish               $70        $80
9  Desserts           $53        $43
10 Beverages          $17        $15
11                          --------------
12                   $1,320   $1,580
```

Make sure the values in B12 and C12 are correct. You will use the worksheet above in the next lesson; save it on disk under the name SEAFOOD.

PART 4 EXERCISES

Part 4 exercises use /Range Name Labels.

4. This exercise demonstrates a trick used to assign several range names in one shot to cells not adjacent to range labels. You will probably not appreciate the procedure until you actually need it.

   Retrieve the SCRANTON file. Name the cell B1 TITLE with /Range Name Create. Insert a column between columns D and E. Copy B5..B7 to the new column, same rows. Use /Range Name Labels to create names for the Total values in column F. Delete the new column. Do a /Range Name Table to range C12. Your worksheet should look like the one below.

```
          A        B              C              D              E
                    SCRANTON HARDWARE COMPANY, INCORPORATED
1
2
3                                 Sales          Tax            Total
4
5    1 Nuts                      $437.50        $26.25         $463.75
6    2 Bolts                     $899.64        $53.98         $953.62
7    3 Screwdrivers               $76.23         $4.57          $80.80
8                    ------------------------------------------------
9            TOTAL             $1,413.37        $84.80       $1,498.17
10
11
12                   BOLTS          E6
13                   NUTS           E5
14                   SCREWDRIVERS   E7
15                   TITLE          B1
```

CUMULATIVE EXERCISES

C1. Create the worksheet below by retrieving TOFUL1 from Lesson 1. Move the range named REPS to A1. Use /Worksheet Delete Row to delete all rows below the Boyle, T. row. Use exactly two /Copy commands to replicate division 3's data in rows 12 through 14 as shown below. Save under TOFU3.

	A	B	C	D	E	F
1	1	Saxe, J.	2	$40,500	$2,430	
2	2	Gress, R.	3	$77,000	$4,620	
3	3	Cosner, L.	3	$23,400	$1,404	
4	4	Smith, A.	1	$150,000	$9,000	
5	5	Smith, B.	1	$54,700	$3,282	
6	6	Kirlin, K.	2	$75,000	$4,500	
7	7	Wodak, F.	1	$29,800	$1,788	
8	8	Reese, J.	3	$111,300	$6,678	
9	9	Gruss, M.	1	$88,200	$5,292	
10	10	Boyle, T.	2	$67,600	$4,056	
11						
12	2	Gress, R.	3	$77,000	$4,620	
13	3	Cosner, L.	3	$23,400	$1,404	
14	8	Reese, J.	3	$111,300	$6,678	
15						

C2.   Create the worksheet below by retrieving the FISH1 worksheet you created in Lesson 1. Copy the 200 items to rows 18 through 22 by issuing exactly 3 /Copy commands. Move the 100 items to rows 24 to 28 by issuing exactly 3 /Move commands. The Total Profit in row 16. Save under FISH3.

	A	B	C	D	E	F	G
1		H A P P Y T R O P I C A L F I S H S T O R E					
2	Item		Quantity	Retail	Wholesale	Profit	Total Pr.
3	#	Item Name	Sold	Price	Price	per Item	per Item
4	---	---	---	---	---	---	---
5	273	7-inch fish net	63	$1.99	$0.70	$1.29	$81.27
6	238	1-lb. decorative rocks	49	$2.99	$1.30	$1.69	$82.81
7							
8	281	40-gallon aquarium	14	$39.99	$22.00	$17.99	$251.86
9							
10							
11	274	2-gallon fish bowl	25	$4.99	$2.00	$2.99	$74.75
12	256	8-vitamin fish food	57	$1.79	$0.80	$0.99	$56.43
13							
14							
15		==					
16							
17							
18	273	7-inch fish net	63	$1.99	$0.70	$1.29	$81.27
19	238	1-lb. decorative rocks	49	$2.99	$1.30	$1.69	$82.81
20	281	40-gallon aquarium	14	$39.99	$22.00	$17.99	$251.86
21	274	2-gallon fish bowl	25	$4.99	$2.00	$2.99	$74.75
22	256	8-vitamin fish food	57	$1.79	$0.80	$0.99	$56.43
23							
24	130	underwater fern	13	$2.29	$0.90	$1.39	$18.07
25	162	goldfish	241	$0.59	$0.10	$0.49	$118.09
26	192	20-inch eel	4	$8.99	$4.00	$4.99	$19.96
27	198	turtle	-1	$3.99	$1.50	$2.49	($2.49)
28	111	piranha	3	$10.99	$5.00	$5.99	$17.97
29							

C3. Modify the BILL1 worksheet that you created in Lesson 1 to look like the worksheet below. Insert a column to the left of Actual and move the Budgeted column into that new column. To save keystrokes, instead of entering the April Actual column cell by cell, copy the March column and change the values that are different. Delete the Over/(Under) column. Save under BILL3.

	A	B	C	D	E
1		MONTHLY BILLS			
2					
3			March	April	
4		Budgeted	Actual	Actual	
5	Food	$220	$238	$222	
6	Rent	$550	$550	$550	
7	Phone	$30	$39	$40	
8	Electric	$50	$43	$45	
9	Gasoline	$45	$56	$52	
10	Car Payment	$345	$345	$345	
11	Insurance	$55	$55	$55	
12	Charge Cards	$100	$250	$170	
13	Entertainment	$100	$150	$150	
14		--------------------------			
15	Total	$1,495	$1,726	$1,629	
16					

C4. Create the worksheet below by retrieving the GOLF1 worksheet that you created in Lesson 1. Copy Joe's and Mike's scores to rows 12 and 13. Move Mary's and Sheila's scores to rows 15 and 16. Erase row 10. Save under GOLF3.

	A	B	C	D	E	F	G	H	I	J	K
1		J & F GOLF COURSE SCORE SHEET									
2	Hole	1	2	3	4	5	6	7	8	9	Total
3	Par	4	5	4	3	5	4	4	3	4	36
4											
5	Joe	8	5	6	4	4	5	6	4	4	46
6											
7	Mike	3	7	6	4	5	5	6	5	4	45
8											
9											
10											
11											
12	Joe	8	5	6	4	4	5	6	4	4	46
13	Mike	3	7	6	4	5	5	6	5	4	45
14											
15	Mary	4	6	5	4	6	4	5	5	3	42
16	Sheila	5	5	6	4	3	3	4	6	5	41
17											

MORE ON FORMATTING VALUES

Contents:

This lesson covers the various formats for the display of values and the concept that the original accuracy of an entered value is not altered because of the format display. /Copy is used with the [End]-Arrow combination several times for practice in using this time-saving feature. Other topics included are resetting format and column-width settings, hiding columns and zero values, on-screen HELP, and /System.

Begin with a blank worksheet and create the worksheet shown in Figure 4-1 by following the steps below.

	A	B	C	D	E	F	G
1	General	Fixed	Scien.	Currency	,	Percent	
2							
3	100	100	100	100	100	100	
4	14.55	14.55	14.55	14.55	14.55	14.55	
5	1.3	1.3	1.3	1.3	1.3	1.3	
6	-25	-25	-25	-25	-25	-25	
7	0.12345	0.12345	0.12345	0.12345	0.12345	0.12345	
8	9.9999	9.9999	9.9999	9.9999	9.9999	9.9999	
9	-0.5	-0.5	-0.5	-0.5	-0.5	-0.5	
10	123456.7	123456.7	123456.7	123456.7	123456.7	123456.7	

Figure 4-1. Worksheet for Formatting Values.

First change the global label-prefix to right.

You enter: **/ Worksheet Global Label Right**

You enter: **Labels in Row 1 of Figure 4-1.**

You enter: **Values in Column A of Figure 4-1.**

Your worksheet should look like Figure 4-2.

```
A10: 123456.7


        A        B        C        D        E        F        G
 1   General    Fixed   Scien.  Currency     ,     Percent
 2
 3      100
 4     14.55
 5      1.3
 6      -25
 7    0.12345
 8    9.9999
 9     -0.5
10   123456.7
```

Figure 4-2. Incomplete Figure 4-1.

Copy the values in column A to the other five columns to finish creating Figure 4-1.

You enter: **/ Copy A3..A10 [Return] B3..F3 [Return]**

Your worksheet should look like Figure 4-1.

In this lesson, you will change your worksheet to look like Figure 4-3.

```
F3: (P1) [W11] 100


        A          B          C          D          E          F
 1   General     Fixed     Scien.    Currency       ,       Percent
 2
 3      100    100.0000  1.00E+02    $100.00      100.0    10000.0%
 4     14.55    14.5500  1.46E+01     $14.55       14.6     1455.0%
 5      1.3      1.3000  1.30E+00      $1.30        1.3      130.0%
 6      -25    -25.0000 -2.50E+01    ($25.00)     (25.0)   -2500.0%
 7    0.12345    0.1235  1.23E-01      $0.12        0.1       12.3%
 8    9.9999     9.9999  1.00E+01     $10.00       10.0     1000.0%
 9     -0.5     -0.5000 -5.00E-01     ($0.50)      (0.5)     -50.0%
10   123456.7 123456.7000 1.23E+05 $123,456.70 123,456.7 12345670.0%
```

Figure 4-3. Worksheet with Different Formats.

General, Fixed, and Currency formats were discussed in Lesson 1. Use /Range Format to change the values' formats under the Fixed and Currency column headers.

You: **Move Pointer to B3.**

You enter: **/ Range Format Fixed 4 [Return] B3..B10 [Return]**

Display Format

A **display format** is shown in the control panel for all cells which have been /Range Formatted and therefore are not under control of the global default format. The display format, (F4), in the control panel indicates Fixed format with 4 decimal places. The accuracy of the number you enter is not lost because of the appearance of the cell. If you had originally entered a number with 5 digits of accuracy and the display format is only 4, the original accuracy remains in the cell. 0.12345 is currently displayed in cell B7 as 0.1235, but .12345 is actually still stored in the cell. In the future, if you change the display format to 5 decimal places, the original number in B7 with all of its accuracy will be displayed. The full accuracy is used in calculations regardless of the display format. The asterisks in B10, you'll recall, show that 123456.7000 cannot fit in the column-width. Widen column B to 12, 11 characters are needed plus 1 for spacing.

You: **Verify pointer is in column B.**

You enter: **/ Worksheet Column Set-Width 12 [Return]**

The column-width indicator, [W12], is shown in the control panel.

[End]-Arrow Key Combination

[End] is a toggle key which can be used in combination with an arrow key to quickly move to the end of a column of numbers. Format the currency column using the [End] key in POINT mode to designate the range.

You: **Move pointer to D3.**

You enter: **/ Range Format Currency [Return] [End]**

An END indicator is shown on the bottom of the screen.

You enter: **[Down] [Return]**

As in this case, if the pointer is in a non-empty cell, [End] followed by an arrow key moves the pointer to the last non-empty cell before an empty cell in the direction of the arrow. If the pointer is in an empty cell, [End] and an arrow key moves the pointer to the first non-empty cell in that direction.

[End] [Home] moves the pointer to the end of the active area, where the active area is defined to be the smallest range beginning at cell A1 containing all non-empty cells in the worksheet.

You enter: **[End] [Home]**

The cell pointer moves to the end of the active area, cell F10.

This key combination is useful when you wish to print the entire worksheet; put the pointer in A1, do a / Print Printer Range, hit [End] [Home] and your range designation is the entire non-empty worksheet.

You: **Move pointer to D10.**

(C2) is the display format shown in the control panel.

Clear those asterisks in D10.

You enter: / **Worksheet Column Set-Width [Right] [Right] [Right] [Return]**

Scientific Format

Format column C in scientific format with 2 decimal places.

You: **Move pointer to C3.**

You enter: / **Range Format Scientific [Return] [End] [Down] [Return]**

You enter: / **Worksheet Column Set-Width [Right] [Return]**

(S2) is the display format. The 2 decimal places are the ones in the mantissa or after the decimal point and before the E. Compare the numbers in column C with the originals in column A. In C3, 1.00E+02 means 1.00 times 10 raised to the positive 2 power. 1.00 times 100 is 100 as in A3. In C9, -5.00 times 10 raised to the negative 1 power is -5 times .1 equals -.5 as in A9.

Comma (,) Format

Comma format inserts commas and shows negative numbers in parentheses.

You: **Move pointer to E3.**

You enter: / **Range Format , 1 [Return] E3..E10 [Return]**

You enter: / **Worksheet Column Set-Width 11 [Return]**

(,1) is the display format.

Percent Format

Percent format displays a percent sign after the number times 100.

You: **Move pointer to F3.**

You enter: / **Range Format Percent 1 [Return] F3..F10 [Return]**

You enter: / **Worksheet Column Set-Width 11 [Return]**

(P1) is the display format. Compare F3 to A3; 100 is 10000%. Compare the others.

Your worksheet should look like Figure 4-3. Use this figure in the future as a reference to decide which formats to use in your worksheets.

Most display formats have 1 character and 1 digit such as (F1), (S2), (C2), etc. The writers of 1-2-3 were clever when they used format names with unique first characters as they did with the menu options.

Save the file under the name FORMATS.

You enter: / **File Save FORMATS [Return]**

- - - **If you need a break, stop at this point.** - - -

Retrieve the SCRANTON file.

You enter: / File Retrieve **SCRANTON [Return]**

Text Format

Text format displays the formulas in the cells, not the results of the computation. Format the values in column E of the worksheet in Text.

You enter into E5: / **Range Format Text E5..E9 [Return]**

Your worksheet should look like Figure 4-4.

```
        A        B            C              D              E
1                    SCRANTON HARDWARE COMPANY, INCORPORATED
2
3                              Sales           Tax          Total
4
5       1 Nuts               $437.50        $26.25  +C5+D5
6       2 Bolts              $899.64        $53.98  +C6+D6
7       3 Screwdrivers        $76.23         $4.57  +C7+D7
8                          ---------------------------------------
9            TOTAL         $1,413.37        $84.80  @SUM(E5..E7)
```

Figure 4-4. Column E in Text Format.

Your pointer should be in E5. Note the display format of (T) in the control panel.

Formatting, whether by local /Range Format or global /Worksheet Global Format, has no effect on labels. Cell E8 contains a label and therefore is not affected by this command. Likewise, values are not affected by label-prefixes whether /Range Label-Prefix or /Worksheet Global Prefix is used.

/Range Format Reset

The /Range Format Reset command "undoes" any previously issued local

/Range Format command on the cells in the designated range and restores the global default format. Change the values in column E back to the global default.

You enter: / **Range Format Reset E5..E9 [Return]**

The display format no longer exists in the control panel for these cells, therefore they are taking the global format.

/Worksheet Column Reset-Width

Another command which changes a local setting to the global default is the /Worksheet Column Reset-Width command. Recall that column A was locally set with the /Worksheet Column Set-Width command to 3.

You enter: **[Home]** / **Worksheet Column Reset**

Column A is now 15 characters wide, the global default. Note that no column-width indicator is shown in the control panel, therefore the global column-width takes effect here. If the global column-width changes, so will column A's width. Change it back to a width of 3 and note that the column-width indicator, [W3], reappears.

You enter: / **Worksheet Column Set-Width 3 [Return]**

Changes in the global column-width will not affect column A now. Of course, the global format can also be Text.

You enter: / **Worksheet Global Format Text**

Your worksheet should look like Figure 4-5.

```
     A      B            C          D          E
1              SCRANTON HARDWARE COMPANY, INCORPORATED
2
3                       Sales        Tax        Total
4
5   1 Nuts              437.5 0.06*C5      +C5+D5
6   2 Bolts            899.64 0.06*C6      +C6+D6
7   3 Screwdrivers      76.23 0.06*C7      +C7+D7
8              ----------------------------------------
9         TOTAL    @SUM(C5..C7)  @SUM(D5..D7)  @SUM(E5..E7)
```

Figure 4-5. Global Format of Text.

Note that the constant values in column C are shown in General format when the format is Text. Column A's format is not affected by this global command because it has been set with the /Range Format.

Change the global format back to (C2).

You enter: **/ Worksheet Global Format Currency [Return]**

/Range Format Hidden

There are times when you might wish to hide some of the data in a worksheet. For example, you may wish not to display names associated with confidential salary information.

To cause values (and labels) to be hidden, use /Range Format Hidden. Hide the cells in the range C3..D7.

You enter: **/ Range Format Hidden C3..D7 [Return]**

Your worksheet should look like Figure 4-6.

```
        A        B             C           D            E
  1              SCRANTON HARDWARE COMPANY, INCORPORATED
  2
  3                                                    Total
  4
  5     1 Nuts                                       $463.75
  6     2 Bolts                                      $953.62
  7     3 Screwdrivers                                $80.80
  8                           ---------------------------------
  9          TOTAL       $1,413.37      $84.80     $1,498.17
```

Figure 4-6. Cells in Columns C and D in Hidden Format.

Note that the contents still exist, because the Total column and TOTAL row are still intact. Bring back the display.

You enter: **/ Range Format Reset C3..D7**

/Worksheet Column Hide

To hide one or more columns, use /Worksheet Column Hide. Hide columns C and D.

You enter: **/ Worksheet Column Hide C3..D9 [Return]**

Only the column letters in the range designation are important. Row numbers, in this case 3 and 9, are irrelevant. Any other row numbers would cause the same results.

Your worksheet should look like Figure 4-7.

```
        A       B           E              F
1                 SCRANTON HARDWARE COMPANY, INCORPORATED
2
3                         Total
4
5       1 Nuts                 $463.75
6       2 Bolts                $953.62
7       3 Screwdrivers          $80.80
8                         ----------------
9            TOTAL           $1,498.17
```

Figure 4-7. Columns C and D Hidden.

The difference between this command and /Range Format Hidden is that the entire column is not displayed, including the column headers C and D. The /Range Format Hidden command hides only a range of cells.

```
        A   B C   D E F G    H    I    J    K    L    M    N    O    P
1    M R P         Prd  0    1    2    3    4    5    6    7    8    9
2    ======        Qty                                               1250
3    |-----|-----|-------------------------------------------------------
4    Lot  | End |GR  |     0    0    0    0    0    0    0    0 1250
5    for  |Item |SR  |     0    0    0    0    0    0    0    0 1250
6    Lot  |     |OH  | 0   0    0    0    0    0    0    0    0    0
7    Only | LT= |NR  |     0    0    0    0    0    0    0    0 1250
8         |  1  |POR |     0    0    0    0    0    0    0 1250    0
9    -----------|----|------------------------------------------------
10   Component 1|GR  |     0    0    0    0    0    0    0 1250    0
11              |SR  |     0    0    0    0    0    0    0  800    0
12      1  times|OH  | 450 450  450  450  450  450  450  450  450    0
13              |NR  |     0    0    0    0    0    0    0  800    0
14   LT=     4  |POR |     0    0    0  800    0    0    0    0   NA
15   -----------|----|------------------------------------------------
16   Component 2|GR  |     0    0    0  800    0    0    0    0   NA
17              |SR  |     0    0    0  550    0    0    0    0   NA
18      1  times|OH  | 250 250  250  250  250    0    0    0    0    0
19              |NR  |     0    0    0  550    0    0    0    0   NA
20   LT=     1  |POR |     0    0  550    0    0    0    0   NA   NA
```

Figure 4-8. Worksheet with Many Zeroes.

```
       A  B  C  D E F G   H    I    J    K    L    M    N    O    P
 1   M R P        Prd      1    2    3    4    5    6    7    8    9
 2   =======      Qty                                            1250
 3      ---------|----|--------------------------------------------
 4   Lot    End  |GR                                             1250
 5   for    Item |SR                                             1250
 6   Lot         |OH
 7   Only   LT=  |NR                                             1250
 8          1    |POR                                       1250
 9   ------------|----|--------------------------------------------
10   Component 1 |GR                                        1250
11               |SR                                         800
12      1  times |OH  450  450  450  450  450  450  450  450  450
13               |NR                                         800
14   LT=     4   |POR             800                              NA
15   ------------|----|--------------------------------------------
16   Component 2 |GR               800                             NA
17               |SR               550                             NA
18      1  times |OH  250  250  250  250  250
19               |NR               550                             NA
20   LT=     1   |POR              550                        NA   NA
```

Figure 4-9. Worksheet with Display of Cells containing Zeroes Suppressed.

/Worksheet Global Zero

The /Worksheet Global Zero command allows you to hide cells containing zeroes. Figure 4-8 is an example of a worksheet containing many zeroes. After a / Worksheet Global Zero is issued, the worksheet looks like Figure 4-9. A view the global settings will show that zeroes are not displayed. (Some of you might recognize the Material Requirements Planning layouts in these figures).

+/- Format

+/- format displays values using the symbols +, ., and - in horizontal bar graphs. Each + represents one positive integer, - represents one negative integer, and zero is represented by a period.

Create the worksheet in Figure 4-10 using /Data Fill and /Copy.

You enter: / **Worksheet Erase Yes**

You enter into A1: / **Data Fill . [PgDn] [Return]**

You enter: **4 [Return] -.5 [Return] -4 [Return]**

You enter: / **Copy [End] [Down] [Return] [Right] [Return]**

Your worksheet should look like Figure 4-10.

```
      A        B        C
1     4        4
2     3.5      3.5
3     3        3
4     2.5      2.5
5     2        2
6     1.5      1.5
7     1        1
8     0.5      0.5
9     0        0
10    -0.5     -0.5
11    -1       -1
12    -1.5     -1.5
13    -2       -2
14    -2.5     -2.5
15    -3       -3
16    -3.5     -3.5
17    -4       -4
```

Figure 4-10. Worksheet before +/- Format.

Now format column B into +/- format.

You enter: / **Range Format + B1..B17 [Return]**

Your worksheet should look like Figure 4-11.

```
      A       B       C
1     4  ++++
2     3.5 +++
3     3   +++
4     2.5 ++
5     2   ++
6     1.5 +
7     1   +
8     0.5 .
9     0   .
10    -0.5 .
11    -1  -
12    -1.5 -
13    -2  --
14    -2.5 --
15    -3  ---
16    -3.5 ---
17    -4  ----
```

Format 4-11. Worksheet with +/- Format.

Note that numbers with fractions are truncated and displayed the same as the integer part of the number. A number like 3.99 would still be displayed as only 3 + signs. Values between -1 and 1 are displayed as if zero.

- - - If you need a break, stop at this point. - - -

[F1/HELP]

Pressing the key marked F1 puts you into on-screen HELP mode.

You enter: **[F1/HELP]**

The **help index** is shown on the screen. In general, you obtain on-screen help on a subject by highlighting the subject in this help index and hitting [Return].   [Backspace] returns you to the previous screen, and [Esc] returns you to READY mode.

Releases 2.3 and 2.4: Hit [F3] for an explanation on the keys used for navigation through help.

Take time now to familiarize yourself with the help utility.

You: **Exit from Help using [Esc].**

Help in MENU Mode

Help can be used in the middle of a command for more information on the command or its options.

You enter: **/ Worksheet Insert [F1/HELP]**

The screen shows information on the /Worksheet Insert command.

You enter: **[Esc]**

[Esc] in the middle of a command takes you back to MENU mode, not READY mode, so that you may continue issuing the command.

You: **Return to READY mode.**

Releases 2.2, 2.3, and 2.4:

In these releases, **settings sheets**, screens with information about certain groups of settings, appear on the screen with the issuance of some commands. [F6/WINDOW] will toggle the screen display between the settings sheet and the worksheet.

You enter: /Worksheet **G**lobal **[F6/WINDOW] [F6/WINDOW]**

/System

To temporarily exit 1-2-3 and go to DOS, /System can be used. This command allows you to issue DOS commands while Lotus is still resident in RAM. To return to 1-2-3, type EXIT.

You enter: / **System**

The DOS prompt should be on your screen. DOS commands can now be issued.

WARNING: Always save your worksheet immediately prior to the issuance of this /System command. Sometimes DOS commands cause RAM's capacity to be exceeded, and you will not be able to return to your worksheet, thereby losing all changes since the most recent /File Save.

You enter: **EXIT [Return]**

While doing the exercises or creating your own worksheets, try to keep in mind this hint. Concentrate first on getting the data into the worksheet. Then, after most of the data is in, focus on adjusting column-widths and formats to make the worksheet clearer, more readable, and more appealing. Your very last step should be the centering of titles.

NEW COMMAND SUMMARY

/Range Format Reset   Restores the global format to a range of cells.

**/Worksheet Column
Reset-Width**   Restores the global column-width to the single column the pointer is
                                            in.

/Range Format Hidden   Turns off the display of a range of cells and makes them look empty.

/Worksheet Column Hide   Hides a range of columns and causes the bordering columns to the left
                                            and right of the hidden range to appear adjacent.

/Worksheet Global Zero   Displays all cells in the worksheet containing zero values (whether
                                            formulas or constants) as empty cells. Does not change or erase the
                                            contents of cells with zeroes.

[F1/HELP]   Causes 1-2-3 to enter the on-screen Help mode.

/System   Temporary exit to DOS. 1-2-3 remains in RAM. Use EXIT to return
                                            to 1-2-3.

EXERCISES

PART 1 EXERCISES

Part 1 Exercises require the use of on-screen HELP to find information about the 10 function keys and @ functions. This is information frequently forgotten by the average Lotus user.

1A.   HELP screens will vary depending on the release you are using. Use HELP to call up information on the 10 function keys similar to the information shown in the screen below:

```
A1:                                         HELP

Function Keys    The ten function keys on the IBM keyboard are
used by 1-2-3 as follows:

F1:  [HELP]      Displays Help screen
F2:  [EDIT]      Switches to/from EDIT mode for current entry
F3:  [NAME]      Displays list of range names or file names
F4:  [ABS]       Makes cell address absolute  Preselects ranges
F5:  [GOTO]      Moves cell pointer to a particular cell
F6:  [WINDOW]    Moves cell pointer to other window.  Turns off settings screen.
F7:  [QUERY]     Repeats most recent /Data Query operation
F8:  [TABLE]     Repeats most recent /Data Table operation
F9:  [CALC]      Recalculates all formulas (READY mode only)
F10: [GRAPH]     Draws graph using current graph settings

To have a macro include a function key, enclose its name in braces,
e.g., {Query} or {QUERY}.
-----------------------------------------------------------------
Ranges    Absolute/Relative Cell Addresses   Keyboard Macros
Help Index
```

The above figure is a nice summary of the 10 functions keys, use it for future reference. If you forget where it is, look up "Function Keys Summary" or "Summary of 10 Function Keys" in the index.

Releases 2.3 and 2.4: Use [Down] arrow in the Help Index to find 1-2-3 Keys, then Function Keys.

Releases 2.2, 3.0, and 3.1+: From the Help Index, choose Function Keys, then Continued to see the entire list.

1B.   Use HELP to find information on two statistical @ functions: @AVG, which computes an average, and @SQRT which computes a square root. (Hint: Look for @Function Index.)

1C.   It is common for beginning users to forget that HELP is available **during** the issuance of a command. Issue /Print Printer and then press [F1/HELP] to produce the HELP screen below.

Practice using HELP during the issuance of other commands, too.

Releases 2.2, 2.3, 2.4, 3.0, and 3.1+:
Your screen will be different but have similar information.

```
Range  Line  Page  Options  Clear  Align  Go  Quit
Advance to top of page

/Print Menu -- Main menu of print settings and operations.

   Select a print setting or a print operation.
            (1-2-3 returns to this menu until you select Quit.)

Print Settings:

   Range              Range to be printed.
   Options            Page layout (margins, headers, footers),
                            cell-formula printing, and so forth.
Print Operations:

   Go                 Print the range with the current options.
   Line, Page, Align  Format the printout with blank space.
   Clear              Cancel some or all print settings.
   Quit               Return to READY mode.


Ranges   Entering Ranges   Printing Cell Formulas   Help Index
```

PART 2 EXERCISES

Part 2 exercises involve formatting ranges. Simple formulas are copied.

2A. Create the worksheet below and save under L4SEA. Enter the proper formulas in D5 and E5 and copy them down the columns. The next lesson explains how formulas are copied.

```
        A          B         C         D         E
1              ART PREACHER'S SEAFOOD RESTAURANT
2
3   Department     1987      1988    Change    % Change
4   ---------------------------------------------------
5   Appetizers     $900    $1,100     $200       22.2%
6   Soup             30        37        7       23.3%
7   Salad           250       305       55       22.0%
8   Fish             70        80       10       14.3%
9   Desserts         53        43      (10)     -18.9%
10  Beverages        17        15       (2)     -11.8%
11                 ---------------------------------------
12               $1,320    $1,580
```

2B. Create the worksheet below and save under L4WTAVG. Enter the proper formula in C3 and copy it into C4..C6. Cell C10 should reference cell C8. The next lesson explains how formulas are copied.

```
        A          B         C
1    Value      Weight    Product
2
3        3       10.5%      0.315
4        2       21.0%      0.420
5        7       28.0%      1.960
6        5       40.0%      2.000
7              ------------------
8               100%       4.695
9
10  Weighted average=      4.70
```

2C. Create the worksheet below and save under L4PROB. Enter the proper formula in D6 and copy it into D7 and D8. The next lesson explains how formulas are copied.

```
         A              B            C            D
1                  EXPECTED VALUE WORKSHEET
2
3                                      Value
4                              ---------------------------
5       Event        Probability  Conditional    Expected
6         A              73.5%       $4,567      $3,356.75
7         B              12.7%        3,529         448.18
8         C              13.8%       (5,000)       (690.00)
9                              ---------------------------
10                         100%                  $3,114.93
11
12        EXPECTED VALUE =         $3,114.9280
```

2D. Create the worksheet below and save under L4DEFECT. Use /Data Fill to enter the run numbers. Enter Total Pieces and Number Good as constants. Enter formulas for the number and percentage defective and the ratio into D3..F3. Copy D3..F3 to D4..F7. The next lesson explains how formulas are copied.

```
       A       B       C       D          E             F
1     Run    Total  Number  Number   Percentage       Ratio
2   Number  Pieces   Good  Defective  Defective   Total-to-Good
3      1      120     78      42        35.00%         1.538
4      2      135     90      45        33.33%         1.500
5      3      117     68      49        41.88%         1.721
6      4      128     81      47        36.72%         1.580
7      5      140     89      51        36.43%         1.573
```

PART 3 EXERCISES

Part 3 exercises show how +/- format can be used in cells to imitate bar graphs. The graphing chapters cover how to create real bar graphs. Cell references and /Data Fill are required.

3A. Create the worksheet below and save under L4GRADE. Column C is blank and used only to space between columns B and D. Use /Data Fill for the first column, the constants shown for the second column, and CELL REFERENCES to the second column for the fourth column. Remember to always use cell references if one value depends on another value in the worksheet. The cell reference in the first cell of column D can be copied down the column. The copying of cell references is covered in detail in the next lesson.

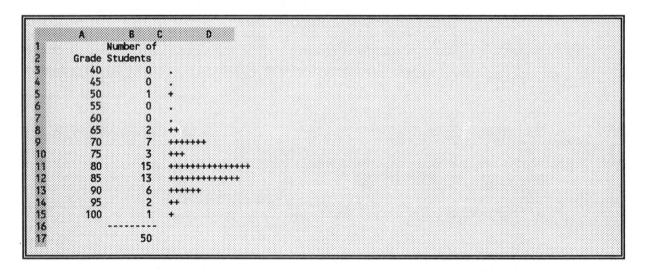

3B. Create the worksheet below and save under L4RAND. Column C is blank and used only to space between columns B and D. Use /Data Fill for the first column, the constants shown for the second column, and CELL REFERENCES to the second column for the fourth column. Remember to always use cell references if one value depends on another value in the worksheet. The cell reference in the first cell of column D can be copied down the column. The copying of cell references is covered in detail in the next lesson.

	A	B	C	D
1	Value of the	Number of		
2	Random Variable	Occurrences		
3	0.50	2		++
4	0.51	10		+++++++++++
5	0.52	7		++++++++
6	0.53	6		+++++++
7	0.54	9		++++++++++
8	0.55	8		+++++++++
9	0.56	5		++++++
10	0.57	3		++++
11		---------------		
12		50		

3C. Create the worksheet below and save under L4SALES. Column C is blank and used only to space between columns B and D. Use /Data Fill for the first column, the constants shown for the second column, and CELL REFERENCES to the second column for the fourth column. Remember to always use cell references if one value depends on another value in the worksheet. The cell reference in the first cell of column D can be copied down the column. The copying of cell references is covered in detail in the next lesson. Total units sold is found by first multiplying each daily demand by it's corresponding number of occurrences and hiding the products in column E. These products are irrelevant; they will clutter the worksheet and cause confusion. Again, the first product formula can be copied down the column. Total units is the sum of the products.

```
          A          B         C     D            E
 1                 SALES HISTORY
 2
 3        Daily    Number of         Graphical Representation
 4        Demand   Occurrences       of Daily Order Occurrences
 5          0          2             ++
 6          1         10             ++++++++++
 7          2          7             +++++++
 8          3          6             ++++++
 9          4          3             +++
10          5          8             ++++++++
11          6          5             +++++
12          7          3             +++
13
14     Total Units Sold =                145
```

PART 4 EXERCISES

Part 4 exercises are common financial statements. They require the student to use /Range Format to incorporate a $ before the first value in a column as is standard in many statements.

Hint to Student: In Part 4 exercises, series of periods (........) are used to help guide the eye to the corresponding number. To get the ...'s as they appear in the figures, enter more periods than you need at the end of the labels. Change the width of the column to its right to 1 and place a single period as a label ('.) in the cells. This will prevent the ...'s after the labels from overflowing into adjacent empty cells. For example, in exercise 4A below, the labels in columns A and B have .....'s much longer than displayed. The single period labels in C5, C8..C12, C14, C15, C17, C18, and C20 truncate the periods to the left leaving a sharp straight edge.

4A.   Create the worksheet below and save under L4STMNT. See Hint to Student at beginning of part 4 exercises.

```
          A                   B                 C    D        E
 1              SCRANTON HARDWARE COMPANY, INCORPORATED
 2              Statement of Income and Retained Earnings
 3                  For Year Ended December 31, 1988
 4
 5  Revenue from sales.........................     $300,000
 6
 7  Expenses:
 8    Cost of goods sold......................$230,000
 9    Selling expenses........................  30,700
10    General and administrative expenses.......  27,600
11    Income taxes expense....................   2,300
12          Total expenses....................--------- 290,600
13                                              ---------
14  Net income...............................     $9,400
15    Add retained earnings, January 1, 1988....    8,600
16                                              ---------
17          Total............................    $18,000
18    Deduct dividends declared...............     4,000
19                                              ---------
20  Retained earnings, December 31, 1988........   $14,000
                                                =========
```

4B. Create the worksheet below and save under L4BALAN. See Hint to Student at beginning of part 4 exercises.

```
            A      B   C     D    E        F      G    H        I
 1                      XYZ CORPORATION
 2                       BALANCE SHEET
 3                     December 31, 1989
 4                          ($000)
 5
 6  Cash........... $4,600        Accounts
 7  Accounts                        payable........ $1,000
 8   receivable.....  1,200       Loans
 9  Inventory.......  1,000         payable........  5,000
10                   --------                       --------
11  Total current                 Total current
12   assets........          $6,800  liabilities....        $6,000
13                                 Long-term
14                                  debt...........          1,000
15  Net plant and                 Equity..........          3,000
16   equipment......   3,200
17                   --------   Total              --------
18  Total Assets....  $10,000   Liabilities....        $10,000
```

4C. Create the worksheet below and save under L4FUNDS. To create vertical line, enter | into column C as a label ('|) and change column C's width to 1.

```
            A           B      C       D           E
 1            SOURCES AND USES OF FUNDS STATEMENT
 2                      XYZ Corporation
 3           December 31, 1988 to December 31, 1989
 4
 5       Sources of Funds            Uses of Funds
 6  --------------------------------+--------------------------------
 7  Cash               $2,000 |Accounts receivable    $2,500
 8  Accounts payable    4,500 |Inventory              3,000
 9  Long-term debt      1,000 |Plant and equipment    5,000
10  Equity              3,000 |
11                   ------------ |             ------------
12  Total sources     $10,500 |Total uses           $10,500
```

4D.   Create the income statement and balance sheet below in the same worksheet and save under L4FLUFFY. See Hint to Student at beginning of part 4 exercises.   For ratios, use named cell references to the income statement and balance sheet.

```
                          A            B    C       D
 1            FLUFFY CARPET MANUFACTURERS
 2                   Income Statement
 3             Year Ended December 31, 1989
 4                      ($000)
 5
 6   Net Sales.............................    $24,000
 7   Cost of goods sold....................     11,500
 8                                            -----------
 9   Gross margin..........................    $12,500
10   Less operating expenses:
11     Selling.............................   1,378
12     General and administrative..........   2,100    3,478
13                                            -----------------
14   Gross operating revenue...............     $9,022
15   Depreciation..........................          0
16                                            -----------
17   Earnings bef. Int. and Taxes (EBIT)....    $9,022
18   Interest expenses.....................        300
19                                            -----------
20   Net income before taxes...............     $8,722
21   Provision for income taxes............      3,489
22                                            -----------
23   Net income............................     $5,233
24                                            ===========
25   Earnings per common share.............      $8.72
26   make note (000) and use 625 below           ===========
27
28   Market price of common stock (12/31/89)->    $27.00
29
30
```

Continued

4D. L4FLUFFY Continued:

```
              A              B   C        D
31         FLUFFY CARPET MANUFACTURERS
32              Balance Sheet
33            December 31, 1989
34
35                  Assets
36   Current assets:
37     Cash and equivalent.................          $450
38     Marketable securities...............             0
39     Receivables.........................  4,200
40                                           1,000    3,200
41     Inventories.........................           5,000
42     Other...............................           1,500
43                                                  ----------
44        Total current assets..........            $10,150
45   Gross Plant........................... 25,678
46   Accumulated depreciation.............  6,543
47                                                  ---------
48     Net plant...........................          19,135
49                                                  ----------
50         Total assets................             $29,285
51                                                  ===========
52                  Equities
53   Current liabilities:
54     Short-term debt.....................          $1,000
55     Accounts payable....................           1,500
56     Accrued expenses....................            900
57     Provisions for taxes................            500
58                                                  ----------
59        Total current liabilities.......          $3,900
60     Long term debt......................           1,700
61                                                  ----------
62         Total liabilities............            $5,600
63                                                  ===========
64   Shareholders' equity:
65     Common stock........................          $7,000
66     (shares outstanding)............... 600,000
67     Retained earnings...................          16,685
68                                                  ----------
69         Total net worth.............             $23,685
70                                                  ----------
71   Total equities.......................           $29,285
72                                                  ===========
```

Continued

4D.   L4FLUFFY Continued Again:

```
              A              B    C        D
73
74  LIQUIDITY RATIOS
75
76  Current assets divided by current liabilities.
77  Current Ratio=                  2.603
78
79  Current assets less inventory divided by total liabilities.
80  Quick Ratio or Acid Test=       0.920
81
82  LEVERAGE RATIOS
83
84  Total liabilities divided by total assets.
85  Debt-to-Asset Ratio=            0.191
86
87  EBIT divided by interest expenses.
88  Times-Interest-Earned-Ratio=   30.073
89
90  ACTIVITY RATIOS
91
92  Net sales divided by inventory.
93  Inventory Turnover Ratio=       4.800
94
95  Receivables divided by sales per day (net sales divided by 365 days).
96  Average Collection Period=        64
97
98  Net sales divided by total assets.
99  Asset Turnover Ratio=           0.820
100
101 PROFITABILITY RATIOS
102
103 Net income divided by net sales.
104 Profit Margin on Sales=        21.80%
105
106 Net income divided by total assets.
107 Return on Total Assets=        17.87%
108
109 Net income divided by net worth.
110 Return on Net Worth=           22.09%
111
112 VALUATION RATIOS
113
114 Market price per share divided by earnings per share.
115 Price-Earnings Ratio=           3.096
116
117 Earnings per share divided by market price per share.
118 Capitalization Ratio=           0.323
```

PART 5 EXERCISES

Part 5 is meant to issue a warning not to do anything "tricky" with numbers in a worksheet.

5.   Create the worksheet below. Here, the formula in the last column cannot be copied. Read the warning below only after you have finished.

```
                              A                     B         C       D
1                        CAPITAL STRUCTURE
2
3     Bonds (at par)................    $500,000    34.5%
4     Preferred stock (at market)....    250,000    17.2
5     Common stock (at market).......    700,000    48.3
6                                        -----------------
7                                      $1,450,000   100.0%
```

WARNING: In order to cause the decimal points in C4..C5 to line up with the rest of the column, the values must be multiplied by 100 and formatted Fixed. This is very poor practice because it is not apparent in the display that the value is stored incorrectly in memory. You may forget the craftiness used here and refer to the value in this cell from a far off formula cell. The results could be catastrophic.

This trick is not worth using.

Cumulative Exercises

C1. Create the worksheet below from TOFU1 that you created in Lesson 1. Hide the Commission column with /Worksheet Column Hide. All sales reps are expected to meet a 1992 sales quota of $90,000. Add the Above/(Below) Quota column as the 92 Sales minus $90,000. Add the Percent of Quota column as 92 Sales divided by $90,000. Format the cells using /Range Format. Save under TOFU4.

	A	B	C	D	F	G
1		IMITATION TOFU, INCORPORATED				
2					Above/(Below)	Percent of
3		SalesRep	Division	92 Sales	Quota	Quota
4		==				
5	1	Saxe, J.	2	$40,500	(49,500)	45.0%
6	2	Gress, R.	3	$77,000	(13,000)	85.6%
7	3	Cosner, L.	3	$23,400	(66,600)	26.0%
8	4	Smith, A.	1	$150,000	60,000	166.7%
9	5	Smith, B.	1	$54,700	(35,300)	60.8%
10	6	Kirlin, K.	2	$75,000	(15,000)	83.3%
11	7	Wodak, F.	1	$29,800	(60,200)	33.1%
12	8	Reese, J.	3	$111,300	21,300	123.7%
13	9	Gruss, M.	1	$88,200	(1,800)	98.0%
14	10	Boyle, T.	2	$67,600	(22,400)	75.1%
15				-----------		
16			Total	$717,500		
17			Average	$71,750		
18						

C2. Create the worksheet below by retrieving the FISH1 worksheet that you created in Lesson 1. Use /Worksheet Column Hide to hide the Retail Price and Wholesale Price columns. Format the profits in comma format in columns F and G. The Profit Margin % is the profit per item divided by the retail price. Enter one formula in cell H5 and copy it down the column. Format the column as percent. Save under FISH4.

	A	B	C	F	G	H
1		H A P P Y T R O P I C A L F I S H S T O R E				
2	Item		Quantity	Profit	Total Pr.	Profit
3	#	Item Name	Sold	per Item	per Item	Margin %
4		---				
5	273	7-inch fish net	63	1.29	81.27	64.8%
6	238	1-lb. decorative rocks	49	1.69	82.81	56.5%
7	130	underwater fern	13	1.39	18.07	60.7%
8	281	40-gallon aquarium	14	17.99	251.86	45.0%
9	162	goldfish	241	0.49	118.09	83.1%
10	192	20-inch eel	4	4.99	19.96	55.5%
11	274	2-gallon fish bowl	25	2.99	74.75	59.9%
12	256	8-vitamin fish food	57	0.99	56.43	55.3%
13	198	turtle	-1	2.49	(2.49)	62.4%
14	111	piranha	3	5.99	17.97	54.5%
15		==				
16					$718.72	
17						

C3. Create the worksheet below by retrieving the BILL3 worksheet that you created in Lesson 3. Change the global format to , and add row 16. Name the range C5..C13 "MARCH" and the range D5..D13 "APRIL". Make the range name table in columns F and G. Save under BILL4.

	A	B	C	D	E	F	G
1		MONTHLY BILLS					
2							
3			March	April			
4		Budgeted	Actual	Actual			
5	Food	220	238	222		APRIL	D5..D13
6	Rent	550	550	550		MARCH	C5..C13
7	Phone	30	39	40			
8	Electric	50	43	45			
9	Gasoline	45	56	52			
10	Car Payment	345	345	345			
11	Insurance	55	55	55			
12	Charge Cards	100	250	170			
13	Entertainment	100	150	150			
14			---------------------------------				
15	Total	1,495	1,726	1,629			
16	Percent of Budgeted		115%	109%			
17							

C4. Create the worksheet below by retrieving the GOLF1 worksheet that you created in Lesson 1. Format row 10 as shown. Name Joe's row "JOE" (range A5..K5) and name Mike's row "MIKE" (range A7..K7). Create the range name table shown. Save under GOLF4.

	A	B	C	D	E	F	G	H	I	J	K
1			J	&	F GOLF	COURSE	SCORE	SHEET			
2	Hole	1	2	3	4	5	6	7	8	9	Total
3	Par	4	5	4	3	5	4	4	3	4	36
4											
5	Joe	8	5	6	4	4	5	6	4	4	46
6	Mary	4	6	5	4	6	4	5	5	3	42
7	Mike	3	7	6	4	5	5	6	5	4	45
8	Sheila	5	5	6	4	3	3	4	6	5	41
9											
10	Average	5.00	5.75	5.75	4.00	4.50	4.25	5.25	5.00	4.00	43.50
11											
12	JOE	A5..K5									
13	MIKE	A7..K7									
14											

RELATIVE AND ABSOLUTE ADDRESSING

Contents:

Copying formulas is an inevitable part of the use of 1-2-3. To copy formulas containing cell references correctly, one must have a knowledge of the cell addressing techniques 1-2-3 uses. By default, cell references are copied relative to the formula cell. This lesson explains how this is done and how to change relative addressing to mixed or absolute addressing schemes.

Clear the worksheet.

You enter into B2: **12 [Return]**

You enter into C4: **+B2 [Return]**

Copy C4 to D4.

You enter: / **Copy C4 [Return] D4 [Return]**

You: **Place pointer in cell D4.**

The control panel shows that the cell reference in D4 is +C2. To understand why +B2 has been changed to +C2 during the /Copy, we must look at how 1-2-3 stores cell references. Change the global format to Text so that you can see the formulas, not the values, in each cell.

You enter: / **Worksheet Global Format Text**

Your screen should look like Figure 5-1.

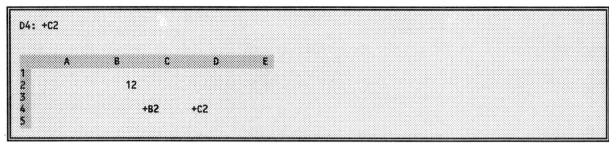

Figure 5-1. Relative Addresses in C4 and D4.

Relative Addressing

The cell address +B2 in cell C4 is actually stored as "the cell one column to the left and 2 rows up" from the formula cell, C4. It is called a relative address because it is stored as an address relative to the formula cell. If this relative address is copied into any other cell, it will be changed to the address of the cell one column to the left and 2 rows up relative to the cell being copied TO. Cell C2 is one column to the left and 2 rows up from D4. What address will be copied if D4 is copied to B10? Which cell is one column to the left and 2 rows up relative to B10?

You enter: / **Copy D4 [Return] B10 [Return]**

The answer is cell A8. (If the referenced cell doesn't exist, as in the case where the address above is copied into column A, the worksheet "wraps around" to the right end of the worksheet.)

Absolute Addressing

There will be times when you want a cell reference to be copied exactly as it is and not relatively. An absolute address should be used in these cases, because it is copied without changes. An absolute address has dollar signs before the column and row references.

You enter into F3: **+$B$2 [Return]**

You enter: / **Copy F3 [Return] F3..H6 [Return]**

Your worksheet should look like Figure 5-2.

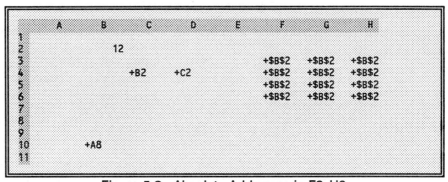

Figure 5-2. Absolute Addresses in F3..H6.

Mixed Addressing

Mixed addresses are half relative and half absolute.

You enter into A6: **+$B2 [Return]**

This mixed address has an absolute column reference, B, which will not be changed when copied. The row reference, 2, is relative and will be changed according to the TO cells' positions.

You enter: **/ Copy A6 [Return] A6..C8 [Return]**

Your worksheet should look like Figure 5-3.

	A	B	C	D	E	F	G	H
1								
2		12						
3						+$B$2	+$B$2	+$B$2
4			+B2	+C2		+$B$2	+$B$2	+$B$2
5						+$B$2	+$B$2	+$B$2
6	+$B2	+$B2	+$B2			+$B$2	+$B$2	+$B$2
7	+$B3	+$B3	+$B3					
8	+$B4	+$B4	+$B4					
9								
10		+A8						
11								

Figure 5-3. Mixed Addresses in A6..C8.

Here the absolute column reference is copied as B. The row changes because it is stored relatively as "the row 4 rows up". Without the $ before the B, the column would have been copied as "the column to the right" and the cell references in column B would have been C2, C3, and C4 and those in column C would have been D2, D3, and D4.

You enter into D12: **+B$2 [Return]**

Before doing the next copy, try to figure out how it will look when complete.

You enter: **/ Copy D12 [Return] D12..F16 [Return]**

Your worksheet should look like Figure 5-4.

	A	B	C	D	E	F	G	H
1								
2		12						
3						+$B$2	+$B$2	+$B$2
4			+B2	+C2		+$B$2	+$B$2	+$B$2
5						+$B$2	+$B$2	+$B$2
6	+$B2	+$B2	+$B2			+$B$2	+$B$2	+$B$2
7	+$B3	+$B3	+$B3					
8	+$B4	+$B4	+$B4					
9								
10		+A8						
11								
12				+B$2	+C$2	+D$2		
13				+B$2	+C$2	+D$2		
14				+B$2	+C$2	+D$2		
15				+B$2	+C$2	+D$2		
16				+B$2	+C$2	+D$2		
17								

Figure 5-4. Mixed Addresses in D12..F16.

The absolute row reference of 2 did not change. The relative column address of "the column 2 columns to the left" is changed accordingly.

- - - If you need a break, stop at this point. - - -

Let's use these addressing concepts in a practical example. You'll create Figure 5-5.

	A	B	C	D
1		PERIODIC LOAN PAYMENTS TABLE		
2				
3	Principal:	$65,000		
4				
5				
6			Term in Years	
7		10	15	20
8	Annual Rate			
9	9.0%	$823.39	$659.27	$584.82
10	9.5%	$841.08	$678.75	$605.89
11	10.0%	$858.98	$698.49	$627.26
12	10.5%	$877.08	$718.51	$648.95
13	11.0%	$895.38	$738.79	$670.92
14	11.5%	$913.87	$759.32	$693.18
15	12.0%	$932.56	$780.11	$715.71
16	12.5%	$951.45	$801.14	$738.49
17				

Figure 5-5. Table of Periodic Loan Payments.

Figure 5-5 shows the payment amounts necessary to pay back a loan of $65,000 for the number of years and interest rates in the corresponding column headers and row borders respectively. For example, to pay off $65,000 at 10½% in 15 years, the monthly payment would be $718.51.

You enter: / **Worksheet Erase Yes**

You enter: / **Worksheet Global Column-Width 19 [Return]**

You enter: / **Worksheet Global Label Right**

Use about 10 spaces before the title.

You enter into B1:   **PERIODIC LOAN PAYMENTS TABLE**

You enter into A3: **Principal: [Return]**

You enter into A3: / **Worksheet Column Set-Width 11 [Return]**

You enter into B3: **65000 [Return]**

You enter into B3: / **Range Format Currency 0 [Return] [Return]**

You enter into A8: **Annual Rate [Return]**

You enter into A9: / **Data Fill A9..A16 [Return]**

You enter: **.09 [Return] .005 [Return] [Return]**

You enter: / **Range Format Percent 1 [Return] A9..A16 [Return]**

You enter into C6: **Term in Years [Return]**

You enter into B7: **10 [Right] 15 [Right] 20 [Return]**

Your worksheet should look like Figure 5-6.

```
            A            B              C              D
 1                    PERIODIC LOAN PAYMENTS TABLE
 2
 3   Principal:      $65,000
 4
 5
 6                               Term in Years
 7                        10             15             20
 8   Annual Rate
 9         9.0%
10         9.5%
11        10.0%
12        10.5%
13        11.0%
14        11.5%
15        12.0%
16        12.5%
17
```

Figure 5-6. Part of Figure 5-5.

@PMT(principal,interest,term)

The @PMT function computes the periodic payment on an installment loan. The three arguments are principal (the amount borrowed), interest (the interest rate per period), and term (the number of payments). For example, @PMT(100000,.12,10) computes to 17698.42 meaning that to pay back $100,000 in 10 payments at an interest rate of 12% per payment, each payment should be $17,698.42.

To complete Figure 5-5, it is necessary to put the @PMT function into each cell in the range B9..D16. Start with cell B9. The principal is $65,000. Recall that we never enter as a constant an entry which depends on another cell. The principal argument should be entered as B3. The interest is in A9 and the term is in B7. First change the global format to text so that you can see the formula.

You enter: / **Worksheet Global Format Text**

You enter into B9: **@PMT(B3,A9,B7) [Return]**

Now copy this formula to the range B9..D16.

You enter: / **Copy B9 [Return] B9..D16 [Return]**

Your worksheet should look like Figure 5-7.

```
          A              B              C              D
1                        PERIODIC LOAN PAYMENTS TABLE
2
3    Principal:        $65,000
4
5
6                                  Term in Years
7                        10              15              20
8    Annual Rate
9        9.0%@PMT(B3,A9,B7)     @PMT(C3,B9,C7)     @PMT(D3,C9,D7)
10       9.5%@PMT(B4,A10,B8)    @PMT(C4,B10,C8)    @PMT(D4,C10,D8)
11      10.0%@PMT(B5,A11,B9)    @PMT(C5,B11,C9)    @PMT(D5,C11,D9)
12      10.5%@PMT(B6,A12,B10)   @PMT(C6,B12,C10)   @PMT(D6,C12,D10)
13      11.0%@PMT(B7,A13,B11)   @PMT(C7,B13,C11)   @PMT(D7,C13,D11)
14      11.5%@PMT(B8,A14,B12)   @PMT(C8,B14,C12)   @PMT(D8,C14,D12)
15      12.0%@PMT(B9,A15,B13)   @PMT(C9,B15,C13)   @PMT(D9,C15,D13)
16      12.5%@PMT(B10,A16,B14)  @PMT(C10,B16,C14)  @PMT(D10,C16,D14)
17
```

Figure 5-7. Incorrect Cell References in Arguments.

Most of the cell references are incorrect. Cell B9 is fine but every copied formula is wrong. Without an understanding of absolute and relative addressing, you would not be able to set up the correct formula to be copied. Do you see that it is possible to create this worksheet by individually entering a different formula into each cell in the range B9..D16? This would indeed be tedious, time-consuming, and with good possibilities for typographical errors. It is much easier to use absolute and relative addressing in the formula to be copied.

Let's edit the formula in B9 and add the proper dollar signs.

You: **Move pointer to B9.**

The principal should be an absolute address because you want neither the row nor column to change during the copy. The interest should be a mixed address with the column absolute and the row relative. The term should be mixed with the column relative and the row absolute. A good rule of thumb is to "put $ before the part of the address that you DON'T want changed".

Take some time now to enter the correct formula without looking at the answer below. You will not learn unless you think for yourself.

The correct cell references are below.

You change B9 to: **@PMT($B$3,$A9,B$7)**

Did you use [F2/EDIT] to make the changes in B9 or did you retype the whole entry?

You enter: / **Copy B9 [Return] B9..D16**

Your worksheet should look like Figure 5-8.

```
         A              B                C                D
1                    PERIODIC LOAN PAYMENTS TABLE
2
3  Principal:        $65,000
4
5
6                                 Term in Years
7                       10               15                20
8  Annual Rate
9      9.0%@PMT($B$3,$A9,B$7) @PMT($B$3,$A9,C$7) @PMT($B$3,$A9,D$7)
10     9.5%@PMT($B$3,$A10,B$7) @PMT($B$3,$A10,C$7) @PMT($B$3,$A10,D$7
11    10.0%@PMT($B$3,$A11,B$7) @PMT($B$3,$A11,C$7) @PMT($B$3,$A11,D$7
12    10.5%@PMT($B$3,$A12,B$7) @PMT($B$3,$A12,C$7) @PMT($B$3,$A12,D$7
13    11.0%@PMT($B$3,$A13,B$7) @PMT($B$3,$A13,C$7) @PMT($B$3,$A13,D$7
14    11.5%@PMT($B$3,$A14,B$7) @PMT($B$3,$A14,C$7) @PMT($B$3,$A14,D$7
15    12.0%@PMT($B$3,$A15,B$7) @PMT($B$3,$A15,C$7) @PMT($B$3,$A15,D$7
16    12.5%@PMT($B$3,$A16,B$7) @PMT($B$3,$A16,C$7) @PMT($B$3,$A16,D$7
17
```

Figure 5-8. Correct Cell References.

Now that you have the correct cell references, change the global format to Currency to display the payment values.

You enter: / **Worksheet Global Format Currency 2 [Return]**

You enter: / **Range Format Fixed 0 [Return] B7..D7 [Return]**

These values are wrong because we want the monthly payment. The interest rate in @PMT is per period, not necessarily per year, and the term is number of payments, not necessarily number of years. Therefore the second argument should be annual interest divided by 12 payments per year and the third argument should be number of years times 12 payments per year. Edit the formula in B9 and recopy.

You enter into B9: **[F2/EDIT]**

You change to formula to: **@PMT($B$3,$A9/12,B$7*12)**

You enter: / **Copy B9 [Return] B9..D16 [Return]**

Your worksheet should finally look like Figure 5-5. Save it on disk under PMT.

You enter: / **File Save PMT [Return]**

Let's say you are going to take out a mortgage for $100,000. Simply change the amount of the principal in the worksheet.

You enter into B3: **100000 [Return]**

With this table you can see the difference a half a percentage point would make in your monthly payments. In my opinion, it's worth shopping around for the bank or savings and loan association or rich uncle which gives the best interest rate.

Of course, the constant percentage rates in column A and the terms in row 7 can be changed to suit your needs.

Absolute Named Range Addressing

Range names used as cell references in formulas are, by default, relative addresses. To made them absolute, simply type a $ before the name. For example, $TOTAL will make the address absolute.

[F4/ABS]

Seasoned users of 1-2-3 use point mode for referencing cells more often than nought. To change the addressing scheme of a cell reference, the fourth function key can be used.

You enter into A18: **+**

You: **Move pointer to B3.**

You: **Repeatedly hit the [F4/ABS] key.**

Note how the four possibilities for absolute, relative, and mixed cell addresses alternate: +$B$3, +B$3, +$B3, and +B3. Simply use [F4/ABS] until the one you want appears in the cell.

Releases 3.0 and 3.1+: The A: before each cell reference indicates a worksheet. (See Appendix.)   In this release, you may have many worksheets in memory at the same time labelled A, B, C, etc. Each worksheet can refer to cells in other worksheets by indicating the corresponding worksheet letter before the cell reference. There are more combinations of relative and absolute references in this case. Keep hitting [F4/ABS] until the one you need is shown in the control panel.

NEW COMMAND SUMMARY

Relative Addressing   An addressing scheme where cell references are stored relative to the formula cell.

Absolute Addressing   An addressing scheme where cell references are absolute and do not depend on the position of the cell relative to the formula cell.

Mixed Addressing   An addressing scheme where part of the cell reference is absolute and part is relative.

[F4/ABS]   This function key alternates between all possibilities of cell addressing schemes in point mode.

EXERCISES

PART 1 EXERCISES

Part 1 exercises use mixed addresses to create tables where the entries refer to the column header above and the row border to the left.

1A. Create the worksheet below using /Data Fill to set up the column header numbers and row border numbers. Create the vertical line by using | as a label in column B and setting column B's width to 1. Enter only one formula - in cell C4 and copy it to C4..N15.

	A	B	C	D	E	F	G	H	I	J	K	L	M	N
1						TIMES TABLES								
2	x			1	2	3	4	5	6	7	8	9	10	11	12
3			-	-	-	-	-	-	-	-	-	-	-	-
4	1			1	2	3	4	5	6	7	8	9	10	11	12
5	2			2	4	6	8	10	12	14	16	18	20	22	24
6	3			3	6	9	12	15	18	21	24	27	30	33	36
7	4			4	8	12	16	20	24	28	32	36	40	44	48
8	5			5	10	15	20	25	30	35	40	45	50	55	60
9	6			6	12	18	24	30	36	42	48	54	60	66	72
10	7			7	14	21	28	35	42	49	56	63	70	77	84
11	8			8	16	24	32	40	48	56	64	72	80	88	96
12	9			9	18	27	36	45	54	63	72	81	90	99	108
13	10			10	20	30	40	50	60	70	80	90	100	110	120
14	11			11	22	33	44	55	66	77	88	99	110	121	132
15	12			12	24	36	48	60	72	84	96	108	120	132	144
16														

1B. Create the worksheet below using /Data Fill to set up the column header numbers and row border numbers. Create the vertical line by using | as a label and setting the column's width to 1. Enter only one formula and copy it throughout the table.

```
                    PECKVILLE FABRIC STORE

                             Yardage
                0.5   1.0   1.5   2.0   2.5   3.0   3.5   4.0
               ------------------------------------------------
       $1.00  | 0.50  1.00  1.50  2.00  2.50  3.00  3.50  4.00
       $1.25  | 0.63  1.25  1.88  2.50  3.13  3.75  4.38  5.00
       $1.50  | 0.75  1.50  2.25  3.00  3.75  4.50  5.25  6.00
Price  $1.75  | 0.88  1.75  2.63  3.50  4.38  5.25  6.13  7.00
per    $2.00  | 1.00  2.00  3.00  4.00  5.00  6.00  7.00  8.00
Yard   $2.25  | 1.13  2.25  3.38  4.50  5.63  6.75  7.88  9.00
       $2.50  | 1.25  2.50  3.75  5.00  6.25  7.50  8.75 10.00
       $2.75  | 1.38  2.75  4.13  5.50  6.88  8.25  9.63 11.00
       $3.00  | 1.50  3.00  4.50  6.00  7.50  9.00 10.50 12.00
       $3.25  | 1.63  3.25  4.88  6.50  8.13  9.75 11.38 13.00
```

Change the formula above to show the addition of a 6% tax on each piece of material. Copy it throughout the table.

1C. Create the worksheet below using /Data Fill to set up the column header numbers and row border numbers. Create the vertical line by using | as a label and setting the column's width to 1. Enter only one formula in C4 and copy it throughout the table.

```
     A B   C       D        E       F       G
1                        Power
2          0.5      2        3       4       5
3       +--------------------------------------
4     2 | 1.41421   4        8       16      32
5     3 | 1.73205   9        27      81      243
6     4 | 2.00000   16       64      256     1024
7     5 | 2.23607   25       125     625     3125
8     6 | 2.44949   36       216     1296    7776
9     7 | 2.64575   49       343     2401    16807
10    8 | 2.82843   64       512     4096    32768
11    9 | 3.00000   81       729     6561    59049
12   10 | 3.16228   100      1000    10000   100000
13
```

PART 2 EXERCISES

Part 2 exercises include the common requirement of % of total. The formula requires a knowledge of absolute and relative addressing.

2A. Create the worksheet below and save under L5BUDGET. Enter one formula in C4 and copy it down the column.

	A	B	C
1		Monthly Household Budget	
2			
3		Amount	% of Total
4	Mortgage	$900	30.1%
5	Car Payment	$450	15.0%
6	Food	$375	12.5%
7	Heat	$200	6.7%
8	Electric	$60	2.0%
9	Phone	$20	0.7%
10	Insurances	$90	3.0%
11	Charity	$300	10.0%
12	Entertainment	$200	6.7%
13	Miscellaneous	$400	13.4%
14		---------------------------------	
15	Total	$2,995	100.0%

2B. Create the worksheet below by entering one formula in C3 and copying it down the column. Column D should contain cell references to column D. Save it under L5RAND. (If you did the L4RAND exercise from the previous lesson, retrieve and modify it to save yourself some typing.)

	A	B	C	D	E
1	Value of the	Number of	Relative		
2	Random Variable	Occurrences	Frequency		
3	0.50	2	4.00%	++++	
4	0.51	10	20.00%	+++++++++++++++++++++	
5	0.52	7	14.00%	+++++++++++++++	
6	0.53	6	12.00%	+++++++++++++	
7	0.54	9	18.00%	+++++++++++++++++++	
8	0.55	8	16.00%	+++++++++++++++++	
9	0.56	5	10.00%	+++++++++++	
10	0.57	3	6.00%	+++++++	
11		----------------------------			
12		50	100%		
13					

2C. Create the worksheet below and save under L5INC. Enter one formula in column C and copy it throughout that column. It may be easier to enter the formula in a bottom cell, perhaps cell C18, and copy it up.

```
              A                  B        C
1                 INCOME STATEMENT
2                   XYZ Corporation
3          Year Ending December 31, 1989
4
5    Net Sales                  $7,000   100.00%
6    Cost of goods sold          5,000    71.43%
7                               ----------------
8    Gross Profit               $2,000    28.57%
9    Selling general administration
10     Expenses                   850     12.14%
11                              ----------------
12   EBIT                       $1,150    16.43%
13   Interest                     110      1.57%
14                              ----------------
15   Profit before tax          $1,040    14.86%
16   Taxes                        490      7.00%
17                              ----------------
18   Profit after tax           $550       7.86%
19
```

2D. Create the worksheet below and save under L5SHARES. Enter only one formula into cell D7 and copy it through D7..D12 and F7..F12.

```
         A         B        C         D        E        F
1                      1989 MARKET SHARES
2
3                        -------U.S.------  -----Canada-----
4                        Number of Market  Number of Market
5    Publisher              Books   Share     Books   Share
6
7    Wise Books            2,000   11.05%    2,500   13.16%
8    Deltan Books          2,300   12.71%    2,000   10.53%
9    Faucett Books         4,500   24.86%    4,200   22.11%
10   Harl-quinn Books      1,000    5.52%    1,100    5.79%
11   Vallantine Books      3,300   18.23%    3,500   18.42%
12   Other                 5,000   27.62%    5,700   30.00%
13                        ----------------------------------
14                        18,100  100.00%   19,000  100.00%
15
```

2E. Create the worksheet below and save under L5DOORKN. Make much use of the /Copy command. The provision for income taxes in the Comparative Income Statement is 49% of total. In the Percentage of Sales bottom half of the worksheet, one formula can be entered into 1987 Net sales and copied throughout the two columns.

A	**B**	**C**	**D**	**E**	**F**	**G**
1		BLAKELY DOORKNOB CORPORATION				
2		Comparative Income Statements				
3	For the Years Ended December 31, 1988, and 1987					
4		($000)				
5					1987	1986
6	Net sales.....................				$32,088	$27,999
7	Cost of goods sold............				26,754	23,000
8					--------------	
9	Gross Margin..................				5,334	4,999
10	Other Expenses:..............					
11	Selling expenses............				1,076	987
12	Administrative expenses......				2,100	1,980
13	Interest expense............				250	243
14					--------------	
15	Total..............				3,426	3,210
16	Income before income taxes.....				1,908	1,789
17	Provision for income taxes.....				1,679	1,573
18					--------------	
19	Net income...................				229	216
20						
21		BLAKELY DOORKNOB CORPORATION				
22	Expenses and Net Income as a Percentage of Sales					
23	For the Years Ended December 31, 1988, and 1987					
24		($000)				
25						
26					1987	1986
27	Net sales.....................				100.0%	100.0%
28	Cost of goods sold............				83.4%	82.1%
29					--------------	
30	Gross Margin..................				16.6%	17.9%
31	Other Expenses:..............					
32	Selling expenses............				3.4%	3.5%
33	Administrative expenses......				6.5%	7.1%
34	Interest expense............				0.8%	0.9%
35					--------------	
36	Total..............				10.7%	11.5%
37	Income before income taxes.....				5.9%	6.4%
38	Provision for income taxes.....				5.2%	5.6%
39					--------------	
40	Net income...................				0.7%	0.8%

PART 3 EXERCISES

Part 3 exercises include formulas which require absolute addressing schemes for referring to cells remote to the formula cell and mixed addressing schemes for referring to a cell in the same row relatively but absolutely to the column.

3A. Create the worksheet below and save under L5VCR. Use your knowledge of absolute and relative addressing to enter one cell and copy it whenever possible. For instance, one formula can be entered into cell C20 and copied to C20..E23.

	A	B	C	D	E
1				INPUT CELLS	
2	First Year Sales in Units--------------			120	
3	Annual Increase Rates:				
4	Sales---------------------------------			12.0%	
5	Costs---------------------------------			4.5%	
6	Expenses------------------------------			5.0%	
7	Cost per VCR - Year 1-----------------			$455.00	
8	Markup on VCR-------------------------			45%	
9	Price per VCR - Year 1---------------			$659.75	
10					
11		FOUR YEAR PROJECTION FOR VCR SALES			
12					
13		1989	1990	1991	1992
14	Sales	$79,170.00	$88,670.40	$99,310.85	$111,228.15
15	Cost of Sales	54,600.00	57,057.00	59,624.57	62,307.67
16		-------------	-------------	-------------	-------------
17	Gross Margin	$24,570.00	$31,613.40	$39,686.28	$48,920.48
18	Expenses:				
19	Rent	2,000.00	2,000.00	2,000.00	2,000.00
20	Advertising	3,500.00	3,675.00	3,858.75	4,051.69
21	Utilities	1,400.00	1,470.00	1,543.50	1,620.68
22	Wages	7,500.00	7,875.00	8,268.75	8,682.19
23	Other	12,630.00	13,261.50	13,924.58	14,620.80
24		-------------	-------------	-------------	-------------
25	Total Exp.	$27,030.00	$28,281.50	$29,595.58	$30,975.35
26					
27	Net Profit	($2,460.00)	$3,331.90	$10,090.71	$17,945.13
28					

3B.   Create the worksheet below and save under L5NAIL. Use your knowledge of absolute and relative addressing to enter one cell and copy it whenever possible. The only constant values are in the B column and C5..C6 and C10..C14. The formula in D5 can be copied to D5..F6 and D10..F14.

	A	B	C	D	E	F
1			FOUR YEAR PROJECTION FOR NAIL CLIPPER SALES			
2						
3		Inc/Dec				
4		Rate	1989	1990	1991	1992
5	Sales	12.0%	$23,896.00	$26,763.52	$29,975.14	$33,572.16
6	Cost of Sales	-5.0%	13,697.19	$13,012.33	$12,361.71	$11,743.63
7			----------	----------	----------	----------
8	Gross Margin		$10,198.81	$13,751.19	$17,613.43	$21,828.53
9	Expenses:					
10	Mortgage	0.0%	$2,000.00	$2,000.00	$2,000.00	$2,000.00
11	Maintenance	2.0%	2,939.21	2,997.99	3,057.95	3,119.11
12	Utilities	4.0%	743.00	772.72	803.63	835.77
13	Wages	7.0%	4,735.00	5,066.45	5,421.10	5,800.58
14	Insurance	10.0%	3,400.00	3,740.00	4,114.00	4,525.40
15			----------	----------	----------	----------
16	Total Exp.		$13,817.21	$14,577.16	$15,396.68	$16,280.86
17						
18	Net Profit		($3,618.40)	($825.97)	$2,216.75	$5,547.67

PART 4 EXERCISES

Part 4 exercises include the idea of cumulative sums. These can be entered as the sum of the value to the left plus the value immediately above. Another way is to use the @SUM function with range argument from the cell to the immediate left up to the top of its column. For a specific example read the directions for exercise 4A below. The @SUM method requires knowledge of relative and absolute addressing.

4A. The Expenditure and Budgeted Amount columns in the worksheet below are constants. There are at least two different formulas which can be entered and copied into the Year-to-Date column. One is where the value two columns to the left is added to the value in the row above, for example $1,173 = $638 + $535. The other is @SUM where the argument is a range with relative and absolute addressing. Use the @SUM formula. Save on disk under L5JESSUP.

```
        JESSUP CORPORATION

                                Expenditure
            Expend-   Budgeted    Year-to-
Month        iture    Amount    Date Total
-------|---------------------------------
Jan    |    $535       $400        $535
Feb    |    $638       $550      $1,173
Mar    |    $422       $450      $1,595
Apr    |    $838       $950      $2,433
May    |    $333       $300      $2,766
Jun    |    $734       $750      $3,500
Jul    |    $744       $750      $4,244
Aug    |    $612       $800      $4,856
Sept   |    $574       $550      $5,430
Oct    |    $568       $600      $5,998
Nov    |    $854       $850      $6,852
Dec    |    $876       $800      $7,728
-------|---------------------------------
TOTAL  |  $7,728     $7,750
```

4B. Create the worksheet below and save under L5CTAX. Columns A, B, and C contain constants. All other cells contain formulas. Total taxes paid is a cumulative sum. Use @SUM and your knowledge of absolute and relative addressing to enter one formula into E5 and copy it down the column.

	A	B	C	D	E	F
1		MARGINAL AND AVERAGE		CORPORATE TAX RATES		
2						
3	Taxable Corp. Income		Marginal	Incremental	Total	Average
4	From	To	Tax Rate	Taxes	Taxes Paid	Tax Rate
5	0	25,000	17%	$4,250	$4,250	17.00%
6	25,001	50,000	20%	$5,000	$9,250	18.50%
7	50,001	75,000	30%	$7,500	$16,750	22.33%
8	75,001	100,000	40%	$10,000	$26,750	26.75%
9	100,001	200,000	46%	$46,000	$72,750	36.38%
10	200,001	1,000,000	46%	$368,000	$440,750	44.08%
11	1,000,001	11,000,000	46%	$4,600,000	$5,040,750	45.83%
12	11,000,001	111,000,000	46%	$46,000,000	$51,040,750	45.98%

4C. Create the worksheet below and save under L5DIE. All are constants except the cumulative frequency. Use @SUM and your knowledge of relative and absolute addressing to enter one formula into C4 and copy it down the column.

	A	B	C
1		Relative	Cumulative
2	Roll of Die	frequency of z	frequency
3			
4	1	10.0%	10.0%
5	2	20.0%	30.0%
6	3	20.0%	50.0%
7	4	10.0%	60.0%
8	5	30.0%	90.0%
9	6	10.0%	100.0%
10		----------	
11		100%	
12			

4D. Create the worksheet below and save under L5CFREQ. If you did the L5RAND exercise, retrieve and modify it to save yourself some typing. Use @SUM and your knowledge of relative and absolute addressing to enter one formula into D3 and copy it down the column.

	A	B	C	D
1	Value of the	Number of	Relative	Cumulative
2	Random Variable	Occurrences	Frequency	Frequency
3	0.50	2	4.00%	4.00%
4	0.51	10	20.00%	24.00%
5	0.52	7	14.00%	38.00%
6	0.53	6	12.00%	50.00%
7	0.54	9	18.00%	68.00%
8	0.55	8	16.00%	84.00%
9	0.56	5	10.00%	94.00%
10	0.57	3	6.00%	100.00%
11		-------------------------------		
12		50	100%	

CUMULATIVE EXERCISES

C1.   Create the worksheet below from TOFU4 which you created in Lesson 4. Delete columns E (Commission column) and column F (the Above/Below Quota column). Add the Percent of 92 Sales column by entering one formula in G5 which references cell D16 and copying it down the column. Change the Percent of Quota formulas to reference cell E19 by entering one formula in H5 and copying it down. Add the Above/(Below) Average column by entering one formula in G5 with a reference to D17 and copying it down the column. Change cell D19 to $70,000 Now how many sales reps meet at least 100% of the quota? Save under TOFU5A.

	A	B	C	D	E	F	G
1				IMITATION TOFU, INCORPORATED			
2					Percent of	Percent of	Above/(Below)
3		SalesRep	Division	92 Sales	92 Sales	Quota	Average
4		======	======	======	======	======	======
5		1 Saxe, J.	2	$40,500	5.6%	57.9%	(31,250)
6		2 Gress, R.	3	$77,000	10.7%	110.0%	5,250
7		3 Cosner, L.	3	$23,400	3.3%	33.4%	(48,350)
8		4 Smith, A.	1	$150,000	20.9%	214.3%	78,250
9		5 Smith, B.	1	$54,700	7.6%	78.1%	(17,050)
10		6 Kirlin, K.	2	$75,000	10.5%	107.1%	3,250
11		7 Wodak, F.	1	$29,800	4.2%	42.6%	(41,950)
12		8 Reese, J.	3	$111,300	15.5%	159.0%	39,550
13		9 Gruss, M.	1	$88,200	12.3%	126.0%	16,450
14		10 Boyle, T.	2	$67,600	9.4%	96.6%	(4,150)
15				--------------------			
16			Total	$717,500	100.0%		
17			Average	$71,750			
18							
19		Sales quota for all Reps=			$70,000		
20							

C2. Create the worksheet below by retrieving the TOFU1 worksheet you created in Lesson 1. Delete columns A, C, and E and rows 17 through 19. First add row 18 and 19 with constant percentage increases. Then add the three projected sales columns by entering one formula in cell C5 and copying it to the range C5..E14. Save under TOFU5B.

	A	B	C	D	E
1		IMITATION TOFU, INCORPORATED			
2			Projected	Projected	Projected
3	SalesRep	92 Sales	93 Sales	94 Sales	95 Sales
4	===				
5	Saxe, J.	$40,500	$42,930	$45,076	$48,232
6	Gress, R.	$77,000	$81,620	$85,701	$91,700
7	Cosner, L.	$23,400	$24,804	$26,044	$27,867
8	Smith, A.	$150,000	$159,000	$166,950	$178,636
9	Smith, B.	$54,700	$57,982	$60,881	$65,143
10	Kirlin, K.	$75,000	$79,500	$83,475	$89,318
11	Wodak, F.	$29,800	$31,588	$33,167	$35,489
12	Reese, J.	$111,300	$117,978	$123,877	$132,548
13	Gruss, M.	$88,200	$93,492	$98,167	$105,038
14	Boyle, T.	$67,600	$71,656	$75,239	$80,506
15		--			
16		$717,500	$760,550	$798,577	$854,478
17					
18	Projected increases				
19	over previous year:		6%	5%	7%
20					

C3. Create the worksheet below by retrieving the FISH1 worksheet that you created in Lesson 1. Delete columns F and G. Create the new F and G columns, Retail Sales and Wholesale Purchases, by entering formulas into F5 and G5 and copying them down the columns. Then enter one formula in H5 using your knowledge of addressing and copy it through the range H5..I14. % of Retail Sales is retail sales divided by total retail sales, % of Wholesale purchases is wholesale purchases divided by total wholesale purchases. Save under FISH5.

	A	B	C	D	E	F	G	H	I
1			H A P P Y	T R O P I C A L		F I S H	S T O R E		
2	Item		Quanti	Retail	Wholesale	Retail	Wholesale	% of R	% of W
3	#	Item N	Sold	Price	Price	Sales	Purchases	Sales	Purchases
4									
5	273	7-inch	63	1.99	0.70	125.37	44.10	9.7%	7.6%
6	238	1-lb.	49	2.99	1.30	146.51	63.70	11.3%	11.0%
7	130	underw	13	2.29	0.90	29.77	11.70	2.3%	2.0%
8	281	40-gal	14	39.99	22.00	559.86	308.00	43.2%	53.4%
9	162	goldfi	241	0.59	0.10	142.19	24.10	11.0%	4.2%
10	192	20-inc	4	8.99	4.00	35.96	16.00	2.8%	2.8%
11	274	2-gall	25	4.99	2.00	124.75	50.00	9.6%	8.7%
12	256	8-vita	57	1.79	0.80	102.03	45.60	7.9%	7.9%
13	198	turtle	-1	3.99	1.50	(3.99)	(1.50)	-0.3%	-0.3%
14	111	piranh	3	10.99	5.00	32.97	15.00	2.5%	2.6%
15			======	======	======	======	======	======	======
16			TOTAL			1,295.42	576.70	100.0%	100.0%
17									

C4. Create the worksheet below by retrieving the BILL4 worksheet that you created in Lesson 4. Erase the range name table and the percentages in C16..D16. Enter one formula in C16 using your knowledge of relative and absolute addressing and copy it to cell D16. Enter one formula into E5 and copy it to range E5..F15. Add the underline in row 14. Save under BILL5A.

	A	B	C	D	E	F
1			MONTHLY BILLS			
2					March	April
3			March	April	Over/	Over/
4		Budgeted	Actual	Actual	(Under)	(Under)
5	Food	220	238	222	18	2
6	Rent	550	550	550	0	0
7	Phone	30	39	40	9	10
8	Electric	50	43	45	(7)	(5)
9	Gasoline	45	56	52	11	7
10	Car Payment	345	345	345	0	0
11	Insurance	55	55	55	0	0
12	Charge Cards	100	250	170	150	70
13	Entertainment	100	150	150	50	50
14		---------	---------	---------	---------	---------
15	Total	1,495	1,726	1,629	231	134
16	Percent of Budgeted		115%	109%		
17						

C5. Create the worksheet below by retrieving the BILL4 worksheet that you created in Lesson 4. Erase the range name table and the percentages in C16..D16. Enter one formula in C16 using your knowledge of relative and absolute addressing and copy it to cell D16.   Enter one formula into E5 and copy it to range E5..F15. Add the underline in row 14. Save under BILL5B.

	A	B	C	D	E	F
1			MONTHLY BILLS			
2					% of	% of
3			March	April	March	April
4		Budgeted	Actual	Actual	Total	Total
5	Food	220	238	222	13.8%	13.6%
6	Rent	550	550	550	31.9%	33.8%
7	Phone	30	39	40	2.3%	2.5%
8	Electric	50	43	45	2.5%	2.8%
9	Gasoline	45	56	52	3.2%	3.2%
10	Car Payment	345	345	345	20.0%	21.2%
11	Insurance	55	55	55	3.2%	3.4%
12	Charge Cards	100	250	170	14.5%	10.4%
13	Entertainment	100	150	150	8.7%	9.2%
14		---------	---------	---------	---------	---------
15	Total	1,495	1,726	1,629	100.0%	100.0%
16	Percent of Budgeted		115%	109%		
17						

C6. Create the worksheet below by retrieving the GOLF1 worksheet you created in Lesson 1 and deleting the rows not shown below. Add the two rows with the differences between Joe's and Mike's scores and par. Use your knowledge of relative and absolute addressing and enter one formula into B8 and copy through the range B8..K9. The 4 in cell B8 designates that on the first hole, Joe was 4 over par. The -1 in cell B9 means Mike was 1 under par. Save under GOLF5.

	A	B	C	D	E	F	G	H	I	J	K
1		J & F GOLF COURSE SCORE SHEET									
2	Hole	1	2	3	4	5	6	7	8	9	Total
3	Par	4	5	4	3	5	4	4	3	4	36
4											
5	Joe	8	5	6	4	4	5	6	4	4	46
6	Mike	3	7	6	4	5	5	6	5	4	45
7											
8	J difference	4	0	2	1	-1	1	2	1	0	10
9	M difference	-1	2	2	1	0	1	2	2	0	9
10											

Lesson 6

MATHEMATICAL @ FUNCTIONS

Contents:

This lesson covers statistical and mathematical @ functions. The complex mathematical @ functions are optional and may be skipped.

Statistical @ Functions

Below are @ functions which do computations on lists of values with brief explanations of the value each returns. The possible arguments for list were explained using the @SUM function in Lesson 1. (See Table 1-1, page 42.)

@AVG(list)
Returns the average of the values in the list.

@COUNT(list)
Returns the number of non-blank entries in the list.

@MAX(list)
Returns the maximum value in the list.

@MIN(list)
Returns the minimum value in the list.

@STD(list)
Returns the population standard deviation for values in the list.

@SUM(list)
Returns the sum of the values in the list.

@VAR(list)
Returns the population variance of the values in the list.

```
              A           B        C        D
1                       Test 1   Test 2   Test 3
2   Alunni, Angelo        82       79       63
3   Carver, Clementine    90       82       75
4   Cicilioni, Fred       72       70       80
5   Cicilioni, John       83       75       70
6   Falzett, Rose         75
7   Killian, Nicholas     64       45       52
8   Minster, Catharine    70       95       88
9   Sesak, Flora          91       99       95
10  Shepard, Gary         30       42
11  Washington, Barbara   82       87       86
12
13           Average    73.9     74.9     76.1
14          St. Dev.    16.8     18.9     13.2
15           Minimum      30       42       52
16           Maximum      91       99       95
17     Number of Tests    10        9        8
```

Figure 6-1. Gradebook Worksheet.

Figure 6-2 shows the @ functions in Text format.

```
              A              B              C              D        E
13        Average  aAVG(TEST1)    aAVG(TEST2)    aAVG(D2..D11)
14       St. Dev.  aSTD(TEST1)    aSTD(TEST2)    aSTD(D2..D11)
15        Minimum  aMIN(TEST1)    aMIN(TEST2)    aMIN(D2..D11)
16        Maximum  aMAX(TEST1)    aMAX(TEST2)    aMAX(D2..D11)
17  Number of Tests aCOUNT(TEST1) aCOUNT(TEST2) aCOUNT(D2..D11)
```

Figure 6-2. Text Format for @ Function Cells for Range A13..D17.

Create the worksheet shown in Figure 6-1. Column A's width is 20; the global column-width remains unchanged at 9. Rose Falzett missed the second and third tests, so leave cells C6 and D6 blank. Name only the first two test columns TEST1 and TEST2 with the /Range Name Create command. Use the statistical @ functions listed above for B13..B17 using the named range TEST1 as the argument. Then /Copy B13..B17 to C13..D13. 1-2-3 automatically uses the named range TEST2 as the arguments in the TO range! D2..D11 was not named so the range designation is used in the arguments.

Releases 3.0 and 3.1+: These releases do not automatically use the named range TEST2.

Format B13..D14 to Fixed with 1 decimal place. Your worksheet should look like Figure 6-1.

Save this file under GRADES because you will be using it in later lessons.

You enter: / File Save **GRADES [Return]**

Precedence of Operations

The result of 3+2*5 is 13 not 25 because the multiplication operation, which has a higher precedence than addition, is done first. 1-2-3 follows the normal algebraic order of operations. The precedence in which 1-2-3 does its computations is shown in the table below. Higher precedence-numbered operations are done before lower ones.

```
Precedence
Number          Operator

7               ^ exponentiation

6               + unary positive, - unary negative

5               * multiplication, / division

4               + addition, - subtraction

3               = equal, <> not equal, < less than, > greater than,
3               <= less than or equal to, >= greater than or equal to,

2               #NOT# logical NOT

1               #AND# logical AND, #OR# logical OR
1               & string combination


Two operations of equal precedence will be done from left to right.  The
order of operations can be changed using parentheses.
```

Table 4-1. Precedence of Operators.

-3^2 + 14 * 2^3

First 3 is squared (9), then 2 is cubed (8). The unary negative before 3 is next (-9), followed by the multiplication (112) and addition (103). Therefore 103 would be the value of the cell containing the above formula.

(((-3)^2 + 14) * 2)^3

Negative 3 squared is positive 9. (9+14)*2 is 46. 46 cubed is 97336. Therefore 97336 would be the value of the cell containing the above formula.

Mathematical @ Functions

Below are listed the @ functions that do calculations using numeric values. Examples of results given specific inputs are given. They are divided into two groups. The first are those math functions widely used. The second are more complex functions used mostly by mathematicians, scientists, and engineers and can be skipped.

Commonly Used Mathematical @ Functions

@ABS(x)

Returns the absolute value of x. The absolute value of a number is the number without the sign or the positive value of the number. In other words, if x is negative, this function returns x without the minus sign or (-1*x). If x is positive or 0, the function returns x.

You enter: **@ABS(-3) [Return]**

3 is displayed in the cell.

@ABS(8) = 8

@ABS may be used to make sure a number is positive before taking a square root with @SQRT. Another use is to display a negative number from a computation as positive. For instance, let's say you're computing inventory and come out with -10 units. This can be displayed as 10 under a column header "Shortage".

In all these functions, the argument x could be a constant, formula, cell reference, or range name (the upper left corner cell of the range would be used).

@INT(x)

Returns the integer part of x. It truncates a number after the decimal point, even if it is larger than .5.

You enter: **@INT(2.945) [Return]**

2 is displayed in the cell.

@INT may be used for something like the computation of ages given the birthdate and today's date. (See @DATE function.) Instead of displaying a person's age as 34.7 years, @INT can be used to show it as 34 years.

@ROUND(x,n)

Returns x rounded to n decimal places. After rounding, the number of digits after the decimal point is equal to n. It is different from truncating in that the last digit is increased by 1 if the digit to its right is greater than or equal to 5.[1]

You enter: **@ROUND(324.695,1) [Return]**

324.7 is displayed in the cell. Note that there is one digit after the decimal point and that digit, previously 6, has been rounded up to 7 because of the 9.

This function is sometimes necessary to correct what seems to be computational problems in 1-2-3. Retrieve the SCRANTON worksheet and change the global format to Currency with 0 decimal digits. The Sales TOTAL (C9) and overall TOTAL (E9) look incorrect! Compare the two worksheets below to see what mathematically caused this problem.

---

[1]Or rounds to a number greater than or equal to 5.

A	B	C	D	E
		SCRANTON HARDWARE COMPANY, INCORPORATED		
		Sales	Tax	Total
1 Nuts		$438	$26	$464
2 Bolts		$900	$54	$954
3 Screwdrivers		$76	$5	$81
		------------	-------	---------
	TOTAL	$1,413	$85	$1,498

A	B	C	D	E
		SCRANTON HARDWARE COMPANY, INCORPORATED		
		Sales	Tax	Total
1 Nuts		$437.50	$26.25	$463.75
2 Bolts		$899.64	$53.98	$953.62
3 Screwdrivers		$76.23	$4.57	$80.80
		------------	-------	---------
	TOTAL	$1,413.37	$84.80	$1,498.17

Figure 6-3. Seemingly Incorrect Additions Due to Format Display.

The addends are displayed as if they are whole integers, but the values in memory are really less. The number displayed as $438 and $900 really are stored in memory as 437.5 and 899.64. The total of the differences, .5 and .36, is enough to decrease the display of the total one full point. Changing the actual contents of memory with @ROUND, i.e. @ROUND(437.5,0) in C5..C7, will cause the value after rounding, 438 to be added to the sum and the problem will be corrected.

If the second argument of @ROUND, n, is negative, the values are rounded to the left of the decimal point.

You enter: **@ROUND(1583.71,-2) [Return]**

1600 is displayed in the cell.

@RAND

Returns a random number between 0 and 1. Each time the worksheet is recalculated, this function returns a new random number. It is useful in probability and statistics and analysis of risk. Let's say you wish to simulate the roll of a die. The possible outcomes are the integers 1 through 6 with equal probability. Because the number returned goes from 0 to 1, it must be mapped with some formula to the numbers 1 through 6.

You enter: **@RAND*5+1 [Return]**

Format the cell as Fixed with 0 decimal digits. [F9/CALC] can be used to recalculate the worksheet.

You enter: **[F9/CALC] [Return]**

Repeatedly hit [F9/CALC] until you are convinced only the integers 1 through 6 will be returned. This may take 30 or 40 times.

If @RAND generates .0000001, @RAND*5+1 will be 1.0000005 displayed as 1. If @RAND generates .45792, @RAND*5+1 will be 3.2896 displayed as 3. If @RAND generates .99999999, @RAND*5+1 will be 5.99999995 displayed as 6. Very importantly, keep in mind that the number in your cell is displayed as an integer. The actual contents is some number with many decimal digits. If you're going to use the cell containing @RAND in other computations, make sure you use @INT to truncate those decimal digits.[2]

The general formula for generating a random number between an upper limit, U, and a lower limit, L is

@INT(@RAND*(U-L+1)+L)

Releases 3.0 and 3.1+:
When entering a function, [F3/NAME] can be entered after the @ to get a list of functions on the third line of the control panel. Hitting [F3/NAME] a second time gives a full screen listing of all @ functions. Pointer movement keys can be used to highlight and choose a function. Try it.

You enter into any cell: @ **[F3/NAME] [F3/NAME] [PgDn] [DOWN] [Return]**

@SUMPRODUCT(should be shown in the cell.

Complex Mathematical @ Functions

Non-mathematicians may skip to the end of this lesson. I am assuming those that read this section understand what these functions are. This section lists @ functions which would be interesting to those using 1-2-3 for more advanced mathematics.

---

[2]A hidden column can be set up containing @INT with argument referring to the original cell. /Range Value (see index) can be used to actually change the contents of the cell to the truncated value.

@ACOS(x)
Returns the arc cosine of angle x.

@ASIN(x)
Returns the arc sine of angle x.

@ATAN(x)
Returns the arc tangent of angle x (2 quadrant).

@ATAN2(x,y)
Returns the arc tangent of angle y/x (4 quadrant).

@COS(x)
Returns the cosine of angle x.

@EXP(x)
Returns the number e raised to the xth power.

@LN(x)
Returns the natural log (base e) of x.

@LOG(x)
Returns the log (base 10) of x.

@MOD(x)
Returns the remainder of x/y.

@PI
Returns the number pi.

@SIN(x)
Returns the sine of angle x.

@SQRT(x)
Returns the positive square root of x.

@TAN(x)
Returns the tangent of angle x.

EXERCISES

PART 1 EXERCISES

Part 1 Exercises require the use of parentheses to change the order of precedence of operations in fairly simple mathematical formulas.

1A. Create the worksheet below and save under L6SALREP. Bonus should be computed on sales over quota.

	A	B	C	D	E	F	G
1			NATIONAL SCAFFOLDING CORPORATION				
2			SALES REPRESENTATIVES' EARNINGS				
3							
4			Sales		Actual	Earned	Total
5	Rep	Salary	Quota	% Bonus	Sales	Bonus	Earnings
6							
7	Nagle	$450.00	3000	0.020	4200.00	24.00	$474.00
8	Cheney	$300.00	2500	0.035	3000.00	17.50	$317.50
9	Shelski	$239.71	1000	0.100	1200.00	20.00	$259.71
10	Zingle	$742.00	5000	0.070	5000.00	0.00	$742.00
11							----------
12							$1,793.21

1B. Create the worksheet below and save under L6PARAB. The vertex of a parabola occurs at -b divided by 2a where b is the coefficient of the linear term and a is the coefficient of the quadratic term.

	A	B
1	FINDING THE VERTEX OF A PARABOLA.	
2		
3	Quadratic Function:	
4	Coefficient of quadratic term (x^2)=	-1.0
5	Coefficient of linear term (x) =	-4.0
6	Constant term =	12.0
7		
8	Vertex occurs at:	
9	x=	-2.0
10	y=	16.0

1C.   Create the worksheet below and save under L6BREVEN. The contribution margin ratio is the difference in selling price and variable cost per unit divided by price (or, equivalently, 1 minus the variable price per unit divided by the selling price per unit). Break-even units sold is the fixed costs divided by the price per unit minus the variable cost per unit. Break-even sales is the fixed cost divided by the contribution margin ratio. The table in A11..D20 is created around the break-even units sold point. The number of units in the first column are as follows: 0 units, half of the break-even units, break-even units, one and a half times the break-even units, two times the break-even units, two and a half times, and so on in a linear fashion. These values can be depicted graphically on the screen or printout. (See Graph lesson exercises.)

	A	B	C	D
1		BREAK-EVEN ANALYSIS		
2				
3	Selling price per unit=			$2.00
4	Total variable cost per unit=			$1.50
5	Total fixed costs per period=			$10,000.00
6				
7	Contribution margin ratio=			$0.2500
8	Break-even quantity of units sold=			20,000
9	Break-even sales=			$40,000.00
10				
11	Units			
12	Sold	Sales	Costs	Profit
13	-------	-------	-------	-------
14	0	$0	$10,000	($10,000)
15	10,000	$20,000	$25,000	($5,000)
16	20,000	$40,000	$40,000	$0
17	30,000	$60,000	$55,000	$5,000
18	40,000	$80,000	$70,000	$10,000
19	50,000	$100,000	$85,000	$15,000
20	60,000	$120,000	$100,000	$20,000

1D. Create the poker game below using the general formula for generating a random number between 1 through 13 inclusive. In the worksheet below, Joe has a pair of jacks and Mary has two pair. Save under CARD6.

	A	B	C	D	E	F
1			FIVE CARD DRAW POKER			
2						
3		Card 1	Card 2	Card 3	Card 4	Card 5
4						
5	Joe	11	11	8	1	9
6						
7	Mary	9	9	7	7	12
8						
9						
10		1 = Ace		12 = Queen		
11		11 = Jack		13 = King		
12						
13		Hit F9 for another deal.				
14						

PART 2 EXERCISES

Part 2 exercises have mathematical formulas which are more complex than Part 1.

2A. Create the worksheet below and save under L6FUNCTI. The only input cells (constant values) are the value of x and the coefficients.

```
          A              B       C              D
1         EVALUATING A FUNCTION AT THE VALUE x.
2
3                     Value of x is                    -11.340
4                     Value of function 61,567,224,127.342
5
6                     Term Coefficient            Term N
7                       N  of Term N              Addend
8    constant term-->   0        6              6.000
9       linear term-->  1        1            (11.340)
10   quadratic term-->  2       -9         (1,157.360)
11          etc.        3        3         (4,374.822)
12                      4       12        198,441.940
13                      5        3       (562,582.900)
14                      6        7     14,885,943.537
15                      7        1    (24,115,228.530)
16                      8        2    546,933,383.051
17                      9        3  (9,303,336,845.696)
18                     10        2  70,333,226,553.463
```

Modify the worksheet above to allow a square root term.

2B. Create the worksheet below and save under L6QUAD. Use the quadratic formula to compute the 2 roots. Assume 2 rational roots exist.

```
                     A                    B
1     FINDING THE ROOTS OF A QUADRATIC EQUATION.
2
3     Quadratic Function:
4       Coefficient of quadratic term (x^2)=    1.0
5       Coefficient of linear term (x) =       -3.0
6       Constant term =                         2.0
7
8                          Roots:
9                            2
10                           1
```

2C. Create the worksheet below and save under L6EOQ. The bottom part of the worksheet gives specific costs for various order sizes around the optimal quantity. The first order size in the column, the 31, is 25% of the optimal, the next is 50%, next 75%, etc. in this linear fashion in increments of .25. Knowledge of relative and absolute addressing is necessary to enter one formula in the other 3 columns and copy each down the corresponding column. This 4-column table is used to create a graph in the first graph lesson exercises.

	A	B	C	D
1		COMPUTING OPTIMAL ORDER QUANTITY		
2	INPUTS:	Annual demand =		3000
3		Annual holding costs=		$4.00
4		Order costs=		$10.00
5	OUTPUTS:			
6	Optimal order quantity=			122
7	Orders per year=			24
8	Ordering Costs=			$244.95
9	Holding Costs=			$244.95
10	Total Costs=			$489.90
11				
12	Order	Ordering	Holding	Total
13	Size	Costs	Costs	Costs
14	31	$979.80	$61.24	$1,041.03
15	61	$489.90	$122.47	$612.37
16	92	$326.60	$183.71	$510.31
17	122	$244.95	$244.95	$489.90
18	153	$195.96	$306.19	$502.15
19	184	$163.30	$367.42	$530.72
20	214	$139.97	$428.66	$568.63

2D. Create the worksheet below and save under L6NORMAL. The two input parameters are mean and standard deviation and are stored in C4..C5 as constants. A8..A12 are set up by /Data Fill and can be modified as needed for specific values of x. The x's in column B are column A multiplied by the mean. The actual function is fairly complex and therefore it is displayed for you in the control panel. This worksheet is actually a subset of one in the first graph lesson exercises. It is introduced here because the mathematics involved in the creation of a graph of a normal distribution is covered in this lesson.

```
C8: (F10) [W15] (1/($C$5*@SQRT(2*@PI)))*@EXP(-0.5*((B8-$C$4)/$C$5)^2)
```

	A	B	C	D	E	F	G
1		NORMAL DISTRIBUTION					
2							
3	INPUT:						
4		Mean=		5.7			
5		St. Dev.=		1.34			
6							
7		x	f(x)				
8	0.00	0.00	0.0000350504				
9	0.05	0.29	0.0000846801				
10	0.10	0.57	0.0001955349				
11	0.15	0.86	0.0004315406				
12	0.20	1.14	0.0009102768				

2E. Create the worksheet below and save under L6PERTAX. Columns A, C, and D are constants; the rest are cell references or formulas.

	A	B	C	D	E
1		MARGINAL AND AVERAGE PERSONAL INCOME TAX RATES				
2						
3	Taxable Personal Income			Excess	Avg. Tax
4	Minimum	Maximum	Tax	over Min.	on Maximum
5	3,400	5,500	0	14%	5.35%
6	5,500	7,600	294	16%	8.29%
7	7,600	11,900	630	18%	11.80%
8	11,900	16,000	1,404	21%	14.16%
9	16,000	20,200	2,265	24%	16.20%
10	20,200	24,600	3,273	28%	18.31%
11	24,600	29,900	4,505	32%	20.74%
12	29,900	35,200	6,201	37%	23.19%
13	35,200	45,800	8,162	43%	27.77%
14	45,800	60,000	12,720	49%	32.80%
15	60,000	85,600	19,678	54%	39.14%
16	85,600	109,400	33,502	59%	43.46%
17	109,400	162,400	47,544	64%	50.16%
18	162,400	215,400	81,464	68%	54.55%
19	215,400	and over	11,504	70%	

2F. Create the worksheet below and save under L6COV. Enter one formula in C6 and copy it down the column. Copy that same formula into E6..E15. Columns D and G are hidden and contain the squares of the predicted and actual deviations, respectively. The covariance is the sum of squares of the predicted deviations divided by one less than the number of periods. The correlation coefficient is the covariance divided by the quantity the square root of the sum of the predicted deviations divided by one less than the number of periods times the square root of the sum of the actual deviations divided by one less than the number of periods.

	A	B	C	E	F	H
1	COVARIANCE AND CORRELATION BETWEEN ACTUAL AND PREDICTED DEMAND					
2						
3		Predicted	Predicted	Actual	Actual	Predicted Deviation
4	Period	Demand	Deviation	Demand	Deviation	* Actual Deviation
5	-----	------	---------	------	---------	------------------
6	1	2,555	(2,286)	2,764	(2,456)	5,613,713.220
7	2	3,421	(1,420)	3,578	(1,642)	2,331,191.820
8	3	2,365	(2,476)	2,413	(2,807)	6,949,356.120
9	4	3,241	(1,600)	4,900	(320)	511,648.020
10	5	6,345	1,504	5,900	680	1,023,088.820
11	6	5,324	483	6,300	1,080	521,844.620
12	7	6,743	1,902	7,145	1,925	3,661,922.920
13	8	7,426	2,585	7,543	2,323	6,005,704.320
14	9	7,777	2,936	8,111	2,891	8,488,852.320
15	10	3,212	(1,629)	3,544	(1,676)	2,729,710.620
16	-----	------	---------	------	---------	------------------
17		48,409	(0)	52,198	(0)	37,837,033
18						
19				Covariance =		4,204,114.756
20			Correlation Coefficient =			0.962816

2G. Create the worksheet below and save under L6BIAS. The bias is the sum of the forecast errors divided by the number of periods. The mean absolute deviation (MAD) is the sum of the absolute forecast errors divided by the number of periods. The mean squared error (MSE) is the sum of the squared forecast errors divided by the number of periods.

	A	B	C	D	E	F
1	CALCULATION OF BIAS, MAD, AND, MSE FOR DEMAND FORECASTS					
2					Absolute	Squared
3		Predicted	Actual	Forecast	Forecast	Forecast
4	Period	Demand	Demand	Error	Error	Error
5	--------	--------	--------	--------	--------	--------
6	1	2,555	2,764	(209)	209	43,681
7	2	3,421	3,578	(157)	157	24,649
8	3	2,365	2,413	(48)	48	2,304
9	4	3,241	4,900	(1,659)	1,659	2,752,281
10	5	6,345	5,900	445	445	198,025
11	6	5,324	6,300	(976)	976	952,576
12	7	6,743	7,145	(402)	402	161,604
13	8	7,426	7,543	(117)	117	13,689
14	9	7,777	8,111	(334)	334	111,556
15	10	3,212	3,544	(332)	332	110,224
16	--------	--------	--------	--------	--------	--------
17					Bias=	-378.900
18					MAD=	467.900
19					MSE=	437,058.900

CUMULATIVE EXERCISES

C1.   Create the worksheet below by retrieving the TOFU1 worksheet that you created in Lesson 1. Name the range D5..D14 SALES and the range E5..E14 COMMIS. Add the standard deviation, maximum, and minimum values for the 92 Sales, using the range names as arguments. Copy the three cells to column E. Note that the named range COMMIS is copied as the argument. Save under TOFU6.

	A	B	C	D	E
1		IMITATION TOFU, INCORPORATED			
2					
3		SalesRep	Division	92 Sales	Commission
4		===			
5	1	Saxe, J.	2	$40,500	$2,430
6	2	Gress, R.	3	$77,000	$4,620
7	3	Cosner, L.	3	$23,400	$1,404
8	4	Smith, A.	1	$150,000	$9,000
9	5	Smith, B.	1	$54,700	$3,282
10	6	Kirlin, K.	2	$75,000	$4,500
11	7	Wodak, F.	1	$29,800	$1,788
12	8	Reese, J.	3	$111,300	$6,678
13	9	Gruss, M.	1	$88,200	$5,292
14	10	Boyle, T.	2	$67,600	$4,056
15			-----------------------------		
16		Total	$717,500	$43,050	
17		Average	$71,750	$4,305	
18		St. Dev.	$36,576	$2,195	
19		Maximum	$150,000	$9,000	
20		Minimum	$23,400	$1,404	
21					

C2. Create the worksheet below by retrieving the FISH4 worksheet that you created in Lesson 4. Display the D and E columns with /Worksheet Column Display. Hide column F. Name the range D5..D14 RETPRICE and enter @ functions into D16..D20 using that name as the argument. Copy the four functions to columns E, F, and H. Save under FISH6.

	A	B	C	D	E	F	H
1		H A P P Y	T R O P I C A L	F I S H	S T O R E		
2	Item		Quantity	Retail	Wholesal	Profit	Profit
3	#	Item Name	Sold	Price	Price	per Item	Margin %
4		---					
5	273	7-inch fish net	63	$1.99	$0.70	1.29	64.8%
6	238	1-lb. decorative rocks	49	$2.99	$1.30	1.69	56.5%
7	130	underwater fern	13	$2.29	$0.90	1.39	60.7%
8	281	40-gallon aquarium	14	$39.99	$22.00	17.99	45.0%
9	162	goldfish	241	$0.59	$0.10	0.49	83.1%
10	192	20-inch eel	4	$8.99	$4.00	4.99	55.5%
11	274	2-gallon fish bowl	25	$4.99	$2.00	2.99	59.9%
12	256	8-vitamin fish food	57	$1.79	$0.80	0.99	55.3%
13	198	turtle	-1	$3.99	$1.50	2.49	62.4%
14	111	piranha	3	$10.99	$5.00	5.99	54.5%
15		===					
16		Number of items		10	10	10	10
17		Maximum		$39.99	$22.00	$17.99	83.1%
18		Minimum		$0.59	$0.10	$0.49	45.0%
19		Average		$7.86	$3.83	$4.03	59.8%
20							

C3. Retrieve the BILL4 worksheet that you created in Lesson 4 and add the Maximum, Minimum, and Count rows at the bottom. First enter column C using the range name MARCH as the argument and copy those three cells to range B16..D16. Save under BILL6.

	A	B	C	D	E	F	G
1		MONTHLY BILLS					
2							
3			March	April			
4		Budgeted	Actual	Actual			
5	Food	220	238	222	APRIL	D5..D13	
6	Rent	550	550	550	MARCH	C5..C13	
7	Phone	30	39	40			
8	Electric	50	43	45			
9	Gasoline	45	56	52			
10	Car Payment	345	345	345			
11	Insurance	55	55	55			
12	Charge Cards	100	250	170			
13	Entertainment	100	150	150			
14		-------------------------------------					
15	Total	1,495	1,726	1,629			
16	Maximum	550	550	550			
17	Minimum	30	39	40			
18	Count	9	9	9			
19							

C4. Create the worksheet below by retrieving the GOLF4 worksheet that you created in Lesson 4. Delete the range name table and add the minimum and maximum rows by entering @ functions in B11..B12 and copying them across the columns. Save under GOLF6.

	A	B	C	D	E	F	G	H	I	J	K
1				J & F GOLF COURSE SCORE SHEET							
2	Hole	1	2	3	4	5	6	7	8	9	Total
3	Par	4	5	4	3	5	4	4	3	4	36
4											
5	Joe	8	5	6	4	4	5	6	4	4	46
6	Mary	4	6	5	4	6	4	5	5	3	42
7	Mike	3	7	6	4	5	5	6	5	4	45
8	Sheila	5	5	6	4	3	3	4	6	5	41
9											
10	Average	5.00	5.75	5.75	4.00	4.50	4.25	5.25	5.00	4.00	43.50
11	Minimum	3	5	5	4	3	3	4	4	3	41
12	Maximum	8	7	6	4	6	5	6	6	5	46
13											

LOGICAL AND SPECIAL @ FUNCTIONS

Contents:

Lesson 7 covers the @IF function and the other logical functions. @IF is necessary when the contents of a cell depends upon the contents of another cell. It is similar to the IF-THEN-ELSE concept in any programming language. Some other special @ functions are also covered.

Logical @ Functions

A logical @ function returns a value or label depending upon the result of some condition.

@IF

The @IF function returns the second argument if the condition is true or the third argument if the condition is false. Clear your worksheet and place a simple example of the @IF function into cell A1.

You enter: **/ Worksheet Erase Yes**

You enter into A1: **@IF(3>4,100,200) [Return]**

The condition 3>4 is false because 3 is not greater than 4. The false-value, 200, is displayed in cell A1. For those familiar with programming, this structure is similar to the IF-THEN-ELSE.

```
                A                    B
1    Number of units purchased           500
2    Price per unit                    $2.99
3                                  ---------------
4                                   $1,495.00
5    Discount (for orders
6            over 200 only)          $149.50
7                                  ===============
8    Total balance due              $1,345.50
```

Figure 7-1. Discount Worksheet.

Without looking below at the formulas in Figure 7-2, create the worksheet in Figure 7-1 using @IF to compute the discount amount. The total price is discounted by 10% if the number of units purchased is greater than 200.

Change the constant in B1 to other numbers to verify that the discount would be 0 for all orders up to and including 200 units and 10% for all orders 201 units and over.

@IF's can be nested (placed one inside of another). Let's say the

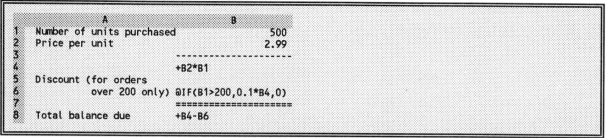

Figure 7-2. Formulas in Discount Worksheet.

discount is 10% for orders between 201 and 500 and 20% for orders greater than 500. Change the formula in B6.

You enter into B6:
@IF(B1>200,@IF(B1>500,.2*B4,.1*B4),0) [Return]

@IF(B1>200,<u>@IF(B1>500,.2*B4,.1*B4)</u>,0)

This formula is easier to understand if you view the underlined function as the one true-value unit which will be performed if B1>200. If B1<=200, the false-value, 0, will be displayed in the cell. If B1>200, then the nested @IF compares it to 500. If it is greater, the discount is computed as 20% of B4; if not, B1 must be between 201 and 500 and the discount is 10% of B4.

There are many other logically equivalent formulas for this structure, some of which are:

@IF(B1>500,.2*B4,@IF(B1>200,.1*B4,0))

@IF(B1<=200,0,@IF(B1<=500,.1*B4,.2*B4))

Below is a list of the other logical @ functions.

@TRUE
Returns the logical value 1.

@FALSE
Returns the logical value 0.

@ISNUMBER(x)
Returns 1 or TRUE if x contains a numeric value, otherwise it returns 0 or FALSE.

@ISSTRING(x)
Returns 1 or TRUE if x contains a string value or label, otherwise it returns 0 or FALSE.

@ISERR(x)

Returns 1 or TRUE if x contains the value ERR (see @ERR function below), otherwise it returns 0 or FALSE.

@ISNA(x)

Returns 1 or TRUE if x contains the value NA (see @NA function below), otherwise it returns 0 or FALSE.

Some Special @ Functions

@NA

Returns the value not available (NA).

@ERR

Returns the value error (ERR).

@ROWS(range)

Returns the number of rows in the range.

@COLS(range)

Returns the number of columns in the range.

Retrieve the file GRADES from the previous lesson.

You enter: **/ File Retrieve GRADES [Return]**

Name the range A2..A11 NAMES. Add a row at the bottom of the worksheet to signify if all students have taken the test.

You enter: **/ Range Name Create NAMES [Return] A2..A11 [Return]**

You enter into A18: **"All Tests Taken? [Return]**

You enter into B18:
@IF(B17=@COUNT(NAMES),"Yes","No") [Return]

Your worksheet should look like Figure 7-3.

```
              A             B       C
 1                       Test 1  Test 2  Test 3
 2  Alunni, Angelo          82      79      63
 3  Carver, Clementine      90      82      75
 4  Cicilioni, Fred         72      70      80
 5  Cicilioni, John         83      75      70
 6  Falzett, Rose           75
 7  Killian, Nicholas       64      45      52
 8  Minster, Catharine      70      95      88
 9  Sesak, Flora            91      99      95
10  Shepard, Gary           30      42
11  Washington, Barbara     82      87      86
12
13            Average     73.9    74.9    76.1
14           St. Dev.     16.8    18.9    13.2
15            Minimum       30      42      52
16            Maximum       91      99      95
17    Number of Tests       10       9       8
18  All Tests Taken? Yes
```

Figure 7-3. Gradebook Worksheet with Added Row 18.

The Yes in B18 would look better if it were right-justified. Because an @IF is a value, you really cannot change the label-prefix of this cell. A possible solution is to add spaces between the " and the Y in the second argument (and the " and the N in the third). Beware if you decrease the width of this column as you may truncate the Yes. We'll simply leave it as is.

Copy B18 to C18.

You enter: / Copy **B18 [Return] C18 [Return]**

You: **Move pointer to C18.**

In the control panel you see that the argument has been changed to TEST1 because of relative addressing. NAMES must be changed to an absolute addressing mode.

You enter into C18: **[F2/EDIT] Add $ before NAMES.**

Note that the range B2..B11 is displayed on the input line instead of TEST1, in case you wish to modify it.

Releases 3.0 and 3.1+: These releases show the range name.

Perhaps the best way to go is with the @ROWS function. Use EDIT mode again to change the condition to the one below.

You enter into C18: **@IF(B17=@ROWS(TEST1),"Yes","No")**

You enter: / Copy **B18 [Return] C18..D18 [Return]**

The not available (@NA) function can be used for the missing test scores.

You enter into C6: **@NA [Return]**

Your worksheet should look like Figure 7-4.

	A	B	C
1		Test 1	Test 2	Test 3
2	Alunni, Angelo	82	79	63
3	Carver, Clementine	90	82	75
4	Cicilioni, Fred	72	70	80
5	Cicilioni, John	83	75	70
6	Falzett, Rose	75	NA	
7	Killian, Nicholas	64	45	52
8	Minster, Catharine	70	95	88
9	Sesak, Flora	91	99	95
10	Shepard, Gary	30	42	
11	Washington, Barbara	82	87	86
12				
13	Average	73.9	NA	76.1
14	St. Dev.	16.8	NA	13.2
15	Minimum	30	NA	52
16	Maximum	91	NA	95
17	Number of Tests	10	10	8
18	All Tests Taken? Yes	Yes	No	

Figure 7-4. Ripple-through Effect of @NA.

Any formula depending on a cell containing the @NA function will also compute to @NA. This phenomenon is called the **ripple-through effect**. It also occurs with the @ERR function. Note that @COUNT counts @NA. All tests taken is now "Yes" in C18.

Erase the @NA.

You enter into C6: **/ Range Erase [Return]**

Add an "Average" column header in E1.

Of course you can use @AVG in column E to compute the average of the 3 tests. But let's say the professor wishes to drop each student's lowest test grade. Take a minute or so to find a formula which will do this without looking below.

You enter into E2:
(@SUM(B2..D2)-@MIN(B2..D2))/(@COUNT(B2..D2)-1)

The outermost parentheses in the numerator and denominator are necessary to insure that the arithmetic operations are done in the proper order. (See precedence of operations.) Both the minimum grade should be subtracted from the sum and the number 1 should be subtracted from the number of tests before the division is done. Therefore the

	A	B	C	D	E
1		Test 1	Test 2	Test 3	Average
2	Alunni, Angelo	82	79	63	
3	Carver, Clementine	90	82	75	
4	Cicilioni, Fred	72	70	80	
5	Cicilioni, John	83	75	70	
6	Falzett, Rose	75			
7	Killian, Nicholas	64	45	52	
8	Minster, Catharine	70	95	88	
9	Sesak, Flora	91	99	95	
10	Shepard, Gary	30	42		
11	Washington, Barbara	82	87	86	
12					
13	Average	73.9	74.9	76.1	
14	St. Dev.	16.8	18.9	13.2	
15	Minimum	30	42	52	
16	Maximum	91	99	95	
17	Number of Tests	10	9	8	
18	All Tests Taken? Yes		No	No	

Figure 7-5. Gradebook Worksheet with 3 Tests.

parentheses are necessary. Copy the formula down the column.

You enter: / Copy **E2 [Return] E3..E11 [Return]**

Copy the statistical functions also.

You enter: / Copy **D13..D16 [Return] E13..E16 [Return]**

Your worksheet should look like Figure 7-6.

	A	B	C	D	E
1		Test 1	Test 2	Test 3	Average
2	Alunni, Angelo	82	79	63	80.5
3	Carver, Clementine	90	82	75	86.0
4	Cicilioni, Fred	72	70	80	76.0
5	Cicilioni, John	83	75	70	79.0
6	Falzett, Rose	75			ERR
7	Killian, Nicholas	64	45	52	58.0
8	Minster, Catharine	70	95	88	91.5
9	Sesak, Flora	91	99	95	97.0
10	Shepard, Gary	30	42		42.0
11	Washington, Barbara	82	87	86	86.5
12					
13	Average	73.9	74.9	76.1	ERR
14	St. Dev.	16.8	18.9	13.2	ERR
15	Minimum	30	42	52	ERR
16	Maximum	91	99	95	ERR
17	Number of Tests	10	9	8	
18	All Tests Taken? Yes		No	No	

Figure 7-6. Gradebook Worksheet with Average Column Added.

Division by zero caused the ERR in E6. The denominator in that fraction computes to zero because the number of tests is 1 and 1-1=0. Even 1-2-3 cannot divide by zero. The ripple-through effect is shown in the statistical functions which depend on E6. Rose Falzett has mononucleosis and the professor is not sure at this point how he's going to handle her grade, so erase cell E6.

You enter: / **Range** Erase **E6 [Return]**

Format the average column.

You enter: / **Range Format Fixed 1 [Return] E2..E11 [Return]**

You could have, of course, named the Test 3 and Average ranges.

The professor decides that students earning an average of 67 or over will pass the course. He may change his mind at a later date, so we'll enter the cut-off value in its own separate cell and use a reference in the formula.

You enter into A20: **Pass-Fail Cut-off [Return]**

You enter into B20: **67 [Return]**

You enter into F2: **@If(E2>=$B$20,"Pass","Fail") [Return]**

You enter: / **Copy F2 [Return] F3..F11 [Return]**

You enter: / **Range** Erase **F6 [Return]**

Your worksheet should look like Figure 7-7.

	A	B	C	D	E	
1		Test 1	Test 2	Test 3	Average	
2	Alunni, Angelo	82	79	63	80.5	Pass
3	Carver, Clementine	90	82	75	86.0	Pass
4	Cicilioni, Fred	72	70	80	76.0	Pass
5	Cicilioni, John	83	75	70	79.0	Pass
6	Falzett, Rose	75				
7	Killian, Nicholas	64	45	52	58.0	Fail
8	Minster, Catharine	70	95	88	91.5	Pass
9	Sesak, Flora	91	99	95	97.0	Pass
10	Shepard, Gary	30	42		42.0	Fail
11	Washington, Barbara	82	87	86	86.5	Pass
12						
13	Average	73.9	74.9	76.1	77.4	
14	St. Dev.	16.8	18.9	13.2	16.3	
15	Minimum	30	42	52	42	
16	Maximum	91	99	95	97	
17	Number of Tests	10	9	8		
18	All Tests Taken?	Yes	No	No		
19						
20	Pass-Fail Cut-off	67				

Figure 7-7. Worksheet with Pass-Fail Column.

Hide the columns containing the tests.

You enter: **/ Worksheet Column Hide B1..D1 [Return]**

You enter into G1: **Failures [Return]**

You enter into G2: **@IF(F2="Fail",@TRUE,@FALSE) [Return]**

You enter: **/ Copy G2 [Return] G3..G11 [Return]**

You enter into G13: **@SUM(G2..G11) [Return]**

The blank cell F6 can cause a problem. We don't know about Rose yet.

You enter into F6: **? [Return]**

Your worksheet should look like Figure 7-8.

```
F6: '?

              A           E        F         G         H
1                       Average         Failures
2   Alunni, Angelo       80.5 Pass        0
3   Carver, Clementine   86.0 Pass        0
4   Cicilioni, Fred      76.0 Pass        0
5   Cicilioni, John      79.0 Pass        0
6   Falzett, Rose           ?             0
7   Killian, Nicholas    58.0 Fail        1
8   Minster, Catharine   91.5 Pass        0
9   Sesak, Flora         97.0 Pass        0
10  Shepard, Gary        42.0 Fail        1
11  Washington, Barbara  86.5 Pass        0
12
13            Average    77.4             2
14           St. Dev.    16.3
15            Minimum     42
16            Maximum     97
17     Number of Tests
18     All Tests Taken?
19
20  Pass-Fail Cut-off
```

Figure 7-8. Gradebook Worksheet with Failures.

Display the 3 test columns.

You enter: **/ Worksheet Column Display B1..D1 [Return]**

Hidden columns are displayed with asterisks after the column header letters. If you are POINTing to ranges (as I strongly suggest you do), you have already observed that hidden columns are also displayed temporarily in POINT mode. Move the pointer to cell A1 and save the file.

You enter: **[Home] / File Save GRADES [Return] Replace**

Figure 7-9 is another example of where the @IF is necessary. The values in E8..G9 depend upon the corporate income and cutoff dollar amounts for tax rates.

```
        A      B      C      D        E        F        G        H
1                      CORPORATION TAXES
2                                   1987     1988     1989
3                                ---------------------------
4      Total corporate income    $20,000  $50,000  $70,000
5
6      Corporation taxes:
7       $25,000  at    17%          3,400    4,250    4,250
8       $25,000  at    20%              0    5,000    5,000
9        Balance at    30%              0        0    6,000
10                               ---------------------------
11     Total corporate tax       $3,400   $9,250  $15,250
```

Figure 7-9. Corporation Tax Example with @IF.

Figure 7-10 shows the formulas for the 1987 taxes in E7..E9. These formulas are copied to F7..G9. The @MIN statistical function is needed in this example. Recall the possibilities for the arguments of the statistical functions as depicted in Table 1-1 in Lesson 1, page 42.

```
        A      B      C      D        E        F        G
1                      CORPORATION TAXES
2                                   1987     1988     1989
3                                ---------------------------
4      Total corporate income    $20,000  $50,000  $70,000
5
6      Corporation taxes:
7       $25,000  at    17%       @MIN(E$4,$A$7)*$C$7
8       $25,000  at    20%       @IF(E$4<=$A$7,0,@MIN(E$4-$A$7,$A$8)*$C$8)
9        Balance at    30%       @IF(E$4<=$A$7+$A$8,0,(E$4-$A$7-$A$8)*$C$9)
10                               ---------------------------
11     Total corporate tax       @SUM(E9..E7)
```

Figure 7-10. Display of Formula Cells in Figure 7-9.

The rest of this lesson is optional and covers special @ functions. They are most commonly used in interactive macros. (See macro lessons.)

@CELL and @CELLPOINTER

@CELL and @CELLPOINTER are two special @ functions which return information about a cell, such as its row, label-prefix, format, etc.

In the GRADES file on your screen, 73.9 is displayed in B13 in Fixed format with one decimal digit.

You enter into A1: **@CELL("format",B13) [Return]**

F1, for Fixed with one decimal digit, is displayed in the cell.

@CELL(attribute,range) returns a piece of information about the cell designated in the second argument.

@CELLPOINTER(attribute) returns a piece of information about the cell in which the pointer currently is displayed.

Below are all possible attribute arguments which can be used with @CELL and @CELLPOINTER and the result of each attribute. They must be enclosed in quotes, as "format" was in the previous example. Upper or lowercase does not matter.

"address" - the address of the cell
"row" - the row number of the cell
"col" - the column number (not letter) of the cell
"contents" - the current value or string in the cell
"type" - the type of data in the cell: b for blank cell; v for value; l for label
"prefix" - current label-prefix of the cell: ', ", ^, \, or blank if the cell does not contain a label
"protect" - returns 1 if cell is protected, 0 if not
"width" - returns the width of the column
"format" - returns the current numeric format as seen in example

@@(cell address) is another special @ function which returns the value or label in the cell at the cell address argument.

You enter into A1: **B13 [Down]**

You enter into A2: **@@(A1) [Return]**

73.9 is displayed in A2 because that is the value in B13 which is the contents of A1. This may be confusing to those who have never dealt with the concept of indirect addressing.

EXERCISES

PART 1 EXERCISES

Part 1 exercises require simple @IF's which are not nested.

1A. Create the worksheet below and save under L7JESSUP. (Modify the L5JESSUP worksheet if you have it on disk to save yourself some typing.) The Overspent and Underspent columns depend on the Expenditure and Budgeted Amount columns, therefore @IF is needed.

Expenditure/Budget Sheet for Jessup Corporation

Month	Expend-iture	Budgeted Amount	Expenditure Year-to-date total	Overspent	Underspent
Jan	$535	$400	$535	$135	NA
Feb	$638	$550	$1,173	$88	NA
Mar	$422	$450	$1,595	NA	$28
Apr	$838	$950	$2,433	NA	$112
May	$333	$300	$2,766	$33	NA
Jun	$734	$750	$3,500	NA	$16
Jul	$744	$750	$4,244	NA	$6
Aug	$612	$800	$4,856	NA	$188
Sept	$574	$550	$5,430	$24	NA
Oct	$568	$600	$5,998	NA	$32
Nov	$854	$850	$6,852	$4	NA
Dec	$876	$800	$7,728	$76	NA
TOTAL	$7,728	$7,750			

1B. Create the worksheet below and save under L7VCR. (Modify the L5VCR worksheet if you have it on disk to save yourself some typing.) There will only be taxes if income before taxes is positive.

	A	B	C	D	E
1				INPUT CELLS	
2	First Year Sales in Units--------------			120.00	
3	Annual Increase Rates:				
4	Sales------------------------------			12.0%	
5	Costs-----------------------------			4.5%	
6	Expenses--------------------------			5.0%	
7	Cost per VCR - Year 1-----------------			$455.00	
8	Markup on VCR-------------------------			45%	
9	Price per VCR - Year 1---------------			$659.75	
10					
11		FOUR YEAR PROJECTION FOR VCR SALES			
12					
13		1989	1990	1991	1992
14	Sales	$79,170.00	$88,670.40	$99,310.85	$111,228.15
15	Cost	54,600.00	57,057.00	59,624.57	62,307.67
16		--			
17	Gross Margin	$24,570.00	$31,613.40	$39,686.28	$48,920.48
18	Expenses:				
19	Rent	2,000.00	2,000.00	2,000.00	2,000.00
20	Advertising	3,500.00	3,675.00	3,858.75	4,051.69
21	Utilities	1,400.00	1,470.00	1,543.50	1,620.68
22	Wages	7,500.00	7,875.00	8,268.75	8,682.19
23	Other	12,630.00	13,261.50	13,924.58	14,620.80
24		--			
25	Total Exp.	$27,030.00	$28,281.50	$29,595.58	$30,975.35
26					
27	Bef. Tax Inc.	(2,460.00)	3,331.90	10,090.71	17,945.13
28	Taxes (50%)	0.00	1,665.95	5,045.35	8,972.56
29		--			
30	Net Income	($2,460.00)	$1,665.95	$5,045.35	$8,972.56

1C. Create the worksheet below and save under L7NAIL. (Modify the L5NAIL worksheet if you have it on disk to save yourself some typing.) There will only be taxes if income before taxes is positive.

	A	B	C	D	E	F
1			FOUR YEAR PROJECTION FOR NAIL CLIPPER SALES			
2						
3		Inc/Dec				
4		Rate	1989	1990	1991	1992
5	Sales	12.0%	$23,896.00	$26,763.52	$29,975.14	$33,572.16
6	Cost of Sales	-5.0%	13,697.19	$13,012.33	$12,361.71	$11,743.63
7						
8	Gross Margin		$10,198.81	$13,751.19	$17,613.43	$21,828.53
9	Expenses:					
10	Mortgage	0.0%	$2,000.00	$2,000.00	$2,000.00	$2,000.00
11	Maintenance	2.0%	2,939.21	2,997.99	3,057.95	3,119.11
12	Utilities	4.0%	743.00	772.72	803.63	835.77
13	Wages	7.0%	4,735.00	5,066.45	5,421.10	5,800.58
14	Insurance	10.0%	3,400.00	3,740.00	4,114.00	4,525.40
15						
16	Total Exp.		$13,817.21	$14,577.16	$15,396.68	$16,280.86
17	Bef. Tax Inc.		($3,618.40)	($825.97)	$2,216.75	$5,547.67
18	Taxes (45%)		0.00	0.00	997.54	2,496.45
19						
20	Net Income		(3,618.40)	(825.97)	1,219.21	3,051.22

1D. Create the worksheet below and save on disk under L7CHECK. All values are constants except those in column F. The returned column contains @TRUE if the check came back to the bank or @FALSE if not. @IF will be needed in the balance formula to be copied down the column and for the service charge. The service charge is $3.00 if the minimum balance for the month drops below $300. You might wish to add a wide column for labels designating to whom each check was written.

	A	B	C	D	E	F
1	MY PERSONAL CHECK REGISTER					
2	September, 1989					
3					Previous Balance	
4					$564.23	
5						
6		Check	Check		Deposit	
7	Date	Number	Amount	Returned?	Amount	Balance
8	09/02/89	180	$40.00	1		$524.23
9	09/02/89	181	$75.21	1		$449.02
10	09/03/89	182	$293.00	1		$156.02
11	09/04/89				$395.68	$551.70
12	09/07/89	183	$22.95	0		$551.70
13	09/07/89	184	$38.75	1		$512.95
14	09/10/89	185	$21.64	0		$512.95
15	09/10/89				$159.77	$672.72
16						
17				Minimum Balance=		$156.02
18				Service Charge=		$3.00
19						
20				New Balance=		$669.72

Hint: The balance formula in F9..F15 will differ from that in F8. The entries in the Returned? column should be either @TRUE, @FALSE, or no entry. The amount subtracted from the balance should be the check amount if the check was returned or 0 if it was not. The product Check Amount*Returned? would produce this amount, but do not use it in the balance formula. Use @IF with first argument Returned? to compute the amount and embed it in the balance formula.

1E. Create the worksheet below and save on disk under L7AGGPLN. The cells in the ranges A4..E15 and F20..F23 and cell F4 are constants input by the user. All other values are formulas.

	A	B	C	D	E	F	G	H	I
1					AGGREGATE PLANNING				
2			Product	Over-	Subcon-		I n v	e n t o r y	
3	Prd	Demand	Regular	time	tract	Beg	End	Avg	Shortages
4	1	250	250			50	50	50	0
5	2	250	300			50	100	75	0
6	3	150	200			100	150	125	0
7	4	300	200			150	50	100	0
8	5	500	350			50	0	25	100
9	6	350	350	70		0	70	35	0
10	7	400	350			70	20	45	0
11	8	700	500	43	50	20	0	10	87
12	9	500	500			0	0	0	0
13	10	600	550	5	100	0	55	28	0
14	11	350	350			55	55	55	0
15	12	250	250			55	55	55	0
16					--				
17				118	150			603	187
18									
19									
20		Overtime cost =				$10.00			
21		Subcontracting cost per unit=				$12.00			
22		Inventory costs per unit =				$1.00			
23		Cost of shortages per unit =				$15.00			
24									
25				COST SUMMARY					
26		Overtime							
27			118 units a $10.00 per unit=				$1,180		
28		Subcontracting							
29			150 units a $12.00 per unit=				$1,800		
30		Inventory costs							
31			603 units a $1.00 per unit=				$603		
32		Shortages							
33			187 units a $15.00 per unit=				$2,805		
34							--------		
35							$6,388		

1F. Create the worksheet below and save under L7INVTBL. @IF and a knowledge of relative and absolute addressing is needed to enter the one formula into D9 and copy throughout the table.

	A	B	C D	E	F	G	H	I	J
1			INVENTORY PAYOFF TABLE						
2									
3	Cost of spoilage per unit =					$2			
4	Profit per unit on sale =					$12			
5									
6				Number of units stocked					
7				0	1	2	3	4	5
8				--					
9			0	$0	($2)	($4)	($6)	($8)	($10)
10	Number		1	$0	$12	$10	$8	$6	$4
11	Demanded		2	$0	$12	$24	$22	$20	$18
12			3	$0	$12	$24	$36	$34	$32
13			4	$0	$12	$24	$36	$48	$46
14			5	$0	$12	$24	$36	$48	$60

1G. Create the worksheet below and save under L7INVTB2. Modify the previous exercise to handle inventory shortage costs by changing the formula and copying it throughout the table again.

	A	B	C D	E	F	G	H	I	J
1			INVENTORY PAYOFF TABLE						
2									
3	Cost of spoilage per unit =					$2			
4	Profit per unit on sale =					$12			
5	Estimated stockout cost per unit =					$4			
6									
7				Number of units stocked					
8				0	1	2	3	4	5
9				--					
10			0	$0	($2)	($4)	($6)	($8)	($10)
11	Number		1	($4)	$12	$10	$8	$6	$4
12	Demanded		2	($8)	$8	$24	$22	$20	$18
13			3	($12)	$4	$20	$36	$34	$32
14			4	($16)	$0	$16	$32	$48	$46
15			5	($20)	($4)	$12	$28	$44	$60

1H. Modify the L6QUAD worksheet from the previous lesson to handle irrational roots. If the discriminant is negative, display "irrational" in cell A9. If the discriminant is zero, display "one root" in cell A10 and the one root in cell A9.

```
                          A                          B
 1    FINDING THE ROOTS OF A QUADRATIC EQUATION.
 2
 3    Quadratic Function:
 4      Coefficient of quadratic term (x^2)=     1.0
 5      Coefficient of linear term (x) =        -3.0
 6      Constant term =                          2.0
 7
 8                                Roots:
 9                                   2
10                                   1
```

PART 2 EXERCISES

Part 2 exercises require require the use of nested @IF's.

2A. Create the worksheet below and save under L7PARK. Cell C3 contains a number input by the person in the ticket booth. Name cell C3 AGE with /Range Name Create. Cell C5's value will be 0 if AGE is 2 years or under, $3.75 if the person is older than 2 years but 12 years or under, and $5.75 if over 12 years.

```
           A        B        C
  1    Hearsch Amusement Park
  2
  3              Age:       14
  4
  5  Price of ticket:     $5.75
  6
```

2B. Create the worksheet below and save under L7REST. Cells C3 and C5 contain numbers input by the waitress. Name cell C3 AGE and C5 PRICE with /Range Name Create. Use @IF to compute the discount. Children 5 years and under receive a 50% discount; senior citizens 65 years and over receive a 10% discount; all others pay full price.

```
            A          B        C        D       E
  1     Felby's Family Restaurant
  2
  3   Age of customer:              66
  4
  5     Price of meal:           $5.99
  6          Discount:           $0.60
  7                           ---------
  8  Discounted Price:            $5.39
  9
```

2C. Create the worksheet below and save under L7POUND. Cells C4 and C5 contain numbers input by the waiter. Name cell C4 AGE and C5 WEIGHT with /Range Name Create. Use @if to compute the discount. If the customer is 65 or over, the senior citizen's discount is 10%. If the customer is a child 5 years or under, the cost of the meal is 1 cent for each pound the child weighs.

```
              A              B        C        D        E
 1         Felby's Family Restaurant
 2  Featuring our Famous Penny-per-Pound Prices!
 3
 4      Age of customer:             4
 5      Weight in lbs.:             32
 6
 7      Price of meal:           $5.99
 8          Discount:            $5.67
 9                             ----------
10  Discounted Price:           $0.32
11
```

Is there a better way to design this worksheet?

CUMULATIVE EXERCISES

C1. Create the worksheet below by retrieving the TOFU1 worksheet that you created in Lesson 1. Delete column A and rows 17 through 20. Modify the commission formula in column D. Sales reps from division 2 receive a 5% commission and reps from all other divisions receive 7%. Enter one formula in cell D5 and copy it down the column. IT, Inc. believes in treating its employees well and decided to pay each rep a commission of $5000 minimum, whether it was earned or not. Add the Additional Unearned Commission column, which is computed as the amount necessary to make up the difference between the minimum $5000 and the employees' commissions. It should be zero IF the commission in column D is greater than or equal to $5000. Enter one formula into cell E5 and copy it down the column. To reward the reps who sold more than quota, a Bonus of 15% of sales over $90,000 was awarded. Add column F to compute this bonus by entering one formula in F5 and copying it down the column. If you are having trouble with the computation, see Precedence of Operations in Lesson 6. Save under TOFU7.

	A	B	C	D	E	F
1		IMITATION TOFU, INCORPORATED			Additional	
2					Unearned	
3	SalesRep	Div	92 Sales	Commission	Commission	Bonus
4	=========	====	========	===========	===========	========
5	Saxe, J.	2	$40,500	$2,025	$2,975	$0
6	Gress, R.	3	$77,000	$5,390	$0	$0
7	Cosner, L.	3	$23,400	$1,638	$3,362	$0
8	Smith, A.	1	$150,000	$10,500	$0	$9,000
9	Smith, B.	1	$54,700	$3,829	$1,171	$0
10	Kirlin, K.	2	$75,000	$3,750	$1,250	$0
11	Wodak, F.	1	$29,800	$2,086	$2,914	$0
12	Reese, J.	3	$111,300	$7,791	$0	$3,195
13	Gruss, M.	1	$88,200	$6,174	$0	$0
14	Boyle, T.	2	$67,600	$3,380	$1,620	$0
15			--------			
16		Total	$717,500	$46,563	$13,292	$12,195
17						

C2. Create the worksheet below by retrieving the FISH4 worksheet that you created in Lesson 4. Delete columns D through H. Add the 3 new columns: Quantity On-hand, Reorder Point, and Reorder?. Enter the Quantities On-hand and Reorder Points as values. Items are ordered when the Quantity On-hand (at last inventory count) minus the Quantity Sold is less than the Reorder Point. Enter one formula using @IF into F5 and copy it down the column. Save under FISH7A.

```
         A          B              C        D        E      F
  1            H A P P Y   T R O P I C A L   F I S H   S T O R E
  2    Item                      Quantity Quantity Reorder
  3     #        Item Name         Sold   On-hand   Point Reorder?
  4    -------------------------------------------------------------
  5    273 7-inch fish net          63       70       10 Yes
  6    238 1-lb. decorative rocks   49       50       20 Yes
  7    130 underwater fern          13       15       10 Yes
  8    281 40-gallon aquarium       14       30       10 No
  9    162 goldfish                241      300      100 Yes
 10    192 20-inch eel              4        7        3 No
 11    274 2-gallon fish bowl       25       30       10 Yes
 12    256 8-vitamin fish food      57       57       50 Yes
 13    198 turtle                  -1        2        5 Yes
 14    111 piranha                  3        4        3 Yes
 15    =============================================================
 16
```

C3. Create the worksheet below by retrieving the FISH 4 worksheet that you created in Lesson 4. Hide columns C through G. Enter one formula into J5 that will display "OK" if the profit margin for each item is greater than or equal to 55% and "Too Low" otherwise and copy it down the column. Save under FISH7B.

```
        A          B                  H    I J
  1   H A P P Y   T R O P I C A L   F I S H   S T O R
  2   Item                        Profit
  3    #        Item Name         Margin %
  4   ------------------------------------------
  5   273 7-inch fish net          64.8% OK
  6   238 1-lb. decorative rocks   56.5% OK
  7   130 underwater fern          60.7% OK
  8   281 40-gallon aquarium       45.0% Too Low
  9   162 goldfish                 83.1% OK
 10   192 20-inch eel              55.5% OK
 11   274 2-gallon fish bowl       59.9% OK
 12   256 8-vitamin fish food      55.3% OK
 13   198 turtle                   62.4% OK
 14   111 piranha                  54.5% Too Low
 15   =============================================
 16
 17
```

C4. Create the worksheet below by retrieving the BILL1 worksheet that you created in Lesson 1. Change the heading "Over/(Under)" to "Difference" as shown below. Enter one formula into E1 which will display "Over" if the Actual bill is greater than the Budgeted bill and will display nothing if it is not. Copy the formula down the column. Save under BILL7.

	A	B	C	D	E
1		MONTHLY BILLS FOR MARCH			
2					
3		Actual	Budgeted	Difference	
4	Food	$238	$220	$18	Over
5	Rent	$550	$550	$0	
6	Phone	$39	$30	$9	Over
7	Electric	$43	$50	($7)	
8	Gasoline	$56	$45	$11	Over
9	Car Payment	$345	$345	$0	
10	Insurance	$55	$55	$0	
11	Charge Cards	$250	$100	$150	Over
12	Entertainment	$150	$100	$50	Over
13		----------	----------	----------	
14	Total	$1,726	$1,495	$231	
15					

C5. Create the worksheet below by retrieving the GOLF4 worksheet that you created in Lesson 4. Delete the range name table. Enter a formula into B12 that will display "Under" if the score on that hole is under par for that hole. Use your knowledge of relative and absolute addressing and copy it through the range B12..K15. If you haven't done the Lesson 5 on addressing, enter four formulas in B12..B15 and copy them through the rows. A bird is one under par. Do the same as with "Under", substituting "Birdie" if the score is one under par. Do the same with "Eagle" which is two under par. Save under GOLF7.

	A	B	C	D	E	F	G	H	I	J	K
1			J & F GOLF COURSE SCORE SHEET								
2	Hole	1	2	3	4	5	6	7	8	9	Total
3	Par	4	5	4	3	5	4	4	3	4	36
4											
5	Joe	8	5	6	4	4	5	6	4	4	46
6	Mary	4	6	5	4	6	4	5	5	3	42
7	Mike	3	7	6	4	5	5	6	5	4	45
8	Sheila	5	5	6	4	3	3	4	6	5	41
9											
10	Average	5.00	5.75	5.75	4.00	4.50	4.25	5.25	5.00	4.00	43.50
11											
12	Joe				Under						
13	Mary									Under	
14	Mike	Under									
15	Sheila				Under	Under					
16											

"WHAT IF" SIMULATION FINANCIAL @ FUNCTIONS

Contents:

Lesson 8 introduces "what if" analysis. Automating the "what if" process is covered in Lesson 20. Financial analysis using financial @ functions is demonstrated. The finance portion of the lesson is optional and may be skipped.

"What-if" Analysis

1-2-3 is great for "what if" analysis, which determines the effect of an input value on a result variable. It answers questions like these:

"What if" my production level is increased by 500 units?

"What if" inventory carrying costs decrease by 5%?

In 1-2-3, you simply type in the new figure and the result variable is automatically recalculated.

Templates

Templates are worksheets containing previously entered formulas. The user enters or modifies input numbers in order to see the results or output from the existing formulas.

Let's say you and your husband wish to sell your current home and purchase a new one, but you're not sure how much house you can afford. It depends on several different variables, including your savings, the sale price of old house, interest rates, the monthly payment on the new mortgage, etc.

Create the template in Figure 8-1, using the formulas displayed in Figure 8-2 as guides. The two @ functions @PV (present value) and @FV (future value) are needed in this worksheet. Please just enter them exactly as shown. They are explained later in the lesson. For now, keep in mind that they are two financial @ functions which take into account interest earned on the savings account and interest paid on the mortgage.

```
      A               B                    C              D
 1          WHAT IF ANALYSIS - HOW MUCH HOUSE CAN WE AFFORD?
 2   Savings per month=                    300
 3       Total savings=                 $1,820
 4   Lottery winnings=                       0
 5   Inheritance=                       10,000
 6   Royalties on books=                     0
 7     Miscellaneous Income=           $10,000
 8          DOWNPAYMENT=                              $11,820
 9   Selling price of old home=        103,000
10   Amount still owed on mortgage=     52,460
11   Cost of selling old home=          1,400
12       PROFIT FROM SALE OF OLD HOME=               $49,140
13   Monthly mortgage payment (new home)=  775
14   Mortgage interest rate=            10.5%
15   Term of new mortgage in years =      25
16       MORTGAGE AMOUNT BORROWED=                    $82,082
17   Number of months until purchase=       6
18   =====================================================
19   MAXIMUM COST OF HOME WE CAN AFFORD=            $143,042
20        (includes closing costs)              ===============
```

Figure 8-1. "What if" Analysis for Home Purchase.

```
                 C                          D
 1
 2                    300
 3   @FV(C2,0.0525/12,C17)
 4                      0
 5                  10000
 6                      0
 7   +C4+C5+C6
 8                                 +C3+C7
 9                 103000
10   @PV(634.19,0.115/12,(14*12+3-C17))
11                   1400
12                                 +C9-C10-C11
13                    775
14                  0.105
15                     25
16                                 @PV(C13,C14/12,C15*12)
17                      6
18   ======================================================
19                                 +D8+D12+D16
20                                 =========================
```

Figure 8-2. Columns C and D from Figure 8-1 in Text Format.

The following assumptions have been made. The amount of house you can afford depends upon many variables, including the number of months from the current date to the date of purchase of the new home. The longer you wait, the more savings you will have and the less you will owe on your current mortgage.

Now that you have the worksheet set up, let's do some "what if" simulation. With the current values for the variables, you can afford a $143,042 home, but this doesn't suit you. You would like to be able to afford a $250,000 home. What if you could save $550 a month instead of $300?

You enter into C2: **550 [Return]**

Wow! Not much difference at all. The amount of house you can afford does not seem to be "sensitive" to monthly savings. At least this is the case if you wait only 6 months to purchase the new home.

Sensitivity Analysis

Sensitivity analysis is a kind of "what if" analysis that tests how sensitive some result value is on one or more input variables. We just found that affordable house price is not very sensitive to savings.

Another example of sensitivity analysis is determining the effect of advertising, level of quality control, and market price on gross sales. Let's say that formulas exist relating the effect of these variables to gross sales. A sensitivity question might be: If the amount spent on advertising is increased a little, say 5%, exactly how much are sales affected? In other words, how sensitive are gross sales to advertising expenses. Maybe a little, maybe a lot. Maybe even a little sometimes and a lot other times depending on the status of other input variables.

Back to the house example. What if you wait a year and a half instead of 6 months to buy your new home?

You enter into C17: **18 [Return]**

That's better, now there's only about $100,000 to go. Because the wait period is longer, the home cost on the bottom line is now more sensitive to changes in the savings per month. Do you see that you must look at both number of months and savings per month? Trying combinations of the two can get tedious, and unless you write the numbers down, you really don't get a good picture of the effect of the combined values of the variables. /Data Table is ideal for sensitivity analysis because is creates tables showing the effect of variables on values. (See /Data Table.)

What if you made $75,000 on royalties from a Lotus book you wrote?

You enter into C6: **75000 [Return]**

This can be fun. We don't have to be realistic. Well, now you can either wait about 4 years or win $22,000 on the lottery and you've got your $250,000 house. Perhaps, instead, you can afford a larger mortgage payment than $775 a month. Could you swing $982, which would be the new home monthly mortgage payment for a $250,000 home? (@PMT was used to find the number 982 and is covered later in the lesson). If interest rates fall or your bank allows a longer term, you can afford more house. Perhaps you'll get more than $103,000 for the old home.

Another assumption is your ability to maintain a more expensive house. After all, the cost of a home doesn't stop at the closing.

- - - If you need a break, stop at this point. - - -

The rest of this lesson covers the financial and depreciation @ functions and is optional. Business majors should definitely go through it.

Financial @ Functions

1-2-3 has financial @ functions which calculate annuities, loans, cash flows, depreciation, and investments. The time value of money is accounted for by interest calculations. LOTUS assumes ordinary annuities.

Compound Interest

Create Figure 8-3. All values are constants except cell D4 which contains the formula +B4*C4and cell E4 which contains the formula +B4+D4.

$100 is deposited into a savings account at the beginning of year 1 at an interest rate of 10%. At the end of the year, the amount in the saving account is the original $100 plus the earned interest of $10 or $110.

The $110 is left in the savings account through year 2. How much interest is earned if the rate is still 10%? Because the amount in the savings account is now $110, not $100, it will be more than the interest of $10 from the first year. The interest from the first year is still there and earning interest. **Compounding** is earning interest on interest.

You enter into B5: **+E4 [Right]**

You enter into C5: **10% [Return]** / Range Format Percent **0 [Return]** **[Return]**

```
D4: +B4*C4


      A         B           C          D            E
1                    COMPOUND INTEREST
2              Amount in     Int.   Int. Earned  Amount Plus
3     Year     Savings       Rate   This Year    Int. Earned
4      1       $100.00       10%      $10.00       $110.00
5      2
6      3
7      4
8      5
9      6
10     7
11     8
12     9
13     10
```

Figure 8-3. First Year Values for Compound Interest Table.

You enter: / Copy **D4..E4 [Return] D5..E5 [Return]**

Your worksheet should look like Figure 8-4.

```
      A         B           C          D            E
1                    COMPOUND INTEREST
2              Amount in     Int.   Int. Earned  Amount Plus
3     Year     Savings       Rate   This Year    Int. Earned
4      1       $100.00       10%      $10.00       $110.00
5      2       $110.00       10%      $11.00       $121.00
6      3
7      4
8      5
9      6
10     7
11     8
12     9
13     10
```

Figure 8-4. Second Year Values for Compound Interest Table.

In this particular example, the amount in the account after two years can be computed using the equation below:

Amount = Beginning Amount * (1 + Rate) $^\wedge$ 2

You enter into B15: **100*1.1 $^\wedge$ 2 [Return]**

$121.00 should be displayed in B15.

Let's let it ride for another eight years.

You enter: / Copy **B5..E5 [Return] B5..B13 [Return]**

Your worksheet should look like Figure 8-5.

	A	B	C	D	E
1			COMPOUND INTEREST		
2		Amount in	Int.	Int. Earned	Amount Plus
3	Year	Savings	Rate	This Year	Int. Earned
4	1	$100.00	10%	$10.00	$110.00
5	2	$110.00	10%	$11.00	$121.00
6	3	$121.00	10%	$12.10	$133.10
7	4	$133.10	10%	$13.31	$146.41
8	5	$146.41	10%	$14.64	$161.05
9	6	$161.05	10%	$16.11	$177.16
10	7	$177.16	10%	$17.72	$194.87
11	8	$194.87	10%	$19.49	$214.36
12	9	$214.36	10%	$21.44	$235.79
13	10	$235.79	10%	$23.58	$259.37
14					
15		$121.00			

Figure 8-5. Ten Years of Compound Interest.

Save this file under COMPOUND.

You enter: / File Save **COMPOUND [Return]**

Banks usually compound or add interest more than once a year. Let's say our bank has an annual interest rate of 10% but compounds quarterly or 4 times a year. Don't have the misconception that the bank is going to take 10% and add it to the amount 4 times a year. That 10% is an annual interest rate. The percentage used each quarter is .10 divided by 4 periods or .025. Change the Int. Rates to .025 and the format to Percent with 1 decimal place. Change A3 to Quarter and Year to Qtr in D3.

Your worksheet should look like Figure 8-6.

	A	B	C	D	E
1			COMPOUND INTEREST		
2		Amount in	Int.	Int. Earned	Amount Plus
3	Quarter	Savings	Rate	This Qtr	Int. Earned
4	1	$100.00	2.5%	$2.50	$102.50
5	2	$102.50	2.5%	$2.56	$105.06
6	3	$105.06	2.5%	$2.63	$107.69
7	4	$107.69	2.5%	$2.69	$110.38
8	5	$110.38	2.5%	$2.76	$113.14
9	6	$113.14	2.5%	$2.83	$115.97
10	7	$115.97	2.5%	$2.90	$118.87
11	8	$118.87	2.5%	$2.97	$121.84
12	9	$121.84	2.5%	$3.05	$124.89
13	10	$124.89	2.5%	$3.12	$128.01
14					
15		$121.00			

Figure 8-6. Compounding Done Quarterly.

The compound interest equation below can be used to find the amount after t periods.

amount = beginning amount * (1 + annual rate/t) ^ (years * t)

where t is the number of periods.

You enter into B17: **100*(1+.10/4) ^ (2.5*4) [Return]**

There are 10 quarters which is equal to 2.5 years. $128.01 should be displayed in the cell which is the same as the computed value in E13. At the end of the fourth quarter, instead of having $110 in the account, there is now $110.38 which leads to the conclusion that the annual interest rate is 10.38% instead of 10%. This is true. 10.38% is the effective rate which differs from the annual rate because compounding is not done once a year. The formula below can be used to find effective interest rates if you are given an annual rate and the number of compounding periods a year.

effective rate = (1 + annual rate/t) ^ t - 1

where t is the number of periods per year.

You enter into A17: **(1+.10/4) ^ 4-1 [Return]**

Format A17 as Fixed with 4 decimal digits and 0.1038 should appear in the cell.

An entirely new table will be generated if the initial investment is changed.

You enter into B4: **400 [Return]**

@CTERM(interest rate,future value,present value)

@CTERM returns the term or number of compounding periods necessary for a single investment earning interest to grow to a certain amount in the future. Interest rate is the rate per period, so if you're given annual rate you must divide it by the number of periods per year. Future value is the amount the investment will be worth in the future, or the amount the investment grows to. Present value is the initial single investment.

How long does it take a single investment of $100 to grow to $194.87 at a periodic interest rate of 10%? If you happen to have the table in Figure 8-5, you can easily find the answer in row 10. @CTERM will answer that kind of question without a table.

You enter anywhere: **@CTERM(.10,194.87,100) [Return]**

A 7 should be displayed in the cell (you may have to format it Fixed with 0 decimal digits). This is consistent with Figure 8-5.

How many compounding periods would it take for $100 invested at 10% compounded quarterly to grow to $120?

You enter: **@CTERM(.10/4,120,100) [Return]**

Around 7.4 compounding periods is the answer. Therefore you would have to wait 8 quarterly periods or 2 years.

@RATE(future value,present value,term)

@RATE returns the interest rate which must be earned for a single investment of present value to grow to future value.

At which rate will $100 grow to $121.84 in 8 compounding periods? We know the answer is 2.5% per period from Figure 8-6.

You enter: **@RATE(121.84,100,8) [Return]**

I recommend that you do the exercises on compound interest at the end of this lesson now, while the material is fresh in your mind.

- - - If you need a break, stop at this point. - - -

Annuities

An **annuity** is a series of payments at equal time intervals which involves an interest rate. Each time interval is called a payment period or period and the number of payment periods is called the term. The interest rate is per period, not necessarily per year. Examples are:

1) Monthly deposits of $300 into a savings account for 6 months earning 5¼% compounded monthly. The payment is $300, the period is a month, the term is 6 months, and the interest rate per period is 5¼% divided by 12 periods per year or .0525/12 = .004375. Refer to C3 in Figure 8-1.

2) Monthly mortgage payments of $775 for 25 years at an interest rate of 10½% per year. The payment is $775, the period is a month, the term is 300 periods = 25 years * 12 periods a year, and the interest rate per period is .105/12 or .00875. Refer to C13..D16 in Figure 8-1.

1-2-3 assumes ordinary annuity, which means that payments are made at the end of the period.

@FV(payment,interest rate,term)

The @FV function computes the future value of an annuity, which is the sum of the compound amounts of all payments. It uses the formula:

future value = payment * (((1+rate)^t) - 1) / rate

where t is the number of periods in the term (not year, necessarily).

Let's say you will deposit $300 at the end of each month for 6 months at an annual interest rate of 5¼%. It's very important to remember that the interest rate argument in the @FV is per period, not per year. Therefore, you must divide 5¼% by the number of periods per year. The third argument, term, is the number of periods (not years).

You enter: **/ Worksheet Erase Yes**

You enter into A1: **@FV(300,.0525/12,6) [Return]**

1819.802 is displayed therefore the savings account would contain $1,819.02 after 6 months. Figure 8-7 shows the interest earned and amount in the savings at the end of each month. Interest does not accrue on a payment until the month after it is made because, in ordinary annuities, the payments are made at the end of the month. You need not create Figure 8-7, it is only displayed for further clarification of the process of finding future values.

```
D3: (F6) 0.0525/12

          A          B          C     D      E        F
1                Future Value of Annuity Table
2
3   Interest Rate/Period          0.004375
4
5                      Payment        Interest      Amount at End
6   Month        End of Month         Earned         of Month
7      1             $300.00           $0.00          $300.00
8      2             $300.00           $1.31          $601.31
9      3             $300.00           $2.63          $903.94
10     4             $300.00           $3.95        $1,207.90
11     5             $300.00           $5.28        $1,513.18
12     6             $300.00           $6.62        $1,819.80
```

Figure 8-7. Future Value of Ordinary Annuity Table.

The big difference between @FV and compound interest (as in Figure 8-5) is that the compound interest table has one single initial lump sum investment which grows into a future value. The @FV function assumes that payment is made each period (not just once in the beginning) and therefore the value grows not only from accruing interest, but also from the additional payments.

The compound interest of an annuity is the difference between the amount of the annuity and the sum of the payments. In the last example, the compound interest is $1819.80 - $1800 = $19.80.

Let's say you invest $100 every 3 months for 5 years at an annual rate of 6 percent compounded quarterly. How much will you have in the account at the end of the term? The payment argument is 100, the interest rate argument is .06/4, and the term or number of periods is 20 (4 per year times 5 years).

You enter anywhere: **@FV(100,.06/4,20) [Return]**

$2312.37 is the amount or future value and $312.37 is the compound interest.

Some "real world" examples of future value are in the exercises at the end of this lesson. Even if you do not do the exercises, take a minute and look at them now.

- - - **If you need a break, stop at this point.** - - -

Loans

You need to borrow $150,000 for a new home. The bank tells you that its current fixed annual interest rate is 10½% for a 15 year mortgage and that the monthly payment will be $1681.42.

You enter: / **Worksheet Erase Yes**

You enter into E1: **150000 [Down]**

You enter into E2: **.1075/12 [Down]**

You enter into E3: **1681.42 [Down]**

You enter into E4: **15*12 [Return]**

Now finish creating Figure 8-8 by entering A1..A4 and formatting as shown. Column E will have to be widened.

```
E2: (P2) [W13] 0.1075/12


        A       B       C       D          E
1   Principal:                        $150,000.00
2   Interest Rate per Period:              0.90%
3   Payment per Period:                $1,681.42
4   Term or Number of Periods:               180
```

Figure 8-8. The Four Values of a Loan.

@PMT(principal,interest rate,term)

1-2-3's @PMT function will calculate the payment, given the amount borrowed or principal, periodic interest rate (not necessarily annual rate), and the number of payment periods or term.

To find the monthly payment for a mortgage of $150,000 at 10¾% for 15 years:

You enter into F3: **@PMT(150000,.1075/12,15*12) [Return]**

1681.421 is displayed; the bank is correct. It is important that you remember that interest rate is per period, not per year. Most of the time you will have to divide the annual rate, here 10.75%, by the number of periods per year, here 12 periods. The term is not necessarily the number of years. Here there are 12 periods per year and 15 years for a total of 180 periods.[1]

A corporation borrows $500,000 at 14% and repays it monthly in 1 year. What is the payment amount?

You enter into E1: **500000 [Down]**

You enter into E2: **.14/12 [Down]**

You enter into E3: **@PMT(E1,E2,E4) [Down]**

You enter into E4: **12 [Return]**

Your worksheet should look like Figure 8-9.

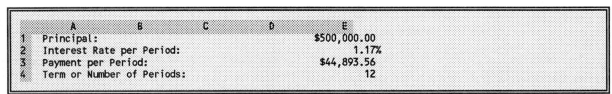

	A	B	C	D	E
1	Principal:				$500,000.00
2	Interest Rate per Period:				1.17%
3	Payment per Period:				$44,893.56
4	Term or Number of Periods:				12

Figure 8-9. Corporation Loan with Monthly Payments.

The payment amount is $44,893.56.

The corporation wishes to compute the amount of interest paid on this loan for tax purposes; interest is deductible. There is no @ function to do this. Although this can be estimated, to get an exact figure, an amortization table must be created.

---

[1]The arguments here should have really been entered as @PMT(E1,E2,E4) if we are to follow the rule that cells dependent on other cells should never be entered as constants.

Amortization Table

An amortization table shows the breakdown of each payment into interest and principal.

```
B20: @SUM(B8..B19)


          A            B            C            D            E
1   Principal:                                           $500,000.00
2   Interest Rate per Period:                                  1.17%
3   Payment per Period:                                   $44,893.56
4   Term or Number of Periods:                                    12
5                      AMORTIZATION TABLE
6                        Applied to
7   Payment    Interest   Principal New Balance
8        1    $5,833.33 $39,060.23 $460,939.77
9        2    $5,377.63 $39,515.93 $421,423.85
10       3    $4,916.61 $39,976.95 $381,446.90
11       4    $4,450.21 $40,443.34 $341,003.55
12       5    $3,978.37 $40,915.18 $300,088.37
13       6    $3,501.03 $41,392.53 $258,695.84
14       7    $3,018.12 $41,875.44 $216,820.40
15       8    $2,529.57 $42,363.99 $174,456.41
16       9    $2,035.32 $42,858.23 $131,598.18
17      10    $1,535.31 $43,358.25  $88,239.93
18      11    $1,029.47 $43,864.09  $44,375.84
19      12      $517.72 $44,375.84      $0.00
20            $38,722.71
```

Figure 8-10. Amortization Table.

The interest paid in the first period (cell B8) is computed as the rate times principal or E2*E1. The amount of payment 1 applied to the principal (C8) is the difference between the payment and the interest for period 1 or E3-B8. The balance after the first payment (D8) is the principal minus the amount applied to the principal or E1-C8. For the second payment, the interest is the interest rate (E2) times the previous payment's new balance (D8). The amount applied to the principal (C9) is the payment (E3) minus interest for this period (B9). The new balance is the previous period's new balance (D8) minus the amount applied to the principal (C9). B9..D9 can then be copied to the next ten rows to finish creating the table. In order to do this copy command, a knowledge of addressing is necessary (Lesson 5). Save Figure 8-9 under the name AMORT. The total interest paid is simply the sum of the interest column (see control panel).

@PV(payment,interest rate,term)

Let's look at the bank's point of view. If a customer will give the bank $44,893.56 starting next month for 12 months and the current interest rate one can expect from an investment is 12%, what amount is due the customer today? In other words, what is the value today of an investment that will return $44,893.56 for the next 12 months if current interest rates are 12%? This value is an example of present value.

Present value is the current value of one or more future payments discounted at a discount interest rate. Techniques in discounting, which can be considered the opposite of compounding, came about when it was realized that a dollar in hand today is better than one in received in the future. Just as one would rather have a bird in the hand than two in the bush, one would rather be handed a little less money today than more in the future because of opportunity cost. Remember, future values are more than the sum of the payments because of interest compounded and present values are less than the sum of the payments because of interest discounted.

You enter into D6: **@PV(44893.56,.14/12,12) [Return]**

500000.01 is displayed in the cell.[2] Note that this is the principal amount or amount borrowed.

Investment Analysis

Given a choice between $2000 now and $300 a year for 10 years, which would you take? The sum of the future payments is 10 * $300 = $3000 which is 50% more than the lump sum. But you have to wait for the money and if you took the $2000 today and invested it, you may make more then $1000 in interest over the 10 years. But you have to wait for the interest! To answer the question, you must have an opportunity cost or interest rate in mind. The rate should be that which can be earned on a safe investment, let's say a CD earning 9%.

You enter: **@PV(300,.09,10) [Return]**

Because the present value of the future $300 payments is only $1925.30, take the $2000 and run. You can be earning more on the lump sum.

---

[2]There are accuracy errors with any computer or calculator. In 1-2-3, the round-off errors are usually negligible and cause no problem.

What if the CD is only paying 8%?

You enter: **@PV(300,.08,10) [Return]**

But, you could be enjoying that stereo system right now. Is the $13.02 really worth waiting for? Well, it's nice to have some future income just in case you hit hard times. But what if the entity doesn't pay you back because of bankruptcy? Numbers alone don't answer the question, but they help.

Remember, the higher the interest rate, the lower the present value of future fixed payments. This should make sense because the more interest you could earn, the more it is likely that you should take the lump sum now.

Increase the future payments to $400.

You enter: **@PV(400,.08,10) [Return]**

The $2684.03 doesn't leave any question in your mind that future is better. If you really want that $2000 right now, go get a loan at 11% for 10 years. Using @PMT, your yearly payments will only be $339.60, which you can pay with the $400 payments and have $60 left over.

Another consideration is ALWAYS taxes. Claiming interest earned as income is painful and I will discuss it no further.

@IRR(initial guess for rate,range of cash flows)

What is the actual rate of return if you give up $2000 now to gain $300 for 10 future yearly payments? We know it's between 8% and 9%. The IRR or internal rate of return is the rate which equates the present value of future cash flows from an investment to the original cost of the investment. Very simply, it is the interest rate you're making. Our cost is $2000 and our future cash flows are 10 payments of $300. 1-2-3 will compute the IRR given a range of figures where the first value in the range is the initial cash outlay (negated) and the rest are the cash flows. Create Figure 8-11. All values are constants.

The first argument is a guess with which 1-2-3 starts its calculations. Finding the IRR is an iterative process and if after 20 iterations the answer is not found, ERR is displayed in the cell. A good rule of thumb is to estimate between 5% and 20%, although any number between 0 and 1 is valid.

You enter into A13: **@IRR(.08,A1..A11) [Return]**

```
        A
1     -2000
2       300
3       300
4       300
5       300
6       300
7       300
8       300
9       300
10      300
11      300
```

Figure 8-11. Range of Cash Flows for @IRR.

Not surprisingly the answer is 8.14%.

Cash Flow Analysis

The cash flows need not all be the same.

You have a choice between two investments. One involves an initial outlay of $3000 and pays back 5 yearly payments of $100, $1700, $40, $2000, and $500. The other's outlay is $3500 and pays back 4 installments of $1000, $0, $2000, and $2000. The cash flow ranges for the two investments are shown in Figure 8-12, as well as the @IRR values.

```
B8: aIRR(0.08,B1..B5)


          A          B
1      -3000      -3500
2        100       1000
3       1700          0
4         40       2000
5       2000       2000
6        500
7
8     0.123331 0.129738
```

Figure 8-12. Analysis of Two Investments.

The second pays slightly more. What if the third payment of the first investment is $200 rather than $40 (cell A4)? Figure 8-13 shows that the first investment is now more profitable.

The @IRR actually assumes an interest rate, finds the present values of each of the cash flows, adds up the present values and compares their sum to the initial outlay. If they are not equal, it adjusts the rate and tries again until the difference between the present values' sum and the outlay is almost zero. This difference is referred to as net present value.

	A	B
1	-3000	-3500
2	100	1000
3	1700	0
4	200	2000
5	2000	2000
6	500	
7		
8	0.136859	0.129738

Figure 8-13. Increase in Third Payment in Investment 1.

@NPV(interest rate,range of cash flows)

The net present value (NPV) is what it sounds like. It is the sum of the present values of each cash flow minus the initial investment. If it is positive, you're making money, because the present value of the cash flows is greater than the cost. If it is negative, you're losing money, because you're investing more than the present value of the future cash flows. The more positive the NPV, the more net gain.

Using Figure 8-13 and assuming a discount rate of 10%, the NPV of the two investments are shown in A9 and B9 of Figure 8-14.

A9: @NPV(0.08,A1..A6)

	A	B
1	-3000	-3500
2	100	1000
3	1700	0
4	200	2000
5	2000	2000
6	500	
7		
8	0.136859	0.129738
9	480.7280	447.8241

Figure 8-14. Net Present Values in A9 and B9.

Investment 1 is more profitable because it has a higher NPV and IRR. These two go together. The higher the better.

The NPV's are both positive, because we are assuming an interest rate less than the IRR. The IRR is the rate of return you're actually making on the investment. If you're assuming a lower rate, then you're ahead of the game here and your net gain is positive. Here's another way of looking at it. The sum of the present values of the future cash flows is some value which is computed with an assumed realistic interest rate. That sum should be equal to the initial outlay. If the initial outlay is less, then you're getting more in the future than you're paying for now. This is good.

What would the NPV be if the assumed interest rate is the IRR? If you cannot answer 0, then re-read this section again until it is clear to you.

Depreciation

1-2-3 has 3 @ functions for computing depreciation: @DDB (double-declining balance method), @SLN (straight-line depreciation), and @SYD (sum-of-the-years' digits method).

@SLN(cost,salvage,life)

The cost argument is the amount paid for the asset, the salvage argument is the salvage value or the amount it's worth at the end of its life, and the life argument is the number of years of its life. The yearly depreciation is the same for all years and therefore year is not necessary as an input argument. It is computed as:

yearly depreciation = (cost - salvage)/life

@DDB(cost,salvage,life,period)

The cost, salvage, and life arguments are the same as for @SLN and the period argument is the period for which you want the depreciation allowance. It is computed as:

depreciation
for this period = (book value * 2) / life

where book value is cost - previous depreciation.

@SYD(cost,salvage,life,period)

The arguments are the same as @DDB. It is computed as:

depreciation for this period =

[(cost-salvage) * (life-period+1)] / [life*(life+1)/2]

	A	B	C	D
1			DEPRECIATION METHODS	
2				
3		Cost:	$10,000.00	
4		Salvage:	$1,000.00	
5		Life:	10	
6				
7			Double-Declining	Sum-of-Years'-
8	Period	Straight Line	Balance	Digits
9	1	$900.00	$2,000.00	$1,636.36
10	2	$900.00	$1,600.00	$1,472.73
11	3	$900.00	$1,280.00	$1,309.09
12	4	$900.00	$1,024.00	$1,145.45
13	5	$900.00	$819.20	$981.82
14	6	$900.00	$655.36	$818.18
15	7	$900.00	$524.29	$654.55
16	8	$900.00	$419.43	$490.91
17	9	$900.00	$335.54	$327.27
18	10	$900.00	$268.44	$163.64
19		-------------	------------------	------------
20	Total	$9,000.00	$8,926.26	$9,000.00

Figure 8-15. Comparison of 3 Depreciation Methods.

Figure 8-15 shows the depreciation schedules of an asset whose original cost was $10,000 with a salvage value of $1000 and a life of 10 periods or years. To create this table using the copy command instead of entering each and every function by hand, a knowledge of addressing is necessary. See Lesson 5.

NEW COMMAND SUMMARY

"What if" Analysis   Using trial-and-error values in a combination of several input variables in order to see the results of the variable changes on output values.

Templates   Worksheets containing user-defined input and process-defined output cells. Templates can be used to perform "What if" simulation.

Summary of Financial @ Functions

@CTERM(interest rate,future value,present value)
Returns the number of periods for an single lump sum investment of present value to grow to future value earning interest rate per period.

@DDB(cost,salvage,life,period)
Uses double-declining balance method to compute depreciation allowance for period.

@FV(payment,interest,term)
Finds future value of an annuity.

@IRR(guess,range)
Returns the internal rate of return for a series of cash flows in the range based on percentage guess.

@NPV(interest,range)
Returns the present value of a series of future cash flows in range discounted at interest.

@PMT(principal,interest rate,term)
Returns the payment amount for each period in the term to pay off principal amount borrowed at interest rate per period.

@PV(payment,interest rate,term)
Finds present value of an annuity.

@RATE(future value,present value,term)
Returns the periodic interest rate necessary for a single lump sum of present value to grow to future value in term or the number of compounding periods.

@SLN(cost,salvage,life)
Uses straight-line depreciation method to compute depreciation allowance for one period.

@SYD(cost,salvage,life,period)
Uses sum-of-the-years'-digits depreciation method to compute depreciation allowance for period.

@TERM(payment,interest,future value)
Returns the number of payment periods for investment to reach future value.

EXERCISES

PART 1 EXERCISES

"What if" Analysis[3]

1. Create the worksheet below and save under the name INCOME. You need only to enter columns A and B. The data that looks like it's in column D is only there to show you the actual formulas in the B column. On your screen, columns C, D, E, and F should be empty.

	A	B		
1	Units Produced..........	100	100	
2	Percentage Sold..........	90%	0.9	
3				
4	Net Sales...............	$72.00	0.8*B1*B2	
5	Costs of Production......	$33.00	0.33*B1	
6				
7	Gross Margin.............	$39.00	+B4-B5	
8				
9	Other Expenses..........			
10	Selling Expenses.......	$0.90	0.0125*B4	
11	Shipping & Handling....	$6.62	0.092*B4	
12	Interest Expense.......	$0.28	0.1/12*B5	
13	Total Expenses..........	$7.80	@SUM(B10..B12)	
14				
15	Net Income.............	$31.20	+B7-B13	

All figures in the worksheet depend upon the units produced and/or the percentage of units sold.

a) If the number of units produced increased to 200, how would net income be affected? Is it a linear relationship?

---

[3]This "What-if" analysis can be automated by using the /Data Table command. The command stores the results of formulas which depend upon other values in the worksheet into tables. (See "What-if" Analysis and /Data Table in index.) Also, the Solver add-in automates this process. (See Add-in Appendix.)

b)   If the percentage sold drops by 10%, does it cause a drop of 10% in net income also?

c)   What effect does a 50% increase on units produced have on total expenses?

d)   If the percentage sold is only 60%, how many units must be produced to net $100? This trial-and-error method is automated by the /Data Table commands. (See index.)

2. Use the L5NAIL worksheet below created in the Lesson 5 exercises.

	A	B	C	D	E	F
1			FOUR YEAR PROJECTION FOR NAIL CLIPPER SALES			
2						
3		Inc/Dec				
4		Rate	1989	1990	1991	1992
5	Sales	12.0%	$23,896.00	$26,763.52	$29,975.14	$33,572.16
6	Cost of Sales	-5.0%	13,697.19	$13,012.33	$12,361.71	$11,743.63
7			---------------	---------------	---------------	---------------
8	Gross Margin		$10,198.81	$13,751.19	$17,613.43	$21,828.53
9	Expenses:					
10	Mortgage	0.0%	$2,000.00	$2,000.00	$2,000.00	$2,000.00
11	Maintenance	2.0%	2,939.21	2,997.99	3,057.95	3,119.11
12	Utilities	4.0%	743.00	772.72	803.63	835.77
13	Wages	7.0%	4,735.00	5,066.45	5,421.10	5,800.58
14	Insurance	10.0%	3,400.00	3,740.00	4,114.00	4,525.40
15			---------------	---------------	---------------	---------------
16	Total Exp.		$13,817.21	$14,577.16	$15,396.68	$16,280.86
17						
18	Net Profit		($3,618.40)	($825.97)	$2,216.75	$5,547.67

a) To what rate must sales increase to show a profit in 1990?

b) If the sales increase rate is 12%, what rate must cost of sales decrease to for a profit in 1990?

c) If cost of sales doesn't change from year to year and sales are increased by 12% each year, in which year will net profit first be positive?

d) How much does an increase or decrease of one percentage point in wages affect net profit in each year?

e) From past data, it has been found that for each percentage point increase in wages, there is a decrease of one percentage point in cost of sales because employees are less wasteful of raw materials. Vary the wage increase from 4% to 8% and decrease the cost of sales accordingly from the figure above. In the best case, what is maximum total net profit for all 4 years? What is the best case wage increase? What is the cost of sales? (Hint: Set up a formula in B5 with a cell reference to B12. To find this formula, use the equation of the line passing through (4%,-2%), (5%,-3%), (6%,-4%), etc. Also, set up a cell to show the sum of the net profits for all 4 years.)

f) Change C5 to 4000 and use the information from part e above. Now what is the best wage increase in terms of net profit over the 4 years? What are the human factors which should be considered here?

3.   Use the L7AGGPLN worksheet below created in Lesson 7.

a)   What would bottom line costs be if the user added 100 units of Subcontract work in period 5?

b)   What would bottom line costs be is the user added 100 units of Overtime work in period 5?

c)   If cost of shortages were $10.00 instead of $15.00, would it be economical to use Overtime in period 5?

Compound Interest

1. Show the amount at the end of each of 5 years of a savings account with a single lump sum deposit of $2000 and an annual interest rate of 6% compounded annually. Create a table similar to those in the Compound Interest section of this lesson using the COMPOUND file you have saved on disk. Change "Year" to "Period" in A3 and D3 to make it more generic. What is the total amount in the account after 5 years? Use the compound interest equation to verify the amount after 5 years. Use @CTERM to see how long it takes $2000 to grow to $3000 at 6%. What is the minimum annual interest rate $2000 would have to earn if you wanted it to grow to $3000 in 6 years instead of 7? (Use @RATE.)

2. Do the same as Exercise 1 but with an original lump sum deposit of $5000 and an annual rate of 7% compounded semi-annually. What is the effective rate? What is the total amount in the account after 4 years (8 periods)? Use the compound interest equation to verify the amount after 4 years. How many years must the initial $5,000 sit in the account before it's worth $10,000? What must the interest rate increase to if you wanted $10,000 in only 8 years? (Don't forget that each period is 6 months and not a year.)

3. Do the same as Exercise 1 but with a lump sum deposit of $3210 and an annual rate of 8% compounded monthly. What is the effective rate? What is the total amount in the account after 10 years? Use the compound interest equation to verify the amount after 10 years. How many years would it take $3210 to grow to $5000 at this rate? (Hint: To get the number of years, divide the entire @CTERM by 12.) At which rate would it take only 4 years to grow to $5000?

4. Do the same as Exercise 1 but with a lump sum of $4300 and an annual rate of 9% compounded daily. What is the effective rate? To get the total amount in the account after 2 years, use the compound interest equation to verify the amount after 2 years. Use of a table would involve over 730 rows because of the daily compounding.

Future Value

(There is no need to create a table for these problems. Just use @FV.)

1. At the end of each quarter, $500 is deposited into a savings account that pays 7% annual interest compounded monthly. What is the balance at the end of 4 years? What is the compounded interest?

2. A sinking fund is a fund into which a series of payments are made to pay for some future obligation. A machine at your factory must be replaced in 5 years. The cost of the new machine will be $70,000 in 5 years. Your company is depositing $1000 at the end of each month into the fund which is earning 5% compounded monthly. Will it have enough to purchase the machine?

3. The cost of a college education in 10 years is estimated to be 5 million dollars.[4] You have triplets who will be graduating high school in 10 years. You deposit $100,000 every month for ten years into a savings account earning 10% compounded monthly. Will you have enough for their educations?

4. What's the future value of an IRA where $2000 is invested annually for 10 years at a rate of 8.5%?

Loans

1. $60,000 is borrowed for 10 years at an annual interest rate of 12%. What should each of the 10 yearly payments be?

2. The borrower would rather pay back the $60,000 from Exercise 1 in monthly payments. What is the payment amount?

---

[4]Just kidding.

3. (Student must have done Lesson 5 Relative and Absolute Addressing.)

    a) Create the amortization table below using the file AMORT from this lesson. (If you did not do the optional financial @ functions, you will not have the file on disk.)

```
B20: @SUM(B8..B19)


          A            B            C           D              E
1   Principal:                                          $500,000.00
2   Interest Rate per Period:                                 1.17%
3   Payment per Period:                                  $44,893.56
4   Term or Number of Periods:                                   12
5                      AMORTIZATION TABLE
6                         Applied to
7   Payment       Interest   Principal New Balance
8         1     $5,833.33 $39,060.23 $460,939.77
9         2     $5,377.63 $39,515.93 $421,423.85
10        3     $4,916.61 $39,976.95 $381,446.90
11        4     $4,450.21 $40,443.34 $341,003.55
12        5     $3,978.37 $40,915.18 $300,088.37
13        6     $3,501.03 $41,392.53 $258,695.84
14        7     $3,018.12 $41,875.44 $216,820.40
15        8     $2,529.57 $42,363.99 $174,456.41
16        9     $2,035.32 $42,858.23 $131,598.18
17       10     $1,535.31 $43,358.25  $88,239.93
18       11     $1,029.47 $43,864.09  $44,375.84
19       12       $517.72 $44,375.84      $0.00
20              $38,722.71
```

    b) If the amount borrowed was $400,000 instead of $500,000, what would the total interest paid be for the year? How much does a decrease of 1% in the annual interest rate affect the total interest paid on the $400,000?

    c) The term has been increased to 24 months with the amount borrowed still $500,000 at an annual interest rate 14%. Expand the table to handle this. What is the new payment per period? What is interest paid in the first year? In the second year?

Present Value

1.   You have just won a million dollars from Ed McMahon. You're given the choice of receiving it in one lump sum or in $140,000 in 10 yearly payments. Which should you choose? Assume an interest rate of 6% which is a likely assumption for those who return those mailers.

2.   A rich uncle of yours just died and left you $40,000. You can either have it all at once or in monthly payments of $500 for 10 years. Which is worth more? Assume an interest rate of 9%.

Internal Rate of Return

1.   Given a choice of two investments, which would you choose. The first has yearly cash flows in order of $400, $500, $300, $0, and $700 and initially costs $1200. The second has flows of $100, $200, $300, and $1000 and costs $2000. What is the IRR on each?

2.   Would your answer to Exercise 1 change if the initial cost of the second investment changed to $1100 and the fourth yearly payment of $0 increased to $100?

Net Present Value

1.   In IRR Exercise 2, what is the NPV of each investment? Assume a 9% discount rate. Which investment is preferable?

2.   For Exercise 1 (of NPV), if a discount rate of 11% is assumed, do you expect the value of the NPV of each investment to be positive or negative? Verify by using @NPV.

Depreciation

1.   Compute the second period depreciation value for an machine originally costing $15,000 with a salvage value of $2000 and a lifetime of 5 years using the 3 depreciation methods covered in this lesson.

2.   You buy a computer costing $20,000 which will become obsolete 2 years. If you're lucky you can sell it for $500. Create a depreciation schedule for the two years with the 3 methods of depreciation. What's the problem with the double-declining balance method?

3. Create the depreciation table in the worksheet below. You must have gone through the optional depreciation methods of this lesson to know what the formulas are. Also required is a knowledge of relative and absolute addressing techniques from Lesson 5.

	A	B	C	D
1			DEPRECIATION METHODS	
2				
3		Cost:	$10,000.00	
4		Salvage:	$1,000.00	
5		Life:	10	
6				
7			Double-Declining	Sum-of-Years'-
8	Period	Straight Line	Balance	Digits
9	1	$900.00	$2,000.00	$1,636.36
10	2	$900.00	$1,600.00	$1,472.73
11	3	$900.00	$1,280.00	$1,309.09
12	4	$900.00	$1,024.00	$1,145.45
13	5	$900.00	$819.20	$981.82
14	6	$900.00	$655.36	$818.18
15	7	$900.00	$524.29	$654.55
16	8	$900.00	$419.43	$490.91
17	9	$900.00	$335.54	$327.27
18	10	$900.00	$268.44	$163.64
19		------------	------------------------	------------
20	Total	$9,000.00	$8,926.26	$9,000.00

a) Which method accelerates the depreciation fastest?

b) Change the original cost from $10,000 to $20,000 and the salvage value to $5,000. Leave the life at 10 years. Print the new amortization table.

ON-SCREEN GRAPHING

Contents:

Lesson 9 is a thorough coverage of on-screen graphing. All aspects of graphs from types of graphs through manual axis scaling are included. PrintGraph is covered in the next lesson. The separation of on-screen and hard copy graphing into two different lessons encourages the liberal use of /Graph Name and /Graph Save commands. The reader gains a full understanding of the difference between the two and hopefully will not forget to name a graph.

Create the worksheet shown in Figure 9-1. All values in the range B5..E8 are constants. The YEARLY SALES and Total values are computed using @SUM. The title is in C1.

	A	B	C	D	E	F	G
1			ATHLETIC SHOES ARE US				
2							
3			QTR1	QTR2	QTR3	QTR4	YEARLY SALES
4							
5		Running	43	57	32	14	146
6		Racquetball	21	9	26	49	105
7		Tennis	46	55	43	28	172
8		Aerobic	37	25	19	13	94
9			----------	----------	----------	----------	--------
10		Total	147	146	120	104	517

Figure 9-1. Worksheet for Graphing.

Save the file under the name SHOES9.

You enter: / File **Save SHOES9 [Return]**

Observe that the quarterly sales for running shoes peaked in QTR2 and had its lowest point in QTR4. Highs and lows in sets of data points are more easily seen in a graphic representation.

/Graph

You enter: / **Graph**

The main graph menu below should be on your screen.

Type X A B C D E F Reset View Save Options Name Group Quit

Releases 2 and 2.01: No Group option.

Data Ranges

Up to six sets of data points (menu options A through F) can be graphed. The quarterly sales for running shoes will be the first set of data points, range A.

You enter: **A**

Computer message: Enter first data range:

You enter: **B5..E5 [Return]**

The graph menu is a sticky menu and remains on the screen. To look at the graph you have so far, choose the View option.

You enter: **View**

Your graph should look like Figure 9-2.

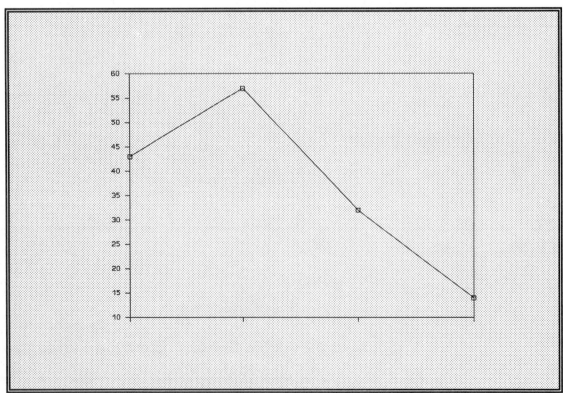

Figure 9-2. Graph of Running Shoes Quarterly Sales.

The maximum and minimum sales are readily seen in the graph. Return to main graph menu with almost any key.

You enter: **[Esc]**

To recall which range is the A graph range, choose A from the graph menu.

You enter: **A**

The current A range is clearly visible.

You enter: **[Return]**

Continue graphing and viewing the quarterly sales for the other 3 types of sneakers.

You enter: **B B6..E6 [Return] View [Esc]**

You enter: **C B7..E7 [Return] View [Esc]**

You enter: **D B8..E8 [Return] View**

Your graph should look like Figure 9-3.

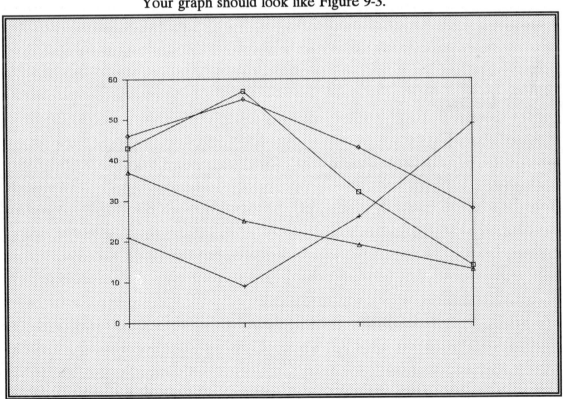

Figure 9-3. Four Data Ranges of Quarterly Sales.

Releases 2.2, 2.3, 2.4, 3.0, and 3.1+:
The first set of data points on left and the last set of data points on right do not touch the graph frame as shown above. Also, the tic marks for the x-axis on the bottom in these releases are inside the frame.

Much has to be added to the graph to clarify for the viewer what each set of points represents.

You enter: **[Esc]**

Releases 2.3 and 2.4: The Graph Settings screen is displayed under the main graph menu. Instead of the method just used to set up data ranges, you may type the data ranges into this screen.

X-Axis Labels

Labels can be added to the x-axis with the X option of the graph menu.

You enter: **X B3..E3 [Return]** View **[Esc]**

/Graph Group

Releases 2 and 2.01: /Graph Group command is not available.

This command makes it unnecessary to set up each individual data range separately. If the data is in consecutive rows, as in this example, the range of all rows can be specified in this command. The top row of the range must be the X-range, the next row the A-range, etc.

In this example you could have simply issued this one command:

/Graph Group B3..E8 Rowwise

instead of the last 5 individual range specifications.

Rowwise tells 1-2-3 to consider each row a data range. If your range is set up column-wise, i.e. the X-range is in the first column of the range, the A-range the next column, etc., the Columnwise option should have been chosen from the last sub-menu.

To verify that the ranges are properly set, choose A, B, etc. from the main graph menu and visually check the highlighted range.

Releases 3.0 and 3.1+:

These releases outdo the Group command with a feature called **automatic graphing**. If absolutely nothing has been set up for a graph, simply hitting [F10/GRAPH] causes a graph to be displayed which contains all data around the position of the cell pointer. Rowwise, the topmost row from the pointer is graphed as the X-range, the next row down the A-range, etc. Columnwise, the left-most column is graphed as the X-range, the next column to the right the A-range, etc. The /Worksheet Global Default Graph Columnwise or Rowwise command determines whether rowwise or columnwise is used as the default.

Legends

Legends found on the Options sub-menu must be added to associate each set of points to its type of shoe.

You enter: **Options Legend A Running [Return]**

It will take a while for you to get used to the fact that these sub-menus are also sticky menus and therefore must be exited with the Quit option.

You enter: **Quit View**

The line graph with the square symbols is associated with running shoes. Your graph should look like Figure 9-4.

Set up the legend for the B range to be "Racquetball".

Releases 2.3 and 2.4: Use the entry screen method:

You enter: **Options Legend [F2/EDIT] Legends B Racquetball B [Return] [Esc] [Esc] View [Esc]**

You enter: **[Esc] Options Legend B Racquetball [Return] Quit View [Esc]**

We have entered the last two legends as constants; legends can also be entered as cell references.

You enter: **Options Legend C**

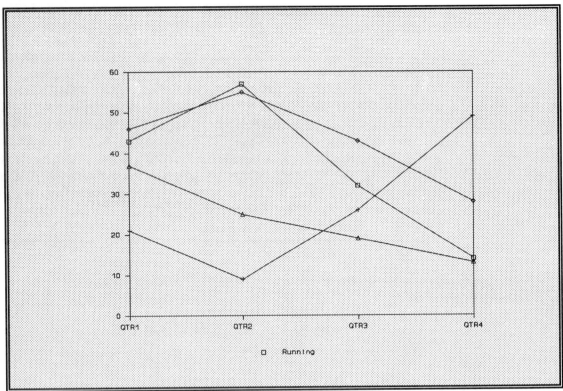

Figure 9-4. Graph with X-Axis Labels and First Legend.

The label Tennis is in cell A7.

You enter: **\A7 [Return] Q**uit View **[Esc]**

The \ was necessary to inform 1-2-3 that this is a cell reference. If the \ was left out, the constant "A7" would have been shown as the legend instead of "Tennis".

WARNING: Cell references are not automatically adjusted if rows or columns are inserted or deleted. (This problem has been corrected in releases 3.x.)

You: **Return to READY mode.**

[F10/GRAPH]

From READY mode, graphs can be viewed without entering the graph menu by using the tenth function key.

You enter: **[F10/GRAPH] [Esc]**

You're back to READY mode.

Releases 3.0 and 3.1+: The problem discussed next has been corrected in Release 3.0, so you may skip to the next section, Graph Titles. First set up the aerobic legend as you did in the last command. One reason for using cell references in legends is to allow changes in legends by simply changing a cell's contents. Change the contents of cell A7 from Tennis to Squash and view the graph. Continue with the next section.

Insert a row above row 5.

You enter: **/ Worksheet Insert Row A5 [Return]**

	A	B	C	D	E	F	G
			ATHLETIC SHOES ARE US				
1							
2							
3		QTR1	QTR2	QTR3	QTR4	YEARLY SALES	
4							
5							
6	Running	43	57	32	14	146	
7	Racquetball	21	9	26	49	105	
8	Tennis	46	55	43	28	172	
9	Aerobic	37	25	19	13	94	
10		-----	-----	-----	-----	-----	
11	Total	147	146	120	104	517	

Figure 9-5. Worksheet with Added Row.

Your worksheet should look like Figure 9-5.

The label Tennis which was in cell A7 is now in cell A8. Racquetball has been moved to cell A7. Recall that the legend for the Tennis range, range C, was entered as \A7. View the graph.

You enter: **[F10/GRAPH]**

Your graph should look like Figure 9-6.

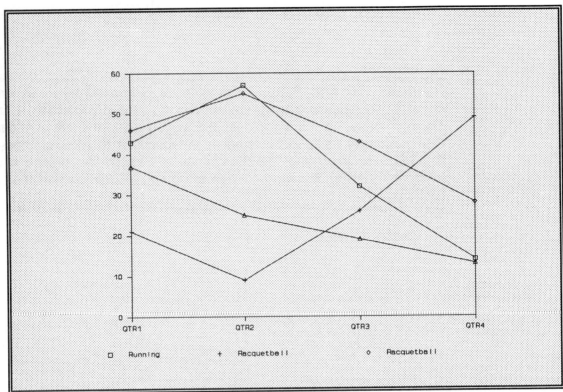

Figure 9-6. Unadjusted Cell Reference for Third Legend.

Surprisingly, 1-2-3 did not adjust the cell reference from A7 to A8, it remains \A7! Therefore the label in cell A7, Racquetball, is displayed as the third legend.

Delete the added row and view the graph.

You enter: **[Esc]** / **Worksheet Delete Row A5 [Return] [F10/GRAPH]**

The third legend is Tennis as it should be. Remember that good worksheets are designed so that they are flexible. You should be able to add and delete rows at anytime without being concerned about messing up cell references.

In the case where you want a cell reference for a legend, name the cell which contains the label and use the range name in the legend. Do this now for the legend for Aerobic shoes.

You enter: **[Esc]** / **Range Name Create Legend4 [Return] A8 [Return]**

The cell A8 is named LEGEND4. Set up the legend for the D range.

You enter: / **Graph Options Legend D \Legend4 [Return] Q**uit **Q**uit

You're back to READY mode. A common mistake, forgetting the \,would cause "Legend4" instead of "Aerobic" to appear as the legend at the bottom of the graph. View the graph.

You enter: **[F10/GRAPH] [Esc]**

Insert a row and verify that the fourth legend is updated.

You enter: / **Worksheet Insert Row A4 [Return]**

You enter: **[F10/GRAPH] [Esc]**

The fourth legend is ok. Of course, the third legend is still incorrect.

You enter: / **Worksheet Delete Row A4 [Return]**

The main purpose in using range names for legends is to have the flexibility to change the label, thereby automatically changing the legend.

You enter into A7: **Squash [Return]**

You enter: **[F10/GRAPH] [Esc]**

The third legend is displayed as Squash, not Tennis. Changing the contents of A5 or A6 would have no effect on the graph, because the first and second legends were entered as constants.

Releases 2.2, 2.3, 2.4, 3.0, and 3.1+: /Graph Options Legend Range can be used to graph all legends in one shot, if they are in consecutive cells. For this example, the range A5..A8 would be the specified range. This command sets up the legend ranges as cell references (like the \A7 we just dealt with), so be wary.

Graph Titles

Two titles can be placed above the graph. All that holds for legends in terms of cell references also holds for titles. Create the main or first title as the label in C1.

You enter: / **Range Name Create Company [Return] C1 [Return]**

You enter: / **Graph Options Title First \Company [Return] Q**uit **V**iew **[Esc]**

Enter the second title as a constant.

You enter: **Options Title Second Quarterly Sales [Return] Q**uit View
[Esc]

Releases 2.3 and 2.4: Use the Graph Legends & Titles screen to enter
the titles for the x and y axes as constants:

You enter: **Options [F2/EDIT] Legends&Titles Titles Xaxis Quarter
[Return] Titles Yaxis Sales [Return] [Return]
[Return] Q**uit View **[Esc]**

Enter the titles for the x and y axes as constants.

You enter: **Options Title X Quarter [Return] Q**uit View **[Esc]**

You enter: **Options Title Y Sales [Return] Q**uit View

Your graph should look like Figure 9-7.

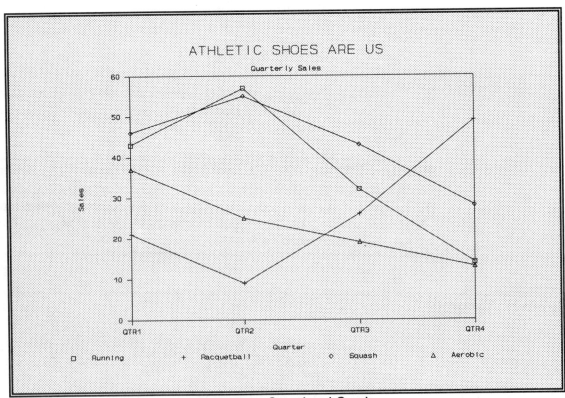

Figure 9-7. Completed Graph.

Releases 3.0 and 3.1+:
Three other options appear on the title sub-menu: 2Y-Axis which allows a title on the second y-axis on the right frame of the graph; Note which allows a footnote to be added below the bottom left corner of the graph; and Other-Note which allows another footnote under the first.

The /File Save command saves all graph settings along with the worksheet.

You enter: **[Esc] Quit / File Save SHOES9 [Return] Replace**

- - - If you need a break, stop at this point. - - -

Graph Types - Line

Figure 9-7 is a line graph. Line graph is the default type graph.

Bar and Stacked-Bar Graphs

Change the graph to a bar graph.

You enter: **/ Graph Type, Bar View**

Your graph should look like Figure 9-8.

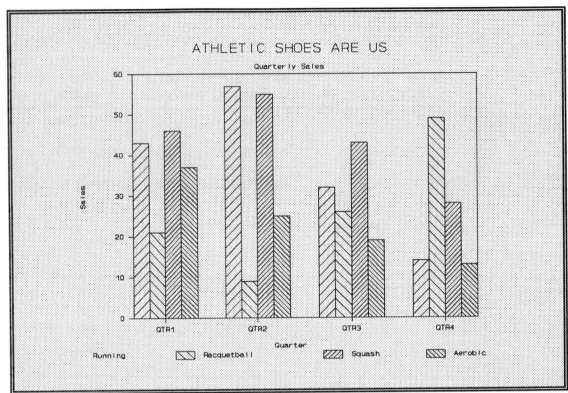

Figure 9-8. Bar Graph.

Releases 2.2, 2.3, and 2.4: There are some improvements to the graph display in these releases. Bar patterns go from dark to light from left to right above each x-axis label. Long legends, which were truncated in earlier releases, are now wrapped to the next line.

Change to a stacked-bar graph.

You enter: **[Esc]** T**ype** **Stacked-Bar** **View**

Your graph should look like Figure 9-9.

Change the graph type back to line.

You enter: **[Esc]** T**ype** **Line** **View** **[Esc]**

Your graph should again look like Figure 9-7.

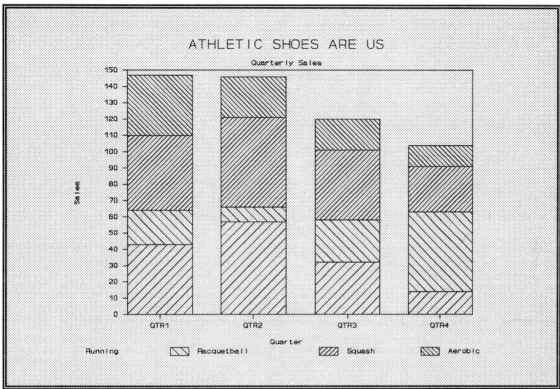

Figure 9-9. Stacked-bar Graph.

/Graph Name Create

The current graph is the graph which will be displayed on issuance of a /Graph View or [F10/GRAPH]. /Graph Name Create saves a picture of the current graph within the worksheet (not to disk). Graph naming is necessary when more than one graph is created within the same worksheet. Name the current graph QTRSALES.

You enter: **Name Create**

Computer message: Enter graph name:

You enter: **QTRSALES [Return]**

WARNING: Don't forget to name your completed graph with /Graph Name Create.

/Graph Reset

To clear all current graph settings and start with a clean slate, use the /Graph Reset Graph command.

You enter: **Reset**

You can clear any individual range, A through F or X, with the menu below which is currently on your screen.

Graph X A B C D E F Range Options Quit

Range resets all graph ranges X, and A through F, and group ranges; Options resets all options set by the /Graph Options sub-menu.

Releases 2 and 2.01: Range and Options are not available.

The Graph option clears all graph settings.

You enter: **Graph**

Try to view the graph.

You enter: **View**

An error beep is issued and the screen is blank.

Releases 3.0 and 3.1+: Due to automatic graphing, an error does not occur.

You enter: **[Esc]**

Pie Charts

Whereas line, bar, and stacked-bar graphs represent values by vertical distances from the x-axis (the horizontal axis), pie charts depict values by arc lengths around the outside of a circle. Only one set of data points, the A range, can be graphed in a pie chart. Graph the yearly sales of the four types of shoes in a pie chart by changing the type to pie and entering the A range.

You enter: **Type Pie A F5..F8 [Return] View [Esc]**

The percentages are found by dividing each value in the A range by the sum of the A range. To label the pieces of the pie, set the X range to the four corresponding label cells.

You enter: **X A5..A8 [Return]** View

Your graph should look like Figure 9-10.

Releases 3.0 and 3.1+: Your screen differs from the figure in that the A-range is at the top with the B, C, and D-ranges following in a counter-clockwise direction. Also, your graph slices might have hatch patterns or be in color.

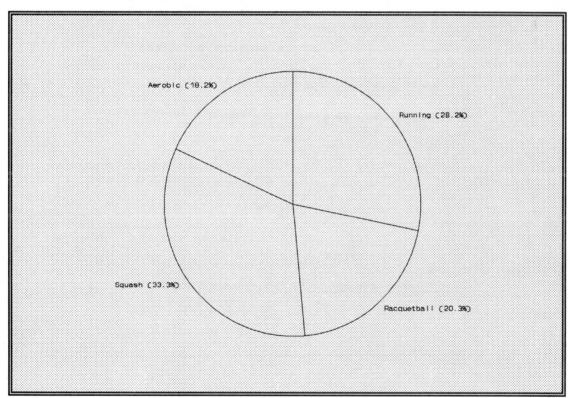

Figure 9-10. Pie Chart of Yearly Sales.

Name the current pie chart PIE.

You enter: **[Esc]** Name Create

Note that the names of previously created graphs are displayed on the third line.

You enter: **PIE [Return]**

Shaded and/or Exploded Pie Charts

The A range of a pie chart can be shaded and/or exploded by setting up a B range the same size as the A range. Set the B range to A15..A19 and return to READY mode.

You enter: **B A15..A19 [Return] Q**uit

Each cell in the B range corresponds to the associated slice of pie from the A range. Code numbers for shading or explosion are entered into the B range cells. Shading codes go from 0 to 7 where 0 is no shading. Enter a code of 1 into cell A15 to shade the first slice of the pie and view the graph.

You enter into A15: **1 [Return] [F10/GRAPH] [Esc]**

Your graph should look like Figure 9-11. The Running slice is shaded.

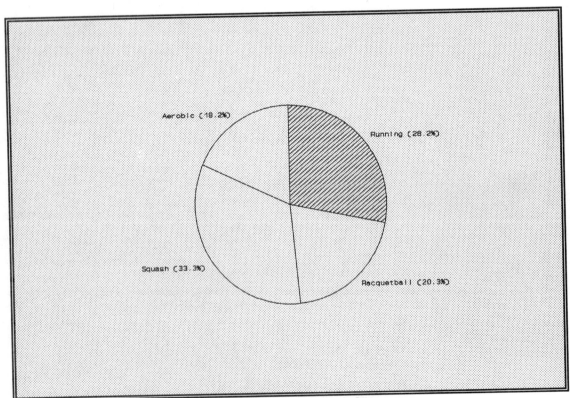

Figure 9-11. Shading in A Slice.

Releases 3.0 and 3.1+: By default, graphs are displayed with shading or in color.

You enter into A16: **2 [Down]**

You enter into A17: **3 [Down]**

You enter into A18: **4 [Return]**

You enter: **[F10/GRAPH] [Esc]**

To explode a slice of the pie, add 100 to the shading code.

You enter into A15: **101 [Return] [F10/GRAPH] [Esc]**

The Running slice is shaded and exploded.

You enter into A17: **100 [Return] [F10/GRAPH] [Esc]**

The Squash slice is exploded and not shaded.

Releases 3.0 and 3.1+: Codes 0 and 100 cause the slice to be hidden.

Your B range should look like cells A15..A18 in Figure 9-12.

	Column A	
15	101	Shading Code 1, Exploded
16	2	Shading Code 2
17	100	Shading Code 0 (no shading), Exploded
18	4	Shading Code 4

Figure 9-12. A15..A18 is B Range for Pie Chart.

Your graph should look like Figure 9-13.

Name this current graph EXPIE.

You enter: **/ Graph Name Create EXPIE [Return]**

(Those with color monitors can come back and experiment with exploded pie charts in color after reading the Graphs in Color section of this lesson.)

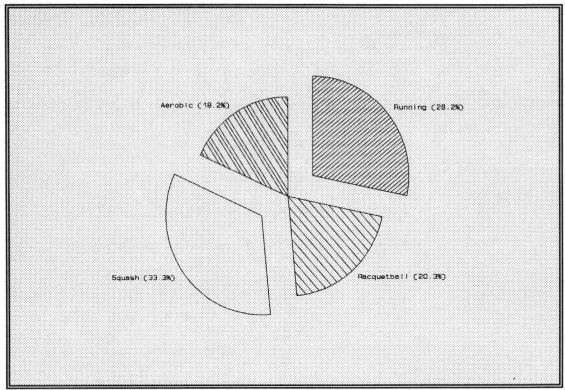

Figure 9-13. A Range Exploded. C Range Exploded and Not Shaded.

/Graph Name Use

You now have three named graphs, EXPIE, PIE, and QTRSALES. To make a named graph the current graph, use /Graph Name Use.

You enter: **Name Use Highlight QTRSALES [Return]**

The graph is displayed on the screen as in Figure 9-7. Make the pie chart current.

You enter: **[Esc] Name Use PIE [Return] [Esc]**

/Graph Name Table

Releases 2 and 2.01: /Graph Name Table is not available.

This command creates a 3-column table where the first column contains all graph names, the second column contains the types of graphs, and the third column contains the first titles of the graphs. Try it.

You enter: **/ Graph Name Table D13 [Return] Q**uit

/Graph Name Delete

/Graph Name Delete erases a named graph from the worksheet.

You enter: **/Graph Name Delete**

Computer message: **Enter name of graph to delete:**

You can either type the graph name you wish to delete or use the highlight and [Return] method. Do not delete any graphs.

You enter: **[Esc] 3 times.**

/Graph Name Reset

/Graph Name Reset erases ALL named graphs. Be very careful not to accidentally issue this command.

Data Labels

Data labels are labels which can be added to line and bar graphs near the data points. Use the line graph, QTRSALES.

You enter: **Name Use QTRSALES [Esc]**

You enter: **Options Data-Labels A**

You enter: **B5..E5 [Return] A**bove **Q**uit **Q**uit **V**iew

Your graph should look like Figure 9-14.

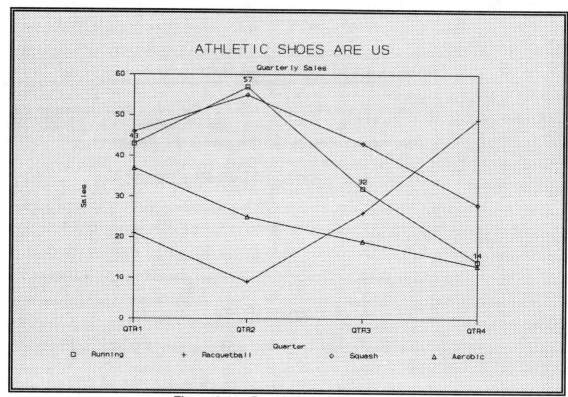

Figure 9-14. Data Labels on A Range.

Data labels can be added to the other 3 sets of data points also. As you saw in one of the sub-menus, the labels can be placed above (as you did), below, centered, to the left, or to the right of the data points.

Replace the old QTRSALES named graph with this graph.

You enter: **[Esc] Name Create Highlight QTRSALES [Return]**

Change the type of graph to bar and stacked-bar to see how the data labels look.

You enter: **Type Bar View [Esc] Type Stacked-Bar View [Esc]**

Some releases don't show data labels on stacked bar graphs. If you like, you may add data labels to the other three ranges now.

Change back to a Line type graph.

You enter: **Type Line**

Be careful when entering the designated range for data labels. It is possible to incorrectly enter a range of labels. Try it.

You enter: **Options Data-Labels B B10..E10 [Return] A Quit Quit View**

Your graph should look like Figure 9-15. 1-2-3 has no "common sense" when it displays data labels.

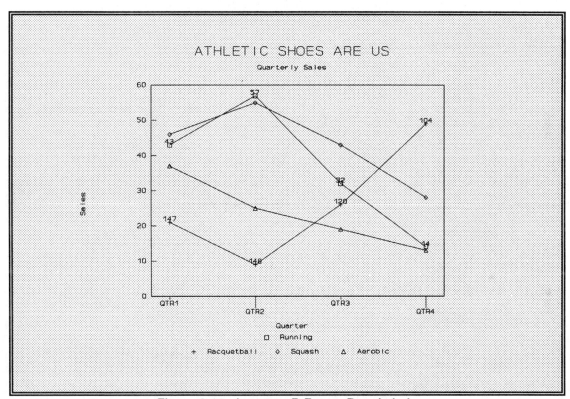

Figure 9-15. Incorrect B Range Data Labels.

Releases 2.2, 2.3, 2.4, 3.0, and 3.1+: The Group option on the Data-labels sub-menu can be used to set up data-labels, if the labels are stored in consecutive cells.

Bring back the QTRSALES line graph.

You enter: **[Esc] Name Use QTRSALES [Esc]**

Grid Lines

Add both horizontal and vertical grid lines to the graph.

You enter: **Options Grid Both Quit View**

Your graph should look like Figure 9-16.

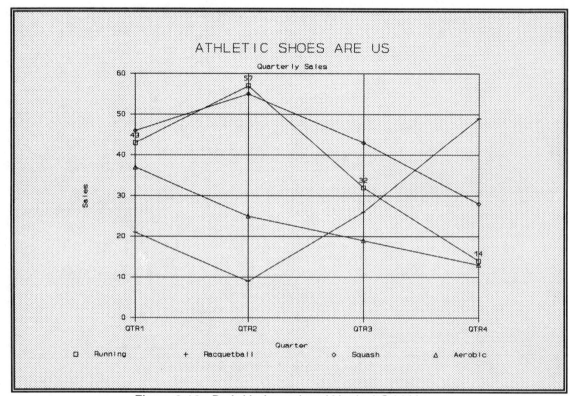

Figure 9-16. Both Horizontal and Vertical Grid Lines.

Grid lines, of course, cannot be added to pie charts. Clear the grid lines.

You enter: **[Esc] Options Grid**

As you can see in this menu, it is possible to have only horizontal or vertical lines in the graph - in other words, you don't have to have both.

Releases 3.0 and 3.1+:
The additional Y-axis option is used if you have another y-axis on the right of the graph.

The Clear option erases both types of grid lines.

You enter: **Clear Quit View [Esc]**

Graph Format -
Lines, Symbols, or Both

The Format option on the Options sub-menu allows you to control the display of data points in line and XY (covered later) graphs. This is the one case where Format does NOT mean the display format of values, such as General, Currency, Scientific, etc.

You enter: **Options Format Graph**

The menu Lines Symbols Both Neither lets you choose lines only, symbols only, both lines and symbols which is the default, and neither lines nor symbols. Choose symbols only.

You enter: **Symbols Quit Quit View**

Your graph should look like Figure 9-17.

Turn to the graph on page 301 and look for the handwriting that says "/Graph Options Format for lines and/or symbols". This will remind you how to get this special effect.

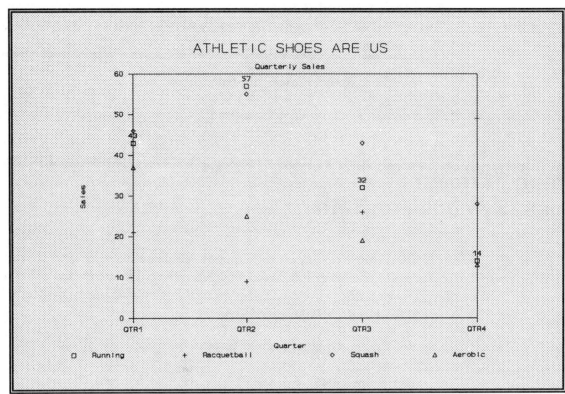

Figure 9-17. Graph Format of Symbols Only.

Change the format to lines only.

You enter: **[Esc] O**ptions **F**ormat

The menu **Graph A B C D E F Quit** allows you to change the format of the entire graph or an individual set of data points. Change the entire graph to lines only.

You enter: **G**raph **L**ines **Q**uit **Q**uit **V**iew

Your graph should look like Figure 9-18.

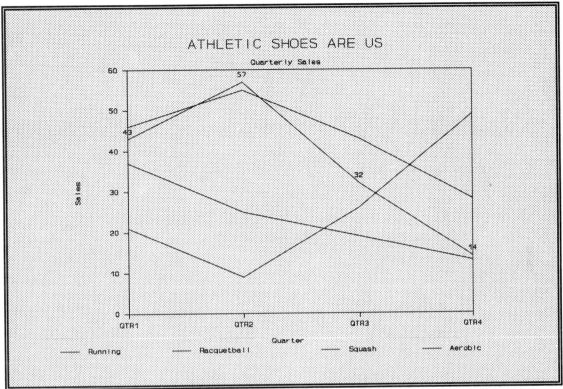

Figure 9-18. Graph with Lines Only.

Choosing neither lines nor symbols would make sense if data labels were present, as they are for the A range on your graph.

You enter: **[Esc] Options Format Graph Neither Quit Quit View**

Your graph should look like Figure 9-19.

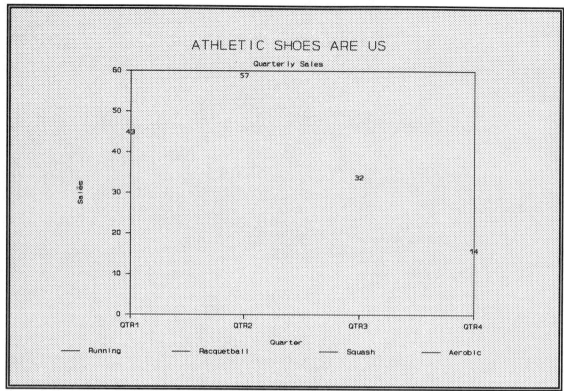

Figure 9-19. Graph Format of Neither Lines nor Symbols.

Reset the format to the default of both lines and symbols.

You enter: **[Esc] Options Format Graph Both Quit Quit Quit**

You should be back to READY mode. View the graph; it should again appear as Figure 9-14.

You enter: **[F10/GRAPH] [Esc]**

Manual Axis Scaling

1-2-3 sets up the y-axis scale so that the maximum and minimum y-axis scale values encompass all values in the graph ranges. In the case where one value is vastly different from the rest, you will probably want to set up the y-axis scale yourself. Change the value in C5 to a very large sales figure.

You enter into C5: **1000 [Return] [F10/GRAPH] [Esc]**

Your graph should look like Figure 9-20.

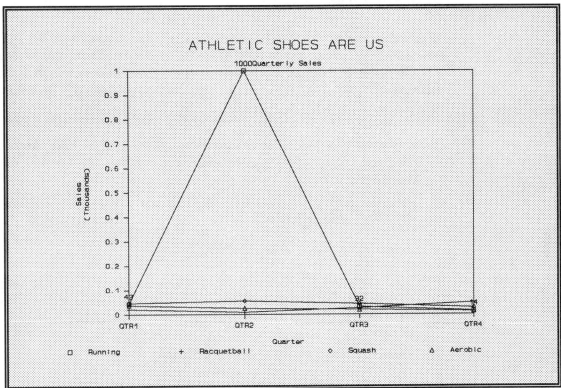

Figure 9-20. Disproportionately Large Value in A Range.

Change the maximum y-axis value to 60, a reasonable number for the set of data points to be graphed.

You enter: / **G**raph **O**ptions **S**cale **Y**-Axis

The following menu should be on your screen.

Automatic Manual Lower Upper Format Indicator Quit

Releases 2.3 and 2.4: The Display option allows the y-axis labels to be displayed on the left (default) or right side of the graph or both sides. The labels can also be hidden.

Releases 3.0 and 3.1+:

Three more options appear on this sub-menu: Type is used for logarithmic scales which are scales which increase logarithmically instead of linearly; exponent which sets an order of magnitude for the scale, i.e. 2 is the order of magnitude if you're graphing numbers between 100 and 1,000; and Width sets the maximum width of the numbers displayed on the axis.

Automatic and Manual are adjacent opposite options with Automatic being the default. The Lower and Upper options are relevant only if Manual is set on.

You enter: **Manual Lower**

Computer message: Enter lower limit: 0

Leave the default lower y-axis label, 0, unchanged by hitting [Return].

You enter: **[Return] U**pper

Computer message: Enter upper limit: 0

You enter: **60 [Return] Q**uit **Q**uit **View**

Your graph should look like Figure 9-21.

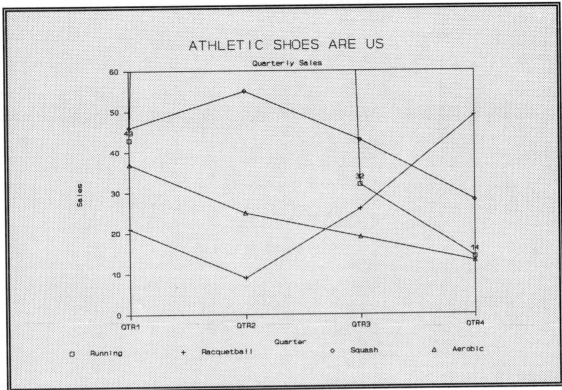

Figure 9-21. Manual Y-Axis Scaling.

You can see by the almost vertical lines that the second value in the Running range is way off the chart.

You enter: **[Esc]**

Y-Scale Format Display

The display values on the y-axis can be formatted like values in cells. Change the y-axis format to Currency with 2 decimal places.

You enter:
Options **S**cale **Y**-Scale **F**ormat **C**urrency **[Return]** **Q**uit **Q**uit **V**iew **[Esc]**

Your graph should look like Figure 9-22.

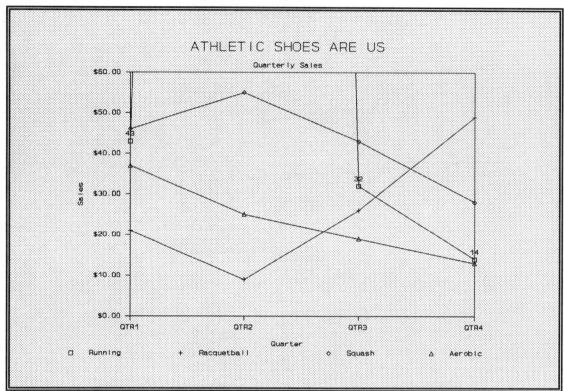

Figure 9-22. Y-Scale Format of Currency with 2 Decimal Places.

You enter: **Options Scale**

The menu Y scale X Scale Skip on your screen has an X Scale option which allows you to manipulate the x-axis similar to the y-axis and is used in XY-type graphs (covered later).

Releases 3.0 and 3.1+: 2Y-Scale is used to set up a second y-axis on the right frame of a graph.

The **Skip** option changes how labels are displayed on the x-axis. It is used in line and bar graphs to display every nth label on the x-axis. This comes in handy when you have so many numbers on the x-axis, they overlap each other and are unreadable. n is called the skip factor. Figure 9-23A shows a worksheet with the row 1 values (A1..T1) being the A graph range and the row 2 values (A2..T2) being the x-axis labels. Figure 9-23B shows only every fourth label on the x-axis.

Releases 2.2, 2.3, 2.4, 3.0, and 3.1+: This may not be necessary in these new releases because the x-axis labels are staggered.

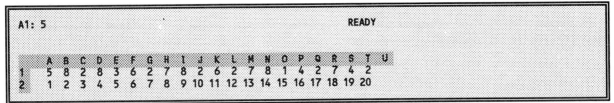

Figure 9-23A. Row 1 is A-Range. Row 2 is X-Range.

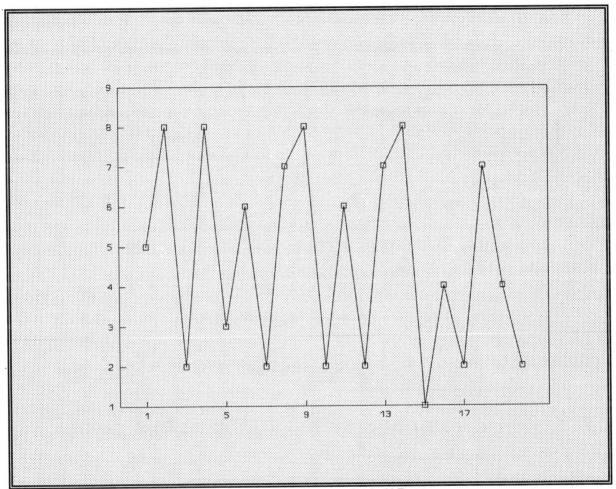

Figure 9-23B. Skip Factor of 4 in X-Range.

Graphs in Color

The graph Options sub-menu below should be on your screen.

Legend Format Titles Grid Scale Color B&W Data-Labels Quit

Releases 3.0 and 3.1+: The Advanced option allows you to select colors, text attributes for titles, and hatch patterns for data ranges.

The Color and B&W are adjacent opposite options with black and white being the default. If you have a color monitor, choose Color from this menu.

You enter if you have a color monitor: **Color Quit View [Esc]**

Take some time and try graphing other types of graphs in color. Experiment.

Save the worksheet file and erase the entire worksheet.

You enter: **[Esc] [Esc] [Esc] / File Save [Return] Replace**

You enter: **/Worksheet Erase Yes**

Do you see that a /Range Erase would not clear the graph settings? To be sure you have a clean worksheet, always use /Worksheet Erase instead of /Range Erase.

- - - If you need a break, stop at this point. - - -

XY Graphs

XY graphs are those that you are probably familiar with from high school algebra classes. The vertical distance from the x-axis and the horizontal distance from the y-axis represent values. XY graphs can be used for scatter diagrams.

Create the simple worksheet in Figure 9-24.

Figure 9-24. Worksheet for XY Graph of 3 data points.

To plot the three points (3,1), (2,4), and (5,6), set up the X range as the x-coordinates in column A and the A range as the y-coordinates of column B.

You enter: **/ Graph Type XY X A1..A3 [Return] A B1..B3 [Return] View**

Your graph should look like Figure 9-25.

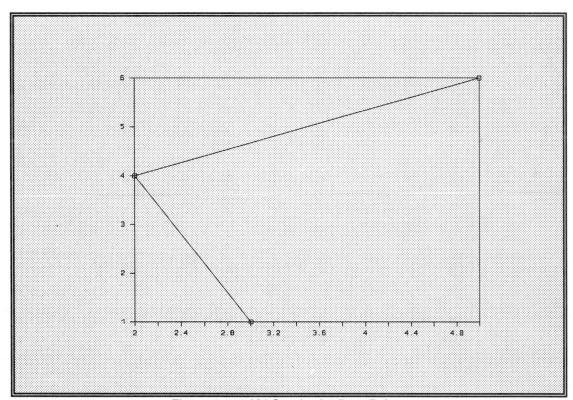

Figure 9-25. XY Graph of 3 Data Points.

The X range corresponds to the x-coordinates; the A range corresponds to the y-coordinates. The B through F ranges can be used to add additional lines.

To refashion the graph to a more familiar form, change the format to symbols only and manually re-scale each axis to go from 0 to 10.

You enter: **[Esc]** **O**ptions **F**ormat **G**raph **S**ymbols **Q**uit

You enter: **Scale Y-Scale Manual Upper 10 [Return] Q**uit

You enter: **Scale X-Scale Manual Upper 10 [Return] Q**uit **Q**uit **View**

Your graph should look like Figure 9-26.

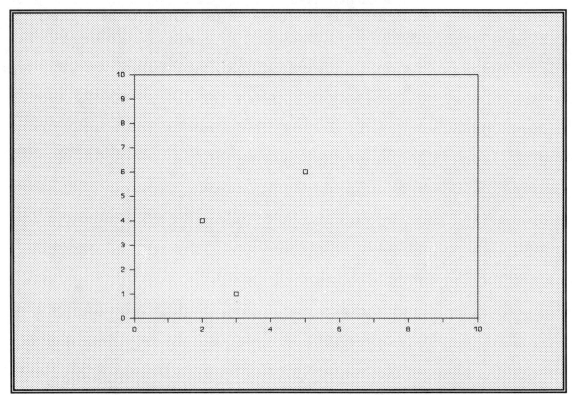

Figure 9-26. XY Graph with Symbols Only and Manual Scaling.

Data-labels can be added to the points. Add the column C entries shown in Figure 9-27 to your worksheet.

	A	B	C	D
1	3	1	Point A	
2	2	4	Point B	
3	5	6	Point C	

Figure 9-27. Data-Labels in Column C.

Add data-labels to the graph.

You enter: **/ G**raph **O**ptions **Data-Labels A C1..C3 [Return] R**ight **Q**uit **Q**uit **View [Esc]**

Your graph should look like Figure 9-28.

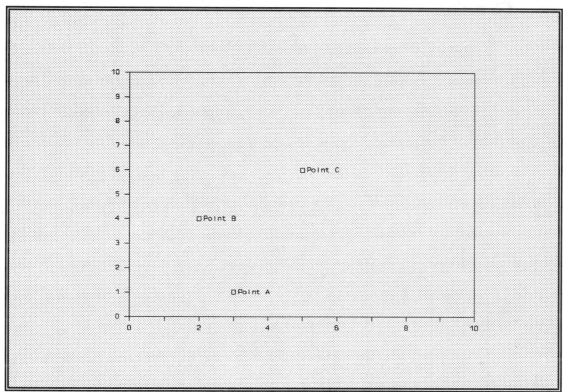

Figure 9-28. XY Graph with Data-Labels.

The rest of this lesson covers more graph features not included in releases 2, 2.01, and 2.2. If you are using one of these releases, skip to the end of the lesson.

Mixed Graphs

Bar and line graphs can be combined in the graph type Mixed. Graph ranges A, B, and C are considered bar graph ranges and graph ranges D, E, and F are the line ranges. Therefore you may have up to three ranges of each type. To get an example of this type graph on your screen, use the SHOES worksheet and change the graph type to Mixed.

You enter: / **Graph Type Mixed View**

Your screen should look like Figure 9-30.

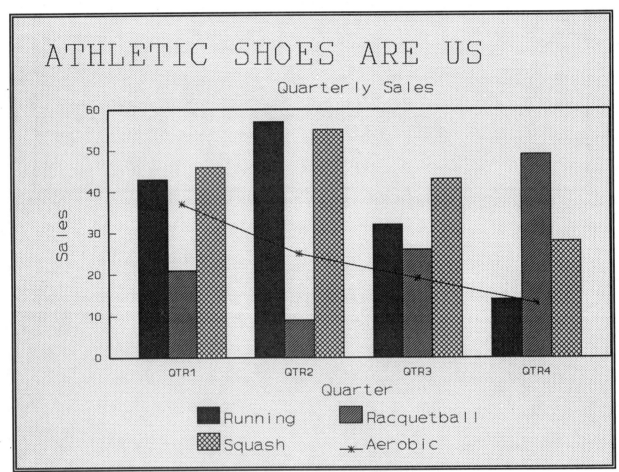

Figure 9-30. Mixed Type Graph.

The first three data ranges are depicted in bar-type graphs and the D-range in a line-type graph. This type of graph is useful for plotting different types of data on the same graph such as trading volumes and stock prices or sales volumes and advertising expenditures.

Area Graphs

Area graphs are line graphs in which the lines are stacked and the areas between the lines are colored or hatched. These graphs are used to show trends in the data; bar graphs which emphasize individual data values. Figure 9-32 is an example using the SHOES worksheet after all data had been modified to show upward trends in shoe sales.

To create an area graph, first make sure that the graph type is Line, then issue:

/Graph **O**ptions **F**ormat **G**raph **A**rea

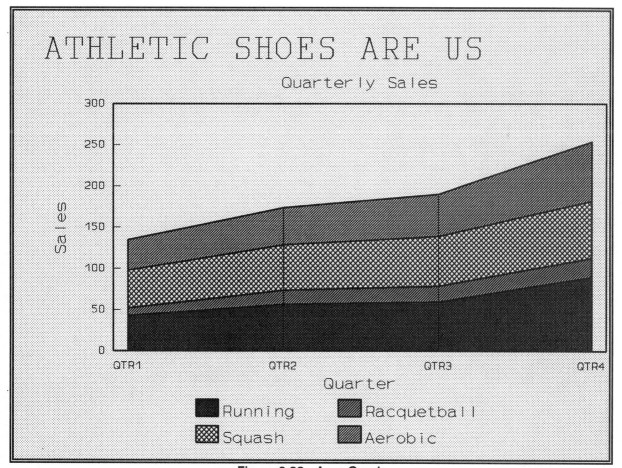

Figure 9-32. Area Graph.

High-Low-Close-Open Graphs (HLCO)

These graphs are usually used to track stock prices. Figure 9-33 is a simple worksheet containing stock prices for three days. Figure 9-34 shows the associated HLCO graph. The vertical line above Mon goes from a low of 14 to a high of 18. Compare this to column B of Figure 9-33. The tick mark at 16 to the left of this vertical line depicts the opening price of 16. The tick mark to the right shows the stock closed at 17. If there were many more days in this graph, the vertical lines would be closer together and the tick marks would almost touch. In a HLCO graph, the A-range contains the high values (in this example B2..D2), the B-range the low values, the C-range the closing values, and the D-range the opening values. These are in order in the first column in Figure 9-33 for your quick reference. The E-range is graphed as bars in the lower part of the graph. The F-range is graphed as a line graph. Rows 7 and 8 are graphed as the E and F ranges, respectively, in Figure 9-35.

A	A	B	C	D
1		Mon	Tue	Wed
2	High	18	23	20
3	Low	14	6	18
4	Close	17	18	20
5	Open	16	17	18
6				
7	Average	15.5	18	19
8		18	23	20

Figure 9-33. Simple Stock Price Tracking Worksheet.

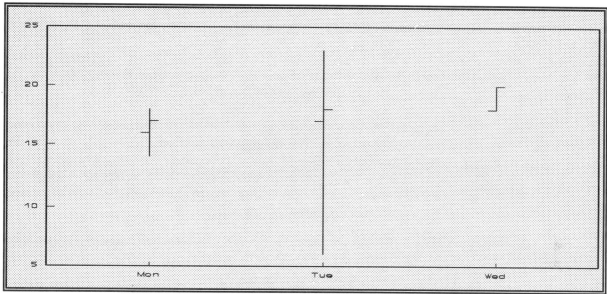

Figure 9-34. HLCO Graph with Graph Ranges A, B, C, and D.

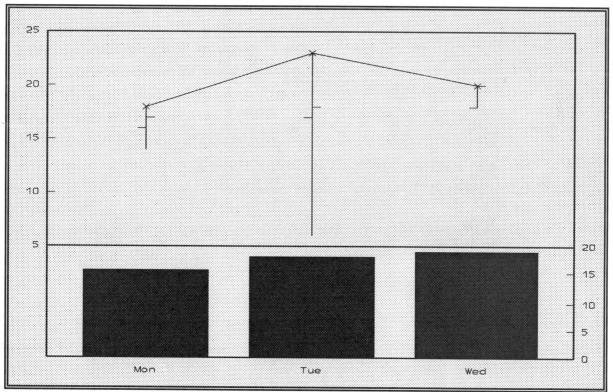

Figure 9-35. HLCO Graph with All Six Data Ranges.

Features

The first three options on the /Graph Type Features sub-menu, Vertical Horizontal Stacked, have not yet been addressed.

The Vertical option is the default that we've used in this lesson. The Horizontal option rotates the graph 90 degrees. The x-axis becomes the vertical axis on the left and the y-axis becomes the horizontal axis on the top. Change the Type to Stacked-Bar in the SHOES worksheet and choose the Horizontal option from the Features sub-menu. Your graph should look like Figure 9-36.

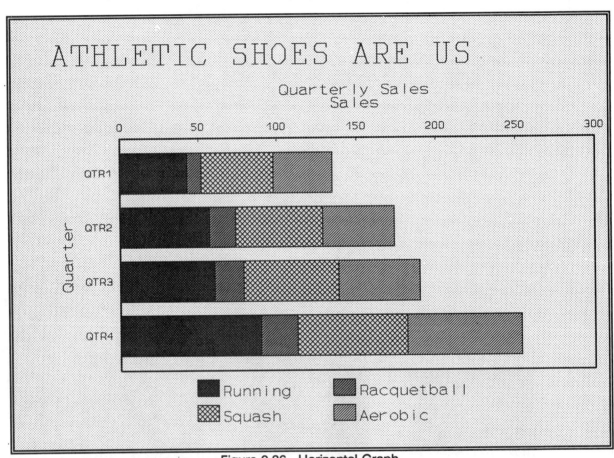

Figure 9-36. Horizontal Graph.

Releases 2.3 and 2.4:
The following two options are on the Features submenu:
Frame, which manipulates how the frame of the graph is displayed, and
3D-Effect, which creates a three dimensional effect in bar graphs.

Releases 3.0 and 3.1+: The 100% option in the Features sub-menu
displays data as a percentage of the total value for ALL ranges.

The last two graph features, /Worksheet Windows Graph and 2Y-Axis are not available in releases 2.3 and 2.4. If you are using one of these releases, skip to the end of this lesson.

/Worksheet Windows Graph

This command allows you to view both the graph and the worksheet at the same time. The screen is divided vertically in the cell pointer column, therefore have the cell pointer in mid-screen before issuing this command. Don't use column A or you'll get an error beep. Changes made to the worksheet are shown in the graph display immediately.

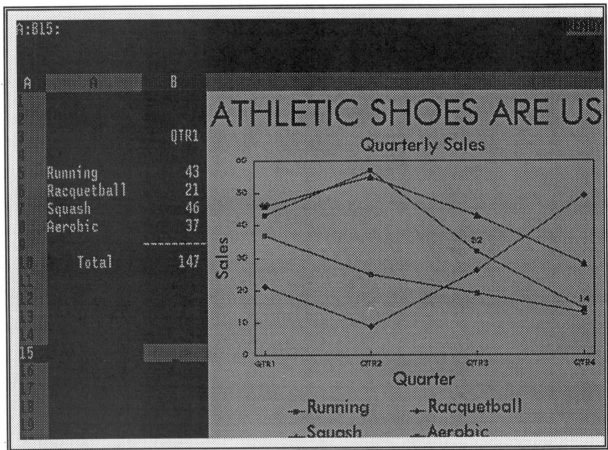

Figure 9-29. /Worksheet Windows Graph Command.

Use /Worksheet Windows Clear to clear the graph from the screen.

2Y-Axis

You may need a different scale for the line graphs than the one used for the bar graphs. Release 3 allows a second y-scale on the right frame of the graph. Figure 9-31 shows a second y-axis scale.

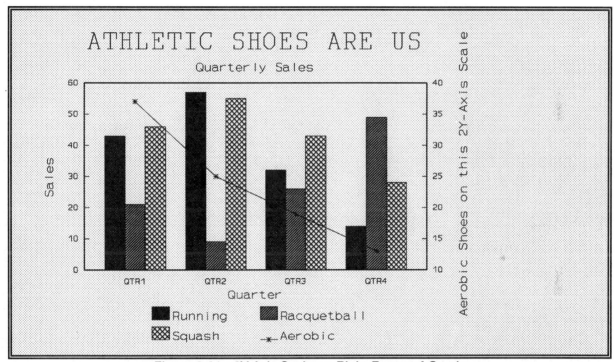

Figure 9-31. 2Y-Axis Scale on Right Frame of Graph.

The commands used to create the second y-scale were:

/Graph Type Features 2Y-Ranges D

You can assign any or all of the graph ranges to the second y-axis from this menu. There is an option on the Features sub-menu, Y-Ranges, to coincide specifically with the first y-axis on the left frame of the graph. The title on the second y-axis in Figure 9-31 was added with the command:

/Graph Options Title 2Y-Axis

Automatic scaling is the default. Manual axis scaling can be set up on the second y-axis with

/Graph Options Scale 2Y-Scale Manual

and continue as you would with the original y-axis. The second y-scale may be assigned to other than mixed type graphs.

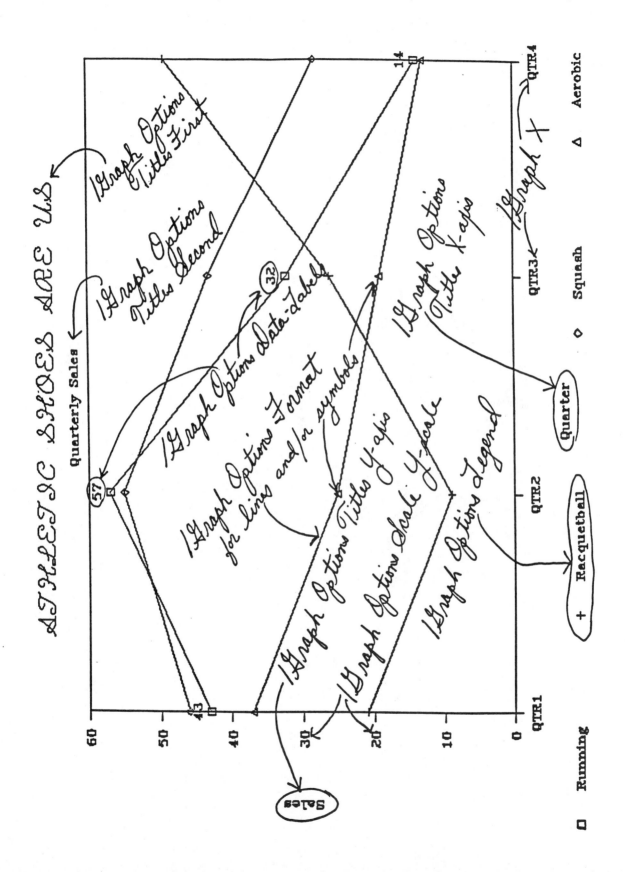

NEW COMMAND SUMMARY

/Graph	Pulls up main graph menu which allows you to create graphs.
/Graph A (through F)	Used to designate up to 6 sets of data points to be graphed.
/Graph X	Sets up the labels on the x-axis for line and bar graphs and labels for pie slices in pie charts.
/Graph Options Legend	Sets up the legends on bottom of graph screen to associate labels with sets of data points.
[F10/GRAPH]	From READY mode, displays current graph on screen.
/Graph Options Title	Creates up to 2 titles displayed above graph or titles for x and y axes.
/Graph Options Type	Changes type of graph to line, bar, stacked-bar, pie, or XY.
/Graph Name Create	Names the current graph and stores it in worksheet.
/Graph Reset	Clears all or some of the current graph settings.
/Graph Name Use	Makes current a previously named graph.
/Graph Name Delete	Deletes a named graph.
/Graph Name Reset	Deletes all named graphs.
/Graph Options Data-Labels	Adds labels near the data points on the graph.
/Graph Options Grid	Adds horizontal, vertical, neither, or both grid lines to the graph.
/Graph Options Format	In line and XY graphs, controls whether lines only, symbols only, neither, or both are included in the graph display.

/Graph Options Scale	Allows for automatic or manual scaling of the y-axis (and x-axis in XY graphs).
/Graph Options Scale Y-Scale Format	Changes the format of the values on the y-axis.
/Graph Options Scale Skip	Displays every nth label on the x-axis.
/Graph Options Color	Displays the graph in color rather than the default of Black & White.
/Graph Options B&W	Displays the graph in black and white.

EXERCISES

PART 1 EXERCISES

1A.   (SHOES9 worksheet) Use the SHOES9 worksheet to create the graph below. Graph the Total figures. (Sales for running shoes in quarter 2 should be 57, not 1000.) Name the graph PIEQTR. Don't forget to save the file after creating and naming the graphs.

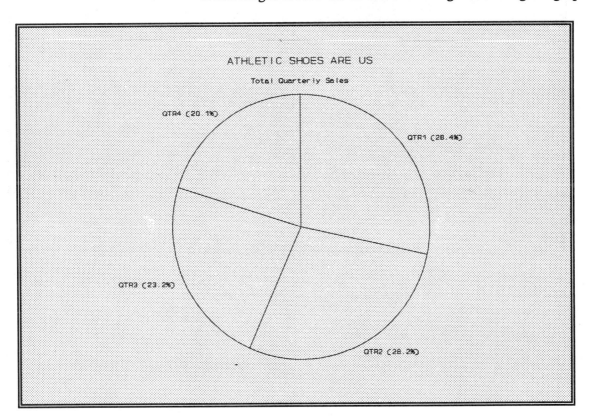

1B. (SHOES9 worksheet) Use the previous exercise's pie chart and explode the QTR2 slice with shading (code 6) to create the graph below. Name it EXPIEQTR. Don't forget to save the file after creating and naming the graphs.

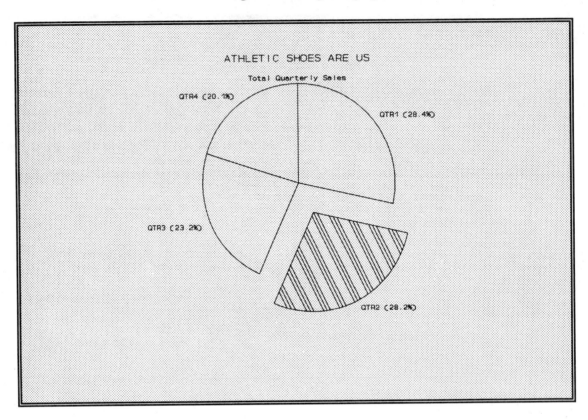

1C. (SHOES9 worksheet) Use the SHOES9 worksheet file to create the graph below. Sales for running shoes in quarter 2 should be 57, not 1000. Change the quarter 1 sales for aerobic shoes to 500. Remember to save the file after creating the graph.

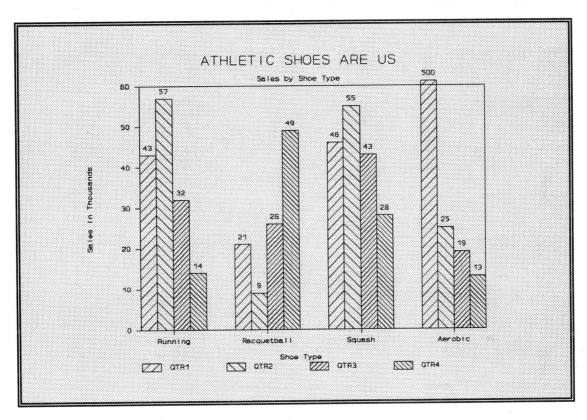

1D. (SHOES9 worksheet) Create the graph below. The only difference between it and the previous exercise graph is the format of the data-labels.

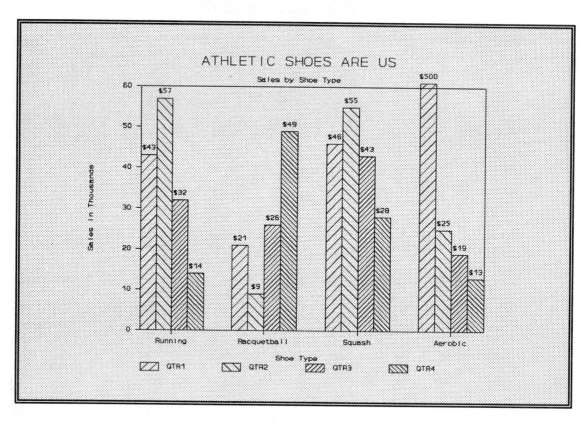

2. The worksheet below will be used in this exercise. (You should have it on disk if you've created L5BUDGET in Lesson 5.)

	A	B
1	Monthly Household Budget	
2		
3	Mortgage	$900
4	Car Payment	$450
5	Food	$375
6	Heat	$200
7	Electric	$60
8	Phone	$20
9	Insurances	$90
10	Charity	$300
11	Entertainment	$200
12	Miscellaneous	$400
13		------------
14		$2,995

2A. Create the pie chart below from the worksheet above. Remember to save the file after the graph has been created.

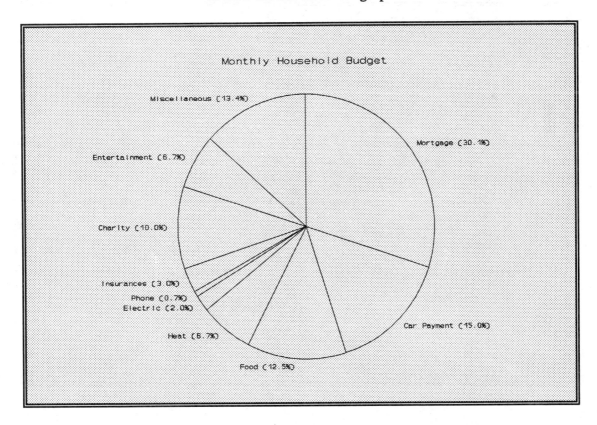

2B. Create a bar graph with the same data.

3. The worksheet below will be used in subsequent exercises. Create it and save under AUTO.

	A	B	C	D	E	F
1		VERY RELIABLE AUTO PARTS, INC.				
2						
3		Company	Sales	Gross	Units	
4		Cost	Price	Margin	Sold	Profits
5		--------	------	------	------	------
6	Radiators	99	150	51	23	1,173
7	Water Pumps	25	49	24	75	1,800
8	Carburetors	29	79	50	34	1,700
9	Defoggers	19	29	10	56	560
10						---------
11						$5,233

3A. (AUTO worksheet) Create the pie chart below. Remember to save the file after the graph has been created.

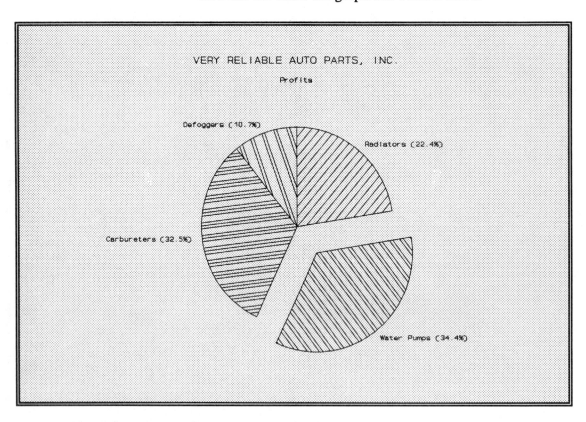

3B. (AUTO worksheet)   Create the bar graph below.   Name the graph AUTOBAR. Remember to save the file after the graph has been created.

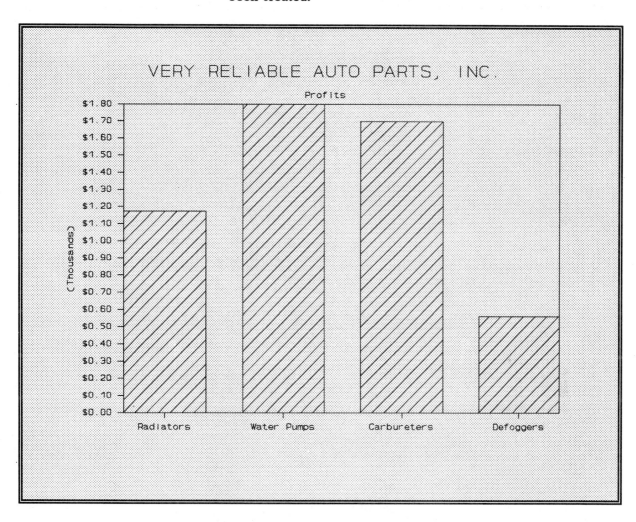

3C. (AUTO worksheet) Create the bar graph below. Name the graph and remember to save the file after the graph has been created.

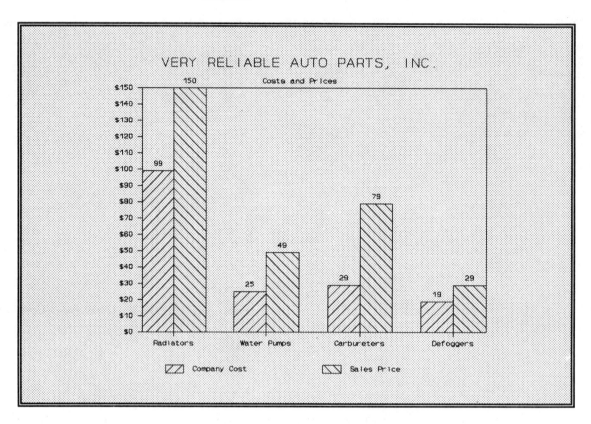

4. The worksheet below will be used in subsequent exercises. Create it and save under L9EOQ, if you do not already have it under L6EOQ.

```
         A         B          C         D
 1            COMPUTING OPTIMAL ORDER QUANTITY
 2   INPUTS:    Annual demand =         3000
 3              Annual holding costs=  $4.00
 4              Order costs=          $10.00
 5   OUTPUTS:
 6   Optimal order quantity=            122
 7   Orders per year=                    24
 8   Ordering Costs=                $244.95
 9   Holding costs=                 $244.95
10   Total Costs=                   $489.90
11
12      Order    Ordering   Holding    Total
13      Size     Costs      Costs      Costs
14       31      $979.80     $61.24  $1,041.03
15       61      $489.90    $122.47    $612.37
16       92      $326.60    $183.71    $510.31
17      122      $244.95    $244.95    $489.90
18      153      $195.96    $306.19    $502.15
19      184      $163.30    $367.42    $530.72
20      214      $139.97    $428.66    $568.63
```

Hint: To get the order sizes in A14..A20, use increments of .25 multiplied by the optimum order quantity.

4. (Continued) Create the graph below using the worksheet above.

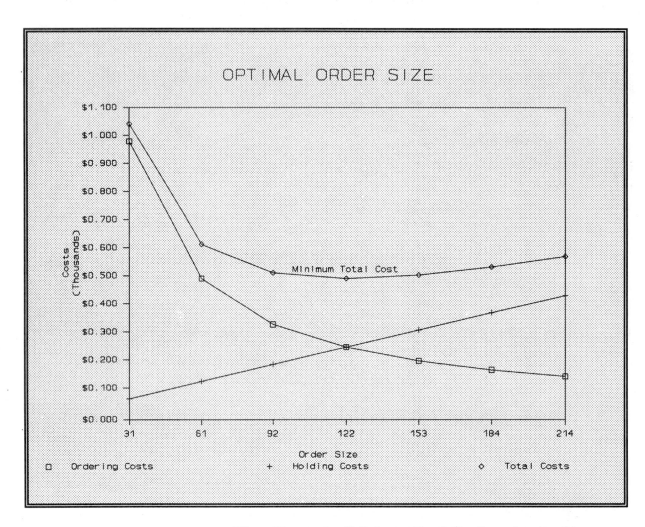

Hint: To get the "Minimum Total Cost" on the graph, set up a range to be used for data-labels for the total cost graph range. It should be blank except for the middle cell containing "Minimum Total Cost".

5. The worksheet below will be used in subsequent exercises. Create it and save under L9BREVEN.

	A	B	C	D
1		BREAK-EVEN ANALYSIS		
2				
3	Selling price per unit=			$2.00
4	Total variable cost per unit=			$1.50
5	Total fixed costs per period=			$10,000.00
6				
7	Contribution margin ratio=			$0.2500
8	Break-even quantity of units sold=			20,000
9	Break-even sales=			$40,000.00
10				
11	Units			
12	Sold	Sales	Costs	Profit
13	-------	-------	-------	-------
14	0	$0	$10,000	($10,000)
15	10,000	$20,000	$25,000	($5,000)
16	20,000	$40,000	$40,000	$0
17	30,000	$60,000	$55,000	$5,000
18	40,000	$80,000	$70,000	$10,000
19	50,000	$100,000	$85,000	$15,000
20	60,000	$120,000	$100,000	$20,000

Hint: The units sold column in A14..A20 can be computed using multiples of .5 multiplied by the break-even units sold.

5A. (L9BREVEN worksheet) Create the graph below and name it
BREVEN.

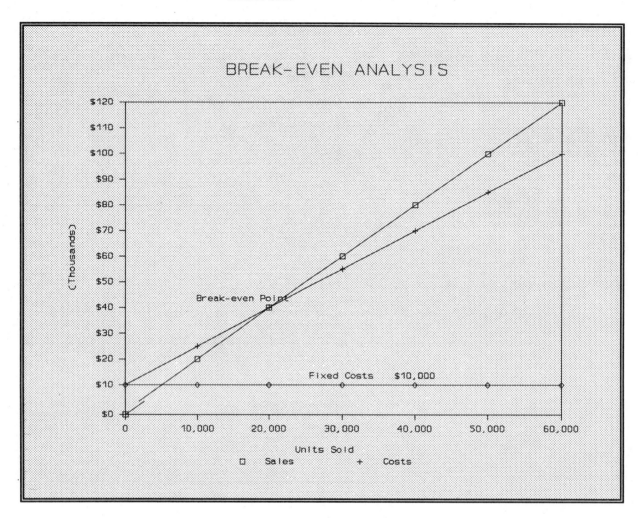

5B.   (L9BREVEN worksheet) Create the graph below and name it
ADDCOSTS.

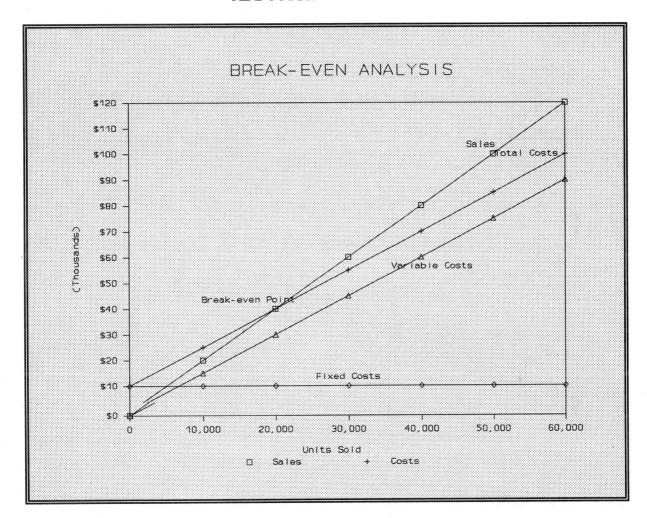

5C.   (L9BREVEN worksheet) Create the graph below and name it COSTS.

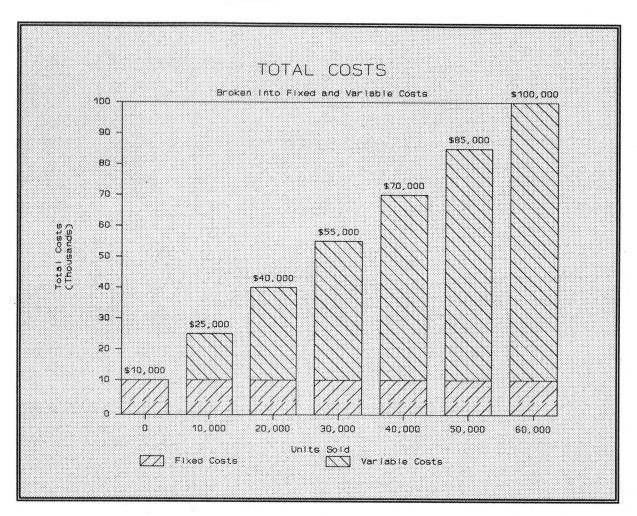

6. Create the worksheet below if you haven't created it Lesson 6 and save under L9NORMAL.

```
C8: (F10) [W15] (1/($C$5*@SQRT(2*@PI)))*@EXP(-0.5*((B8-$C$4)/$C$5)^2)
```

	A	B	C	D	E	F	G
1	GRAPH OF NORMAL DISTRIBUTION						
2							
3	INPUT:						
4	Mean=		5.7				
5	St. Dev.=		1.34				
6							
7		x	f(x)				
8	0.00	0.00	0.0000350504				
9	0.05	0.29	0.0000846801				
10	0.10	0.57	0.0001955349				
11	0.15	0.86	0.0004315406				
12	0.20	1.14	0.0009102768				
13	0.25	1.43	0.0018351842				
14	0.30	1.71	0.0035362283				
15	0.35	2.00	0.0065126144				
16	0.40	2.28	0.0114637017				
17	0.45	2.57	0.0192862960				
18	0.50	2.85	0.0310118174				
19	0.55	3.14	0.0476606595				
20	0.60	3.42	0.0700079428				
21	0.65	3.71	0.0982854032				
22	0.70	3.99	0.1318818923				
23	0.75	4.28	0.1691358831				
24	0.80	4.56	0.2073197992				
25	0.85	4.85	0.2428847474				
26	0.90	5.13	0.2719657067				
27	0.95	5.42	0.2910599745				
28	1.00	5.70	0.2977181197				
29	1.05	5.99	0.2910599745				
30	1.10	6.27	0.2719657067				
31	1.15	6.56	0.2428847474				
32	1.20	6.84	0.2073197992				
33	1.25	7.13	0.1691358831				
34	1.30	7.41	0.1318818923				
35	1.35	7.70	0.0982854032				
36	1.40	7.98	0.0700079428				
37	1.45	8.27	0.0476606595				
38	1.50	8.55	0.0310118174				
39	1.55	8.84	0.0192862960				
40	1.60	9.12	0.0114637017				
41	1.65	9.41	0.0065126144				
42	1.70	9.69	0.0035362283				
43	1.75	9.98	0.0018351842				
44	1.80	10.26	0.0009102768				
45	1.85	10.55	0.0004315406				
46	1.90	10.83	0.0001955349				
47	1.95	11.12	0.0000846801				
48	2.00	11.40	0.0000350504				

6. (Continued)   Create the graph below from the previous worksheet.

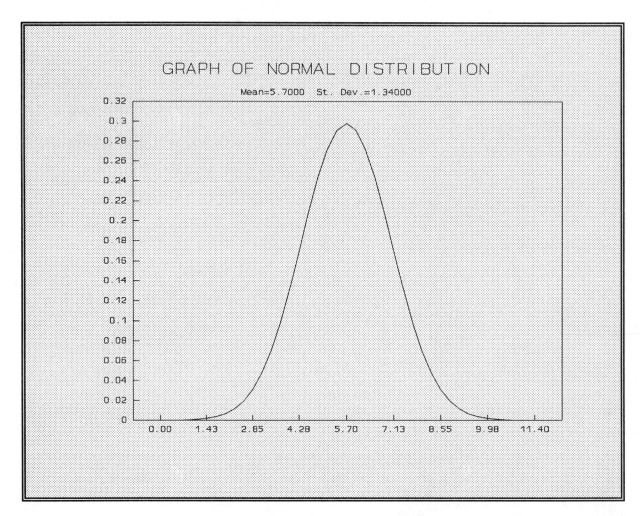

Set options up to lines only with a skip factor of 5. The A range is F(x). Change the mean to 10 and standard deviation to 15 and view the graph with [F10/GRAPH]. Your screen should look like the next graph.

Try several combinations of different means and standard deviations. How does the standard deviation change the shape of the curve?

The second title must be created using the @STRING function. (See page 548.)

6.   (Continued Again)

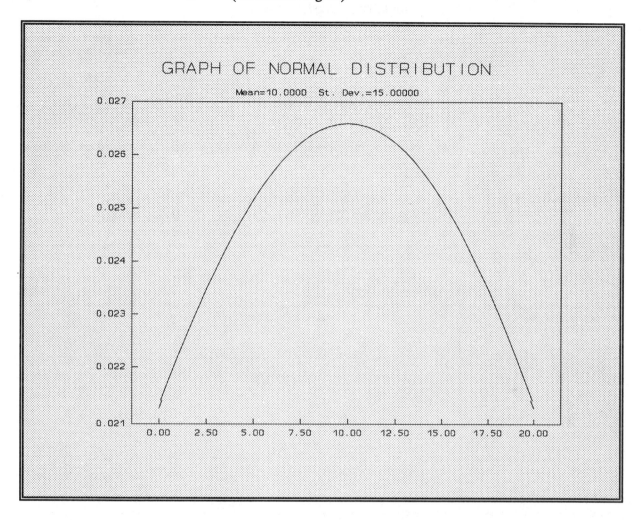

7.   Create the worksheet below.

```
         A          B         C
1    International YoYo Corp.
2
3    Plant A        12        58
4    Warehouse      52        27
5    Plant B        34         6
6    Warehouse      20        41
```

Create the XY graph below using the above worksheet.

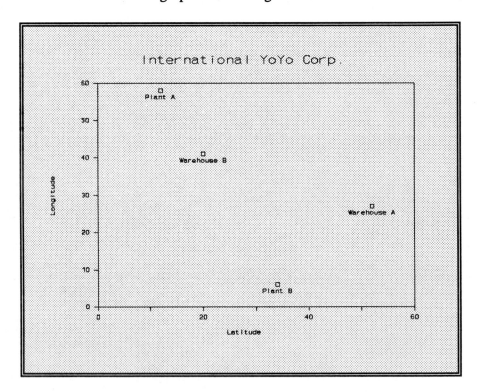

CUMULATIVE EXERCISES

C1.   Create the graphs below from the TOFU1 worksheet.

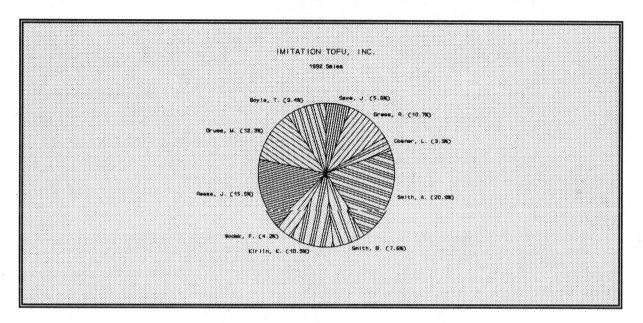

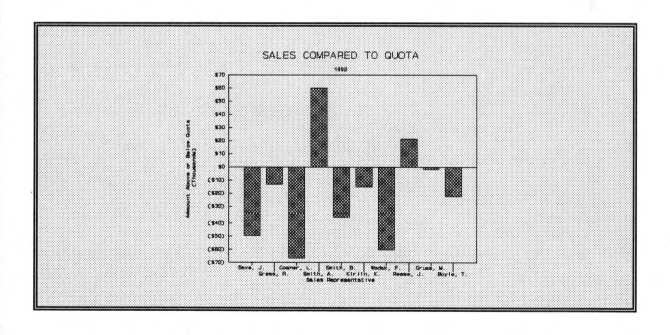

C2. Create the graph below from the FISH1 worksheet.

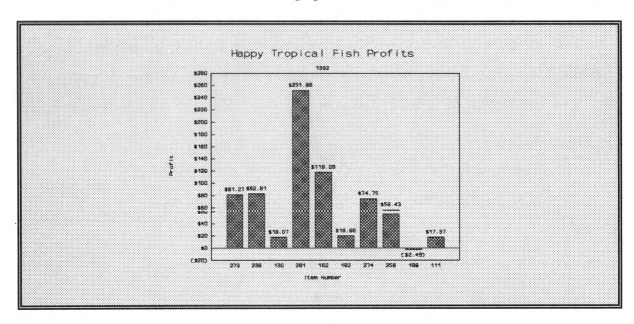

C3. Create the graph below from the GOLF1 worksheet.

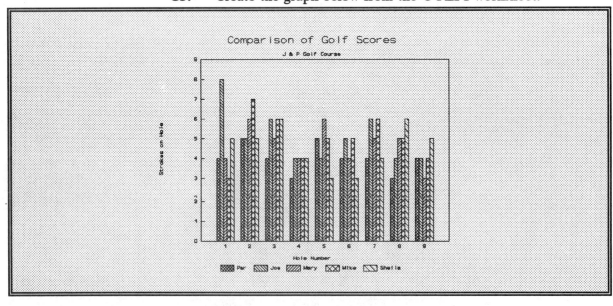

C4.   Create the graphs below from the BILL1 worksheet.

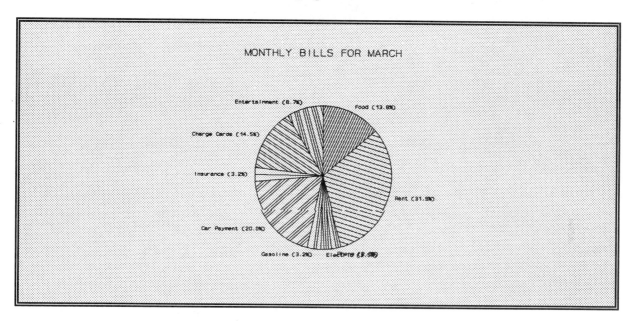

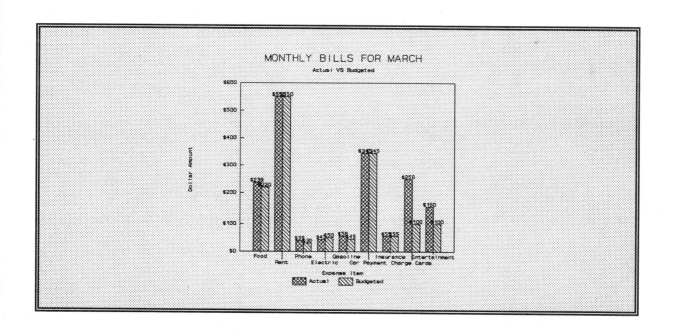

PRINTGRAPH

Contents:

Lesson 10 is a comprehensive discussion of the PrintGraph program. It explains how to get printouts of graphs created in worksheets using 1-2-3.

Releases 2.2, 2.3, 2.4, and 3.1+: WYSIWYG and ALLWAYS make this lesson obsolete. All features in this lesson do still exist in these releases. You may do this lesson if you wish, but I would suggest you use the time to do the appendix on WYSIWYG or ALLWAYS instead.

Releases 3.0 and 3.1+: These releases allow you to print graphs directly from 1-2-3. PrintGraph no longer exists. Skip to the end of this lesson for information on how to print graphs in Release 3.x

---

Begin this lesson with the SHOES worksheet on the screen as in Figure 10-1.

	A	B	C	D	E	F
1			ATHLETIC SHOES ARE US			
2						
3		QTR1	QTR2	QTR3	QTR4	YEARLY SALES
4						
5	Running	43	1000	32	14	1089
6	Racquetball	21	9	26	49	105
7	Squash	46	55	43	28	172
8	Aerobic	37	25	19	13	94
9		--------	--------	--------	--------	--------
10	Total	147	1089	120	104	1460

Figure 10-1. SHOES Worksheet.

Change the second quarter sales for running shoes back to 57.

You enter into C5: **57 [Return]**

Make the QTRSALES graph the current graph.

You enter: **/ Graph Name Use QTRSALES [Return]**

Your graph should look like Figure 10-2.

You enter: **[Esc]**

/Graph Save

To print a graph, you must save a .PIC file to disk. From the print menu on your screen now, choose the Save option.

You enter: **Save**

Computer message: Enter graph file name:

Save it under the name QTRSALES.

You enter: **QTRSALES [Return]**

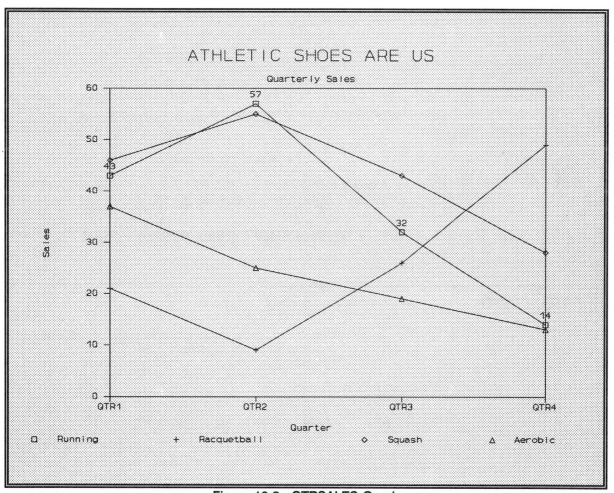

Figure 10-2. QTRSALES Graph.

Beginning 1-2-3 users frequently get confused with /Graph Save and /Graph Name Create. /Graph Save is used when you want to print a graph. It stores a picture of the graph on disk in a separate file (not inside the worksheet file) and gives the separate file the extension .PIC. /Graph Name Create is used to name the graph or store it internally to the worksheet file, so that it may be pulled onto the screen for use later. /Graph Name Create is used when more than one graph is created from the same worksheet. Named graphs are saved inside the .WK1 files by the /File Save command.

Save the pie chart under the name PIE.PIC.

You enter: **Name Use PIE [Return] [Esc] Save PIE [Return] Quit**

/File List Graph

To see a directory of .PIC files residing on disk, use /File List Graph.

You enter: **/ File List Graph**

The screen format is similar to that of /File List Worksheet. Use the arrow keys to highlight a filename. Return to the worksheet.

You enter: **[Return]**

You must now exit 1-2-3 and return to the Lotus Access System menu to print these two graphs you saved. Save the file before you exit.

You enter: **/ File Save SHOES [Return] Replace / Quit Yes**

PrintGraph

The Lotus Access System menu is on your screen. Enter the PrintGraph part of Lotus.

You enter: **PrintGraph**

Your screen should be similar to Figure 10-3.

```
Copyright 1985 Lotus Development Corp.  All Rights Reserved.  Release 2    MENU
-----------------------------------------------------------------------------
Select graphs for printing
Image-Select  Settings  Go  Align  Page  Exit
=============================================================================
   GRAPH       IMAGE OPTIONS                        HARDWARE SETUP
   IMAGES       Size               Range Colors      Graphs Directory:
   SELECTED      Top      .395     X Black             B:\
                 Left     .750     A Black           Fonts Directory:
                 Width   6.500     B Black             A:\
                 Height  4.691     C Black           Interface:
                 Rotate   .000     D Black             Parallel 1
                                   E Black           Printer Type:
                 Font              F Black             IBM/Lo
                  1  BLOCK1                          Paper Size
                  2  BLOCK1                            Width     13.000
                                                       Length    11.000

                                                    ACTION OPTIONS
                                                    Pause: No
                                                    Eject: No
```

Figure 10-3. Main PrintGraph Screen.

The options in the main PrintGraph menu are on your screen as below.

Image-Select Settings Go Align Page Exit

The brief explanations of each option are shown above the option line.

Image-Select

The first step in printing the two graphs is designating the .PIC files.
Choose the option Image-Select.

You enter: Image-Select

Your screen should look like Figure 10-4.

```
Copyright 1985 Lotus Development Corp.  All Rights Reserved.  Release 2     POINT

Select graphs for output


   PICTURE      DATE      TIME      SIZE
   ------------------------------------------          [SPACE] turns mark on and off
   PIE        02-15-88   13:54      1244               [RETURN] selects marked pictures
   QTRSALES   02-15-88   13:52      1172               [ESCAPE] exits, ignoring changes
                                                       [HOME] goes to beginning of list
                                                       [END] goes to end of list
                                                       [UP] and [DOWN] move cursor
                                                           List will scroll if cursor
                                                           moved beyond top or bottom
                                                       [GRAPH] displays selected picture
```

Figure 10-4. Image-Select Menu.

The help column on the right of the screen lists possible keystrokes and their functions. The bottom key, [Graph], displays the highlighted graph on the screen. [Graph] means [F10/GRAPH] or the tenth function key.

You enter: **[F10/GRAPH] [Esc]**

Select both graphs for printing. The [SpaceBar] is used to place a mark, #, by the graphs to be printed.

You enter: **[SpaceBar] [Down] [SpaceBar]**

A # should be seen at the left of both graphs. Select both marked graphs by hitting [Return].

You enter: **[Return]**

WARNING: Don't make the mistake of highlighting the graph you want and pressing [Return], as the graph will not be selected. The # mark must be placed before the graph with [SpaceBar]. Always verify that your graphs have been selected correctly by checking the list under the GRAPHS TO PRINT (or GRAPH IMAGES SELECTED) heading on the main graph menu.

Back on this main graph menu, PIE and QTRSALES are listed under the column header GRAPH TO PRINT or GRAPH IMAGES SELECTED. The graphs will be printed in the order they appear in this vertical list. The graph at the top of the list, PIE, will be printed first and QTRSALES will be printed second. The order is determined by the order in which the .PIC files were marked with # in the Image-Select menu. Change the order so that QTRSALES will be printed first.

You enter: Image-Select

Delete the #'s by the graphs by using the [SpaceBar].

You enter: **[SpaceBar] [Down] [SpaceBar]**

Now mark QTRSALES first, then PIE and select the marked graphs.

You enter: **[SpaceBar] [Up] [SpaceBar] [Return]**

Go

In the main menu, QTRSALES is first in the list and will be printed first. Print the two graphs by choosing the Go command.

You enter: **G**o

It may take several minutes before the prints come out. If you are on a network, you may have to exit Lotus before your graphs are printed.

Your printed graphs should look like Figures 9-14 and 9-10.

Graph Size

By default, graphs are printed half-size, or approximately half of a standard sheet of 8½ by 11 paper. Next you'll print the full-size graph in Figure 10-6, which takes a full sheet of standard paper. First delete the PIE graph from the selected graphs.

You enter: Image-Select

You: **Delete # before PIE using [SpaceBar].**

You enter: **[Return]**

From the main PrintGraph menu choose Settings.

You enter: **S**ettings **I**mage **S**ize **F**ull **Q**uit **Q**uit **Q**uit

On the main PrintGraph screen now on your screen, note the Size column.

```
Size
  Top        .250
  Left       .500
  Width     6.852
  Height    9.445
  Rotate   90.000
```

The Top and Left lines show the number of inches in the top and left margins. Width is the horizontal page width in inches. Height is the vertical length of the graph in inches. The full-size graph is rotated 90 degrees on the paper as shown in Figure 10-6. Half-size graphs are rotated 0 degrees.

You enter: **Settings Image Size**

The menu Full Half Manual Quit on your screen now has a Manual option which allows you to manually set up graph placement on the page.

You enter: **Manual**

Each variable can be set up via this menu on your screen:
Top Left Width Height Rotation Quit.

You enter: **Quit Quit**

Graph Fonts

A font is a type of print. The fonts shown in Figure 10-5 can be used in printing the text portions of graphs.

Choose Font from the menu.

You enter: **Font**

Now you must set up font 1 or 2. Font 1 is used for the first title on top of the graph only. Font 2 is used for all other graph text.

You enter: **1**

The mark is before BLOCK1, the default font. Change to SCRIPT1 by highlighting SCRIPT1, moving the mark, and selecting the marked font:

You enter: **[End] [Up] [SpaceBar] [Return]**

Under Font on the main graph screen you see:

1 SCRIPT1
2 SCRIPT2

Unless Font 2 is specifically changed, it takes Font 1. Change Font 2 to ROMAN2.

You enter: **Font 2 Highlight ROMAN2. [SpaceBar] [Return]**

The screen shows the fonts below.

1 SCRIPT1
2 ROMAN2

You enter: **Quit**

ABCDEFGHIJKLM
NOPQRSTUVWXYZ
abcdefghijklm .
nopqrstuvwxyz
1234567890
!@#$%^&*()
_-+={}[]:;'~
""?/<>,.'\

Block 1

ABCDEFGHIJKLM
NOPQRSTUVWXYZ
abcdefghijklm
nopqrstuvwxyz
1234567890
!@#$%^&*()
_-+={}[]:;'~
""?/<>,.'\

Block 2

ABCDEFGHIJKLM
NOPQRSTUVWXYZ
abcdefghijklm
nopqrstuvwxyz
1234567890
!@#$%^&*()
_-+={}[]:;'~
""?/<>,.'

Bold

ABCDEFGHIJKLM
NOPQRSTUVWXYZ
abcdefghijklm
nopqrstuvwxyz
1234567890
!@#$%^&*()
_-+={}[]:;'~
""?/<>,.'

Forum

ABCDEFGHIJKLM
NOPQRSTUVWXYZ
abcdefghijklm
nopqrstuvwxyz
1234567890
!@#$%^&()*
_-+={}[]:;'~
""?/<>,.'

Italic 1

ABCDEFGHIJKLM
NOPQRSTUVWXYZ
abcdefghijklm
nopqrstuvwxyz
1234567890
!@#$%^&()*
_-+={}[]:;'~
""?/<>,.'

Italic 2

ABCDEFGHIJKLM
NOPQRSTUVWXYZ
abcdefghijklm
nopqrstuvwxyz
1234567890
!@#$%^&()*
_-+={}[]:;'~
""?/<>,.'

Lotus

ABCDEFGHIJKLM
NOPQRSTUVWXYZ
abcdefghijklm
nopqrstuvwxyz
1234567890
!@#$%^&*()
_-+={}[]:;'~
""?/<>,.'\

Roman 1

ABCDEFGHIJKLM
NOPQRSTUVWXYZ
abcdefghijklm
nopqrstuvwxyz
1234567890
!@#$%^&*()
_-+={}[]:;'~
""?/<>,.'\

Roman 2

ABCDEFGHIJKLM
NOPQRSTUVWXYZ
abcdefghijklm
noopqrstuvwxyz
1234567890
!@#$%^&*()
_-+={}[]:;'~
""?/<>,.'\

Script 1

ABCDEFGHIJKLM
NOPQRSTUVWXYZ
abcdefghijklm
nopqrstuvwxyz
1234567890
!@#$%^&*()*
_-+={}[]:;'~
""?/<>,.'\

Script 2

Figure 10-5. PrintGraph Fonts.

Paper Size

The HARDWARE SETUPs can be changed from this menu beginning Image Hardware.... If you are using other than standard size paper, use the Hardware option from this menu to change the paper size.

You enter: **Hardware Size-Paper Quit Quit**

Action

The ACTION OPTIONS are currently set so that PrintGraph does not pause after each graph printed. It printed the two graphs QTRSALES and PIE one right after the other. To force PrintGraph to stop after each graph print, so that perhaps you could insert another single sheet of paper, use the Action option from this menu.

You enter: **Action Pause [Esc]**

Eject

The Eject option will eject the page after each graph, if it is set to Yes. By default, PrintGraph will print as many graphs as can fit on the page before ejecting, as it did with the half-size QTRSALES and PIE graphs.

You enter: **Eject [Esc] Quit**

Save and Reset

The current PrintGraph settings can be saved by using the Save option from this menu. Reset "retrieves" the last set of saved PrintGraph settings.

You enter: **Quit**

Page

The Page option from this main menu will eject the page.

Align

Align, as in printing worksheets, resets the line counter to 1.

Releases 2.x+: The rest of this lesson covers printing graphs in Release 3.x. Skip to the end of this lesson if you are not using this release.

/Print Printer Image

From 1-2-3, this command allows you to print a graph. The next sub-menu, Current   Named-Graph, lets you choose the current graph or a named graph.

/Print Printer Range *

An alternate way to print a graph is to do a /Print Printer Range and type an asterisk followed by the name of the graph and hit [Return].

Printing Ranges and Graphs on the Same Paper

Because you don't have to leave 1-2-3 to get a graph printout in Release 3.x, printing a graph and range consecutively on the same sheet of paper is now possible. (Allways and WYSIWYG is better for this, see appendices.)

/Print Printer Options Advanced Image

This command allows you to print the graph sideways, change the size of the printed graph, and change the density of the printed graph.

If you are interested in doing something more elaborate, read the lesson on Advanced Worksheet Printing.

NEW COMMAND SUMMARY

/Graph Save	Saves the current graph in a .PIC file for later printing with PrintGraph.
/File List Graph	Lists .PIC files on disk.
Image-Select	Allows the selection of graphs in .PIC files to be printed.
Go	Prints the selected graphs.
Settings Image Size	Changes the size of the graph prints to full-size, half-size or manually set-up size.
Settings Image Font	Changes the font used for text in graph prints. Font 1 is used for the main title. Font 2 is used for all other text.
Hardware Size-Paper	Changes the size of the paper.
Action Pause	Controls whether PrintGraph pauses between graph prints.
Action Eject	Controls whether the paper is ejected between graph prints.
Settings Save	Saves the current PrintGraph settings to a file.
Settings Reset	Sets the PrintGraph settings to a previously saved settings file with Settings Save.
Page	Ejects the page.
Align	Resets the line counter to 1. Should be used after paper has been adjusted to the top of the page in the printer.

EXERCISES

1. Print half-size the PIEQTR graph created in Lesson 9, Exercise 1 using Bold for font 1 and Forum for font 2.

2. Print full-size the EXPIEQTR graph created in Lesson 9, Exercise 1 using Italic 1 for font 1 and Italic 2 for font 2.

3. Print two half-size graphs from Lesson 9 on the same sheet of paper. Use Script 1 for both font 1 and 2 on the first graph and Roman 2 for both font 1 and 2 on the second graph.

4. Print one of the graphs from Lesson 9 full-size. Use the Lotus fonts for both fonts 1 and 2.

5. Print the quarter-size graph below using the QTRSALES line graph from Lesson 9. Change the size manually to a left margin of 4.15 and a width of 3.25. Do this by beginning at the main PrintGraph menu and entering the keystrokes below.

You enter:
Settings Image Size Manual Left 4.15 [Return] Width 3.25 [Return] Quit Quit Quit Quit

Your graph print should be the size of the one to the right.

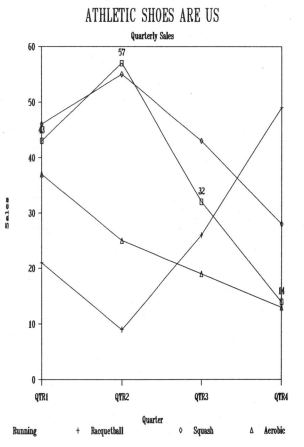

CUMULATIVE EXERCISES

If your release has the WYSIWYG add-in, I would suggest that you do the exercises at the end of the WYSIWYG appendix instead of, or in addition to, these exercises.

C1. Print the pie chart that you created in Lesson 9 from the TOFU1 worksheet half-size using Lotus for font 1 and Script 1 for font 2.

Print the bar graph that you created in Lesson 9 from the TOFU1 worksheet full-size using Italic 2 for both fonts 1 and 2.

Retrieve the TOFU1 worksheet. Use WYSIWYG or ALLWAYS to pull both the pie chart and bar graph into the worksheet and print.

C2. Print the bar graph that you created in Lesson 9 from the FISH1 worksheet full-size using Roman 2 for font 1 and Roman 1 for font 2.

Retrieve the FISH1 worksheet. Use WYSIWYG or ALLWAYS to pull the bar graph into the worksheet and print.

C3. Print the bar graph that you created in Lesson 9 from the BILL1 worksheet full-size using Forum for boths font 1 and 2.

Print the pie chart that you created in Lesson 9 from the BILL1 worksheet half-size using Lotus for font 1 and Script 1 for font 2.

Retrieve the BILL1 worksheet. Use WYSIWYG or ALLWAYS to pull both the pie chart and bar graph into the worksheet and print.

C4. Print the bar graph that you created in Lesson 9 from the GOLF1 worksheet full-size using Roman 2 for font 1 and Roman 1 for font 2.

Retrieve the GOLF1 worksheet. Use WYSIWYG or ALLWAYS to pull the bar graph into the worksheet and print.

DATA
SORT

Contents:

In this lesson, the hierarchy of a database including fields and records is discussed. Sorting records of a database with both primary and secondary keys is illustrated.

Database

A **database** is a collection of data concerning some subject. It is actually a group of logically related **files.** An employee database might consist of two files: a full-time employee file and a part-time employee file. A file in a database is made up of records. In an employee file, a **record** exists for each employee and contains all data on that particular employee such as name, social security number, address, etc. Records are made up of **fields** or **data elements.** The fields in the employee records would be the name field, social security number field, address fields, etc. Fields are further broken down into **characters.** In summary, characters make up fields which make up records which make up files which make up databases.

Create Figure 11-1 and save under the name ALLSHOP if you have not already done so in another lesson. If you have, retrieve the file. Do not modify the file on disk by saving it with the modifications you will make in this lesson. You will need it, as is, in other lessons.

```
         A            B          C        D
  1          ALLSHOP RESTAURANT SERVICE, INC.
  2
  3    ITEM #   DESCRIPTION     PRICE    CLASS
  4
  5       1048 GROUND GINGER    $1.29 SPICE
  6       2668 TIDAL LIQUID     $3.99 DETERGENT
  7       3555 PICKLING SPICE   $1.39 SPICE
  8       4874 ARROWROOT        $2.19 SPICE
  9       4913 WOODITE          $2.49 DETERGENT
 10       5104 DILL WEED        $1.79 SPICE
 11       6125 JEST SOAP        $2.09 DETERGENT
 12       6270 CELERY SEED      $1.35 SPICE
```

Figure 11-1. ALLSHOP Worksheet.

This worksheet can be considered a part of a database of items sold by Allshop. In the table A3..D12, each line or row is considered a record. Each column is called a field or data element. The column headers in row 3 are called field names. The characters DILL WEED make up the DESCRIPTION field of the sixth record of this file.

/Data Sort

/Data Sort is used to change the order of records in a database. The ALLSHOP file is currently sorted by the item number field in ascending order. Change the sort order to ascending by DESCRIPTION.

You enter: **/ Data Sort**

and the main sort menu appears on the screen:

Data-Range Primary-Key Secondary-Key Reset Go Quit

Releases 3.0 and 3.1+: An additional Extra-Key option is on this menu.

Data-Range

The range containing the records to be sorted is specified with the Data-Range option above.

You enter: **Data-Range**

Computer message: **Enter data range:**

Do not include the fields names in row 3 or the blank record in row 4.

You enter or point to: **A5..D12 [Return]**

WARNING: Be very careful to include in the range all fields or columns of the database, not just the field you want sorted. Save the file immediately BEFORE doing the sort. If an error is made, the file can be easily restored.

The main sort menu is a sticky menu and has returned to the screen.

Primary-Key

The primary key is the field to be used for sorting. The DESCRIPTION field, column B, will be our primary key.

You enter: **Primary-Key**

Computer message: Primary sort key:

Enter any cell address in column B.

You enter: **B5 [Return]**

The row number is not important, therefore you could have entered B1 or B287 with the same result.

Computer message: Sort order (A or D): D

The sort order is either ascending or descending. Ascending is smallest to largest for values and alphabetical order for labels. Descending is largest to smallest for values and reverse alphabetical order for labels. The default is descending order. Change it to ascending order:

You enter: **A [Return]**

Go

The Data-Range and Primary-Key are set up and you're ready to sort. Choose Go from the main sort menu on the screen.

You enter: **Go**

Your worksheet should look like Figure 11-2.

```
          A          B          C       D
1              ALLSHOP RESTAURANT SERVICE, INC.
2
3    ITEM #   DESCRIPTION       PRICE   CLASS
4
5     4874  ARROWROOT          $2.19  SPICE
6     6270  CELERY SEED        $1.35  SPICE
7     5104  DILL WEED          $1.79  SPICE
8     1048  GROUND GINGER      $1.29  SPICE
9     6125  JEST SOAP          $2.09  DETERGENT
10    3555  PICKLING SPICE     $1.39  SPICE
11    2668  TIDAL LIQUID       $3.99  DETERGENT
12    4913  WOODITE            $2.49  DETERGENT
```

Figure 11-2. Records Sorted by DESCRIPTION Field, Ascending Order.

Note that the DESCRIPTION field is in alphabetical order.

If your worksheet doesn't match Figure 11-2, retrieve the ALLSHOP file and do the sort again.

Do a sort on the DESCRIPTION field again, but this time in descending order.

You enter: **/ Data Sort Data-Range [Return]**

You need not enter the data range again, 1-2-3 remembers the last data range set up. It's a good idea to check it by choosing it from the main data sort menu and visually verifying the range. In fact, 1-2-3 remembers all of the most recent sort settings.

You enter: **Primary-Key [Return]**

The only thing you must change is order of the primary key.

You enter: **D [Return] G**o

Your worksheet should look like Figure 11-3.

```
         A          B              C        D
1               ALLSHOP RESTAURANT SERVICE, INC.
2
3    ITEM #    DESCRIPTION      PRICE   CLASS
4
5       4913  WOODITE           $2.49 DETERGENT
6       2668  TIDAL LIQUID      $3.99 DETERGENT
7       3555  PICKLING SPICE    $1.39 SPICE
8       6125  JEST SOAP         $2.09 DETERGENT
9       1048  GROUND GINGER     $1.29 SPICE
10      5104  DILL WEED         $1.79 SPICE
11      6270  CELERY SEED       $1.35 SPICE
12      4874  ARROWROOT         $2.19 SPICE
```

Figure 11-3. Records Sorted by DESCRIPTION Field, Descending Order.

Do a sort by the CLASS field in ascending order.

You enter: / **Data Sort Primary-Key D10 [Return] A [Return] G**o

The CLASS fields in your worksheet be like that of Figure 11-4.

```
         A          B              C        D
1               ALLSHOP RESTAURANT SERVICE, INC.
2
3    ITEM #    DESCRIPTION      PRICE   CLASS
4
5       6125  JEST SOAP         $2.09 DETERGENT
6       2668  TIDAL LIQUID      $3.99 DETERGENT
7       4913  WOODITE           $2.49 DETERGENT
8       3555  PICKLING SPICE    $1.39 SPICE
9       1048  GROUND GINGER     $1.29 SPICE
10      5104  DILL WEED         $1.79 SPICE
11      6270  CELERY SEED       $1.35 SPICE
12      4874  ARROWROOT         $2.19 SPICE
```

Figure 11-4. Sort by CLASS with Ties in Primary-Key.

Releases 2.3 and 2.4: Under the main data sort menu is displayed the Sort Settings screen. [F2/EDIT] and the mouse can be used to change settings. Try it with the next sort setting - Secondary-Key.

Secondary-Key

When there is a tie in the primary-key field, the Secondary-Key can be used to break it. Sort the three DETERGENT records and the five SPICE records in ascending order by item number:

You enter: / **Data Sort Secondary-Key A1 [Return] A [Return] G**o

Your worksheet should look like Figure 11-5. Note that records with the same CLASS are now in order by ITEM #.

```
          A              B              C        D
1              ALLSHOP RESTAURANT SERVICE, INC.
2
3      ITEM #     DESCRIPTION         PRICE    CLASS
4
5         2668 TIDAL LIQUID          $3.99 DETERGENT
6         4913 WOODITE               $2.49 DETERGENT
7         6125 JEST SOAP             $2.09 DETERGENT
8         1048 GROUND GINGER         $1.29 SPICE
9         3555 PICKLING SPICE        $1.39 SPICE
10        4874 ARROWROOT             $2.19 SPICE
11        5104 DILL WEED             $1.79 SPICE
12        6270 CELERY SEED           $1.35 SPICE
```

Figure 11-5. Secondary-Key is Item Number.

Think about how the records would be sorted if the secondary-key was DESCRIPTION in descending order. Try it.

You enter: / **Data** **S**ort **S**econdary-Key **B5 [Return] D [Return] G**o

Your worksheet should look like Figure 11-6.

```
          A              B              C        D
1              ALLSHOP RESTAURANT SERVICE, INC.
2
3      ITEM #     DESCRIPTION         PRICE    CLASS
4
5         4913 WOODITE               $2.49 DETERGENT
6         2668 TIDAL LIQUID          $3.99 DETERGENT
7         6125 JEST SOAP             $2.09 DETERGENT
8         3555 PICKLING SPICE        $1.39 SPICE
9         1048 GROUND GINGER         $1.29 SPICE
10        5104 DILL WEED             $1.79 SPICE
11        6270 CELERY SEED           $1.35 SPICE
12        4874 ARROWROOT             $2.19 SPICE
```

Figure 11-6. Secondary Key is DESCRIPTION, Descending.

Releases 3.0 and 3.1+:
The Extra-Key option allows the use of up to 253 more keys.

You enter: **/ Data Sort**

The option Reset clears all sort settings: the range and the keys. The Quit option is used to return to READY mode.

You enter: **Quit**

EXERCISES

1. Sort the records in the ALLSHOP file by ITEM # in descending order as in the worksheet below:

```
           A              B               C        D         E
 1              ALLSHOP RESTAURANT SERVICE, INC.
 2
 3     ITEM #    DESCRIPTION      PRICE    CLASS
 4
 5       6270 CELERY SEED        $1.35 SPICE
 6       6125 JEST SOAP          $2.09 DETERGENT
 7       5104 DILL WEED          $1.79 SPICE
 8       4913 WOODITE            $2.49 DETERGENT
 9       4874 ARROWROOT          $2.19 SPICE
10       3555 PICKLING SPICE     $1.39 SPICE
11       2668 TIDAL LIQUID       $3.99 DETERGENT
12       1048 GROUND GINGER      $1.29 SPICE
```

2. Sort the records in the ALLSHOP file by CLASS in ascending order, and in case of ties, secondarily by PRICE in ascending order as in the worksheet below.

```
           A              B               C        D         E
 1              ALLSHOP RESTAURANT SERVICE, INC.
 2
 3     ITEM #    DESCRIPTION      PRICE    CLASS
 4
 5       6125 JEST SOAP          $2.09 DETERGENT
 6       4913 WOODITE            $2.49 DETERGENT
 7       2668 TIDAL LIQUID       $3.99 DETERGENT
 8       1048 GROUND GINGER      $1.29 SPICE
 9       6270 CELERY SEED        $1.35 SPICE
10       3555 PICKLING SPICE     $1.39 SPICE
11       5104 DILL WEED          $1.79 SPICE
12       4874 ARROWROOT          $2.19 SPICE
```

For exercises 3, 4, and 5, create the worksheet below and save under the name JOURNAL if you have not already done so in another lesson. If you have, retrieve the file. Do not modify the file on disk by saving it with modifications as you will need it in other lessons.

```
        FROGGIE'S BAR CHECK DISBURSEMENTS JOURNAL
CHECK    DATE      AMOUNT         TO              CLASS
    283 12-Jan-89 $147.00 HARVEY COOK        LABORKROOM
    284 12-Jan-89 $230.00 FRED BARTENDER     LABORBROOM
    285 12-Jan-89 $945.38 FROZEN PACKERS     FOOD
    286 13-Jan-89 $533.99 BETTER BEVERAGE    BEER KEG
    287 14-Jan-89 $168.00 BEST FOODS         FOOD
    288 14-Jan-89 $203.41 FROZEN PACKERS     FOOD
    289 14-Jan-89 $230.00 FRED BARTENDER     LABORBROOM
    290 14-Jan-89 $217.00 FLOYD DISHWASHER   LABORKROOM
    291 16-Jan-89 $768.03 FROZEN PACKERS     FOOD
    292 17-Jan-89 $602.50 BOAT BOTTLING      BEER CAN
    293 17-Jan-89 $125.86 BETTER BEVERAGE    BEER KEG
```

3.   Sort the JOURNAL file by CLASS in ascending order and secondarily by TO in ascending order as in the figure below.

```
        FROGGIE'S BAR CHECK DISBURSEMENTS JOURNAL
CHECK    DATE      AMOUNT         TO              CLASS
    292 17-Jan-89 $602.50 BOAT BOTTLING      BEER CAN
    286 13-Jan-89 $533.99 BETTER BEVERAGE    BEER KEG
    293 17-Jan-89 $125.86 BETTER BEVERAGE    BEER KEG
    287 14-Jan-89 $168.00 BEST FOODS         FOOD
    291 16-Jan-89 $768.03 FROZEN PACKERS     FOOD
    288 14-Jan-89 $203.41 FROZEN PACKERS     FOOD
    285 12-Jan-89 $945.38 FROZEN PACKERS     FOOD
    284 12-Jan-89 $230.00 FRED BARTENDER     LABORBROOM
    289 14-Jan-89 $230.00 FRED BARTENDER     LABORBROOM
    290 14-Jan-89 $217.00 FLOYD DISHWASHER   LABORKROOM
    283 12-Jan-89 $147.00 HARVEY COOK        LABORKROOM
```

4.   Look at the figure below and sort the JOURNAL file to match it.

```
        FROGGIE'S BAR CHECK DISBURSEMENTS JOURNAL
CHECK    DATE      AMOUNT           TO            CLASS
    283 12-Jan-89 $147.00 HARVEY COOK        LABORKROOM
    290 14-Jan-89 $217.00 FLOYD DISHWASHER   LABORKROOM
    284 12-Jan-89 $230.00 FRED BARTENDER     LABORBROOM
    289 14-Jan-89 $230.00 FRED BARTENDER     LABORBROOM
    285 12-Jan-89 $945.38 FROZEN PACKERS     FOOD
    287 14-Jan-89 $168.00 BEST FOODS         FOOD
    288 14-Jan-89 $203.41 FROZEN PACKERS     FOOD
    291 16-Jan-89 $768.03 FROZEN PACKERS     FOOD
    286 13-Jan-89 $533.99 BETTER BEVERAGE    BEER KEG
    293 17-Jan-89 $125.86 BETTER BEVERAGE    BEER KEG
    292 17-Jan-89 $602.50 BOAT BOTTLING      BEER CAN
```

5.   Look at the figure below and sort the JOURNAL file to match it.

```
        FROGGIE'S BAR CHECK DISBURSEMENTS JOURNAL
CHECK    DATE      AMOUNT           TO            CLASS
    287 14-Jan-89 $168.00 BEST FOODS         FOOD
    293 17-Jan-89 $125.86 BETTER BEVERAGE    BEER KEG
    286 13-Jan-89 $533.99 BETTER BEVERAGE    BEER KEG
    292 17-Jan-89 $602.50 BOAT BOTTLING      BEER CAN
    290 14-Jan-89 $217.00 FLOYD DISHWASHER   LABORKROOM
    289 14-Jan-89 $230.00 FRED BARTENDER     LABORBROOM
    284 12-Jan-89 $230.00 FRED BARTENDER     LABORBROOM
    288 14-Jan-89 $203.41 FROZEN PACKERS     FOOD
    291 16-Jan-89 $768.03 FROZEN PACKERS     FOOD
    285 12-Jan-89 $945.38 FROZEN PACKERS     FOOD
    283 12-Jan-89 $147.00 HARVEY COOK        LABORKROOM
```

6. Create the worksheet below and save under the name EMPLOYEE if you have not already done so in another lesson. If you have, retrieve the file. Do not modify the file on disk by saving it with modifications as you will need it in other lessons.

	A	B	C	D	E
1	NAME	DEPT	SALARY	CODE	DATE HIRED
2	ABBOTT	CLOTHING	$15,000	1	03/26/85
3	BENTON	SPORTS	$21,000	1	07/03/86
4	GAVERN	CLOTHING	$30,000	2	02/15/81
5	KRAMER	RECORDS	$13,000	1	06/29/88
6	LOVEN	TOYS	$49,000	2	06/29/88
7	SIRKO	DOMESTICS	$10,000	2	02/20/83
8	SMITH	TOYS	$25,000	3	09/07/85
9	THOMAS	TOYS	$28,000	1	12/19/84
10	WELLS	DOMESTICS	$17,000	2	03/26/85

6A. Sort the above database by code. For records with the same code, sort alphabetically by last name.

6B. Sort the above database by department and secondarily in decreasing order by salary.

CUMULATIVE EXERCISES

C1. Create the worksheet below by retrieving the TOFU1 worksheet which you created in Lesson 1 and deleting rows 15 through 19.

   A. Sort the data alphabetically by last name and print.
   B. Sort the data first by Division number and then by decreasing order of 92 Sales. Sort the data by division number and print.
   C. Sort alphabetically by last name and print.

C2. Retrieve the FISH1 worksheet that you created in Lesson 1.
   A. Sort by item number and print.
   B. Sort by Total Profit per item in decreasing order and print.

C3. Retrieve the BILL3 worksheet you created in Lesson 3.
   A. Sort the proper range alphabetically by expense item name and print.
   B. Sort by descending order of Actual April amount and print.

C4. Retrieve the GOLF1 worksheet that you created in Lesson 1.
   A. Sort rows 5 through 8 by decreasing order of total scores and print.
   B. Sort the names alphabetically and print.

Lesson 12

DATA QUERY

Contents:

If you have not done Lesson 13, please read the first few paragraphs for a discussion on databases, fields, and records. This lesson will cover querying, or asking questions, about a database.

Create Figure 12-1 and save under the name JOURNAL, if you have not already done so in another lesson. If you have, retrieve the file. Do not modify the file on disk by saving it with the modifications you will make in this lesson as you will need it, as is, in other lessons.

	A	B	C	D	E
1		FROGGIE'S BAR CHECK DISBURSEMENTS JOURNAL			
2	CHECK	DATE	AMOUNT	TO	CLASS
3	283	12-Jan-89	$147.00	HARVEY COOK	LABORKROOM
4	284	12-Jan-89	$230.00	FRED BARTENDER	LABORBROOM
5	285	12-Jan-89	$945.38	FROZEN PACKERS	FOOD
6	286	13-Jan-89	$533.99	BETTER BEVERAGE	BEER KEG
7	287	14-Jan-89	$168.00	BEST FOODS	FOOD
8	288	14-Jan-89	$203.41	FROZEN PACKERS	FOOD
9	289	14-Jan-89	$230.00	FRED BARTENDER	LABORBROOM
10	290	14-Jan-89	$217.00	FLOYD DISHWASHER	LABORKROOM
11	291	16-Jan-89	$768.03	FROZEN PACKERS	FOOD
12	292	17-Jan-89	$602.50	BOAT BOTTLING	BEER CAN
13	293	17-Jan-89	$125.86	BETTER BEVERAGE	BEER KEG

Figure 12-1. JOURNAL Database.

This database is a check disbursements journal for Froggie's Bar and includes for each check: a field to indicate its number, the date it was written, the amount, to whom it was paid, and a class field to categorize its purpose or type of expense.

/Data Query

The /Data Query command allows you to ask questions of, or query, a database in order to locate records which fit certain criteria.

You enter: / **Copy E2 [Return] A15 [Return]**

You enter into A16: **FOOD [Return]**

/Data Query Find

The /Data Query Find command highlights records which meet specific criteria. You must first specify the input range, or the range containing the database. (Unlike the Data-Range in the /Data Sort command, the input range DOES include the field names.) In the JOURNAL worksheet, the input range is A2..E13. You must also specify a criteria range which informs 1-2-3 of the tests a record must pass in order to be found. "Find" all checks used to purchase food by looking for records whose CLASS field is FOOD.

First, set up the input range.

You enter: / **Data Query Input**

Computer message: Enter Input range:

You enter: **A2..E13 [Return]**

You could have, of course, entered a name for a range previously named with the /Range Name Create command.

The /Data Query menu, shown below, is a sticky menu and remains on the screen.

Input Criteria Output Find Extract Unique Delete Reset Quit

Releases 3.0 and 3.1+: Modify is a new option between Delete and Reset and is explained on page 380.

The criteria range's first row, in this case, CLASS, contains the names of those fields which will be tested to fit certain criteria. The rows under the field name row, in this case, FOOD, will contain specifications or criteria for the records sought. In other words, this particular query will find all records whose CLASS field contains the entry FOOD. You can visually pick out the four records that fit this criteria.

Set up the Criteria range:

You enter: **Criteria**

Computer message: Enter Criteria range:

You enter or point to: **A15..A16 [Return]**

Of course, this range can be a named range.

Now that the input and criteria ranges are set up, the Find can be executed.

You enter: **Find**

Note that the mode indicator shows FIND.

The record for check number 285 is highlighted on your screen. This is the first record to fit the criteria. Movement keys can used to find other records meeting the criteria.

You enter: **[Down]**

Check 287's record is highlighted.

You enter: **[Down] [Down] [Down]**

A beep is heard when a movement key does not find any more records to fit the criteria.

You enter: **[Up] [Up] [Up] [Up]**

[Home] and [End] will take you to the first and last records in the database even though they do not necessarily fit the criteria.

You enter: **[Home] [End]**

Releases 3.0 and 3.1+: [Home] and [End] highlight the first and last record that fit the criteria.

[Right] and [Left] move the cell pointer horizontally from field to field in the currently highlighted record, and can be used to move off the screen if the records are too long to fit in one screen width.

You enter: **[Right] and [Left] several times.**

Let's now search for all checks written to pay laborers in the kitchen. LABORKROOM, emphasis on the K, is the category for people who work in the kitchen. The criteria under CLASS in the criteria range must be changed. To change an entry, you must get back to READY mode with the [Esc] key. The mode indicator still shows FIND.

You enter: **[Esc] 4 times.**

You enter into A16: **LABORKROOM [Return]**

The case of the letters is ignored, therefore upper and lower case letters are treated identically. The criteria range is now set up so that only check numbers 283 and 290 will be found.

You enter: **/ Data Query**

There is no need to set up the input and criteria ranges again, 1-2-3 remembers all previous settings. They can be verified by choosing the proper option and noting the range highlighted:

You enter: Input **[Return]**

You enter: Find **[Down]**

The first and eighth records are highlighted.

You enter: **[Esc]** Quit

You enter into A16: **BEER CAN [Return]**

[F7/QUERY]

The seventh function key can be used to repeat the most recent query. In this case, [F7/QUERY] repeats the command /Data Query Find.

You enter: **[F7/QUERY]**

BEER CAN is found in the second to the last record's CLASS field.

You enter: **[Esc]**

The label in A16 must be entered exactly (excluding upper or lower case) or the records will not be found. Be especially careful with spaces. If you accidentally typed [SpaceBar] twice between BEER and CAN, the record would not have been found.

You enter into A16: **BEER [SpaceBar] [SpaceBar] CAN [Return]**

You enter: **[F7/QUERY]**

An error beep is heard signifying that no records were found.

You enter: **/Data Query Find**

No highlighting is shown on the screen and the error beep is heard again.

You enter: **Quit**

If the entry under a field name in the criteria range is empty, ANY ENTRY in the input records' field name passes the test and is found.

Releases 2.3 and 2.4: A blank entry will cause NO records to be found.

You enter: / Range Erase **A16 [Return]**

You enter: **[F7/QUERY]**

You enter: **[Down] several times. [Esc]**

Let's suppose you wish to find records with a CLASS of either BEER CAN or FOOD.

You enter into A16: **BEER CAN [Return]**

Add another criteria under the CLASS field name.

You enter into A17: **FOOD [Return]**

The criteria range must be expanded to include the added row.

You enter: / **Data Query Criteria A15..A17 [Return]** Find

You enter: **[Down] 5 times.**

The five records containing FOOD or BEER CAN in the CLASS field have been found.

You enter: **[Esc] Q**uit

Two or more criteria rows under a field name in the criteria range causes the logical operator OR to be performed.

/Data Query Extract

/Data Query Extract creates a list in an output range which consists of the subset of records which fit the criteria. The output range's top row is a horizontal list of field names, as in the input and criteria ranges. The labels have to be exact, but they do not have to be in the same order as the input range, and they don't have to comprise the complete list of field headers. In other words, you can have any subset of the field names from the input range's top row, and they can be in any order from left to right in the output range. Set up your output list so that it contains only the fields TO, AMOUNT, and CLASS, in that order.

You enter: / Copy **D2 [Return] D15 [Return]**

You enter: / **Copy C2 [Return] E15 [Return]**

You enter: / **Copy E2 [Return] F15 [Return]**

Your worksheet should look like Figure 12-2.

	A	B	C	D	E	F
1		FROGGIE'S BAR CHECK DISBURSEMENTS JOURNAL				
2	CHECK	DATE	AMOUNT	TO	CLASS	
3		283	12-Jan-89	$147.00 HARVEY COOK	LABORKROOM	
4		284	12-Jan-89	$230.00 FRED BARTENDER	LABORBROOM	
5		285	12-Jan-89	$945.38 FROZEN PACKERS	FOOD	
6		286	13-Jan-89	$533.99 BETTER BEVERAGE	BEER KEG	
7		287	14-Jan-89	$168.00 BEST FOODS	FOOD	
8		288	14-Jan-89	$203.41 FROZEN PACKERS	FOOD	
9		289	14-Jan-89	$230.00 FRED BARTENDER	LABORBROOM	
10		290	14-Jan-89	$217.00 FLOYD DISHWASHER	LABORKROOM	
11		291	16-Jan-89	$768.03 FROZEN PACKERS	FOOD	
12		292	17-Jan-89	$602.50 BOAT BOTTLING	BEER CAN	
13		293	17-Jan-89	$125.86 BETTER BEVERAGE	BEER KEG	
14						
15	CLASS			TO	AMOUNT	CLASS
16	BEER CAN					
17	FOOD					

Figure 12-2. JOURNAL Database with Output Range.

It is very important to copy the field headers from the input range to the criteria range or the output range, as you just did, even though it's a pain. This ensures that the label is exactly the same in both cells. Label-prefixes are irrelevant.

Set up the output range:

You enter: / **Data Query Output D15..F20 [Return]**

You enter: **Extract**

Your worksheet should look like Figure 12-3.

```
           A        B        C          D              E           F
          ▓▓▓▓▓▓▓▓▓▓▓▓▓▓▓▓▓▓▓▓▓▓▓▓▓▓▓▓▓▓▓▓▓▓▓▓▓▓▓▓▓▓▓▓▓▓▓▓▓▓▓▓▓▓▓
 1              FROGGIE'S BAR CHECK DISBURSEMENTS JOURNAL
 2      CHECK     DATE    AMOUNT          TO            CLASS
 3        283 12-Jan-89 $147.00 HARVEY COOK      LABORKROOM
 4        284 12-Jan-89 $230.00 FRED BARTENDER   LABORBROOM
 5        285 12-Jan-89 $945.38 FROZEN PACKERS   FOOD
 6        286 13-Jan-89 $533.99 BETTER BEVERAGE  BEER KEG
 7        287 14-Jan-89 $168.00 BEST FOODS       FOOD
 8        288 14-Jan-89 $203.41 FROZEN PACKERS   FOOD
 9        289 14-Jan-89 $230.00 FRED BARTENDER   LABORBROOM
10        290 14-Jan-89 $217.00 FLOYD DISHWASHER LABORKROOM
11        291 16-Jan-89 $768.03 FROZEN PACKERS   FOOD
12        292 17-Jan-89 $602.50 BOAT BOTTLING    BEER CAN
13        293 17-Jan-89 $125.86 BETTER BEVERAGE  BEER KEG
14
15 CLASS                      TO            AMOUNT    CLASS
16 BEER CAN                   FROZEN PACKERS $945.38 FOOD
17 FOOD                       BEST FOODS     $168.00 FOOD
18                            FROZEN PACKERS $203.41 FOOD
19                            FROZEN PACKERS $768.03 FOOD
20                            BOAT BOTTLING  $602.50 BEER CAN
```

Figure 12-3. JOURNAL Worksheet after Extract Command.

The five appropriate records' fields have been copied. output range.

The output range can now be printed separately.

Our next query will list all records for purchases of beer of any type, such as cans or kegs.

You enter: **Quit**

You enter into A17: **BEER KEG [Return]**

You enter: **[F7/QUERY]**

Your worksheet should look like Figure 12-4.

```
           A        B         C              D                 E           F
 1                 FROGGIE'S BAR CHECK DISBURSEMENTS JOURNAL
 2         CHECK    DATE     AMOUNT          TO                CLASS
 3           283 12-Jan-89 $147.00 HARVEY COOK          LABORKROOM
 4           284 12-Jan-89 $230.00 FRED BARTENDER       LABORBROOM
 5           285 12-Jan-89 $945.38 FROZEN PACKERS       FOOD
 6           286 13-Jan-89 $533.99 BETTER BEVERAGE      BEER KEG
 7           287 14-Jan-89 $168.00 BEST FOODS           FOOD
 8           288 14-Jan-89 $203.41 FROZEN PACKERS       FOOD
 9           289 14-Jan-89 $230.00 FRED BARTENDER       LABORBROOM
10           290 14-Jan-89 $217.00 FLOYD DISHWASHER     LABORKROOM
11           291 16-Jan-89 $768.03 FROZEN PACKERS       FOOD
12           292 17-Jan-89 $602.50 BOAT BOTTLING        BEER CAN
13           293 17-Jan-89 $125.86 BETTER BEVERAGE      BEER KEG
14
15 CLASS                              TO                  AMOUNT   CLASS
16 BEER CAN                           BETTER BEVERAGE     $533.99 BEER KEG
17 BEER KEG                           BOAT BOTTLING       $602.50 BEER CAN
18                                    BETTER BEVERAGE     $125.86 BEER KEG
```

Figure 12-4. All-type Beer Purchases Query.

The last two rows of the output range are empty, indicating that 1-2-3 first erases the output range rows (under the field names) before copying any fields.

If a field name in the output range does not match any of the input range fields, the extract command leaves that column blank.

You enter into E15: **AMONT [Return]**

You enter: **[F7/QUERY]**

Your worksheet should look like Figure 12-5.

```
           A        B         C              D                 E           F
 1                 FROGGIE'S BAR CHECK DISBURSEMENTS JOURNAL
 2         CHECK    DATE     AMOUNT          TO                CLASS
 3           283 12-Jan-89 $147.00 HARVEY COOK          LABORKROOM
 4           284 12-Jan-89 $230.00 FRED BARTENDER       LABORBROOM
 5           285 12-Jan-89 $945.38 FROZEN PACKERS       FOOD
 6           286 13-Jan-89 $533.99 BETTER BEVERAGE      BEER KEG
 7           287 14-Jan-89 $168.00 BEST FOODS           FOOD
 8           288 14-Jan-89 $203.41 FROZEN PACKERS       FOOD
 9           289 14-Jan-89 $230.00 FRED BARTENDER       LABORBROOM
10           290 14-Jan-89 $217.00 FLOYD DISHWASHER     LABORKROOM
11           291 16-Jan-89 $768.03 FROZEN PACKERS       FOOD
12           292 17-Jan-89 $602.50 BOAT BOTTLING        BEER CAN
13           293 17-Jan-89 $125.86 BETTER BEVERAGE      BEER KEG
14
15 CLASS                              TO                  AMONT    CLASS
16 BEER CAN                           BETTER BEVERAGE              BEER KEG
17 BEER KEG                           BOAT BOTTLING                BEER CAN
18                                    BETTER BEVERAGE              BEER KEG
```

Figure 12-5. Invalid Field Name in Output Range.

You enter: /Copy **C2 [Return] E15 [Return] [F7/QUERY]**

Your worksheet should look like Figure 12-4 again.

Wildcards

The two wildcard characters in /Data Query are * and ?. The * matches all characters and any number of characters at the end of a label. BEER* would match BEER CAN, BEER KEG, and any other label beginning with BEER. The * must be the last character in the label.

You enter: **/Range Erase A17 [Return]**

You enter into A16: **BEER* [Return] [F7/QUERY]**

The result in the output range should be the same as that of Figure 12-4.

? is a wildcard character which matches any single character. Find all records having to do with labor payments.

You enter into A16: **LABOR?ROOM [Return]**

You enter: **[F7/QUERY]**

Your worksheet should look like Figure 12-7.

	A	B	C	D	E	F
1		FROGGIE'S BAR CHECK DISBURSEMENTS JOURNAL				
2	CHECK	DATE	AMOUNT	TO	CLASS	
3	283	12-Jan-89	$147.00	HARVEY COOK	LABORKROOM	
4	284	12-Jan-89	$230.00	FRED BARTENDER	LABORBROOM	
5	285	12-Jan-89	$945.38	FROZEN PACKERS	FOOD	
6	286	13-Jan-89	$533.99	BETTER BEVERAGE	BEER KEG	
7	287	14-Jan-89	$168.00	BEST FOODS	FOOD	
8	288	14-Jan-89	$203.41	FROZEN PACKERS	FOOD	
9	289	14-Jan-89	$230.00	FRED BARTENDER	LABORBROOM	
10	290	14-Jan-89	$217.00	FLOYD DISHWASHER	LABORKROOM	
11	291	16-Jan-89	$768.03	FROZEN PACKERS	FOOD	
12	292	17-Jan-89	$602.50	BOAT BOTTLING	BEER CAN	
13	293	17-Jan-89	$125.86	BETTER BEVERAGE	BEER KEG	
14						
15	CLASS			TO	AMOUNT	CLASS
16	LABOR?ROOM			HARVEY COOK	$147.00	LABORKROOM
17				FRED BARTENDER	$230.00	LABORBROOM
18				FRED BARTENDER	$230.00	LABORBROOM
19				FLOYD DISHWASHER	$217.00	LABORKROOM

Figure 12-7. Query Using ? Wildcard Character.

Wildcards are used for labels only and won't work with values. For example, using 29* to find all check numbers beginning with 29 won't work. (The Querying with Values section below will cover how to handle extracting records with 29*.)

Please note that LABOR?ROOM would match LABOR3ROOM, LABOR%ROOM, and LABOR ROOM, but not LABORROOM or LABORXXROOM. It does not match the null string or more than one character; it will match exactly one character for each ?

Change the criteria field name to TO.

You enter: / Copy **D2 [Return] A15 [Return]**

You enter into A16: **B??T* [Return]**

Before querying, what results do you expect?

You enter: **[F7/QUERY]**

Your worksheet should look like Figure 12-8.

```
A16: 'B??T*

         A        B         C             D              E          F
1                 FROGGIE'S BAR CHECK DISBURSEMENTS JOURNAL
2        CHECK    DATE     AMOUNT         TO             CLASS
3          283 12-Jan-89  $147.00 HARVEY COOK       LABORKROOM
4          284 12-Jan-89  $230.00 FRED BARTENDER    LABORBROOM
5          285 12-Jan-89  $945.38 FROZEN PACKERS    FOOD
6          286 13-Jan-89  $533.99 BETTER BEVERAGE   BEER KEG
7          287 14-Jan-89  $168.00 BEST FOODS        FOOD
8          288 14-Jan-89  $203.41 FROZEN PACKERS    FOOD
9          289 14-Jan-89  $230.00 FRED BARTENDER    LABORBROOM
10         290 14-Jan-89  $217.00 FLOYD DISHWASHER  LABORKROOM
11         291 16-Jan-89  $768.03 FROZEN PACKERS    FOOD
12         292 17-Jan-89  $602.50 BOAT BOTTLING     BEER CAN
13         293 17-Jan-89  $125.86 BETTER BEVERAGE   BEER KEG
14
15  TO                              TO              AMOUNT  CLASS
16  B??T*                           BETTER BEVERAGE  $533.99 BEER KEG
17                                  BEST FOODS       $168.00 FOOD
18                                  BOAT BOTTLING    $602.50 BEER CAN
19                                  BETTER BEVERAGE  $125.86 BEER KEG
```

Figure 12-8. Query Using * and ?.

You need not change the input, criteria, or output ranges unless they move or change sizes. Here, changing the contents of a field name does not require any range changes.

You enter into A16: **B??T * [Return]**

You enter: **[F7/QUERY]**

The two records with BETTER BEVERAGE are not extracted this time because there is no space after the T. Remember that spaces are treated as any other character and must be matched accordingly.

Another special character for use with labels in querying is the ~ (tilde). It is the logical equivalent of the NOT operator. Placed at the beginning of a label, it matches all labels that are different from the characters following it. For example, ~SMITH would match any non-empty cell containing a label not equal to SMITH, or, in other words, everyone except SMITH.

You enter into A16: **~F* [Return] [F7/QUERY]**

Your worksheet should look like Figure 12-9.

```
A16: '~F*


      A         B        C              D              E           F
1             FROGGIE'S BAR CHECK DISBURSEMENTS JOURNAL
2     CHECK     DATE     AMOUNT          TO             CLASS
3       283 12-Jan-89  $147.00 HARVEY COOK       LABORKROOM
4       284 12-Jan-89  $230.00 FRED BARTENDER    LABORBROOM
5       285 12-Jan-89  $945.38 FROZEN PACKERS    FOOD
6       286 13-Jan-89  $533.99 BETTER BEVERAGE   BEER KEG
7       287 14-Jan-89  $168.00 BEST FOODS        FOOD
8       288 14-Jan-89  $203.41 FROZEN PACKERS    FOOD
9       289 14-Jan-89  $230.00 FRED BARTENDER    LABORBROOM
10      290 14-Jan-89  $217.00 FLOYD DISHWASHER  LABORKROOM
11      291 16-Jan-89  $768.03 FROZEN PACKERS    FOOD
12      292 17-Jan-89  $602.50 BOAT BOTTLING     BEER CAN
13      293 17-Jan-89  $125.86 BETTER BEVERAGE   BEER KEG
14
15    TO                       TO                AMOUNT    CLASS
16    ~F*                      HARVEY COOK        $147.00 LABORKROOM
17                             BETTER BEVERAGE    $533.99 BEER KEG
18                             BEST FOODS         $168.00 FOOD
19                             BOAT BOTTLING      $602.50 BEER CAN
20                             BETTER BEVERAGE    $125.86 BEER KEG
```

Figure 12-9. Query with Special Exception Character ~.

All records with TO field entry not starting with the letter F are extracted.

You enter: **/ Range Erase A14..F20 [Return]**

If you need a break, save the current file under LES12, (not JOURNAL).

- - - **If you need a break, stop at this point.** - - -

If you are returning from a break, retrieve the LES12 file.

/Data Query Unique

The /Data Query Unique command extracts records without any duplicate rows in the output range.

You: **Copy E2 into A15 and D15.**

You enter: / **Data Query Output D15..F21 [Return] U**nique

Your worksheet should look like Figure 12-10.

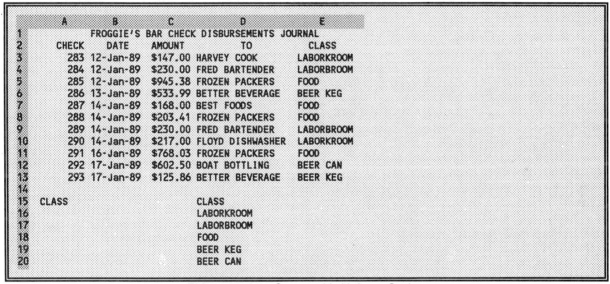

	A	B	C	D	E
1		FROGGIE'S BAR CHECK DISBURSEMENTS JOURNAL			
2	CHECK	DATE	AMOUNT	TO	CLASS
3	283	12-Jan-89	$147.00	HARVEY COOK	LABORKROOM
4	284	12-Jan-89	$230.00	FRED BARTENDER	LABORBROOM
5	285	12-Jan-89	$945.38	FROZEN PACKERS	FOOD
6	286	13-Jan-89	$533.99	BETTER BEVERAGE	BEER KEG
7	287	14-Jan-89	$168.00	BEST FOODS	FOOD
8	288	14-Jan-89	$203.41	FROZEN PACKERS	FOOD
9	289	14-Jan-89	$230.00	FRED BARTENDER	LABORBROOM
10	290	14-Jan-89	$217.00	FLOYD DISHWASHER	LABORKROOM
11	291	16-Jan-89	$768.03	FROZEN PACKERS	FOOD
12	292	17-Jan-89	$602.50	BOAT BOTTLING	BEER CAN
13	293	17-Jan-89	$125.86	BETTER BEVERAGE	BEER KEG
14					
15	CLASS			CLASS	
16				LABORKROOM	
17				LABORBROOM	
18				FOOD	
19				BEER KEG	
20				BEER CAN	

Figure 12-10. Query with Unique Option.

Releases 3.0 and 3.1+: The extracted records are in alphabetical order.

This command is useful if you wish to get a list of all the different entries in a field with no duplicates. For example, you may want all zip codes in a mail order catalog's current mailing list, or a list of all states served by a distribution center, or a list of all customers who regularly order from your company.

You enter: **Quit**

/Data Query Delete

The Delete option deletes from the database all records fitting the criteria.

You enter into A16: **FOOD [Return]**

You enter: / **Data Query Delete Delete Quit**

Your worksheet should look like Figure 12-11.

Figure 12-11. Deletion of Records from Database.

All records with a CLASS of FOOD are deleted from the database. 1-2-3 automatically contracts the input range.

WARNING: Delete commands are almost always dangerous. Issue a /File Save command just before a /Data Query Delete. If you mess up, a simple /File Retrieve will restore all deleted records.

It should be clear that an output range is necessary for the Unique and Extract options, but not for the Find option or the Delete option.

- - - If you need a break, stop at this point. - - -

You enter: / **File Retrieve JOURNAL [Return]**

Querying with Values

Finding records with value entries is similar to those with label entries.

You enter: / Copy **C2 [Return] A15 [Return]**

You enter into A16: **945.38 [Return]**

You enter: / Copy **A2 [Return] D15 [Return]**

You enter: / Copy **C2 [Return] E15 [Return]**

You enter: / Copy **D2 [Return] F15 [Return]**

You enter: / Data Query Input **A2..E13 [Return]** Criteria **A15..A16 [Return]**

You enter: Output **D15..F20 [Return]** Extract Quit

Your worksheet should look like Figure 12-12.

```
         A         B         C             D                E         F
1                  FROGGIE'S BAR CHECK DISBURSEMENTS JOURNAL
2        CHECK    DATE      AMOUNT        TO               CLASS
3          283 12-Jan-89  $147.00 HARVEY COOK         LABORKROOM
4          284 12-Jan-89  $230.00 FRED BARTENDER      LABORBROOM
5          285 12-Jan-89  $945.38 FROZEN PACKERS      FOOD
6          286 13-Jan-89  $533.99 BETTER BEVERAGE     BEER KEG
7          287 14-Jan-89  $168.00 BEST FOODS          FOOD
8          288 14-Jan-89  $203.41 FROZEN PACKERS      FOOD
9          289 14-Jan-89  $230.00 FRED BARTENDER      LABORBROOM
10         290 14-Jan-89  $217.00 FLOYD DISHWASHER    LABORKROOM
11         291 16-Jan-89  $768.03 FROZEN PACKERS      FOOD
12         292 17-Jan-89  $602.50 BOAT BOTTLING       BEER CAN
13         293 17-Jan-89  $125.86 BETTER BEVERAGE     BEER KEG
14
15  AMOUNT                        CHECK               AMOUNT  TO
16    945.38                         285 $945.38 FROZEN PACKERS
```

Figure 12-12. Querying with Value Criteria.

Only record has an amount of 945.38. To display A16 in Currency format you must use /Range Format, of course.

The 285 under CHECK in the output range looks like it's not in the same column because of the column's width. These examples are set up so that they will fit on one screen for ease of comprehension. Ideally, you would use a much bigger part of the total worksheet. It is likely that you would set up more than one criteria range and more than one output range in the same worksheet to pull different sets of records from the same database input range. They should be named CRITER1, CRITER2, OUTPUT1, OUTPUT2, etc. or something appropriate. Naming ranges almost always makes setting up easier. Be wary that deleting columns or rows from one part of the worksheet can mess up other parts of your worksheet not visible on the screen at that time. I suggest you expand your worksheet diagonally to prevent this problem, i. e., the input range A1..N100, a criteria range AA200..AD204, another criteria range BA300..BC303, etc. Deleting or adding rows or columns in any range should not then pose a problem.

Querying with Formulas

It's probably rare to pull records with an exact numerical value, as in the last example. For example, you might want to extract all records of checks with amounts over $500. A formula in the criterion field is necessary to do this. The formula's referenced cells should always point to the first row in the database. For checks greater than $500, the referenced cell in the formula should point to column C, where AMOUNT is stored. The cell reference should point to the row of the first record in the database, row 3.

You enter into A16: **+C3>500 [Return]**

WARNING: Do not forget that + before the C. Without it, 1-2-3 would think that this entry was a label because of the first character, the letter C. If this does not make sense to you, re-read page 35.

Releases 2.3 and 2.4: In these releases, shorthand criteria formulas (formulas that don't require the column cell reference) are possible. For this operation, >500 is equivalent; the cell reference +C3 is not required.

A logical 0 is displayed in cell A16, because the result of the condition C3>500 is false ($147.00 is not greater than 500). For clarity, always format the criteria cells containing formulas as Text.

You enter: **/ Range Format Text A16 [Return]**

You enter: **[F7/QUERY]**

Your worksheet should look like Figure 12-13.

```
A16: (T) +C3>500
```

```
         A         B         C              D                E         F
1                FROGGIE'S BAR CHECK DISBURSEMENTS JOURNAL
2        CHECK     DATE    AMOUNT          TO               CLASS
3          283 12-Jan-89  $147.00 HARVEY COOK       LABORBROOM
4          284 12-Jan-89  $230.00 FRED BARTENDER    LABORBROOM
5          285 12-Jan-89  $945.38 FROZEN PACKERS    FOOD
6          286 13-Jan-89  $533.99 BETTER BEVERAGE   BEER KEG
7          287 14-Jan-89  $168.00 BEST FOODS        FOOD
8          288 14-Jan-89  $203.41 FROZEN PACKERS    FOOD
9          289 14-Jan-89  $230.00 FRED BARTENDER    LABORBROOM
10         290 14-Jan-89  $217.00 FLOYD DISHWASHER  LABORBROOM
11         291 16-Jan-89  $768.03 FROZEN PACKERS    FOOD
12         292 17-Jan-89  $602.50 BOAT BOTTLING     BEER CAN
13         293 17-Jan-89  $125.86 BETTER BEVERAGE   BEER KEG
14
15  AMOUNT                       CHECK              AMOUNT   TO
16  +C3>500                        285   $945.38 FROZEN PACKERS
17                                 286   $533.99 BETTER BEVERAGE
18                                 291   $768.03 FROZEN PACKERS
19                                 292   $602.50 BOAT BOTTLING
```

Figure 12-13. Querying with a Formula Criterion.

1-2-3 compares the field contents in column C of the first record in the database to 500. If the condition is true, the record is extracted. It then goes to the second record and recalculates the condition with this record's value, etc.

To make your formulas easier to understand, use the /Range Name Down command to name all of the first record's cells with the field names directly over them. In this case the formula in A16 would then read +AMOUNT>500. That + is still necessary or the first character, A, would cause 1-2-3 to think it is a label and use the value 0 instead of a condition.

If your formula contains a reference to a cell outside of the database, use absolute addressing for that cell reference.

You enter into F1: **500 [Return]**

You enter into A16: **+C3>$F$1 [Return]**

You enter: **[F7/QUERY]**

You get the same results as in Figure 12-13.

If cell F1 had a name, you would use it in absolute form with a $ before the range name. (See absolute named range addressing.)

You enter into F1: **600 [Return] [F7/QUERY]**

Your worksheet should look like Figure 12-14.

```
A16: (T) +C3>$F$1


          A         B         C           D              E           F
1              FROGGIE'S BAR CHECK DISBURSEMENTS JOURNAL              600
2      CHECK    DATE     AMOUNT         TO            CLASS
3        283  12-Jan-89  $147.00  HARVEY COOK        LABORKROOM
4        284  12-Jan-89  $230.00  FRED BARTENDER     LABORBROOM
5        285  12-Jan-89  $945.38  FROZEN PACKERS     FOOD
6        286  13-Jan-89  $533.99  BETTER BEVERAGE    BEER KEG
7        287  14-Jan-89  $168.00  BEST FOODS         FOOD
8        288  14-Jan-89  $203.41  FROZEN PACKERS     FOOD
9        289  14-Jan-89  $230.00  FRED BARTENDER     LABORBROOM
10       290  14-Jan-89  $217.00  FLOYD DISHWASHER   LABORKROOM
11       291  16-Jan-89  $768.03  FROZEN PACKERS     FOOD
12       292  17-Jan-89  $602.50  BOAT BOTTLING      BEER CAN
13       293  17-Jan-89  $125.86  BETTER BEVERAGE    BEER KEG
14
15   AMOUNT                        CHECK           AMOUNT   TO
16   +C3>$F$1                         285        $945.38  FROZEN PACKERS
17                                    291        $768.03  FROZEN PACKERS
18                                    292        $602.50  BOAT BOTTLING
```

Figure 12-14. Querying with a Cell Reference out of the Database.

Multiple Criteria Fields

Let's say you wish to extract all records written for food purchases whose amounts are over $600. For this there are two criteria: AMOUNT must be greater than 600 and CLASS must be FOOD.

You enter: / Copy **E2 [Return] B15 [Return]**

You enter into B16: **FOOD [Return]**

You enter: / **Data Query Criteria A15..B16 [Return] Extract**

Your worksheet should look like Figure 12-15.

```
B16: (D2) [W10] 'FOOD


        A           B          C             D              E          F
1                 FROGGIE'S BAR CHECK DISBURSEMENTS JOURNAL          600
2        CHECK     DATE     AMOUNT           TO             CLASS
3          283  12-Jan-89  $147.00  HARVEY COOK        LABORKROOM
4          284  12-Jan-89  $230.00  FRED BARTENDER     LABORBROOM
5          285  12-Jan-89  $945.38  FROZEN PACKERS     FOOD
6          286  13-Jan-89  $533.99  BETTER BEVERAGE    BEER KEG
7          287  14-Jan-89  $168.00  BEST FOODS         FOOD
8          288  14-Jan-89  $203.41  FROZEN PACKERS     FOOD
9          289  14-Jan-89  $230.00  FRED BARTENDER     LABORBROOM
10         290  14-Jan-89  $217.00  FLOYD DISHWASHER   LABORKROOM
11         291  16-Jan-89  $768.03  FROZEN PACKERS     FOOD
12         292  17-Jan-89  $602.50  BOAT BOTTLING      BEER CAN
13         293  17-Jan-89  $125.86  BETTER BEVERAGE    BEER KEG
14
15   AMOUNT    CLASS              CHECK            AMOUNT   TO
16   +C3>$F$1  FOOD                         285   $945.38  FROZEN PACKERS
17                                          291   $768.03  FROZEN PACKERS
```

Figure 12-15. Multiple Criteria in Same Row (AND).

You enter: **Quit**

Placing criteria in the same column, one under the other, in the criteria range executes a logical OR database operation. Logical OR is when the record has to meet one OR the other criteria, but not necessarily both. Recall the example where BEER CAN and FOOD (Figure 12-3) were in the same column the criteria range. All records with either BEER CAN or FOOD in the CLASS field were extracted.

Placing criteria in different columns causes a logical AND to execute, where all criteria must be met. Here AMOUNT must be greater than 600 and CLASS must be FOOD.

Extract records with amounts greater than 600 OR with a category of FOOD.

You enter: **/ Range Erase B16 [Return]**

You enter into B17: **FOOD [Return]**

Hold it! You've got to expand that criteria range.

You enter: **/ Data Query Criteria [Down] [Return]** Extract

Your worksheet should look like Figure 12-16.

Compare Figures 12-15 and 12-16. In summary, criteria in different rows effect logical ORs and criteria in the same row perform logical ANDs.

```
           A         B         C           D            E         F
1                 FROGGIE'S BAR CHECK DISBURSEMENTS JOURNAL       600
2      CHECK     DATE     AMOUNT          TO           CLASS
3        283 12-Jan-89  $147.00 HARVEY COOK        LABORKROOM
4        284 12-Jan-89  $230.00 FRED BARTENDER     LABORBROOM
5        285 12-Jan-89  $945.38 FROZEN PACKERS     FOOD
6        286 13-Jan-89  $533.99 BETTER BEVERAGE    BEER KEG
7        287 14-Jan-89  $168.00 BEST FOODS         FOOD
8        288 14-Jan-89  $203.41 FROZEN PACKERS     FOOD
9        289 14-Jan-89  $230.00 FRED BARTENDER     LABORBROOM
10       290 14-Jan-89  $217.00 FLOYD DISHWASHER   LABORKROOM
11       291 16-Jan-89  $768.03 FROZEN PACKERS     FOOD
12       292 17-Jan-89  $602.50 BOAT BOTTLING      BEER CAN
13       293 17-Jan-89  $125.86 BETTER BEVERAGE    BEER KEG
14
15   AMOUNT    CLASS               CHECK          AMOUNT  TO
16   +C3>$F$1                        285  $945.38 FROZEN PACKERS
17             FOOD                  287  $168.00 BEST FOODS
18                                   288  $203.41 FROZEN PACKERS
19                                   291  $768.03 FROZEN PACKERS
20                                   292  $602.50 BOAT BOTTLING
```

Figure 12-16. Multiple Criteria in Different Rows (OR).

You enter: **Quit**

You enter into B16: **FOOD [Down]**

You enter into B17: **BEER KEG [Return]**

Before querying, which records do you expect to be extracted?

You enter: **[F7/QUERY]**

Your worksheet should look like Figure 12-17.

The records extracted fit the criteria in the first row OR the criteria in the second row. AMOUNT greater than 600 and CLASS is FOOD (checks 285 and 291) or CLASS is BEER KEG (checks 286 and 293).

Perhaps thinking about it this way will help. To figure out which records will be extracted, start with the first row. Simply concentrate on the first row and ignore all others rows for now. If a record fits all criteria in that row, it's extracted. Move to the next row and do the same.

―――

WARNING: Make sure the criteria range does not include any blank rows. In the older releases, a blank row means anything goes and all records from the database will be extracted.

―――

```
          A        B         C            D              E         F
 1                FROGGIE'S BAR CHECK DISBURSEMENTS JOURNAL            600
 2       CHECK    DATE     AMOUNT         TO            CLASS
 3         283 12-Jan-89 $147.00 HARVEY COOK        LABORKROOM
 4         284 12-Jan-89 $230.00 FRED BARTENDER     LABORBROOM
 5         285 12-Jan-89 $945.38 FROZEN PACKERS     FOOD
 6         286 13-Jan-89 $533.99 BETTER BEVERAGE    BEER KEG
 7         287 14-Jan-89 $168.00 BEST FOODS         FOOD
 8         288 14-Jan-89 $203.41 FROZEN PACKERS     FOOD
 9         289 14-Jan-89 $230.00 FRED BARTENDER     LABORBROOM
10         290 14-Jan-89 $217.00 FLOYD DISHWASHER   LABORKROOM
11         291 16-Jan-89 $768.03 FROZEN PACKERS     FOOD
12         292 17-Jan-89 $602.50 BOAT BOTTLING      BEER CAN
13         293 17-Jan-89 $125.86 BETTER BEVERAGE    BEER KEG
14
15  AMOUNT    CLASS            CHECK              AMOUNT    TO
16  +C3>$F$1  FOOD                          285  $945.38 FROZEN PACKERS
17            BEER KEG                      286  $533.99 BETTER BEVERAGE
18                                          291  $768.03 FROZEN PACKERS
19                                          293  $125.86 BETTER BEVERAGE
20
```

Figure 12-17. Multiple Criteria in Rows and Columns.

You enter: **[Esc]**

WARNING: There should be no blank line between the field name header row and the first record in the database. Unexpected results might occur if a blank line exists. Cell references should always refer to the first row directly beneath the field name row.

Querying by Dates

For you who have done the date and time lesson, there is something you must know about querying dates. First, make sure the dates in column B were entered with the @DATE function and not as labels.

Let's extract all checks written on January 14. The criteria field:

DATE
@DATE(89,1,14)

does not work. The criteria must be entered as a formula with a cell reference to the first record's date field. The correct criteria field is:

DATE
+B3=@DATE(89,1,14)

To extract records for checks written from Jan 13 through Jan 16 the criteria range would be:

DATE
+B3>=@DATE(89,1,13)#AND#B3<=@DATE(89,1,16)

- - - If you need a break, stop at this point. - - -

You enter: / File Retrieve **JOURNAL [Return]**

Database Statistical @ Functions

@ functions used on databases are similar to the statistical @ functions, but the computations are done on only the records which fit the criteria in the criteria range argument.

Let's say you wish to add all food purchases from the JOURNAL database. This entails adding the AMOUNT fields of all records whose CLASS field is FOOD.

First set up a criteria range.

You enter: / Copy **E2 [Return] B17 [Return]**

You enter into B18: **FOOD [Return]**

@DSUM(input range,offset,criteria range)

@DSUM and all database statistical @ functions use the ranges in their arguments and ignore the any ranges associated with the /Data Query command.

You enter into D16: **@DSUM(A2..E13,2,B17..B18) [Return]**

Your worksheet should look like Figure 12-18.

The sum 2084.82 is the sum of the four food records' AMOUNT fields. The first argument, A2..A13, is the input range. The second argument, offset, designates the column or field to be summed. It is the field number, or the number of columns to move right from the upper left corner of the database. The counting begins at 0, not 1, therefore the

```
D16: [W18] @DSUM(A2..E13,2,B17..B18)


      A        B        C               D              E
1            FROGGIE'S BAR CHECK DISBURSEMENTS JOURNAL
2    CHECK     DATE    AMOUNT            TO           CLASS
3      283 12-Jan-89 $147.00 HARVEY COOK        LABORBROOM
4      284 12-Jan-89 $230.00 FRED BARTENDER     LABORBROOM
5      285 12-Jan-89 $945.38 FROZEN PACKERS     FOOD
6      286 13-Jan-89 $533.99 BETTER BEVERAGE    BEER KEG
7      287 14-Jan-89 $168.00 BEST FOODS         FOOD
8      288 14-Jan-89 $203.41 FROZEN PACKERS     FOOD
9      289 14-Jan-89 $230.00 FRED BARTENDER     LABORBROOM
10     290 14-Jan-89 $217.00 FLOYD DISHWASHER   LABORKROOM
11     291 16-Jan-89 $768.03 FROZEN PACKERS     FOOD
12     292 17-Jan-89 $602.50 BOAT BOTTLING      BEER CAN
13     293 17-Jan-89 $125.86 BETTER BEVERAGE    BEER KEG
14
15
16                            2084.82
17         CLASS
18         FOOD
```

Figure 12-18. @DSUM for Food Purchases.

field with offset 0 is CHECK, the field with offset 1 is DATE, the field with offset 2 is AMOUNT which is our applicable field in this example, etc. The third argument, B17..B18, is the criteria range. The criteria range is, of course, not limited to two cells, and can be as large and complicated as you like.

The database statistical @ functions are listed below and all have the three arguments as @DSUM does - (input range,offset,criteria range).

@DAVG
Returns the average of the offset field values in the records which meet the criteria.

@DCOUNT
Returns a count of all non-blank cells in the offset field of the records which meet the criteria.

@DMAX
Returns the maximum value of the offset field values from the records which meet the criteria.

@DMIN
Returns the minimum value of the offset field values from the records which meet the criteria.

@DSTD
Returns the standard deviation of the offset field values in the

records which meet the criteria.

@DSUM

Returns the sum of the offset field values in the records which meet the criteria.

@DVAR

Returns the variance of the offset field values in the records which meet the criteria.

Turn to /Data Table (see index) for more examples of the database statistical functions.

Releases 3.0 and 3.1+:

The Modify option on the /Data Query menu allows you to

Extract: extracts records and stores their addresses for later reinsertion after modification.

Insert: adds records to the output range from the input range.

Replace: replaces original records in the input range with corresponding modified records previously extracted with Extract.

Extract and Replace above go hand-in-hand. First Extract the records that fit the criteria, then modify them in the output range, then Replace to have 1-2-3 put them back into the input range with the modifications. It's an easy way of looking at a subset of data for modification.

In this release, data can be extracted from multiple input ranges. When specifying the Input range, use commas between the specified ranges. A correspondence between fields can be set up with a join formula. For example, let's say you have two Input ranges, EMPLOYEES and PERSONNEL. The EMPLOYEES database has a field named SOCSEC and the PERSONNEL database has a field name SSN, each containing social security numbers. You want to extract a record for each person with data from both databases. For the Input range, specify EMPLOYEE,PERSONNEL. In the criteria range under a field name SSN (or SOCSEC) enter the join formula +SSN=SOCSEC. The join formula tells 1-2-3 to search for the criteria and consider SSN and SOCSEC keys to both sets of records. The Output range may have fields from both Input databases.

EXERCISES

Create the worksheet below for exercises 1 through 6 and save under the name ALLSHOP if you have not already done so in another lesson. If you have, retrieve the file. Do not modify the file on disk by saving it with modifications as you will need it in other lessons.

```
        A           B              C        D
1          ALLSHOP RESTAURANT SERVICE, INC.
2
3    ITEM #    DESCRIPTION      PRICE    CLASS
4
5      1048 GROUND GINGER       $1.29 SPICE
6      2668 TIDAL LIQUID        $3.99 DETERGENT
7      3555 PICKLING SPICE      $1.39 SPICE
8      4874 ARROWROOT           $2.19 SPICE
9      4913 WOODITE             $2.49 DETERGENT
10     5104 DILL WEED           $1.79 SPICE
11     6125 JEST SOAP           $2.09 DETERGENT
12     6270 CELERY SEED         $1.35 SPICE
```

1. Find all spices in the ALLSHOP worksheet.

2. Extract the ITEM # and PRICE fields of all spices in the ALLSHOP worksheet.

3. Extract the ITEM # and DESCRIPTION fields of the three records whose DESCRIPTION has I as a second character, i.e. TIDAL LIQUID, PICKLING SPICE, AND DILL WEED.

4. Extract the ITEM # and DESCRIPTION fields of records whose DESCRIPTION begins with the character A or J.

5. Extract the ITEM # and DESCRIPTION fields of items which cost more than $2.00.

6. Extract the ITEM # and DESCRIPTION fields of spices which cost more than $1.29.

7. Use the JOURNAL worksheet to create a list without duplicates of all different parties to whom checks were written by FROGGIE'S.

8. Clear from the JOURNAL database all records of checks written to BETTER BEVERAGE. Do not modify the original JOURNAL worksheet on disk as you will need it in other lessons. When you save, use another file name.

9. Extract from the JOURNAL database the CHECK, TO, and AMOUNT fields (in that order) of records whose checks are numbered between 286 and 290 inclusive.

10. Use the JOURNAL file and add an input cell for a check number out of the range of the database. When the user inputs a check number and presses [F7/QUERY], all information on that check number will be placed in a range directly under the input cell. Use labels to document the information for the user.

11. If you've done the date and time lesson, extract the CHECK, DATE, and TO fields of records whose checks were written on Jan 12. Of those records whose checks were written after Jan 14.

CUMULATIVE EXERCISES

C1. Create the worksheet below by retrieving the TOFU1 worksheet which you created in Lesson 1 and deleting rows 15 through 19 first and then row 4.

A. Find the records for all sales reps in division 2. Extract the names of all sales reps in division 1.

B. Extract the names of all sales reps in division 1 or 3.

C. Extract then names of all sales reps in division 2 whose commission is greater than $3,000.

D. Extract the names of all sales reps who are either in division 2 or whose commission is greater than $3,000.

Save under TOFU12.

	A	B	C	D	E
1		IMITATION TOFU, INCORPORATED			
2					
3		SalesRep	Division	92 Sales	Commission
4	1	Saxe, J.	2	$40,500	$2,430
5	2	Gress, R.	3	$77,000	$4,620
6	3	Cosner, L.	3	$23,400	$1,404
7	4	Smith, A.	1	$150,000	$9,000
8	5	Smith, B.	1	$54,700	$3,282
9	6	Kirlin, K.	2	$75,000	$4,500
10	7	Wodak, F.	1	$29,800	$1,788
11	8	Reese, J.	3	$111,300	$6,678
12	9	Gruss, M.	1	$88,200	$5,292
13	10	Boyle, T.	2	$67,600	$4,056
14					

C2. Retrieve the FISH1 worksheet that you created in Lesson 1. Change the field headers to those shown in the worksheet below.

A. Find all living items (item # is less than 200) using /Data Find.

B. Extract the quantity sold and item name of those records found in part A.

C. Extract the item number and item name of items whose retail price is greater than $5.00.

Save under FISH12.

	A	B	C	D	E	F
1		HAPPY TROPICAL FISH STORE				
2	Item #	Item Name	Sold	Retail	Wholesale	Profit
3	273	7-inch fish net	63	$1.99	$0.70	$1.29
4	238	1-lb. decorative rocks	49	$2.99	$1.30	$1.69
5	130	underwater fern	13	$2.29	$0.90	$1.39
6	281	40-gallon aquarium	14	$39.99	$22.00	$17.99
7	162	goldfish	241	$0.59	$0.10	$0.49
8	192	20-inch eel	4	$8.99	$4.00	$4.99
9	274	2-gallon fish bowl	25	$4.99	$2.00	$2.99
10	256	8-vitamin fish food	57	$1.79	$0.80	$0.99
11	198	turtle	-1	$3.99	$1.50	$2.49
12	111	piranha	3	$10.99	$5.00	$5.99
13						

C3. Retrieve the BILL1 worksheet that you created in Lesson 1 and add the Class column as shown below. N indicates "Necessity" and L indicates "Luxury".

    A. Find the records that are luxuries.

    B. Extract the expense item name of those records that are luxuries.

    C. Extract the expense item name and amount over/(under) of all expense items that were over budget. Sum the amounts over budget in a separate cell and label it properly.

Save under BILL12.

	A	B	C	D	E
1		MONTHLY BILLS FOR MARCH			
2					
3	Expense Item	Actual	Budgeted	Over/(Under)	Class
4	Food	$238	$220	$18	N
5	Rent	$550	$550	$0	N
6	Phone	$39	$30	$9	N
7	Electric	$43	$50	($7)	N
8	Gasoline	$56	$45	$11	N
9	Car Payment	$345	$345	$0	N
10	Insurance	$55	$55	$0	N
11	Charge Cards	$250	$100	$150	L
12	Entertainment	$150	$100	$50	L
13		--------------------------------			
14	Total	$1,726	$1,495	$231	
15					

C4. Retrieve the GOLF1 worksheet that you created in Lesson 1. Use the /Data Query command to extract the names and scores the best and worst scores of the four players. You will have to modify the worksheet and set up a range with field headers. Save under GOLF12.

Lesson 13

DATA TABLE 1 AND 2

Contents:

This lesson covers the use of /Data Table 1 and 2 commands. It also explains how they are used in combination with a database.

Sensitivity Analysis

Sensitivity analysis is a form of "what if" analysis which determines the sensitivity of some output to one or more input values. It asks variation-type questions like "What increase in the cost of raw material A would cause us to operate in the red?" and elasticity-type questions like "What is the highest price we could set for product 1 before the drop in demand would cause an overall decline in profits?" and range-type questions like "What can the price range be for product 1 if we want a profit margin of x?" In these questions, one input value is varying (cost of raw material A and price of product 1). Often, sensitivity questions contain two variables: "What cholesterol level combined with what age would cause the probability of a heart attack within the next year to rise to 56%?" and "What rate of population growth combined with what death rate would cause the population to double in 5 years?" and "What interest rate and initial downpayment would allow for a maximum monthly payment of x dollars, given a constant term?" Finding answers to these questions could get tedious, unless you have a tool like 1-2-3's /Data Table command.

/Data Table

/Data Table displays, in table form, the results of formulas with varying input values.

/Data Table 1 (One Input, One or More Formulas)

The first example is a very simple one. Create the worksheet shown in Figure 13-1 following the instructions below.

You enter into A1: **45 [Return]**

You enter into C2: **2*A1 [Return]**

You enter into C2: **/ Range Format Text C2 [Return]**

The last /Range Format command has no effect on the outcome of the /Data Table command. Text format will allow you to easily see the formula in cell C2.

You enter: / **Data Fill B3..B7 [Return] 10 [Return] 10 [Return] [Return]**

Figure 13-1. Simple Data Table 1.

The /Data Table 1 command answers this question in table form: To what will C2's formula evaluate if 10 or 20 or 30 or 40 or 50 were placed in A1? The five answers will be placed in the range C3..C7.

You enter: / **Data Table 1**

Computer message: Enter table range:

You enter: **B2..C7 [Return]**

The table range consists of the formula, the column of variables 10 through 50, and the output range where the five answers will be placed.

Computer message: Enter Input cell 1:

You enter: **A1 [Return]**

Your worksheet should look like Figure 13-2.

Figure 13-2. Worksheet after /Data Table 1.

The results in C3..C7 are the values of the formula in C2, if the input cell, A1, was replaced with the input values in column B. If A1 contained 10, the formula in C2 would evaluate to 20, if it contained 20, C2 would evaluate to 40, etc.

You may be wondering why you had to enter the input cell, A1. The formula might contain several cell references. For instance, the formula in C2 could have just-as-well been something like 2*B4-A1+30*Q78. 1-2-3 needs to know which of them, B4, A1 or Q78, should be varied or replaced with the input values 10, 20, 30, 40, 50.

The input cell does not have to be directly in the formula - a referenced cell in the formula could depend upon the input cell value. The input cell would thereby affect the formula cell indirectly.

Note that the current value in A1 is irrelevant. /Data Table ignores it and substitutes only the input values from the table range.

/Data Table 1 can have more than one formula; others should be placed to the right of the first formula.

You enter into D2: **1+A1-A2 [Return]**

You enter: / **Range Format Text D2 [Return]**

You enter into A2: **10 [Return]**

Expand the Table range to include the new column.

You enter: / **Data Table 1 [Right] [Return] [Return]**

Your worksheet should look like Figure 13-3.

	A	B	C	D
1	45			
2	10		2*A1	1+A1-A2
3		10	20	1
4		20	40	11
5		30	60	21
6		40	80	31
7		50	100	41

Figure 13-3. More than One Formula in /Data Table 1.

What if A2 were the input cell instead of A1? Think about it before doing the next command.

You enter: / **Data Table 1 [Return] A2 [Return]**

Your worksheet should look like Figure 13-4.

```
          A         B         C         D
1        45
2        10                 2*A1    1+A1-A2
3                  10        90        36
4                  20        90        26
5                  30        90        16
6                  40        90         6
7                  50        90        -4
```

Figure 13-4. New Input Cell is A2. First Formula is Not Dependent.

In Data Table 1, only the input cell (A1) varies; all other cells are held constant. The output values in column C are all 90 because its associated formula in B2 (2*A1) does not reference the varying cell, A2.

For future reference, a summarization of the Table range setup for /Data Table 1 is shown in Figure 13-5.

```
        blank           formula1   formula2   formula3   etc.
        value1
        value2
        value3
          etc.

The values are substituted into ONE input cell (somewhere else
in the worksheet) in order to see the effect on the formulas.
```

Figure 13-5. Table Range Setup for /Data Table 1.

For a practical example, create the worksheet in Figure 13-6 and save it under the name DATATABL. All numbers are constant values except B6 which contains the formula @SUM(B4..B5) and B8 which contains the formula +B1-B6. Make the global format Currency with 0 decimal digits.

```
B8: +B1-B6

          A         B
1  Total Sales   $5,000
2
3  Costs
4    Labor       $2,300
5    Material    $1,900
6  Total Costs   $4,200
7
8  Profit          $800
```

Figure 13-6. DATATABL Worksheet.

What if labor costs were only $2000? What would Total Costs be? What would Profit be? What if labor costs were $2100? How much must labor costs decrease for profits to rise to $1500? /Data Table 1 is great for "what if" analysis.

You enter into D11: **+B6 [Right]**

You enter into E11: **+B8 [Return]**

You enter: **/ Data Fill C12..C20 [Return] 1500 [Return] 100 [Return] [Return]**

You enter: **/ Data Table 1 C11..E20 [Return] B4 [Return]**

Your worksheet should look like Figure 13-7.

	A	B	C	D	E
1	Total Sales	$5,000			
2					
3	Costs				
4	Labor	$2,300			
5	Material	$1,900			
6	Total Costs	$4,200			
7					
8	Profit	$800			
9					
10					
11				$4,200	$800
12			$1,500	$3,400	$1,600
13			$1,600	$3,500	$1,500
14			$1,700	$3,600	$1,400
15			$1,800	$3,700	$1,300
16			$1,900	$3,800	$1,200
17			$2,000	$3,900	$1,100
18			$2,100	$4,000	$1,000
19			$2,200	$4,100	$900
20			$2,300	$4,200	$800

Figure 13-7. Data Table 1 - Labor Costs as Input.

It is common for the /Data Table formulas to be simple references to other formula cells, as +B6 and +B8 are here.

The table shows the effect of labor costs on Total Costs (column D) and Profit (column E). For example, look at row 16. If labor costs are $1,900, then Total Costs are $3,800 and Profit is $1,200.

The numbers are more understandable if you add some labels and hide the formula row.

You enter into D10: **"Costs [Right]**

You enter into E10: **"Profit [Return]**

You enter: / **Range Format Hidden D11..E11 [Return]**

What effect on Costs and Profit would an increase in Total Sales have? Change the input values in the table and the input cell:

You enter: / **Data Fill [Return] 5000 [Return] [Return] [Return]**

You enter: / **Data Table 1 [Return] B1 [Return]**

Your worksheet should look like Figure 13-8.

```
        A           B        C        D        E
1   Total Sales   $5,000
2
3   Costs
4    Labor        $2,300
5    Material     $1,900
6   Total Costs   $4,200
7
8   Profit         $800
9
10                               Costs    Profit
11
12                     $5,000   $4,200     $800
13                     $5,100   $4,200     $900
14                     $5,200   $4,200   $1,000
15                     $5,300   $4,200   $1,100
16                     $5,400   $4,200   $1,200
17                     $5,500   $4,200   $1,300
18                     $5,600   $4,200   $1,400
19                     $5,700   $4,200   $1,500
20                     $5,800   $4,200   $1,600
```

Figure 13-8. Total Sales as Input Cell in /Data Table 1.

Note that the costs don't depend on Total Sales and remain constant. (This is obviously a very simple example.) Not surprisingly, the profit increases with total sales.

The 1 in the /Data Table 1 signifies that one variable is varying.

What if Total Sales increased AND Labor Costs changed? Two inputs are varying here; this is a job for /Data Table 2.

/Data Table 2 (Two Inputs, One Formula)

What if Total Sales were $5500 AND Labor Costs were $2000? What if Total Sales were $6000 and Labor Costs were $1500? What would Profit be? There are two input variables in these questions.

The setup for the Table range for /Data Table 2 is shown in Figure 13-9.

```
formula  value2A  value2B  value2C etc.
value1A
value1B
value1C
  etc.

  Value1's and value2's are substituted into input cells 1 and 2,
  respectively.  ONE formula contains references to the input cells.
```

Figure 13-9. Table Range Setup for /Data Table 2.

There are 2 input cells (Total Sales and Labor Costs) and only one formula (the Profit formula).

You enter: / File Retrieve **DATATABL [Return]**

Your worksheet should look like Figure 13-6.

You enter into C10: **+B8 [Return]**

You enter into C10: / **R**ange Format **H**idden **C10 [Return]**

Hiding the formula is not necessary and will not effect the outcome of the /Data Table command.

You enter: / **D**ata **F**ill **D10..G10 [Return] 2000 [Return] 100 [Return] [Return]**

You enter into E9: **"Labor [Return]**

You enter: / **D**ata **F**ill **C11..C18 [Return] 5000 [Return] 500 [Return] [Return]**

You enter into B13: **Sales [Return]**

Your worksheet should look like Figure 13-10.

```
C10: (H) +B8


         A          B           C       D       E       F       G
 1   Total Sales   $5,000
 2
 3   Costs
 4    Labor        $2,300
 5    Material     $1,900
 6   Total Costs   $4,200
 7
 8   Profit         $800
 9                                              Labor
10                             $2,000  $2,100  $2,200  $2,300
11                     $5,000
12                     $5,500
13           Sales     $6,000
14                     $6,500
15                     $7,000
16                     $7,500
17                     $8,000
```

Figure 13-10. Before Issuance of /Data Table 2.

You enter: / **Data Table 2 C10..G17 [Return]**

The labels Sales and Labor are only for clarification and should not be included in the table range.

Computer message: Enter Input cell 1:

This is the cell which will take the values in the left-most column of the table range and should be set to Total Sales.

You enter: **B1 [Return]**

Computer message: Enter Input cell 2:

This is the cell which will take the values in the top row of the table range and should be set to Labor Costs.

You enter: **B4 [Return]**

Your worksheet should look like Figure 13-11.

```
C10: (H) +B8


          A          B         C         D         E         F         G
1    Total Sales  $5,000
2
3    Costs
4      Labor      $2,300
5      Material   $1,900
6    Total Costs  $4,200
7
8    Profit         $800
9                                             Labor
10                                  $2,000    $2,100    $2,200    $2,300
11                        $5,000    $1,100    $1,000      $900      $800
12                        $5,500    $1,600    $1,500    $1,400    $1,300
13             Sales      $6,000    $2,100    $2,000    $1,900    $1,800
14                        $6,500    $2,600    $2,500    $2,400    $2,300
15                        $7,000    $3,100    $3,000    $2,900    $2,800
16                        $7,500    $3,600    $3,500    $3,400    $3,300
17                        $8,000    $4,100    $4,000    $3,900    $3,800
```

Figure 13-11. After Issuance of /Data Table 2.

The values in D11..G17 are the values of the Profit function in B8, if values in the row for Total Sales and column for Labor Costs are substituted. Maximum profit of $4100 in D17 occurs for these values when Total Sales are $8000 and Labor Costs are $2000. (@MAX(D11..G17) can be used to find maximum profit.)

[F8/TABLE]

The eighth function key recalculates the output values in the table range, using the latest /Data Table settings for the table range and input cells.

You enter into C11: **10000 [Return]**

You enter: **[F8/TABLE]**

Your worksheet should look like Figure 13-12.

	A	B	C	D	E	F	G
1	Total Sales	$5,000					
2							
3	Costs						
4	Labor	$2,300					
5	Material	$1,900					
6	Total Costs	$4,200					
7							
8	Profit	$800					
9					Labor		
10				$2,000	$2,100	$2,200	$2,300
11			$10,000	$6,100	$6,000	$5,900	$5,800
12			$5,500	$1,600	$1,500	$1,400	$1,300
13		Sales	$6,000	$2,100	$2,000	$1,900	$1,800
14			$6,500	$2,600	$2,500	$2,400	$2,300
15			$7,000	$3,100	$3,000	$2,900	$2,800
16			$7,500	$3,600	$3,500	$3,400	$3,300
17			$8,000	$4,100	$4,000	$3,900	$3,800

Figure 13-12. [F8/TABLE] used for /Data Table Recalculation.

The output range D11..G17 are the only cells changed by the recalculation.

The values column C10..C17 and row D10..G10 need not be in order. I've been using /Data Fill commands to minimize typing.

[F8/TABLE] can be used in either /Data Table 1 or 2.

- - - If you need a break, stop at this point. - - -

/Data Tables with Databases

For this part of the lesson, you must have knowledge of /Data Query. If you do not wish to do the lesson on Data Query, skip to the end of this lesson.

Retrieve the file JOURNAL created with the Data Query lesson. Your worksheet should look like Figure 13-13.

```
        A        B        C              D                    E
1            FROGGIE'S BAR CHECK DISBURSEMENTS JOURNAL
2   CHECK    DATE     AMOUNT          TO                  CLASS
3      283 12-Jan-89  $147.00 HARVEY COOK          LABORKROOM
4      284 12-Jan-89  $230.00 FRED BARTENDER       LABORBROOM
5      285 12-Jan-89  $945.38 FROZEN PACKERS       FOOD
6      286 13-Jan-89  $533.99 BETTER BEVERAGE      BEER KEG
7      287 14-Jan-89  $168.00 BEST FOODS           FOOD
8      288 14-Jan-89  $203.41 FROZEN PACKERS       FOOD
9      289 14-Jan-89  $230.00 FRED BARTENDER       LABORBROOM
10     290 14-Jan-89  $217.00 FLOYD DISHWASHER     LABORKROOM
11     291 16-Jan-89  $768.03 FROZEN PACKERS       FOOD
12     292 17-Jan-89  $602.50 BOAT BOTTLING        BEER CAN
13     293 17-Jan-89  $125.86 BETTER BEVERAGE      BEER KEG
```

Figure 13-13.   JOURNAL File.

/Data Table 1 with a Database

You enter: / **Copy E2 [Return] A15 [Return]**

You enter into D16: **FOOD [Down]**

You enter into D17: **BEER KEG [Return]**

You enter into E15: **@DSUM(A2..E13,2,A15..A16) [Right]**

You enter into F15: **@DAVG(A2..E13,2,A15..A16) [Return]**

You enter: / **R**ange **F**ormat **T**ext **E15..F15 [Return]**

Your worksheet should look like Figure 13-14.

```
F15: (T) @DAVG(A2..E13,2,A15..A16)


      A         B         C            D               E           F
1          FROGGIE'S BAR CHECK DISBURSEMENTS JOURNAL
2     CHECK     DATE     AMOUNT          TO             CLASS
3       283 12-Jan-89  $147.00 HARVEY COOK       LABORKROOM
4       284 12-Jan-89  $230.00 FRED BARTENDER    LABORBROOM
5       285 12-Jan-89  $945.38 FROZEN PACKERS    FOOD
6       286 13-Jan-89  $533.99 BETTER BEVERAGE   BEER KEG
7       287 14-Jan-89  $168.00 BEST FOODS        FOOD
8       288 14-Jan-89  $203.41 FROZEN PACKERS    FOOD
9       289 14-Jan-89  $230.00 FRED BARTENDER    LABORBROOM
10      290 14-Jan-89  $217.00 FLOYD DISHWASHER  LABORKROOM
11      291 16-Jan-89  $768.03 FROZEN PACKERS    FOOD
12      292 17-Jan-89  $602.50 BOAT BOTTLING     BEER CAN
13      293 17-Jan-89  $125.86 BETTER BEVERAGE   BEER KEG
14
15    CLASS                                      @DSUM(A2 @DAVG(A2
16                               FOOD
17                               BEER KEG
```

Figure 13-14. Table and Criterion Ranges for /Data Table 1 with Database.

The formulas in E15..F15 are only partially displayed because of the column-widths, but the entire formulas are stored and will work.

You enter: / **Data Table 1 D15..F17 [Return] A16 [Return]**

Your worksheet should look like Figure 13-15.

```
      A         B         C            D               E           F
1          FROGGIE'S BAR CHECK DISBURSEMENTS JOURNAL
2     CHECK     DATE     AMOUNT          TO             CLASS
3       283 12-Jan-89  $147.00 HARVEY COOK       LABORKROOM
4       284 12-Jan-89  $230.00 FRED BARTENDER    LABORBROOM
5       285 12-Jan-89  $945.38 FROZEN PACKERS    FOOD
6       286 13-Jan-89  $533.99 BETTER BEVERAGE   BEER KEG
7       287 14-Jan-89  $168.00 BEST FOODS        FOOD
8       288 14-Jan-89  $203.41 FROZEN PACKERS    FOOD
9       289 14-Jan-89  $230.00 FRED BARTENDER    LABORBROOM
10      290 14-Jan-89  $217.00 FLOYD DISHWASHER  LABORKROOM
11      291 16-Jan-89  $768.03 FROZEN PACKERS    FOOD
12      292 17-Jan-89  $602.50 BOAT BOTTLING     BEER CAN
13      293 17-Jan-89  $125.86 BETTER BEVERAGE   BEER KEG
14
15    CLASS                                      @DSUM(A2 @DAVG(A2
16                               FOOD            2084.82   521.205
17                               BEER KEG         659.85   329.925
```

Figure 13-15. /Data Table 1 Results with JOURNAL Database.

The 2084.82 is the sum of all check amounts written for FOOD, 521.205 is the average of all check amounts written for FOOD, 659.85 is the sum of all checks written for BEER KEGs, and 329.925 is the average of all check amounts written for BEER KEGs.

Let's remember how /Data Table 1 works and try to follow the steps necessary to get the 2084.82. Look back at Figure 13-5 and compare it on your screen to D15..F17, the /Data Table range. In Figure 13-5, value1 is substituted into the input cell to compute formula1. On your screen, FOOD (value1) is substituted into A16 (the input cell) to compute @DSUM(A2..E13,2,A15..A16) (formula1). @DSUM sums the AMOUNT field (offset 2) for records fitting the criteria in range A15..A16. /Data Table computes 2084.82 by plugging FOOD into A16 and computing formula1, @DSUM. Likewise, for 329.925, BEER KEG is plugged into A16 and @DAVG is computed.

In the real world, there would be dozens of CLASSes. The /Data Query Unique command can be used to set up the values range in the data table so that it contains all CLASSes.

You enter into A16: ***[Return]**

You enter: **/ Copy E2 [Return] D15 [Return]**

You enter: **/ Data Query Input A2..E13 [Return]**

You enter: **Criterion A15..A16 [Return] Output D15..D21 [Return]**

You enter: **Unique Quit**

All CLASSes are listed for you. If it didn't work, check your ranges.

You enter: **/ Range Erase D15 [Return]**

You enter: **/ Data Table 1 D15..F20 [Return] [Return]**

Your worksheet should look like Figure 13-16.

```
      A      B        C           D              E        F
 1         FROGGIE'S BAR CHECK DISBURSEMENTS JOURNAL
 2   CHECK    DATE    AMOUNT          TO           CLASS
 3     283 12-Jan-89 $147.00 HARVEY COOK        LABORKROOM
 4     284 12-Jan-89 $230.00 FRED BARTENDER     LABORBROOM
 5     285 12-Jan-89 $945.38 FROZEN PACKERS     FOOD
 6     286 13-Jan-89 $533.99 BETTER BEVERAGE    BEER KEG
 7     287 14-Jan-89 $168.00 BEST FOODS         FOOD
 8     288 14-Jan-89 $203.41 FROZEN PACKERS     FOOD
 9     289 14-Jan-89 $230.00 FRED BARTENDER     LABORBROOM
10     290 14-Jan-89 $217.00 FLOYD DISHWASHER   LABORKROOM
11     291 16-Jan-89 $768.03 FROZEN PACKERS     FOOD
12     292 17-Jan-89 $602.50 BOAT BOTTLING      BEER CAN
13     293 17-Jan-89 $125.86 BETTER BEVERAGE    BEER KEG
14
15   CLASS                               @DSUM(A2 @DAVG(A2
16   *                    LABORKROOM            364     182
17                        LABORBROOM            460     230
18                        FOOD              2084.82 521.205
19                        BEER KEG           659.85 329.925
20                        BEER CAN            602.5   602.5
```

Figure 13-16. Use of /Data Query Unique in /Data Table.

E16..F20 should be formatted to Currency. Now you have a summary of expenses according to CLASS. /Data Sort can be used to list the CLASSes in alphabetical order.

Releases 3.0 and 3.1+: The CLASSes are automatically listed in alphabetical order.

BEER* can be used in the values range as a CLASS instead of, or in addition to, the BEER KEG and BEER CAN to give a total and average for all beer. Same goes with LABOR* or LABOR?ROOM.

/Data Table 2 with a Database

You enter: / **Range Erase D15..F20 [Return]**

You enter into E2: / **Worksheet Column Set-Width 12 [Return]**

You enter into F2: **BOUNCED? [Return]**

You enter: / **Copy F2 [Return] B15 [Return]**

You enter into D15: **@DSUM(A2..F13,2,A15..B16) [Return]**

After formatting D15 as Text, entering the YES's and NO's in F3..F13, and completing the table range D15..F20 (see control panel for formula), your worksheet should look like Figure 13-17. Be careful not to type 0 (zero) instead of O (capital letter O).

```
D15: (T) [W18] @DSUM(A2..F13,2,A15..B16)


          A       B       C          D              E            F
1           FROGGIE'S BAR CHECK DISBURSEMENTS JOURNAL
2    CHECK     DATE    AMOUNT          TO          CLASS      BOUNCED?
3      283 12-Jan-89 $147.00 HARVEY COOK        LABORKROOM   NO
4      284 12-Jan-89 $230.00 FRED BARTENDER     LABORBROOM   NO
5      285 12-Jan-89 $945.38 FROZEN PACKERS     FOOD         YES
6      286 13-Jan-89 $533.99 BETTER BEVERAGE    BEER KEG     YES
7      287 14-Jan-89 $168.00 BEST FOODS         FOOD         YES
8      288 14-Jan-89 $203.41 FROZEN PACKERS     FOOD         NO
9      289 14-Jan-89 $230.00 FRED BARTENDER     LABORBROOM   NO
10     290 14-Jan-89 $217.00 FLOYD DISHWASHER   LABORKROOM   YES
11     291 16-Jan-89 $768.03 FROZEN PACKERS     FOOD         NO
12     292 17-Jan-89 $602.50 BOAT BOTTLING      BEER CAN     NO
13     293 17-Jan-89 $125.86 BETTER BEVERAGE    BEER KEG     NO
14
15   CLASS BOUNCED?           @DSUM(A2..F13,2,A YES          NO
16                            BEER CAN
17                            BEER KEG
18                            FOOD
19                            LABORBROOM
20                            LABORKROOM
```

Figure 13-17. Table and Criterion Ranges for /Data Table 2 with Database.

The four checks 285, 286, 287, and 290 were returned for insufficient funds. (This has been a bad month for Froggie's.)

The two input cells will be A16, where the left column in the table range will be substituted, and B16, where the top row of the table range will be substituted. Review Figure 13-9.

You enter: **/Data Table 2 D15..F20 [Return] A16 [Return] B16
[Return]**

Your worksheet should look like Figure 13-18.

```
          A        B        C            D              E          F
 1           FROGGIE'S BAR CHECK DISBURSEMENTS JOURNAL
 2    CHECK    DATE     AMOUNT          TO            CLASS      BOUNCED?
 3      283 12-Jan-89 $147.00 HARVEY COOK         LABORKROOM   NO
 4      284 12-Jan-89 $230.00 FRED BARTENDER      LABORBROOM   NO
 5      285 12-Jan-89 $945.38 FROZEN PACKERS      FOOD         YES
 6      286 13-Jan-89 $533.99 BETTER BEVERAGE     BEER KEG     YES
 7      287 14-Jan-89 $168.00 BEST FOODS          FOOD         YES
 8      288 14-Jan-89 $203.41 FROZEN PACKERS      FOOD         NO
 9      289 14-Jan-89 $230.00 FRED BARTENDER      LABORBROOM   NO
10      290 14-Jan-89 $217.00 FLOYD DISHWASHER    LABORKROOM   YES
11      291 16-Jan-89 $768.03 FROZEN PACKERS      FOOD         NO
12      292 17-Jan-89 $602.50 BOAT BOTTLING       BEER CAN     NO
13      293 17-Jan-89 $125.86 BETTER BEVERAGE     BEER KEG     NO
14
15   CLASS BOUNCED?              @DSUM(A2..F13,2,A YES          NO
16                               BEER CAN              0      602.5
17                               BEER KEG         533.99     125.86
18                               FOOD            1113.38     971.44
19                               LABORBROOM            0        460
20                               LABORKROOM          217        147
```

Figure 13-18. /Data Table 2 Results with JOURNAL Database.

In E16, the amount of bounced checks for the purchase of BEER CANs is zero. In E17, checks totaling $533.99 bounced for the purchase of BEER KEGs, etc. The total amount of checks that did not bounce for the purchase of FOOD was $971.44.

Let's look at how /Data Table 2 computed the 533.99. First, it substituted BEER KEG into A16 and YES into B16. Then it computed the @DSUM(A2..F13,2,A15..B16) by summing the AMOUNT field of all records fitting the criteria in A15..B16. Therefore, all checks for BEER KEGs that bounced were totalled.

Perhaps a better statistic for this case instead of the sum would be the number or count of checks which did or did not bounce in each CLASS. Perhaps instead of CLASS the field should be TO. These changes are left as an exercise at the end of this lesson.

Save this file under LES13.

Releases 3.0 and 3.1+:

/Data Table 3 (3 Inputs, One Formula) allows 3 inputs to any one formula. The table becomes 3 dimensional. Release 3 allows more than worksheet in memory simultaneously. Imagine several worksheets overlaying each other. The data table becomes three-dimensional, like a cube. Rows hold values for input 1, columns hold values for input 2, and stacked worksheets hold values for input 3 in the upper left corner of the table.

/Data Table Labeled allows more flexibility in creating data tables. Three variables can be used with more than one formula and much more. This command is beyond the scope of this text.

EXERCISES

1. Create the worksheet below and save under the name INCOME if you have not already done so in another lesson. If you have, retrieve the file. Do not modify the file on disk by saving it with modifications as you will need it in other lessons. You only need to enter columns A and B. The data that looks like it's in column D is only there to show you the actual formulas in the B column. On your screen, columns C, D, E, and F should be empty.

	A	B	
1	Units Produced..........	100	100
2	Percentage Sold.........	90%	0.9
3			
4	Net Sales...............	$72.00	0.8*B1*B2
5	Costs of Production......	$33.00	0.33*B1
6			
7	Gross Margin............	$39.00	+B4-B5
8			
9	Other Expenses..........		
10	Selling Expenses.......	$0.90	0.0125*B4
11	Shipping & Handling....	$6.62	0.092*B4
12	Interest Expense.......	$0.28	0.1/12*B5
13	Total Expenses..........	$7.80	@SUM(B10..B12)
14			
15	Net Income..............	$31.20	+B7-B13

1a. Create a list of figures as in C14..D15 in the worksheet below which show net income if the number of units produced were increased from current production level of 100 to a level in the range 200 through 1300 (multiples of 100 units).

```
D3: +B15

         A                 B       C      D
1  Units Produced..........   100
2  Percentage Sold.........   90%
3                                         $31.20
4  Net Sales...............  $72.00    200  $62.40
5  Costs of Production.....  $33.00    300  $93.60
6                                      400  $124.80
7  Gross Margin............  $39.00    500  $156.01
8                                      600  $187.21
9  Other Expenses..........            700  $218.41
10   Selling Expenses.......  $0.90    800  $249.61
11   Shipping & Handling....  $6.62    900  $280.81
12   Interest Expense.......  $0.28   1000  $312.01
13 Total Expenses..........  $7.80    1100  $343.21
14                                    1200  $374.41
15 Net Income..............  $31.20   1300  $405.61
```

1b. If maximum production capacity of the current plant is 1000 units for the time period which could be a day, month or year, what is maximum net income for that period if all other variables stay at their current values?

1c. Using the INCOME worksheet, create the list of figures below with the explanatory column header labels and hide any formula cells you deem necessary.

	C	D	E	F	G	H	I
1	Units	Net	Prod.	Selling	Ship &	Interest	Net
2	Produced	Sales	Costs	Expenses	Handling	Expense	Income
3							
4	200	$144.00	$66.00	$1.80	$13.25	$0.55	$62.40
5	300	$216.00	$99.00	$2.70	$19.87	$0.83	$93.60
6	400	$288.00	$132.00	$3.60	$26.50	$1.10	$124.80
7	500	$360.00	$165.00	$4.50	$33.12	$1.38	$156.01
8	600	$432.00	$198.00	$5.40	$39.74	$1.65	$187.21
9	700	$504.00	$231.00	$6.30	$46.37	$1.93	$218.41
10	800	$576.00	$264.00	$7.20	$52.99	$2.20	$249.61
11	900	$648.00	$297.00	$8.10	$59.62	$2.48	$280.81
12	1000	$720.00	$330.00	$9.00	$66.24	$2.75	$312.01
13	1100	$792.00	$363.00	$9.90	$72.86	$3.03	$343.21
14	1200	$864.00	$396.00	$10.80	$79.49	$3.30	$374.41
15	1300	$936.00	$429.00	$11.70	$86.11	$3.58	$405.61

1d. At what production level do the production costs reach $300? (The production level is the number of units produced.)

1e. For tax purposes, this company does not want to make a profit of more than $200 per time period. What is the highest production level that would fulfill this requirement?

1f. How many units must be produced if the company's owners want to make at least $100 per time period?

1g. Percentage of units sold is actually a variable and does not stay constant at 90%. Create the table of net income values in the worksheet below. Units produced varies in the range 100 to 1000 (multiples of 100) and the percentage of units sold varies in the range 90% to 95%.

```
D3: (H) +B15

        C      D      E      F      G      H      I      J
1
2                     Percentage of Units Sold
3              90%    91%    92%    93%    94%    95%
4             100     $31    $32    $33    $33    $34    $35
5             200     $62    $64    $65    $67    $68    $70
6             300     $94    $96    $98    $100   $102   $104
7  Units      400     $125   $128   $131   $133   $136   $139
8  Produced   500     $156   $160   $163   $167   $170   $174
9             600     $187   $192   $196   $200   $204   $209
10            700     $218   $223   $228   $233   $238   $243
11            800     $250   $255   $261   $267   $273   $278
12            900     $281   $287   $294   $300   $307   $313
13            1000    $312   $319   $326   $334   $341   $348
```

1h. Due to a labor shortage, the maximum production level possible is 700 units for the next few time periods. Marketing studies have shown that an increase in advertising expenses by 10 dollars in the current time period increases the percentage sold by 1 percentage point in the current time period and 2 percentage points over the current percentage sold in the next time period. Currently the product is selling at 91% of units produced. Should advertising expenses be increased by $10 in this time period if the production level is at its maximum with the labor shortage? What effect would it have on net income over the next two time periods? If the production level dropped to 600 units in the next two time periods, what would your answers be?

2. Modify Figure 13-18 (saved under LES13) to show a count for the number of checks which did and did not bounce to each party in the TO field of the database.

3. Use the WHATIF worksheet (Figure 8-1) and the /Data Table 1 command to list affordable home costs associated with savings from $100 to $500 a month.

Use /Data Table 2 to list affordable home costs associated with savings ranging from $100 to $500 a month coupled with mortgage interest rates ranging from 9% to 11% in increments of 1/2 %.

4. Create a worksheet portraying the same data in Figure 5-5. Use /Data Table 2.

CUMULATIVE EXERCISES

C1.   Create the worksheet below by retrieving the TOFU1 worksheet which you created in Lesson 1 and deleting rows 15 through 19 first and then row 4. Find the sum and average of 92 Sales for all three divisions by using /Data Table 1 and the @DSUM and @DAVG functions. Save under TOFU13.

	A	B	C	D	E
1		IMITATION TOFU, INCORPORATED			
2					
3		SalesRep	Division	92 Sales	Commission
4	1	Saxe, J.	2	$40,500	$2,430
5	2	Gress, R.	3	$77,000	$4,620
6	3	Cosner, L.	3	$23,400	$1,404
7	4	Smith, A.	1	$150,000	$9,000
8	5	Smith, B.	1	$54,700	$3,282
9	6	Kirlin, K.	2	$75,000	$4,500
10	7	Wodak, F.	1	$29,800	$1,788
11	8	Reese, J.	3	$111,300	$6,678
12	9	Gruss, M.	1	$88,200	$5,292
13	10	Boyle, T.	2	$67,600	$4,056
14					

C2.   Retrieve the BILL1 worksheet that you created in Lesson 1 and add the Class column as shown below. N indicates "Necessity" and L indicates "Luxury". (Or retrieve BILL12 from Lesson 12 if you did it.) Use /Data Table 1 and @DSUM and @DCOUNT to add the amounts spent on necessities and luxuries. Save under BILL13.

	A	B	C	D	E
1		MONTHLY BILLS FOR MARCH			
2					
3	Expense Item	Actual	Budgeted	Over/(Under)	Class
4	Food	$238	$220	$18	N
5	Rent	$550	$550	$0	N
6	Phone	$39	$30	$9	N
7	Electric	$43	$50	($7)	N
8	Gasoline	$56	$45	$11	N
9	Car Payment	$345	$345	$0	N
10	Insurance	$55	$55	$0	N
11	Charge Cards	$250	$100	$150	L
12	Entertainment	$150	$100	$50	L
13		-------	-------	-------	
14	Total	$1,726	$1,495	$231	
15					

TITLES, WINDOWS, AND RECALCULATION

Contents:

Large worksheets require some special handling in terms of viewing them on the screen. Titles and windows commands can be used to juxtapose two remote parts of the worksheet for comparison or other purposes. Recalculation methods are also explained.

Create the partial worksheet shown in Figure 14-1.

```
A1: [W15]


            A           B       C       D       E       F
1                         FROGGIE'S BAR & GRILL
2                       Jan     Feb     Mar     Apr     May
3    Beer
4    Liquor
5    Food
6    Total Income
7
8    Labor
9    Beer
10   Liquor
11   Food
12   Mortgage
13   Utilities
14   Phone
15   Insurance
16   Taxes
17   Total Expenses
18
19   Net Income
20
```

Figure 14-1. Partial Froggie's Bar Worksheet.

Continue entering all months as column headers until cell M2 contains Dec. The idea here is to create a worksheet too large to fit on one screen. For this lesson the numbers are irrelevant, so to save typing, use /Data Fill and /Copy to complete the worksheet.

You enter: **/ Data Fill B3..M5 [Return]**

          9000 [Return] 100 [Return] 99999 [Return]

You enter: **/ Data Fill B8..M16 [Return]**

          1000 [Return] -1 [Return] -99999 [Return]

You enter into B6: **@SUM(B3..B5) [Return]**

You enter: **/ Copy B6 [Return] C6..M6 [Return]**

You enter into B17: **@SUM(B8..B16) [Return]**

You enter: / Copy **B17 [Return] C17..M17 [Return]**

You enter into B19: **+B6-B17 [Return]**

You enter: / Copy **B19 [Return] C19..M19 [Return]**

Your worksheet should look like Figure 14-2.

	A	B	C	D	E	F
1			FROGGIE'S BAR & GRILL			
2		Jan	Feb	Mar	Apr	May
3	Beer	9000	9300	9600	9900	10200
4	Liquor	9100	9400	9700	10000	10300
5	Food	9200	9500	9800	10100	10400
6	Total Income	27300	28200	29100	30000	30900
7						
8	Labor	1000	991	982	973	964
9	Beer	999	990	981	972	963
10	Liquor	998	989	980	971	962
11	Food	997	988	979	970	961
12	Mortgage	996	987	978	969	960
13	Utilities	995	986	977	968	959
14	Phone	994	985	976	967	958
15	Insurance	993	984	975	966	957
16	Taxes	992	983	974	965	956
17	Total Expenses	8964	8883	8802	8721	8640
18						
19	Net Income	18336	19317	20298	21279	22260
20						

Figure 14-2. Froggie's Worksheet.

Place the cell pointer home and save under the name FROGGIES.

You enter: **[Home] / File Save FROGGIES [Return]**

What did food cost in October?

You: **Position pointer to column K.**

Because column A is not shown on the screen, you cannot tell which number is the food expense.

You enter: **[Home]**

/Worksheet Titles

A title is a set of adjacent columns (or rows) frozen on the left (or top) of the screen.

To prevent column A from scrolling off the screen, freeze it with /Worksheet Titles.

You: **Position pointer in column B.**

You enter: / **Worksheet Titles Vertical**

You: **Position pointer in column K.**

The scroll lock key can be used to easily position the relevant column next to the titles.

You enter: **[Home] [ScrollLock] [Right] [Right] [Right]**

Try to position the pointer in column A.

You enter: **[Home] [Left]**

An error beep is issued to inform you that the pointer cannot be moved into a title column. Sometimes beginning Lotus users accidentally set up a Title and are clueless when they cannot move the pointer into some cell.

You enter: / **Worksheet Titles Clear**

Now the pointer can be moved into column A.

Turn off the SCROLL indicator at the bottom of the screen.

You enter: **[ScrollLock]**

The position of the pointer before issuance is important because it tells 1-2-3 how many columns to freeze. All columns to the left of the pointer column will be frozen. Position the pointer in column D.

You enter: **[Home] [Right] [Right] [Right]**

You enter: / **Worksheet Titles Vertical**

You: **Position pointer into column K.**

Columns A, B, and C are frozen.

You enter: / Worksheet Titles **C**lear

The same rules apply for horizontal titles.

You enter: **[Home] [Down] [Down]** / Worksheet Titles **H**orizontal

You enter: **[Down] [Down] [ScrollLock] [Down] [Down] [ScrollLock]**

You enter: / Worksheet Titles **C**lear

You can have both horizontal and vertical titles simultaneously.

You enter: **[Home] [Down] [Down] [Right]**

You enter: / Worksheet Titles **B**oth

You enter: **[ScrollLock] [Down] [Down] [Right] [Right]**

You enter: **[ScrollLock]** / Worksheet Titles **C**lear **[Home]**

- - - If you need a break, stop at this point. - - -

Retrieve the FROGGIES file if you are returning from a break.

/Worksheet Window

Until now, we've been working with one window into the worksheet, the screen. 1-2-3 allows you to view the worksheet through two windows at once with the /Worksheet Window command.

You: **Position the cell pointer in column D.**

You enter: / Worksheet Window **V**ertical

The screen is split into two vertical windows about the same size. Virtually all 1-2-3 commands are valid in a window.

You enter: **[Right] [Right]**

Use the sixth function key to jump between windows.

You enter: **[F6/WINDOW] [Left] [Left]**

By default, the two windows move vertically in synchrony.

You enter: **[Down] many times until row 25.**

To turn off synchronization:

You enter: / **Worksheet Window Unsync**

You enter: **[Up] many times until row 1.**

Your worksheet should look like Figure 14-3.

	C	D	E		B	C	D	E
6	28200	29100	30000	1		FROGGIE'S BAR & GRILL		
7				2		Jan	Feb	Mar	Apr
8	991	982	973	3	9000	9300	9600	9900
9	990	981	972	4	9100	9400	9700	10000
10	989	980	971	5	9200	9500	9800	10100
11	988	979	970	6	27300	28200	29100	30000
12	987	978	969	7				
13	986	977	968	8	1000	991	982	973
14	985	976	967	9	999	990	981	972
15	984	975	966	10	998	989	980	971
16	983	974	965	11	997	988	979	970
17	8883	8802	8721	12	996	987	978	969
18				13	995	986	977	968
19	19317	20298	21279	14	994	985	976	967
20				15	993	984	975	966
21				16	992	983	974	965
22				17	8964	8883	8802	8721
23				18				
24				19	18336	19317	20298	21279
25				20				

Figure 14-3. Vertical Windows Unsynchronized.

The windows now scroll independently; different row numbers are on the left of the windows. Turn synchronization back on.

You enter: / **Worksheet Window Sync**

In the menu Horizontal Vertical Sync Unsync Clear, the options Sync and Unsync are adjacent opposite options.

Releases 3.0 and 3.1+: The additional options Map, Perspective, Graph, and Display are discussed at the end of this section.

The Clear option returns the screen back to one window. No matter which window the cell pointer is in, the single window that returns is the one on the left.

You enter: / **Worksheet Window Clear**

You enter: **[Home]**

The screen can also be split horizontally.

You: **Position the cell pointer in row 10.**

You enter: **/ Worksheet Window Horizontal**

The [F6/WINDOW] key again moves the cell pointer to the alternate window.

You enter: **[F6/WINDOW] [F6/WINDOW] [F6/WINDOW]**

You enter: **[Down] several times.**

You enter: **[Right] several times.**

The windows are synchronized and therefore the same columns in each window are kept on the screen.

You enter: **/ Worksheet Window Unsync**

You enter: **[Left] several times.**

Your worksheet should look like Figure 14-4.

	E	F	G	H	I	J
1	ILL					
2	Apr	May	June	July	Aug	Sept
3	9900	10200	10500	10800	11100	11400
4	10000	10300	10600	10900	11200	11500
5	10100	10400	10700	11000	11300	11600
6	30000	30900	31800	32700	33600	34500
7						
8	973	964	955	946	937	928
9	972	963	954	945	936	927

	A	B	C	D	E
15	Insurance	993	984	975	966
16	Taxes	992	983	974	965
17	Total Expenses	8964	8883	8802	8721
18					
19	Net Income	18336	19317	20298	21279
20					

Figure 14-4. Unsynchronized Horizontal Windows.

In the case of horizontal windows, Clear returns the screen to the single window on top.

You enter: **/ Worksheet Window Clear**

Don't be misled to believe that the two windows must divide the screen equally as in the last two examples. You may position the cell pointer before the issuance of the /Worksheet Window command to have one thin and one large window.

You cannot divide the screen into more than two windows.

Releases 3.0 and 3.1+:
There are 4 new options on the /Worksheet Window sub-menu:

/Worksheet Window Map gives you a large overview of the worksheet by temporarily shrinking each column-width to 2. " is displayed in cells containing tables, # in cells containing values, and + in cells containing formulas. Try it. Hit [Esc] to return to the normal display.

/Worksheet Window Perspective displays 3 stacked worksheets at a time. Release 3.0 allows more than one worksheet or worksheet file in memory at once. (See Release 3 Appendix.)

/Worksheet Window Graph is discussed in Lesson 9 On-Screen Graphing, page 298. It allows a graph and worksheet to be simultaneously displayed side by side on the same screen.

/Worksheet Window Display allows you to select another screen display, if two displays were set up with the Install program.

- - - If you need a break, stop at this point. - - -

Retrieve the FROGGIES worksheet if you have just returned from a break.

Recalculation

To demonstrate the recalculation feature of 1-2-3, create a very large worksheet by copying a formula through a large range.

You enter into A21: **@SUM(B19..M19) [Return]**

You enter: **/ Copy A21 to A21..Z200**

You enter: **[Home]**

You now have a fairly large worksheet in memory. Change an entry in the worksheet and see what happens.

You enter into B3: **8000 [Return]**

WAIT flashes in the mode indicator and it takes a while for READY to return. What is happening here and why does it take so long to make an entry? With the WAIT after each entry, imagine how long it would take to enter a whole column of numbers. By default, 1-2-3 recalculates the entire worksheet after each and every new entry or change.

Releases 3.0 and 3.1+:
The wait for you is less than a second. This release recalculates only cells which were affected by a change in the worksheet. Recalculation time is greatly reduced.   You may also continue entering data, even if recalculation has not been completed.

In larger worksheets, these calculations take a while to do. Let's say your task is to change every month's beer entry to 8000.

You enter into C3: **8000 [Return]**

You enter into D3: **8000 [Right]**

You enter into E3: **8000 [Right]**

In this case, it is really not necessary for 1-2-3 to do any calculations until you are done entering all the changes.

/Worksheet Global Recalculation

To turn off this automatic recalculating, the /Worksheet Global Recalculation command can be issued.

You enter: / **Worksheet** **G**lobal **R**ecalculation

In this recalculation menu on your screen now

Natural Columnwise Rowwise Automatic Manual Iteration

Automatic and Manual are adjacent opposite options with Automatic being the default. In automatic recalculation, the entire worksheet is recalculated any time an entry or change occurs. In manual recalculation, the worksheet isn't recalculated until you command.

You enter: **Manual**

Note beforehand that the F6 entry will not change with the next entry.

You enter into F3: **8000 [Return]**

There's no wait for READY mode now. This could be quite dangerous if you don't realize that the values are not correct because they have not been updated. The CALC indicator at the bottom of the screen is a warning that none of the values on the screen can be taken seriously yet.

[F9/CALC]

To tell 1-2-3 to recalculate the worksheet, the ninth function key is used.

You enter: **[F9/CALC]**

The WAIT indicator flashes. When READY mode returns, the CALC indicator will disappear to signal that all numbers are up to date.

WARNING: Never leave a worksheet in manual recalculation mode. Immediately after you finish making entries, change recalculation back to automatic.

I have at times used and printed data that was not up to date because I forgot to hit [F9/CALC] after entering data. This mistake is more likely to occur in a worksheet created some time before and saved with the recalculation setting as manual.

You enter: **/ Worksheet Global Recalculation Automatic**

Save the file as is for an exercise at the end of the lesson.

You enter: **/ File Save FROGGY2 [Return]**

You: **View the global settings.**

Note that Recalculation is shown as Automatic.

You may choose the order of cell recalculation as one of three options: Natural, Columnwise, or Rowwise. In the /Worksheet Global Recalculation sub-menu, these three are adjacent opposite options. Rowwise recalculates the cells in this order: A1, B1, C1,..., A2, B2, C2, ..., A3, etc. or first row, second row, etc. Columnwise recalculates in this order: A1, A2, A3, ..., B1, B2, B3, ..., C3, etc. or column A, column B, etc. Natural is the default. If cell A2 depends on the contents of cell B6, B6 is calculated first and then A2. In other words, before calculating a formula, it first calculates the contents of its referenced cells. You use columnwise or rowwise only when you must control the order of the recalculation.

Iteration sets the number of times the worksheet is recalculated. It is used if the recalculation method is rowwise or columnwise or if the method is natural with a circular reference (see below).

Circular References

Below are three worksheets with circular references. The global format is Text so that the formulas can be seen.

Figure 14-5. Circular Reference - Cell Depends on Itself.

Figure 14-6. Circular Reference - Two Cells Depend on Each Other.

Figure 14-7. Circular Reference - Chain of Dependent Cells.

Create Figure 14-5.

You enter: / **Worksheet Erase Yes**

You enter into A1: **+A1 [Return]**

A CIRC indicator is shown on the bottom of the screen. How can 1-2-3 possibly compute cell A1 when it depends on itself? (Some mathematical applications use circular references with a number of iterations.) When a formula cell contains a cell reference which depends directly (as in Figure 14-6) or indirectly (as in Figure 14-7) on the formula cell, a circular reference occurs. Look at the three previous figures to see how this could happen. More complicated formulas make circular references difficult to find. The Auditor add-in is helpful in finding circular references. See page 680.

EXERCISES

1. Retrieve the FROGGIES file and display it on the screen as in the worksheet below. Start with the pointer in D4 and use /Worksheet Titles. Use the row numbers on the left and column letters on top as a reference.

	A	B	C	K	L	M
1			FROGGIE'S			
2		Jan	Feb	Oct	Nov	Dec
3	Beer	9000	9300	11700	12000	12300
17	Total Expenses	8964	8883	8235	8154	8073
18						
19	Net Income	18336	19317	27165	28146	29127
20						

2. Retrieve the FROGGIES file and display it on the screen as in the worksheet below. Use both titles and windows and go by the row numbers and column letters.

	A	M	N	O		C	D
1					1	FROGGIE'S BAR & GR	
2		Dec			2	Feb	Mar
12	Mortgage	897			3	9300	9600
13	Utilities	896			4	9400	9700
14	Phone	895			5	9500	9800
15	Insurance	894			6	28200	29100
16	Taxes	893			7		
17	Total Expenses	8073			8	991	982
18					9	990	981
19	Net Income	29127			10	989	980
20					11	988	979
21					12	987	978
22					13	986	977
23					14	985	976
24					15	984	975
25					16	983	974
26					17	8883	8802
27					18		
28					19	19317	20298

3. Retrieve FROGGY2 and change cells B8..B16 to those in the worksheet below. To save time, change the recalculation method. Don't forget to change it back to automatic when you're done.

	A	B	C	D	E	F
1			FROGGIE'S BAR & GRILL			
2		Jan	Feb	Mar	Apr	May
3	Beer	9000	9300	9600	9900	10200
4	Liquor	9100	9400	9700	10000	10300
5	Food	9200	9500	9800	10100	10400
6	Total Income	27300	28200	29100	30000	30900
7						
8	Labor	200	991	982	973	964
9	Beer	400	990	981	972	963
10	Liquor	200	989	980	971	962
11	Food	300	988	979	970	961
12	Mortgage	100	987	978	969	960
13	Utilities	170	986	977	968	959
14	Phone	340	985	976	967	958
15	Insurance	222	984	975	966	957
16	Taxes	999	983	974	965	956
17	Total Expenses	2931	8883	8802	8721	8640
18						
19	Net Income	24369	19317	20298	21279	22260

4. Retrieve FROGGIES and compare the food costs in February to those in October. Use windows.

LOOKUP @ FUNCTIONS

Contents:

This lesson covers the process of looking up numbers in tables. The vertical and horizontal lookup functions use the contents of cells as search numbers. The index function uses offsets into tables to retrieve the number.

Create Figure 15-1 and save under the name ALLSHOP if you have not already done so in another lesson. If you have, retrieve the file. Do not modify the file on disk by saving it with modifications, as you will need it, as is, in other lessons.

```
           A          B          C        D
 1              ALLSHOP RESTAURANT SERVICE, INC.
 2
 3     ITEM #   DESCRIPTION    PRICE   CLASS
 4
 5       1048 GROUND GINGER    $1.29 SPICE
 6       2668 TIDAL LIQUID     $3.99 DETERGENT
 7       3555 PICKLING SPICE   $1.39 SPICE
 8       4874 ARROWROOT        $2.19 SPICE
 9       4913 WOODITE          $2.49 DETERGENT
10       5104 DILL WEED        $1.79 SPICE
11       6125 JEST SOAP        $2.09 DETERGENT
12       6270 CELERY SEED      $1.35 SPICE
```

Figure 15-1. ALLSHOP Worksheet.

@VLOOKUP(x,table range,offset)

@VLOOKUP(x,table range,offset) performs a lookup by vertically searching down the first column of a table until the search number is found. It then moves "offset" number of columns to the right and returns the value in that cell.

You enter into A15: **@VLOOKUP(3555,A5..D12,2) [Return]**

1.39 is displayed in A15 as is shown in Figure 15-2.

The column being searched must be in ascending order. (See /Data Sort for the command used to sort a database.)

```
A15: [W8] @VLOOKUP(3555,A5..D12,2)


          A          B              C       D
 1            ALLSHOP RESTAURANT SERVICE, INC.
 2
 3     ITEM #    DESCRIPTION        PRICE  CLASS
 4
 5        1048 GROUND GINGER        $1.29 SPICE
 6        2668 TIDAL LIQUID         $3.99 DETERGENT
 7        3555 PICKLING SPICE       $1.39 SPICE
 8        4874 ARROWROOT            $2.19 SPICE
 9        4913 WOODITE              $2.49 DETERGENT
10        5104 DILL WEED            $1.79 SPICE
11        6125 JEST SOAP            $2.09 DETERGENT
12        6270 CELERY SEED          $1.35 SPICE
13
14
15        1.39
16
```

Figure 15-2. @VLOOKUP Function.

The table in which the lookup is performed is the second argument, A5..D12. Note that you do not include titles or column headers as part of the table. The search for the first argument, 3555, is begun at cell A5, which is the first entry in the first column of the table. The search moves vertically down the first column until 3555 is found in A7. The entry returned is 2 columns (third argument) to the right of 3555 or $1.39. If you want A15 in Currency format, you must format it.

Let's set up a cleaner way to look up prices of items. First name the table range.

You enter: / **Range Name Create ITEMTBL [Return] A5..D12 [Return]**

Add a few rows above the table.

You enter: / **Worksheet Insert Row A2..A4 [Return]**

You enter into A3: **Item: [Return]**

You enter into C3: **Price: [Return]**

You enter into A4: **3555 [Return]**

You enter into C4: **@VLOOKUP(A4,ITEMTBL,2) [Return]**

You enter into C4: / **Range Format Currency 2 [Return] [Return]**

Your worksheet should look like Figure 15-3.

```
C4: (C2) @VLOOKUP(A4,ITEMTBL,2)


        A          B           C       D
1            ALLSHOP RESTAURANT SERVICE, INC.
2
3    Item:                  Price:
4       3555                  $1.39
5
6    ITEM #   DESCRIPTION     PRICE   CLASS
7
8       1048 GROUND GINGER    $1.29 SPICE
9       2668 TIDAL LIQUID     $3.99 DETERGENT
10      3555 PICKLING SPICE   $1.39 SPICE
11      4874 ARROWROOT        $2.19 SPICE
12      4913 WOODITE          $2.49 DETERGENT
13      5104 DILL WEED        $1.79 SPICE
14      6125 JEST SOAP        $2.09 DETERGENT
15      6270 CELERY SEED      $1.35 SPICE
16
17
18      1.39
19
```

Figure 15-3. @VLOOKUP with First Argument as Cell Reference.

By having the first argument set up as a cell reference (A4) instead of a constant as before, a quick price look-up of any item number is now possible by simply changing the referenced cell.

Let's assume there are really several hundred items in this list and most cannot be seen on the screen.

You enter into A4: **5104 [Return]**

You can look up any entry in the right-most 3 columns of the table.

You enter into B3: **Description: [Down]**

You enter into B4: **@VLOOKUP(A4,ITEMTBL,1) [Return]**

You enter into D3: **Class: [Down]**

You enter into D4: **@VLOOKUP(A4,ITEMTBL,3) [Return]**

Your worksheet should look like Figure 15-4.

```
           A           B              C        D
1              ALLSHOP RESTAURANT SERVICE, INC.
2
3   Item:      Description:   Price:   Class:
4       5104 DILL WEED         $1.79 SPICE
5
6   ITEM #    DESCRIPTION      PRICE    CLASS
7
8       1048 GROUND GINGER     $1.29 SPICE
9       2668 TIDAL LIQUID      $3.99 DETERGENT
10      3555 PICKLING SPICE    $1.39 SPICE
11      4874 ARROWROOT         $2.19 SPICE
12      4913 WOODITE           $2.49 DETERGENT
13      5104 DILL WEED         $1.79 SPICE
14      6125 JEST SOAP         $2.09 DETERGENT
15      6270 CELERY SEED       $1.35 SPICE
16
17
18      1.39
19
```

Figure 15-4. @VLOOKUP with Different Offsets.

One very important fact to remember about @VLOOKUP functions is that the first or search column in the table must be sorted in ascending order. If the table is not in order, /Data Sort will quickly do it for you. (See index.)

If the search number does not exist in the table, the greatest number less than the search number is "found". To make this clearer:

You enter into A4: **2670 [Return]**

Moving vertically down the first column of the table, the first number greater than the 2670 search number is 3555. The previous entry, 2668, is found; it is the greatest number less than the search number 2670. As you can see, this simply will not do. In some cases, this is perfectly ok, such as postage cost for a range of package weights or a letter grade for a range of number grades. (See exercises at the end of this lesson.) But here, an order for item # 2670 will cause Tidal Detergent to be mistakenly shipped.

To display an error message in the case of a non-existent item number, the @IF function can be used.

You enter into B4:

@IF(A4=@VLOOKUP(A4,ITEMTBL,0),@VLOOKUP(A4,ITEMTBL,1) ,"Item #Not Found") [Return]

Your worksheet should look like Figure 15-5.

```
B4: [W16] @IF(A4=@VLOOKUP(A4,ITEMTBL,0),@VLOOKUP(A4,ITEMTBL,1),"Item # Not Found")
              A          B          C       D        E        F        G
   1          ALLSHOP RESTAURANT SERVICE, INC.
   2
   3     Item:   Description:   Price:   Class:
   4        2670 Item # Not Found   $3.99 DETERGENT
   5
   6     ITEM #   DESCRIPTION      PRICE   CLASS
   7
   8        1048 GROUND GINGER      $1.29 SPICE
   9        2668 TIDAL LIQUID       $3.99 DETERGENT
  10        3555 PICKLING SPICE     $1.39 SPICE
  11        4874 ARROWROOT          $2.19 SPICE
  12        4913 WOODITE            $2.49 DETERGENT
  13        5104 DILL WEED          $1.79 SPICE
  14        6125 JEST SOAP          $2.09 DETERGENT
  15        6270 CELERY SEED        $1.35 SPICE
  16
  17
  18        1.39
  19
```

Figure 15-5. @IF to Warn of Non-existent Search Number.

If A4 is the same as the entry in the ITEM # column (0 offset), then the description is returned, otherwise "Item # Not Found" is returned. A similar function can be placed into C4 and D4.

If the search number is less than the first entry in the search column, ERR is returned.

You enter into A4: **1047 [Return]**

ERR is displayed in B4, C4, and D4 because the first entry in the table, 1048, is greater than the search number, 1047, and @VLOOKUP cannot return the previous value because there is none.

ERR will also be displayed if the offset argument is outside the table range.

- - - If you need a break, stop at this point. - - -

@HLOOKUP(x,table range,offset)

@HLOOKUP(x,table range,offset) is similar to @VLOOKUP except the search proceeds horizontally across the top row of the table. It then moves down "offset" number of rows into the table to get the entry to be returned.

Retrieve the SHOES worksheet from the graph lessons and modify row 3 to make it look like Figure 15-6.

```
A13: [W13]

            A         B         C         D         E         F
1                     ATHLETIC SHOES ARE US
2
3                     1         2         3         4         5
4
5    Running         43      1000        32        14      1089
6    Racquetball     21         9        26        49       105
7    Squash          46        55        43        28       172
8    Aerobic         37        25        19        13        94
9    ----------------------------------------------------------
10      Total       147      1089       120       104      1460
```

Figure 15-6. SHOES Worksheet Slightly Modified.

Set up @HLOOKUP to do a look-up of the quarter 4 sales of racquetball shoes.

You enter into A13: **@HLOOKUP(4,B3..F10,3) [Return]**

Your worksheet should look like Figure 15-7.

```
A13: [W13] @HLOOKUP(4,B3..F10,3)


          A          B         C         D         E         F
 1                      ATHLETIC SHOES ARE US
 2
 3                      1         2         3         4         5
 4
 5    Running          43      1000        32        14      1089
 6    Racquetball      21         9        26        49       105
 7    Squash           46        55        43        28       172
 8    Aerobic          37        25        19        13        94
 9                 -----------------------------------------------
10       Total        147      1089       120       104      1460
11
12
13            49
14
```

Figure 15-7. @HLOOKUP Function.

Displayed in A13 is 49. The search starts in the first cell, B3, of the
search row B3..F3 and continues horizontally until the first argument 4 is
found in E3. The offset should be 3 for racquetball, not 2, because you
must count the blank row, row 4, in the offset count.

The rules for the horizontal lookups are similar to vertical lookups. The
numbers in the horizontal search row must be sorted in ascending order
from left to right. A non-existent search number will cause the return of
the greatest number less than it. Both functions' search argument must
be of type value, although the entry returned can be of type label (as
"Item # Not Found"). This is why the label entries QTR1, QTR2, etc.
had to be changed to the values 1, 2, etc.

Retrieve the original SHOES file as shown in Figure 15-8.

```
          A          B         C         D         E         F         G
 1                      ATHLETIC SHOES ARE US
 2
 3                    QTR1      QTR2      QTR3      QTR4   YEARLY SALES
 4
 5    Running          43      1000        32        14      1089
 6    Racquetball      21         9        26        49       105
 7    Squash           46        55        43        28       172
 8    Aerobic          37        25        19        13        94
 9                 -----------------------------------------------
10       Total        147      1089       120       104      1460
```

Figure 15-8. Original SHOES Worksheet.

@INDEX(range,column offset,row offset)

@INDEX(range,column offset,row offset) returns the entry in the cell where the column offset and the row offset intersect.

You enter into A13: **@INDEX(A3..F10,4,2) [Return]**

14 is the entry 4 columns to the right and 2 rows down from the upper left corner of the table. The top row of the table is counted as row 0 and the left-most column is considered column 0. The last 2 arguments are not search numbers, but offsets. If they are not whole numbers, the integer part is used. As you probably suspect, ERR is returned if they are out of the range. ERR is also returned if either is negative.

The next example is a trick you can use with @INDEX.

	A	B	C	D	E	F	G
1			XYZ REVENUES				
2							
3				Period			
4		1	2	3	4		
5	1988	$4,592	$2,394	$9,123	$7,654	Enter year number:	1989
6	1989	$4,730	$2,466	$9,397	$7,884	Enter period number:	3
7	1990	$4,872	$2,540	$9,679	$8,120		
8	1991	$5,018	$2,616	$9,969	$8,364	Revenues are:	$9,379
9	1992	$5,168	$2,694	$10,268	$8,615		

Figure 15-9. @INDEX Function.

In the figure above, @INDEX(A4..E9,3,2) would return $9,397 because it is 3 columns over and 2 columns down from the upper left corner of range, cell A4. It is associated with period 3 of 1989.

When the first column or row of an index table has increasing values with a difference of 1 (as in the years 1888 through 1992 above), a simple arithmetic expression can adjust the index arguments to allow a value input instead of an offset.

In the figure above, cells G5 and G6 are value inputs into the @INDEX function in G8: @INDEX(A4..E9,G6,G5-1988+1). The user can change the contents of G5 and G6 to retrieve other revenue figures.

EXERCISES

1. Create the worksheet below and save under the name JOURNAL
    if you have not already done so in another lesson. If you have,
    retrieve the file. Do not modify the file on disk by saving it with
    modifications as you will need it in other lessons.

```
         A         B          C              D                E
              FROGGIE'S BAR CHECK DISBURSEMENTS JOURNAL
      CHECK    DATE     AMOUNT          TO               CLASS
        283 12-Jan-89  $147.00 HARVEY COOK         LABORKROOM
        284 12-Jan-89  $230.00 FRED BARTENDER      LABORBROOM
        285 12-Jan-89  $945.38 FROZEN PACKERS      FOOD
        286 13-Jan-89  $533.99 BETTER BEVERAGE     BEER KEG
        287 14-Jan-89  $168.00 BEST FOODS          FOOD
        288 14-Jan-89  $203.41 FROZEN PACKERS      FOOD
        289 14-Jan-89  $230.00 FRED BARTENDER      LABORBROOM
        290 14-Jan-89  $217.00 FLOYD DISHWASHER    LABORKROOM
        291 16-Jan-89  $768.03 FROZEN PACKERS      FOOD
        292 17-Jan-89  $602.50 BOAT BOTTLING       BEER CAN
        293 17-Jan-89  $125.86 BETTER BEVERAGE     BEER KEG
```

Add the entries in the first 4 rows in the worksheet below. C1 is
an input cell and will be changed by the user to look up the
information in C3..C4 which contain formulas.

```
          A         B          C              D                E
   1  Check Number:         286
   2
   3  Amount:            $533.99
   4  Written to:        BETTER BEVERAGE
   5
   6
   7        FROGGIE'S BAR CHECK DISBURSEMENTS JOURNAL
   8  CHECK    DATE     AMOUNT          TO               CLASS
   9    283 12-Jan-89  $147.00 HARVEY COOK         LABORKROOM
  10    284 12-Jan-89  $230.00 FRED BARTENDER      LABORBROOM
  11    285 12-Jan-89  $945.38 FROZEN PACKERS      FOOD
  12    286 13-Jan-89  $533.99 BETTER BEVERAGE     BEER KEG
  13    287 14-Jan-89  $168.00 BEST FOODS          FOOD
  14    288 14-Jan-89  $203.41 FROZEN PACKERS      FOOD
  15    289 14-Jan-89  $230.00 FRED BARTENDER      LABORBROOM
  16    290 14-Jan-89  $217.00 FLOYD DISHWASHER    LABORKROOM
  17    291 16-Jan-89  $768.03 FROZEN PACKERS      FOOD
  18    292 17-Jan-89  $602.50 BOAT BOTTLING       BEER CAN
  19    293 17-Jan-89  $125.86 BETTER BEVERAGE     BEER KEG
```

Shipping Weight	1	2	3	4
2 lbs. or under	$3.00	$3.25	$3.50	$3.75
2 lbs. 1 oz. to 4 lbs.	$5.00	$5.50	$6.00	$6.50
4 lbs. 1 oz. to 10 lbs.	$7.00	$7.50	$8.00	$8.50
over 10 lbs.	$16.00	$18.00	$20.00	$25.00

2. Given the table of delivery rates above, set up a worksheet for VPS Overnight Delivery Co. to determine the cost of shipping a package given its weight and the zone number of its destination. Your worksheet should be similar to the setup below.

```
            QPS OVERNIGHT DELIVERY CO.

Weight:          Zone:          Cost:


table range.................................
      .                                    .
      .                                    .
      .                                    .
      .                                    .
.............................................
```

	A	B	C	D	E	F
1		Test Average		Grade	Point Value	
2	Alunni, Angelo	80.5				
3	Carver, Clementine	86.0				
4	Cicilioni, Fred	76.0				
5	Cicilioni, John	79.0				
6	Falzett, Rose					
7	Killian, Nicholas	58.0				
8	Minster, Catharine	91.5				
9	Sesak, Flora	97.0				
10	Shepard, Gary	42.0				
11	Washington, Barbara	86.5				
12						
13						
14						
15	Cutoff	0	60	70	80	90
16	Letter Grade	F	D	C	B	A
17	Point Value	0.0	1.0	2.0	3.0	4.0

3. Given the worksheet above where all cells contain constants, use your knowledge of lookup @ functions to enter two formulas and copy them down the Grade and Point Value columns in order to produce the worksheet below. (Retrieving the GRADES file and using /Range Erase and /Range Value will save some typing, however don't modify the original file on disk by saving over the name GRADES.)

	A	B	C	D	E	F
1		Test Average		Grade	Point Value	
2	Alunni, Angelo	80.5		B	3	
3	Carver, Clementine	86.0		B	3	
4	Cicilioni, Fred	76.0		C	2	
5	Cicilioni, John	79.0		C	2	
6	Falzett, Rose			F	0	
7	Killian, Nicholas	58.0		F	0	
8	Minster, Catharine	91.5		A	4	
9	Sesak, Flora	97.0		A	4	
10	Shepard, Gary	42.0		F	0	
11	Washington, Barbara	86.5		B	3	
12						
13						
14						
15	Cutoff	0	60	70	80	90
16	Letter Grade	F	D	C	B	A
17	Point Value	0.0	1.0	2.0	3.0	4.0

4. Set up a tax table with column headers as number of dependents and row borders on left as wage cut-offs. Use @INDEX to pull from the table an amount of income tax associated with an employee's wages and exemptions.

5.   A.   Create the worksheet below and save under CARD15A. There are two lookup functions. One, in A5, looks up the number in cell A4 in the table range D4..E7. The other, in C5 looks up the number in cell C4 in the table range D9..E21.

```
      A    B    C    D    E
1
2   Draw a card:
3
4      13        3    1 Hearts
5   King of Spades    2 Diamonds
6                     3 Spades
7                     4 Clubs
8
9                     1 Ace
10                    2   2
11                    3   3
12                    4   4
13                    5   5
14                    6   6
15                    7   7
16                    8   8
17                    9   9
18                   10  10
19                   11 Jack
20                   12 Queen
21                   13 King
22
```

B.   If you have done Lesson 6, use @RAND to randomly generate a number from 1 to 13 in cell A4 and to randomly generate a number from 1 to 4 in cell C4. Use /Worksheet Column Hide and /Range Format Hidden to hide most cells in the worksheet so that it looks like the one below. Use [F9/CALC] to draw a new card. Save under CARD15B.

```
      A    B    C
1
2   Draw a card:
3
4
5   King of Spades
6
7        Hit F9 to draw another card.
8
```

CUMULATIVE EXERCISES

C1. Create the worksheet below by retrieving the TOFU1 worksheet which you created in Lesson 1 and deleting rows 15 through 19. Create rows 16 and 17 by using the vertical lookup @ function. When a the employee number (a number from 1 to 10) is input into A17, the four output cells in B17..E17 should show the data associated with the number of that rep. Save under TOFU15.

```
        A           B           C         D          E
1               IMITATION TOFU, INCORPORATED
2
3           SalesRep      Division   92 Sales   Commission
4       ================================================
5          1 Saxe, J.        2        $40,500     $2,430
6          2 Gress, R.       3        $77,000     $4,620
7          3 Cosner, L.      3        $23,400     $1,404
8          4 Smith, A.       1       $150,000     $9,000
9          5 Smith, B.       1        $54,700     $3,282
10         6 Kirlin, K.      2        $75,000     $4,500
11         7 Wodak, F.       1        $29,800     $1,788
12         8 Reese, J.       3       $111,300     $6,678
13         9 Gruss, M.       1        $88,200     $5,292
14        10 Boyle, T.       2        $67,600     $4,056
15
16  Input: SalesRep      Division   92 Sales   Commission
17         4 Smith, A.       1       $150,000     $9,000
18
```

C2. Create the worksheet below by retrieving the FISH1 worksheet which you created in Lesson 1 and deleting rows 15 and 16. Change the field headers as shown. Sort the data by item number. This is one case where you had to do a previous lesson (the /Data Sort Lesson) before doing this exercise. Actually, you can re-enter the data in order which would be a ridiculous waste of time.

A. Create rows 16 and 17 by using the vertical lookup @ function. When the item number is input into A17, the four output cells in B17..E17 should show the data associated with that item. Save under FISH15A.

```
          A              B          C       D       E        F
1              H A P P Y   T R O P I C A L   F I S H   S T O R E
2    Item #        Item Name      Sold   Retail Wholesale  Profit
3       111 piranha                  3   $10.99    $5.00   $5.99
4       130 underwater fern         13    $2.29    $0.90   $1.39
5       162 goldfish               241    $0.59    $0.10   $0.49
6       192 20-inch eel              4    $8.99    $4.00   $4.99
7       198 turtle                  -1    $3.99    $1.50   $2.49
8       238 1-lb. decorative rocks  49    $2.99    $1.30   $1.69
9       256 8-vitamin fish food     57    $1.79    $0.80   $0.99
10      273 7-inch fish net         63    $1.99    $0.70   $1.29
11      274 2-gallon fish bowl      25    $4.99    $2.00   $2.99
12      281 40-gallon aquarium      14   $39.99   $22.00  $17.99
13
14
15
16   Item #        Item Name      Sold   Retail Wholesale
17      256 8-vitamin fish food    57    $1.79    $0.80
18
```

B. Insure that an invalid input number will not cause invalid output. Let the output from an invalid number be similar to the output shown below. Save under FISH15B.

```
          A              B          C       D       E
15
16   Item #        Item Name      Sold   Retail Wholesale
17      170 Invalid item #, re-enter.
```

C3. Create the worksheet below by retrieving the BILL1 worksheet which you created in Lesson 1 and deleting rows 13 and 14. Sort the data by Expense Item. This is one case where you had to do a previous lesson (the /Data Sort Lesson) before doing this exercise. Actually, you can re-enter the data in order which would be a ridiculous waste of time. Create rows 14 and 15 by using the vertical lookup @ function. When the expense item name is input into A15, the three output cells in B15..D15 should show the data associated with that expense. Save under BILL15.

	A	B	C	D
1		MONTHLY BILLS FOR MARCH		
2				
3	Expense Item	Actual	Budgeted	Over/(Under)
4	Food	$238	$220	$18
5	Rent	$550	$550	$0
6	Phone	$39	$30	$9
7	Electric	$43	$50	($7)
8	Gasoline	$56	$45	$11
9	Car Payment	$345	$345	$0
10	Insurance	$55	$55	$0
11	Charge Cards	$250	$100	$150
12	Entertainment	$150	$100	$50
13				
14	Expense Item	Actual	Budgeted	Over/(Under)
15	Phone	$39	$30	$9
16				

C4. Retrieve the GOLF1 worksheet that you created in Lesson 1 and modify it to look like the worksheet below. Use a lookup function in cell B10, the output cell. When a name is entered into A10, the input cell, cell B10 should show the person's total score. Save under GOLF15.

	A	B	C	D	E	F	G	H	I	J	K
1			J & F GOLF COURSE SCORE SHEET								
2	Name	1	2	3	4	5	6	7	8	9	Total
3	Joe	8	5	6	4	4	5	6	4	4	46
4	Mary	4	6	5	4	6	4	5	5	3	42
5	Mike	3	7	6	4	5	5	6	5	4	45
6	Sheila	5	5	6	4	3	3	4	6	5	41
7											
8											
9	Name	Total									
10	Mary	42									
11											

FILE
OPERATIONS

Contents:

This lesson covers file manipulations, including combining worksheets in different files together and storing parts of worksheets to separate files on disk. The importing of files created by other software into a 1-2-3 worksheet is discussed. Creating generic text or ASCII files from a 1-2-3 worksheet which can be used in other software is discussed in the Advanced Printing Lesson.

/File Erase

/File Erase deletes files from disk. The sub-menu:

Worksheet Print Graph Other

will appear. Choosing any of these four options will cause a list of files to appear on the third line of the screen. [F3/NAME] will cause a full screen list of files.

Releases 2 and 2.01: [F3/NAME] doesn't work in this command.

Choosing Worksheet will list only worksheet files; Print will list only .PRN files created with the /Print File command; Graph will list only .PIC files created with the /Graph Save command; and Other will list files of all types including those not created with Lotus.

/File Directory

/File Directory allows you to change the default directory. Enter the path after the prompt. (See your DOS manual for more information on directories.) This command must be used to change default disks.

When you do a /File Save or any other file operation, this current directory is the default. You need not change the current directory if you wish to save a file to another directory. Files can be saved to directories other than the default by typing the directory before the filename. Use [Esc] to clear the default directory first.

/Worksheet Global Default Directory

This command sets up the default directory upon entry into 1-2-3. This command must be followed with a /Worksheet Global Default Update in order to change the 123.CNF file on disk.

What is the difference between /File Directory and /Worksheet Global Default Directory? If you change the default directory with /File Directory, that directory is in effect for the rest of the session. When you Exit Lotus, it goes away. Upon entry into Lotus next time, the directory set up by the /Worksheet Global Default Directory is in effect.

Combining Files

/File Combine superimposes one worksheet over another beginning at the position of the cell pointer.

You: **Retrieve the SCRANTON file.**

You: **Position the pointer to A11.**

You enter: **/File Combine Copy Entire-File**

Computer message: Enter name of file to combine:

You: **Choose any file.**

The file you chose is added to the bottom of the SCRANTON file. /File Combine is different from /File Retrieve in that it does not erase the existing worksheet. It overlays the combined worksheet beginning at the cell pointer position (not necessarily home), and leaves the previously existing worksheet's global settings intact.

You can combine a part of one file into another, but you must name the part of the worksheet you wish to combine.

You enter: **/File Combine Copy**

This menu Entire-File Named/Specified-Range is where you specify the named range to be combined.

You: **Return to READY mode.**

```
         A          B          C          D          E          F          G
1   January                  Paid       Total
2                   Wages   Holidays  Gross Pay                 1989
3   Joe            $1,400      $40      $1,440              New Year's Day
4   Mary           $1,300      $30      $1,330
5   Fred            $400      none       $400               one paid holiday
```

Figure 16-1. JAN Worksheet.

```
         A          B          C          D          E          F
1   FEBRUARY                 PAID       TOTAL                   1988
2                  WAGES   HOLIDAYS  GROSS PAY
3   JOE           $900.00    NONE     $900.00
4   MARY          $700.00   $0.00     $700.00              NO PAID
5   FRED          $200.00   $0.00     $200.00              HOLIDAYS
```

Figure 16-2. FEB Worksheet.

```
         A          B          C          D          E          F
1   FEBRUARY                 PAID       TOTAL                   1988
2                  WAGES   HOLIDAYS  GROSS PAY                  1989
3   JOE          $2,300.00   NONE    $2,300.00
4   MARY         $2,000.00  $30.00   $2,030.00              NO PAID
5   FRED          $600.00   $0.00     $600.00               HOLIDAYS
```

Figure 16-3. JAN Worksheet Combine Added to FEB Worksheet.

```
         A          B          C          D          E          F
1   FEBRUARY                 PAID       TOTAL                   1988
2                  WAGES   HOLIDAYS  GROSS PAY                 -1989
3   JOE          ($500.00)   NONE    ($500.00)
4   MARY         ($600.00) ($30.00)  ($630.00)              NO PAID
5   FRED         ($200.00)  $0.00    ($200.00)              HOLIDAYS
```

Figure 16-4. JAN Worksheet Combine Subtracted to FEB Worksheet.

Figure 16-3 is the result of combine adding Figure 16-1 and Figure 16-2. First the FEB file was retrieved, then the JAN file was added to it with the /File Combine Add Entire-File command. Note that the global defaults were retained from the original file, FEB, and the settings from the added file, JAN, were not considered. Only values have been added, labels in JAN are ignored; New Year's Day has not been "added". Formulas from the file being added are computed to values and then added.

Figure 16-4 is the result of combine subtracting Figure 16-1 and Figure 16-2. First the FEB file was retrieved, then the JAN file was subtracted from it with the /File Combine Subtract Entire-File command. Note that 1989 was subtracted from cell F2 in the FEB file.

Named ranges can be combine added and subtracted to worksheets.

A file can be combined with itself.

Xtracting Files

/File Xtract is the inverse of /File Combine. It writes part of the worksheet to a file on disk.

You enter: **/File Xtract**

This menu **Formulas Values** requires you to specify how you want formulas handled. Choosing Formulas saves the formulas, as is, out to disk. Values saves the formulas as the constant values to which they currently compute.

Global settings in the existing worksheet are saved in the file with the xtracted part. Named ranges and graphs are also saved.

Importing Files

The /File Import command combines a standard ASCII file into the existing worksheet beginning at the cell pointer position. The ASCII file must be named with an extension of .PRN. (New releases don't require this extension.)

Word processors usually have commands to write files to disk in standard ASCII (or generic) format. Make sure when you write the file you give it the extension .PRN.

While in 1-2-3

You enter: **/ File Import**

The Text option in this sub-menu **Text Numbers** sub-menu will read the lines from the .PRN file and place them into long consecutive labels down the column beginning at the pointer position. See /Data Parse to break up the labels into individual cells.

You enter: **Text**

Computer message: **Enter name of file to import:**

Now enter the name of the .PRN file.

The Numbers option in the sub-menu is for .PRN files containing numerical data and labels, where the labels are enclosed in quotes. As an example, the records of the file may look like this:

"Sam Jones" 29 "accountant"
"Marie Smith" 27 "financial analyst"

If the cell pointer was in the home position, the label Sam Jones would be put in A1, the number 29 in B1, the label accountant in C1. Marie Smith in A2, 27 in B2, financial analyst in C2, etc.

/File View

Releases 2, 2.01, 2.2, 3.0, and 3.1+: Not available in these releases.

/File View invokes the Viewer add-in, if it is attached. The Viewer add-in allows you to look into worksheet files on disk. You can then retrieve one of them. See the Add-in Appendix for other features of the Viewer.

EXERCISES

1.   Create the worksheet below by manually typing A1..A5 and combining the SCRANTON file.

```
A1: [W3] 'Dear Mr. President:


      A        B            C            D            E
1  Dear Mr. President:
2
3  Below are the sales figures for our division
4  for February, 1988.  I hope you are pleased
5  with the increase from January's figures.
6
7           SCRANTON HARDWARE COMPANY, INCORPORATED
8
9                         Sales         Tax         Total
10
11  1 Nuts                $437.50      $26.25       $463.75
12  2 Bolts               $899.64      $53.98       $953.62
13  3 Screwdrivers         $76.23       $4.57        $80.80
14                     -------------------------------------
15          TOTAL       $1,413.37      $84.80     $1,498.17
```

2.

```
January Sales

Nuts            $400.00
Bolts           $800.00
Screwdrivers     $67.00
                ----------
              $1,267.00
```

```
February Sales

Nuts            $437.50
Bolts           $899.64
Screwdrivers     $60.00
                ----------
              $1,397.14
```

Create the two worksheets above in two different files named JANSALES and FEBSALES. Use /File Combine to generate the two worksheets below.

```
Yearly Sales to Date 3/1/89

Nuts            $837.50
Bolts         $1,699.64
Screwdrivers    $127.00
                ----------
              $2,664.14

------------------------------------------

Increase in Sales from Jan to Feb

Nuts             $37.50
Bolts            $99.64
Screwdrivers     ($7.00)
                ----------
                $130.14
```

3. Retrieve the FROGGIES worksheet created in Lesson 14. Create a column N consisting of the totals of all 12 months. Title it 1989 TOTALS.   Extract column A and save under FROGTITL. Extract column N and save under FROGTOT.   Extract the January column and save under FROGJAN.   Combine FROGTITL and FROGTOT so they look like the worksheet below:

	A	B
1		1989
2		TOTAL
3	Beer	127800
4	Liquor	129000
5	Food	130200
6	Total Income	387000
7		
8	Labor	11406
9	Beer	11394
10	Liquor	11382
11	Food	11370
12	Mortgage	11358
13	Utilities	11346
14	Phone	11334
15	Insurance	11322
16	Taxes	11310
17	Total Expenses	102222
18		
19	Net Income	284778

It's January 1 of 1990 and the owner of Froggie's wishes to estimate a total of figures for 13 months: from last January through December and the month yet to come - January, 1990. Adding last January's figures to the total will give a good 13 month total sale forecast.   Combine FROGJAN with the worksheet above to get the worksheet below:

	A	B
1		13-month
2		Estimate
3	Beer	136800
4	Liquor	138100
5	Food	139400
6	Total Income	414300
7		
8	Labor	12406
9	Beer	12393
10	Liquor	12380
11	Food	12367
12	Mortgage	12354
13	Utilities	12341
14	Phone	12328
15	Insurance	12315
16	Taxes	12302
17	Total Expenses	111186
18		
19	Net Income	303114

4. Create one worksheet combining the balance sheet from Lesson 4, Exercise 4B with the sources and uses of funds statement from Lesson 4, Exercise 4C.

5. Use Exercise 4C from Lesson 4. Create a similar statement for sources and uses of funds for the next year - period Dec. 31, 1989 to Dec. 31, 1990. Print the two statements and then print the sum of the two statements.

6. Use the L4FLUFFY worksheet from Lesson 4, Exercise 4D. Split it into 3 different worksheet files: an income statement file, a balance sheet file, and a file containing the ratios. Be careful of cell references.

7. Create two worksheet files from Lesson 5, Exercise 2E: a comparative income statement file and an expense and net income as a percentage of sales file. Be careful with cell references.

ADVANCED PRINTING

Contents:

Lesson 17 is an optional continuation of Lesson 2. It demonstrates how to get fancier printouts which include font changes, headers, footers, page numbering, and automatic dating. Possible problems with printing and how to solve them are explained.

Releases 2.3, 2.4, and 3.1+: The big thing in these new releases is an add-in called WYSIWYG. WYSIWYG pretty much makes this lesson obsolete. I suggest you do only the first part of this lesson (up to, but not including, the Options sub-menu) and forget the rest. Instead, read the WYSIWYG Appendix.

```
       A        B              C           D              E
  1                SCRANTON HARDWARE COMPANY, INCORPORATED
  2
  3                        Sales         Tax          Total
  4
  5      1 Nuts             $437.50      $26.25        $463.75
  6      2 Bolts            $899.64      $53.98        $953.62
  7      3 Screwdrivers      $76.23       $4.57         $80.80
  8              ----------------------------------------------
  9          TOTAL        $1,413.37      $84.80      $1,498.17
```

Figure 17-1. SCRANTON Worksheet.

Retrieve the SCRANTON file in Figure 17-1 and clear all print settings.

You enter: / File **Retrieve SCRANTON [Return]**

You enter: / **Print Printer Clear All Quit**

/Print File

You enter: / **Print**

The sub-menu Printer File is on the screen. You've been using the Printer option which sends the output to the printer. The option **File** sends the output to a file on disk. You may wish to send the output to a file in order to verify the output on the screen before printing it to paper. This saves time and paper. The DOS command TYPE can be used to display the output file on the screen. (See your DOS manual for more information.)

Release 2.3 and 2.4: The two additional options, Encoded and Background, allow printing to an encoded file and background printing. See encoded file and background printing in index.

Release 3.0 and 3.1+: There are four additional options on the menu: Encoded, Suspend, Resume, and Cancel. /Print Encoded creates an encoded file. See encoded file in index. Suspend temporarily suspends printing, Resume resumes printing, and Cancel aborts a print job.

Perhaps the most common use of the /Print File command is the creation of an ASCII file on disk for use in other software packages. For example, database packages can pull ASCII files into their database files. Word processing programs can retrieve ASCII files into their text files. Some database and word processing programs, like FoxPro 2.0® and WordPerfect 5.1®, can even pull worksheet files directly into them, thereby eliminating the need for /Print File for this purpose. Transporting data between software packages is common.

You enter: **File**

Computer message: Enter print file name:

1-2-3 is asking what the output file on disk is to be named.

You enter: **SCRANTON [Return]**

Output will now go to a file named SCRANTON.PRN on disk. The extension used on all print files is .PRN. If SCRANTON.PRN already exists on disk, 1-2-3 will now issue the Cancel Replace menu to verify an overwrite.

Set up the range and print.

You enter: **Range A1..E9 [Return] Go Quit**

The drive's light goes on showing that there is activity to the disk.
To verify that the file SCRANTON.PRN had been saved, list all files of type .PRN.

You enter: / **File List Print**

You enter: **[Return]**

To view the contents of the SCRANTON.PRN file, temporarily exit to DOS and use the TYPE command.

You enter: / **System**

Enter the TYPE command and followed by the subdirectory and the filename.

You enter: **TYPE \123R24\SCRANTON.PRN [Return]**

Figure 17-1 should be typed on the screen. As with the printer, the column headers A, B, and C and row number borders are not printed. Worksheet or .WK1 files are in a special format which cannot legibly be TYPEd on the screen or PRINTED using DOS. Try it.

You enter: **TYPE B:SCRANTON.WK1 [Return]**

Funny looking characters and noises should come out of your computer.

Return to 1-2-3.

You enter: **EXIT [Return]**

The rest of this lesson will cover the Options sub-menu.

You enter: / **Print Printer Options**

The Options menu is on your screen as below:

Header Footer Margins Borders Setup Pg-Length Other Quit

Releases 3.0 and 3.1+: The Name option allows you to assign a name to a group of print settings. The Advanced option allows you to setup colors, fonts, devices, and more for your print jobs.

Margins

The default margins are left margin, 4 spaces; right margin, 76; top margin, 2 lines; and bottom margin, 2 lines.

You enter: **Margins**

The sub-menu Left Right Top Bottom is displayed.

Releases 2.2, 2.3, 2.4, 3.0, and 3.1+:
None is an additional option which clears all margin settings. It initializes the left, top, and bottom margins to 0 and the right margin to 1000.

Choose one of these margin options and the current margin setting will be displayed. The maximum values for left or right margins is 240, for bottom or top margins it is 32.

Releases 3.0 and 3.1+: The maximum value for left and right margin is 1000. For top and bottom, it's 240.

A common problem with printing wide worksheets is the truncation of one or more columns on the right side of the page. The right-most columns are then printed a page-length below. This occurs when the columns in the print range cannot fit between the left and right margins. To see what I mean, return to READY mode and do the following.

You enter: / **Worksheet Global Column-Width 25 [Return]**

You enter: / **Print Printer Range A1..E9 [Return] Go Quit**

Your printout should be similar to Figure 17-2.

```
              SCRANTON HARDWARE COMPANY, INCORPORATED

                                Sales              Tax

1 Nuts                        $437.50           $26.25
2 Bolts                       $899.64           $53.98
3 Screwdrivers                 $76.23            $4.57
                       -------------------------------------
      TOTAL                 $1,413.37           $84.80




            Total

          $463.75
          $953.62
           $80.80
-------------------------------
          $1,498.17
```

Figure 17-2. Print Range Too Wide for Margins.

A solution to this problem is to widen the margins if your paper is wide enough or to change the size of the print (Print Setup is covered later in this lesson.) A software package called Sideways exists on the market which turns the print 90 degrees and allows almost an unlimited number of columns to be printed adjacently. (See Sideways Appendix.)

When printing to a file, several blank lines are placed in the file before the actual data. This number of blank lines can be changed with the Top option; also, blank lines can be deleted entirely by printing unformatted. (See Unformatted Printing in Lesson 2.)

Another possible problem you may run into is shown in Figure 17-3. It occurs when the margins are too wide for the paper width. Either use wider paper, thin the margins, or change the size of the print (see Print Setup below).

```
                        FROGGIE'S BAR & GRILL
                  Jan    Feb    Mar    Apr    May    June   July   Aug    Sept   Oct
    Nov    Dec
    Beer          9000   9300   9600   9900   10200  10500  10800  11100  11400  11700
12000  12300
    Liquor        9100   9400   9700   10000  10300  10600  10900  11200  11500  11800
12100  12400
    Food          9200   9500   9800   10100  10400  10700  11000  11300  11600  11900
12200  12500
    Total Income  27300  28200  29100  30000  30900  31800  32700  33600  34500  35400
36300  37200
```

Figure 17-3. Margins Too Wide for Paper.

You enter: / **Worksheet G**lobal **C**olumn-Width **15 [Return]**

Page-Length

The default page-length is 66 lines and can be changed with the Pg-Length option from the Options menu.

You enter: /**Print Printer O**ptions **P**g-Length

Computer message: Enter Lines per Page (10..100): 66

As you can see the page length can go from 10 to 100 lines.

Release 2.01, 2.2, 2.3, and 2.4: from 1 to 100
Releases 3.0 and 3.1+: from 1 to 1000

To save paper during the rest of this lesson, let's change the page length to 20.

You enter: **20 [Return]**

Borders

Borders are columns that are printed to the left of the print range on each page or rows that are printed above the print range on each page. Choose a print range consisting of only part of the worksheet.

You enter: **Quit Range D5..E9 [Return]**

You enter: **Options Borders Columns A1..B1 [Return] Quit**

It is good practice to use the Align option when you are beginning at the top of a new page to prevent the Page-Break problem mentioned in Lesson 2.

You enter: **Page Align Go**

Your printout should look like Figure 17-4.

```
1 Nuts               $26.25       $463.75
2 Bolts              $53.98       $953.62
3 Screwdrivers        $4.57        $80.80
                    --------------------------------
            TOTAL    $84.80     $1,498.17
```

Figure 17-4. Column Borders.

The first two columns of Figure 17-4 are actually the borders. The print range consists of the last two columns on the right.

If you include in the print range the columns which are also borders, you will get two copies of these columns. Change the range to include the column borders.

You enter: **Range A1..E9 [Return] Page Align Go**

The first part of your printout should be similar to Figure 17-5. The first two columns are the border. The next 2 identical columns are part of the print range. (The borders in your printout may have caused the problem shown in Figure 17-2.) Note SCRANT in the second column is a truncation of the title due to the comparatively short width of the second column.

```
        SCRANT           SCRANTON HARDWARE COMPANY, INCORPORATED

                                       Sales        Tax        Total
    1 Nuts            1 Nuts          $437.50      $26.25      $463.75
    2 Bolts           2 Bolts         $899.64      $53.98      $953.62
    3 Screwdrivers    3 Screwdrivers   $76.23       $4.57       $80.80
                                    --------------------------------------
        TOTAL            TOTAL       $1,413.37     $84.80     $1,498.17
```

Figure 17-5. Print Range includes Borders.

Column borders are useful for worksheets with many columns.

Row borders are printed at the top of each page. They will also be printed twice if also included in the print range. They are useful for worksheets with more rows than can fit on a page.

Recall that the Clear option resets settings to the default settings. Clear the border.

You enter: **Clear Borders**

Headers and Footers

A header is one line of text printed below the top margin of each page. Let's create a simple one.

You enter: **Options Header**

Computer message: Enter Header Line:

You may enter up to 240 characters if your page width and margins allow.

Releases 3.0 and 3.1+: up to 512 characters but cannot continue beyond right margin.

You enter:
This header will appear at the top of each page. [Return]

You enter: **Quit Page Align Go**

Your printout should look like Figure 17-6.

There are always two blank lines printed after the header and before the print range text.

```
This header will appear at the top of each page.

            SCRANTON HARDWARE COMPANY, INCORPORATED

                    Sales          Tax          Total

1 Nuts             $437.50       $26.25        $463.75
2 Bolts            $899.64       $53.98        $953.62
3 Screwdrivers      $76.23        $4.57         $80.80
            -------------------------------------------
      TOTAL       $1,413.37      $84.80      $1,498.17
```

Figure 17-6. Header in Printout.

A footer is a line of text printed above the bottom margin and two blank lines below the text from the print range.

Two special characters used in headers and footers, the at sign @ and the pound sign #. @ is replaced in the header or footer with the current date from DOS. # is replaced with the current page number.

You enter: **Options Footer**

Computer message: Enter Footer Line:

You enter: **This is the footer line. Date: @   # [Return] Q**uit

Issue a Page so that the worksheet will not be half on the bottom of this page and half on the top of the next.

You enter: **Page Go**

Your printout should be similar to Figure 17-7.

```
This header will appear at the top of each page.

          SCRANTON HARDWARE COMPANY, INCORPORATED

                    Sales         Tax         Total

1 Nuts             $437.50      $26.25       $463.75
2 Bolts            $899.64      $53.98       $953.62
3 Screwdrivers      $76.23       $4.57        $80.80
                 -------------------------------------------
        TOTAL    $1,413.37      $84.80     $1,498.17


This is the footer line. Date: 21-Dec-88          1



This header will appear at the top of each page.

          SCRANTON HARDWARE COMPANY, INCORPORATED

                    Sales         Tax         Total

1 Nuts             $437.50      $26.25       $463.75
2 Bolts            $899.64      $53.98       $953.62
3 Screwdrivers      $76.23       $4.57        $80.80
                 -------------------------------------------
        TOTAL    $1,413.37      $84.80     $1,498.17
```

Figure 17-7. Footer with Date (@) and Page Number (#).

The 1 in the footer line after the date is the page number. If your date is incorrect, you probably did not enter it correctly after booting up the system.

Another special character used in headers and footers is the split vertical bar |, usually found above the backslash. (It looks like ¦ on your keyboard, but on some printers it is printed |). | allows text to be centered and right justified in the header or footer. Clear the current header with [Esc] and re-enter it as follows.

You enter: **Options Header [Esc] @ | Page # | right-aligned [Return]**

Text following the first | will be centered in the header. Text following the second | will be right-aligned. Try it.

You enter: **Quit Page Go**

The Go should have caused Figure 17-8 to be added to the printout. Again, the 2 after the date in the footer is the page number.

```
This is the footer line. Date: 21-Dec-88        2



21-Dec-88                    Page 3                  right-aligned


          SCRANTON HARDWARE COMPANY, INCORPORATED

                         Sales          Tax         Total

1 Nuts                  $437.50       $26.25       $463.75
2 Bolts                 $899.64       $53.98       $953.62
3 Screwdrivers           $76.23        $4.57        $80.80
                      -------------------------------------------
        TOTAL         $1,413.37       $84.80     $1,498.17
```

Figure 17-8. Header with Centered and Right-aligned Text.

In the new header, the date is left-aligned, the Page # (current page number is 3) typed between the |'s is centered, and the "right-aligned" is flush right.

You need not have all three parts in order to use |, you can have just a right-aligned part, or a centered part, or a left-aligned and right-aligned part, etc. The table below shows examples.

```
Header or Footer                Printed Result
abc¦def¦ghi                     abc          def         ghi
abc¦¦ghi                        abc                      ghi
abc¦def                         abc          def
¦def                                         def
¦def¦ghi                                     def         ghi
¦¦ghi                                                    ghi
```

Table 17-1. Center and Right-Alignment Operator (|) in Headers/Footers.

Note in Figure 17-8 that no footer is printed on the bottom because the end of the page has not yet been reached. Your page length should still be 20 and we have not yet printed 20 lines. In a case like this, the issuance of a Page command will cause the footer to be printed at the bottom of the page.

You enter: **Page Quit**

/Worksheet Page

The /Worksheet Page command forces a page to be ejected, even if the text printed thus far on the page has not been enough to fill it or make a complete page. It places a page break marker in the worksheet to designate where the page should be ejected.

You enter into A11:
This text will be printed at the top of the next page. [Return]

You enter into A11: **/ Worksheet Page**

Your worksheet should look like Figure 17-9.

```
A12: [W3] "This text will be printed at the top of the next page.


        A        B              C            D            E
 1              SCRANTON HARDWARE COMPANY, INCORPORATED
 2
 3                            Sales          Tax         Total
 4
 5       1 Nuts               $437.50       $26.25      $463.75
 6       2 Bolts              $899.64       $53.98      $953.62
 7       3 Screwdrivers        $76.23        $4.57       $80.80
 8                        ------------------------------------
 9            TOTAL         $1,413.37       $84.80    $1,498.17
10
11     ::
12  This text will be printed at the top of the next page.
```

Figure 17-9. Page Break in Row 11.

The double colon is the indicator for the page break. A row has been inserted into which nothing should be entered as it will not be printed. Extend the print range to include the new cells and print.

You enter: **/ Print Printer Page Range A1..E12 [Return] Align Go**

Your printout should look like Figure 17-10.

```
21-Dec-88                    Page 1                    right-aligned


            SCRANTON HARDWARE COMPANY, INCORPORATED

                          Sales           Tax           Total

      1 Nuts             $437.50        $26.25         $463.75
      2 Bolts            $899.64        $53.98         $953.62
      3 Screwdrivers      $76.23         $4.57          $80.80
                         ---------------------------------------
           TOTAL        $1,413.37       $84.80       $1,498.17



  This is the footer line.  Date:  21-Dec-88        1




  21-Dec-88                    Page 2                    right-aligned

  This text will be printed at the top of the next page.
```

Figure 17-10. Print with Page Break.

To remove a page break, /Worksheet Delete Row can be used. /Range Erase (or a new entry in the cell with the page break) will remove the page break but not the inserted row.

Note that page numbering is initialized to 1 because of the Align.

You enter: **Quit**

Setup

A setup string is usually a string of 3 or 4 digits prefaced with a backslash (\) which changes the size of the print or the font. Your printer manual will indicate which printer control codes are applicable.

The Setup option is commonly used to decrease the size of printed characters so that more of them can fit across a line of print as in Figure 17-11.

FROGGIE'S BAR & GRILL

	Jan	Feb	Mar	Apr	May	June	July	Aug	Sept	Oct	Nov	Dec
Beer	9000	9300	9600	9900	10200	10500	10800	11100	11400	11700	12000	12300
Liquor	9100	9400	9700	10000	10300	10600	10900	11200	11500	11800	12100	12400
Food	9200	9500	9800	10100	10400	10700	11000	11300	11600	11900	12200	12500
Total Income	27300	28200	29100	30000	30900	31800	32700	33600	34500	35400	36300	37200

Figure 17-11. Print is Compressed with Setup Option.

Note that these thirteen columns fit across a standard sheet of paper when print is compressed.

Look for your printer's code which will produce compressed print (15 characters per inch). For example, an Epson printer's compressed code is 15. To change to compressed print, use the Setup option and enter the code with a backslash followed by three digits. The code 15 in this example should therefore be entered as \015. Print will now be done in a compressed form. To return to normal print of 10 characters per inch, the setup string is \018. To change to another setup string, it is usually necessary to turn the printer off and on.

Printer	Compressed	Normal
Epson, IBM, Star, Panasonic, Victor	\015	\018
BMC, C. Itoh, PMC, TEC	\027\081	\027\078
Brother, Comrex	\027\077	\027\080
Okidata 92, 93	\029	\030
Okidata 2350,3410	\027\066	\027\054
IDS	\031	\029

Figure 17-12. Setup Codes for Compressed and Normal Print.

You will most likely have to expand the right margin to prevent the problem in Figure 17-2.

You can also change the height of the characters by changing the line spacing from the default of 6 lines per inch to 8 lines per inch by changing the setup string. (Commonly \0270 for 8 lines and \0272 to go back to 6 lines). Another font possible with most printers is expanded or large print (See below).

Setup strings can be entered into worksheet cells to give you more than one size print or font in the same printout. Enter the setup string preceded by two split vertical bars (only one bar will be displayed on the screen). For example, you enter ||\015 [Return] into the cell where compressed printing is to begin and ||\018 [Return] where normal print is to be resumed. Figure 17-13 shows the contents of a worksheet and corresponding printout with the title in expanded print and the rest in compressed print.

```
A1: [W15] ||015


            A           B         C         D         E         F
1    |015
2                       FROGGIE'S BAR & GRILL
3    |018
4                       Jan       Feb       Mar       Apr       May
5    Beer              9000      9300      9600      9900     10200
6    Liquor            9100      9400      9700     10000     10300
7    Food              9200      9500      9800     10100     10400
8    Total Income     27300     28200     29100     30000     30900
```

Figure 17-13 A. Setup Codes as Entries in A1 and A2.

	Jan	Feb	Mar	Apr	May	June	July	Aug	Sept	Oct	Nov	Dec
Beer	9000	9300	9600	9900	10200	10500	10800	11100	11400	11700	12000	12300
Liquor	9100	9400	9700	10000	10300	10600	10900	11200	11500	11800	12100	12400
Food	9200	9500	9800	10100	10400	10700	11000	11300	11600	11900	12200	12500
Total Income	27300	28200	29100	30000	30900	31800	32700	33600	34500	35400	36300	37200

FROGGIE'S BAR & GRILL

Figure 17-13 B. Printout of Worksheet Containing Setup Codes.

The title is printed in expanded print and the rest of the text is compressed.

So either you can use the Setup option to change the font or size of all printing or you can enter setup strings directly into a cell of the worksheet to have more than one size or type of font in the same printout.

Releases 3.0 and 3.1+:
Additional options on the main print menu are:

Image - prints a graph, see Lesson 10.

Sample - shows current print settings and samples of your printer's capabilities. Try it.

Hold - takes you back to READY mode and allows you to continue working with worksheet, even if printing has not been completed.

/Worksheet Global Default Printer

Recall that the default page-length setting is 66 lines. You issued a /Print Printer Options Pg-Length command during this lesson and changed the current setting to 20 lines. This really is not the "default" setting which is still 66 lines. To verify this, Clear the setting and change it back to the default of 66 lines.

You enter: / **Print Printer Clear**

Now either All or Format will reset the page length to the 66 line default. Highlight Format and note the third line explanation.

You enter: **Format**

You enter: **Options Pg-Length**

Computer message: Enter Lines per Page (10..100): 66

The setting has indeed been reset to a default of 66.

There are also default settings for the 4 margins which can be changed with the /Print Printer Options Margins command.

Although /Print Printer Options will work for a single worksheet, it will not change the default settings (the ones you get initially or the ones to which settings are Cleared) nor will it affect other worksheet files.

It is possible to change a default margin or page-length setting from this SCRANTON worksheet so that it affects all other worksheet files as well as this one. A special configuration file, 123.CNF, exists on the Lotus diskette which initializes default settings for all worksheets. The print settings in this file can be changed with the /Worksheet Global Default Printer commands.

Let's say you wish the default page length setting for all worksheet files to be 20.

You enter: / **Worksheet Global Default Printer**

The sub-menu below is on your screen:

Interface Auto-LF Left Right Top Bottom Pg-Length Wait Setup Name Quit

You enter: **Pg-Length 20 [Return] Quit Quit**

To actually change the 123.CNF file, a /Worksheet Global Default Update command is necessary. (Don't do this Update command now because you probably don't want future worksheets to have a default page length of 20.)

To summarize, the defaults used for all future retrieved worksheets can be set from any worksheet with the use of two commands: 1) /Worksheet Global Default Printer to set the particular defaults and 2) /Worksheet Global Default Update to permanently set the new defaults in the 123.CNF file on disk.

Choosing Left, Right, Top, or Bottom from the menu shown above will allow a change to the default margins.

The other sub-menu options are:

Interface - To specify parallel or serial connection to printer. If serial, baud rate must be specified. Default is Parallel 1.

Auto-LF - To specify whether printer should automatically issue a line feed after a carriage return. Default is No.

Wait - To specify whether printer should pause after each page to let you change the paper in the case of single sheet feed printers. Default is No.

Setup - To specify a setup string in case your printer needs to be initialized. Default is blank.

Name - To select a printer if you installed with more than one. Default is the first printer selected during installation.

NEW COMMAND SUMMARY

/Print File

Sends output to file on disk rather than the printer. The file on disk is in ASCII format which is capable of being retrieved into most other proprietary software programs such as word processing programs. This can be used to merge a table of numbers created in Lotus into a text file.

/Print Printer Options Margins

Allows the top, bottom, left, and right margins to be changed from their current values.

/Print Printer Options Pg-Length

Allows the length of the page to be changed from its current value. Useful for other than standard size paper such as mailing labels and legal size paper.

/Print Printer Options Borders

Creates borders either at the top or on the left of each printed page consisting of designated rows or columns from the worksheet. The borders should not be included in the print range.

/Print Printer Options Header

Prints a one line header at the top of each page which may contain the page number or date if # or @ is used. | is used to space parts of the header.

/Print Printer Options Footer

Prints a one line footer at the top of each page. Also may contain #, @, and | mentioned in /Print Printer Options Header above.

/Worksheet Page

Inserts a special character into a cell in the worksheet to force a page eject at that row even though the current page has not been filled up with printed data.

/Print Printer Options Setup

Sends a setup string to the printer which changes the way the characters are printed. The size of the character or the font can be changed with this command.

/Worksheet Global Default Printer

Changes the default print settings in the 123.CNF file if /Worksheet Global Default Update is issued subsequently.

/Worksheet Global Default Update

Permanently changes the default settings on disk in the 123.CNF file with the current settings created with /Worksheet Global Default Printer. Other worksheet files will take on these new default settings.

EXERCISES

1. Print the GRADES file As-Displayed to disk. Temporarily exit 1-2-3 and view the .PRN file with the TYPE command.

2. Retrieve the GRADES file from disk and print the entire active part of the worksheet in As-Displayed format on the first page and Cell-Formulas format beginning at the top of the second page. The header "Calculus I Section A" should be centered at the top of each page. The footer should have today's date on the left and the page number on the right of the bottom of each page. Make sure the footer appears at the bottom of the last page.

3. Print the GRADES file As-Displayed using the same header and footer in Exercise 2 with a page eject forced between Catharine Minster and Flora Sesak. Make sure the footer appears at the bottom of each page.

4. Change the left margin to 20 and the right margin to 50 and print the GRADES file.

5. With all print settings back to the defaults, change the print size to compressed print on your printer using the Setup option. Print the GRADES file.

OTHER DATA COMMANDS

Contents:

475

This lesson will cover the following /Data commands:

Data Distribution sets up a frequency distribution of values in a specified range.

Data Parse breaks apart long labels in a single column and places them into separate columns with labels and/or values.

Data Matrix multiplies or inverts a matrix.

Data Regression performs regression analysis.

Each section is independent of the others so that you can cover any individual section or cover the sections in a different order.

/Data Distribution

You enter: **/ File Retrieve GRADES [Return]**

You enter: **/ Range Erase E1..G20 [Return]**

You enter: **/ Range Erase A13..D20 [Return]**

You enter: **/ Range Format Reset A1..G20 [Return]**

Your worksheet should look like Figure 18-1.

	A	B	C	D
1		Test 1	Test 2	Test 3
2	Alunni, Angelo	82	79	63
3	Carver, Clementine	90	82	75
4	Cicilioni, Fred	72	70	80
5	Cicilioni, John	83	75	70
6	Falzett, Rose	75		
7	Killian, Nicholas	64	45	52
8	Minster, Catharine	70	95	88
9	Sesak, Flora	91	99	95
10	Shepard, Gary	30	42	
11	Washington, Barbara	82	87	86

Figure 18-1. Part of GRADES Worksheet.

To create a frequency distribution using /Data Distribution, you must specify two ranges: the values range, containing the input values which will be counted as falling within certain numeric intervals, and the bin range, containing the values designating the cutoffs in the intervals.

Let's say you wish to count how many values in the range B2..B11 are less than or equal to 60, greater than 60 but less than or equal to 70, greater than 70 but less than or equal to 80, etc. These are the typical cutoffs for letter grades F, D, C, etc. The values range should be specified as B2..B11.

There are two adjacent columns in a bin range. The left column contains the cutoffs for the intervals, which must be in ascending order. The right column contains the bins, where 1-2-3 outputs the counts for each value interval.

Put the numbers in the bin range.

You enter:
/ Data Fill B13..B16 [Return] 60 [Return] 10 [Return] [Return]

Your worksheet should look like Figure 18-2.

	A	B	C	D
1		Test 1	Test 2	Test 3
2	Alunni, Angelo	82	79	63
3	Carver, Clementine	90	82	75
4	Cicilioni, Fred	72	70	80
5	Cicilioni, John	83	75	70
6	Falzett, Rose	75		
7	Killian, Nicholas	64	45	52
8	Minster, Catharine	70	95	88
9	Sesak, Flora	91	99	95
10	Shepard, Gary	30	42	
11	Washington, Barbara	82	87	86
12				
13		60		
14		70		
15		80		
16		90		

Figure 18-2. Bin Range for /Data Distribution.

It happens that the cutoffs differ by a constant number, 10, so you can use /Data Fill instead of entering each number manually.

You enter: / **Data Distribution**

Computer message: **Enter values range:**

You enter: **B2..B11 [Return]**

Actually you could have entered TEST1 which, you recall, is the name for the above range.

Computer message: **Enter bin range:**

You enter: **B13..C16 [Return]**

Your worksheet should look like Figure 18-3.

	A	B	C	D
1		Test 1	Test 2	Test 3
2	Alunni, Angelo	82	79	63
3	Carver, Clementine	90	82	75
4	Cicilioni, Fred	72	70	80
5	Cicilioni, John	83	75	70
6	Falzett, Rose	75		
7	Killian, Nicholas	64	45	52
8	Minster, Catharine	70	95	88
9	Sesak, Flora	91	99	95
10	Shepard, Gary	30	42	
11	Washington, Barbara	82	87	86
12				
13		60	1	
14		70	2	
15		80	2	
16		90	4	
17			1	
18				

Figure 18-3. Worksheet after /Data Distribution.

There is 1 value less than or equal to 60 (30 in B10); 2 values greater than 60 but less than or equal to 70 (64 in B7 and 70 in B8); etc. The cell below the right column in the bin range, in this case C17, is used by 1-2-3 to store the count for values greater than the last cutoff value, in this case 90 in B16. So there is 1 value greater than 90 in the values range (91 in B9). Be careful not to have unexpendable data in that cell, as it will be erased.

Do a frequency distribution of all 3 tests by setting up the values range as the three columns.

You enter: **/ Data Distribution B2..D11 [Return] [Return]**

Your worksheet should look like Figure 18-4.

	A	B	C	D
1		Test 1	Test 2	Test 3
2	Alunni, Angelo	82	79	63
3	Carver, Clementine	90	82	75
4	Cicilioni, Fred	72	70	80
5	Cicilioni, John	83	75	70
6	Falzett, Rose	75		
7	Killian, Nicholas	64	45	52
8	Minster, Catharine	70	95	88
9	Sesak, Flora	91	99	95
10	Shepard, Gary	30	42	
11	Washington, Barbara	82	87	86
12				
13		60	4	
14		70	5	
15		80	6	
16		90	8	
17			4	
18				

Figure 18-4. Frequency Distribution of All Test Scores.

Empty cells or cells containing labels have a count value of zero, they're simply not counted.

Of course the values in the values range do not have to be all constants, as in this example. They can also contain formulas and/or @functions which evaluate to values.

/Data Matrix

The two operations you can do on matrices are inversion and multiplication. (To transpose a matrix, use /Range Transpose.)

Create the worksheet in Figure 18-31.

	A	B
1	1	6
2	3	9
3		

Figure 18-31. Matrix to be Inverted.

You enter: / **Data Matrix Invert A1..B2 [Return] C4 [Return]**

Your worksheet should look like Figure 18-32.

Of course, only square matrices can be inverted.

You enter: / **Data Matrix Multiply A1..B2 [Return]**

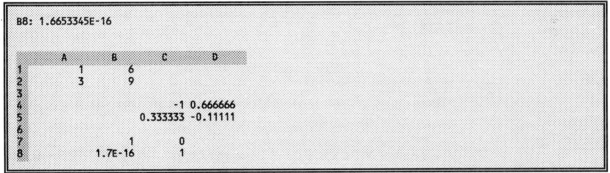

Figure 18-32. Inverted Matrix.

You enter: **C4..D5 [Return] B7 [Return]**

Your worksheet should look like Figure 18-33.

```
B8: 1.6653345E-16

        A        B        C        D
1        1        6
2        3        9
3
4                         -1  0.666666
5                  0.333333  -0.11111
6
7                  1        0
8         1.7E-16          1
```

Figure 18-33. Multiplication of Inverse Matrices is Identity Matrix.

As with calculators, accuracy problems exist. The value in B8 is certainly close enough to zero.

You enter: **/ Worksheet Global Format Fixed 2 [Return]**

Of course, the number of columns of the first matrix must equal the number of rows of the second for multiplication.

The maximum matrix size for inversion or multiplication is 90 x 90.

/Data Regression

/Data Regression does regression analysis.

Create Figure 18-34.

```
          A        B
    1     X        Y
    2     2        5
    3     1        1.3
    4     4        6.7
    5     3        6
    6
```

Figure 18-34. Four Points for Regression Analysis.

You enter: **/ Data Regression X**-Range **A2..A5 [Return]**

The x-range contains the values of the independent variable; the y-range - the dependent variable.

You enter: **Y**-Range **B2..B5 [Return] Output**-Range **A7 [Return] Go**

Your worksheet should look like Figure 18-35.

```
          A        B          C        D
    1     X        Y
    2     2        5
    3     1        1.3
    4     4        6.7
    5     3        6
    6
    7            Regression Output:
    8   Constant                    0.45
    9   Std Err of Y Est        1.126499
   10   R Squared               0.853548
   11   No. of Observations            4
   12   Degrees of Freedom             2
   13
   14   X Coefficient(s)     1.72
   15   Std Err of Coef.  0.503785
```

Figure 18-35. Result of /Data Regression.

The constant .45 is the y-intercept. By default, the y-intercept is computed. The Intercept option forces it to be 0. The X Coefficient is the slope. The rest of the output is self-explanatory.

To create a graph, first compute y-estimates and use an XY type graph.

You enter into D1: **Y-Estimate [Down]**

You enter into D2: **+$C$14*A2+$D$8 [Return]**

You enter: **/ Copy D2 [Return] D3..D5 [Return]**

Your worksheet should look like Figure 18-36.

```
D2: +$C$14*A2+$D$8


          A        B        C        D
1         X        Y                 Y-Estimate
2         2        5                 3.89
3         1        1.3               2.17
4         4        6.7               7.33
5         3        6                 5.61
6
7              Regression Output:
8    Constant                        0.45
9    Std Err of Y Est         1.126499
10   R Squared                0.853548
11   No. of Observations             4
12   Degrees of Freedom              2
13
14   X Coefficient(s)     1.72
15   Std Err of Coef.  0.503785
```

Figure 18-36. Y-Estimates.

The X and A ranges of the XY graph will both be the y-estimates, the B range will be the actual y's and will be shown as symbols only.

You enter: **/ Graph Type XY X D2..D5 [Return] A D2..D5 [Return]**

You enter:
B B2..B5 [Return] Options Format B Symbols Quit Quit View

Your graph should look like Figure 18-37.

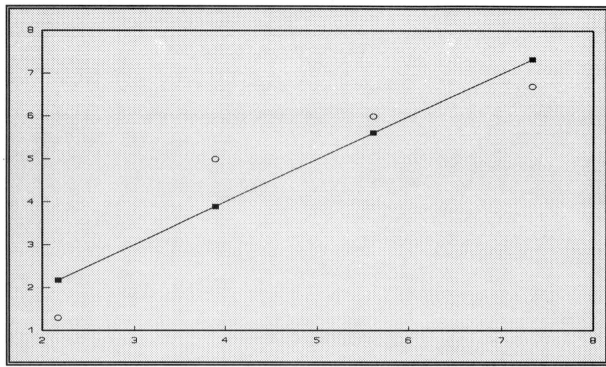

Figure 18-37. Regression Analysis Graph.

You can do multiple regression with up to 16 different independent variables. The X-range should be a range with the number of columns equal to the number of independent variables. For example, in Figure 18-38, the X-Range should be specified as A2..B5.

	A	B	C	D
1	X1	X2	Y	
2	5	2	5	
3	2	1	1.3	
4	7	4	6.7	
5	4	3	6	
6				
7		Regression Output:		
8	Constant		0.15	
9	Std Err of Y Est		1.5	
10	R Squared		0.870167	
11	No. of Observations		4	
12	Degrees of Freedom		1	
13				
14	X Coefficient(s)	0.3	1.3	
15	Std Err of Coef.	0.838525	1.352081	

Figure 18-38. Multiple Regression with 2 Independent Variables.

/Data Parse

/Data Parse breaks apart long labels into columns across a row.

You enter: / **Worksheet Erase Yes**

You enter into A1:

**Smith, John 123 Main St. Akron, OH 56789 (717) 555-1234 10/12/56
07:45 [Return]**

Your worksheet should look like Figure 18-23.

```
A1: 'Smith, John 123 N Main St. Akron, OH 56789 (717) 555-1234 10/12/56 7:4READY


       A        B        C        D        E        F        G        H
1   Smith, John 123 N Main St. Akron, OH 56789 (717) 555-1234 10/12/56 7:45
2
```

Figure 18-23. Long Label in Cell A1 for /Data Parse Command.

All this data is in cell A1, although it looks as if it were in the individual
cells A1, B1, C1, etc. See control panel in figure. You really cannot do
much with the label's parts or fields if they are not in individual cells.

You enter into A1: / **Data Parse**

The Parse menu below is now on the screen:

Format-Line Input-Column Output-Range Reset Go Quit

The first step in parsing a long label is the creation of a format line, which
specifies how the label should be taken apart and put into individual cells.

You enter: **Format-Line Create**

Your worksheet should look like Figure 18-24.

Releases 2.3 and 2.4: The Parse Settings screen is superimposed on
Figure 18-24. Hit [F6/WINDOW] to clear it.

```
A1: |L>>>>>*L>>>*V>>*L*L>>>*L>>*L>>>>>*L>*V>>>>*V>>>>*L>>>>>>*D>>>>>>>*T>> MENU
Format-Line  Input-Column  Output-Range  Reset  Go  Quit
Create or edit format line at current cell
          A         B         C         D         E         F         G         H
1   L>>>>>*L>>>*V>>*L*L>>>*L>>*L>>>>>*L>*V>>>>*V>>>>*L>>>>>>*D>>>>>>>*T>>>
2   Smith, John 123 N Main St. Akron, OH 56789 (717) 555-1234 10/12/56 7:45
3
```

Figure 18-24. Format-Line Created in Cell A1.

The row that has been inserted contains the format line. The pointer position must be on the cell to be parsed before the issuance of the command.

Figure 18-25 explains the characters in the format line.

```
L the first character of data for a cell containing a label
V the first character of data for a cell containing a value
D the first character of data for a cell containing a date
T the first character of data for a cell containing a time
> usually one or more of these follow the letters to indicate
  the length of the data for that cell
* indicates a blank in the label being parsed (if subsequent
  labels using the same format line have non-blank characters
  in these positions, the characters will become part of the
  data)
S characters will be skipped or ignored
```

Figure 18-25. List of Format Line Symbols.

Compare the format line in A1 to the symbols listed in Figure 18-25. /Data Parse assumes that spaces are delimiters between individual data items.

Break the label apart into cells according to the format line.

You enter: Input-Column **A1..A2 [Return]**

You must include the format line in the column range.

You enter: Output-Range **A4 [Return] Go**

Your worksheet should look like Figure 18-26.

```
A1:  |L>>>>>*L>>>*V>>*L*L>>>*L>>*L>>>>>*L>*V>>>>*V>>>>*L>>>>>>>*D>>>>>>>*T>>READY


          A        B       C       D       E       F        G        H
1   L>>>>>*L>>>*V>>*L*L>>>*L>>*L>>>>>*L>*V>>>>*V>>>>*L>>>>>>>*D>>>>>>>*T>>>
2   Smith, John 123 N Main St. Akron, OH 56789 (717) 555-1234 10/12/56 7:45
3
4   Smith,    John         123 N      Main   St.      Akron,  OH
5
```

Figure 18-26. Results of /Data Parse with Default Format Line.

Move the pointer through row 4 and note the control panel to see the type of data in each cell. The -717 results because the parentheses (717) around the area code of the phone number are taken to mean negativity. You must have done the Date and Time lesson to understand the last two cells associated with 10/12/56 and 07:45.

1-2-3 does its best to guess how you want the label to be broken up, but you almost always have to clean it up. 1-2-3 assumes that each blank means another cell which is certainly not true here.

The edit command on the Format-Line sub-menu is used to clean up the format line. Position the pointer into the cell with the format line before issuing this command, otherwise you will get the error message "Invalid format line" on the bottom of the screen.

You enter into A1: / **Data Parse Format-Line Edit**

Now use [Right], [Left], [Del], and > and the other character keys to change the format line to that in Figure 18-27. (The part of the line after the phone number which cannot be seen in the figure doesn't need to be modified.) The OVR indicator on the bottom of the screen indicates typeover mode. Type [Return] when done.

```
A1:  |L>>>>>>>>>>*L>>>>>>>>>>>>>>*SSSSSSSSS*V>>>>*L>>>>>>>>>>>>>>*D>>>>>>>*T>>  MENU
Format-Line  Input-Column  Output-Range  Reset  Go  Quit
Create or edit format line at current cell
          A        B       C       D       E       F        G        H
1   L>>>>>>>>>>*L>>>>>>>>>>>>>>*SSSSSSSSS*V>>>>*L>>>>>>>>>>>>>>*D>>>>>>>*T>>>
2   Smith, John 123 N Main St. Akron, OH 56789 (717) 555-1234 10/12/56 7:45
3
4   Smith,    John         123 N      Main   St.      Akron,  OH
5
```

Figure 18-27. Modified Format Line.

The S's over Akron, OH indicate that the characters below should be ignored and not placed into any cell. (Databases with zipcodes sometimes make it unnecessary to store cities and states.) Now parse again with the new format line into another Output-Range beginning at B7.

You enter: **Output-Range B7 [Return] Go**

Your worksheet should look like Figure 18-28.

```
      A            B          C          D         E        F          G        H
1 L>>>>>>>>>>*L>>>>>>>>>>>>*SSSSSSSSS*V>>>>*L>>>>>>>>>>>>>*D>>>>>>>*T>>>
2 Smith, John 123 N Main St. Akron, OH 56789 (717) 555-1234 10/12/56 7:45
3
4 Smith,      John       123 N        Main      St.      Akron,   OH
5
6
7         Smith, Jo123 N Mai    56789 (717) 555    20740 0.322916
8
```

Figure 18-28. Results of /Data Parse with Modified Format Line.

Thin columns cause only part of the labels to be displayed. To ensure that they are copied correctly, position the pointer through B7..G7 and note the control pane. If you've done the lesson on dates and times, you can format the date and time cells as Date-4 and Date Time-4 respectively.

When you're done parsing, the format lines can be deleted with /Worksheet Delete Row.

We've parsed in this example one cell of data. Usually, /Data Parse is used on a long column of data. One format line above the column will parse the whole column if the input range is adjusted to include it.

/Data Parse is usually used on ASCII data which has been loaded into 1-2-3 with /File Import Text. The ASCII file could have been created with a database package, a word processing package, or from a file downloaded from a mainframe to a PC over a network.

Parsing Imported Text Data

The rest of this section is optional. It may be unclear if you have not used the /File Import command (in the File Operations Lesson) or the /Print File command (in the Advanced Worksheet Printing Lesson). If you wish, you can still continue because all necessary keystrokes are stated.

To create a standard ASCII file in order to import it and parse it, retrieve the SCRANTON file and print part of it to the file PARSE.PRN.

You enter: / File Retrieve **SCRANTON [Return]**

You enter: / Print File **PARSE [Return]**

You enter: **Range A3..E7 [Return] G**o **Q**uit

You enter: / **Worksheet E**rase **Y**es

You enter: / File Import Text **PARSE [Return]**

Your worksheet should look like Figure 18-29.

	A	B	C	D	E	F	G
1							
2							
3							
4							
5							
6				Sales	Tax	Total	
7							
8	1 Nuts			$437.50	$26.25	$463.75	
9	2 Bolts			$899.64	$53.98	$953.62	
10	3 Screwdrivers			$76.23	$4.57	$80.80	

Figure 18-29. Imported ASCII File Created from Print.

The blank rows correspond to the .PRN file's top margin. To prevent these blank lines, do the print unformatted with /Print File Options Other Unformatted.Quit Go.

Move the pointer down through column A and note that all data is stored in column A only. Although it is in long labels, it looks as though columns B through G contain data.

You enter into A6: / **Data Parse Format-Line Create Q**uit

You enter into A9: / **Data Parse Format-Line Create**

You enter: **Input-Column A6..A12 [Return]**

You enter: **Output-Range C15 [Return] G**o

Your worksheet should look like Figure 18-30.

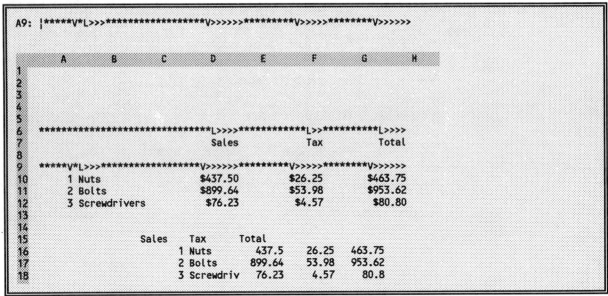

Figure 18-30. Result of /Data Parse Command.

Note that the Go caused both format lines to parse the data below them. Screwdrivers was copied in its entirety even though there are *'s above it in the format line. See * in Figure 18-25.

If you modified the first format line by adding two labels before the label above Sales in A6, the column headers in row 15 would go over the correct columns.

You enter into A9: / **Data Parse Format-Line Edit**

You: **Hit [Down] several times.**

If you had dozens of lines to parse instead of only three, it might be necessary for you to see rows below the screen while you're editing the format line. [Down], [Up], [PgDn], and [PgUp] can be used to scroll the screen. [Home] returns you to the first row. [Esc] erases the entire format line. [Ctrl]+[Break] returns you directly to READY mode. Try the keys now in the order that they are mentioned in this paragraph.

NEW COMMAND SUMMARY

/Data Distribution	Creates a frequency distribution of values occurring in the specified range.
/Data Matrix	Finds inverses and transposes matrices. Multiplies matrices.
/Data Parse	Uncouples data from long labels into individual cells containing values or constants.
/Data Regression	Performs linear regression or multiple regression analysis.

EXERCISES

1.   **Data Distribution.** Create the worksheet below and save under the name JOURNAL, if you have not already done so in this or another lesson. If you have, retrieve the file. Do not modify the file on disk by saving it with modifications as you will need it in other lessons.

	A	B	C	D	E
1		FROGGIE'S BAR CHECK DISBURSEMENTS JOURNAL			
2	CHECK	DATE	AMOUNT	TO	CLASS
3	283	12-Jan-89	$147.00	HARVEY COOK	LABORBROOM
4	284	12-Jan-89	$230.00	FRED BARTENDER	LABORBROOM
5	285	12-Jan-89	$945.38	FROZEN PACKERS	FOOD
6	286	13-Jan-89	$533.99	BETTER BEVERAGE	BEER KEG
7	287	14-Jan-89	$168.00	BEST FOODS	FOOD
8	288	14-Jan-89	$203.41	FROZEN PACKERS	FOOD
9	289	14-Jan-89	$230.00	FRED BARTENDER	LABORBROOM
10	290	14-Jan-89	$217.00	FLOYD DISHWASHER	LABORBROOM
11	291	16-Jan-89	$768.03	FROZEN PACKERS	FOOD
12	292	17-Jan-89	$602.50	BOAT BOTTLING	BEER CAN
13	293	17-Jan-89	$125.86	BETTER BEVERAGE	BEER KEG

A.   Create a frequency distribution for the number of checks for amounts greater than $1000, from $901 to $1000 inclusive, from $801 to $900 inclusive, ..., from $101 to $200 inclusive, and $100 or less.

B.   If you've done the date and time lessons, create a list of dates with the number of checks written on those dates from the JOURNAL file. (If you've done the Data Query lesson, use /Data Query Unique to set up bin range cutoffs in order to save yourself some typing.)

2. **Data Distribution.** Create the worksheet below and save under the name EMPLOYEE if you have not already done so in another lesson. If you have, retrieve the file. Do not modify the file on disk by saving it with modifications as you will need it in other lessons.

	A	B	C	D	E
1	NAME	DEPT	SALARY	CODE	DATE HIRED
2	ABBOTT	CLOTHING	$15,000	1	03/26/85
3	BENTON	SPORTS	$21,000	1	07/03/86
4	GAVERN	CLOTHING	$30,000	2	02/15/81
5	KRAMER	RECORDS	$13,000	1	06/29/88
6	LOVEN	TOYS	$49,000	2	06/29/88
7	SIRKO	DOMESTICS	$10,000	2	02/20/83
8	SMITH	TOYS	$25,000	3	09/07/85
9	THOMAS	TOYS	$28,000	1	12/19/84
10	WELLS	DOMESTICS	$17,000	2	03/26/85

A. Create a frequency distribution for the number of employees having each of the 3 codes.

B. Create a list of the number of employees who make more than $30,000, between $20,000 and $30,000, and less than $20,000.

3. **Data Matrix.** Solve these equations simultaneously:

$2x+3y= 14$
$2x+6y= -6$

by inverting the coefficient matrix

2 3
2 6

and multiplying that inverse by the constant matrix

14
-6

4.　　**Data Regression.** Do regression analysis on the data below:

X	Y
10	80
21	150
66	250
11	90
44	230
12	100

5.　　**Data Parse.** Practice parsing data by printing the JOURNAL file (or any worksheet file) to a file on disk. Import the .PRN file and parse it so that it looks exactly like the original worksheet file.

CUMULATIVE EXERCISES

C1. Create the worksheet below by retrieving TOFU1 that you created in Lesson 1. Delete rows 15 through 17. Create the distribution table shown below using /Data Distribution. Delete the 0 in cell E21. Save under TOFU18.

	A	B	C	D	E	F
1		IMITATION TOFU, INCORPORATED				
2						
3		SalesRep	Division	92 Sales	Commission	
4		===				
5	1	Saxe, J.	2	$40,500	$2,430	
6	2	Gress, R.	3	$77,000	$4,620	
7	3	Cosner, L.	3	$23,400	$1,404	
8	4	Smith, A.	1	$150,000	$9,000	
9	5	Smith, B.	1	$54,700	$3,282	
10	6	Kirlin, K.	2	$75,000	$4,500	
11	7	Wodak, F.	1	$29,800	$1,788	
12	8	Reese, J.	3	$111,300	$6,678	
13	9	Gruss, M.	1	$88,200	$5,292	
14	10	Boyle, T.	2	$67,600	$4,056	
15						
16						
17				Division	Number of SalesReps	
18				1	4	
19				2	3	
20				3	3	
21					0	

C2. Create the worksheet below by retrieving the FISH1 worksheet that you created in Lesson 1. Use /Data Distribution to create the distribution table. (Hint: Create a new column that has the first digit of the item number in it. 1 indicates alive, 2 indicates not living. Use @INT(cellreference/100) to pull off the digit. Hide the bin range values of 1 and 2 in range E17..E18 with /Range Format Hidden.) Save under FISH18.

	A	B	C	D	E	F	G
1		H A P P Y T R O P I C A L F I S H S T O R E					
2	Item		Quantity	Retail	Wholesale	Profit	Total Pr.
3	#	Item Name	Sold	Price	Price	per Item	per Item
4	--						
5	273	7-inch fish net	63	$1.99	$0.70	$1.29	$81.27
6	238	1-lb. decorative rocks	49	$2.99	$1.30	$1.69	$82.81
7	130	underwater fern	13	$2.29	$0.90	$1.39	$18.07
8	281	40-gallon aquarium	14	$39.99	$22.00	$17.99	$251.86
9	162	goldfish	241	$0.59	$0.10	$0.49	$118.09
10	192	20-inch eel	4	$8.99	$4.00	$4.99	$19.96
11	274	2-gallon fish bowl	25	$4.99	$2.00	$2.99	$74.75
12	256	8-vitamin fish food	57	$1.79	$0.80	$0.99	$56.43
13	198	turtle	-1	$3.99	$1.50	$2.49	($2.49)
14	111	piranha	3	$10.99	$5.00	$5.99	$17.97
15							
16						Number of Items	
17				Alive		5	
18				Not living		5	
19						0	

C3. Create the worksheet below by retrieving the BILL1 worksheet that you created in Lesson 1. Add column E by entering each value or, if you did Lesson 7, by entering an @IF formula in E4 and copying it down the column. Create the distribution table. (Hint: Enter 1 into D17 and 2 into D18 and use /Range Format Hidden to hide those two cells.) Delete the 0 in cell E19. Save under BILL18.

	A	B	C	D	E
1		MONTHLY BILLS FOR MARCH			
2				Over/(Under)	1=Over
3		Actual	Budgeted	Amount	2=Not Over
4	Food	$238	$220	$18	1
5	Rent	$550	$550	$0	2
6	Phone	$39	$30	$9	1
7	Electric	$43	$50	($7)	2
8	Gasoline	$56	$45	$11	1
9	Car Payment	$345	$345	$0	2
10	Insurance	$55	$55	$0	2
11	Charge Cards	$250	$100	$150	1
12	Entertainment	$150	$100	$50	1
13		-------	-------	-------	---
14	Total	$1,726	$1,495	$231	
15					
16					Number of Expenses
17		Over Budget			5
18		Not Over Budget			4
19					0

C4. Create the worksheet below by retrieving the GOLF1 worksheet that you created in Lesson 1. Delete rows 10 down. Create the distribution for the scores per hole for all four players in columns A and B. Do the other distributions for each of the four players individually. Save under GOLF18.

	A	B	C	D	E	F	G	H	I	J	K
1			J & F	GOLF	COURSE	SCORE	SHEET				
2	Hole	1	2	3	4	5	6	7	8	9	Total
3	Par	4	5	4	3	5	4	4	3	4	36
4											
5	Joe	8	5	6	4	4	5	6	4	4	46
6	Mary	4	6	5	4	6	4	5	5	3	42
7	Mike	3	7	6	4	5	5	6	5	4	45
8	Sheila	5	5	6	4	3	3	4	6	5	41
9											
10	All										
11	Scores	Number			Joe:		Mary:		Mike:	Sheila:	
12	--------	--------	--------	--------	--------	--------	--------	--------	--------	--------	
13	3	4			3	0	3	1	3	1	3	2
14	4	11			4	4	4	3	4	2	4	2
15	5	11			5	2	5	3	5	3	5	3
16	6	8			6	2	6	2	6	2	6	2
17	7	1			7	0	7	0	7	1	7	0
18	over 7	1		over 7	1	over 7	0	over 7	0	over 7	0
19											

Lesson 19

OTHER RANGE COMMANDS

Contents:

This lesson covers:

Commands which protect against accidental modification of cells: /Range Protect, /Range Unprotect, /Worksheet Global Protection.

/Range Value makes a copy of a range. It copies any cells in the FROM range containing formulas to the TO range as constants.

/Range Transpose copies a range transposing the columns and rows.

/Range Justify reformats labels within a range.

/Range Search finds characters within ranges and optionally replaces them with other characters.

/Range Input restricts cell pointer movement.

Each section is independent of the others so that you can cover any individual section or cover the sections in a different order.

Protection

You enter: / **File Retrieve SCRANTON [Return]**

Your worksheet should look like Figure 19-1.

	A	B	C	D	E
1		SCRANTON HARDWARE COMPANY, INCORPORATED			
2					
3			Sales	Tax	Total
4					
5		1 Nuts	$437.50	$26.25	$463.75
6		2 Bolts	$899.64	$53.98	$953.62
7		3 Screwdrivers	$76.23	$4.57	$80.80
8			-----------	-----------	-----------
9		TOTAL	$1,413.37	$84.80	$1,498.17

Figure 19-1. SCRANTON Worksheet.

After creation of this worksheet, it's reasonable that only the sales figures in C5..C7 should be considered cells that can change or "input cells". To prevent accidental modification of non-input cells, protection can be set on them. I've gnashed my teeth several times after accidentally deleting a long carefully thought-out formula. Cell protection is particularly useful if other people are using your worksheets, and you're concerned they may destroy some data by accident or ignorance.

Think about a security system at a bank or home. Two things must be done: 1) it must be installed properly, and 2) it must be powered on by electricity or battery.

Two things must be done for cell protection: 1) the cells to protect must be specified (protection must be installed around certain cells), and 2) protection must be powered on (or enabled).

Let's do step 1 - specify the cells to protect. By default, every cell in the worksheet has protection installed on it. In this example, all cells should be protected except the input cells, C5..C7.

You enter: / **Range Unprotect C5..C7 [Return]**

The unprotected cells may be shown on your screen in boldface or another color.

You: **Position pointer in C5..C7.**

Not that the control panel shows a U indicator for each of these three cells. U, of course, stands for Unprotect.

We're ready for step 2 - turn protection on.

You enter: / **Worksheet Global Protection Enable**

You enter into C5: **400 [Return]**

No problem changing the unprotected cell C5.

You enter into D5: **20 [Return]**

Your worksheet should look like Figure 19-2.

```
D5: PR 0.06*C5                              ERROR
20

        A        B              C              D              E
1                  SCRANTON HARDWARE COMPANY, INCORPORATED
2
3                             Sales           Tax           Total
4
5        1 Nuts                $400.00       $24.00         $424.00
6        2 Bolts               $899.64       $53.98         $953.62
7        3 Screwdrivers         $76.23        $4.57          $80.80
8                        ----------------------------------------
9              TOTAL          $1,375.87       $82.55       $1,458.42
10
Protected cell
```

Figure 19-2. Failed Attempt to Modify a Protected Cell.

An error beep is heard, ERROR flashes in the mode indicator, and an error message "Protected cell" is shown somewhere on the screen.

You enter: **[Esc]**

Note that a PR indicator is displayed in the control panel. This indicator is present for protected cells only when protection is globally enabled. The U indicator for cells unprotected is always present in the control panel, whether protection is enabled or not.

To change a protected cell, turn off protection with /Worksheet Protection Disable and turn it back on immediately after the modification.

View the global settings.

Save the file under L19PROT in order to be used later for /Range Input.

/Range Value

The /Range Value command is a /Copy command that copies formulas as constants.

Use the SCRANTON worksheet.

You enter: **/ Range Value E5..E9 [Return] C12 [Return]**

Position the pointer in C12 and note that the value is a constant.
As with the /Copy, numeric formats move with the contents of each cell. You can do a /Range Value with identical FROM and TO ranges to change the contents of cells containing formulas to constant values.

You enter: **/ Range Value D5..D9 [Return] D5 [Return]**

Check the control panel and note that the formulas are gone. These constants will not be updated if modifications occur in the range C5..C9. The rule "Never use a constant if a cell depends on another cell" still stands. /Range Value is used when the referenced cells must be deleted. It is also used before transposing a range (next section) containing formulas.

/Range Transpose

Create the worksheet in Figure 19-3 using /Data Fill.

You enter:
/Data Fill A1..B6 [Return] 10 [Return] 10 [Return] [Return]

	A	B
1	10	70
2	20	80
3	30	90
4	40	100
5	50	110
6	60	120

Figure 19-3. Worksheet before /Range Transpose.

The /Range Transpose command is similar to a matrix transpose operation. It does a copy of the specified range, changing the rows to columns and the columns to rows.

You enter: / **Range Transpose A1..B6 [Return] B9 [Return]**

Your worksheet should look like Figure 19-4.

	A	B	C	D	E	F	G
1	10	70					
2	20	80					
3	30	90					
4	40	100					
5	50	110					
6	60	120					
7							
8							
9		10	20	30	40	50	60
10		70	80	90	100	110	120

Figure 19-4. Worksheet after /Range Transpose.

This command can be used for transposing a single row range to a column range or vice versa.

If formulas exist in the FROM range, /Range Transpose copies them as constants.

Releases 2 and 2.01: This is not true in these releases. If there are relative cell references in the FROM range, they will be copied as in the /Copy or /Move commands. This problem can be remedied with the /Range Value command.

/Range Justify

The word "justify" may remind you of the justification feature in a word processor. 1-2-3's very limited word processing capabilities consist of EDIT mode, /Range Search, and the /Range Justify command. (WYSIWYG has additional capabilities. See appendix.)

/Print File can store labels in a file which can be brought into your word processor. /File Import Text can bring files created by your word processor into worksheets. (See index.)

You enter: / **Worksheet Erase Yes**

You enter into A1: **Four score and seven years ago [Down]**

You enter into A2: **our fathers brought forth a new nation [Down]**

You enter into A3: **conceived in liberty and that all men [Down]**

You enter into A4: **are created equal. [Return]**

Your worksheet should look like Figure 19-6.

```
A4: 'are created equal.


       A        B        C        D
1   Four score and seven years ago
2   our fathers brought forth a new nation
3   conceived in liberty and that all men
4   are created equal.
5
```

Figure 19-6. Four labels in the Range A1..A4.

/Range Justify takes a range of consecutive cells down a column containing labels, and rewrites the characters within a given width.

You enter: / **Range Justify A1..C1 [Return]**

Your worksheet should look like Figure 19-7.

```
A1: 'Four score and seven years


       A        B        C
1   Four score and seven years
2   ago our fathers brought
3   forth a new nation
4   conceived in liberty and
5   that all men are created
6   equal.
```

Figure 19-7. Labels Justified into 3 Columns of Specified Range.

The first blank cell causes the command to stop. Observe the control panel and note that instead of having four labels in four consecutive cells, there are now six labels in six consecutive cells. All labels are given the left-align label-prefix (').

/Range Justify is useful if you modify a label.

You enter into A4:

conceived in liberty and dedicated to the proposition [Return]

(I hope you used [F2/EDIT] and added the last 4 words.)

Your worksheet should look like Figure 19-8.

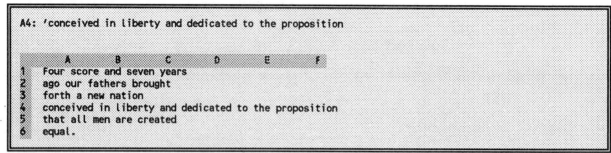

Figure 19-8. Modified Label Cell A4.

You enter: / **Range Justify A1..C1 [Return]**

Your worksheet should look like Figure 19-9.

Figure 19-9. Modified Text Re-justified.

WARNING: If data exists below the justified range, it is /Moved up or down to accommodate for the adjustment in the number of cells containing labels. Save the file just before doing a /Range Justify in case unexpected moves occur in the data below.

/Range Search

This command allows you to search for a string within a specified range. It gives the option of searching labels only, formulas only, or both. The string could be found only or found and replaced with another string. After one occurrence of the string is completed, the command asks if you wish to do the next occurrence.

Retrieve the SCRANTON worksheet and search the entire active area for "ts".

You enter: **[Home] /Range Search . [End] [Home] [Return]**

You enter: **ts [Return] Labels Find**

ts was found in B5 and is highlighted in the control panel.

You enter: **Next Next**

Let's try the search and replace feature. Replace all s's with q's. Get back to READY mode.

You enter:
/Range Search Replace [Esc] s [Return] Labels Replace q [Return]

You: **Hit Replace for each s.**

You enter: **[Esc]**

Releases 2.3 and 2.4: Wildcards can be used in the search string. The asterisk, *, matches any string and the question mark, ?, matches any single character.

/Range Input

/Range Input restricts movement of the cell pointer to unprotected cells in the specified range. It is commonly used in macros to position the cell pointer for user input.

You must have done the section on Protection in this lesson first.

You enter: **/File Retrieve L19PROT**

You enter: **/Range Input A1..E9 [Return]**

You enter: **[Down] 4 times. [Left] [Right]**

The pointer is restricted to the unprotected cells, C5..C7, in the specified range A1..E9. This command is useful for positioning the the cell pointer for data entry into templates.

You enter: **[Esc]**

Enter [Esc] to cancel /Range Input. (Hitting [Return] without any data also cancels /Range Input.)

You enter: **/ Range Input B5..E9 [Return]**

The upper left corner of the specified range is placed in the home position. This could be useful if you have several forms in the same worksheet.

You enter: **/ Range Input B5..E6 [Return]**

Your worksheet should look like Figure 19-10.

```
C5: U "/riB5..E6

              B               C           D           E
5   Nuts            /riB5..E6          ERR          ERR
6   Bolts             $899.64       $53.98      $953.62
7   Screwdrivers       $76.23        $4.57       $80.80
8                  --------------------------------------
9       TOTAL         $975.87          ERR          ERR
```

Figure 19-10. In /Range Input Mode, Command Entered as Data.

You are still in "/Range Input" mode and every key typed is taken as data to be input into the current unprotected cell. Don't forget to hit [Esc] to exit.

You enter: **[Esc]**

You enter into C5: **500 [Return]**

You enter: / **Range Input B5..E6 [Return]**

You enter: **[Down] [Down] [Left] [Right]**

The unprotected cell C7 cannot be modified because it is not in the specified range B5..E6.

The /Range Input command used with macros is a powerful combination.

NEW COMMAND SUMMARY

/Range Input	Restricts cell pointer movement to unprotected cells in the specified range.
/Range Justify	Reformats consecutive labels down a column in the worksheet.
/Range Protect (Unprotect)	Sets (or clears) protection on individual cells in the worksheet. Used in combination with /Worksheet Global Protection.
/Range Search	Releases 2.2, 2.3, 2.4, 3.0, and 3.1+: Searches and allows optional replacement of strings in worksheet cells.
/Range Transpose	Changes the rows and columns of one range to the columns and rows of another range, similar to matrix transpose.
/Range Value	Copies one range to another, changing formulas to constants.
/Worksheet Global Protection Enable (Disable)	Enables (or disables) protection or prohibits modification of cells set with /Range Protect.

EXERCISES

1. Retrieve the SCRANTON file. Use /Range Value and /Range Transpose to create the worksheet below. Do not save the new worksheet under SCRANTON. Use another name.

```
           A           B            C            D            E
 1                       SCRANTON HARDWARE COMPANY, INCORPORATED
 2
 3                                 Sales         Tax         Total
 4
 5            1 Nuts              $437.50      $26.25       $463.75
 6            2 Bolts            $899.64      $53.98       $953.62
 7            3 Screwdrivers      $76.23       $4.57        $80.80
 8                              ----------------------------------
 9                 TOTAL       $1,413.37      $84.80     $1,498.17
10
11
12   $437.50     $899.64       $76.23 -------------     $1,413.37
13    $26.25      $53.98        $4.57 -------------        $84.80
14   $463.75     $953.62       $80.80 -------------     $1,498.17
```

2. Create the worksheet below by retrieving the SCRANTON file and entering one long label into A3. Use /Range Justify.

```
       A        B            C            D            E
 1  Dear Mr. President:
 2
 3  Below are the sales figures for our division
 4  for February, 1988.  I hope you are pleased
 5  with the increase from January's figures.
 6
 7            SCRANTON HARDWARE COMPANY, INCORPORATED
 8
 9                         Sales         Tax         Total
10
11  1 Nuts                $437.50      $26.25       $463.75
12  2 Bolts              $899.64      $53.98       $953.62
13  3 Screwdrivers        $76.23       $4.57        $80.80
14                      ----------------------------------
15       TOTAL         $1,413.37      $84.80     $1,498.17
```

3. Retrieve the GRADES file. Set up appropriate protection on the file. Use /Range Input to Change Catharine Minster's grades to those in the worksheet below. Print columns A through E in Cell-Formulas as well as As-Displayed format.

	A	B	C	D	E
1		Test 1	Test 2	Test 3	Average
2	Alunni, Angelo	82	79	63	80.5 Pass
3	Carver, Clementine	90	82	75	86.0 Pass
4	Cicilioni, Fred	72	70	80	76.0 Pass
5	Cicilioni, John	83	75	70	79.0 Pass
6	Falzett, Rose	75			?
7	Killian, Nicholas	64	45	52	58.0 Fail
8	Minster, Catharine	85	90	70	87.5 Pass
9	Sesak, Flora	91	99	95	97.0 Pass
10	Shepard, Gary	30	42		42.0 Fail
11	Washington, Barbara	82	87	86	86.5 Pass
12					
13	Average	75.4	74.3	73.9	76.9
14	St. Dev.	17.0	18.3	12.5	15.9
15	Minimum	30	42	52	42
16	Maximum	91	99	95	97
17	Number of Tests	10	9	8	
18	All Tests Taken? Yes		No	No	
19					
20	Pass-Fail Cut-off	67			

DATE AND TIME @ FUNCTIONS

Contents:

This lesson covers dates and times and how they are entered and stored in 1-2-3. Dates and times are stored as numbers so that they may be used in computations. Applications using date computations are numerous and include finding due dates and ages. Time computations include determining amount of time passed, given a start time and an end time.

You: **Create Figure 20-1.**

	A	B
1	Name:	Herbert Firmstone
2		
3	Birthdate:	
4		
5	Age:	
6		
7	Today's Date:	
8		

Figure 20-1. Birthdate and Age Worksheet.

Change the global column-width to 15.

You enter: **/ Worksheet Global Column-Width 15 [Return]**

Herbert was born on April 9, 1956. To enter this birthdate, do not just type it in as you would any label. Use the @DATE function.

@DATE(year,month,day)

The year is actually the year minus 1900, so for Herbert's birthday the year is 1956-1900 or 56. The month is a number from 1 through 12. The day is a number from 1 through 31; 1-2-3 will display error (ERR) if a number is not valid for a particular month.

You enter into B3: **@DATE(56,4,9) [Return]**

The value 20554 is displayed in the cell. Dates are stored as serial numbers which can be used in calculations. The value 1 corresponds to the date January 1, 1900; 2 corresponds to January 2, 1900; up to a maximum date value of 73050 corresponding to December 31, 2099. Therefore Herbert was born on the 20554th day since the beginning of the 20th century.

Date Formats

To display the date in a more familiar manner, use one of the Date formats.

You enter into C3: / **R**ange **F**ormat **D**ate **1** **[Return]**

Your worksheet should look like Figure 20-2.

B3: (D1) @DATE(56,4,9)

	A	B
1	Name:	Herbert Firmstone
2		
3	Birthdate:	09-Apr-56
4		
5	Age:	
6		
7	Today's Date:	
8		

Figure 20-2. Date1 Format in B3.

The display format in the control panel is D1. Date display formats and a sample of each format are shown in Table 20-1.

Display Format	Date Format	Display of Herbert's Birthdate	
(D1)	(DD-MMM-YY)	09-Apr-56	
(D2)	(DD-MMM)	09-Apr	
(D3)	(MMM-YY)	Apr-56	
(D4)	MM/DD/YY	04/09/56	Not permanent.
(D5)	MM/DD	04/09	Not permanent.

Table 20-1. Date Formats.

The "Not permanent" indicates that these formats can be changed by the /Worksheet Global Default Other International Date command. In the United States, 04/09/56 means April 9, 1956. In other countries, it means September 4, 1956.

Change the format of B3 to Date4 (D4).

You enter into B3: / **R**ange **F**ormat **D**ate **4** **[Return]**

04/09/56 is displayed in B3.

@NOW

The @NOW function returns the serial number for today's date (and time).

You enter into B7: **@NOW [Return]**

A value of approximately 34,000 should be displayed, depending on the current date. The fraction in the value relates to the time of day.

Time Formats

A fraction of .0 represents midnight, .5 represents noon, .75 represents 6 pm, etc. Display the current time in cell B7.

You enter into B7: **/ Range Format Date Time 1 [Return]**

(D6) is the display format in the control panel. B7 shows the time of day in hours, minutes, and seconds. As seconds pass, the time displayed becomes more and more inaccurate. It is updated each time the worksheet is recalculated. By default, recalculation occurs each time a cell is modified. (See recalculation.) Also, [F9/CALC] causes recalculation.

You enter: **[F9/CALC]**

Four time formats are possible and can be seen on the time sub-menu.

You enter into B7: **/ Range Format Date Time**

Cell B7 in your worksheet is in the first time format, HH:MM:SS AM/PM. Change the format of @NOW back to (D1).

You enter into B7: **/ Range Format Date 1 [Return]**

Today's date should be shown in D1 format.

To summarize, the integer part of the value designates the date and the fractional part designates the time of day.

Age Computation

Herbert's age will computed from today's date from the cell containing @NOW.

You enter into B5: **+B7-B3 [Return]**

@NOW-B3 could have been used as the formula.

The number shown in B5 is the number of days since Herbert was born. Why? Because @NOW returns the number of days since the beginning of the 20th century until today, B3 contains the number of days from the beginning of the 20th century until the day Herbert was born.

Divide this number of days by the number of days in a year (365.25) and you have Herbert's age in years.

You enter into B5: **(B7-B3)/365.25 [Return]**

You enter: **/ Range Format Fixed 0 [Return] [Return]**

1-2-3 rounds values in Fixed format by default so that if Herbert is 31.79 years old, 32 would be displayed in the cell. The mathematical function @INT can be used to truncate the fraction of a year. Use [F2/EDIT] to change the formula.

You enter into B5: **[F2/EDIT] [HOME] @INT([END]) [Return]**

The control panel should read B5: (F0) @INT((B7-B3)/365.25)

Enter your birthdate into B3 with @DATE and see if the age formula works.

My worksheet looks like Figure 20-3.

```
B5: (F0) @INT((B7-B3)/365.25)


              A              B
1   Name:          Herbert Firmstone
2
3   Birthdate:        04/09/56
4
5   Age:                    36
6
7   Today's Date:    30-Aug-92
8
9
10
11
12
13
14
15
16
17
18
19
20
30-Aug-92  03:40 PM
```

Figure 20-3. Age Computation Worksheet.

Save the file under HERBAGE.

You enter: / File Save **HERBAGE [Return]**

- - - If you need a break, stop at this point. - - -

It is good practice to compute ages rather than enter them as constants. Ages change from day to day. If you use @NOW to compute ages, you will never have to change an age entry.

There are many uses for date computations. Some credit card payments are due 30 days from date of purchase. If a purchase was made on credit on 04/12/92, the due date would be @DATE(92,4,12)+30. In a dentist's office, postcards are mailed to patients to remind them of their six month clean and check. For a patient visit today, the next patient visit should be @NOW + (365/2). In a veterinarian's office where dogs should receive their shots once a year, the reminder postcards can be mailed on the date-of-last-shot + 365 days. Perhaps a number of days should be subtracted to allow ample time to set up the appointment.

@DATEVALUE(date string)

@DATEVALUE is very similar to @DATE in that it returns a value equal to the number of days since the beginning of the 20th century. The difference between the two functions is the argument. @DATE has three arguments separated by commas, the year, month, and day. @DATEVALUE has one argument, a character string in one of the five date formats shown in Table 20-1.

Let's say your co-worker, not skillful at Lotus, has typed into a worksheet a whole column of dates as labels. No need to re-enter all of those dates, instead, use @DATEVALUE.

You enter into A12: **'04/09/56 [Return]**

You enter into B12: **@DATEVALUE(A12) [Return]**

20554 is displayed.

You enter into B12: **/Range Format Date 1 [Return]**

09-Apr-56 is displayed.   Now the date in B12 can be used in computations, whereas cell A12 cannot.

To correct your co-worker's mistake, you can use @DATEVALUE, copy it down the adjacent column, use /Range Value to copy the @DATEVALUE cells over themselves, and delete the column with the labels the co-worker typed in.

If the @DATEVALUE is not a cell reference, as above, and is a constant string, the string must be enclosed in double quotes.

You enter into A14: **@DATEVALUE("04/09/56")**

20554 is displayed. If the quotes weren't there, 04/09/56 would mean 4 divided by 9 divided by 56 to Lotus.

@DATEVALUE will take as its argument any of the five date formats shown in Table 20-1. Table 20-2 shows the results of the five formats as arguments in @DATEVALUE.

```
Cell Contents          Serial Number Returned    Date of Serial Number

@DATEVALUE("09-Apr-56")        20554             April 9, 1956

@DATEVALUE("09-Apr")           32242*            April 9, 1988*

@DATEVALUE("Apr-56")           20546+            April 1, 1956+

@DATEVALUE("04/09/56")         20554             April 9, 1956

@DATEVALUE("04/09")            32242*            April 9, 1988*

* If the year is omitted in the string, the current year is assumed.
+ If the day of the month is omitted, 1 is assumed.
```

Table 20-2. Examples of @DATEVALUE's Serial Numbers.

The @DATE, @NOW, @DATEVALUE generate serial date numbers. The next two date functions also generate serial numbers.

@TIME(hour,minute,second)
> Returns the serial time number of hour (between 0 and 23), minute (between 0 and 59), and second (between 0 and 59). ERR is returned if an argument is invalid.

You enter into D4: **@TIME(12,0,0) [Return]**

The serial time number of noon (12 hours, no minutes, no seconds) is 0.5, as mentioned in the paragraph under Time Formats.

@TIMEVALUE(time string)
> Similar to @DATEVALUE. Returns the serial time number of time string. Time string must be one of the 4 time formats enclosed in double quotes. Time string can be a cell reference to a cell containing a time string.

Recall the @ function @CHOOSE introduced in Lesson 7.

@CHOOSE(x,value0,value1,value2,...,valueN)
Returns value0 if x is 0, value1 if x is 1, etc.

Example:
@CHOOSE(2,100,101,102,103,104) = 102
Because the first argument is 2 the fourth argument corresponding to value2, 102, is the value returned by the function.

You: **Create the worksheet in Figure 20-4, entering dates as labels.**

```
C4: [W8] '1/21/88


      A       B       C       D       E        F         G           H
1            Hours   Date    Day Regular Overtime  Overtime      Gross
2     Name  Worked  Worked  of Wk Rate/Hr  Factor   Rate/Hr        Pay
3
4     Joe      3 1/21/88           $6.75
5     Sally    5 2/14/88           $5.00
6     Mike     8 3/11/88           $3.80
7     Gloria   6 4/16/88           $7.50
```

Figure 20-4. Payroll Worksheet.

Let's create the completed payroll worksheet for your company shown in Figure 20-5.

Your employees get paid time and a half on Saturdays and double time on Sundays.

```
D4: @CHOOSE(@MOD(@DATEVALUE(C4),7),"Sat","Sun","Mon","Tue","Wed","Thu","Fri"


      A       B       C       D       E        F        G         H
1            Hours   Date    Day Regular Overtime Overtime    Gross
2     Name  Worked  Worked of Wk Rate/Hr  Factor  Rate/Hr      Pay
3
4     Joe      3 1/21/88 Thu    $6.75       1      $6.75    $20.25
5     Sally    5 2/14/88 Sun    $5.00       2     $10.00    $50.00
6     Mike     8 3/11/88 Fri    $3.80       1      $3.80    $30.40
7     Gloria   6 4/16/88 Sat    $7.50     1.5     $11.25    $67.50
```

Figure 20-5. Completed Payroll Worksheet.

To compute the day of the week of the date worked, you must first change the labels in the Date Worked column to serial date numbers.

@DATEVALUE(C4) = 32163

To find the day of the week, the @MOD function can be used to get a number between 0 and 6.

@MOD(32163,7) = 5

1/21/88 was a Thursday, therefore 5 should correspond to Thursday, 6 to Friday, 0 to Saturday, 1 to Sunday, ... , and 4 to Wednesday. The dayofweeknumber below is a number between 0 and 6 inclusive.

@CHOOSE(dayofweeknumber,"Sat","Sun","Mon","Tue","Wed","Thu","Fri")

Put these 3 functions together and you have your day of the week.

You enter into D4:
**@CHOOSE(@MOD(@DATEVALUE(C4),7),"Sat","Sun","Mon","Tue",
"Wed","Thu","Fri")**

You enter: **/ Copy D4 [Return] D5..D7 [Return]**

The overtime factor should be 2 for double time on Sundays, 1.5 for time and a half on Saturdays, and 1 for weekdays.

You enter into F4: **@IF(D4="Sat",1.5,@IF(D4="Sun",2,1)) [Return]**

You enter into G4: **+E4*F4 [Return]**

You enter into H4: **+B4*G4 [Return]**

You enter: **/ Copy F4..H4 [Return] F5..F7 [Return]**

Your worksheet should look like Figure 20-5. Save the file under PAYROLL.

You enter: **/ File Save PAYROLL [Return]**

- - - If you need a break, stop at this point. - - -

The date functions below have arguments that are serial numbers.

@DAY(serial date number)
>   Returns the day number of serial date number.

@MONTH(serial date number)
>   Returns the month number of serial date number.

@YEAR(serial date number)
>   Returns the year number of serial date number.

@HOUR(serial time number)
>   Returns the hour number of serial time number.

@MINUTE(serial time number)
>   Returns the minute number of serial time number.

@SECOND(serial time number)
>   Returns the second number of serial time number.

The serial number 20554.523 corresponds to April 9, 1956 12:33:07 PM.

@DAY(20554.523) = 9

@MONTH(20554.523) = 4

@YEAR(20554.523) = 56

@HOUR(20554.523) = 12

@MINUTE(20554.523) = 33

@SECOND(20554.523) = 7

Create the worksheet in Figure 20-6. It is shown in Text format so that you can see the formulas.

```
        A       B                           C
1  Electronic Reminder
2
3  Date:
4  @NOW
5  Time:   @IF(@DAY(A4)=1,"Monthly Report Due"," ")
6  +A4     @IF(@MONTH(A4)=9 #AND# @DAY(A4)=28,"Junior's Birthday"," ")
7          @IF(@YEAR(A4)>=100,"21st Century"," ")
8          @IF(@HOUR(A4)=12,"Lunch Time"," ")
```

Figure 20-6. Electronic Reminder Worksheet in Text Format.

(The formula in B7 would not work into the 22nd century or beyond. A better formula is @YEAR(A4)>=100 #AND# @YEAR(A4)<200. Current versions of Lotus only handle dates up to 2099.)

Figure 20-7 shows how your screen should look after formatting A4 in Date1 format and A6 in Time2 format. Your date and time should be different from mine, of course.

```
        A       B                       C
1  Electronic Reminder
2
3  Date:
4  26-Sep-88
5  Time:
6   12:00 AM
```

Figure 20-7. Screen Display of Electronic Reminder Worksheet.

To see how the date functions work, change the date in cell A4 to those dates shown in the next figures. Use the control panel to see the contents of cell A4.

```
A4: (D1) [W12] @DATE(88,10,1)

        A        B
1   Electronic Reminder
2
3   Date:
4     01-Oct-88
5   Time:            Monthly Report Due
6     12:00 AM
```

```
A4: (D1) [W12] @DATE(88,9,28)

        A        B
1   Electronic Reminder
2
3   Date:
4     28-Sep-88
5   Time:
6     12:00 AM    Junior's Birthday
```

```
A4: (D1) [W12] @DATE(100,1,1)

        A        B
1   Electronic Reminder
2
3   Date:
4   01-Jan-2000
5   Time:            Monthly Report Due
6     12:00 AM
7                21st Century
```

```
A4: (D1) [W12] @DATE(88,3,31)+.514

        A        B
1   Electronic Reminder
2
3   Date:
4     31-Mar-88
5   Time:
6     12:20 PM
7
8                Lunch Time
```

Releases 3.0 and 3.1+:
The @DATE function does not have to be used to enter dates. It is possible to enter them as they are displayed in Table 20-1, under column 3, Display of Herbert's Birthdate.

You enter into any cell: **09-Apr-56 [Return]**

20554 is displayed. You still must format them with /Range Format or /Worksheet Global Format.

Dates can be entered with the /Data Fill command. The increments below can be used:

an integer - number of days

an integer followed by a d - number of days

an integer followed by an m - number of months

an integer followed by a q - number of quarters

an integer followed by a y - number of years

For example,

/Data Fill A1..A7 09-Apr-89 [Return] 2m [Return] 9999999 [Return]

would cause the following to appear in a range formatted D1:

```
09-Apr-89
09-Jun-89
09-Aug-89
09-Oct-89
09-Dec-89
09-Feb-90
09-Apr-90
```

EXERCISES

1. Create the worksheet below and save on disk under LIBRARY. Columns D, E, and F contain formulas. The current date should normally be @NOW but for now keep it as @DATE. The Late? cells should contain @TRUE or @FALSE. Use zero suppression (/Worksheet Global Zero). Compute the late fees as 10 cents a day for adult books and 5 cents a day for children's books. To determine the type of book, look at the first digit in the book number. If it is 1, it's an adult book. If it is 7, it's a child's. The late days should include holidays and weekends. Of course, there should be a column with the library card number of the person who took out the book, but let's leave it out this time.

	A	B	C	D	E	F
1		DICKSON PUBLIC LIBRARY				
2						
3		Current Date:	29-Aug-88			
4						
5		Book	Book	Date	Due		Fees
6		Number	Title	Borrowed	Date	Late?	Owed
7							
8		19540	Computers and You	12-Aug	26-Aug	1	$0.30
9		13925	War and Peace	18-Aug	01-Sep		
10		12884	Good Earth	06-Jul	20-Jul	1	$4.00
11		72043	Woof Woof Barks	08-Aug	22-Aug	1	$0.35
12		79355	Jack Gets Lost	24-Aug	07-Sep		
13		11453	Gone with the Wind	17-Aug	31-Aug		

2. Create a worksheet showing current time in 5 different time zones. Use @NOW for your geographical time zone and add and subtract hours for the other 4.

Hint: A day is equivalent to 1, therefore one hour is equivalent to the fraction 1/24.

3. A. Calculate an employee's weekly wages. Base it on a time in and a time out for 7 days a week and the hourly wage.

B. On Saturday, the employee makes time and a half; on Sunday, double time. Calculate the equivalent number of hours worked for the week and multiply by the hourly wage.

4. A. Create a database of purchases on Mary Smith's credit card. Calculate the finance charge for a month based on a modifiable interest rate per day and the average balance of purchases for each day of the month.

B. Add to the calculations a finance charge for cash advances. The interest rate for cash advances should be a different input cell and is usually less than the interest rate for purchases.

5. Create the worksheet below and save on disk under ABC. The Age and Year Starting Kindergarten are formulas. A child starts kindergarten in the first year in which s/he is 5 on Nov. 1. Therefore add 5 to the birth year if the birthdate is before November 2 and 6 if it is on or after November 2. For now, use @DATE in A3 although it should be @NOW.

```
A3: (D1) [W10] @NOW


          A          B          C          D          E       F
1                        ABC PRE-SCHOOL
2    Current Date:
3    02-Mar-89
4                                   Year Starting  Birthday
5    Student     Birthdate  Age     Kindergarten   This Month?
6
7    Joey        31-Oct-85   3          1991
8    Mary        01-Nov-85   3          1990
9    Freddie     26-Mar-85   3          1991         Yes
10   Alfie       31-Aug-85   3          1991
11   Chrissy     31-Jul-84   4          1990
12   Missy       02-Nov-85   3          1991
```

6. Create the worksheet below and save on disk under PLEDGE. Column A contains labels and column B constants. Use zero suppression (/Worksheet Global Zero). The purpose of column C is to keep track of phone pledges that came in during the special Peter, Paul, and Marie's 25th Anniversary Celebration which was broadcast during the hour from 9 to 10 pm. Therefore column C should use @TIMEVALUE because column A's entries are labels and @HOUR to determine if the time of the pledge was within the hour beginning at 9 pm.

```
              A                  B                 C
1                   WVIO EDUCATIONAL PUBLIC TELEVISION
2
3    Time of Pledge   Amount of Pledge   Special Broadcast Pledges
4    -----------------------------------------------------------
5    10:48 AM               $15
6    7:12 AM                $20
7    4:04 PM                $35
8    9:36 PM                $35                    $35
9    3:36 PM                $20
10   5:31 AM                $15
11   9:21 PM                $20                    $20
12   9:26 AM                $15
13   2:09 AM                $50
14   9:07 PM                $10                    $10
15   11:02 AM               $25
16                   --------------------------------
17                         $260                    $65
```

STRING
@ FUNCTIONS

Contents:

This lesson covers the manipulation of string data. Pulling off characters from strings, concatenation, and finding and replacing substrings are covered. ASCII codes are included.

String

A string is a series of characters enclosed in quotes. Entries in cells that are of the label data type are also strings. "TOTAL" is a constant or literal string which, because it is enclosed in quotes, is differentiated from the range named TOTAL. Quotes cue 1-2-3 that the string should be taken literally. References to cells containing strings should not be enclosed in quotes. A1 means cell A1; "A1" designates the 2-character constant string uppercase A followed by the character 1.

String @ Functions

1-2-3 has many @ functions that manipulate strings.

Retrieve the GRADES file and erase most of the cells leaving only the names, as in Figure 21-1.[1]

	A	B
1	Alunni, Angelo	
2	Carver, Clementine	
3	Cicilioni, Fred	
4	Cicilioni, John	
5	Falzett, Rose	
6	Killian, Nicholas	
7	Minster, Catharine	
8	Sesak, Flora	
9	Shepard, Gary	
10	Washington, Barbara	

Figure 21-1. Names from GRADES Worksheet.

---

[1]The proper way to pull out a range of cells from a worksheet is with the /File Xtract command. (See index.)

@LENGTH(string)

@LENGTH(string) returns the number of characters in a string. A blank cell or the null string has length 0.

Examples:

@LENGTH("TOTAL")=5
@LENGTH(TOTAL)=the number of characters in the string entered in the cell named TOTAL.

You enter into B1: **@LENGTH(A1) [Return]**

14 is displayed in B1 because the Angelo, Alunni has 14 characters including the space. Copy the formula down the column.

You enter: / **Copy B1 [Return] B2..B10 [Return]**

Your worksheet should look like Figure 21-2.

```
B1: @LENGTH(A1)


          A              B
1   Alunni, Angelo       14
2   Carver, Clementine   18
3   Cicilioni, Fred      15
4   Cicilioni, John      15
5   Falzett, Rose        13
6   Killian, Nicholas    17
7   Minster, Catharine   18
8   Sesak, Flora         12
9   Shepard, Gary        13
10  Washington, Barbara  19
```

Figure 21-2. @LENGTH Function.

@LEFT(string,n) and @RIGHT(string,n)

@LEFT(string,n) returns the first n characters in the string. @RIGHT(string,n) returns the last n characters in the string.
These functions can be used to pull off the first name and last name and place them in separate cells. Put the first name in column C and last name in column D.

You enter into C1: **@RIGHT(A1,6) [Return]**

You enter into D1: **@LEFT(A1,6) [Return]**

The last 6 characters, "Angelo", are pulled off and stored in C1 as the first name. The 6 character string "Alunni" is stored in D1 as the last name. These two functions cannot be copied down their respective columns because the length of each first and last name varies.

Entering each individual function with a constant second argument is not practical. It is possible to use @ string functions to pull off the first and last names, when they are of variable lengths.

@FIND(search string,string,start number)

Just as your eye must search for the comma and the space separating the first and last name, so also must 1-2-3 in order to carry out this procedure.

@FIND(search string,string,start number) returns the position at which search string is found in string. If the search string is not found, ERR is returned. The start number is the position in string where the search for search string begins; its purpose is explained later.

The first character in a string is position 0, not 1 as you might expect. Therefore, the last position in the string is always one less than the length of the string. Figure 21-3 shows the positions in the string "Alunni, Angelo" underneath the corresponding characters.

```
Alunni, Angelo
01234567890123
```

Figure 21-3. Character Positions Begin at 0.

Pulling off the last name from any name in the database requires finding the position of the comma.

You enter into E1: **@FIND(",",A1,0) [Return]**

Beginning at position 0, "," is searched for. The comma is at position 6 in the string as is shown in Figure 21-3. 6 should be displayed in cell E1 on your screen. (You may have to reset the format display with /Range Format Reset on that column.)

The last name column, column D, can now be set up using the information from the @FIND.

You enter into D1: **@LEFT(A1,E1) [Return]**

It pulled the leftmost 6 characters from the string in A1. Copy these formulas through columns D and E.

You enter: / Copy **D1..E1 [Return] D1..D10 [Return]**

Adjust your column widths if necessary.

For column C, in order to calculate the number of characters to be pulled off for the first name, both the comma (or space) position and the length of the string must be used. Observing Figure 21-3, the number of characters in Angelo (6) can be computed as the length of the string (14) minus the comma position (6) minus 1 to account for the space after the comma minus another 1 to adjust for a first position of 0 instead of one.

You enter into C1: **@RIGHT(A1,B1-E1-2) [Return]**

You enter: / Copy **C1 [Return] C2..C10 [Return]**

Your worksheet should look like Figure 21-4.

```
C1: [W11] @RIGHT(A1,B1-E1-2)


              A              B      C          D         E
1   Alunni, Angelo          14 Angelo     Alunni     6
2   Carver, Clementine      18 Clementine Carver     6
3   Cicilioni, Fred         15 Fred       Cicilioni  9
4   Cicilioni, John         15 John       Cicilioni  9
5   Falzett, Rose           13 Rose       Falzett    7
6   Killian, Nicholas       17 Nicholas   Killian    7
7   Minster, Catharine      18 Catharine  Minster    7
8   Sesak, Flora            12 Flora      Sesak      5
9   Shepard, Gary           13 Gary       Shepard    7
10  Washington, Barbara     19 Barbara    Washington 10
```

Figure 21-4. @LENGTH, @RIGHT, @LEFT, and @FIND Examples.

The functions would be clearer if cells B1 and E1 were named LENGTH and COMMAPOS, respectively. The formulas would then look like:

@RIGHT(A1,LENGTH-COMMAPOS-2)

@LEFT(A1,COMMAPOS)

I personally prefer not using columns to hold numbers pertaining to lengths of and positions of characters in strings in my databases. I think it's cleaner to combine the @ string functions into one cell.

For first name: @RIGHT(A1,@LENGTH(A1)-@FIND(",",A1,0)-2)

For last name: @LEFT(A1,@FIND(",",A1,0))

Two advantages exist in entering the formulas this way and doing away with the length column and comma position column. First, these formulas are not dependent on the length and comma position columns. If, in the future, you wish to delete those two columns, there will be no ERRor in the first and last names. This independence leads to a more flexible, modifiable worksheet. Second, the length and comma positions show irrelevant information which clutters up the screen. Of course, /Worksheet Column Hide can easily be used to hide the length and comma position columns for a cleaner screen display. It's really up to you.

@MID(string,start number,n)

@MID(string,start number,n) returns n characters from the string beginning at position start number.

@MID("193-47-8765 Harry Jones",12,5) returns Harry.

In strings with varying word lengths, @FIND can be used to find the position of the spaces. The combination of @MID and @FIND will allow you to pull off any information you need.

As the worksheet stands now, column A's information seems redundant. Deleting it would cause errors in the first and last name columns because there are cell references to it. The /Range Value command can be used to change the formulas to constants. (See Lesson 19.)

You enter: **/ Range Value C1..D10 [Return] C1..D10 [Return]**

This command copied the range over itself changing all formulas to the string constants to which the formulas evaluated. Look at the control panel displays for the cells in that range. The formulas are gone and now column A can be deleted.

Generic files created by other software such as word processors and database management systems can be imported into a Lotus worksheet. (See /File Import.) String manipulation is often needed to separate the data into individual cells.

The /Data Parse command (see index), breaks apart long labels into separate cells. It would not be useful in this application, where the names are of variable length and overlapping, because it cues on vertical position. In other words, the commas aren't under one another, so it won't work.

The third argument in the @FIND, start number, is not always 0. It is used to bypass inapplicable first occurrences of a search string. The @FIND below finds the position of the space between the first and last names in order to be used later to pull out the last name.

@FIND(" ","193-47-8765 Harry Jones",12) returns 17.

```
193-47-8765 Harry Jones
01234567890123456780123
          1         2
```

The search is started at position 12, the position of the first character in the first name. This position doesn't vary because of the constant length of the social security number. In the case where data would vary before this position, @FINDs should be used in combination.

In the next example, the department name's length varies and therefore the position of the first space is not known.

Cell B3 contains: Personnel Joe McDonald

```
Personnel Joe McDonald
0123456789012345678901
         1        2
```

@FIND(" ",B3,@FIND(" ",B3,0)+1) returns 13.

In this example, the above @FIND is equivalent to @FIND(" ",B3,10), because the @FIND(" ",B3,0)+1 returns 10.

13 is the position of the second space separating the first and last name. It seeks a space in B3, starting the search right after the position of the first space, yielding the second space.

A flaw will exist in most of the previous @FIND examples if extra spaces exist at the end of the string, which would not be evident in the display. Extra spaces between the words would cause problems also. To prevent this problem of too many spaces, the @TRIM function can be used and is explained later in this lesson.

@REPLACE(original string,start number,n,new string)

@REPLACE(original string,start number,n,new string) replaces a substring of n characters in original string with new string beginning at start number. Think about it this way: look at the original string, find the "start number" position, beginning there pull off n characters and discard them, and insert the new string at that position.

@REPLACE("ABCDEFGHIJKLMNOP",5,4,"zz")= ABCDEzzJKLMNOP

The fifth position is F, 4 characters (FGHI) are pulled off and discarded, and the new string "zz" replaces the discarded characters.

@REPLACE("John Robert Smith",5,6,"Michael") changes Robert to Michael.

For a general formula in finding a middle name in cell E10 and replacing it with "Michael":

```
@REPLACE(E10,@FIND(" ",E10,0),@FIND(" ",E10,@FIND(" ",E10,0)+1)-@FIND(" ",E10,0)-1,"Michael")
```

The second argument is the position of the first space. The third argument (underlined) is the number of characters of the middle name to be pulled off and can be thought of as the position of the second space minus the position of first space minus 1.

Delete all columns except C and D so that your worksheet looks like Figure 21-5.

You enter: / **Worksheet Delete Column A1..B1 [Return]**

You enter: / **Worksheet Delete Column C1 [Return]**

Save the worksheet in order to be used in the exercises after this lesson.

You enter: / **File Save STRINGEX [Return]**

&

The old deleted column A can be rebuilt using &.

Figure 21-5. First and Last Name Columns Only.

Strings can be concatenated or linked together with &. Spaces should not be typed before or after &.

Examples:

"John "&"Smith" yields the string John Smith.
"John"&"Smith" yields the string JohnSmith.
"John"&E5 yields the string John concatenated with the string in cell E5.
D5&E5 concatenates the strings in cells D5 and E5.

You enter into C1: **+A1&B1 [Return]**

AngeloAlunni should be displayed in C1. A space should be added.

You enter into C1: **+A1&" "&B1 [Return]**

Restore the old column A with the column before looking on the next page.

You should have entered into C1: **+B1&", "&A1 [Return]**

That + is necessary because 1-2-3 uses the first character entered to cue it to the data type, value or label. "John "&"Smith" would actually have to be entered into a cell preceded by a + also or else the first " would be taken as a left-aligned label-prefix.

Cell C1 can now be copied down the column.

Clear the worksheet.

- - - If you need a break, stop at this point. - - -

@TRIM(string)

@TRIM(string) removes all excess spaces from a string; spaces before the string, after it, and consecutive spaces in between are deleted.

You enter into A1: **[Spacebar] [Spacebar] Lotus [Spacebar] [Spacebar] [Spacebar] 1-2-3 [Spacebar] [Spacebar] [Return]**

You enter into A2: **@TRIM(A1) [Return]**

The two spaces before Lotus and two of the three spaces between Lotus and 1-2-3 are removed. Although not readily apparent, the two spaces after 1-2-3 are deleted also.

You enter into A3: **@LENGTH(A2) [Return]**

The length of A2 is 11 which confirms that no unseen characters exist after 1-2-3.

Your worksheet should look like Figure 21-6.

```
        A        B
1     Lotus    1-2-3
2   Lotus 1-2-3
3       11
```

Figure 21-6. @TRIM Function.

Data imported form other software programs (See /File Import) may sometimes contain extra problematic spaces which can be quickly and easily deleted with @TRIM and a /Range Value command.

Clear the worksheet.

@REPEAT(string,n)

@REPEAT(string,n) duplicates the string n times.

You enter into A1: **@REPEAT("IGM",20) [Return]**

IBM is repeated 20 times across the top of the worksheet.

You enter into A2: **@REPEAT("IGM ",3) [Return]**

Again, be careful with spaces; they are treated as characters just as any other letter or digit. There is a trailing space after the third M which makes the length of the string 12, not 11 as it seems.

Your worksheet should look like Figure 21-7.

```
A2: @REPEAT("IGM ",3)


     A        B        C        D        E        F        G
1 IGMIGMIGMIGMIGMIGMIGMIGMIGMIGMIGMIGMIGMIGMIGMIGMIGMIGMIGMIGM
2 IGM IGM IGM
3
```

Figure 21-7. @REPEAT Function.

@EXACT(string1,string2)

@EXACT(string1,string2) returns a 1 if string1 is exactly the same as string2 and returns a 0 otherwise.

You enter anywhere: **@EXACT("Hi","Hi") [Return]**

A 1 or logical true is displayed.

You enter anywhere: **@EXACT("Hi","hi") [Return]**

A 0 or logical false is displayed.

The equal operator (=) ignores the case of letters. Therefore +"hi"="Hi" is true.

@EXACT is used when you must distinguish between upper and lowercase characters.

Clear the worksheet.

Enter the label below into cell A1 paying particular attention to upper and lowercase characters.

You enter into A1: **Four score and SEVEN Years ago.**

@LOWER(string) and @UPPER(string)

@LOWER(string) converts all characters in the string to lowercase characters. @UPPER(string) converts all characters in the string to uppercase characters.

You enter into A4: **@LOWER(A1) [Down]**

You enter into A5: **@UPPER(A1) [Down]**

@PROPER(string)

@PROPER(string) changes the capitalization in the string so that each word's first letter is uppercase and the rest of the characters in each word are lowercase.

You enter into A6: **@PROPER(A1) [Return]**

Your worksheet should look like Figure 21-8.

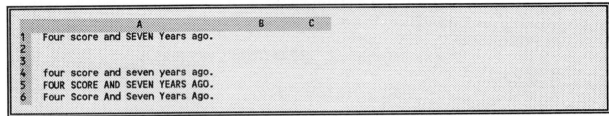

Figure 21-8. @LOWER, @UPPER, and @PROPER functions.

- - - If you need a break, stop at this point. - - -

@STRING(value,n)

@STRING(value,n) converts a value into a string with n decimal digits. If C1 contains the value 15.2, @STRING(C1,3) returns the label 15.200. One application of this function is in a graph title to display in the title a value from a cell in the worksheet. For example, to get the title

Section=63

where 63 is the value in the cell G3. Enter +"Section="&@STRING(G3,0) into a cell, name the cell, and use the backslash cell reference technique. (See Lesson 9 On-Screen Graphing, specifically, the second graph title in Exercise 6, page 320.)

@VALUE(string)

@VALUE(string) is the inverse of @STRING. It converts a label which looks like a number to its value. If B1 contains the label '3.72, @VALUE(B1) returns the value 3.72.

@N(range)

Retrieve the file SEAFOOD. Your worksheet should look like Figure 21-9.

```
              A        B       C       D       E
1                ART PREACHER'S SEAFOOD RESTAURANT
2
3   Department    1987    1988   Change  % Change
4   ------------------------------------------------
5   Appetizers    $900  $1,100    $200     22.2%
6   Fish            70      80      10     14.3%
7   Desserts        53      43     (10)   -18.9%
8   Beverages       17      15      (2)   -11.8%
9   Soup            30      37       7     23.3%
10  Salad          250     305      55     22.0%
11  ------------------------------------------------
12              $1,320  $1,580    $260     19.7%
```

Figure 21-9. SEAFOOD Worksheet.

The @N(range) function returns the number found in the upper left corner cell of the range argument.

You enter into A14: **@N(B3..B12) [Return]**

1987 is returned.

You enter into A15: **@N(C3..G7) [Return]**

1988 is returned.

You enter into A16: **@N(A3..E12) [Return]**

0 is returned because the contents of A3 is a string, not a label.
Single cell ranges should be entered with both endpoints or proceeded by an !. For example, the single cell B12 should be entered as B12..B12 or !B12 and not as B12.

You enter into A17: **@N(!B12) [Return]**

1320 is returned and can be changed into currency format with the /Range Format command if you wish.

Your worksheet should look like Figure 21-10.

```
A17: [W11] @N(B12..B12)


            A         B       C        D         E
1                  ART PREACHER'S SEAFOOD RESTAURANT
2
3     Department    1987     1988    Change    % Change
4     ------------------------------------------------
5     Appetizers    $900   $1,100     $200      22.2%
6     Fish            70       80       10      14.3%
7     Desserts        53       43      (10)    -18.9%
8     Beverages       17       15       (2)    -11.8%
9     Soup            30       37        7      23.3%
10    Salad          250      305       55      22.0%
11                  ------------------------------------
12                 $1,320   $1,580     $260      19.7%
13
14        1987
15        1988
16           0
17        1320
```

Figure 21-10. @N Function.

This function would more likely be used with named ranges as arguments. For instance, if the range B3..B12 were named LASTYEAR and C3..C12 were named THISYEAR, @N(LASTYEAR) would return 1987 and @N(THISYEAR) would return 1988. If the single cell B12 had the name LASTSUM, @N(!LASTSUM) would return 1320.

@S(range)

@S(range) returns the string in the upper left corner of the range argument.

You enter into C14: **@S(D3..D12) [Return]**

"Change" is returned.

You enter into C15: **@S(E3..E12) [Return]**

"% Change" is returned.

You enter into C16: **@S(C3..C12) [Return]**

The null string is returned because C3 contains a value.

Your worksheet should look like Figure 21-11.

```
C16: @S(C3..C12)
              .

           A          B          C          D          E
1                 ART PREACHER'S SEAFOOD RESTAURANT
2
3     Department     1987       1988      Change    % Change
4     --------------------------------------------------------
5     Appetizers     $900      $1,100      $200       22.2%
6     Fish            70         80         10        14.3%
7     Desserts        53         43        (10)      -18.9%
8     Beverages       17         15         (2)      -11.8%
9     Soup            30         37          7        23.3%
10    Salad          250        305         55        22.0%
11                 --------------------------------------------
12                  $1,320     $1,580      $260       19.7%
13
14         1987               Change
15         1988               % Change
16            0
17         1320
```

Figure 21-11. @S Function.

- - - If you need a break, stop at this point. - - -

The rest of this lesson is optional.

Alphanumeric Data

Letters, digits, and special characters such as !, ", #, etc. with which we are familiar, are referred to as alphanumeric or alpha data. Numeric data generally refers to digits only. The simplest cash registers for small businesses handle only numeric data, whereas more powerful registers include alphanumeric data. Note the receipt given to you next time you purchase something. You may see something like

```
1 0138 MILK   1.19
2 4122 EGGS   1.49
     SUBTOTAL  2.68
```

which obviously handles alpha data or

```
1   1.19
2   1.49
       2.68
```

which includes only numerics.

ASCII

American Standard Code for Information Interchange or ASCII is a universal code used in computers to represent characters. Table 21-1 shows each character's numeric representation.

```
32 space  48 0   64 @   80 P   96 `   112 p
33 !      49 1   65 A   81 Q   97 a   113 q
34 "      50 2   66 B   82 R   98 b   114 r
35 #      51 3   67 C   83 S   99 c   115 s
36 $      52 4   68 D   84 T   100 d  116 t
37 %      53 5   69 E   85 U   101 e  117 u
38 &      54 6   70 F   86 V   102 f  118 v
39 '      55 7   71 G   87 W   103 g  119 w
40 (      56 8   72 H   88 X   104 h  120 x
41 )      57 9   73 I   89 Y   105 i  121 y
42 *      58 :   74 J   90 Z   106 j  122 z
43 +      59 ;   75 K   91 [   107 k  123 {
44 ,      60 <   76 L   92 \   108 l  124 |
45 -      61 =   77 M   93 ]   109 m  125 }
46 .      62 >   78 N   94 ^   110 n  126 ~
47 /      63 ?   79 O   95 _   111 o  127 delete

Code 32 is the [SpaceBar] and Code 127 is the [Del] key.
```

Table 21-1. ASCII Codes.

The ASCII code for A is 65, for g is 103, for (is 40. A space or

[SpaceBar] is a character with code 32. The [Del] key has code 127. The ASCII character set is actually a subset of the LICS or Lotus International Character Set. LICS codes go from 0 to 255. Codes 1 through 31 represent characters pressed simultaneously with [Ctrl]. Codes 32 to 127 are the same as the ASCII codes in Table 21-1. Codes 128 through 255 are for international characters found in other languages besides English, including Japanese and German and characters such as the British pound sign, Japanese yen sign, and Greek characters such as delta and pi. A blank cell has no LICS code.

The reason for these codes is that computers understand only numbers. Actually they understand only two states - on and off. Perhaps you are familiar with the binary number system which has only two digits - 0 and 1. If you could look into memory, you would see nothing but strings of 0's and 1's. Keystrokes from the keyboard and characters on printers and CRT screens are encoded into the LICS codes and converted mathematically from the decimal number system to the binary number system.

Labels are strings of ASCII characters. Values are actually decimal numbers represented by equivalent binary numbers. Remember that values and labels are treated differently. The 1 in the label "Series 1" is a character with LICS or ASCII code 49, whereas the number 1 stored in a cell as a value is stored as the equivalent binary number 1.

Clear the worksheet.

You enter: **/ Worksheet Erase Yes**

@CODE(string)

@CODE(string) returns the LICS or ASCII code number of the first character of the string.

Again, in Table 21-1, uppercase A's ASCII code is 65.

You enter into A1: **@CODE("A") [Return]**

Your worksheet should look like Figure 21-12.

A1: @CODE("A")

	A	B
1	65	
2		

Figure 21-12. @CODE Function.

You enter into A3: **A [Return]**

You enter into B3: **@CODE(A3) [Return]**

65 is shown in B3.

You enter: **/ Copy B3 to B4..B6**

@CODE(A4) is in cell B4. ERR is displayed because cell A4 is empty and no LICS or ASCII code exists for an empty cell. Likewise for A5 and A6.

You enter into A4: **America [Return]**

65 is displayed in B4 because @CODE returns the code for the first character only.

You enter into A5: **1 [Return]**

For @CODE to return a code, the argument must be a label or character string. Perhaps it will help if, when you see @CODE, to think to yourself "this will give me a code or number (value); I must give it a label". These codes can be used in computations just as any other value.

You enter into A6: **'1 [Return]**

The label-prefix ' before the 1 makes the entry in A6 a label or character string. Code 49 is displayed in B6 for the character 1 in A6.

Your worksheet should look like Figure 21-13.

A6: '1

	A	B
1	65	
2		
3	A	65
4	America	65
5	1	ERR
6	1	49

Figure 21-13. More on @CODE Function.

@CHAR(x)

The inverse function of @CODE is @CHAR(x). @CHAR returns the character associated with that LICS or ASCII code argument. Think to yourself "@CHAR gives me a character; I must give it a number or code".

You enter into A8: **@CHAR(65) [Return]**

The character or label uppercase A is shown in A8.

You enter into A10: **65 [Return]**

You enter into B10: **@CHAR(A10) [Return]**

Uppercase A is displayed in B10.

You enter: / **Copy B10** to **B11..B12**

ERR's are shown because there are no values in the empty cells in column A.

You enter into A11: **49 [Return]**

The label "1" is displayed in B11.

You enter into A12: **63 [Return]**

As Table 21-1 shows, code 63 is a ?.

Your worksheet should look like Figure 21-14.

```
A12: 63


           A         B
 1        65
 2
 3   A              65
 4   America        65
 5          1       ERR
 6   1              49
 7
 8   A
 9
10        65 A
11        49 1
12        63 ?
```

Figure 21-14. @CHAR Function.

For a list of characters associated with LICS codes 128 through 255, fill cells A1..A123 with the values 128 to 255.

You enter: / **Worksheet Erase Yes**

You enter:
/ **Data Fill A1..A128 [Return] 128 [Return]** 1 [Return] 255 [Return]

Now place the characters associated with those codes in column B.

You enter into B1: **@CHAR(A1) [Return]**

You enter: / **Copy B1 to B2..B128**

Perhaps you recognize some of the characters. Code 162 is the cent sign, 163 the pound sign, 165 the yen sign, 172 is delta, 173 is pi, 174 >=, 177 plus or minus, 181 micro sign, 182 paragraph sign, 188 is 1/4, 189 is 1/2.

A list of each can be found in the Lotus 1-2-3 Reference Manual.

Use @CHAR to display those characters not found on your keyboard.

EXERCISES

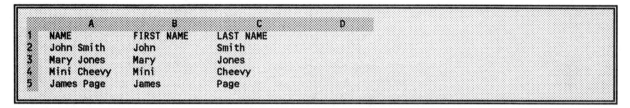

	A	B	C	D
1	NAME	FIRST NAME	LAST NAME	
2	John Smith	John	Smith	
3	Mary Jones	Mary	Jones	
4	Mini Cheevy	Mini	Cheevy	
5	James Page	James	Page	

1. Create the worksheet above by entering the names as shown in column A. Use @RIGHT and @LEFT to place the first and last names into individual cells as above. The @FIND command will have to be used to determine where the last name begins. @LENGTH will also be needed in the computation of the number of characters to pull off for the LAST NAME.

	A	B	C	D
1	NAME	FIRST NAME	LAST NAME	
2	John Smith	John	Smith	Dr. Smith
3	Mary Jones	Mary	Jones	Dr. Jones
4	Mini Cheevy	Mini	Cheevy	Dr. Cheevy
5	James Page	James	Page	Dr. Page

2. Add column D to the worksheet by using the concatenation operator & and column C.

```
         A          B          C          D
 1   Angelo     Alunni     Mr.       Mr. Angelo Alunni
 2   Clementine Carver     Prof.     Prof. Clementine Carver
 3   Fred       Cicilioni  Dr.       Dr. Fred Cicilioni
 4   John       Cicilioni  Mr.       Mr. John Cicilioni
 5   Rose       Falzett              Rose Falzett
 6   Nicholas   Killian    Pres.     Pres. Nicholas Killian
 7   Catharine  Minster    Dr.       Dr. Catharine Minster
 8   Flora      Sesak      Prof.     Prof. Flora Sesak
 9   Gary       Shepard    Mr.       Mr. Gary Shepard
10   Barbara    Washington Ms.       Ms. Barbara Washington
```

3. Enter column C into the STRINGEX worksheet shown above, which you saved during the lesson. Create column D with the concatenation operator and the three other columns. The @TRIM function can be used to delete the extra space before Rose Falzett.

Hint: column C and the concatenated space after it as a quantity would have to be trimmed.

```
         A                  B          C          D
 1   Mr. Angelo Alunni      Mr.      Angelo     Alunni
 2   Prof. Clementine Carve Prof.    Clementine Carver
 3   Dr. Fred Cicilioni     Dr.      Fred       Cicilioni
 4   Mr. John Cicilioni     Mr.      John       Cicilioni
 5   Rose Falzett                    Rose       Falzett
 6   Pres. Nicholas Killian Pres.    Nicholas   Killian
 7   Dr. Catharine Minster  Dr.      Catharine  Minster
 8   Prof. Flora Sesak      Prof.    Flora      Sesak
 9   Mr. Gary Shepard1      Mr.      Gary       Shepard
10   Ms. Barbara Washington Ms.      Barbara    Washington
```

4. Create column A of the worksheet above by using /Range Value on column D from the previous exercise's worksheet. Use string functions to pull off the title, first name, and last name as shown in columns B, C, and D above. Rose Falzett with no title will be a little involved, an @IF testing for a second space will be needed. You may assume that no space follows Falzett. Using @TRIM, of course, would eradicate this assumption.

5.   Create the worksheet below.

```
         A              B                    C
1    DICKSON PUBLIC LIBRARY
2
3    Book          Book                 Type of
4     ID           Title                 Book
5
6    A9264    Computers and You         Adult
7    A4678    Gone with the Wind        Adult
8    R3000    Anteaters of Modern America  Reference
9    A2015    Good Earth                Adult
10   C2345    Woof Woof Barks           Children's
11   C0271    Jack Gets Lost            Children's
```

A book id beginning with the letter A is an Adult book (meant in the most decent sense of the word), one beginning with C is Children's, and R is reference. All entries are constant except those in column C. The @IF and @LEFT functions will be needed. The string constants in the @IF arguments must be enclosed in double quotes.

6.   Use /Data Fill and @CHAR to create the worksheet below in a few easy keystrokes.   Do not enter any letters manually.

```
       A       B       C       D       E       F       G
1      65              A
2      66              B
3      67              C
4      68              D
5      69              E
6      70              F
7      71              G
8      72              H
9      73              I
10     74              J
11     75              K
12     76              L
13     77              M
14     78              N
15     79              O
16     80              P
17     81              Q
18     82              R
19     83              S
20     84              T
```

7.   Create the worksheet below.

```
A1: 'abcdefghijklmnopqrstuvwxyz

            A           B           C         D         E         F         G
1   abcdefghijklmnopqrstuvwxyz
2
3           1 a
4           2 ab
5           3 abc
6           4 abcd
7           5 abcde
8           6 abcdef
9           7 abcdefg
10          8 abcdefgh
11          9 abcdefghi
12         10 abcdefghij
13         11 abcdefghijk
14         12 abcdefghijkl
15         13 abcdefghijklm
16         14 abcdefghijklmn
17         15 abcdefghijklmno
18         16 abcdefghijklmnop
19         17 abcdefghijklmnopq
20         18 abcdefghijklmnopqr
```

Use /Data Fill for column A. Enter one formula into B3 and copy it down the column.

8.   Create the worksheet below.

```
         A              B                         C
 1  abcdefghijklmnopqrstuvwxyz
 2
 3         0 .bcdefghijklmnopqrstuvwxyz   abcdefghijklmnopqrstuvwxyz
 4         1 a.cdefghijklmnopqrstuvwxyz   .bcdefghijklmnopqrstuvwxyz
 5         2 ab.defghijklmnopqrstuvwxyz   ..cdefghijklmnopqrstuvwxyz
 6         3 abc.efghijklmnopqrstuvwxyz   ...defghijklmnopqrstuvwxyz
 7         4 abcd.fghijklmnopqrstuvwxyz   ....efghijklmnopqrstuvwxyz
 8         5 abcde.ghijklmnopqrstuvwxyz   .....fghijklmnopqrstuvwxyz
 9         6 abcdef.hijklmnopqrstuvwxyz   ......ghijklmnopqrstuvwxyz
10         7 abcdefg.ijklmnopqrstuvwxyz   .......hijklmnopqrstuvwxyz
11         8 abcdefgh.jklmnopqrstuvwxyz   ........ijklmnopqrstuvwxyz
12         9 abcdefghi.klmnopqrstuvwxyz   .........jklmnopqrstuvwxyz
13        10 abcdefghij.lmnopqrstuvwxyz   ..........klmnopqrstuvwxyz
14        11 abcdefghijk.mnopqrstuvwxyz   ...........lmnopqrstuvwxyz
15        12 abcdefghijkl.nopqrstuvwxyz   ...........mnopqrstuvwxyz
16        13 abcdefghijklm.opqrstuvwxyz   .............nopqrstuvwxyz
17        14 abcdefghijklmn.pqrstuvwxyz   ..............opqrstuvwxyz
18        15 abcdefghijklmno.qrstuvwxyz   ...............pqrstuvwxyz
19        16 abcdefghijklmnop.rstuvwxyz   ................qrstuvwxyz
20        17 abcdefghijklmnopq.stuvwxyz   .................rstuvwxyz
```

Column B needs only @REPLACE.   Column C will use @REPLACE and @REPEAT.

CUMULATIVE EXERCISES

C1. Create the worksheet below by retrieving the TOFU1 worksheet and deleting the Division, 92 Sales, and Commission columns. Use @ string functions to create the new columns shown below. Save under TOFU21.

```
         A        B         C        D          E
1                 IMITATION TOFU, INCORPORATED
2
3                          First    Last     First Initial &
4                 SalesRep  Initial  Name     Last Name
5                 =================================================
6            1 Saxe, J.     J.       Saxe     J. Saxe
7            2 Gress, R.    R.       Gress    R. Gress
8            3 Cosner, L.   L.       Cosner   L. Cosner
9            4 Smith, A.    A.       Smith    A. Smith
10           5 Smith, B.    B.       Smith    B. Smith
11           6 Kirlin, K.   K.       Kirlin   K. Kirlin
12           7 Wodak, F.    F.       Wodak    F. Wodak
13           8 Reese, J.    J.       Reese    J. Reese
14           9 Gruss, M.    M.       Gruss    M. Gruss
15          10 Boyle, T.    T.       Boyle    T. Boyle
16
```

C2. Create the worksheet below by retrieving the FISH1 worksheet that you created in Lesson 1 and deleting rows 9 through 16. Use @ string functions to create one formula in cell A10 that produces the displayed sentence. Copy the formula to the range A12..A14. (Hint: The only @ string function you need is @STRING.) Save under FISH21.

```
    A          B                 C        D        E        F        G        H
1          H A P P Y  T R O P I C A L  F I S H  S T O R E
2   Item                        Quantity  Retail  Wholesale  Profit  Total Pr.
3    #        Item Name          Sold    Price    Price   per Item  per Item
4   ---------------------------------------------------------------------------
5   273 7-inch fish net          63      $1.99    $0.70    $1.29    $81.27
6   238 1-lb. decorative rocks   49      $2.99    $1.30    $1.69    $82.81
7   130 underwater fern          13      $2.29    $0.90    $1.39    $18.07
8   281 40-gallon aquarium       14     $39.99   $22.00   $17.99   $251.86
9
10  63 of item # 273, 7-inch fish net, were sold at a price of $1.99.
11  49 of item # 238, 1-lb. decorative rocks, were sold at a price of $2.99.
12  13 of item # 130, underwater fern, were sold at a price of $2.29.
13  14 of item # 281, 40-gallon aquarium, were sold at a price of $39.99.
14
15
```

C3. Create the worksheet below by retrieving the BILL1 worksheet that you created in Lesson 1 and deleting rows 8 through 14. Enter one formula using string @ functions into A9 and copy it to A10..A12. Save under BILL21.

	A	B	C	D	E
1		MONTHLY BILLS FOR MARCH			
2					
3		Actual	Budgeted	Over/(Under)	
4	Food	$238	$220	$18	
5	Rent	$550	$550	$0	
6	Phone	$39	$30	$9	
7	Electric	$43	$50	($7)	
8					
9	MARCH: Food bill was $238.				
10	MARCH: Rent bill was $550.				
11	MARCH: Phone bill was $39.				
12	MARCH: Electric bill was $43.				
13					

C4. Create the worksheet below by retrieving the GOLF1 worksheet that you created in Lesson 1 and deleting rows 9 down. Enter one formula using string @ functions into A11 and copy it to A12..A14. Save under GOLF21.

	A	B	C	D	E	F	G	H	I	J	K
1			J & F GOLF COURSE SCORE SHEET								
2	Hole	1	2	3	4	5	6	7	8	9	Total
3	Par	4	5	4	3	5	4	4	3	4	36
4											
5	Joe	8	5	6	4	4	5	6	4	4	46
6	Mary	4	6	5	4	6	4	5	5	3	42
7	Mike	3	7	6	4	5	5	6	5	4	45
8	Sheila	5	5	6	4	3	3	4	6	5	41
9											
10											
11	Joe's score was 46 for 9 holes.										
12	Mary's score was 42 for 9 holes.										
13	Mike's score was 45 for 9 holes.										
14	Sheila's score was 41 for 9 holes.										
15											

Contents:

This lesson covers macros. It begins with quick macros created with the Learn (Releases 2.x) or Record (Releases 3.x) feature. Simple macros are then entered into the worksheet manually and executed. The more commonly used advanced macro commands are then introduced and integrated into simple examples. User-defined menus are illustrated.

Macros

Macros are sets of keystrokes or instructions saved in consecutive cells in the worksheet, which can be easily and repeatedly executed. Macros are generally used to automate a procedure, to store keystrokes used frequently, or in cases where the same keystrokes are done repetitively.

Creating a macro involves entering keystrokes or commands into cells. You can type the commands in manually or you can use the quick macro feature of 1-2-3 to enter them for you. First we'll create a quick macro and then move to manually created macros.

Releases 2 and 2.01: These releases have no quick macros facility. Continue reading at Manually Created Macros.

The quick macro feature in Releases 2.x is the Learn feature; the quick macro feature in Releases 3.x is the Record feature. If you're using Release 2.2, 2.3, or 2.4, read the section Quick Macros with Learn Releases 2.x and then continue reading at Manually Created Macros. If you're using Releases 3.0 or 3.1+, read the section Quick Macros with Record Releases 3.x and continue reading at Manually Created Macros.

Quick Macros with Learn Releases 2.x

The steps necessary for creating and executing a quick macro with **Learn** are:

1. Use /Range Name Create to name the Learn range with a name or with backslash and a letter.
2. Set up the Learn range with /Worksheet Learn Range.
3. Turn on the recording of keystrokes with [Alt]+[F5].
4. Type the keystrokes to be stored.
5. Turn off the recording of keystrokes with [Alt]+[F5].
6. Execute the macro. If you used a name to name the Learn range, type [Alt]+[F3] and the name. If you used backslash and a letter to name the the Learn range, type [Alt]+the letter.

You will use the quick macro Learn feature of 1-2-3 to build a macro beginning in cell E1 which enters your name and address into three consecutive cells in a column. First clear the worksheet:

You enter: **/ Worksheet Erase Yes**

Step 1. Name the Learn range.

You enter:
/Range Name Create ADDRESS [Return] E1..E20 [Return]

Step 2. Set up the location of the Learn range, or where the keystrokes will be stored:

You enter: **/Worksheet Learn Range ADDRESS [Return]**

Move the pointer to cell A1:

You enter: **[Home]**

Step 3. Turn on the recording of keystrokes.

You enter: **[Alt]+[F5]**

A LEARN indicator is shown on the bottom of the screen. All keystrokes will now be recorded beginning in cell E1.

Step 4. Type the keystrokes to be stored for macro execution. I'm going to type my name and address, you type yours:

You enter into A1: **Ruth Yaron [Down]**

You enter into A2: **University of Scranton [Down]**

You enter into A3: **Scranton, PA 18510 [Return]**

Step 5. Turn off the recording of keystrokes:

You enter: **[Alt]+[F5]**

Move the pointer into E1 and E2 and note the keystrokes saved there. {D} indicates that [Down] was typed. The ~ indicates that [Return] was typed. If you made any typing errors and corrected them with [BackSpace] or [Esc], {BS} and {ESC} will be in the cells. See Table 1 in this lesson on page 574. These keystrokes are explained in the next section on Manually Creating a Macro.

Your screen should look something like the figure below:

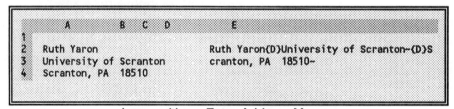

Learn with an Enter Address Macro.

Step 6. Execute the macro.

You: **Move the cell pointer to B6.**

You enter: **[Alt]+[F3] ADDRESS [Return]**

The macro has typed your name and address into B6..B8.

You may execute this macro as many times as you like. The MacroManager add-in is great for keeping macros in a library that you can use with other worksheets. See the Add-In Appendix.

In my opinion, this is a quick and dirty way of creating temporary macros to be used once and thrown away. Macros that will be used again should be well-documented manually and saved in a macro library.

Quick Macros with Record Releases 3.x

All keystrokes that you type are constantly being recorded into a Record Buffer. These recorded keystrokes can then be copied into a range in the worksheet and executed as a macro. The record buffer menu, which allows you to manipulate the recorded keystrokes, is brought up with [Alt]+[F2].

The steps necessary for creating and executing a quick macro with Record are:

1. Clear the record buffer by typing [Alt]+[F2] and choosing Erase. (This step isn't really necessary, but I like working with a clean slate.)
2. Type the keystrokes you wish to record for a macro.
3. Copy the keystrokes to a range in the worksheet. Type [Alt]+[F2] and choose Copy. Hit [Tab] and use the arrow keys to highlight all of the keystokes you wish to copy. Type [Return]. Specify a range in the worksheet to contain the copied keystrokes and hit [Return].
4. Name the worksheet range containing the keystrokes with either a name or a backslash and a letter.
5. Execute the macro. If you used a name to name the Learn range, type [Alt]+[F3] and the name. If you used backslash and a letter to name the the Learn range, type [Alt]+the letter.

You will now use the record feature to create a macro which enters your name and address into three consecutive cells in a column.

First clear the worksheet:

You enter: **/ Worksheet Erase Yes**

Step 1. Clear the record buffer:

You enter: **[Alt]+[F2] Erase**

Step 2. Type the keystrokes to be recorded for macro execution. I'm going to type my name and address, you type yours:

You enter into A1: **Ruth Yaron [Down]**

You enter into A2: **University of Scranton [Down]**

You enter into A3: **Scranton, PA 18510 [Return]**

Step 3. Copy the keystrokes into the range E1..E20:

You enter: **[Alt]+[F2] C**opy

You enter: **[Tab]**

You enter:
[Left] until the first letter in your first name.

{D} indicates that [Down] was typed. The ~ indicates that [Return] was typed. If you made any typing errors and corrected them with [BackSpace] or [Esc], {BS} and {ESC} will be in the cells. See Table 1 in this lesson on page 574. These keystrokes are explained in the next section on Manually Creating a Macro.

You enter: **[Return]**

Specify the range in the worksheet to copy the keystrokes to:

You enter: **E1..E20 [Return]**

Step 4. Name the range containing the macro.

You enter: **/R**ange **N**ame **C**reate **ADDRESS [Return]** E1..E20 [Return]

Before you execute the macro, move the cell pointer to a position in the worksheet where you would like a copy of your name and address.

You: **Position cell pointer to B6.**

Step 5. Execute the macro.

You enter: **[Alt]+[F3] ADDRESS [Return]**

Voila! Your address is entered into B6..B8.

You may execute this macro as many times as you like. The MacroManager add-in is great for keeping macros in a library that you can use with other worksheets. See the Add-In Appendix.

There are two other options on the record buffer menu. Playback is used to run highlighted keystrokes directly from the record buffer. Try it.

Step mode plays back the keystrokes one at a time and requires you to hit [Return] between each keystroke. It is used for debugging purposes. Try it by choosing Step and running a macro.

In my opinion, the record buffer is a quick and dirty way of creating temporary macros to be used once and thrown away. Macros that will be used again should be well-documented manually and saved in a macro library.

Manually Created Macros

Why would you want to create macros manually? Because there are many commands, similar to programming language commands, that could be added to a macro. These are summarized in Lesson 23 Advanced Macro Commands. Some of the commands are used in examples in this lesson.

The 3 steps for manually creating a macro are:

1. Enter the keystrokes and commands into consecutive cells.

2. Name the first cell containing the macro backslash (\) followed by one of the 26 letters of the alphabet using /Range Name Create.[1]

3. Execute the macro by holding down the [Alt] key while typing the letter in its name.

Let's say you work for XYZ Corporation and you find yourself constantly typing the name of the company over and over again into cells of a 1-2-3 worksheet. To save yourself some keystroking, you decide to create a macro.

Start with a clean worksheet.

You enter: / **Worksheet Erase Yes**

---

[1]In all releases except 2 and 2.01, macros can be named with labels up to 15 characters long. Use /Range Name Create and name the first cell containing macro instructions. To execute the macro, type [Alt]+[F3] and you will be prompted for the name of the macro to run.

Do step 1. Enter the macro into some cell.

You enter into A1: **XYZ Corporation [Return]**

Do step 2. Name the macro. We'll name it with the letter N for Name.

You enter: / **Range Name Create \N [Return] A1 [Return]**

Just as a check, issue the create command again and note that \N is listed on the third line in the control panel.

You enter: / **Range Name Create**

Your worksheet should look like Figure 22-1.

```
A1: 'XYZ Corporation
Enter name:
\N
           A          B
1   XYZ Corporation
2
```

Figure 22-1. Macro Named \N.

You enter: **[Esc] 5 times.**

Before executing the macro, move the cell pointer to where you want the company name to be entered, let's say cell C5.

You: **Position pointer in C5.**

Do Step 3. Execute the macro.

Executing the \N macro entails holding down the [Alt] key while typing N (upper or lower case doesn't matter).

You enter: **[Alt]+N**

Recall that the + between [Alt] and N means to hold down the [Alt] key while simultaneously pressing the N key once.

The keystrokes XYZ Corporation are shown on the second line of your control panel as shown in Figure 22-2.

XYZ Corporation is displayed only in the control panel of Figure 12-2 and not yet in cell C5 because a [Return] is necessary.

Figure 22-2. Results of \M Macro Execution.

You enter: **[Return]**

Think about it. How do you get a [Return] keystroke into a macro if, when you hit [Return], 1-2-3 thinks you're done typing the entry?
To get a simulated [Return] keystroke into a macro, the tilde (~) character is used.

You enter into A1: **XYZ Corporation~ [Return]**

You: **Position pointer into D1.**

You execute the macro: **[Alt]+N**

The ~ worked as a [Return] keystroke.

There are many other keys in the same predicament as [Return], such as the [Down] arrow key, which need special characters to simulate them in macros. Below is an alphabetized list of them.

```
In Macro                    When executed, the result is the same as:

~                      [Return]
{ABS}                  [F4/ABS]
{BACKSPACE}            [BackSpace]
or {BS}
{BIGLEFT}              [Shift]+[Tab] or [Ctrl]+[Left]
{BIGRIGHT}             [Tab] or [Ctrl]+[Right]
{CALC}                 [F9/CALC]
{DELETE}               [Del]
or {DEL}
{DOWN} or {D}          [Down]
{EDIT}                 [F2/EDIT]
{END}                  [End]
{ESCAPE}               [Esc]
or {ESC}
{GOTO}                 [F5/GOTO]
{GRAPH}                [F10/GRAPH]
{HOME}                 [Home]
{HELP}                 [F1/HELP]
{LEFT} or {L}          [Left]
{MENU}                 /
{NAME}                 [F3/NAME]
{PGDN}                 [PgDn]
{PGUP}                 [PgUp]
{QUERY}                [F7/QUERY]
{RIGHT} or {R}         [Right] arrow key.
{TABLE}                [F8/TABLE]
{UP} or {U}            [Up] arrow key.
{WINDOW}               [F6/WINDOW]

A repetition factor can be added inside the braces to repeat a keystroke.
For instance {RIGHT 3} would be equivalent to {RIGHT}{RIGHT}{RIGHT}.
```

Table 22-1. Special Macro Keys.

In the special cases where you would really and truly want a ~, {, or } in the macro, enclose them in braces. For example, XYZ{~}Corporation in a macro would result in XYZ~Corporation with the tilde being executed as the typed character tilde and not the [Return] keystroke. {{}x+y{}}*2 would result in {x+y}*2.

Clear the worksheet.

You enter: / **Worksheet Erase Yes**

You'll now create a macro to enter the company's return address,

XYZ Corp.
Main St.
Abctown, PA 10000

into the three consecutive cells B11, B12, and B13.

Step 1. Enter the macro.

You enter into A1:
{GOTO}B11~XYZ Corp.{DOWN}Main St.{DOWN} Abctown, PA 10000~ [Return]

Your worksheet should look like Figure 22-3.

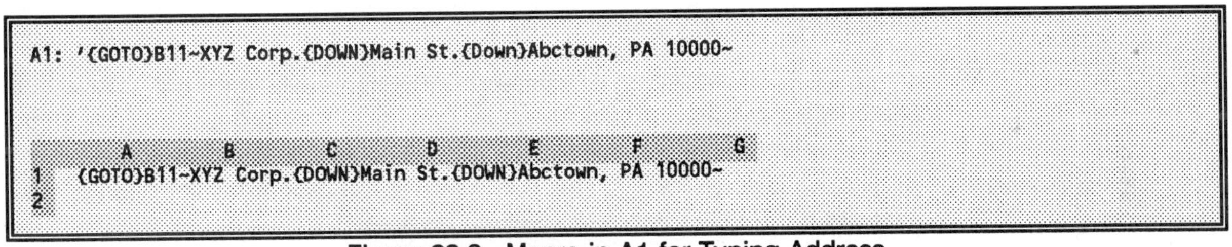

```
A1: '{GOTO}B11~XYZ Corp.{DOWN}Main St.{Down}Abctown, PA 10000~



       A        B        C        D        E        F        G
1   {GOTO}B11~XYZ Corp.{DOWN}Main St.{DOWN}Abctown, PA 10000~
2
```

Figure 22-3. Macro in A1 for Typing Address.

Step 2. Name the macro.

You enter: / **Range Name Create \A [Return] A1 [Return]**

Step 3. Execute the macro.

You enter: **[Alt]+A**

Your worksheet should look like Figure 22-4.

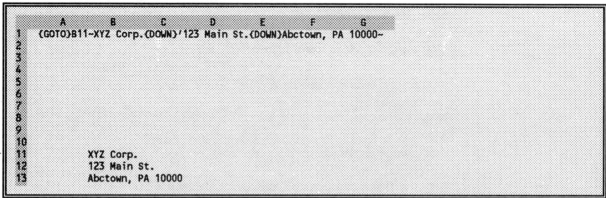

Figure 22-4. Worksheet after Execution of \A Macro.

The ~ after B11 is the [Return] keystroke necessary after the [F5/GOTO] key.

For more involved macros, it is best to do the keystrokes by hand on the computer while writing down each one on a piece of paper. Then do Step 1, Enter the macro, while referring to the paper. It is very easy to forget little things if you don't.

The maximum number of characters that could be entered into a cell containing a macro is 240. However, an entire macro does not have to be entered in one cell. In fact, it is easier to understand and modify a macro if several cells are used. This last macro is rather lengthy for one cell and should be broken down into several cells.

1-2-3 begins macro execution in the named cell (\A). When the commands in that cell have been executed, it continues by moving down a cell. Therefore, cells for a macro must go consecutively down the same column.

Create the same \A again using several cells. You'll use some conventional standards in creating well-written macros, such as placing the name of the macro to the left of its starting cell and adding a column of documentation to the right.

You enter: / **Worksheet Erase Yes**

Step 1. Enter the macro.

You enter into B1: **{GOTO}B11~[Down]**

Don't get confused with {DOWN} and [Down]; the latter means the arrow key, just as we've been using throughout this text. {DOWN} is the macro command from Table 22-1 which causes the pointer to move down during macro execution.

You enter into B2: **XYZ Corp.{DOWN}[Down]**

You enter into B3: **Main St.{DOWN}[Down]**

You enter into B4: **Abctown, PA 10000~[Return]**

Your worksheet should look like Figure 22-5.

```
B4: 'Abctown, PA  10000~


          A         B         C
1                   {GOTO}B11~
2                   XYZ Corp.{DOWN}
3                   Main St.{DOWN}
4                   Abctown, PA  10000~
```

Figure 22-5. Macro in Consecutive Cells in the Same Column.

Step 2. Name the macro.

You enter: **/ Range Name Create \A [Return] B1 [Return]**

You need only specify the first cell address when naming the range of the macro.

Step 3. Execute the macro.

You enter: **[Alt]+A**

The macro starts at the named first cell and continues down until it reaches a blank cell or executes the advanced macro command {QUIT}. (Explained later.)

Now for the good macro programming skills. It is good practice to place the name of the macro in the column to the left of the first macro cell, in this case, cell A1.

You enter into A1: **'\A [Return]**

If you did not include the ', \A would cause a string of A's to be displayed in the cell. (If you don't recall this, see repeat label-prefix in index.)

To the right of the macro cells, comments should be entered to explain the purpose of the macro and anything else the user should know. Good documentation, as in all computer programming, is absolutely necessary.

You enter into E1: **This macro enters the [Down]**

You enter into E2: **company's name and address [Down]**

You enter into E3: **into cells B11, B12, and [Down]**

You enter into E4: **B13. [Return]**

This can much more easily be done by just entering the entire sentence into cell E1 and using /Range Justify. (See index.) The comments to the right should give a quick explanation of the purpose of the macro. The name to the left gives your eye a quick reference.

Placing the name of the macro to the left of the first instruction cell makes possible the use of /Range Name Labels Right to quickly name a whole series of macros and variables. Lesson 23 has many examples of more advanced macros where /Range Name Labels Right was used for this cell naming. Observe the first exercise at the end of this lesson. The macro library contains several macros. /Range Name Labels Right can name each of the 9 macros all at once. Extensive macro use usually entails a worksheet file containing frequently used macros. Using /File Combine, the macro file on disk can be added to any worksheet. One issuance of /Range Name Labels Right and the worksheet is ready to go.

The MacroManager add-in is great for organizing often-used macros in a library. See Add-Ins Appendix.

```
      A       B       C        D       E       F       G
1   \A    {GOTO}B11~              This macro enters the
2         XYZ Corp.{DOWN}         company's name and address
3         Main St.{DOWN}          into cells B11, B12, and
4         Abctown, PA  10000      B13.
```

Figure 22-6. Macro with Range Name to Left and Comments to Right.

Let's further modify the macro to enter the address in any cell (not just cell B11, B12, and 13). The macro will let the user specify the cell where the address is to be entered by asking the user for input. This can be done in many ways, the easiest of which is {?}.

{?}

Modify the macro using {?} which will stop execution of the macro and wait for the user to enter data.

You enter into B1: **{GOTO}{?}~[Return]**

(I hope you are using the [F2/EDIT] key when you modify a cell like this. It's easier than retyping the whole entry.)

You enter: **[Alt]+A**

CMD appears at the bottom of the screen indicating that a macro command is in effect. The POINT mode indicator designates that you can either enter an address at this time or use pointer movement keys to indicate a cell address.

Computer message: **Enter address to go to:**

The message is the same as that from the [F5/GOTO] function key. Remember, whether you type it or the macro does, you get the same results on the screen.

You enter: **F10 [Return]**

Your worksheet should look like Figure 22-7.

	A	B	C	D	E	F	G
1	\A	{GOTO}{?}~			This macro enters the		
2		XYZ Corp.{DOWN}			company's name and address		
3		Main St.{DOWN}			into cells B11, B12, and		
4		Abctown, PA 10000~			B13.		
5							
6							
7							
8							
9							
10					XYZ Corp.		
11		XYZ Corp.			Main St.		
12		Main St.			Abctown, PA 10000		
13		Abctown, PA 10000					

Figure 22-7. Macro with {?}.

The ~ in B1 is still necessary to finish the GOTO command, the [Return] key you typed after F10 was only to inform 1-2-3 you were finished with the input data. The comments in column E should be changed to correspond to the modification in the macro.

If you'd like to save this file, please do.

- - - If you need a break, stop at this point. - - -

You enter: / **Worksheet Erase Yes**

You enter: / **Data Fill A1..C10 [Return] 10 [Return] 5 [Return] [Return]**

Your worksheet should look like Figure 22-8.

	A	B	C
1	10	60	110
2	15	65	115
3	20	70	120
4	25	75	125
5	30	80	130
6	35	85	135
7	40	90	140
8	45	95	145
9	50	100	150
10	55	105	155

Figure 22-8. Worksheet for Insert Rows Macro.

Let's say for some reason you have this worksheet and would like to add a blank row between all existing rows of data so that the worksheet will look like Figure 22-9.

	A	B	C
1	10	60	110
2			
3	15	65	115
4			
5	20	70	120
6			
7	25	75	125
8			
9	30	80	130
10			
11	35	85	135
12			
13	40	90	140
14			
15	45	95	145
16			
17	50	100	150
18			
19	55	105	155
20			

Figure 22-9. Worksheet with Inserted Rows.

The command necessary to add a row is /Worksheet Insert Row [Return]. The actual keystrokes (if not using highlight and [Return] method) are / W I R [Return]. These keystrokes would have to be done for every row of data.

A macro can be set up to add a row.

Step 1. Enter the macro.

You enter into D1: **'\R [Right]**

You enter into E1: **'/wir~[Right]**

You enter into F1: **Macro to insert a row. [Return]**

The ' in E1 is necessary to prevent entering menu mode when the / is typed. Be careful to type forward slash / and not backward slash \.

Step 2. Name the macro.

You enter: **/ Range Name Create \R [Return] E1 [Return]**

Step 3. Execute the macro.

You: **Position the pointer in A2 (or anywhere in row 2).**

You enter: **[Alt]+R**

Your worksheet should look like Figure 22-10.

	A	B	C	D	E	F
1	10	60	110	\R	/wir~	Macro to insert a row.
2						
3	15	65	115			
4	20	70	120			
5	25	75	125			
6	30	80	130			
7	35	85	135			
8	40	90	140			
9	45	95	145			
10	50	100	150			
11	55	105	155			

Figure 22-10. Worksheet after Execution of Macro to Insert a Row.

To insert another row, the pointer must be moved down two rows and the macro must be executed again.

You enter: **[Down] [Down] [Alt]+R**

The two [Down] keystrokes can be added to the macro. {DOWN}{DOWN} can be used but a repetition factor of 2 is cleaner.

You enter into E1: **'/wir~{DOWN 2} [Return]**

You widen column E: / **Worksheet** Column **Set-Width 15 [Return]**

You: **Position pointer to A6.**

You enter: **[Alt]+R [Alt]+R**

Now it's just a matter of typing [Alt]+R for the rest of the worksheet data, which could be time-consuming. Actually, if the macro in E1 would just repeat itself over and over, we wouldn't have to repeat any keystrokes.

{BRANCH location}

{BRANCH} will be the first of the advanced macro commands which we will cover. A complete list can be found at the end of this lesson. {BRANCH} is one command which controls the flow of execution of a macro. For those familiar with computer programming, it is similar to an unconditional go to command. It causes the control to branch to the macro command located at the location argument which can be either a named range or a cell address.

You enter into E2: **{BRANCH E1} [Return]**

Your worksheet should look like Figure 22-11.

	A	B	C	D	E	F
1	10	60	110	\R	/wir~{DOWN 2}	Macro to insert a row
2					{BRANCH E1}	
3	15	65	115			
4						
5	20	70	120			
6						
7	25	75	125			
8						
9	30	80	130			
10	35	85	135			
11	40	90	140			
12	45	95	145			
13	50	100	150			
14	55	105	155			

Figure 22-11. Macro with {BRANCH} Advanced Macro Command.

You: **Position pointer to A10.**

When the macro is executed, the keystrokes in E1 will be done, control will move consecutively down to E2 whose {BRANCH} will send control back to E1, etc.

Don't confuse {BRANCH} with {GOTO}. {BRANCH} transfers control of the macro to another instruction within the macro. {GOTO} moves the cell pointer on the screen.

Break

Before executing the macro, find the [Break] key. You must hold down [Ctrl] while you press [Break]. Now execute the macro, watch it for a while, and then break.

You enter: **[Alt]+R [Ctrl]+[Break]**

Break is shown on the bottom of the screen and ERROR is flashing in the mode indicator.

You enter: **[Esc] [Home]**

That was what was known as an infinite loop or a set of instructions which will repeat indefinitely. (Yes, they would have kept repeating even if row 8192 was reached.)

Put some data back in those rows:

You enter: **/ Data Fill [Return] 10 [Return] 5 [Return] [Return]**

Let's execute it again from the top.

You: **Position pointer in A2.**

You enter: **[Alt]+R**

The first rows of your worksheet should look like Figure 22-12.

	A	B	C	D	E	F
1	10	105	200	\R	/wir~(DOWN 2}	Macro to insert a row
2						
3	15	110	205		{BRANCH E1}	
4	20	115	210			
5	25	120	215			
6	30	125	220			
7	35	130	225			
8	40	135	230			
9	45	140	235			
10	50	145	240			

Figure 22-12. Accidental Modification of Macro Cells.

Only the keystrokes in cell E1 were executed because, by the time control moved down a row to cell E2, it was blank because of the inserted row.

WARNING: Store macros in parts of the worksheet where they will not be affected by themselves, other macros, or your manual keystrokes.

Again I suggest expanding your worksheet diagonally as shown below so that inserted and deleted columns and rows pose no problem. A macro library worksheet file, a file containing a collection of frequently used macros, can be easily combined into a worksheet with /File Combine. (Or forget all of this and use the MacroManager add-in.) It should be added into the worksheet as shown below:

```
Worksheet
```

```
Macros
```

You enter: **/ Worksheet Delete Row A2 [Return]**

You enter: **[Home]**

You enter: **[Alt]+R**

The first rows of your worksheet should look like Figure 22-13.

```
           A          B          C          D          E              F
1
2         10        105        200  \R    /wir~{DOWN 2}  Macro to insert a row
3         15        110        205         {BRANCH E1}
4         20        115        210
5         25        120        215
6         30        125        220
7         35        130        225
8         40        135        230
9         45        140        235
10        50        145        240
```

Figure 22-13. Unadjusted Cell Reference in Macro.

Row 1 is blank but the macro is still in consecutive cells. So what caused the macro to incorrectly halt this time? Look where it's branching. The cell address, E1, was not adjusted to cell E2. We've seen this problem in the graph lesson and the same solution exists here.

WARNING: Never use cell references in macros; always use named ranges.

Here the cell reference is to a cell within the macro. Here you can name cell E1 something like TOPLOOP with /Range Name Create. The second macro cell would then contain {BRANCH TOPLOOP}. My first examples in this lesson did use specified cell references instead of named cells to keep them as simple as possible.

- - - If you need a break, stop at this point. - - -

You enter: / **Worksheet Erase Yes**

You enter: / **Worksheet Global Column-Width 14 [Return]**

Create the worksheet shown in Figure 22-14. See control panel for contents of B6.

Figure 22-14. Worksheet for Macro to Enter Data.

Enter a macro beginning at B12 to allow the user to enter sales data into the range B2..B4 which will have the name SALES.

You enter: **/ Range Name Create SALES [Return] B2..B4 [Return]**

Step 1. Enter the macro.

You enter into B12: **{GOTO}SALES~[Down]**

You enter into B13: **{?}{DOWN}[Down]**

You enter into B14: **{?}{DOWN}[Down]**

You enter into B15: **{?}~[Return]**

You enter into A12: **'\E [Return]**

You enter into C12: **Macro to enter sales data. [Return]**

Your worksheet should look like Figure 22-15.

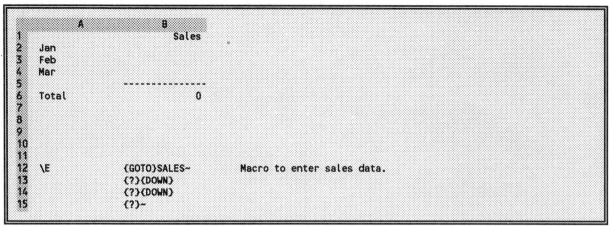

Figure 22-15. Worksheet with Macro.

Step 2. Name the macro.

You enter: **/ Range Name Create \E [Return] B12 [Return]**

Step 3. Execute the macro.

You enter: **[Alt]+E**

You enter: **200 [Return] 215 [Return] 248 [Return]**

Perhaps a command should be added to the macro to erase the range B2..B4 before data is entered.

You: **Position pointer in B13.**

You enter: **/ Worksheet Insert Row B13 [Return]**

The /Range Erase can be used to clear the range.

You enter into B13: **'/reB2..B4~[Return]**

You enter: **[Alt]+E**

You enter: **300 [Return] 315 [Return] 348 [Return]**

Your worksheet should look like Figure 22-16.

```
              A              B
1                          Sales
2      Jan                  300
3      Feb                  315
4      Mar                  348
5                      -----------------
6      Total                963
7
8
9
10
11
12     \E           {GOTO}SALES~         Macro to enter sales data.
13                  /reB2..B4~
14                  {?}{DOWN}
15                  {?}{DOWN}
16                  {?}~
```

Figure 22-16. Added Command to Erase Range.

What's wrong with that macro? It is potentially dangerous in that it contains not only a specified range instead of a named range, but also an erase command on a specified range! Remember my warning that cell references in macros are not adjusted automatically by 1-2-3. A few deleted or inserted rows or columns and this macro has just wiped out some other data almost randomly. Actually, commands other than erase with a specified range can be just as dangerous - copies, moves, and {?} to input data can possibly overwrite existing data.

You enter into B13: **'/reSALES~[Return]**

Texts like this one usually show the first characters of options in macros in lowercase, such as the re is here. Range names and cell references are typed in uppercase. The case of the letter doesn't matter to 1-2-3. Standardized case use makes macros more readable to humans. You can use a different convention, just remember to be consistent with upper and lower cases in your macros.

You enter: **[Alt]+E 400 [Return] 415 [Return] 448 [Return]**

The range is cleared before input is begun.

Always verify a modification to a macro soon after it is made by executing it with some test data. If a bug or error was accidentally added with the modification, it is more easily found now than at a later date.

{BLANK location}

{BLANK location} erases cells; location can be a single cell or range. Change the /Range Erase in the macro to {BLANK} and execute the macro.

You enter into B13: **{BLANK SALES} [Return] [Alt]+E**

Your worksheet should look like Figure 22-17.

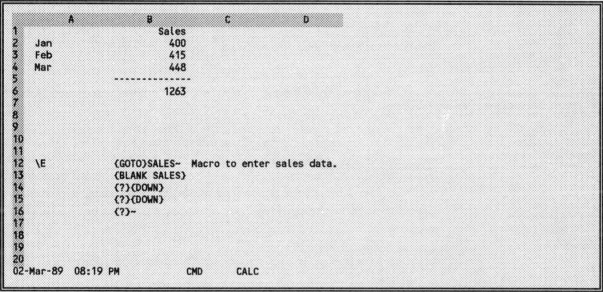

```
            A              B           C             D
1                       Sales
2      Jan               400
3      Feb               415
4      Mar               448
5                     -------------
6                       1263
7
8
9
10
11
12   \E            {GOTO}SALES~  Macro to enter sales data.
13                {BLANK SALES}
14                {?}{DOWN}
15                {?}{DOWN}
16                {?}~
17
18
19
20
02-Mar-89  08:19 PM           CMD        CALC
```

Figure 22-17. Recalculation Necessary before {BLANK} Takes Effect.

{BLANK} does not erase until the worksheet is recalculated. (See Recalculation.) Note the CALC indicator at the bottom of the screen indicating recalculation is necessary; some values are not valid because they haven't been recalculated yet.

Releases 3.0 and 3.1+:   Recalculation is done after the {BLANK} command automatically. Skip to the next section on the Auto-Execute Macro.

The worksheet will be recalculated with a [Return] or pointer movement key. The {DOWN} in B14 will cause recalculation to occur and the range will not be blanked until it's executed. Placing a tilde (~) after the {BLANK SALES} will solve this problem in a quick and dirty fashion. However, to clarify that a recalculation is necessary at that point, {CALC} would be more explanatory.

You enter: **400 [Return] 415 [Return] 448 [Return]**

You enter into B13: **[F2/EDIT] {CALC} [Return]**

Cell B13 should now contain {BLANK SALES}{CALC}

You enter: **[Alt]+E**

Now the cells are blanked immediately.

You enter: **400 [Return] 415 [Return] 448 [Return]**

Many advanced macro commands require a recalculation of the worksheet before the results of the commands are actually obtained. They are marked in the summary in Lesson 23 with "Recalculation required."

Auto-Execute Macro \0

Besides the 26 possible backslash names for macros, \A to \Z, there is one more called the **auto-execute macro**. The auto-exec macro is always named \0 (the number zero, not the letter o). When a file is retrieved, 1-2-3 always searches for a macro named \0. If it exists, it is executed immediately after the retrieve. Set up the \E macro to be the auto-exec macro.

You enter: **/ Range Name Create \0 [Return] B12 [Return]**

Recall that it is legal for a cell to have more than one name. B12 now has two names - \E and \0. In fact, usually the auto-exec macro does have another name just in case you need to execute it while working on the worksheet file. [Alt]+0 doesn't work in READY mode.

Now the file must be saved so that it can be retrieved.

You enter: **/ File Save MACFILE1 [Return]**

You enter: **/ Worksheet Erase Yes**

The erase wasn't really necessary but it make things clearer.

You enter: **/ File Retrieve MACFILE1 [Return]**

The CMD indicator says that a macro is currently executing.

You enter: **500 [Return] 515 [Return] 548 [Return]**

This macro couldn't really be called "user-friendly" because it assumes the user knows what to do with no prompting.

{GETNUMBER prompt-string,location}

{GETNUMBER prompt-string,location} pauses execution of the macro, types the prompt-string in the control panel, takes value the user inputs, and places it in location.

You enter into B14:

{GETNUMBER "Enter January sales: ",SALES}{DOWN} [Return]

Your worksheet should look like Figure 22-18.

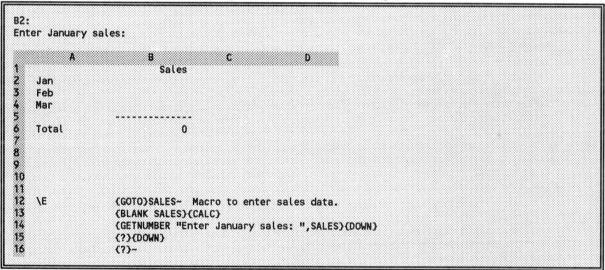

```
B2:
Enter January sales:

              A              B              C              D
1                         Sales
2     Jan
3     Feb
4     Mar
5                      --------------
6     Total                 0
7
8
9
10
11
12    \E           {GOTO}SALES~  Macro to enter sales data.
13                 {BLANK SALES}{CALC}
14                 {GETNUMBER "Enter January sales: ",SALES}{DOWN}
15                 {?}{DOWN}
16                 {?}~
```

Figure 22-18. {GETNUMBER} Prompt in Control Panel.

You enter: **[Alt]+E 600 [Return] 615 [Return] 648 [Return]**

{GETNUMBER} commands can be used to prompt for the Feb and Mar sales, too, if you name cells B3 and B4 and use the names as the location arguments of the {GETNUMBER}s.

{GETNUMBER} requires recalculation which the {DOWN} takes care of.

For the next example, change cell B14 back to its original entry and erase cells A12 and C12.

You enter into B14: **{?}{DOWN}[Return]**

You enter: / **Range Erase A12 [Return]**

You enter: / **Range Erase C12 [Return]**

You enter: **[Alt]+E 700 [Return] 715 [Return] 748 [Return]**

The last execution was to make sure your macro is still working properly.

Get rid of the auto-execute macro.

You enter: / **Range Name Delete \0 [Return]**

You enter: / **File Save MACFILE2 [Return]**

Your worksheet should look like Figure 22-19.

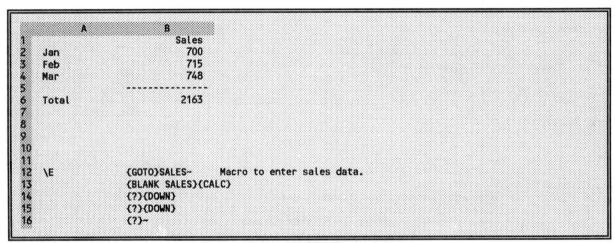

```
              A              B
1                          Sales
2     Jan                   700
3     Feb                   715
4     Mar                   748
5                    -----------------
6     Total                2163
7
8
9
10
11
12    \E          {GOTO}SALES~      Macro to enter sales data.
13                {BLANK SALES}{CALC}
14                {?}{DOWN}
15                {?}{DOWN}
16                {?}~
```

Figure 22-19. MACFILE2 Worksheet.

- - - If you need a break, stop at this point. - - -

Retrieve MACFILE2 if you've just returned from a break.

User-Defined Menus

Lotus is a menu-driven program. You can make up your own menus using the advanced macro commands {MENUBRANCH} and {MENUCALL}. These menus will be displayed in the control panel, as 1-2-3 menus have been all along.

The first step in creating a user-defined menu is to set up the menu range with the options and their corresponding macro instructions. The menu range consists of at least 3 rows: the first row contains the options, the second row contains the control panel's explanations, and the rest of the rows contain macro instructions.

```
Option1            Option2            Option3            ...      Option 8
Explanation1       Explanation2       Explanation3       ...      Explanation 8
InstructionSet1    InstructionSet2    InstructionSet3    ...      InstructionSet8
```

Let's add a user-defined menu to this worksheet. It will have three options:

Input will allow the user to enter sales data.
Graph will graph the current sales data.
Save will save the file to disk.

First let's do some preliminary work on the graph.

You enter: / Graph **A SALES [Return] X A2..A4 [Return]**

             View [SpaceBar] Quit

The graph is minimal; this lesson is not about graphs.

Now you're ready to set up the menu range. First, the top row which will contain the labels for the options.

You enter into B10: **Input [Right]**

You enter into C10: **Graph [Right]**

You enter into D10: **Save [Return]**

Next the second row which will contain the labels for the third line explanations.

You enter into B11: **Input sales data for all months. [Right]**

You enter into C11: **Display graph of sales data on screen. [Right]**

You enter into D11: **Save copy of this screen on disk. [Return]**

The third row will contain the macro commands for each option.

B12..B16 is already set up.

You enter into C12: **{GRAPH} [Right]**

You enter into D12: **'/fsSALES~[Return]**

The menu range is set up. Name it.

You enter into A10: **MENU1 [Return]**

You enter: **/ Range Name Create MENU1 [Return] B10 [Return]**

{MENUBRANCH location}

{MENUBRANCH location} executes a user-defined menu. Location is the upper left corner of the menu range, in this case, cell B10 named MENU1.

You enter into B8: **{MENUBRANCH MENU1} [Return]**

Instead of MENU1, B10 could have been used as the location. Again, it's better to used named cells in case you rearrange the worksheet.

Executing a macro with {MENUBRANCH} follows the same three steps in creating and executing macros.

Step 1. You have just entered it.

Step 2. Name the macro with the {MENUBRANCH} command.

You enter into A8: **'\M [Return]**

You enter: **/ Range Name Create \M [Return] B8 [Return]**

Your worksheet should look like Figure 22-20.

```
          A          B          C          D          E
1                   Sales
2    Jan            700
3    Feb            715
4    Mar            748
5                  --------------
6    Total          2163
7
8    \M             {MENUBRANCH MENU1}
9
10   MENU1          Input       Graph       Save
11                  Input sales daDisplay graph Save copy of this screen on di
12                  {GOTO}SALES~ {GRAPH}      /fsSALES~
13                  {BLANK SALES}{CALC}
14                  {?}{DOWN}
15                  {?}{DOWN}
16                  {?}~
```

Figure 22-20. User-Defined Menu.

Step 3. Execute the macro with the {MENUBRANCH} command.

You enter: **[Alt]+M**

Your worksheet should look like Figure 22-21.

```
A8: '\M
Input  Graph  Save
Input sales data for all months.
          A          B          C          D          E
1                   Sales
2    Jan            700
3    Feb            715
4    Mar            748
5                  --------------
6    Total          2163
7
8    \M             {MENUBRANCH MENU1}
9
10   MENU1          Input       Graph       Save
11                  Input sales daDisplay graph Save copy of this screen on di
12                  {GOTO}SALES~ {GRAPH}      /fsSALES~
13                  {BLANK SALES}{CALC}
14                  {?}{DOWN}
15                  {?}{DOWN}
16                  {?}~
17
18
19
20
12-Jul-88  03:30 AM              CMD
```

Figure 22-21. Execution of User-Defined Macro.

Looks like any other Lotus menu, doesn't it?

You enter: **[Right] [Right] [Left] [Left]**

The explanations are shown on the third line of control panel as usual. You choose options by highlight and [Return] or by typing the first character of the option.

You enter: **Input**

You enter: **800 [Return] 815 [Return] 848 [Return]**

With {MENUBRANCH}, control returns to READY mode after the chosen option's instructions are complete.

You enter: **[Alt]+M Graph**

The graph should be on your screen. It is assumed the user knows enough to type any key to get back to the worksheet. If not, you can set always set up a prompt in the x-axis title of the graph like "Type any key to return to worksheet."

Releases 3.0 and 3.1+: The new footnote feature on graph display can be employed here. Use /Graph Options Titles Note. See footnotes in graphs in index.

If you're writing macros for yourself, you needn't be that concerned about these things. However, if your inexperienced-in-Lotus secretary is using your worksheets, you've got to look at all angles.

{MENUCALL location}

{MENUCALL location} is like {MENUBRANCH} except control transfers back to the next macro command after the {MENUCALL} command instead of just ending with the last command in the chosen option's macro. To those familiar with programming, {MENUCALL} can be considered a subroutine call to a menu.

You enter into B8: **{MENUCALL MENU1}[Return]**

In this case, control will transfer to B9 which is blank and the macro stops. If you want to loop or keep repeating the menu, a {BRANCH} instruction should be placed in B9.

You enter into B9: **{BRANCH \M}**

You enter: **[Alt]+M Input 900 [Return] 915 [Return] 948 [Return]**

After execution of MENU1, control transfers to the {BRANCH}

instruction which transfers to {MENUCALL} again. The menu executes again.

You enter: **Graph [SpaceBar] S**ave

And again. You're in another one of those infinite loops where even [Esc] won't get you out.

You enter: **[Ctrl]+[Break] [Esc]**

Another option is needed to stop the loop.

You enter into E10: **Quit [Down]**

You enter into E11: **Return to READY mode. [Down]**

You enter into E12: **{QUIT} [Return]**

Your worksheet should look like Figure 22-22.

```
         A              B              C              D              E
 1                    Sales
 2   Jan              900
 3   Feb              915
 4   Mar              948
 5                --------------
 6   Total           2763
 7
 8   \M          {MENUCALL MENU1}
 9               {BRANCH \M}
10   MENU1       Input         Graph         Save          Quit
11               Input sales daDisplay graph Save copy of tReturn to READY
12               {GOTO}SALES~  {GRAPH}       /fsSALES~     {QUIT}
13               {BLANK SALES}{CALC}
14               {?}{DOWN}
15               {?}{DOWN}
16               {?}~
```

Figure 22-22. Quit Option Added to User-defined Menu.

You enter: **[Alt]+M [Right] [Right] [Right] [Return]**

The Save option macro in this worksheet works properly only if the file SALES does not exist on disk. A Replace would be necessary after the ~ if it were. Although it may be dangerous, we're going to assume that the user always wants to replace the file. (An example of a macro which warns the user of an already existing file is given at the end of Lesson 23.)

The macro must contain commands which will work in two cases - the file exists or does not exist. In general, /fsSALES~r{ESC} will work in both cases. If the file exists, Replace is issued, the file is overwritten and the

{ESC} is an extra keystroke which causes no problem at this point. If the file does not exist, READY mode is entered and the Cancel Replace menu is not brought up. An R typed in READY mode will be taken as the first character of a label entry; {ESC} will undo it and return control to READY mode. "In general", this will work.

You should issue a warning in the third line explanation that the previous file will be overwritten.

You enter into D13: **r{ESC}**

Delete the currently existing SALES file from disk.

You enter: **/ File Erase Worksheet SALES [Return] Yes**

You enter: **[Alt]+M Save Save**

The file was saved ok in both cases.

You enter: **Quit**

The {MENUBRANCH} and {MENUCALL} commands can be anywhere in the worksheet and need not be two rows above the left corner of the menu range as it is here. The same menu may even be called from many different {MENUBRANCH}s or {MENUCALL}s in several different macros.

You have been entering menus in the part of the worksheet close to the home position to help you see the effects of menu executions on one screen. Menus should generally be stored off the screen so you will have more room for your worksheet and to be invisible from non-Lotus people. I use AA100 for the beginning cell of my macros. You may not wish to move that far right and down.[2] It is good practice to use a consistent cell as the start of the macro part of your worksheets for easy reference.

You enter: **/ Move A8..E16 [Return] AA100 [Return] [Home]**

Set the \M menu macro up as the auto-execute macro.

You enter: **/ Range Name Create \0 [Return] \M [Return]**

---

[2]Version 1A does not manage memory efficiently as the newer versions of Lotus do. It uses memory for each cell in the active area, even if the cells are empty. Memory may become filled quite easily, especially if you are working with less than 640K. If this occurs, an "insufficient memory" error message will be shown on the bottom of the screen. Therefore, if you are using Version 1A, store your macros closer to the main part of your worksheet. In this case, cell L30 would be reasonable.

You enter: / File Save **SALES [Return]** Replace

Instead of the /File Save you could have run the M macro and chosen the Save option.

You enter: / **Worksheet Erase Yes**

Unnecessary again but a blank screen will make things clearer.

You enter: / **File Retrieve SALES [Return]**

The auto-exec menu macro takes over and you have a menu-driven worksheet.

You enter: **Quit**

The AUTO123 File

When 1-2-3 is started (either from the Lotus Access System menu or from the 123 command to DOS), 1-2-3 searches the default directory for a file named AUTO123.WK1. If it exists, it is automatically retrieved.

Save this file under AUTO123.WK1.

You enter: / **File Save AUTO123 [Return]**

Now leave 1-2-3 and return.

You enter: / **Quit Yes**

The Lotus Access System menu should be on your screen.   Re-enter 1-2-3.

You enter: **[Return]**

With a little experience, you can create quite elaborate menu-driven systems for users with no knowledge of Lotus. Basically they would need to boot up, get to the Access menu, choose 1-2-3 and follow the on-screen instructions you have set up. (A DOS batch file could do this form them.) I strongly recommend protection on template cells which should not be modified by the user. You can set up a complete database system with an AUTO123 file containing only a user-defined menu macro to retrieve other files. Macros in the retrieved files can transfer the user anywhere with a simple option choice. A Quit option can return the user to the Lotus Access System menu or retrieve another worksheet with an automatic menu to other files.

Delete the AUTO123.WK1 file unless you automatically wish to enter this worksheet every time you enter 1-2-3.

You enter: **/ File Erase Worksheet AUTO123 [Return] Yes**

Releases 3.0 and 3.1+: You must clear the worksheet with a /Worksheet Erase before 1-2-3 will allow you to erase the file on disk.

- - - If you need a break, stop at this point. - - -

Single Step Execution

No doubt you will end up with some errors in your macros and debugging will be necessary.

Save the file just before Step 3, macro execution, so that if the macro messes something up, a /File Retrieve will get the worksheet back intact. Of course, don't save the file with a macro named \0.

The STEP ([Alt]+[F2]) key toggles single step execution mode on and off and is helpful for debugging macros.[3] Single step execution mode pauses execution of a macro after each character or step to allow you to see the results. You hit [Return] after each step to continue execution.

Let's debug a macro by first creating one with an error.

You enter: **/ Worksheet Erase Yes**

You enter into A1: **'/rncTOTAL [Return]**

You enter into A2: **C10~ [Return]**

Your worksheet should look like Figure 22-23.

You enter: **/ Range Name Create \C [Return] A1 [Return]**

You enter: **[Alt]+C**

Your worksheet should look like Figure 22-24.

---

[3]In Lotus version 1A, STEP is [Alt]+[F1].

Figure 22-23. Macro with Error.

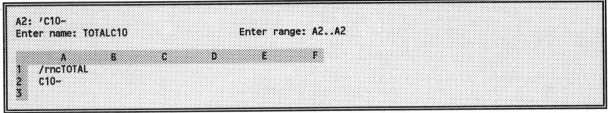

Figure 22-24. Missing ~ in Cell A1.

There should be a ~ after the /rncTOTAL in A1.

You enter: **[Ctrl]+[Break]**

You enter: **[Alt]+[F2]**

Releases 3.0 and 3.1+: Choose the STEP option from the menu.

The STEP indicator is shown at the bottom of the screen. All macros will now be executed in STEP mode. Begin the macro:

You enter: **[Alt]+C**

The cell address and contents of the cell containing the currently executing macro instruction is displayed at the bottom of the screen.

Releases 2, 2.01, 3.0, and 3.1+: SST is flashing on the bottom of the screen indicating Single STep execution is on.

You must now type [Return] to execute the /, r, n, c, etc.

You enter: **[Return] slowly several times.**

When

TOTALc

is in the control panel, you realize that the ~ is missing. You've found the bug. Stop execution:

You enter: **[Ctrl]+[Break]**

Releases 3.0 and 3.1+: Hit [Esc].

Now you may add ~ if you wish and execute the macro again. You must turn off STEP mode as it is not automatically done for you. The STEP key is actually a toggle switch.

You enter: **[Alt]+[F2]**

Releases 3.0 and 3.1+: Choose STEP.

The STEP indicator is gone from the bottom of the screen.

Forgetting keystrokes is probably the most common error in creating macros. Also be careful with blanks in your macro instructions - only hit that [SpaceBar] if it's absolutely needed.

The next lesson covers advanced macro commands.

EXERCISES

```
        AA      AB        AC        AD      AE       AF       AG
100 MACROS TO FORMAT A VALUE IN A CELL.
101 The pointer must be in the cell to be formatted.
102
103 \C      /rfc0~~  Currency with no digits. (C=Currency)
104
105 \M      /rfc~~   Currency with 2 decimal digits. (M=Money)
106
107 \I      /rff0~~  Fixed with no decimal digits. (I=Integer)
108
109 \F      /rff~~   Fixed with 2 decimal digits.  (F=Fixed)
110
111 \G      /rfg~    General format. (G=General)
112
113 \P      /rfp1~~  Percent with 1 decimal digit.  (P=Percent)
114
115 \O      /rf,2~~  , with 2 decimal digits.  (C=cOmma)
116
117 \S      /rfs3~~  Scientific with 3 decimal digits. (S=Scientific)
118
119 \R      /rfr~    Reset to global format.  (R=Reset)
```

1A. Modify the library of macros above to change global formats. Use /Range Name Labels Right to name all the macros in one shot.

1B. Modify each macro above to format a column of numbers instead of just one cell. Assume the cell pointer is in the top cell of the column. (Hint: Make use of {END} and {DOWN}.)

---

2. Create and execute a macro to name the range B2..B10 QTR2.

---

3. Retrieve the GRADES file and create a macro to help the instructor enter the three columns of grades in the test columns. The macro should move the pointer through the input cells so that all the instructor need do is type each grade and hit [Return]. All pointer positioning should be done by the macro.

---

4. Retrieve the SCRANTON worksheet and create a macro to prompt the user to enter the sales data for the three products. After the last datum is entered the macro then graphs the three values in a bar graph.

5A. Create a macro to reset the current pointer column and the next 4 to the right back to the global default column width.

5B. Instead of resetting the 5 columns, have the user input the number of columns to be reset beginning at the current pointer column.

	A	B	C
1	Joe Smith	Main St.	Newtown, Pa 10000
2			

6A. Create a macro in the worksheet above to copy the three labels in the first row to three consecutive cells in the same column as in the figure below so that they may be used to print a mailing label.

	A	B	C
1	Joe Smith	Main St.	Newtown, Pa 10000
2			
3			
4		Joe Smith	
5		Main St.	
6		Newtown, Pa 10000	

6B. Modify the macro to copy several rows of data instead of only one to the same three cells. Print the three cells before copying the next row of data. Spacing will be needed between each mailing label.

---

7. Create a macro to take an employee payroll database and print payroll checks. The checks should be similar to the format below:

YOUR CORPORATION'S NAME GOES HERE

Today's Date

Pay to the order of: EMPLOYEE NAME GOES HERE

The Amount of: NET PAY AMOUNT GOES HERE

----

president will sign here

Leave that last line blank for the authorized signature.

8. Create a macro to call up the main print menu and change the print settings to print mailing labels. The settings should be: left margin,1; right margin, 30; top margin, 1; and bottom margin,1.

	A	B	C	D	E	F	G
4	Mike	Mellen	301 Penn Ave.	Huntsville	PA	12345	
5	Frank	Palonis	410 Montgo Ave.	Biltmon	NJ	43215	
6	Rose	Apple	84 River St.	Smalltown	NY	98765	

	AA	AB	AC	AD	AE	AF	AG
100	MACRO TO PRINT MAILING LABELS.						
101	Pointer must be in first label's first name cell before executing.						
102							
103	\L	/ppop7~qq		Set page-length to 7 lines.			
104	PRLABEL	/ppcrr.{RIGHT}~gq	Print first and last name.				
105		{RIGHT 2}		Position to street address.			
106		/ppcrr~gq		Print street address.			
107		{RIGHT}		Position to city.			
108		/ppcrr.{RIGHT 2}~gq	Print city, state, and zip.				
109		{DOWN}{LEFT 3}		Position to next row's first name.			
110		{CALC}		Recalculate now for @CELLPOINTER.			
111		{IF @CELLPOINTER("type")="b"}{QUIT} If blank cell, done.					
112		/pppq		Eject to next label.			
113		{BRANCH PRLABEL}	Print next label.				

9A. Instead of separate cells for the first and last names, the database changes to so that the first and last names are in the same cell. (Cell A4: Mike Mellon; cell A5: 301 Penn Ave., etc.) The name change is the only change in the database. Modify the macro above to handle the change.

9B. Change the macro so that it prints the city, a comma, and the

9B. Change the macro so that it prints the city, a comma, and the state and zip. For example, "Huntsville, PA 12345".

9C. Your boss, Edwin Macmannon, wishes to print form letters to advertise his ski resort in the Pocono Mountains. Create a macro to print a letter with a return address, each person's name and mailing address, and a come on which promises to pay one lucky winner 10 million dollars in a sweepstakes.

ADVANCED MACRO COMMANDS

Contents:

Advanced Macro Commands

Along with the keystrokes which can be entered in a macro, several advanced macro commands allow programming capabilities. We have seen the {GETLABEL} and {GETNUMBER} which could be considered input commands, {BRANCH} which could be considered a go to command, and others. Below is a complete list of the advanced macro commands divided into categories of related commands. The general grammatical structure of the commands is:

{KEYWORD argument1,argument2,argument3,...argumentn}

where the argument list is optional. Note that there is one space between the keyword and the first argument. The arguments are separated by a commas and no spaces should be added before or after each comma. A semicolon may be used instead of the comma as argument delimiters.[1]

Examples:

{BLANK SALES}

{MENUBRANCH MENU1}

{GETNUMBER "Enter January sales: ",SALES}

The entire command from { to } must be in the same cell. For example, it is not valid to put something like {BLANK in cell AA115 and SALES} in cell AA116.

The keywords of the three commands above are BLANK, MENUBRANCH, and GETNUMBER. {BLANK} has one argument as does {MENUBRANCH}, {GETNUMBER} has two arguments. There are other commands which need no arguments.

---

[1]Use /Worksheet Global Default Other International Punctuation to configure a different argument separator.

Each argument must be the correct type for its keyword. The four types of arguments are:

number - constant number or formula which can contain cell references, named or cell address. (Always use named cells in case the worksheet is rearranged.)

string - a sequence of characters up to a length of 240. If the string contains an argument separator (comma or semicolon) or a colon, it must be enclosed in quotes. Also enclose in quotes any string which may be confused with a range name or formula.

location - a cell range, named or cell address. (Always use named cells in case the worksheet is rearranged.) In most cases, if a named range contains more than one cell, only the upper left corner of the range is actually used.

condition - a logical expression which evaluates to true or false.

In some commands arguments are followed by suffixes. Suffixes explicitly define the argument type. See {LET} for examples.

Many advanced macro commands which change the contents of cells require a recalculation of the worksheet before the results of the commands are actually seen on the screen. They will be marked with "Recalculation required." Although four[2] of the commands require only a [Return] or other pointer movement key to cause the recalculation, most require a {CALC} keystroke command. I suggest that you use {CALC} after all, even the four exceptions, to make your macros more clear and flexible.

Macro Commands to Control the Screen

{BEEP}
{BEEP number}
Sounds the computer's bell. The optional number argument can be added to modify the tone and is an integer from 1 to 4 inclusive. If the argument is omitted, 1 is the default.
Examples:
{BEEP} sounds computer's bell with a tone of 1.
{BEEP 4} sounds computer's bell with a tone of 4.

---

[2]The four are {BLANK}, {GETLABEL}, {GETNUMBER}, AND {LET}.

{BREAK}

Not available in Releases 2 and 2.1. Simulates [Ctrl]+[Break] which returns control to READY mode. It does not interrupt a macro execution.

{FRAMEOFF}
{FRAMEON}

Not available in Releases 2 and 2.1. Turns off and on the display of the worksheet frame. The frame is the column border with letters and the left border with row numbers.

{GRAPHOFF}
{GRAPHON}

Not available in Releases 2 and 2.1. {GRAPHON} produces a display of graph and continues with macro execution. Display returns to worksheet when {GRAPHOFF} or other command which displays a prompt is executed, such as {GETLABEL}, {MENUCALL}, etc.

{INDICATE}
{INDICATE string}

Changes the mode indicator to the first 5 characters in the string. To return the mode indicator to normal (READY mode indicator, etc.) use no argument.
Examples:
{INDICATE START} displays START in the mode indicator.
{INDICATE "Press RETURN"} displays Press in the mode indicator.
{INDICATE Ent} displays Ent followed by 2 spaces.
{INDICATE " Ent "} centers Ent in the mode indicator.
{INDICATE ""} displays a blank mode indicator.
{INDICATE} returns back to normal mode indicator controlled by 1-2-3.

{PANELOFF}

Does not display the executing macro commands' menus in the control panel. For instance, turning the panel off before the macro execution of /reSALES~ will prevent the main menu, the Range menu, and the prompt Enter range to erase: to be flashed in the control panel.
Example:
{PANELOFF} suppresses display in control panel.
{PANELON} restores the normal display of the control panel.

{WINDOWSOFF}

Suppresses the display of the screen (except the control panel) during macro execution. The modifications made to cells in the worksheet by the macro are not displayed on the screen during execution which speeds it up.

{WINDOWSON}
Restores normal display of the screen.

Macro Commands which Allow Keyboard Interaction

{?}
Pauses macro execution and waits for user to enter keystrokes. Execution is resumed when the user types [Return]. The user's [Return] is taken to mean resumption of macro execution; if a [Return] is actually needed as a macro keystroke to be executed, ~ should be placed in the macro.

{BREAKOFF}
If BREAK is off, [Ctrl]+[Break] will not abort execution of a macro. This command can be used when you do not wish the user to interrupt a macro, either by accident or on purpose. It stays in effect until the macro ends or {BREAKON} is issued. If an infinite loop occurs in the macro, the only way out if {BREAKOFF} is in effect is to reboot the system.

{BREAKON}
Allows macro interruption with [Ctrl]+[Break].

{FORM input-range,call-table,include-list,exclude-list}
Not available in Releases 2, 2.1, and 2.2. The last 3 parameters are optional; use , to keep positions. This command is similar to /Range Input. Input-range must contain some unprotected cells. Call-table is a two column range where the first column contains a macro name of a key on the keyboard and the second column contains macro instructions to execute if the corresponding key is pressed. Include-list is a range specification of a range containing allowable input keystrokes. Exclude-list is a range specification of a range containing keystrokes to be ignored.

{FORMBREAK}
Not available in Releases 2, 2.1, 2.2, and 3.0. Ends a {FORM} command.

{GET location}
Accepts from the user a single character or 1-2-3 standard key as input and stores it at location as a label. If location is a range, the character is stored in the upper left corner. Recalculation required.
Examples:
{GET B10} and user types S: stores S in cell B10. (Use only named ranges as location in case of worksheet rearrangement and not cell references as in this example.)
{GET KEY} and user types [Return]: stores ~ in the range named KEY.
{GET FUNCTION} and user types [F5/GOTO]: stores {GOTO} in range named FUNCTION.

{GETLABEL prompt-string,location}

Displays prompt-string in control panel, accepts keystrokes from user, and stores them in location as a left-aligned label. Prompt-string must be typed right into the command; a named range containing a string cannot be used. Recalculation required.

Example:

{GETLABEL "Enter company name: ",NAMECOMP}

{GETNUMBER prompt-string,location}

Displays prompt-string in control panel, accepts a number, formula, or a range name containing a value from the user, and stores it in location. (If input is invalid, 0 is entered into location.) Prompt-string must be typed right into the command; a named range containing a string cannot be used. Recalculation required.

Example:

{GETNUMBER "Enter number of employees: ",TOTEMPL}

{LOOK location}

Checks to see if the user has typed any keys since the beginning of macro execution. If so, the first character is stored at location. If not, location is erased. {LOOK} does not pause and wait for the user to input as did {?}, {GET}, {GETLABEL}, and {GETNUMBER}. {LOOK} leaves this first character in the type-ahead buffer so that it may be used by other commands or as data by the rest of the macro. Recalculation required.

{MENUBRANCH location}

Executes the user-defined macro beginning at location. It is, in effect, a {BRANCH} to a user-defined menu. The macro ends with the last command in the column associated with the option chosen from the user-defined menu.

{MENUCALL location}

First executes the user-defined macro beginning at location and then transfers control to the macro command following the {MENUCALL}. It treats the user-defined macro as a subroutine.

{WAIT time}

Causes macro execution to halt until time is reached.

Example:

{WAIT @NOW+@TIME(0,0,5)} waits five seconds and resumes execution of the macro.

{WAIT @TODAY+@TIME(12,0,0)} waits until noontime of the current day and resumes execution.

Macro Commands which Manipulate Data

{APPENDBELOW target-location,source-location}
Not available in Releases 2, 2.1, and 2.2. Copies source-location to the row immediately following target-location. Can be used to append records to a database and in combination with {FORM} or /Range Input. Expands target-location range to include these new appended rows.

{APPENDRIGHT target-location,source-location}
Not available in Releases 2, 2.1, and 2.2. Similar to {APPENDBELOW} except works with columns, not rows.

{BLANK location}
Erases the cells in location without affecting format or protection settings. Recalculation required.

{CONTENTS destination-location,source-location,width-number, format-number}
Changes a value from source-location to a left-aligned label and stores it in destination-location. Use it when you need a label which looks like a number. The width-number argument is optional and specifies the number of characters to be in the label. If omitted, the column-width of the source-location is used. The format-number is also optional and specifies how the label should look according to Table 23-1. If omitted, the display format of the source-location cell is used. If a format-number is specified, it must be preceded by a width-number. Recalculation required.

```
Format Number              Format Display

0                  Fixed with 0 decimal places
1                  Fixed with 1 decimal place
2-15               Fixed 2 through 15 decimal places
16-31              Scientific, 0 to 15 places
32-47              Currency, 0 to 15 places
48-63              Percent, 0 to 15 places
64-79              , (Comma), 0 to 15 places
112                +/-
113                General
114                D1 (dd-mm-yy)
115                D2 (dd-mmm)
116                D3 (mmm-yy)
121                D4 Long Int'l Date (Usually mm/dd/yy)
122                D5 Short Int'l Date (Usually mm/dd)
119                D6 (hh:mm:ss AM/PM)
120                D7 (hh:mm AM/PM)
123                D8 Long Int'l Time (Usually hh:mm:ss)
124                D9 Short Int'l Time (Usually hh:mm)
117                Text
118                Hidden
127                Global default display format
```

Table 23-1. Format-Number Codes for {CONTENTS} Macro Command.

Examples:
Cell SOURCE1 contains the value 43.5
Cell SOURCE2 contains the value 20554 or @DATE(56,4,9).

{CONTENTS DEST,SOURCE1}
Results: DEST contains '   43.5
(Column width of SOURCE1 column is 9.)

{CONTENTS DEST,SOURCE1,5}
Results: Dest contains '43.5

{CONTENTS DEST,SOURCE1,4,0}
Results: DEST contains '44

{CONTENTS DEST,SOURCE1,7,34}
Results: DEST contains '$43.50

{CONTENTS DEST,SOURCE2,10,114}
Results: DEST contains '09-Apr-56

{CONTENTS DEST,SOURCE2,10,120}
Results: DEST contains ' 12:00 AM

Not evident after each of these labels is a space at the right end. If a
value is to be transferred as a label into a cell of a macro instruction, the
space is a problem which has to be dealt with.

{LET location,number} or
{LET location,string}
Stores the number or string at location. An optional suffix of string or value can be added to the second argument.
{LET location,number:value}
{LET location,string:string}
Recalculation required.
Examples:
{LET STRTNUM,1} stores the value 1 in upper left corner of range STRTNUM.
{LET TOTAL,1000} stores the value 1000 in TOTAL.
{LET TOTAL,1000:value} does same as previous.
{LET TOTAL,1000:string} stores the string '1000 in TOTAL.
{LET NAME,Smith} stores 'Smith in NAME.
{LET TOTAL,Smith:value} stores the value contents of named cell SMITH in TOTAL.

{PUT location,column-number,row-number,number}
{PUT location,column-number,row-number,string}
Stores the number or string in the location range's column and row numbers given in the arguments. Beginning at the upper left cell of location range, it moves column-number columns to the right and row-number rows down and stores the number or string in that cell. Recalculation required.
Example:
TOPRNG is the range A1..E10.
{PUT TOPRNG,2,5,43.5} stores 43.5 in cell C6.
{PUT TOPRNG,0,0,-21.9} stores -21.9 in cell A1.
{PUT TOPRNG,4,9,300} stores 300 in cell E10.
{PUT TOPRNG,5,10,-99} causes an error because column-number and row-number just enough to be out of location range.[3]

{RECALC location,condition,iteration-number}
{RECALCCOL location,condition,iteration-number}
Recalculates cells in location. {RECALC} recalculates in a row-by-row manner and {RECALCCOL} in a column-by-column manner. Condition and iteration-number are optional. Useful in very large worksheets where recalculation of all cells takes too much time. Allows recalculation of only a small portion of the worksheet which is currently being worked on. Recalculation required.

---

[3]{ONERROR} will not trap an out of range error in a {PUT}.

Macro Commands which Control Program Flow

{subroutine-name}
Executes a subroutine call to the named range and continues with the macro instruction in the next cell below.

{BRANCH location}
A "go to" instruction which transfers control to and resumes macro execution at location.

{DEFINE location1:type1,location2:type2,...location:typen}
Must be the first command a subroutine macro if arguments are being passed. Specifies the cells to be used for the storage of arguments passed to the subroutine and their data types. If :typen is omitted, string is the default type. Recalculation required. (See Subroutine Macros - next section.)

{DISPATCH location}
Transfers control, not to location, but to the address stored in location. (Indirect addressing.)
Example:
{DISPATCH WHERETO}
If the single cell range[4] WHERETO contains the label TOTALIT, control is transferred to the cell having the range name TOTALIT.

{FOR counter-location,start-number,stop-number,step-number,-starting-location}
This looping mechanism commonly known as the FOR-NEXT structure calls the subroutine at starting-location repeatedly until the counter-location value is greater than the stop-number value.
The steps taken are:
1. Counter-location is initialized to start-number. Therefore, it is not necessary for you to set up counter-location.
2. If counter-location<=stop-number, the subroutine at starting-location is executed.
3. The step-number value is added to counter-location.
4. Step 2 is then done again, followed by Step 3, etc. until counter-location>stop-number.

{FORBREAK}
Aborts the {FOR} loop and continues execution with the next command following the {FOR} command.

---

[4]The range name must refer to a single cell only. If the range contains more than one cell, a {BRANCH} instruction rather than a {DISPATCH} is executed.

{IF condition}

Executes the commands after the {IF} in the same cell if condition is true (has non-zero numeric value). Otherwise executes the command in the cell below. This is commonly known as the IF-THEN-ELSE structure: the THEN clause follows the {IF} command in the same cell and the ELSE clause is in the cell immediately below the {IF}THEN cell.

Example:

{IF SPENT>BUDGET}{BRANCH TOOMUCH}
{BRANCH OK}

{ONERROR branch-location,message-location}

Transfers control to branch-location if an error occurs during macro execution. The error message which usually gets shown on the bottom of the screen is stored in message-location instead. The message-location argument is optional. The command stays in effect until another {ONERROR} command is encountered or until the macro ends. Typing [Ctrl]+[Break] during macro execution causes an error[5]; {ONERROR} can transfer control to an interrupt handling subroutine if the user breaks instead of aborting the macro. Recalculation required.

Note: After an error occurs, the {ONERROR} is cancelled. To continue trapping errors, another {ONERROR} must be issued. This is done in the first example below where the {BRANCH \P} transfers to the {ONERROR} so that it is re-issued in case another error needs to be trapped.

Example:

```
This print macro is at location \P:
{ONERROR PRINT_ERR}
/ppg
...
```

```
with PRINT_ERR location containing
{GETLABEL "Printer error occurred.  Correct and type [Return]",DUMMY}
{BRANCH \P}
```

Example:

```
{ONERROR BRKRTN,ERRMSG}
{WAIT @NOW+@TIME(0,1,0)}
...
```

```
with BRKRTN location containing
```

```
{IF ERRMSG<>"Break"}{BRANCH ANOTH_ERR}
{GETLABEL "Do you want to continue? (Y/N)",STOP_OR_NO}
...
```

----

[5]Unless {BREAKOFF} is in effect.

{QUIT}
Terminates macro execution. If {QUIT} is issued in a subroutine macro, all macro execution is terminated not just that of the containing subroutine.

{RESTART}
When executed in a subroutine macro, it clears the subroutine stack and causes macro execution to terminate after completing commands in that subroutine. Normally when {RETURN} or a blank cell are encountered in a subroutine macro, control is transferred back to the calling macro. If a {RESTART} was issued during the execution of the subroutine macro, the subroutine commands between the {RESTART} and {RETURN} are executed and then macro execution is terminated. In short, {RESTART} logically changes the {RETURN} or blank cell in that subroutine to a {QUIT}. (See Subroutine Macros - next section.)

{RETURN}
Used in a subroutine macro, it transfers control back to the calling macro. (See Subroutine Macros - next section.)

{SYSTEM command}
Release 2.2 and 3.0 only. Similar to /System. Temporarily exits 1-2-3, executes the operating system command specified in the parameter, and returns to macro execution.

Subroutine Macros

The first cell of a macro can be named and called as a subroutine to another macro.[6] The name of the macro enclosed in braces with optional arguments is the command used to invoke the macro:

{subroutine-macro-name argument1,argument2,...,argumentn}

Control is returned to the calling macro at the cell immediately below the calling command when {RETURN} or a blank cell is reached in the macro.

Refer to the {DEFINE}, {RESTART}, and {RETURN} commands under the previous section Macro Commands which Control Program Flow.

If arguments are being passed to the subroutine, {DEFINE} must be the first command in the subroutine and a cell must be set aside as storage for

---

[6]Don't name the subroutine with any of the special macro keys listed in Table 23-1.

each of the passed arguments.

/X Macro Commands

To be compatible with files created in Lotus Version 1A, the /X commands are executable in Version 2. Below is shown the advanced macro commands which correspond to the old /X commands.

```
Advanced
Macro Command              /X Command
/XClocation~               {subroutine-macro-name}
/XGlocation~               {BRANCH}
/XIcondition~              {IF}
/XLmessage~location~       {GETLABEL}
/XMlocation~               {MENUBRANCH}
/XNmessage~location~       {GETNUMBER}
/XR                        {RETURN}
/XQ                        {QUIT}
```

Table 23-2. Comparison of Version 1A and 2 Macro Commands.

Macro Commands which Manipulate ASCII Files

{CLOSE}
Terminates read and write access to the currently open file. No argument is necessary because only one file can be open at a time.

{FILESIZE location}
Stores the number of bytes in the currently open file into location. Recalculation required.

{GETPOS location}
Stores the current position of the file pointer of the currently open file into location. The first position in a file is 0. Recalculation required.

{OPEN filename,access-mode}
Opens a file. Filename is a string, single-cell named range containing a string, or a string expression. If the file on disk has an extension, it must be included in the string. The drive and directory must be specified if the file is not in the current directory. If the {OPEN} succeeds, execution continues in the next cell down. If the {OPEN} fails due to a nonexistent file, execution continues in the same cell as that containing the {OPEN}.

Access-mode is one of the following single character strings:

R opens filename for reading only,

W opens a new file called filename (erases filename from disk if it exists) for reading or writing,

M opens an existing file for reading or writing in order to modify it.

Examples:

{OPEN EMPDATAB,R} opens EMPDATAB in current directory and allows {READ} or {READLN} commands only.

{OPEN C:\DBASE\XYCORP\EMPLOYEES.DAT,W} opens a new file EMPLOYEES.DAT in the directory C:\DBASE\XYCORP and allows reading to and writing from it.

{READ bytecount,location}

Reads bytecount characters from the currently open file beginning with the file pointer position and stores them in the single cell in the upper left corner of location range. Bytecount can be any expression which results in a number between 0 and 240. The file pointer advances bytecount characters after the {READ}. If no file is open, execution continues in the same cell as the {READ}; otherwise it continues in the next cell down. Recalculation required.

{READLN location}

Reads a line of characters from the currently open file beginning at the file pointer position and stores them into the single cell in the upper left corner of location range. The carriage return is not copied with the line of text. The file pointer moves to the beginning of the next line. Recalculation required.

{SETPOS file-position}

Moves the file pointer to the character at file-position in the currently open file. The first character of a file is position 0. File-position must be an expression which results in a number. If no file is open, execution continues in the same cell as {SETPOS}; otherwise execution continues in the next cell down.

{WRITE string}

Copies string to the currently open file at the file pointer position. String may be a literal string, a single cell named range, or a string expression. The file pointer advances to just beyond the string.

{WRITELN string}

Similar to {WRITE} with a carriage-return line-feed added after the string. {WRITELN ""} can be used to add a carriage-return line-feed sequence to the end of a line.

Release 3.1+: Listed below are new macro key names.

{ADDIN}
Brings up the add-in menu, similar to [Alt]+[F10].

{CE}
Clears prompts from 1-2-3. For example, the default file name after a /File Save is issued.

{FILE}
Shows the FILE indicator on the screen. Used in conjunction with movement keys between files.

{FC} or **{FIRSTCELL}**
Causes cell pointer to jump to the home cell in worksheet A of the current file, cell A:A1.

{FF} or **{FIRSTFILE}**
Moves pointer to the first file into the cell the pointer was last in.

{HELP}
Brings up on-screen Help during macro execution.

{LC} or **{LASTCELL}**
Moves pointer to the end of the active area in the current file.

{LF} or **{LASTFILE}**
Moves pointer to the last file into the cell the pointer was last in.

{NF} or **{NEXTFILE}**
Moves pointer to the next file into the cell the pointer was last in.

{NS} or **{NEXTSHEET}**
Moves pointer to the next active worksheet.

{PF} or **{PREVFILE}**
Moves pointer to the previous active file into the cell the pointer was last in.

{PS} or **{PREVSHEET}**
Moves pointer to the previous worksheet.

{ZOOM}
Toggles between full-screen worksheet size and normal size.

Macro Examples and Exercises

In general, I find it useful to have a standard setup for more involved macros. My personal preference is as below:

```
BRIEF DESCRIPTION OF PURPOSE OF MACRO.
Notes, requirements, and assumptions made about the
worksheet before macro execution.

CELLNAME1       [ ]       These cells named with cellname to their
CELLNAME2       [ ]       left are memory variables used in the
...             ...       macros.
CELLNAMEN       [ ]

MACRO-NAME      command1       Comment on command1.
                command2       Comment on command2.
                ...
                commandn       Comment on commandn.
                {QUIT}


SUBROUTINE1     commands       Comments.
                {RETURN}

SUBROUTINE2     commands       Comments.
                {RETURN}

...

SUBROUTINEN     commands       Comments.
                {RETURN}
```

The macro below is rather extensive for a first example. The it's here is to show an example of the standard setup on the previous page. It should be reviewed again after the examples in the exercises are studied.

```
         AA        AB        AC        AD        AE        AF        AG        AH
100 THIS MACRO SAVES TO A FILE, ASKING USER TO VERIFY OVERWRITE IF
101 A FILE OF THE SAME NAME ALREADY EXISTS.
102
103 EXISTS              Will contain "c" if file did NOT exist.
104 YESORNO             User input. Yes means do the overwrite.
105
106 \S          {BLANK EXISTS}              Clear exists/doesn't exist flag.
107             {GETLABEL "Enter file name: ",FILENAME}
108             {CALC}
109             {GOTO}EXISTS~
110             {ALMOSTSAVE}c~              If file exists, cancel the save.
111             {IF EXISTS<>""}{QUIT}       If file didn't exist, it's saved.
112             {GETLABEL "File exists. Overwrite? (Y/N)  ",YESORNO}
113             {IF @UPPER(YESORNO)<>"Y"}{CALC}{QUIT}
114             {ALMOSTSAVE}r~              User said Yes, save with replace.
115             {QUIT}
116
117 ALMOSTSAVE  /fs                         If doesn't exist, saves file.
118 FILENAME                                If exists, almost saves it, but
119             ~                               stops before the Replace.
```

The macro above has two variable cells: AB103 named EXISTS and AB104 named YESORNO. Their contents will be changed during macro execution. The actual macro named \S is stored in cells AB106..AB115 with a subroutine macro at AB117..AB119 named ALMOSTSAVE. Another variable cell is at AB118 named FILENAME; it is not stored above the macro like the other two because its contents is part of the macro commands.

Writing "Cautious" Macros

When designing macros, you should always ask yourself "what could possibly go wrong?" Consider the consequences if something does go wrong, and try to put preventative measures in the code. For example, in AB113 the {IF @UPPER(YESORNO)<>"Y"} is seemingly logically equivalent to {IF @UPPER(YESORNO)="N"}. However, in the latter {IF}, if the user accidentally typed something other than yes or no and meant to type no, the existing file would be inadvertently overwritten. The condition in the macro as it stands will not overwrite the file in the case of invalid input.

Several examples are shown in the exercises which follow. Even if you don't do every exercise, you should look at all the examples in the exercises, in the order that they occur, in order to see some practical uses of macros and applications of the advanced macro commands.

EXERCISES

1.

```
        AA          AB          AC          AD          AE          AF          AG
100 MACRO TO ENTER MONTHS'S NAMES ACROSS A ROW.
101 The pointer must be in the first cell or the cell to hold January.
102
103 \M          January{RIGHT}
104             February{RIGHT}
105             March{RIGHT}
106             April{RIGHT}
107             May{RIGHT}
108             June{RIGHT}
109             July{RIGHT}
110             August{RIGHT}
111             September{RIGHT}
112             October{RIGHT}
113             November{RIGHT}
114             December~
115
```

1A. Which modifications must be made to the macro above so that it will enter the months down a column instead of across a row? Make the changes using a macro instead of typing the change into each cell.

1B. Use the {FOR} loop to make the change 11 times.

2.

```
        AA          AB          AC          AD          AE          AF          AG          AH
100 MACRO TO DATE AND TIME STAMP A WORKSHEET.
101
102 \T          aTODAY~              Enter the aTODAY function into cell.
103 .           /rfd1~               Format it into day-month-year.
104             {DOWN}               Move down to enter time.
105             aNOW~                Enter aNOW to get time fraction.
106             /rfdt2~              Format to hours:minutes AM/PM.
107             {IF aCELLPOINTER("width")<10}/wcs10~
108             {QUIT}               For date, col must be at least 10 wide.
109                                  (For dates>=1/1/2000 must be 12 wide.)
```

2. Change the macro above to print yesterday's date in day-month format. Leave the time as it is so that the date-time stamp enter the time and date of exactly 24 hours ago.

3.

```
        AA        AB        AC        AD        AE        AF
100 MACRO TO SET COLUMN WIDTH OF CURRENT POINTER COLUMN.
101
102 \W        {GETLABEL "Enter new column width:",WIDTH}
103           /wcs              Set column width to
104 WIDTH                       width user input.
105           ~
106           {QUIT}
```

3A. Create a macro similar to the one above. Instead of having the user input a number for the column width, have him/her use arrow keys to widen or thin column.

3B. Modify the macro to use {GETNUMBER} and {CONTENTS} to accept as input a number for the column width.

4.

```
        AA        AB        AC        AD        AE        AF        AG        AH
100 MACRO TO SET UP FIELD NAMES AND SET COLUMN WIDTHS.
101 Assumption is that database begins in home position.
102 A fieldname of "quit" will stop macro.
103
104 FLDNAME
105
106 \F        {HOME}            Position pointer to home cell.
107 FLDLOOP   {GETLABEL "Enter field name or ""Quit"":",FLDNAME}
108           {IF @UPPER(FLDNAME)="QUIT"}{CALC}{RETURN}     Quit?
109           /cFLDNAME~~       Copy fieldname to current pointer cell.
110           {GETLABEL "Enter column width:",WIDTH}
111           /wcs              Set column width to
112 WIDTH                       this number input by user.
113           ~
114           {RIGHT}           Position to top of next field.
115           {BRANCH FLDLOOP}  Loop and continue until "quit" is entered.
```

Change the macro above so that the macro commands which handle the column width setting are in a subroutine macro to be called from the \F macro.

5.

```
        AA       AB       AC       AD       AE       AF       AG       AH
100 MACRO TO ALLOW USER TO ADD A RECORD TO A DATABASE.
101 Assumes database begins at home position.  Field names are in row 1.
102 No blank cells should exist in a record.
103
104 NUMFLDS                                Number of fields.
105 CURRFLD                                Current field being entered.
106
107 \E      {HOME}
108         /rndSIZE~                      Clear SIZE from previous \E
109         /rncSIZE~.{END}{RIGHT}~        Name for top row of database.
110         {LET NUMFLDS,@COLS(SIZE)}      Store width of range in NUMFLDS.
111         {HOME}{DOWN}                   Move pointer to second row.
112         /wth~                          Keep field names as title.
113         {END}{DOWN 2}                  Find first blank record.
114         {FOR CURRFLD,1,NUMFLDS,1,ENTER} Loop to enter into fields.
115         /wtc                           Clear title.
116         {HOME}
117
118 ENTER   {?}{RIGHT}
```

5A. This macro adds only one record to the end row of the database. Add a loop to add any number of records. Accept as input from the user the number of records to be added.

5B. Three cases must be handled by this macro. 1. No records exist in the database, only the field names in row 1. 2. One record exists. 3. Two or more records exist. Does this macro handle all 3 cases? If not, modify it so that it does.

———————————

6.

```
        AA       AB       AC       AD       AE       AF       AG       AH
100 MACRO TO DISPLAY A MESSAGE ON THE CONTROL PANEL.
101
102 DUMMY
103
104
105 \M      {GETLABEL "Message to be displayed.  Press RETURN.",DUMMY}
106         {CALC}                  Must recalculate worksheet after GETLABEL.
107
```

6. What's the purpose of the DUMMY cell? Is its contents relevant?

7.

```
        AA        AB        AC        AD        AE        AF        AG        AH
100 MACRO TO DISPLAY A MESSAGE PASSED AS ARGUMENT ON THE CONTROL PANEL.
101
102 DUMMY                           DUMMY cell holds RETURN pressed by
103                                 user after reading message.  Its
104                                 contents is irrelevant.
105
106 PANELMSG {DEFINE MESSAGE:string}
107 MESSAGE                         Message to be displayed.
108             Press RETURN.       Spaces after message are needed.
109             {GET DUMMY}         Lets user read message & press RETURN.
110             {ESC}{CALC}         {ESC} prevents message from being
111             {RETURN}            entered into current cell. Must
112                                 recalculate worksheet after GET.
```

The calling macro to the above macro would look similar to:

\P   ...
          {PANELMSG "Turn printer on."}   ...

7. Modify the above macro to look at the input form the user. If the input is the letter "Q" for quit, issue a {QUIT} to stop all macro execution.

8. This macro is very useful for allowing non-Lotus personnel to enter dates into a worksheet.

```
MACRO TO ENTER A DATE AND FORMAT IT ACCORDING TO USER'S CHOICE.

MONTH          5             Month number input by user.
DAY            18            Day number input by user.
YEAR           1989          Four digit year input by user.
DATEFMT        4             Number of date format input by user.

\D       {GETNUMBER "Enter month number:",MONTH}
         {GETNUMBER "Enter day:  ",DAY}
         {GETNUMBER "Enter year:   ",YEAR}
         {CALC}
         aDATE(
         89,        aSTRING(YEAR-1900,0)&","   Actual contents of
         5,         aSTRING(MONTH,0)&","       cells to the
         18)        aSTRING(DAY,0)&")"         left.
         ~
         {LET ADDR,aCELLPOINTER("address")}    Save pointer position.
DISPLAY  {GOTO}DATESCRN~    Display screen to help user choose format.
         {GETNUMBER "Enter 1, 2, 3, 4, or 5: ",DATEFMT}
         {IF (DATEFMT>5#OR#DATEFMT<1)}{BRANCH DISPLAY}
         {GOTO}            Return to pointer cell before macro began.
ADDR     $A$2             Saved pointer position.
         ~                Move previous pointer cell to mid screen.
         {CONTENTS DATEFMT2,DATEFMT,2,0}      Change value to string.
         {CALC}
         /rfd             Format date.
DATEFMT2 4                Use format which user has input.
         {ESC}{ESC}~      See text for explanation of {ESC}'s.
         {IF aCELLPOINTER("width")<10}/wcs10~
         {QUIT}           Column must be at least 10 wide.
                          (For dates >= 1/1/2000 must be 12 wide.)




DATESCRN PLEASE CHOOSE THE FORMAT IN WHICH TO DISPLAY THE DATE.

         1             day-month-year

         2             day-month

         3             month-year

         4             month/day/year

         5             month/day
```

8. Modify the macro so that a user-defined menu instead of the screen display prompts the user for the format of the date. How does this improve the screen position of the cell to contain the date?

9.

MACRO A:

```
          AA          AB          AC          AD          AE          AF
100 MACRO WITH USER-DEFINED MENU TO DISPLAY GRAPH.
101
102 \G           {MENUBRANCH GMENU}         Execute "choose graph type" menu.
103
104 GMENU        Bar-Graph   Line-Graph  Stacked-Bar Pie-Chart   Quit
105              Display Bar Display LineDisplay StacDisplay Pie Return to RE
106              /gnuBAR~q   /gnuLINE~q  /gnuSTBAR~q /gnuPIE~q   {QUIT}
107              {QUIT}      {QUIT}      {QUIT}      {QUIT}
```

MACRO B:

```
          AA          AB              AC                  AD
100 MACRO WITH USER-DEFINED MENU TO DISPLAY GRAPH.
101
102 \G       {MENUCALL GMENU}     Execute "choose graph type" menu.
103          /gnu                 Use a named graph.
104 TYPE PIE                      Name of graph that GMENU set up.
105          ~q                   q returns to READY mode.
106          {QUIT}
107
108 GMENU Bar-Graph              Line-Graph          Stacked-Bar
109       Display Bar Graph.     Display Line Graph. Display Stacked Bar
110       {LET TYPE,"BAR"}       {LET TYPE,"LINE"}   {LET TYPE,"STBAR"}
111       {RETURN}               {RETURN}            {RETURN}
```

9.   The two macros basically accomplish the same task. Assuming that the graphs have been previously set up and named, which macro do you think is better in terms of flexibility and good macro design? Why?

10.

MACRO A:

```
        AA        AB        AC        AD        AE        AF        AG        AH
100 MACRO TO PLACE ONE OF TWO PARTS OF THE WORKSHEET ON THE SCREEN.
101
102 \P      {GETLABEL "Which page?  Enter ""One"" or ""Two"":  ",PAGE}
103         {IF @UPPER(PAGE)<>"ONE"#AND#@UPPER(PAGE)<>"TWO"}{BEEP}{BRANCH \P}
104         {GOTO}
105 PAGE
106         ~
107         {QUIT}
```

MACRO B:

10A. What is the purpose of the ""'s in the {GETLABEL} prompt?

10B. Which macro has a better error handling method in the case that user input is invalid?

10C. Modify macro B to verify that the error trapped by {ONERROR} is, indeed, an invalid cell or range address. If not, display a message to the user.

---

11. Create a subroutine macro to be branched to in the occurrence of an error. The routine should display the error message and display several alternatives: continue execution, stop execution and return to READY mode, restart macro execution, etc. Accept the user's input and branch to the proper macro segment.

12. The macro below cannot be stored in AA100 or it will erase itself.

```
         AA        AB        AC        AD        AE        AF        AG        AH
100 MACRO TO COMBINE INTO CURRENT WORKSHEET A MACRO LIBRARY FILE.
101 Macros in library file must begin at home position.
102
103 \C       {PANELOFF}                      Turn control panel display off.
104          {WINDOWSOFF}                    Turn screen display off.
105          {BLANK AA100..AZ200}            Clear macro range.
106          {GETLABEL "Name of macro library file: ",FILENAME}
107          {GOTO}AA100~                    Position pointer for combine.
108          /fcce                           Combine file.
109 FILENAME                                 Filename that user input.
110          ~{HOME}                         Position pointer to home.
111          /rnlrAA100..AA200~              Create range names.
112          {PANELON}                       Return control panel display.
113          {WINDOWSON}                     Return screen display.
114          {QUIT}
```

12A. Modify the macro so that the restriction that the macro library in the file to be combined must begin at the home position no longer applies. (Hint: Combine a named range instead of the entire file.)

12B. A limitation of this macro is that it can only combine one macro library into a worksheet file. Modify it so that it will be able to combine any number of macro files consecutively below each other. This macro should be stored at AA100 and macro files should be combined below it in the same columns so that /Range Name Labels Right will work. (Hint: Use {END}{UP} combination from the last row of the worksheet to find the first available row in macro storage columns AA, AB, AC, ...)

13. All cells which may be modified by a macro must be unprotected if the macro exists in a worksheet with protection enabled.

```
        AA       AB       AC       AD       AE       AF       AG       AH
100 MACRO TO CHANGE CONTENTS OF PROTECTED CELLS.
101
102 SURE                      These cells must be
103 DUMMY                     range unprotected.
104
105 \C     {GETLABEL "Are you sure you want to make changes? (Y/N) ",SURE}
106        {IF @UPPER(SURE)<>"Y"}{QUIT}
107        /wgpd
108        {GETLABEL "Remember to Alt-P after changes. Press RETURN.",DUMMY}
109        {CALC}
110        {QUIT}
111
112 \P     /wgpe
113        {QUIT}
```

13. Instead of asking the user if s/he is sure, require the user to input a password. Verify that it is the correct one before allowing protected cells to be changed.

14.

MACRO A:

```
         AA        AB       AC       AD      AE      AF       AG       AH
100 MACRO TO PRINT ONE RANGE N TIMES WHERE N IS INPUT BY USER.
101 Print range PRNRANGE must be previously named.
102
103 NUMPRN                        Number of times to print range.
104 COUNT                         Counter variable for FOR loop.
105
106 \P      {GETNUMBER "How many copies?  ",NUMPRN}
107         {FOR COUNT,1,NUMPRN,1,PRINTIT}   Print range NUMPRN times.
108         {CALC}                Recalculate worksheet.
109         {RETURN}              Return to calling program (or quit).
110
111 PRINTIT  /pprPRNRANGE~gpq  Print the range named PRNRANGE & eject page.
```

MACRO B:

```
         AA        AB       AC       AD      AE       AF      AG       AH
100 MACRO TO PRINT ONE OF THREE NAMED RANGES TO BE INPUT BY USER.
101 Only one copy of the chosen range is printed.
102
103 NUMPAG                        Number of page to print.
104
105 \P      {GETNUMBER "Which page to print? Enter 1, 2, or 3.  ",NUMPAG}
106         {CALC}                Recalculate after GETLABEL.
107         {IF NUMPAG=1}{LET PAGENUM,"PAGE1"}{BRANCH PRINTIT}
108         {IF NUMPAG=2}{LET PAGENUM,"PAGE2"}{BRANCH PRINTIT}
109         {IF NUMPAG=3}{LET PAGENUM,"PAGE3"}{BRANCH PRINTIT}
110         {BRANCH \P}           If invalid entry, ask again.
111 PRINTIT  /ppr                 Bring up print menu and choose Range option.
112 PAGENUM                       Range name of page to be printed.
113         ~gq                   Go and quit print menu.
114         {RETURN}              Return to calling macro or quit.
```

14. In macro B, if many different pages were named in order to be printed, the {IF} statements would be too numerous. Modify the macro so that a few commands will handle from 1 to 99 pages. (Hint: Concatenate "PAGE" with the input number and store in the single-cell range PAGENUM.)

15.

MACRO A:

```
         AA          AB          AC          AD          AE          AF          AG          AH
100 MACRO TO PRINT N COPIES OF ONE OF THREE NAMED RANGES.
101 User inputs the number of copies and the range to be printed.
102
103 NUMPAG                         Number of page to print.
104 NUMPRN                         Number of times to print range.
105 COUNT                          Counter variable for FOR loop.
106
107 \P        {GETNUMBER "Which page to print? Enter 1, 2, or 3.  ",NUMPAG}
108           {CALC}               Recalculate after GETLABEL.
109           {IF NUMPAG=1}{LET PAGENUM,"PAGE1"}{BRANCH GTCOPIES}
110           {IF NUMPAG=2}{LET PAGENUM,"PAGE2"}{BRANCH GTCOPIES}
111           {IF NUMPAG=3}{LET PAGENUM,"PAGE3"}{BRANCH GTCOPIES}
112           {BRANCH \P}          If invalid entry, ask again.
113 GTCOPIES {GETNUMBER "How many copies?  ",NUMPRN}
114           {FOR COUNT,1,NUMPRN,1,PRINTIT}      Print range NUMPRN times.
115           {CALC}               Recalculate worksheet.
116           {RETURN}             Return to calling program (or quit).
117
118 PRINTIT  /ppr                  Bring up print menu and choose Range option.
119 PAGENUM                        Range name of page to be printed.
120          ~gq                   Go and quit print menu.
```

15.   The macro above is a "combination" of the two macros from the previous exercise. Before looking at the next exercise example, modify the macro above so that it contains two subroutines: one to set up the page to print and one to print the n copies. Use {DEFINE} when necessary.

16. Combination of the two macros in exercise 14.

```
MACRO TO PRINT A RANGE N TIMES.
User inputs the number of copies and the range to be printed.

NUMPRN                      Number of times to print range.

\P       {RNGGET}           Get range to be printed into RNGPR.
         {GETNUMBER "How many copies?  ",NUMPRN}
         {NPRINTS NUMPRN,RNGPR}      Print RNGPR range NUMPRN times.
         {QUIT}
-----
MACRO TO GET RANGE TO PRINT FROM USER.

RNGPR                       Name of range to be printed.
RNGNUM                      Number of page input by user.

RNGGET   {GETNUMBER "Which page to print? Enter 1, 2, or 3.   ",RNGNUM}
         {CALC}             Recalculate after GETNUMBER.
         {IF RNGNUM=1}{LET RNGPR,"PAGE1"}{BRANCH RNGDONE}
         {IF RNGNUM=2}{LET RNGPR,"PAGE2"}{BRANCH RNGDONE}
         {IF RNGNUM=3}{LET RNGPR,"PAGE3"}{BRANCH RNGDONE}
         {BRANCH RNGGET}    If invalid entry, ask again.
RNGDONE  {RETURN}
-----
MACRO TO PRINT A RANGE N TIMES.

NPR                         Number of times to print range.
NPRCOUNT       3            Counter in FOR loop.

NPRINTS  {DEFINE NPR:value,NPRNRNG:string}
         /c
NPRNRNG                     Name of range to be printed.
         ~NPRANGE~
         {FOR NPRCOUNT,1,NPR,1,NPRINTIT}      Print range NPR times.
         {CALC}             Recalculate worksheet.
         {RETURN}           Return to calling program.

NPRINTIT /ppr               Bring up print menu and choose Range option.
NPRANGE                     Name of range to be printed.
         ~gq                Print range and quit print menu.
         {RETURN}
```

16. Note that each subroutine's named cells begin with the same 3 letters. This technique can prevent using the same name for more than one cell and make clearer which routine a named cell is coming from. It is necessary to develop consistency in range naming when several macro subroutines exist in the same worksheet.

Appendix A

SUMMARY OF RELEASES

Contents:

This appendix summarizes the requirements for each release of Lotus, the add-ins included in each release, each release's file extension, and compatibility of worksheet files among releases.

Memory, Hardware, and Software Requirements

A summary of each release's memory and hardware requirements is shown in the table below:

Release	RAM	Hard Disk Space	Hardware Requirements	Mouse Support	Operating System
1A	256K	need floppy System disk in drive	8086 or higher	no	DOS 2.0 or higher
2	256K	1 to 1.5 MB	8086 or higher	no	DOS 2.0 or higher
2.01	256K	1 to 1.5 MB	8086 or higher	no	DOS 2.0 or higher
2.2	320K (512 K for Allways)	2 MB recommended	8086 or higher	no	DOS 2.0 or higher
2.3	384K (512 K for WYSIWYG)	5 MB	8086 or higher	yes	DOS 2.1 or higher
2.4	384K (512 K for WYSIWYG)	5 MB	8086 or higher	yes	DOS 2.1 or higher
3.0	1 MB under DOS, 3 MB under OS/2	5 MB recommended	286 or higher	no	DOS 3.0 or higher or OS/2 1.0 or 1.1
3.1+	1 MB	5 MB	286 or higher	with WYSIWYG	DOS 3.0 or higher
Windows	2 MB	5 MB	286 or higher	yes	Microsoft Windows 3.0 or higher, standard or enhanced mode.

Add-Ins Included in Each Release

Below is listed each release and its included add-ins. The main Add-in menu is brought up with /Add-in or [Alt]+[F10] in Releases 2.x and with [Alt]+[F10] in Releases 3.x. The Add-Ins Appendix explains how to use the add-ins.

Release 2.2   Allways and Macro Manager.

Release 2.3   Auditor, Macro Manager, Tutor, Viewer, and WYSIWYG.

Release 2.4   Auditor, Backsolver, Icons, Macro Manager, Tutor, Viewer and WYSIWYG.

Release 3.0   None, uses third party add-ins. Call a software house for available add-ins.

Release 3.1+   Auditor, Backsolver, DataLens, Solver, Viewer, and WYSIWYG. All but WYSIWYG and DataLens are Enhancement add-ins and must be installed separately with AINSTALL on the Enhancement Add-ins Disks.

Windows   There are no add-ins, some previous add-ins are built right into the program. Backsolver and Solver are under the Tools option of the menu bar and DataLens is under the Data option under Connect to External. WYSIWYG features exist throughout the menus; 1-2-3 Classic can also be used to pull up WYSIWYG.

Worksheet File Compatibility

Release 1A saved files with a .WKS extension. Releases 2.x save .WK1 files only. Releases 3.x and Windows save .WK3 files, but will create .WK1 files if you give it that extension.

Sometimes you may wish to save a worksheet file with one release which will later be retrieved into another release. Worksheets created with previous releases are simply retrieved into subsequent releases, automatic translation takes place. To go backwards, save the file with a .WK1 extension and it will be automatically translated for Releases 2.x. For instance, to create a worksheet with Release 3.0 for use in Release 2.4, save it by typing a filename with extension .WK1. Release 2.4 will then be able to retrieve it.

RELEASE 2.2

Contents:

This appendix summarizes at a glance the enhancements in Release 2.2 over prior releases 2 and 2.01. Use the index to find illustrations of these enhancements throughout the text.

File Linking

File linking allows two or more worksheet files to share data. A link is created from the worksheet on the screen to a worksheet on disk by setting up a cell reference. When a cell is modified, so are all references to that cell in other worksheets.

To access cell C9 in the worksheet SCRANTON.WK1 on disk from the current worksheet in on the screen, use the cell reference +<<SCRANTON>>C9.

In general the link formula is:

+<<file reference>>cell reference

Cell reference can be the name of a cell. If necessary, a path including a drive and subdirectory, can be added to the link formula. Example:

+<<F:\123FILS\SALES>>A4

The path would be necessary if the worksheet on disk is not in the directory specified by /File Directory.

/File List Linked gives a display of all files linked to the current worksheet.

Linked cells are updated when you retrieve the worksheet file. /File Admin Link-Refresh will recalculate link formulas while you are working on the file.

UNDO

[Alt]+[F4] will UNDO or cancel any changes made since the time the worksheet was last in READY mode. /Worksheet Global Default Other Undo Enable is used to enable the UNDO feature. An UNDO indicator is displayed on the bottom of the screen when enabled. Be wary that this feature uses a lot of RAM memory; if you're having memory problems, disable UNDO with /Worksheet Global Default Other Undo Disable.

[F3/NAME]

Can be used when entering a formula to get a display of named ranges in the worksheet. Pressing it twice will display a full screen of range names. Highlighting a name displays its address.

Graphing

The /Graph Group command allows the specification of all graph ranges, X and A-F, in one step. The ranges must be in consecutive columns or rows of a range. /Graph Options Data-Labels Group and /Graph Options Legend Range similarly set all data-labels and legends in one step.

/Graph Name Table is similar to /Range Name Table in Lesson 3. It creates a 3-column table of the named graphs in the worksheet. The information given is: name of graph, type of graph, and first line of graph title.

/Graph Reset now allows the resetting of any individual graph range (X,A,B,C,D,E, or F). /Graph Reset Options clears options without resetting the graph ranges.

Search and Replace

/Range Search lets you find a string in a range and optionally replace it with another string. The cells in the range searched can be limited to only those containing formulas or labels. A Next option allows the re-issuance of the command without re-entering it.

Recalculation

Only cells whose values depend upon worksheet modifications are recalculated. This **minimal recalculation** feature decreases recalculation time.

Macro Names

Macros can have range names up to 15 characters long. (Macros can still be named with a backslash and a letter of the alphabet.) They are executed with [Alt]+[F10] followed by the name range of the macro.

File Tables

/File Admin Table creates a table in the worksheet with information about files on disk. The type of file must be specified: Worksheet, Print, Graph, Other, or Linked. The four-column table created contains the file name, date, time, and size.

Backup File

The /File Save (and /File Xtract) command allows the creation of a backup file on disk. Before a file save is done, an existing file of the same name on disk is copied to a file with extension .BAK. The Backup option must be chosen from the /File Save sub-menu.

Network

Files can now be shared on a local area network (LAN). /File Admin Reservation Releases or sets up a file reservation of a shared file on a network.

Settings Sheets

A **settings sheet** is a display of all settings of a particular command which appears on the screen in place of the worksheet. The sheet is displayed during the issuance of the command. Example: /Worksheet Global will display all current global settings on the screen starting from the line below the control panel. The [F6/WINDOW] key will toggle the screen display between the settings sheet and the worksheet.

Learn

[Alt]+[F5] toggles on and off the recording of keystrokes into consecutive cells down a column of a worksheet for later macro execution. The range where keystrokes are to be stored must be previously set with /Worksheet Learn.

Single Step Macro Execution

Instead of "SST", the cell address and contents of the currently executing macro instruction are displayed on the bottom of the screen.

Automatic File Retrieval

Without going through the Lotus Access System Menu, 1-2-3 can be executed directly from the operating system prompt by typing 123.

A>123 [Return]

If the 123 command is followed by with a space, a hyphen, the lowercase letter w, and the name of the worksheet file to be retrieved, the worksheet file will be retrieved . For example:

A>123 -wSCRANTON

A path name can be typed in front of the filename.

Add-in Applications

The new main menu option /Add-in pulls up the add-in menu, whose options are:

Attach - loads an add-in program into RAM
Detach - removes an add-in program into RAM
Invoke - activates a resident add-in program
Clear - deletes all add-in programs in RAM

[Alt]+[F10] invokes the attached add-in program. If none is attached, it pulls up the /Add-In sub-menu.

See Summary of Releases Appendix for available add-ins.

Appendix C

RELEASE 2.3

Contents:

This appendix summarizes at a glance the enhancements in Release 2.3 over prior Release 2.2. Release 2.3 incorporates all features in Release 2.2, so if you have not used 2.2, read the appendix on it. Use the index to find illustrations of these enhancements throughout the text.

WYSIWYG

The most evident addition to Release 2.3 over 2.2 is the WYSIWYG add-in, which is covered in its own appendix. See Summary of Releases Appendix for other available add-ins.

Mouse Support

A mouse can be used to click on menu options, point to ranges, and selecting help topics, changing items in a dialog box, and for some graphing features.

Delete

Typing the delete key in READY mode is equivalent to a /Range Erase on the current cell.

Graphing

Three new types of graphs have been added: mixed graphs, area graphs, and HLCO (stock market) graphs.

Bar and stacked-bar graphs can be drawn horizontally with the new /Graph Type Features Horizontal.

The y-axis can be displayed on the left, right, or both sides of the graph frame with /Graph Options Scale Y-Scale Display. /Graph Type Features Frame allows many options for the display of the graph frame. /Graph Type Features 3D-Effect displays a three-dimensional bar graph.

[F10/GRAPH] shows the graph in almost any mode, you don't have to be in READY mode in this release.

Printing

Background printing lets you continue working while printing. You no longer need to wait for the printer to finish to get back to READY mode.

Encoded files allow you to create files for a printer not attached to your PC.

There are print preview and automatic print compression features in WYSIWYG.

Preselecting Ranges

The fourth function key [F4/POINT] allows you to preselect a range before the issuance of a command. 1-2-3 automatically performs the command on the preselected range. This is useful if you must issue several commands on the same range.

Search and Replace

Wildcards can be used in the search and replace commands. Question mark (?) matches any single character, and asterisk (*) matches any sequence of characters.

Dialog Boxes

A dialog box is similar to a settings sheet in Release 2.2. You can specify settings directly in the dialog box. [F6/WINDOW] will turn off and on the display of dialog boxes.

Shorthand Criteria Formulas

You no longer need to use a cell reference in criteria formulas. Entries in a criterion cell beginning with one of the six operators, > < = >= <= <>, refer to the column under the field header. For instance, instead of +C3>500 under a field header, >500 is sufficient.

/File View Commands

If the Viewer add-in is attached, /File View Browse will allow you to view files on disk, /File View Link will link cells in worksheets on disk, and /File View Retrieve will allow you to view files on disk in order to find the one you wish to retrieve. The Viewer add-in is discussed in the Add-Ins Appendix.

Help

On-screen help has been expanded and improved.

[Ctrl]+[F1] displays the last Help screen you viewed and comes in handy when you are going back and forth from the worksheet to the Help screens to follow a sequence of steps.

RELEASE 2.4

Contents:

This appendix summarizes at a glance the enhancements in Release 2.4 over prior Release 2.3. Release 2.4 incorporates all features in Releases 2.2 and 2.3, so if you have not used 2.2 or 2.3, read the appendices on them. Use the index to find illustrations of these enhancements throughout the text.

SmartIcons Add-In

The mouse can be used to click on these icons to issue frequently used commands. See appendix on SmartIcons.

Backsolver Add-In

This add-in is used to solve problems backwards. See Add-Ins Appendix.

SmartPics

These graphics, included and automatically installed for you, can be accessed with the :Graph Add Metafile command in WYSIWYG. There are several pictures including one of an airplane, an arrow, and the Statue of Liberty.

Printing

You no longer need Sideways (see Sideways appendix) because this release does landscape printing to a dot matrix printer. In WYSIWYG, issue the :Print Config Orientation command.

Included in this release is a driver for printing encapsulated PostScript files with extension .EPS which can be brought into word processing programs. Use the :Print Config Printer and :Print File commands in WYSIWYG.

Appendix E

RELEASE 3.0

Contents:

This appendix summarizes at a glance the enhancements in Release 3.0 over prior releases 2 , 2.01, and 2.2. Use the index to find illustrations of these enhancements throughout the text.

Release 3.0 contains most of the enhancements of Release 2.2 and much more. Please turn to the appendix on Release 2.2 and read the first 10 sections (up to and including Network). These ten are included in Release 3.0. Other additions are as follows:

Multiple Worksheets

One of the most significant updates in this release is the capacity to have multiple worksheets in memory simultaneously. /Worksheet Insert Sheet is used to add another worksheet to the currently active worksheet(s). /Worksheet Window Perspective displays 3 active worksheets simultaneously as in Figure E-1.

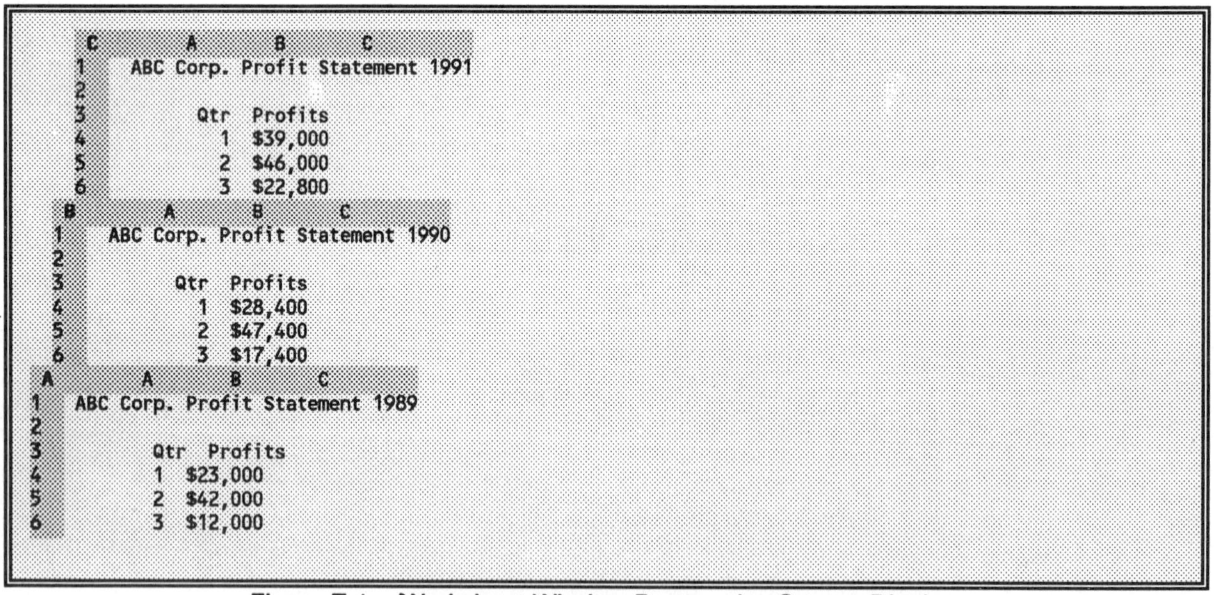

```
C          A        B        C
1    ABC Corp. Profit Statement 1991
2
3         Qtr  Profits
4           1  $39,000
5           2  $46,000
6           3  $22,800
B          A        B        C
1    ABC Corp. Profit Statement 1990
2
3         Qtr  Profits
4           1  $28,400
5           2  $47,400
6           3  $17,400
A          A        B        C
1    ABC Corp. Profit Statement 1989
2
3         Qtr  Profits
4           1  $23,000
5           2  $42,000
6           3  $12,000
```

Figure E-1. /Worksheet Window Perspective Screen Display.

/Worksheet Window Clear changes the display back to a single worksheet; all worksheets remain in memory.

Refer the Figure E-1. Worksheet A is the 1989 statement, worksheet B is the 1990, and worksheet C is the 1991. Cell references have a worksheet letter and a colon appended before the column letter and row number. $39,000, the Qtr 1 profit for 1991, is in cell C:B4. Ranges can become three dimensional. @SUM(A:B4..C:B4) is the result of $23,000+$28,400+$39,000. POINT mode can still be used to designate ranges.

To move the cell pointer from one worksheet to another, special keys are used.

[Ctrl]+[PgUp] moves the cell pointer to the next worksheet.
[Ctrl]+[PgDn] moves the cell pointer to the previous worksheet.
[Ctrl]+[Home] moves the cell pointer to A:A1.
[End] followed by **[Ctrl]+[Home]** moves the cell pointer to the end of
        the last sheet's active area.

1-2-3 remembers the last pointer position of all worksheets and returns the pointer to that row and column.

These keystrokes work whether you're in the perspective display or displaying one worksheet at a time.

To create the worksheets in Figure E-1, follow the steps below.

Erase the worksheet.
Create worksheet A.
Insert 2 worksheets after worksheet A with
       /Worksheet Insert Sheet After 2.
Copy A:A1..A:B6 to B:A1..C:A1.
Move to worksheet B with [Ctrl]+[PgUp].
Change the label to read 1990.
Change the profit values.
Move to worksheet C with [Ctrl]+[PgUp].
Change the label to read 1991.
Change the profit values.

A worksheet can now be added to create the sum of the 3 years' profits.

Insert a worksheet.
Enter appropriate labels.
Use @SUM and 3 dimensional ranges to create sum values for each quarter.

/Worksheet Global Group Enable causes all worksheets in memory to take on the settings of the current worksheet.

/Worksheet Delete Sheet is used to delete files from active memory.

Multiple Files

In addition to multiple worksheets, you can have multiple worksheet files in memory simultaneously. Each of the files can have one or more worksheets. The /File Open command brings in another worksheet file. They are layered similarly to multiple worksheets. The current worksheet's file name is displayed on the bottom of the screen. In addition to the pointer movement keys for moving between worksheets, special sets of keystrokes are used to move between files.

[Ctrl] + [End] followed by **[Ctrl] + [PgUp]** moves the cell pointer to the next file.

[Ctrl] + [End] followed by **[Ctrl] + [PgDn]** moves the cell pointer to the previous file.

[Ctrl] + [End] followed by **[End]** again moves the cell pointer to the last file.

[Ctrl] + [End] followed by **[Home]** moves the cell pointer to the first file.

In all four of these cases, 1-2-3 remembers the last cell pointer position in each file.

/File Save allows you to save one or all of the active files in memory.

/Worksheet Delete File deletes a file from memory.

Graphing

Besides the graph enhancements mentioned in the appendix for Release 2.2, a new feature, **automatic graphing**, has been added. From READY mode, [F10/GRAPH] creates a graph from the values around the cell pointer position. By default the data around the cell pointer is graphed column-wise. The leftmost column with values is the A range, the next column to the right of the A range is the B range, etc. If there's a column with labels to the left of the A range, it is the X range. For example, in Figure E-2 below, if the cell pointer was in any cell in the range A1..C4, the X range would be A1..A4, the A range would be B1..B4, and the B range would be C1..C4.

For example:

	A	B	C	D	E	F	G
1	Qtr1	43	35				
2	Qtr2	30	41				
3	Qtr3	25	48				
4	Qtr4	36	40				

/Worksheet Global Default Rowwise will change the graphing to row-wise. All other settings are taken from the current graph settings.

New graph types - Mixed, Area, and HLCO - have been added. The Area type is actually a Line graph set up with /Graph Options Format Graph Area.

/Worksheet Window Graph allows you to view the worksheet and the current graph simultaneously.

2Y-Axis allows a second y-scale on the right frame of the graph.

Database

Sorting can be done with up to 255 sort keys instead of 2. (See /Data Sort.)

Release 3.0 now has relational database capabilities; data can be extracted from multiple databases using a join formula. (See /Data Query.)

Other data from commonly used database packages, called **external tables**, can be accessed.

A new database feature called **computed column** allows you to enter formulas into field headers in the output range. For example, SALARY+RAISE, will add the SALARY field to the RAISE field and place the products in the output range. An **aggregate column** is a computed column which calculates totals for a group of related values. @AVG, @COUNT, @MAX, @MIN, and @SUM can be used in the field headers of the output range. For example, @SUM(AMOUNT) would sum all values in the AMOUNT field for each unique record pulled according to the criteria range. In a checking account database, amounts of all checks to Joe Smith would be added and displayed in the one extracted record in the output range for Joe Smith.

/Data Table 3 can calculate tables using 3 variables.

Printing

/Print Sample Go will give you a sample printout of the capabilities of your particular printer. Different fonts and colors can be used for your printouts. Background printing (see index) is done automatically.

Record Buffer

Keystrokes are recorded into a buffer in order to be played back or copied into macro instruction cells in the worksheet.

Dates

/Data Fill with increments of days, months, quarters, and years can be used to enter a series of dates. See Date and Time Lesson.

Setting Column Widths in a Range

With /Worksheet Column Column-Range Set-Width, widths of adjacent columns can be set all at once.

Long Labels

When labels are long enough to go off the right edge of the screen, this release lowers the worksheet and gives the label room to wrap.

RELEASE 3.1+

Contents:

This appendix summarizes at a glance the enhancements in Release 3.1+ over prior release 3.0. Read the appendix on Release 3.0, if you haven't used 3.0, because 3.1+ has all of 3.0's features. Use the index to find illustrations of these enhancements throughout the text.

Add-ins

The major additions to 3.1+ over 3.0 are the add-ins, in particular, the WYSIWYG add-in, which has its own appendix. The Summary of Releases lists the add-ins included with each release and the Add-ins Appendix explains how to use each add-in.

Unlike Releases 2.x, you must install the add-ins separately (except WYSIWYG) using AInstall and the Enhancement Add-ins Disk which come with the package; the regular Install program does not do it for you.

Other Enhancements

Release 3.1+ includes broader printer support which means more printers can be used with 3.1+ than with 3.0.

Release 3.1+ has a new indicator at the bottom of the screen, PRT, which is displayed during print operations.

[F10/GRAPH] shows the graph in almost any mode, you don't have to be in READY mode in this release.

Appendix G

LOTUS FOR WINDOWS

Contents:

This appendix covers Lotus for Windows®. It is assumed that you are familiar with the basics of Windows and a mouse.

What is Windows?

Although some refer to Windows as an operating system, Microsoft Windows® is actually an operating environment that sits on top of DOS. Windows offers a friendly graphical user interface for interacting with the PC and provides more functions than DOS does. It allows several programs to run simultaneously in different windows. These programs are specifically written for the Windows environment and have the same fundamental look and feel. Lotus for Windows is one of these programs; other examples include Microsoft Word for Windows® and WordPerfect for Windows®, which are both word processors.

Lotus for Windows

To enter Lotus for Windows, start Windows, open the Program Manager, then the Lotus Applications window, and then 1-2-3 for Windows. The main Lotus for Windows screen as shown in Figure G-1 should be on your screen. The **menu bar**, directly under the 1-2-3 for Windows title, is:

File Edit Worksheet Range Graph Data Style Tools Window Help

Icons, called **SmartIcons,** are shown toward the top of the screen. A blank worksheet named "Untitled" is below the SmartIcons.

Lotus for Windows's commands are similar to other releases of Lotus. In fact, all commands and menus from Release 3.1+ are executable from **1-2-3 Classic**, a feature in 1-2-3 for Windows which allows full compatibility with previous releases. To issue 3.1+ commands, type the usual forward slash from Windows READY mode, and a little "1-2-3 Classic" box will appear with the familiar main menu. The colon will bring up the 3.1+ WYSIWYG main menu. The mouse won't work in 1-2-3 Classic.

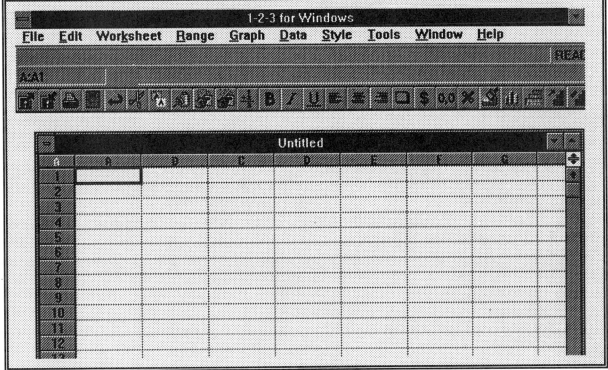

Figure G-1. Initial Lotus for Windows Screen.

To bring up the 1-2-3 Classic main menu, use the forward slash key:

You enter: /

The Classic menu shown in a small window at the top of your screen is:

Worksheet Range Copy Move File Print Graph Data System Quit

This is the menu you will use to do the first four lessons of this text. Type the key with "Esc" written on it to clear the Classic menu. Turn to Figure 1-1 of Lesson 1 and begin reading at that point. You should follow the instructions for Release 3.1+, as this is the release Lotus for Windows is most like. When you're finished with the first four lessons, return here and continue.

Now that you have completed the last four lessons and know the basics of Classic 1-2-3, using Lotus for Windows will be easy.

Clear the worksheet:

You enter: /**W**orksheet **E**rase **Y**es

Select the Range option from the menu bar and the Range pulldown menu will appear as in Figure G-2.

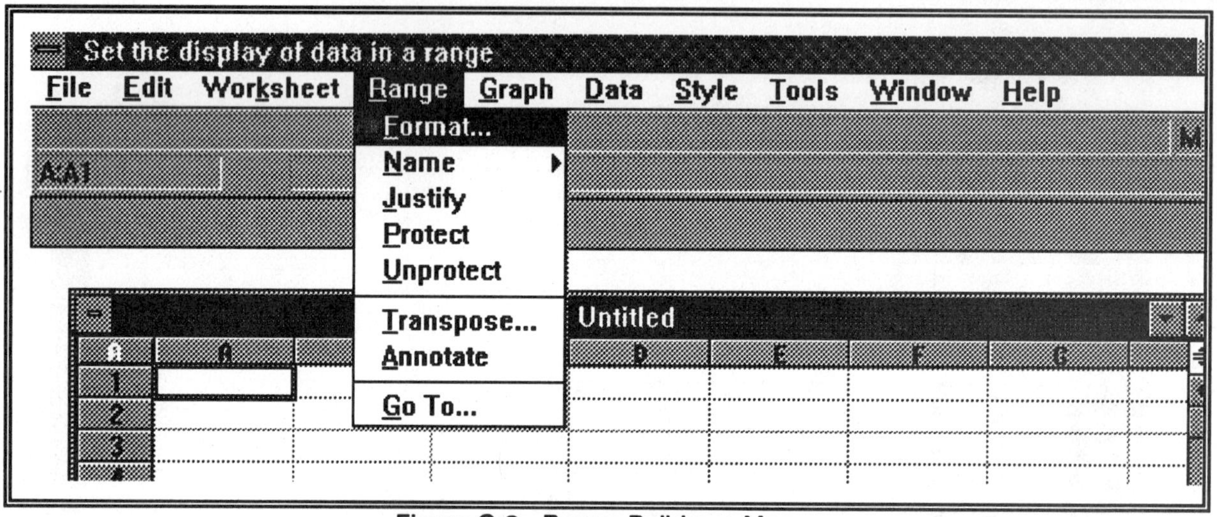

Figure G-2. Range Pulldown Menu.

The /Range Format and /Range Name commands, with which you are now familiar, are issued using this pull-down menu. The ▸ after the Name option designates that another menu, called a **cascade menu**, will appear if you choose the option. Do so and your screen should look like Figure G-3.

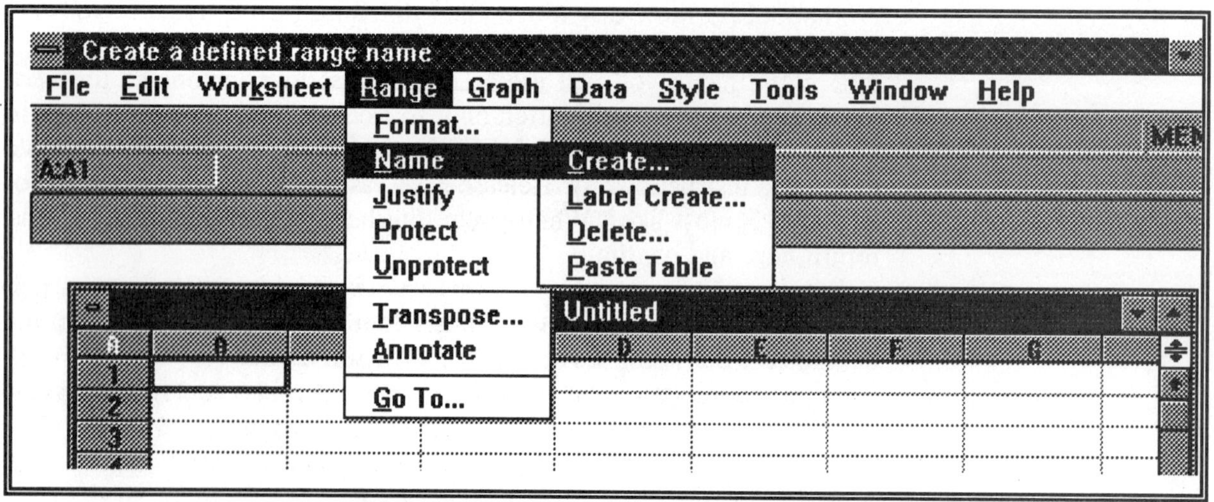

Figure G-3. Range Name Cascade Menu.

The ellipsis (...) designates that a **dialog box** will appear to allow you to complete the command. Issue the familiar /Range Name Create command in Classic 1-2-3 by selecting Create from the cascade menu. The dialog box in Figure G-4 should appear on your screen.

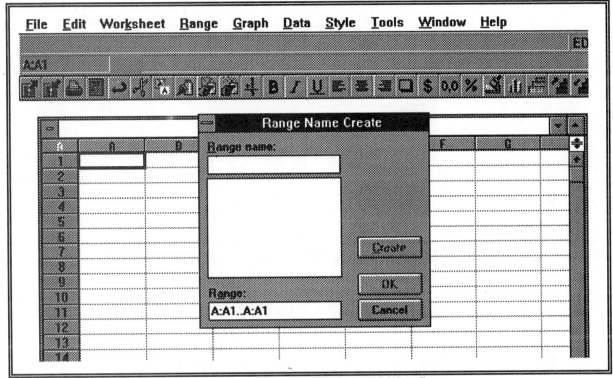

Figure G-4. Range Name Create Dialog Box.

The rectangular boxes allow you to enter the **Range name** and designate the **Range** to name. The largest rectangular box contains a list of all existing range names.

Try naming a few ranges now. Click and drag the mouse to "box" a range before issuing the Range Name Create command.

Corresponding Classic Command

Let's say you wish to do the /Copy command with which you are now familiar. You can always use Classic 1-2-3 to issue the command, but Windows has all new commands which are more efficient and allow the use of a mouse. A quick way to determine the new associated command corresponding to an old familiar command is to use on-screen Help. Click on Help from the menu bar, choose For Upgraders, Choose Search, type "Copy", click on Show Topics, highlight Copying Data in 1-2-3 in the bottom box, and click on the Go To box.

SmartIcons

You can use the mouse to click on SmartIcons to issue commonly used commands. Click the right mouse button to get a description of the SmartIcon under the mouse pointer. Also, see the SmartIcons appendix.

More SmartIcons exist than are currently on your screen. The current ones can be replaced with the Tools SmartIcons Customize command.

The command summaries that follow briefly describe all options on the pulldown menus. Use the mouse to click on the options. If you're using the keyboard instead of the mouse, the underlined letters are the hot keys that will invoke the option.

Summary of Worksheet Window Commands

New	Creates a new blank worksheet.
Open	Retrieves a worksheet into a window.
Close	Closes the active window.
Save	Saves worksheets to disk under current filename.
Save As	Saves worksheets to disk after you specify a filename.
Combine From	Copies, adds, or subtracts all or part of a worksheet file on disk to the current worksheet file.
Import From	Retrieves an ASCII file on disk into the current worksheet file.
Extract To	Saves part of an active worksheet file to disk.
Administration	Recalculates link formulas, creates a table about linked worksheets, handles reservation settings, and seals files.
Preview	Displays on the screen a formatted print of the print range as it will appear on paper.
Page Setup	Sets page settings such as margins, headers, footers, orientation, borders, etc. Saves page settings.

Print	Prints the print range.
Printer Setup	Sets up the printer destination.
Exit	Exits from the 1-2-3 session.

Edit Commands

Undo	Undoes the most recently executed command.
Cut	Deletes the specified worksheet range and copies it to the Clipboard.
Copy	Copies the specified worksheet range to the Clipboard.
Paste	Copies the Clipboard contents to the worksheet.
Clear	Deletes the designated range.
Clear Special	Deletes the data, graph, format, or style from the designated range.
Paste Link	Creates a link to the worksheet using the Clipboard link reference.
Link Options	Creates, deletes, edits, or updates links between worksheet files or other Windows applications.
Find	Searches for and/or replaces characters within a given range.
Move Cells	Moves a range of cells within the same worksheet file.
Quick Copy	Copies a range of cells within the same worksheet file.

Worksheet Commands

Global Settings	Sets up global settings such as format, label-prefix, column-width, etc.
Insert	Adds blank columns, rows, and worksheets to the current worksheet file.
Delete	Deletes columns, rows, and worksheets from the current worksheet file.
Hide	Hides columns and worksheets.
Unhide	Displays columns and worksheets that have previously been hidden.

Column Width	Sets width of columns. Resets column-width to the global setting.
Row Height	Sets the height of rows in the worksheet. Resets row height to global setting.
Titles	Freezes rows at the top edge of the worksheet screen or columns at the left edge of the worksheet screen.
Page Break	Causes a page break during a print operation at a row or column.

Range Commands

Format	Sets the format of data in a range.
Name	Creates and deletes range names. Creates range name tables.
Justify	Formats long labels to fit paragraph-style within a designated width.
Protect	Sets protection on a specified range so that data can not be modified. Global protection must be enabled.
Unprotect	Turns protection off for a specified range.
Transpose	Transposes the rows and columns of a specified range into columns and rows. Changes values to constants.
Annotate	Adds an annotation to a specified range.
Go to	Causes the cell pointer to jump to the designated range.

Graph Commands

New	Creates a new graph and names it.
View	Shows current graph in the graph window.
Add to Sheet	Adds a graph to the worksheet. Brings up Graph Window Commands.
Name	Lists graphs. Deletes graphs not added to the worksheet.
Import	Brings into the current file a graph in a .PIC or .CGM disk file.
Size	Changes the size of a current worksheet graph.
Refresh	Updates all worksheet graphs after data range recalculation.

<u>G</u>o To	Moves cell pointer to range of specified graph.

Data Commands

<u>F</u>ill	Enters values into a range in sequence with a constant increment value.
<u>S</u>ort	Sorts data in a specified range.
What-if <u>T</u>able	Creates a table of output results of a formula, given different input numbers.
<u>D</u>istribution	Does a frequency distribution from a specified range.
<u>M</u>atrix	Inverts and multiplies matrices.
<u>R</u>egression	Does regression analysis.
<u>P</u>arse	Breaks up long labels into separate columns of cells containing values and labels.
<u>Q</u>uery	Does database operations on a specified table within the worksheet or on an external table.
<u>C</u>onnect to External	Sets up a connection between an external database table and 1-2-3.
<u>E</u>xternal Options	Shares data between an external database table and 1-2-3.

Style Commands

<u>F</u>ont	Sets up fonts in ranges in the worksheet. Saves font libraries.
<u>A</u>lignment	Aligns text across the specified columns.
<u>B</u>order	Outlines and does drop shadows around a specified range.
<u>C</u>olor	Sets up colors in ranges for printing or display on the screen. Displays negative values in red.
<u>S</u>hading	Shades or removes shading from a range.
<u>N</u>ame	Sets up a named style from the format of the specified cell.
<u>1</u> through <u>8</u>	Formats a specified range to a named style.

Tools Commands

Backsolver	Starts the Backsolver add-in. See Add-in appendix.
Solver	Starts the Solver add-in.
SmartIcons	Moves and customizes SmartIcons.
User Setup	Sets up the display for windows and the configuration settings.
Macro	Records and runs macros. Allows STEP and TRACE mode.
Add-in	Runs add-ins and opens add-in files. Creates a table of active add-ins.

Window Commands

Split	Divides a window in two. Displays three adjacent worksheets from the current file.
Display Options	Sets up colors, grid lines, and look of the worksheet frame.
Tile	Sizes open windows and places them side by side.
Cascade	Cascades or displays all open windows side by side.
1 through **n**	List open windows and shows a check next to the active one. Makes a window active.
More Windows	Lists windows 10 and up, if there are that many open windows.

Help Commands

Index	Displays all help topics available to you.
Using Help	Explains how to use help.
Keyboard	Displays help on function keys, accelerator keys, and navigation keys.
@Functions	Displays descriptions of @ functions.
Macros	Provides help on macros and macro commands.
How Do I?	Provides help on frequently used commands.

For Upgraders	Displays 3.1 commands and the commands in Windows that are comparable.
About 1-2-3	Displays version number, copyright notice, and other information about 1-2-3.

Summary of Help Window Commands

File	Opens help files. Prints help topics.
Edit	Copies Help text to the clipboard and adds text to Help.
Bookmark	Puts bookmarks in the help text.
Help	Displays Windows help.

Summary of Transcript Window Commands

The Transcript window records keystrokes for creating macros. Tools Macro Show Transcript displays the Transcript window.

File	Closes the current file. Exits 1-2-3.
Edit	Copies data to and from the Clipboard.
Macro	Records keystrokes and runs macros.
Window	Tiles or cascades windows. Lists open windows.
Help	Displays 1-2-3 help.

Summary of Graph Window Commands

The Graph window appears when you're working with a graph.

File	Exits 1-2-3 or closes the current file.
Edit	Selects and edits objects in a graph.
Chart	Does the basic set up commands of a graph: type, ranges, legends, data-labels, etc.

Draw	Adds lines, rectangles, polygons, text, and free-hand drawings to a graph.
Layout	Moves objects forward or back in a graph. Locks graph objects.
Rearrange	Sizes graph objects. Changes orientation of graph objects.
Style	Sets up graph fonts, alignment of text, line-style, color and display options.
Tools	Moves and customizes SmartIcons.
Window	Changes graph window display.
Help	Displays on-screen help.

Cross-Reference to 3.1+ Commands

This section associates 3.1+ commands with the new Windows commands.

Release 3.1+ Command	**Windows Command**
/Copy	Edit Quick Copy
/Data	Data
/Data Table	Data What-if Table
/File	File
/File Dir	Tools User Setup
/File Retrieve	File Open
/Graph View	Graph View
/Graph Type	Chart Type on Graph Window Menu
/Graph Name	Graph Name
/Graph Name Create	Graph New
/Graph Name Use	Graph View

/Graph--setting up ranges	Chart Ranges on Graph Window Menu
/Graph Options	Chart Options on Graph Window Menu
/Graph Options Data-Labels	Chart Data Labels on Graph Window Menu
/Graph Reset	Chart Clear on Graph Window Menu
/Graph Save	none
/Graph Type	Chart Type
/Move	Edit Move Cells
/Print Printer	File Print
/Range Erase	Edit Clear
/Range Label	Style Alignment
/Range Name	Range Name
/Range Search	Edit Find
/Range Value	Edit Quick Copy
/System	/System
/Quit	File Exit
/Worksheet	Worksheet
/Worksheet Delete File	File Close
/Worksheet Erase	File Close
/Worksheet Global Column-Width, Label, Protection, Format	Worksheet Global Settings
/Worksheet Global Default Other	Tools User Setup
/Worksheet Titles	Worksheet Titles
/Worksheet Window	Window Split
/Worksheet Window Graph	Graph View

WYSIWYG 3.1+ Command	Windows Command
:Display	Window Display
:Format	Style
:Format Reset	Edit Clear Special Style
:Graph	Graph
:Print Configuration	File Printer Setup
:Print Go	File Print
:Print Layout	File Page Setup
:Print Preview	File Preview
:Print Range	File Print
:Text Align	Style Alignment
:Text Reformat	Range Justify
Add-in 3.1+ Command	**Windows Command**
Load, Remove, Clear	Tools Add-in
Invoke, Settings, Table	[Alt]+[F10]

Appendix H

ADD-INS

Contents:

An add-in is a program which extends the features of 1-2-3. This appendix covers the two steps necessary to ready an add-in for use - attaching and invoking. Included for each add-in is a brief overview of its commands and a short sample session. WYSIWYG, Allways, and Sideways are covered in their own separate appendices. Refer to the Summary of Releases Appendix to see which of the add-ins are included in your release.

If you run into memory problems, try detaching any unneeded add-ins and/or disabling the UNDO feature with /Worksheet Global Default Other Undo Disable.

Attaching Add-ins

An add-in must first be attached or loaded into conventional memory before it can be used or invoked. [Alt]+[F10] (or /Add-in in Releases 2.2, 2.3, and 2.4) pulls up the main add-in menu:

Attach   Detach   Invoke   Clear   Quit

Attach pulls an add-in program into conventional memory.
Detach deletes a current add-in program from conventional memory.
Invoke starts up an add-in program. The program must have been
      previously attached.
Clear deletes all attached add-in programs from RAM.
Quit returns to READY mode.

Choose Attach from this menu and highlight and choose the add-in you wish to use. The menu No-Key 7 8 9 10 sets up future keystrokes necessary to run or invoke the add-in. Choosing one of the numbers allows the add-in to be invoked with [Alt]+ the function key with that number. For example, choosing 7 will cause the key sequence [Alt]+[F7] to invoke the add-in. Keys set to invoke add-in programs are called **hot keys**. The WYSIWYG add-in's hot key is set up by default to be the colon.

Automatic Attachment of Add-ins

Add-ins can be set up to automatically attach upon entrance into 1-2-3. In Releases 2.2, 2.3, and 2.4, use the /Worksheet Global Default Other Add-In Set followed by a /Worksheet Global Default Update. In Release 3.1+, bring up the main add-in menu with [Alt]+[F10] and choose Settings; System sets up automatic attaching upon retrieval of all worksheets, File sets it up for this individual worksheet only.

Invoking Add-ins

Once attached, add-ins can be invoked or started in one of three ways:

[Alt]+[F10], choose Invoke.

[Alt]+ a function key
    This function key method can be used if you chose 7, 8, 9, or 10 when you attached the add-in.

/Add-in Invoke
    (Releases 2.2, 2.3, and 2.4 only.)

Typing the colon will invoke WYSIWYG.

Viewer

Command Summary

The Viewer add-in allows you to view the contents of worksheet files on disk without having to retrieve them. It also looks into text files and lists directories. Links can be created from one worksheet to another through the Viewer. (/File View will invoke the Viewer in Releases 2.3 and 2.4)

The main menu for Viewer has the three options below:

Retrieve Link Browse

Retrieve is actually a fancy /File Retrieve. It's helpful for finding a worksheet whose name you forgot. It brings up two windows to help you find the file to retrieve. The List window lists the names of the worksheet files on disk in the current directory. The View window displays the contents of the highlighted file in the List window. Hitting [Return] retrieves the highlighted file.

Link creates a link from the current worksheet to a file on disk. (See File Linking in appendix.)

Browse allows you to view the contents of any file in the current directory, including non-worksheet files.

Sample Session

Attach and Invoke the Viewer. (Release 2.3 and 2.4 users can use /File View to invoke the Viewer.) Choose Retrieve from the main menu. Use the down arrow keys to highlight the worksheet file names and note that the contents of the highlighted name is displayed in the window. Hit [Return] to retrieve a file.

Create a link to the SCRANTON worksheet (or actually any worksheet you have handy). Invoke the Viewer and choose Link from the main menu. Highlight the SCRANTON file and type [Right] to enter its contents. Move to the sales value for Nuts and hit [Return]. Choose Yes to allow an overwrite of the cell, if necessary. The link formula is displayed in the control panel. Format the cell as Currency with 2 decimal digits.

Invoke the Viewer and choose Browse from the main menu. Use the arrow keys to view the contents of the listed files. Note that all files are listed, not just worksheet files as in the Retrieve command.

Tutor

The Tutor or 1-2-3 Go! is an interactive tutorial with lessons on 1-2-3. Attach and Invoke it. There is a lesson on building a worksheet, using graphs, using a database, and working with macros. Included is a tutorial on WYSIWYG called **WYSIWYG-Go!** The time it will take to complete the highlighted lesson is displayed on the right. Highlight the lesson you wish to do and hit [Return] to begin.

Macro Library Manager

Command Summary

This add-in allows you to store a set of macros in a library which can be run from any worksheet. First you create the macros in a worksheet, then save them to a library file. 1-2-3 clears them from the worksheet. Run the macros as usual.

The main menu for the Macro Library Manager is shown below:

Load Save Edit Remove Name-List Quit

Load retrieves a macro library into memory so that you can run the
macros in that library.
Save moves the specified range containing macros to a macro library file
on disk with extension .MLB. The macros are removed from the
worksheet and range names now refer to the ranges in the library
file.
Edit moves macros in a library file to the worksheet so you can modify
them.
Remove clears a macro library from memory, freeing up space in memory.
It does NOT delete the library file from disk.
Name-List lists in the worksheet the macro names in a library file.

Sample Session

From READY mode, erase the worksheet and create two very simple
macros: one to move the cell pointer 3 cells down and one to move the
cell pointer two cells right. Name them \D and \R. Test them to make
sure they work.

Attach and Invoke the Macro Library Manager Add-in
(MACROMGR.ADN). The main menu should be on your screen.

Save to the file MOVEIT the range with the two macros with no
password. The macros have disappeared from the worksheet.

Enter [Alt]+D to run the down macro and [Alt]+R to run the other
macro.

Exit Lotus. Get back into 1-2-3 and try running the macros again. You
must attach and invoke again and Load the library file MOVEIT. Now
the macros will run.

Try the other commands on the main menu while referring to the
command summary.

Auditor

Command Summary

The Auditor add-in helps you to find interrelationships between cells in your worksheet. It will give you all referenced cells necessary for a given formula cell and vice versa, identifies cells involved in a circular reference, and identifies formulas in order of recalculation.

The main menu for the Auditor Add-in is:

Precedents Dependents Formulas Recalc-List Circs Options Quit

Precedents identifies all reference cells associated with a specified formula cell.
Dependents identifies all formula cells associated with a specified cell.
Formulas identifies all formula cells within a specified audit range.
Recalc-List identifies formulas in order of recalculation.
Circs identifies cells associated with a circular reference.
Options allows you to specify an audit range, resets highlighting, and allows you to set up the method of identification of cells (highlight, list, or trace).
Quit returns you to READY mode.

Sample Session

Retrieve the SCRANTON worksheet. Attach and Invoke the Auditor. The Auditor Settings screen shows that the default audit range is the entire worksheet and the reporting method is highlighting. Hit [F6/WINDOW] to clear the settings screen.

Let's say we wish to know which cells depend on the Sales of Nuts value in cell C5, $437.50. Choose Dependents from the main menu and specify C5. The five cells which depend on $437.50 are highlighted.

Clear the highlighting by choosing Options Reset Highlight Quit. The main menu should be on your screen.

Which cells are needed for the formula for the Total value $463.75 in the Nuts row? Choose Precedents and specify cell E5. The Nuts Sales and Tax values in C5..D5 are highlighted. Clear the highlighting again.

To determine which cells within the audit range (by default the entire worksheet) are formula cells, choose Formulas. All formula cells are now highlighted.

Instead of being highlighted, cells can be identified by listing them. Choose Options List Quit. From the main menu, choose Formulas again and specify B12 as the range for the list. Under the heading "Formulas in Audit Range A1..IV8192" in cell B12 is a list of formulas and the cells that contain them.

Cells can also be identified by the trace method. Choose Options Trace Quit. Choose Formulas again. The cell pointer moves to the first cell containing a formula (column-major order) in the audit range. Choose Forward several times to trace to the next formula cells.

Recalc-List traces through the formulas in the order of recalculation. Choose Recalc-List and trace through the order with Forward.

Backsolver

Command Summary

The Backsolver add-in solves a problem in a backwards fashion. Basically, you tell it the value you want and it tells you the input number needed to make a formula cell give you that value. It works with two cells: a formula cell and a input cell referenced by the formula cell.

The Backsolver main menu is:

Formula-Cell   Value   Adjustable   Solve   Quit

Formula-cell specifies the cell containing the formula.
Value specifies the value you want the formula cell to compute to.
Adjustable specifies an input cell or referenced cell in the formula.
Solve finds the value needed in the adjustable cell which causes the
     formula to compute to the value you want.
Quit returns to READY mode.

Sample Session

Erase the worksheet. Let's use a ridiculously easy formula to discover how Backsolver works. Enter the value 3 into cell A1 and the formula 1+A1 into cell A2. A 4 is now displayed in cell A2.

Let's pretend we cannot figure out what value in cell A1 will cause the formula in cell A2 to compute to 10. Backsolver can be used to solve for the value that we need in cell A1, 9. Attach and invoke BSOLVER.

Choose Formula-Cell from the main menu and specify cell A2. Choose Value and specify the result we want the formula to compute to, 10.

Choose Adjustable to specify the input cell, A1. Choose Solve. Note that Backsolver has figured out that a 9 is needed in the input or adjustable cell to give a result of 10 in the formula cell.

Let's use a more realistic example. Erase the worksheet and enter the 4 test scores, 67, 75, 45, and 89 into A1..A4. Leave A5 blank and enter the formula @AVG(A1..A5) into cell A6. A6 displays 69. Your question is "What do I have to get on the fifth test to pull my average up to a 70?" Invoke BSOLVER and enter A6 as the Formula-Cell, A5 as the Adjustable cell, and 70 as the Value, and Solve. And the answer is 74.

Solver

The Solver is an add-in that does what-if analysis. It displays solutions to a problem with many possible answers, depending on the constraints you set up. You can use the Solver to go through many different solutions until you find one that suits your needs.

DataLens

DataLens® is an add-in which allows 1-2-3 to access and query data in other database software, such as Paradox® and DBASE IV®.

WYSIWYG

Contents:

WYSIWYG is an add-in that is supplied with releases 2.3, 2.4, and 3.1+. It produces presentation-quality printouts directly from 1-2-3. Worksheet printouts can be combined with graph printouts. Data can be printed in various fonts and sizes, boldfaced, underlined, shaded, and in color if you have a color printer. There are word processing capabilities for text in the worksheet. WYSIWYG, what-you-see-is-what-you-get, means that the special effects are seen directly on your screen; you don't have to do a print to see them.

To use this appendix, first look at Figure I-1, which is a rather cluttered example of almost every WYSIWYG feature. The WYSIWYG Command Summary below is meant to be a reference for the future. Skim it and proceed to the Using WYSIWYG with Lotus - Sample Session. The session steps you through each special effect in Figure I-1.

Allways compatibility: When Release 2.2 worksheet files with Allways format files are retrieved, 1-2-3 converts the formats into WYSIWYG formats wherever possible. Unlike Allways, WYSIWYG allows you to move cells and insert data without having to redo the formatting because it moves the formatting with the cells.

WYSIWYG Commands Summary

To bring up the main menu for WYSIWYG below, type the colon (:) character.

The main menu is also displayed when the mouse is moved into the control panel. Click on the right mouse button to toggle between the main 1-2-3 menu and the WYSIWYG menu.

Worksheet Format Graph Print Display Special Text Named-Style Quit

The sub-menus of each option and their purposes are summarized below.

:Worksheet

Column - specifies column width of a range of columns.
Row - specifies row height of a range of rows.
Page - inserts and removes page breaks at rows and columns.

:Format

Font - assigns a font to a range of cells. There are initially eight default fonts, which can be changed with the Replace option. Modified font selections can be saved as the Default or stored in a Library. Bold - boldfaces a range.

Italics - adds italics from a range.

Underline - underlines a range in single, double, or wide underlining style.

Color - sets text and background colors. Colors can also be reversed and set up for negative values in a range.

Lines - draws lines in cells on the left, right, top, or bottom. outlines and adds drop shadows to ranges. Line style can be single, double, or wide.

Shade - shades a range with light or dark shading or blackens a range.

Reset - restores default font and clears all format settings in a range.

:Graph

Add - overlays a graph over a worksheet range. The graph can be the current graph, a named graph, a .PIC or .CGM file on disk, or a blank box for a placeholder.

Remove - deletes a graph from the worksheet.

Goto - moves the cell pointer to the upper left corner of the range containing the specified graph.

Settings - Replaces a graph in the worksheet with another graph, moves a graph, changes a graph size, hides a graph. The Opaque option lets worksheet cells show through a graph, making it transparent. By default, graphs are redrawn to show modifications to worksheet cells; the Sync option turns automatic redrawing of graphs off.

Move - moves a graph in the worksheet

Zoom - displays a graph in the worksheet full-screen.

Compute - Used to redraw graphs when automatic redrawing of graphs is disabled with the Sync option in the Settings menu.

View - Shows a full-screen picture of a .PIC or .CGM file on disk.

Edit - Adds objects, such as text, lines, arrows, rectangles, ellipses, polygons, and freehand drawings, to a graph. Edits, centers, and changes the font of text in a graph. Changes colors in a graph. Sizes, rotates, flips, and transforms a graph. Many more editing features exist.

:Print

Go - prints the current print range.

File - prints to an **encoded file** on disk with extension .ENC. Encoded files are different from ASCII files created by the /Print File command in that they contain printer codes and setup strings. You can create an encoded file for another printer than the one currently hooked up to your PC by 1) using /Worksheet Global Default Printer Name to specify the other printer and 2) creating an encoded file with this command :Print File. For example, you can create a file at home (where you have a cruddy old dot-matrix) for printing at work (on your company's top-of-the-line laser).

Background - Printing a fancy file in WYSIWYG takes time if you do just a /Print Go; you've got to wait quite a while until it's finished printing before you can continue working. :Print Background does **Background printing**, which allows you to work on your worksheet while the printer is working in the background. It prints to an encoded file on disk, returns you fairly quickly to the worksheet so that you can work or print again, and then ships the encoded file to the printer. You must run **BPrint** from the DOS prompt before entering Lotus to use this feature.

Range - specifies print range.

Config - specifies printer device, interface, and cartridge. Sets print orientation to landscape or portrait, resolution, or paper tray/manual paper feed.

Settings - specifies the first and last pages to be printed, number of copies, page-numbering, beginning page number, inclusion of grid lines, inclusion of frame, and pause for manual paper feed.

Layout - specifies page-size, margins, headers, footers, borders, and compression of print range to one page. Settings can be stored in a Library or as the Default.

Preview - :Print Preview will probably be the command you use most often. It puts a picture of the print on a full screen.

Info - Same effect as [F6/WINDOW]. It removes or restores the Print Settings dialog box.

:Display

Mode - the Text option switches the display to look like plain 1-2-3 without WYSIWYG. The Graphics options switches it back to WYSIWYG. In Graphics mode, the display can be set to black and white only.

Zoom - enlarges or reduces display on the screen. For a close-up view of a few cells, choose Huge. For a view of a large range in the worksheet, choose Tiny (or see Rows below).

Colors - changes colors of the background, foreground, unprotected cells, grid, frame, and more.

Options - changes the worksheet display of the frame, grid, page-breaks, cell-pointer, screen brightness intensity, and specifies the graphics display adapter to use.

Font-Directory - Changes the default fonts directory for the WYSIWYG fonts.

Rows - specifies the number of rows to display on the screen.

Default - Restores the default settings for the display or allows you to save the current settings as the default.

:Special

Copy - copies the format settings of one range to another.

Move - moves the format settings of one range to another.

Import - changes format settings of current worksheet to those settings of another worksheet.

Export - saves the current format settings for importing into another worksheet file.

:Text

Edit - edits text in a range in the worksheet instead of the control panel.

Align - aligns text left, right, centered, or left-and-right (even).

Reformat - formats cells with long text into a range to look like a paragraph.

Set - specifies a range. Subsequent Text commands will be affected on this range.

Clear - clears the alignment and other text attributes from a range.

:Named-Style

Names a group of WYSIWYG format settings for use in other cells. First, set up a cell in the worksheet with WYSIWYG commands. Second, name the style of that cell by issuing :Named-Style Define. Each worksheet can contain up to 8 named styles. The description will be shown in the control panel on the third line. Third, use the same style in another cell by issuing :Named-Style and the number.

Formatting Sequences

Formatting sequences are used to format text when :Format won't work, such as in headers and footers, for specific characters in a cell, and in text added to a graphic. Special effects are turned on by typing [Ctrl]+a and the formatting sequence before the text to be formatted. The special effect is turned off by typing [Ctrl]+e followed by the formatting sequence. To terminate sequences with two characters (a digit followed by a character), use only the character after [Ctrl]+e. [Ctrl]+n turns off all sequences. Formatting sequences are case-sensitive, for example, use lowercase i for italics, not uppercase I and uppercase F for font changes, not lowercase f. Do the sample session for practice in formatting sequences.

Case-Sensitive Formatting Sequence	Special Effect
i	Italics
b	Bold
d	Subscript
u	Superscript
x	Backwards (flipped on x-axis)
y	Upside down (flipped on y-axis)
f	Flashing
1_	Single underline
2_	Double underline
3_	Wide underline
4_	Rectangular outline
5_	Strike-through
1F	Font 1 from current font set
2F	Font 2 from current font set
3F	Font 3 from current font set
4F	Font 4 from current font set
5F	Font 5 from current font set
6F	Font 6 from current font set
7F	Font 7 from current font set
8F	Font 8 from current font set
o	Special effect outline in Figure I-1's title.
1o to 255o	Special effect outline with size change.

To use on-screen help when you forget a formatting sequence, bring up the main help index with [F1/HELP], go right to the bottom and highlight WYSIWYG Main Help Index and hit [Return], highlight Formatting Sequences and hit [Return] and scroll down with [Down] until you find the one you're looking for.

Using WYSIWYG with Lotus -
Sample Session

In this session, you will create Figure I-1. Retrieve the SCRANTON worksheet. Shorten the title to SCRANTON HARDWARE and delete the row with the dashes above the totals (row 8) and the row between Sales Tax and Total and Nuts (row 4).

If you wish to do the graphs part of this session, create the two graphs in Figure I-1. Lesson 9 explains how to create graphs. Both graphs have Nuts, Bolts, and Screwdrivers as the three X range labels and the three Sales figures in the C column as the A range. Don't be too fussy about the graphs. Create one similar the bar graph in Figure I-1 and name it BAR, then change the type to Pie and keep it current.

Attaching WYSIWYG

Add-ins must first be attached (or loaded into RAM). In Release 2.4, WYSIWYG is automatically attached when you enter 1-2-3. In any release, WYSIWYG and other add-ins can be set up to automatically attach with the /Worksheet Global Default Other Add-In Set followed by a /Worksheet Global Default Update. (If you're not sure whether WYSIWYG is attached, just attach it as explained next; clear the "Add-in already attached" error message with [Esc] if it occurs.)

To attach WYSIWYG, bring up the Add-in main menu below by using [Alt]+[F10]. (Release 2.x users can also use /Add-in.)

Attach Detach Invoke Clear Quit

Attach (or Load in Release 3.1+) loads an add-in program into RAM.
Detach deletes a current add-in program from RAM.
Invoke starts up an add-in program. The program must have been
        previously attached.
Clear deletes ALL attached add-in programs from RAM.
Quit returns to READY mode.

To attach the WYSIWYG add-in:

Choose Attach (Load in Release 3.1+), highlight WYSIWYG.ADN (or WYSIWYG.PLC in Release 3.1+), and hit [Return]. Choose No-Key.

Note: If WYSIWYG is not shown in the control panel, Exit Lotus and re-run the INSTALL program from the DOS prompt.

Invoking WYSIWYG

The standard way to invoke WYSIWYG is by simply typing the colon. The mouse can also be used; move the mouse pointer into the control panel and use the right button to toggle between the main 1-2-3 menu and the WYSIWYG menu.

You type :

The WYSIWYG main menu below should now be on your screen.

Worksheet Format Graph Print Display Special Text Named-Style Quit

Special Effects

To create Figure I-1, let's start with shading. Issue the following:

Format Shade Light A3..E3 [Return]

:Format Shade Dark B7 [Return]

Compare your screen to the figure.[1] Note the {S1} and {S2} in the control panel which designates light and dark shading, respectively. These control panel indicators are helpful if you are not in Graphics Display Mode; see :Display Mode Text in Command Summary. As you go through this session, note the control panel indicators that get added with each command. Also compare your screen after each command to the figure.

The shading in B34..B35 was done with :Format Shade Solid.

Italicize the total figures in row 7:

:Format Italics Set C7..E7 [Return]

---

[1]If you're having problems with a black and white monitor, as with a laptop or notebook, re-run INSTALL from the DOS prompt. Do a Change Selected Equipment, Modify Current DCF, Change Selected Display, and choose Enhanced Graphics Adapter, 80x25 monochrome.

Boldfacing is done with :Format Bold Set.

Add some lines:

> **:Format Lines Bottom A3..E3 [Return]**
> **:Format Lines Top A7..E7 [Return]**
> **:Format Lines Wide Bottom B1..E1 [Return]**

To get the shadowed box around A3..E7, you must Outline the range and Shadow it. Use the fourth function key to save keystrokes whenever you have to perform more than one command on the same range:

> **Position pointer in A3.**
> **[F4/RANGE]   [Down] 4 times. [Right] 4 times.   [Return]**
> **:Format Lines Outline**
> **:Format Lines Shadow Set**
> **Hit [Esc] to clear the range.**

Print Preview

This will probably be the command you use most. It saves a lot of trees by allowing you to preview the print on the screen. Try it.

> **:Print Range Set A1..F35 [Return] Preview**

[Esc] returns you to READY mode. I used :Print Settings Frame Yes to get the row numbers and column headers into Figure I-1.

Fonts

The two font styles which always seem to be included with software are Swiss and Dutch. In Figure I-1, the bar graph's title is Dutch and the pie chart's title is Swiss. Dutch looks rounder with more serifs and Swiss looks plainer and more square. The Fonts header above this paragraph is Swiss, the text in this paragraph is Dutch.

In row 3 of the figure, "Sales" and "Tax" are Swiss 14 and "Total" is Dutch 16. Change them now.

> **:Format Font**

The WYSIWYG font selections are listed.

> **Choose the number associated with Swiss 14 Point.**
> **C3..D3 [Return]**

Other fonts in the figure ranges are:

Dutch 16 in range A4..A6 and cell E3,
Dutch 14 in cell A27,
Dutch 12 in range B4..B6,
Swiss 12 in range C4..E7,
Swiss 14 in cell E7.

If no :Format Font was issued on a range, the default font, font 1, is used.

Bring up the WYSIWYG Font Replacement box by issuing:

:Format Font Replace

The default set of eight fonts can be changed with this Replace option.
Let's replace Swiss 14 with Courier 10.

Number associated with Swiss 14.
Courier 10 [Return] Quit

Note that range C3..D3 has been updated to Courier 10 point.

Change the font of the title to Swiss 24 or some other large font.

Underline the title with the wide-style line.

:Format Lines Wide Bottom B1..E1 [Return]

Center the title above the box.

:Text Align Center B1..E1 [Return]

Enter the text in B9..B12 by entering the four long labels into B9, B10,
B11, and B12. Don't worry about the special effects for now.

Text can be aligned in several ways. Create the straight right and left
borders on the text range B9..E12 as shown in the figure:

:Text Align Even B9..E12 [Return]

Do the same command again using Right and Center alignment.

:Text Align Right [Return]
:Text Align Center [Return]

Return the text back to even alignment.

Formatting Sequences

The special effects, such as italics, bold, underlining, etc. are created with the :Format command if the entire contents of a cell are to be effected. Formatting sequences make it possible to put a special effect on part of the text in a cell, as is seen in range B9..E12 in Figure I-1.

You may now skip to the Graphs section with no loss of continuity in this session, if you're not interested in the rather advanced topic of formatting sequences.

In general, to embed a formatting sequence, type [Ctrl]+a and the sequence to initialize the effect and [Ctrl]+e to terminate it. [Ctrl]+n terminates **all** formatting sequences.

Refer to the Formatting Sequence Summary, page 688.

Create the italics effect on "all items" in B9 (it looks like it's in cell D9) by editing the cell and inserting a [Ctrl]+a followed by a lowercase i:

> **Position pointer to B9. [F2/EDIT] Move cursor before "all items." [Ctrl]+a**

▲ appears before "all" in the control panel. <u>Formatting sequences are case sensitive.</u> Type a lowercase i for italics.

> **i [Return]**

The rest of the characters beginning at the formatting sequence, "all items, but a marked," are italicized. Turn off the italics after items.

> **[F2/EDIT] Move cursor after "all items." [Ctrl]+e i**

▲ appears followed by i to designate the end of the italics. [Ctrl]+n can also be used; it turns off **all** formatting sequences in the cell. For example, if you have some text which is both italicized and underlined and wish to turn off italics only, use [Ctrl]+e i. [Ctrl]+n would turn off both underlining and italics. The symbol ▼ appears to designate a [Ctrl]+n. Try it.

Experiment with the other formatting sequences. The "all is well" text and the SCRANTON HARDWARE title are creating with the outline formatting sequence (see the bottom of the Formatting Sequences list in reference). The word "Backwards" is in cell D13 with the backwards formatting sequence (x). The upside down formatting sequence is y.

You can change to a different font by using [Ctrl]+a followed by the number of the font and uppercase F. The footer example contains two font changes. If you're not using [Ctrl]+n to terminate a font, use [Ctrl]+e followed by an uppercase F. (The font number is not entered.) Likewise, for underlining, use [Ctrl]+e followed by the underscore (_) -- no need for the digit. The general rule for terminating sequences that contain a digit and another character, such as 1_, 2_, or 1F, 2F, etc., is to use the character after the [Ctrl]+e and leave out the digit.

Formatting sequences are necessary when you want special effects in headers or footers. The footer was created with :Print Layout Titles Footer and was entered this way:

[Ctrl]+a4_Scranton Hardware[Ctrl]+e_
[Ctrl]+a5F[Ctrl]+a2_[Ctrl]+aiAnnual Report[Ctrl]+n | |
[Ctrl]a2FPage [Ctrl]+ab#[Return]

4_ created the outline around Scranton Hardware. Three formatting sequences are at work on "Annual Report" - 5F gives it the fifth font, 2_ double underlines it, and i italicizes it. | | and # are covered in the advanced printing lesson -- | | flushes text to the right margin, # inserts the current page number (see headers and footers in Advanced Printing Lesson). 2F formats "Page" and the page number in the second font and b boldfaces the # page number.

Issue a :Print Preview to check your footer.

Graphing

The current graph should be a pie chart. Add it to the worksheet:

:Graph Add Current A15..D27 [Return]

Position the pointer through the graph range and note that the control panel states CURRENT. Modifying cells with values used in worksheet graphs causes the graphs to be redrawn with the updates.

Graphs in the worksheet can be edited. Position the cell pointer into the graph area.

:Graph Edit [Return]

The graph editing screen appears with the pie chart. Add the "Increase here" text object shown in Figure I-1.

Add Text Increase here [Return]

Use the arrow keys or the mouse to move the text and hit [Return]. The squares around the added text signify that the text object is selected. Change the font:

Edit Font   Choose a font number.

The control panel displays the font name associated with the highlighted number. Change the font of the graph text.

Select Graph

The graph has squares around it.

Edit Font   Choose a font number.

Unfortunately, all text in the graph takes the same settings; in other words, you cannot change an individual piece of text in a graph.

Add an arrow from "Increase here" to the bolts pie slice. Use the mouse or the arrow keys to place the arrow. Try adding other objects such as a rectangle and an ellipse now. Each command of these edit commands is listed and briefly explained in the command summary.

The shading under the graph titles is actually in cells B15..D16 in the worksheet. Return to READY mode and set up the shading:

:Format Shade Light B15..D16 [Return]

To make the shading "show through" the graph, make the graph transparent:

:Graph Settings Opaque No B15 [Return]

The title looks shaded now. Add the other named graph to the worksheet.

:Graph Add Named BAR   D26..F34 [Return]

The wide line around this graph in Figure I-1 was put there with :Format Lines Wide Outline and not a graph command. Position the cell pointer within the bar graph range. The worksheet cells D34..D35 contain text "showing through" the bar graph in the figure.

	A	B	C	D	E	F

Scranton Hardware

		Sales	Tax	Total
1 Nuts		$437.50	$26.25	$463.75
2 Bolts		$899.64	$53.98	$953.62
3 Screwdrivers		$76.23	$4.57	$80.80
TOTAL		$1,413.37	$84.80	$1,498.17

Sales were up from 1991 on *all items*, but a marked increase existed in the **Bolt department**. Stock price has increased by 90% and all is well at Scranton Hardware. See graph below.

Bɒɔʍɒɿɔƨ

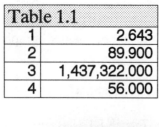

SCRANTON HARDWARE COMPANY
1992 Sales

Screwdrivers (5.4%)

Nuts (31.0%)

Increase here

Bolts (63.7%)

Table 1.1	
1	2.643
2	89.900
3	1,437,322.000
4	56.000

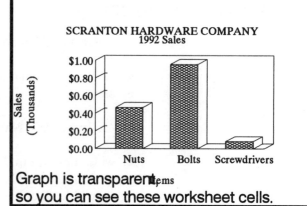

SCRANTON HARDWARE COMPANY
1992 Sales

Graph is transparent so you can see these worksheet cells.

Figure I-1. WYSIWYG Printout.

CUMULATIVE EXERCISES

On the next four pages are printouts in WYSIWYG of the four cumulative exercises. If you did the graph lesson, add the graphs; if not, just format the text data and tables.

IMITATION TOFU, INCORPORATED

SalesRep	Division	92 Sales	Commission
1 Saxe, J.	2	$40,500	$2,430
2 Gress, R.	3	$77,000	$4,620
3 Cosner, L.	3	$23,400	$1,404
4 Smith, A.	1	$150,000	$9,000
5 Smith, B.	1	$54,700	$3,282
6 Kirlin, K.	2	$75,000	$4,500
7 Wodak, F.	1	$29,800	$1,788
8 Reese, J.	3	$111,300	$6,678
9 Gruss, M.	1	$88,200	$5,292
10 Boyle, T.	2	$67,600	$4,056
	Total	$717,500	$43,050
	Average	$71,750	$4,305

<u>Anne Smith</u> had the highest amount of 1992 sales. John Reese has the second highest amount. Frank Wodak will have to be fired.

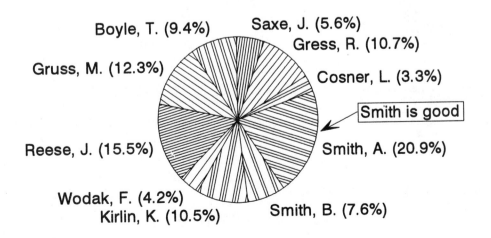

IMITATION TOFU, INC.
1992 Sales

Boyle, T. (9.4%)
Saxe, J. (5.6%)
Gress, R. (10.7%)
Gruss, M. (12.3%)
Cosner, L. (3.3%)
Smith is good
Reese, J. (15.5%)
Smith, A. (20.9%)
Wodak, F. (4.2%)
Kirlin, K. (10.5%)
Smith, B. (7.6%)

Happy Tropical Fish Store

Item #	Item Name	Quantity Sold	Retail Price	Wholesale Price	Profit per Item	Total Pr. per Item
273	7–inch fish net	63	$1.99	$0.70	$1.29	$81.27
238	1–lb. decorative rocks	49	$2.99	$1.30	$1.69	$82.81
130	underwater fern	13	$2.29	$0.90	$1.39	$18.07
281	40–gallon aquarium	14	$39.99	$22.00	$17.99	$251.86
162	goldfish	241	$0.59	$0.10	$0.49	$118.09
192	20–inch eel	4	$8.99	$4.00	$4.99	$19.96
274	2–gallon fish bowl	25	$4.99	$2.00	$2.99	$74.75
256	8–vitamin fish food	57	$1.79	$0.80	$0.99	$56.43
198	turtle	−1	$3.99	$1.50	$2.49	($2.49)
111	piranha	3	$10.99	$5.00	$5.99	$17.97
					Total Profit	**$718.72**

The forty gallon *aquariums* were real
profit makers. Goldfish were good too.
Turtles will be discontinued.

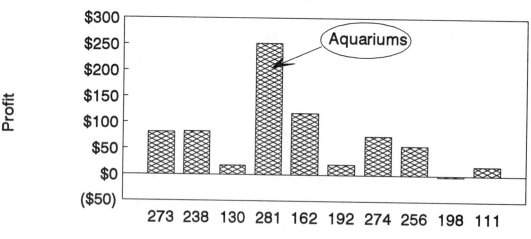

MONTHLY BILLS FOR MARCH

	Actual	Budgeted	Over/(Under)
Food	$238	$220	$18
Rent	$550	$550	$0
Phone	$39	$30	$9
Electric	$43	$50	($7)
Gasoline	$56	$45	$11
Car Payment	$345	$345	$0
Insurance	$55	$55	$0
Charge Cards	$250	$100	$150
Entertainment	$150	$100	$50
Total	$1,726	$1,495	**$231**

In March, too much was spent in the areas of entertainment and charge cards. Only the electric bill was under budget.

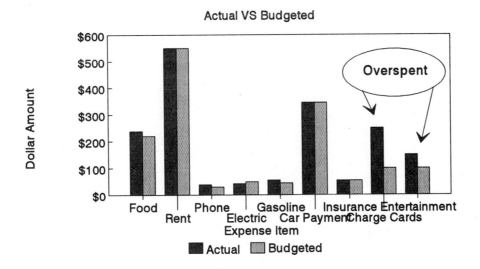

Actual VS Budgeted

J & F GOLF COURSE SCORE SHEET

Hole	1	2	3	4	5	6	7	8	9	Total
Par	4	5	4	3	5	4	4	3	4	36
Joe	8	5	6	4	4	5	6	4	4	46
Mary	4	6	5	4	6	4	5	5	3	42
Mike	3	7	6	4	5	5	6	5	4	45
Sheila	5	5	6	4	3	3	4	6	5	41
Average	5	5.75	5.75	4	4.5	4.25	5.25	5	4	43.5

J&F Golf Course is one of the most beautiful courses in the world. Nestled in the majestic Pocono Mountains, this 7127-yard championship layout is a golfer's paradise.

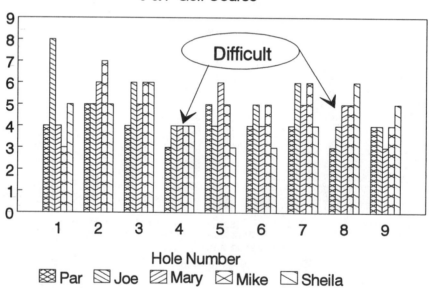

Use the SHOES worksheet from Lesson 9 to create the worksheet below. Print in landscape orientation.

ATHLETIC SHOES ARE US

	QTR1	QTR2	QTR3	QTR4	YEARLY SALES
Running	43	57	32	14	146
Racquetball	21	9	26	49	105
Squash	46	55	43	28	172
Aerobic	500	25	19	13	557
Total	$610	$146	$120	$104	$980

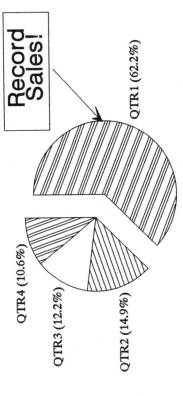

ATHLETIC SHOES ARE US
Total Quarterly Sales

Record Sales!

QTR1 (62.2%)

QTR2 (14.9%)

QTR3 (12.2%)

QTR4 (10.6%)

There was a phenomenal sales record set in quarter 1 in *aerobic footwear*. The profits carried us through the rest of the year.

ALLWAYS

Contents:

Allways^{TM},the Spreadsheet Publisher, is an add-in program produced by Funk Software. It produces presentation-quality printouts directly from 1-2-3. Worksheet printouts can be combined with graph printouts. Data can be printed in various fonts and sizes, boldfaced, underlined, shaded, and in color if you have a color printer. See Figure J-1. Allways supports WYSIWYG (what-you-see-is-what-you-get) screen display. In other words, special effects such as fonts, shading, etc. are shown directly on your screen; you don't have to print to see them.

Allways can be bought separately for Releases 2 and 2.01. It comes with Release 2.2! (Releases 2.3, 2.4, and 3.1+ have WYSIWYG, an upgrade of Allways. Release 3.0 has no comparable add-ins, although IMPRESS^{TM} by PC Publishing, Massachusetts can be purchased.) An IBM PC, PC-compatible, XT, AT or PS/2 is needed. A hard disk with at least 1.1M of free space and at least 512K RAM are needed. Disabling the UNDO feature (see note in this appendix) or clearing some memory resident software might prevent memory problems.

The basics of Allways could be learned in minutes if you have a little previous Lotus experience. The next few sections of this appendix are meant to be a reference. Skim them and go to the Using Allways with Lotus - Sample Session.

Allways Commands Summary

The main menu for Allways is pulled up using the forward slash:

Worksheet Format Graph Layout Print Display Special Quit

The sub-menus of each option and their purposes are summarized below.

Worksheet

Column - specifies column width.
Row - specifies row height.
Page - inserts and removes page breaks at rows and columns.

Format

Font - assigns a font to a range of cells. The two fonts, Triumvirate and
      Times, are available in sizes 10, 14, and 20 point. Ten point Italics
      is available for each font.

Bold - boldfaces a range.

Underline - underlines a range in single or double underlining style.

Color - sets one of 8 colors to a range.

Lines - draws lines or boxes around a range.

Shade - shades a range with light or dark shading or blackens a range.

Reset - restores default font and clears all format settings.

Graph

Add - overlays a graph (a .PIC file) over a worksheet range.

Remove - deletes a graph from the worksheet.

Goto - moves the cell pointer to the upper left corner of the range
      containing the specified graph.

Settings - sets up fonts, colors, and margins in the specified graph.
      Changes the range of a graph which, in effect, moves the graph to
      another location in the worksheet or changes its size in the
      worksheet. Replaces a current graph with another .PIC file

Layout

Page-Size - changes the length or width settings of the paper.

Margins - sets the margins on the printed paper.

Title - sets up headers and footers.

Borders - sets up top, left, or bottom borders.

Options - creates grid lines or sets the thickness of lines created with
      /Format Lines.

Default - resets current layout settings.

Library - saves, retrieves, or erases layout settings on disk.

Print

Go - prints the current print range.

File - prints to a file on disk.

Range - specifies print range.

Configuration - specifies printer device, interface, and cartridge. Sets
      print orientation to landscape or portrait, resolution, or paper
      tray/manual paper feed.

Setting - specifies the first and last pages to be printed, number of copies,
      page-numbering, and pause for manual paper feed.

Display

Mode - switches between text and graphics mode.
Zoom - enlarges or reduces display on the screen. For a close up view of a few cells, choose Huge. For a view of a large range in the worksheet, choose Tiny.
Graphs - turns the display of graphs on and off.
Colors - changes the background and foreground colors and the color of the cell pointer.

Special

Copy - copies the format settings of one range to another.
Move - moves the format settings of one range to another.
Justify - justifies text within a range.
Import - changes format settings of current worksheet to those settings of another worksheet.

Attaching Allways

Allways must be attached or pulled into RAM before it can be used or Invoked. [Alt]+[F10] (or /Add-in in Release 2.2) pulls up the necessary menu:

Attach   Detach   Invoke   Clear   Quit

Attach pulls an add-in program into RAM.
Detach deletes a current add-in program from RAM.
Invoke starts up an add-in program. The program must have been previously attached.
Clear deletes all attached add-in programs from RAM.
Quit returns to READY mode.

Choose Attach from this menu and highlight and choose the ALLWAYS.ADN. The menu No-Key 7 8 9 10 sets up the future keystrokes necessary to run or invoke Allways. Choosing one of the numbers allows Allways to be invoked with [Alt]+ the function key with that number. For example, choosing 7 will cause the key sequence [Alt]+[F7] to invoke Allways. Keys set to invoke add-in programs are called **hot keys**.

Invoking Allways

Allways can be Invoked or started in one of three ways:

[Alt]+[F10], choose Invoke.

[Alt]+ a function key
> This function key method can be used if you chose 7, 8, 9, or 10 when you attached Allways.

/Add-in Invoke
> (Not on Release 2 or 2.01.)

Exiting Allways

To exit from Allways to get back to 1-2-3, use /Quit from the Allways main menu or hit [Esc].

Installing Allways

Place the Allways Setup Disk in drive A:, change the default drive to A:, and type

awsetup

Give the name of the directory on your hard disk where Lotus is installed. Follow the instructions.

Using Allways with Lotus - Sample Session

Using Allways is easy if you know a little bit about Lotus. In this sample session, Figure J-1 or one similar to it will be created. I used a Hewlett Packard LaserJet Series II printer. Allways must be installed on your hard disk before you start this session. (See Installing Allways section above.)

Get into 1-2-3 and retrieve a worksheet file:

/File Retrieve SHOES9.

This session will use the SHOES9 worksheet. Actually, you can use any worksheet handy. Save any graph created from the worksheet to a .PIC file.

/Graph Save QSALES [Return]

Note: If you are using Release 2.2 and receive an Out of Memory error, try disabling the UNDO feature to free up some RAM: /Worksheet Global Default Other Undo Disable.

Attach Allways (bring it into memory) and Invoke it (run it):

[Alt]+[F10] (or /Add-in), Choose Attach, Highlight ALLWAYS.ADN and [Return], Choose 7 to make [F7] a hot key. Choose Invoke. Choose ALLWAYS.

The mode indicator displays ALLWAYS. At the top of the screen is displayed the default font, Triumvirate 10 point, FONT(1). Change the font of a range to Triumvirate Italics 10 point.

/Format Font Use Triumvirate Italic 10 B3..F3 [Return]

Note that the results of the font change can be seen on the screen.

Shade a range:

/Format Shade Light A5..A8.

Try other formats: underline, lines, etc.

Pull the .PIC file into the worksheet:

/Graph Add QSALES A12..F25 [Return]

Turn the graph display on:

/Display Graph Yes

Enlarge the number of cells which can be viewed on the screen:

/Display Zoom Tiny

Print the worksheet and graph:

/Print Range Set A1..F25 [Return]

Experiment.

Note: Make sure you have your worksheet as final as possible before using Allways. Inserting a row or moving cells does not update the Allways formatting.

ATHLETIC SHOES ARE US

	QTR1	QTR2	QTR3	QTR4	LY SALES
Running	43	57	32	14	146
Racquetball	21	9	26	49	105
Squash	46	55	43	28	172
Aerobic	37	25	19	13	94
Total	147	146	120	104	517

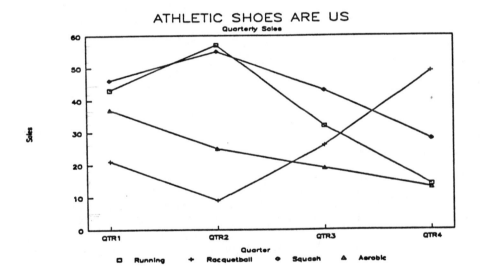

Figure D-1. ALLWAYS Printout.

SIDEWAYS

Contents:

Sideways™ is a program produced by Funk Software which will print your worksheet in landscape mode (turned 90 degrees) on a dot matrix printer.

This "sideways" printing, as in Figure K-1, allows you to print a worksheet of infinite width. Sideways is used to handle the common problem in printing worksheets depicted in Figure 17-2, on page 457.

Start sideways by entering at the DOS prompt:
sideways

Sideways looks and feels like Lotus; its menus are similar to 1-2-3's. The backslash brings up the main menu below:

Range Go Options Clear File Interface Defaults Quit

Options

Form-size - changes the dimensions of the paper: vertical form size is the length of each sheet of paper, from perforation to perforation; horizontal is the width of each paper from one side with holes to the other.

Margins - changes the top (from holes to first vertical line of print), bottom (from last vertical line of print to holes), and left (from first perforated top of form to first column of print) margins.

Character - changes the font (Sideways has 9 fonts which you can choose by increasing or decreasing the size of the current font), density (single or double), spacing (size of separation between characters), and line-spacing (separation of vertical lines). In Figure K-2, the size has been decreased one level.

Borders - sets up borders similar to the print menu in 1-2-3. Top and bottom margins and margins to the left can be set and cleared.

Special-effects - ranges can be set to print in bold, expanded, or underlined format. Choose Add and specify the range to which the special-effect should be set. Edit will allow you to change your mind later. Clear cancels all special-effects ranges. Figure K-2 shows the results of the these special effects. The title is expanded, the first column is in bold, the month column headers are underlined.

Current print settings can be saved with /File Save and are associated with the worksheet.

FRUGGIE'S BAR & GRILL

	Jan	Feb	Mar	Apr	May	June	July	Aug	Sept
Beer	9000	9300	9600	9900	10200	10500	10800	11100	11400
Liquor	9100	9400	9700	10000	10300	10600	10900	11200	11500
Food	9200	9500	9800	10100	10400	10700	11000	11300	11600
Total Income	27300	28200	29100	30000	30900	31800	32700	33600	34500
Labor	1000	991	982	973	964	955	946	937	928
Beer	999	990	981	972	963	954	945	936	927
Liquor	998	989	980	971	962	953	944	935	926
Food	997	988	979	970	961	952	943	934	925
Mortgage	996	987	978	969	960	951	942	933	924
Utilities	995	986	977	968	959	950	941	932	923
Phone	994	985	976	967	958	949	940	931	922
Insurance	993	984	975	966	957	948	939	930	921
Taxes	992	983	974	965	956	947	938	929	920
Total Expenses	8964	8883	8802	8721	8640	8559	8478	8397	8316
Net Income	18336	19317	20298	21279	22260	23241	24222	25203	26184

Figure K-1. Landscape Printout from Sideways.

RIBES DR&GLL

	Jan	Feb	Mar	Apr	May	June	July	Aug	Sept	Oct	Nov
Beer	9000	9300	9600	9900	10200	10500	10800	11100	11400	11700	12000
Liquor	9100	9400	9700	10000	10300	10600	10900	11200	11500	11800	12100
Food	9200	9500	9800	10100	10400	10700	11000	11300	11600	11900	12200
Total Income	27300	28200	29100	30000	30900	31800	32700	33600	34500	35400	36300
Labor	1000	991	932	973	964	955	946	937	928	919	910
Beer	999	990	931	972	963	954	945	936	927	918	909
Liquor	998	989	980	971	962	953	944	935	926	917	908
Food	997	988	979	970	961	952	943	934	925	916	907
Mortgage	996	987	978	969	960	951	942	933	924	915	906
Utilities	995	986	977	968	959	950	941	932	923	914	905
Phone	994	985	976	967	958	949	940	931	922	913	904
Insurance	993	984	975	966	957	948	939	930	921	912	903
Taxes	992	983	974	965	956	947	938	929	920	911	902
Total Expenses	8964	8883	8302	8721	8640	8559	8478	8397	8316	8235	8154
Net Income	18336	19317	20298	21279	22260	23241	24222	25203	26184	27165	28146

Figure K-2. Special-Effects: Bold, Underline and Expanded Print. Decrease in Size.

MENU COMMANDS QUICK REFERENCE

Contents:

Release 2.4's commands are graphically summarized:

Add-In Commands

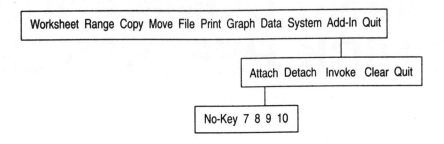

```
┌─────────────────────────────────────────────────────────────────┐
│ Worksheet Range Copy Move File Print Graph Data System Add-In Quit │
└─────────────────────────────────────────────────────────────────┘
                              ┌──────────────────────────────────┐
                              │ Attach Detach Invoke Clear Quit │
                              └──────────────────────────────────┘
                        ┌──────────────────┐
                        │ No-Key 7 8 9 10 │
                        └──────────────────┘
```

Data Commands

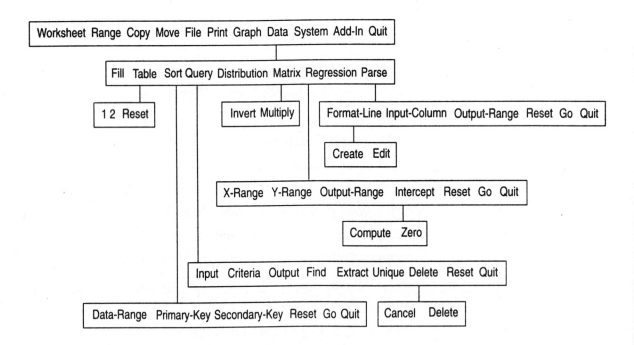

```
┌─────────────────────────────────────────────────────────────────┐
│ Worksheet Range Copy Move File Print Graph Data System Add-In Quit │
└─────────────────────────────────────────────────────────────────┘
    ┌──────────────────────────────────────────────────────┐
    │ Fill Table Sort Query Distribution Matrix Regression Parse │
    └──────────────────────────────────────────────────────┘
        ┌──────────┐      ┌─────────────────┐   ┌───────────────────────────────────────────────┐
        │ 1 2 Reset │      │ Invert Multiply │   │ Format-Line Input-Column Output-Range Reset Go Quit │
        └──────────┘      └─────────────────┘   └───────────────────────────────────────────────┘
                                                        ┌──────────────┐
                                                        │ Create Edit │
                                                        └──────────────┘
                              ┌───────────────────────────────────────────────────────┐
                              │ X-Range Y-Range Output-Range Intercept Reset Go Quit │
                              └───────────────────────────────────────────────────────┘
                                                        ┌──────────────────┐
                                                        │ Compute Zero │
                                                        └──────────────────┘
                    ┌────────────────────────────────────────────────────────────────┐
                    │ Input Criteria Output Find Extract Unique Delete Reset Quit │
                    └────────────────────────────────────────────────────────────────┘
        ┌───────────────────────────────────────────────────────────┐   ┌──────────────────┐
        │ Data-Range Primary-Key Secondary-Key Reset Go Quit │   │ Cancel Delete │
        └───────────────────────────────────────────────────────────┘   └──────────────────┘
```

File Commands

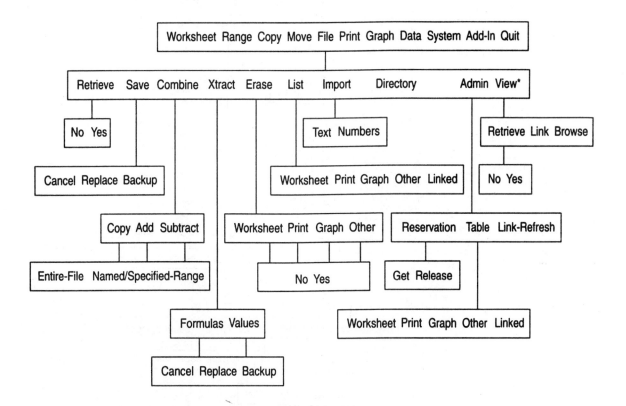

*When Viewer is attached, you can select the View command to activate the Viewer menu.

Graph Commands

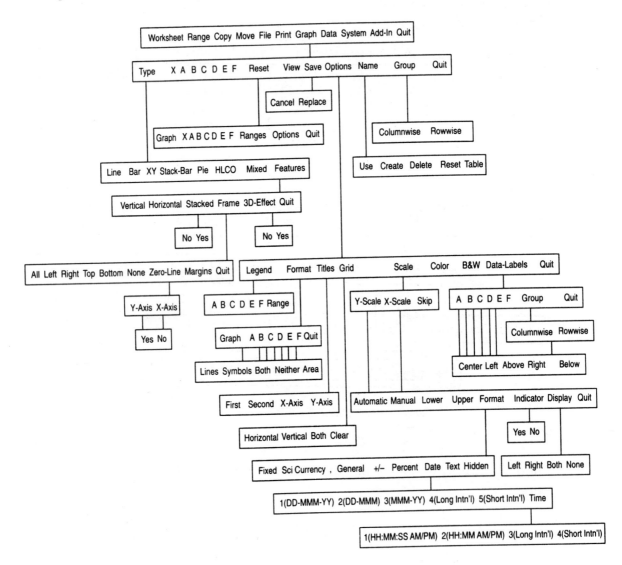

Print Commands

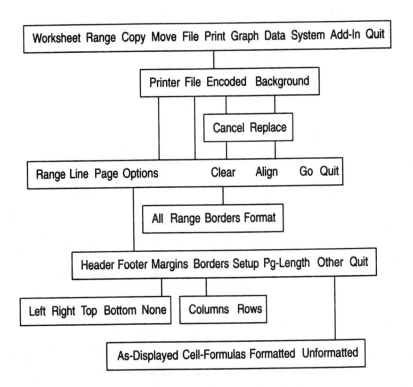

```
Worksheet Range Copy Move File Print Graph Data System Add-In Quit
```

```
Printer File Encoded  Background
```

```
Cancel  Replace
```

```
Range Line  Page  Options          Clear      Align      Go  Quit
```

```
All  Range Borders Format
```

```
Header Footer Margins Borders Setup Pg-Length  Other  Quit
```

```
Left  Right  Top  Bottom  None        Columns   Rows
```

```
As-Displayed Cell-Formulas Formatted  Unformatted
```

Range Commands

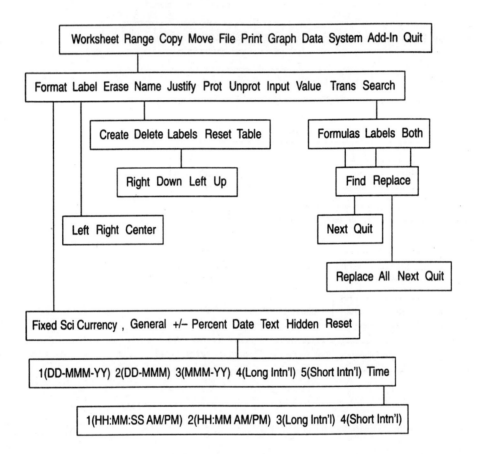

Worksheet Commands

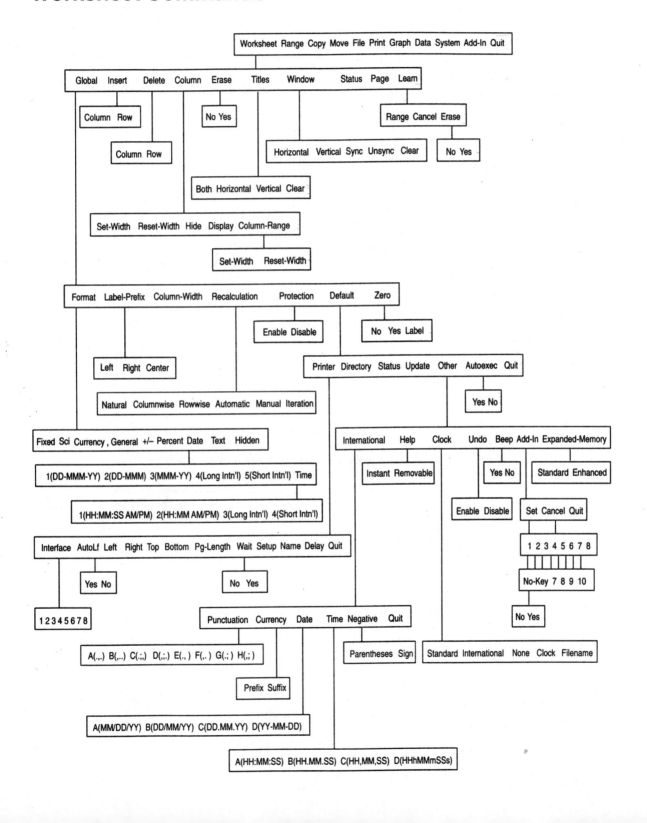

Wysiwyg Menu Trees

The following pages provide graphic representations of the Wysiwyg commands.

Display Commands

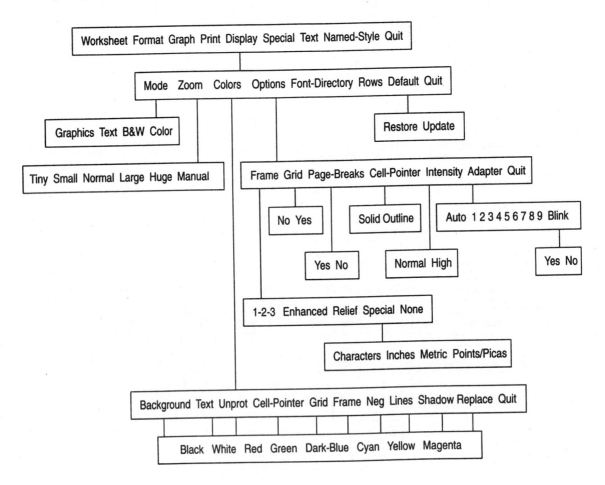

Format Commands

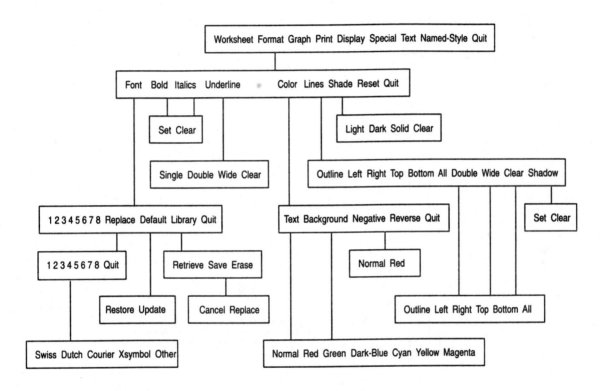

Graph Commands

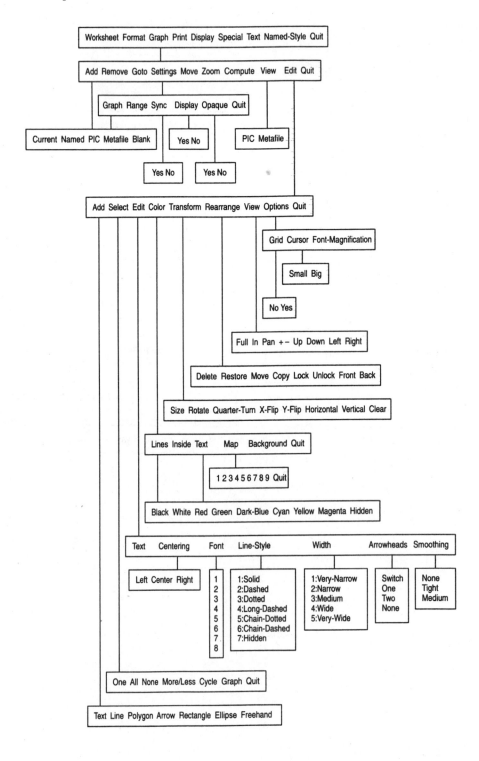

Named-Style Commands

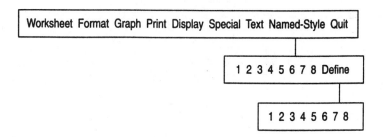

Print Commands

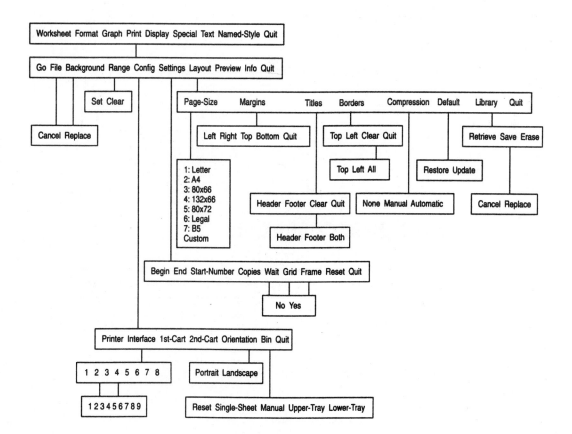

Special Commands

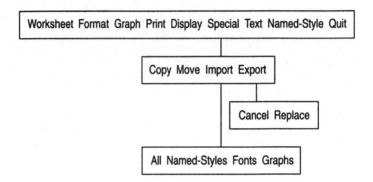

Text Commands

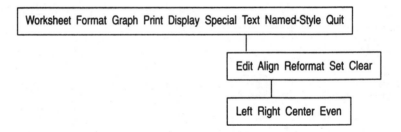

Worksheet Commands

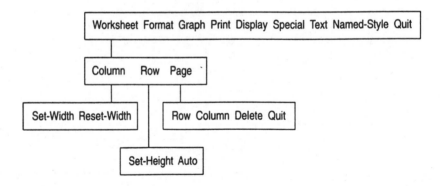

Appendix M

SMARTICONS QUICK REFERENCE

This appendix shows pictures of the SmartIcons, lists the default SmartIcons, and briefly describes their functions.

1-2-3 for Windows

SmartIcons Quick Reference

You can select commonly used commands and macros by clicking SmartIcons™ on the icon palette. SmartIcons provide immediate and easy access to powerful 1-2-3 for Windows functionality.

The default SmartIcons below are available when a Worksheet window is active.

When a Graph window is active, 1-2-3 displays the default SmartIcons below.

To display the description of one of the SmartIcons, position the mouse pointer on the icon and press the right mouse button. The description appears in the first line (the title bar) of the 1-2-3 window.

Using SmartIcons

1. If the icon acts on a range, select the range.
2. Click the icon.

Moving the SmartIcons

1. Choose Tools Icon Palette.
2. Under Palette position, select Left, Right, Top, Bottom, or Floating.
3. To hide the icon palette, select the Hide palette check box.
4. Select OK.

Customizing SmartIcons

Use Tools Icon Palette Customize to change available SmartIcons, group SmartIcons in libraries, and assign a macro to a custom icon.

Getting Help about SmartIcons

For more information about using and moving SmartIcons, changing available SmartIcons, using named palettes, and creating a custom icon and assigning a macro to it, choose Tools Icon Palette and press F1 (HELP).

Worksheet SmartIcons

The following SmartIcons are available when a Worksheet window is active:

Opens a new worksheet file.

Lets you open an existing worksheet file.

Saves the current worksheet file.

Prints the highlighted cell or range.

Displays a preview of the print range as 1-2-3 for Windows formats it for printing.

Undoes the most recent command, action, or macro.

Cuts the highlighted cell or range from the worksheet and places it on the Clipboard.

Copies the highlighted cell or range from the worksheet to the Clipboard.

Pastes the contents of the Clipboard to the worksheet.

Permanently deletes the highlighted cell or range from the worksheet.

Lets you specify a range to move the selected range to.

Lets you specify a range to copy the selected range to.

Lets you find or replace specified characters in labels and formulas in a cell or range.

Lets you move the cell pointer to a specified range.

Creates, names, and displays a graph, using the data in the highlighted range.

Left-aligns labels in a cell or range.

Centers labels in a cell or range.

Right-aligns labels in a cell or range.

Evenly-aligns labels with both the left and right edges of a range.

Displays data in a cell or range in boldface.

Displays data in a cell or range in italic.

Worksheet SmartIcons

U	Underlines data in a cell or range.
U (double)	Double-underlines data in a cell or range.
N	Removes bold, italic, and underlining from a cell or range.
A→A	Displays data in a cell or range in the next available font.
A→A	Displays data in a cell or range in the next available color.
AA	Displays the background of a cell or range in the next available color.
□	Draws an outline around a cell or range.
□	Draws an outline around a cell or range and draws a drop shadow below and to the right of a cell or range.
▦	Lets you add light shading to a cell or range.
$	Formats values in a cell or range with 2 decimal places, the default currency symbol, and the default thousand separators.
0,0	Formats values in a cell or range with the default thousand separators and no decimal places.
%	Formats values in a cell or range as % (percent) with 2 decimal places.
16	Enters today's date in the highlighted cell.
▦	Recalculates the highlighted range.
+2 3	Sums values in the highlighted or adjacent range, if you include empty cells below or to the right of the range.
A→N	Sorts a database table in ascending order (A–Z and smallest to largest values), using the selected column as the key.
N→A	Sorts a database table in descending order (Z–A and largest to smallest values), using the selected column as the key.
◀	Fills the highlighted range with a sequence of values.
◀	Repeats the contents of the current cell in all selected cells.
▥	Tiles all open Worksheet, Graph, and Transcript windows.
▦	Cascades all open Worksheet, Graph, and Transcript windows.
▦	Displays three contiguous worksheets in perspective view.
↖	Moves the cell pointer to the next worksheet.
↙	Moves the cell pointer to the previous worksheet.
↙	Moves the cell pointer to cell A1 in the current worksheet.
↘	Moves the cell pointer to the bottom right corner of the worksheet's active area.
↑	Moves the cell pointer up to the next cell that contains data and is next to a blank cell.
↓	Moves the cell pointer down to the next cell that contains data and is next to a blank cell.
→	Moves the cell pointer right to the next cell that contains data and is next to a blank cell.
←	Moves the cell pointer left to the next cell that contains data and is next to a blank cell.
@	Lets you select an @function from the list of 1-2-3 @functions.
{..}	Lets you select a macro command from the list of 1-2-3 macro commands.
◀	Turns on STEP and TRACE modes.
▦	Lets you select and run a macro.
+	Lets you specify a cell to reference or link to.
▦	Inserts one or more rows above the highlighted rows.
▦	Inserts one or more columns to the left of the highlighted columns.
▦	Deletes all rows in the highlighted range.
▦	Deletes all columns in the highlighted range.
▦	Inserts a new worksheet after the current worksheet.
▦	Deletes all worksheets in the highlighted range.
✎	Lets you specify a range to apply the styles and formats in the current cell or range.
?=	Starts the Solver.
▦	Lets you select and rearrange available SmartIcons.

Copies an object or the entire graph to the Clipboard.

Creates a copy of an object or the entire graph and displays the copy superimposed on the original.

Permanently deletes an object or the entire graph.

Lets you freely rotate an object or the entire graph around its center.

Rotates an object or the entire graph around its center in 90-degree increments.

Horizontally flips an object or the entire graph so that it appears backwards.

Vertically flips an object or the entire graph so that it appears upside down.

Places selected objects in front of all other objects.

Places selected objects behind all other objects.

Tiles all open Worksheet, Graph, and Transcript windows.

Cascades all open Worksheet, Graph, and Transcript windows.

Enlarges the entire contents of the Graph window.

Zooms in on an area of the Graph window to fill the window.

Reduces the enlarged contents of the Graph window.

Lets you select a graph type.

Lets you select and rearrange available SmartIcons.

Graph SmartIcons

The following SmartIcons are available when a Graph window is active:

Displays a bar graph.

Displays a 3-D bar graph.

Displays a pie chart.

Displays a 3-D pie chart.

Displays a line graph.

Displays an area graph.

Displays a 3-D area graph.

Displays a horizontal bar graph.

Displays an XY graph.

Displays an HLCO graph.

Displays a mixed graph.

Displays a 3-D line graph.

Use the following SmartIcons to add objects to a graph. You must anchor the mouse pointer to draw and place the object, and then double-click the left mouse button to complete the object.

Lets you draw a line with an arrowhead.

Lets you draw a line.

Lets you add an ellipse.

Lets you add a polygon.

Lets you add a rectangle.

Lets you add text.

Lets you create a freehand drawing.

Index